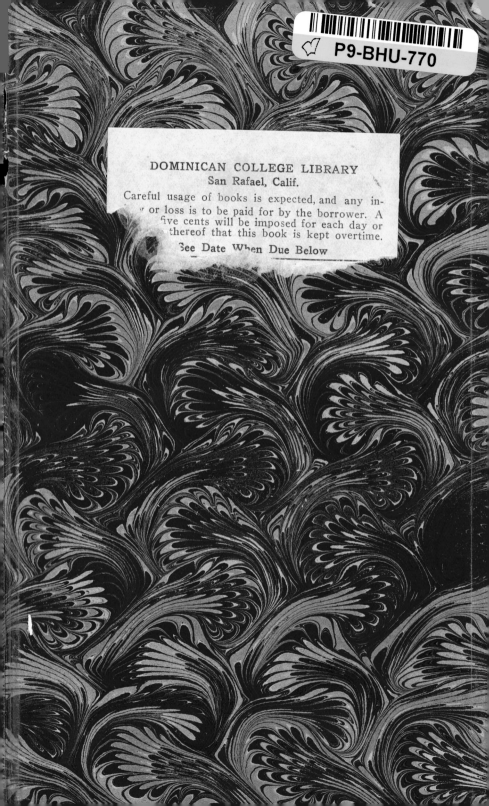

MOMMSEN'S

HISTORY OF ROME

VOL. II.

LONDON: PRINTED BY
SPOTTISWOODE AND CO., NEW-STREET SQUARE
AND PARLIAMENT STREET

THE

HISTORY OF ROME

BY

THEODOR MOMMSEN

TRANSLATED

WITH THE AUTHOR'S SANCTION AND ADDITIONS

BY

THE REV. WILLIAM P. DICKSON, D.D.

REGIUS PROFESSOR OF BIBLICAL CRITICISM IN THE UNIVERSITY OF GLASGOW
LATE CLASSICAL EXAMINER IN THE UNIVERSITY OF ST. ANDREWS

WITH A PREFACE BY DR. LEONHARD SCHMITZ

NEW EDITION, IN FOUR VOLUMES

VOLUME II.

LONDON

RICHARD BENTLEY, NEW BURLINGTON STREET

𝔓𝔲𝔟𝔩𝔦𝔰𝔥𝔢𝔯 𝔦𝔫 𝔒𝔯𝔡𝔦𝔫𝔞𝔯𝔶 𝔱𝔬 𝔥𝔢𝔯 𝔐𝔞𝔧𝔢𝔰𝔱𝔶

1868

937
M739d
v. 2

CONTENTS

OF

THE SECOND VOLUME.

———•◦•———

BOOK THIRD.

FROM THE UNION OF ITALY TO THE SUBJUGATION OF CARTHAGE AND THE GREEK STATES.

———

CHAPTER VII.

CHAPTER VIII.

CHAPTER IX.

CHAPTER X.

CHAPTER XI.

CHAPTER XII.

CHAPTER XIII.

CHAPTER XIV.

BOOK THIRD.

---+---

FROM THE UNION OF ITALY

TO THE

SUBJUGATION OF CARTHAGE AND THE GREEK STATES.

Arduum res gestas scribere.—Sallust.

CHAPTER I.

CARTHAGE.

THE Semitic stock occupied a place amidst, and yet aloof *The Phoe-*
from, the nations of the ancient classical world. The true *nicians.*
centre of the former lay in the East, that of the latter in
the region of the Mediterranean; and, however wars and
migrations may have altered the line of demarcation and
thrown the races across each other, a deep sense of diversity
has always severed, and still severs, the Indo-Germanic
peoples from the Syrian, Israelite, and Arabic nations. This
diversity was no less marked in the case of that Semitic
people, which spread more than any other in the direction of
the west—the Phoenicians. Their native seat was the
narrow border of coast bounded by Asia Minor, the high-
lands of Syria, and Egypt, and called Canaan, that is, the
" plain." This was the only name which the nation itself
made use of; even in Christian times the African farmer
called himself a Canaanite. But Canaan received from the
Hellenes the name of Phoenike, the " land of purple," or
" land of the red men," and the Italians also were accustomed to call the Canaanites Punians, as we are accustomed
still to speak of them as the Phoenician or Punic race.

The land was well adapted for agriculture; but its excel- *Their com-*
lent harbours and the abundant supply of timber and of *merce.*
metals eminently favoured the growth of commerce, and it
was there perhaps, where the opulent eastern continent
abuts on the wide-spreading Mediterranean so rich in
harbours and islands, that commerce first dawned in all
its greatness upon man. The Phoenicians directed all the

resources of courage, acuteness, and enthusiasm to the full
development of commerce and its attendant arts of navigation, manufacturing, and colonization, and thus connected
the East and the West. At an incredibly early period we
find them in Cyprus and Egypt, in Greece and Sicily, in
Africa and Spain, and even on the Atlantic Ocean and the
North Sea. The field of their commerce reached from Sierra
Leone and Cornwall in the west, eastward to the coast of
Malabar. Through their hands passed the gold and pearls
of the East, the purple of Tyre, slaves, ivory, lions' and
panthers' skins from the interior of Africa, frankincense
from Arabia, the linen of Egypt, the pottery and fine wines
of Greece, the copper of Cyprus, the silver of Spain, tin
from England, and iron from Elba. The Phoenician mariners
supplied every nation with whatever it needed or was likely
to purchase; and they roamed everywhere, yet always
returned to the narrow home to which their affections
clung.

Their in-
tellectual
endow-
ments.

The Phoenicians are entitled to be commemorated in history by the side of the Hellenic and Latin nations; but
their case affords a fresh proof, and perhaps the strongest
proof of all, that the development of national energies in
antiquity was of a one-sided character. Those noble and
enduring creations in the field of intellect, which owe their
origin to the Aramaean race, did not emanate from the
Phoenicians. While faith and knowledge in a certain sense
were the especial property of the Aramaean nations and
reached the Indo-Germans only from the East, neither the
Phoenician religion nor Phoenician science and art ever, so
far as we can see, held an independent rank among those
of the Aramaean family. The religious conceptions of the
Phoenicians were rude and uncouth, and it seemed as if their
worship was meant to foster rather than to restrain lust and
cruelty. No trace is discernible, at least in times of clear
historical light, of any special influence exercised by their
religion over other nations. As little do we find any Phoenician architecture or plastic art at all comparable even to
those of Italy, to say nothing of the lands where art was
native. The most ancient seat of scientific observation and
of its application to practical purposes was Babylon, or at

any rate the region of the Euphrates.   It was there probably
that men first followed the course of the stars ; it was there
that they first distinguished and expressed in writing the
sounds of language ; it was there that they began to reflect
on time and space and on the powers at work in nature : the
earliest traces of astronomy and chronology, of the alphabet,
and of weights and measures, point to that region.   The
Phoenicians doubtless availed themselves of the artistic and
highly developed manufactures of Babylon for their industry,
of the observation of the stars for their navigation, of the
writing of sounds and the adjustment of measures for their
commerce, and distributed many an important germ of civilization along with their wares ; but it cannot be demonstrated
that the alphabet or any other ingenious product of the
human mind belonged peculiarly to them, and such religious
and scientific ideas as they were the means of conveying to
the Hellenes were scattered by them more after the fashion
of a bird dropping grains than of the husbandman sowing
his seed.   The power which the Hellenes and even the
Italians possessed, of civilizing and assimilating to themselves the nations susceptible of culture with whom they came
into contact, was wholly wanting in the Phoenicians.   In
the field of Roman conquest the Iberian and the Celtic languages have disappeared before the Romanic tongue ; the
Berbers of Africa speak at the present day the same language as they spoke in the times of the Hannos and the
Barcides.

Above all, the Phoenicians, like the rest of the Aramaean   Their
nations as compared with the Indo-Germans, lacked the   political
qualities.
instinct of political life—the noble idea of self-governed
freedom.   During the most flourishing times of Sidon and
Tyre the land of the Phoenicians was a perpetual apple of
contention between the powers that ruled on the Euphrates
and on the Nile, and was subject sometimes to the Assyrians,
sometimes to the Egyptians.   With half its power Hellenic
cities had achieved their independence ; but the prudent
Sidonians calculated that the closing of the caravan-routes
to the East or of the ports of Egypt would cost them more
than the heaviest tribute, and so they punctually paid their
taxes, as it might happen, to Nineveh or to Memphis, and

even gave their ships, when they could not avoid it, to help to fight the battles of the kings. And, as at home the Phoenicians patiently submitted to the oppression of their masters, so also abroad they were by no means inclined to exchange the peaceful career of commerce for a policy of conquest. Their colonies were factories. It was of more moment in their view to deal in buying and selling with the natives than to acquire extensive territories in distant lands, and to carry out there the slow and difficult work of colonization. They avoided war even with their rivals; they allowed themselves to be supplanted in Egypt, Greece, Italy, and the east of Sicily almost without resistance; and in the great naval battles, which were fought in early times for the supremacy of the western Mediterranean, at Alalia (217) and at Cumae (280), it was the Etruscans, and not the Phoenicians, that bore the brunt of the struggle with the Greeks. If rivalry could not be avoided, they compromised the matter as best they could; no attempt was ever made by the Phoenicians to conquer Caere or Massilia. Still less, of course, were the Phoenicians disposed to enter on aggressive war. On the only occasion in earlier times when they took the field on the offensive—in the great Sicilian expedition of the African Phoenicians which terminated in their defeat at Himera by Gelo of Syracuse (274)—it was simply as dutiful subjects of the great king and in order to avoid taking part in the campaign against the Hellenes of the east, that they entered the lists against the Hellenes of the west; just as their Syrian kinsmen were in fact obliged in that same year to share the defeat of the Persians at Salamis (i. 358).

This was not the result of cowardice; navigation in unknown waters and with armed vessels requires brave hearts, and that such were to be found among the Phoenicians, they often showed. Still less was it the result of any lack of tenacity and idiosyncracy of national feeling; on the contrary the Aramaeans defended their nationality with spiritual weapons as well as with their blood against all the allurements of Greek civilization and all the coercive measures of eastern and western despots, and that with an obstinacy which no Indo-Germanic people has ever equalled, and which to us who belong to the West seems to be sometimes more sometimes less than human. It was the result of that want of political instinct, which amidst all their lively sense of the ties of race, and amidst all their faithful attachment to the city of their fathers, formed the most essential feature in the character of the Phoenicians. Liberty had no charms for them, and they aspired not after dominion; "quietly they lived," says the Book of Judges, " after the manner of the Sidonians, careless and secure, and in possession of riches."

Of all the Phoenician settlements none attained a more Carthage. rapid and secure prosperity than those which were established by the Tyrians and Sidonians on the south coast of Spain and the north coast of Africa—regions that lay beyond the reach of the arm of the great king and the dangerous rivalry of the mariners of Greece, and in which the natives held the same relation to the strangers as the Indians in America held to the Europeans. Among the numerous and flourishing Phoenician cities along these shores, the most prominent by far was the " new town," Karthada or, as the Occidentals called it, Karchedon or Carthago. Although not the earliest settlement of the Phoenicians in this region, and originally perhaps a dependency of the adjoining Utica the oldest of the Phoenician towns in Libya, it soon outstripped its neighbours and even the motherland through the incomparable advantages of its situation and the energetic activity of its inhabitants. It was situated not far from the (former) mouth of the Bagradas (Mejerda), which flows through the richest corn district of northern Africa, and was placed on a fertile rising ground, still occupied with country houses and covered with groves of olive and orange trees, falling off in a gentle slope towards the plain, and terminating towards the sea in a sea-girt promontory. Lying in the heart of the great North-African roadstead, the Gulf of Tunis, at the very spot where that beautiful basin affords the best anchorage for vessels of larger size, and where drinkable spring water is got close by the shore, the place proved singularly favourable for agriculture and commerce and for the exchange of their respective commodities—so favourable, that not only was the Tyrian settlement in that quarter the first of Phoenician mercantile cities, but even in the Roman period Carthage was no sooner restored than it became the third city in the empire, and still, under circumstances far from favourable and on a site far less judiciously chosen, there exists and flourishes in that quarter a city of a hundred thousand inhabitants. The prosperity, agricultural, mercantile, and industrial, of a city so situated and so peopled, needs no explanation; but the question requires an answer—In what way did this settlement come to attain such a development of political power as no other Phoenician city possessed?

Carthage heads the western Phoenicians in opposition to the Hellenes.

That the Phoenician stock did not even in Carthage renounce its passive policy, there is no lack of evidence to prove. Carthage paid, even down to the times of its prosperity, a ground-rent for the space occupied by the city to the native Berbers, the tribe of Maxitani or Maxyes; and although the sea and the desert sufficiently protected the city from any assault of the eastern powers, Carthage appears to have recognized—although but nominally—the supremacy of the great king, and to have paid tribute to him occasionally, in order to secure its commercial communications with Tyre and the East.

But with all their disposition to be submissive and cringing, circumstances occurred which compelled these Phoenicians to adopt a more energetic policy. The stream of Hellenic migration was pouring ceaselessly towards the west: it had already dislodged the Phoenicians from Greece proper and Italy, and it was preparing to supplant them also in Sicily, in Spain, and even in Libya itself. The Phoenicians had to make a stand somewhere, if they were not willing to be totally crushed. In this case, where they had to deal with Grecian traders and not with the great king, submission did not suffice to secure the continuance of their commerce and industry on its former footing, liable merely to tax and tribute. Massilia and Cyrene were already founded; the whole east of Sicily was already in the hands of the Greeks; it was full time for the Phoenicians to think of serious resistance. The Carthaginians undertook the task; after long and obstinate wars they set a limit to the advance of the Cyrenaeans, and Hellenism was unable to establish itself to the west of the desert of Tripolis. With Carthaginian aid, moreover, the Phoenician settlers on the western point of Sicily defended themselves against the Greeks, and readily and gladly submitted to the protection of the powerful cognate city (i. 162). These important successes, which occurred in the second century of Rome, and which saved for the Phoenicians the south-western portion of the Mediterranean, served of themselves to give to the city which had achieved them the hegemony of the nation, and to alter at the same time its political position. Carthage was no longer a mere mercantile city : it aimed at the dominion of Libya and of a part of the Mediterranean, because it could not avoid doing so. It is probable that the custom of employing mercenaries contributed materially to these successes. That custom came into vogue in Greece somewhere about the middle of the fourth century of Rome, but among the Orientals and the Carians more especially it was far older, and it was perhaps the Phoenicians themselves that began it. By the system of foreign recruiting war was converted into a grand pecuniary speculation, which was quite in keeping with the character and habits of the Phoenicians.

It was probably the reflex influence of these successes abroad, that first led the Carthaginians to change the character of their occupation in Africa from a tenure of hire and sufferance to one of proprietorship and conquest. It appears to have been about the year 300 of Rome that the Carthaginian merchants got rid of the rent for the soil, which they had hitherto been obliged to pay to the natives. This change enabled them to prosecute husbandry on a great scale. The Phoenicians were at all times anxious to employ their capital as landlords as well as traders, and to practise agriculture on a large scale by means of slaves or hired labourers ; a large portion of the Jews in this way served the merchant-princes of Tyre for daily wages. The Carthaginians could now without restriction extract the produce of the rich Libyan soil by a system akin to that of the modern planters; slaves in chains cultivated the land—we find single citizens possessing as many as twenty thousand of them. Nor was this all. The agricultural villages of the surrounding

The Carthaginian dominion in Africa.

450.

region—agriculture appears to have been introduced among the Libyans at a very early period, probably anterior to the Phoenician settlement, and in all likelihood from Egypt— were subdued by force of arms, and the free Libyan farmers were transformed into fellahs, who paid to their lords a fourth part of the produce of the soil as tribute, and were subjected to a regular system of recruiting for the formation of a home Carthaginian army. Hostilities were constantly occurring with the roving pastoral tribes (νόμαδες) on the borders; but a chain of fortified posts secured the territory enclosed by them, and the Nomades were slowly driven back into the deserts and mountains, or were compelled to recognize Carthaginian supremacy, to pay tribute, and to furnish contingents. About the period of the first Punic war their great town Theveste (Tebessa, at the sources of the Mejerda) was conquered by the Carthaginians. These formed the "towns and tribes (ἔθνη) of subjects," which appear in the Carthaginian state-treaties; the former being the non-free Libyan villages, the latter the subject Nomades.

Libyphoe-
nicians.

To this fell to be added the sovereignty of Carthage over the other Phoenicians in Africa, or the so-called Libyphoenicians. These included, on the one hand, the smaller settlements sent forth from Carthage along the whole north and part of the north-west coast of Africa—which must have been not unimportant, for on the Atlantic alone there were settled at one time 30,000 such colonists—and, on the other hand, the old Phoenician settlements especially numerous along the coast of the present province of Constantine and Beylik of Tunis, such as Hippo afterwards called Regius (Bona), Hadrumetum (Susa), Little Leptis (to the south of Susa)—the second city of the Phoenicians in Africa—Thapsus (in the same quarter), and Great Leptis (near Tripoli). In what way all these cities came to be subject to Carthage —whether voluntarily, for their protection perhaps from the attacks of the Cyrenaeans and Numidians, or by constraint —cannot be now ascertained; but it is certain that they are designated as subjects of the Carthaginians even in official documents, that they had to pull down their walls, and that they had to pay tribute and furnish contingents to Carthage. They were not liable however to the recruiting

system or to the land-tax, but contributed a definite amount
of men and money, Little Leptis for instance paying the
enormous sum annually of 365 talents (90,000*l.*) ; moreover
there was equality of law between them and the Carthaginians, and they could contract marriage on equal terms.*
Utica alone escaped a similar fate and had its walls and
independence preserved to it, less perhaps from its own power
than from the pious feeling of the Carthaginians towards
their ancient protectors ; in fact the Phoenicians cherished a
remarkable feeling of reverence for such relations, presenting
a thorough contrast to the indifference of the Greeks. Even
in intercourse with foreigners " Carthage and Utica " always
stipulate and promise in conjunction ; which, of course, did
not preclude the far more important " new town " from practically asserting its hegemony over Utica. Thus the Tyrian
factory was converted into the capital of a mighty North-
African empire, which extended from the desert of Tripoli
to the Atlantic Ocean, contenting itself in its western portion (Morocco and Algiers) with the occupation, and that
to some extent superficial, of a belt along the coast, but in
the richer portion to the east (the present districts of Constantine and Tunis) stretching its sway over the interior
also and constantly pushing its frontier farther to the south.
The Carthaginians were, as an ancient author significantly
expresses it, converted from Tyrians into Libyans. Phoenician civilization prevailed in Libya just as Greek civilization

---

* The clearest description of this important class occurs in the Carthaginian
treaty (Polyb. vii. 9), where in contrast
to the Uticenses on the one hand, and
to the Libyan subjects on the other, they
are called οἱ Καρχηδονίων ὕπαρχοι ὅσοι
τοῖς αὐτοῖς νόμοις χρῶνται. Elsewhere
they are spoken of as cities allied (συμ-
μαχίδες πόλεις, Diod. xx. 10) or tributary
(Liv. xxxiv. 62 ; Justin, xxii. 7, 3). Their
conubium with the Carthaginians is mentioned by Diodorus, xx. 55 ; the *commer-
cium* is implied in the "equal laws."
That the old Phoenician colonies were
included among the Libyphoenicians, is
shown by the designation of Hippo as a
Libyphoenician city (Liv. xxv. 40) ; on
the other hand as to the settlements derived from Carthage it is said in the
Periplus of Hanno : "the Carthaginians

resolved that Hanno should sail beyond
the Pillars of Hercules and found cities
of Libyphoenicians." In substance the
word "Libyphoenicians" was used by
the Carthaginians not as a national designation, but as a term denoting a class
in constitutional law. This view is quite
consistent with the fact that grammatically the name denotes Phoenicians
mingled with Libyans (Liv. xxi. 22, an
addition to the text of Polybius) ; in
reality, at least in the institution of
very exposed colonies, Libyans were
frequently associated with Phoenicians
(Diod. xiii. 79 ; Cic. *pro Scauro*, 42).
The analogy in name and constitutional
relations between the Latins of Rome
and the Libyphoenicians of Carthage is
unmistakeable.

prevailed in Asia Minor and Syria after the campaigns of
Alexander, although not with the same intensity. Phoenician
was spoken and written at the courts of the Nomad sheiks,
and the more civilized native tribes adopted for their language the Phoenician alphabet; * to Phoenicise them completely suited neither the genius of the nation nor the policy
of Carthage.

The epoch, at which this transformation of Carthage into
the capital of Libya took place, admits the less of being
determined, because the change doubtless took place gradually. The author just mentioned names Hanno as the re-
former of the nation. If the Hanno is meant who lived at
the time of the first war with Rome, he can only be regarded
as having completed the new system, the carrying out of
which probably occupied the fourth and fifth centuries of
Rome.

The flourishing of Carthage was accompanied by a parallel
decline in the great cities of the Phoenician mother-country,
in Sidon and especially in Tyre, the prosperity of which
was destroyed partly by internal commotions, partly by the
pressure of external calamities, particularly of its sieges by
Salmanassar in the first, Nebuchodrossor in the second, and
Alexander in the fifth century of Rome. The noble families
and the old firms of Tyre emigrated for the most part to the
secure and flourishing daughter-city, and carried thither
their intelligence, their capital, and their traditions. At the
time when the Phoenicians came into contact with Rome,
Carthage was as decidedly the first of Canaanite cities as
Rome was the first of the communities of Latium.

Naval
power of
Carthage.

But the empire of Libya was only half of the power of
Carthage; its maritime and colonial dominion had acquired,
during the same period, a not less powerful development.

---

* The Libyan or Numidian alphabet,
by which we mean that which was and
is employed by the Berbers in writing
their non-Semitic language—one of the
innumerable alphabets derived from the
primitive Aramaean one—certainly appears to be more closely related in several of its forms to the latter rather than
the Phoenician alphabet; but it by no
means follows from this, that the Libyans
derived their writing not from Phoenicians but from earlier immigrants, any
more than the partially older forms of
the Italian alphabets prohibit us from
deriving these from the Greek. We
must rather assume that the Libyan
alphabet has been derived from the
Phoenician at a period of the latter
earlier than the time at which the records of the Phoenician language that
have reached us were written.

In Spain the chief station of the Phoenicians was the Spain.
primitive Tyrian settlement at Gades (Cadiz). Besides this
they possessed to the west and east of it a chain of factories,
and in the interior the region of the silver mines ; so that
they had occupied nearly the modern Andalusia and Granada,
or at least the coasts of these provinces. They made no effort
to acquire the interior from the warlike native nations; they
were content with the possession of the mines and of stations
for traffic and for shell and other fisheries ; and they had
difficulty in maintaining their ground even in these against
the adjoining tribes. It is probable that these possessions
were not strictly Carthaginian but Tyrian, and Gades was
not reckoned among the cities tributary to Carthage ; but
practically, like all the western Phoenicians, it was under
Carthaginian hegemony, as is shown by the aid sent by
Carthage to the Gaditani against the natives, and by the
institution of Carthaginian trading settlements to the westward of Gades. Ebusus and the Baleares, again, were
occupied by the Carthaginians even at an early period, partly
for the fisheries, partly as advanced posts against the Massiliots, with whom furious conflicts were waged from these
stations.

In like manner the Carthaginians already at the end of Sardinia.
the second century of Rome, established themselves in Sardinia, which was turned to account by them precisely in the
same way as Libya. While the natives withdrew into the
mountainous interior of the island to escape from the bondage
of agricultural serfs, just as the Numidians in Africa withdrew to the borders of the desert, Phoenician colonies were
conducted to Caralis (Cagliari) and other important points,
and the fertile districts along the coast were rendered productive by the introduction of Libyan cultivators.

In Sicily the straits of Messana and the larger eastern Sicily.
half of the island had fallen at an early period into the
hands of the Greeks ; but the Phoenicians, with the help of
the Carthaginians, retained the smaller adjacent islands, the
Aegates, Melita, Gaulos, Cossyra—the settlement in Malta
especially was rich and flourishing—and they kept the west
and north-west coast of Sicily, whence they maintained
communication with Africa by means of Motya and after-

wards of Lilybaeum and with Sardinia by means of Panormus and Soluntum. The interior of the island remained in the possession of the native Elymi, Sicani, and Siceli. After the further advance of the Greeks was checked, a state of comparative peace had prevailed in the island, which even the campaign undertaken by the Carthaginians at the instigation of the Persians against their Greek neighbours in

480.   the island (274) did not permanently interrupt, and which continued on the whole to subsist till the Attic expedition to

415–413.   Sicily (339–341). The two competing nations made up their minds to tolerate each other, and confined themselves in the main each to its own field.

Maritime supremacy.   All these settlements and possessions were important enough in themselves; but they were of still greater moment, inasmuch as they became the pillars of the Carthaginian maritime supremacy. By their possession of the south of Spain, of the Baleares, of Sardinia, of western Sicily and Melita, and by their prevention of Hellenic colonies on the east coast of Spain, in Corsica, and in the region of the Syrtes, the masters of the north coast of Africa rendered their sea a closed one, and monopolized the western straits. In the Tyrrhene and Gallic seas alone the Phoenicians were obliged to admit the rivalry of other nations. This state of things might be endured so long as the Etruscans and the Greeks served to counterbalance each other in these waters; with the former as the less dangerous rivals Carthage

Rivalry with Syracuse.   even entered into an alliance against the Greeks. But when, on the fall of the Etruscan power—a fall which, as is usually the case in such forced alliances, Carthage had hardly exerted all her power to avert—and after the miscarriage of the great projects of Alcibiades Syracuse stood forth as indisputably the first Greek naval power, not only did the rulers of Syracuse naturally begin to aspire to dominion over Sicily and lower Italy and at the same time over the Tyrrhene and Adriatic seas, but the Carthaginians also were compelled to adopt a more energetic policy. The immediate result of the long and obstinate conflicts between them and their equally powerful and infamous antagonist, Dionysius of

406–365.   Syracuse (348–389), was the annihilation or weakening of the intervening Sicilian states—a result which both parties

had an interest in accomplishing—and the division of the
island between the Syracusans and Carthaginians. The most
flourishing cities in the island—Selinus, Himera, Agrigentum, Gela, and Messana—were thoroughly destroyed by
the Carthaginians in the course of these unhappy conflicts:
and Dionysius was not displeased to see Hellenism destroyed
or suppressed there, so that, leaning for support on foreign
mercenaries enlisted from Italy, Gaul and Spain, he might
rule in greater security over provinces which lay desolate or
which were occupied by military colonies. The peace, which
was concluded after the victory of the Carthaginian general
Mago at Kronion (371), and which subjected to the Cartha-   383.
ginians the Greek cities of Thermae (the ancient Himera),
Segesta, Heraclea Minoa, Selinus, and a part of the territory
of Agrigentum as far as the Halycus, was regarded by the
two powers contending for the possession of the island as
only a temporary accommodation; on both sides the rivals
were ever renewing their attempts to dispossess each other.
Four several times—in 360 in the time of Dionysius the   394.
elder; in 410 in that of Timoleon; in 445 in that of 344. 309.
Agathocles; in 476 in that of Pyrrhus—the Carthaginians   278.
were masters of all Sicily excepting Syracuse, and were
baffled by its solid walls; almost as often the Syracusans,
under able leaders, such as were the elder Dionysius,
Agathocles, and Pyrrhus, seemed equally on the eve of
dislodging the Africans from the island. But more and
more the balance inclined to the side of the Carthaginians,
who were, as a rule, the aggressors, and who, although they
did not follow out their object with Roman steadfastness, yet
conducted their attack with far greater method and energy
than the Greek city, vexed and torn by factions, conducted
its defence. The Phoenicians might with reason expect
that a pestilence or a foreign *condottiere* would not always
snatch the prey from their hands; and for the time being,
at least at sea, the struggle was already decided (i. 453): the
attempt of Pyrrhus to restore the Syracusan fleet was the
last. After the failure of that attempt, the Carthaginian
fleet commanded without a rival the whole western Mediterranean; and their endeavours to occupy Syracuse, Rhegium,
and Tarentum, showed the extent of their power and the

shofetes and gerusiasts also when circumstances required, to
a reckoning on resigning office, and inflicted even capital
punishment at pleasure, often with the most reckless cruelty.
Of course in this as in every instance, where administrative
functionaries are subjected to the control of another body,
the reality of power was transferred from the controlled to
the controlling authority; and it is easy to understand on the
one hand how the latter came to interfere in all matters of
administration—the Gerusia for instance submitted important despatches first to the judges, and then to the people—
and on the other hand how fear of the control at home, which
regularly meted out its award according to success, hampered the Carthaginian statesman and general in council and
action.

Citizens.   The body of citizens in Carthage, though not expressly
restricted, as in Sparta, to the attitude of passive bystanders
in the business of the state, appears to have had but a very
slight amount of practical influence on it. In the elections
to the Gerusia a system of open corruption was the rule; in
the nomination of a general the people were consulted, but
only after the nomination had really been made by proposal
on the part of the Gerusia; and other questions only went to
the people when the Gerusia thought fit or could not otherwise
agree. Assemblies of the people with judicial functions were
unknown in Carthage. The powerlessness of the citizens
was probably in the main occasioned by their political organization; the mess-associations, which are mentioned among
the Carthaginian institutions and compared with the Spartan
Pheiditia, were probably guilds under oligarchical management. Mention is made even of a distinction between
"burgesses of the city" and "manual labourers," which
leads us to infer that the latter held a very inferior position,
perhaps approaching to servitude.

Character
of the go-
vernment.   On a comprehensive view of its several elements, the Carthaginian constitution appears to have been a government of
capitalists, such as would naturally arise in a civic community which had no opulent middle class but consisted on the
one hand of a city rabble without property and living from
hand to mouth, and on the other hand of great merchants,
planters, and overseers of quality. The system of enriching

decayed grandees at the expense of the subjects, by despatching them as tax-assessors and overseers to the dependent communities—that infallible token of a rotten civic oligarchy —was not wanting in Carthage ; Aristotle describes it as the main cause of the tried durability of the Carthaginian constitution.   Up to his time no revolution worth mentioning had taken place in Carthage either from above or from below. The multitude remained without leaders in consequence of the material advantages which the governing oligarchy was able to offer to all ambitious or necessitous men of rank, and was satisfied with the crumbs, which in the form of electoral corruption or otherwise fell to it from the table of the rich. A democratic opposition indeed could not fail with such a government to emerge ; but at the time of the first Punic war it was still quite powerless.   At a later period, partly under the influence of the defeats which were sustained, its political influence appears on the increase, and that far more rapidly than the influence of the similar party at the same period in Rome ; the popular assemblies began to assume the final decision in political questions, and broke down the omnipotence of the Carthaginian oligarchy.   After the termination of the second Punic war it even was enacted, on the proposal of Hannibal, that no member of the council of a Hundred could hold office for two consecutive years ; and thereby a complete democracy was introduced, which certainly was under existing circumstances the only means of saving Carthage, if there still was time to do so.   The opposition was swayed by a strong patriotic and reforming enthusiasm ; but the fact cannot withal be overlooked, that it rested on a corrupt and rotten basis.   The body of citizens in Carthage, which is compared by well-informed Greeks to the people of Alexandria, was so disorderly that on that account it well deserved to be powerless ; and it might well be asked, what good could arise from revolutions, where, as in Carthage, the boys helped to make them.

From a financial point of view, Carthage held in every respect the first place among the states of antiquity.   At the time of the Peloponnesian war this Phoenician city was, according to the testimony of the first of Greek historians, financially superior to all the Greek states, and its revenues

Capital and its power in Carthage.

were compared to those of the great king; Polybius calls it
the wealthiest city in the world.   The intelligent character
of the Carthaginian husbandry—which, as was the case subsequently in Rome, generals and statesmen did not disdain
scientifically to practise and to teach—is attested by the
agricultural treatise of the Carthaginian Mago, which was
universally regarded by the later Greek and Roman rural
authors as the fundamental code of rational husbandry, and
was not only translated into Greek, but was edited also in
Latin by command of the Roman senate and officially recommended to the Italian landholders.   A characteristic feature
was the close connection between this Phoenician agriculture and capital: it was quoted as a leading maxim of Phoenician husbandry that one should never acquire more land
than he could thoroughly manage.   The rich resources of
the country in horses, oxen, sheep, and goats, in which
Libya by reason of its Nomad husbandry perhaps excelled at
that time, as Polybius testifies, all other lands of the earth,
were of great advantage to the Carthaginians.   As these
were the instructors of the Romans in the art of profitably
working the soil, they were so likewise in the art of turning
to good account their subjects; by virtue of which Carthage
reaped indirectly the rents of the "best part of Europe," and
of the rich—and in some portions, such as in Byzacitis
and on the lesser Syrtis, surpassingly productive—region of
northern Africa.   Commerce, which was always regarded
in Carthage as an honourable pursuit, and the shipping
and manufactures which commerce rendered flourishing,
brought even in the natural course of things golden
harvests annually to the settlers there; and we have
already indicated how skilfully, by an extensive and ever-
growing system of monopoly, not only all the foreign but also
all the inland commerce of the western Mediterranean, and
the whole carrying trade between the west and east, were
more and more concentrated in that single harbour.

  Science and art in Carthage, as afterwards in Rome, seem
to have been mainly dependent on Hellenic influences, but
they do not appear to have been neglected.   There was a
respectable Phoenician literature; and on the conquest of
the city there were found rich treasures of art—not created,

it is true, in Carthage, but carried off from Sicilian temples —and considerable libraries. But even intellect there was in the service of capital ; the prominent features of its literature were chiefly agricultural and geographical treatises, such as the work of Mago already mentioned and the account by the admiral Hanno of his voyage along the west coast of Africa, which was originally deposited publicly in one of the Carthaginian temples, and which is still extant in a translation. Even the general diffusion of certain attainments, and particularly of the knowledge of foreign languages,* as to which the Carthage of this epoch probably stood almost on a level with Rome under the empire, forms an evidence of the thoroughly practical turn given to Hellenic culture in Carthage. It is absolutely impossible to form an idea of the mass of capital accumulated in this London of antiquity, but some notion at least may be gained of the public revenues from the fact, that, in spite of the costly system on which Carthage organized its wars and in spite of the careless and faithless administration of the state property, the contributions of its subjects and the customs-revenue completely covered the expenditure, so that no direct taxes were levied from the citizens ; and further, that even after the second Punic war, when the power of the state was already broken, the current expenses and the payment to Rome of a yearly instalment of £48,000 could be met, without levying any tax, merely by a somewhat stricter management of the finances, and fourteen years after the peace the state proffered immediate payment of the thirty-six remaining instalments. But it was not merely the sum total of its revenues that evinced the superiority of the financial administration at Carthage. The economical principles of a later and more advanced epoch are found by us in Carthage alone of all the more considerable states of antiquity. Mention is made of foreign state-loans, and in the monetary system we find along with gold and silver mention of a token-money having no intrinsic value—a species of currency

---

* The steward on a country estate, although a slave, ought, according to the precept of the Carthaginian agricultural writer Mago (*ap.* Varro, *R. R.* i. 17), to be able to read, and ought to possess some culture. In the prologue of the "Poenulus" of Plautus, it is said of the hero of the title :—

Et is omnes linguas scit ; sed dissimulat sciens
Se scire ; Poenus plane est ; quid verbis opus't ?

not used elsewhere in antiquity. In fact, if government had resolved itself into mere mercantile speculation, never would any state have solved the problem more brilliantly than Carthage.

Compa-
rison
between
Carthage
and Rome.

Let us now compare the respective resources of Carthage and Rome. Both were agricultural and mercantile cities, and nothing more; art and science had substantially the same altogether subordinate and altogether practical character in both, except that in this respect Carthage had

In their
economy.

made greater progress than Rome. But in Carthage the moneyed interest preponderated over the landed, in Rome at this time the landed still preponderated over the moneyed; and, while the agriculturists of Carthage were universally large landlords and slave-holders, in the Rome of this period the great mass of the burgesses still tilled their fields in person. The majority of the population in Rome held property, and was therefore conservative; the majority in Carthage held no property, and was therefore accessible to the gold of the rich as well as to the cry of the democrats for reform. In Carthage there already prevailed all that opulence which marks powerful commercial cities, while the manners and police of Rome still maintained at least externally the severity and frugality of the olden times. When the ambassadors of Carthage returned from Rome, they told their colleagues that the relations of intimacy among the Roman senators surpassed all conception; that a single set of silver plate sufficed for the whole senate, and had reappeared in every house to which the envoys had been invited. The sneer is a significant token of the difference in their economic condition.

In their
constitu-
tion.

In both the constitution was aristocratic; the Judges governed in Carthage, as did the senate in Rome, and both on the same system of police-control. The strict state of dependence in which the governing board at Carthage held the individual magistrate, and the injunction to the citizens absolutely to refrain from learning the Greek language and to communicate with a Greek only through the medium of a public interpreter, originated in the same spirit as the system of government at Rome; but in comparison with the cruel harshness and the categorical precision, bordering on silliness, of this Carthaginian state-tutelage, the Roman system of fining and censure appears mild and reasonable. The Roman senate, which was open to eminent ability and represented in the best sense the nation, was able also to trust the nation, and had no need to fear the magistrates. The Carthaginian senate, on the other hand, was based on a jealous control of administration by the government, and represented exclusively the leading families; its essence was mistrust of all above and below it, and therefore it could neither be confident that the people would follow whither it led, nor free from the dread of usurpations on the part of the magistrates. Hence the steady course of Roman policy, which never receded a step in times of misfortune, and never threw away the favours of fortune by negligence or indifference; whereas the Carthaginians desisted from the struggle when a last effort might perhaps have saved all, and weary or forgetful of their great duties as a nation allowed the half-completed building to fall to pieces, only to begin it in a few years anew. Hence the able magistrate in Rome was ordinarily on a good understanding with his government; in Carthage he was frequently at decided feud with his masters at home, and was forced to resist them by unconstitutional means and to make common cause with the reform party which constituted the opposition.

Both Carthage and Rome ruled over communities of lineage kindred with their own, and over numerous others of alien race. But Rome had thrown open her citizenship to one district after another, and had rendered it even legally accessible to the Latin communities; Carthage from the first maintained her exclusiveness, and did not permit the dependent districts even to cherish a hope of being some day placed upon an equal footing. Rome granted to the communities of kindred lineage a share in the fruits of victory, especially in the acquired domains; and sought, by conferring material advantages on the rich and noble, to gain over at least a party to her own interest in the other subject states. Carthage not only retained for herself the produce of her victories, but even deprived the most privileged cities of their freedom of trade. Rome did not wholly take away the independence of even the lowest grade of her subject communities, and

In the treatment of their subjects.

imposed a fixed tribute on none; Carthage despatched her
overseers everywhere, and loaded even the old Phoenician
cities with a heavy tribute, while her subject tribes were
practically treated as state-slaves. In this way there was
not in the compass of the Carthagino-African state a single
community, with the exception of Utica, that would not
have been politically and materially benefited by the fall of
Carthage; in the Romano-Italic there was not one that had
not much more to lose than to gain in rebelling against a
government, which was careful to avoid injuring material
interests, and which never at least by extreme measures challenged political opposition to conflict. If Carthaginian
statesmen believed that they had attached to the interests of
Carthage her Phoenician subjects by their greater dread of
a Libyan revolt and all the landholders by means of token-
money, they transferred mercantile calculation to a sphere
to which it did not apply. Experience proved that the
Roman symmachy, notwithstanding its seemingly looser
bond of connection, held out against Pyrrhus like a wall of
rock, whereas the Carthaginian fell to pieces like a gossamer
web as soon as a hostile army set foot on African soil. It
was so on the landing of Agathocles and of Regulus, and
likewise in the mercenary war; the spirit that prevailed in
Africa is illustrated by the fact, that the Libyan women
voluntarily contributed their ornaments to the mercenaries
for their war against Carthage. In Sicily alone the Carthaginians appear to have exercised a milder rule, and to
have attained on that account better results. They granted
to their subjects in that quarter comparative freedom in
foreign trade, and allowed them to conduct their internal
commerce, probably from the outset and exclusively, with a
metallic currency; far greater freedom of movement generally was allowed to them than was permitted to the Sardinians
and Libyans. Had Syracuse fallen into Carthaginian hands,
their policy would doubtless soon have changed. But that
result did not take place; and so, owing to the well-calcu-
lated mildness of the Carthaginian government and the unhappy distractions of the Sicilian Greeks, there actually
existed in Sicily a party really friendly to the Phoenicians;
for example, even after the island had passed to the Romans,

Philinus of Agrigentum wrote the history of the great war
in a thoroughly Phoenician spirit. Nevertheless on the
whole the Sicilians must, both as subjects and as Hellenes,
have been at least as averse to their Phoenician masters as
the Samnites and Tarentines were to the Romans.

In a financial point of view the state revenues of Carthage   In finance
doubtless far surpassed those of Rome; but this advantage
was partly neutralized by the facts, that the sources of the
Carthaginian revenue—tribute and customs—dried up far
sooner (and just when they were most needed) than those of
Rome, and that the Carthaginian mode of conducting war was
far more costly than the Roman.

The military resources of the Romans and Carthaginians   In their
were very different, yet in many respects not unequally   military
balanced. The citizens of Carthage still at the conquest   system.
of the city amounted to 700,000, including women and
children,* and were probably at least as numerous at the
close of the fifth century; in that century they were able in
case of need to set on foot a burgess army of 40,000 hoplites.
At the very beginning of the fifth century, Rome had in
similar circumstances sent to the field a burgess army equally
strong (i. 465); after the great extension of the Roman domain in the course of that century the number of full burgesses capable of bearing arms must at least have doubled.
But far more than in the number of men capable of bearing
arms, Rome excelled in the effective condition of the burgess-
soldier. Anxious as the Carthaginian government was to
induce its citizens to take part in military service, it could
neither furnish the artisan and the manufacturer with the
bodily vigour of the husbandman, nor overcome the native
aversion of the Phoenicians to warfare. In the fifth century

---

* Doubts have been expressed as to
the correctness of this number, and the
highest possible number of inhabitants,
taking into account the available space,
has been reckoned at 250,000. Apart
from the uncertainty of such calculations, especially as to a commercial city
with houses of six stories, we must re-
member that the numbering is doubtless
to be understood in a political, not in an
urban, sense, just like the numbers in
the Roman census, and that thus all
Carthaginians would be included in it,
whether dwelling in the city or its neighbourhood, or resident in its subject territory or in other lands. There would,
of course, be a large number of such
absentees in the case of Carthage; indeed it is expressly stated that in Gades,
for the same reason, the burgess-roll
always showed a far higher number than
that of the citizens who had their fixed
residence there.

there still fought in the Sicilian armies a "sacred band" of 2500 Carthaginians as a guard for the general; in the sixth not a single Carthaginian, officers excepted, was to be met with in the Carthaginian armies such as that of Spain. The Roman farmers, again, took their places not only in the muster-roll, but also in the field of battle. It was the same with the cognate dependencies of both communities; while the Latins rendered to the Romans no less service than their own burgess-troops, the Libyphoenicians were as little adapted for war as the Carthaginians, and, as may easily be supposed, still less desirous of it, and so they too disappeared from the armies; the towns bound to furnish contingents probably redeemed their obligation by a payment of money. In the Spanish army just mentioned, composed of some 15,000 men, only a single troop of cavalry of 450 men consisted, and that but partly, of Libyphoenicians. The flower of the Carthaginian armies was formed by the Libyans, whose recruits were capable of being trained under able officers into good infantry, and whose light cavalry was unsurpassed in its kind. To these were added the forces of the more or less dependent tribes of Libya and Spain and the famous slingers of the Baleares, who seem to have held an intermediate position between allied contingents and mercenary troops; and finally, in case of need, the hired soldiery raised abroad. So far as numbers were concerned, such an army might without difficulty be raised almost to any desired strength; and in the ability of its officers, in acquaintance with arms, and in courage it might be capable of coping with that of Rome. Not only, however, did a dangerously long interval elapse, in the event of mercenaries being required, ere they could be got ready, while the Roman militia was able at any moment to take the field, but—which was the main matter—there was nothing to keep together the armies of Carthage but military honour and profit, while the Romans were united by all the ties that bound them to their common fatherland. The average Carthaginian officer estimated his mercenaries, and even the Libyan farmers, very much as men in modern warfare estimate cannon-balls; hence such disgraceful proceedings as the betrayal of the Libyan troops by their general Himilco in 358, which was followed by a

396.

dangerous insurrection of the Libyans, and hence that proverbial cry of " Punic faith," which did the Carthaginians no
small injury.   Carthage experienced in full measure all the
evils which armies of fellahs and mercenaries could bring
upon a state, and more than once she found her paid serfs
more dangerous than her foes.

The Carthaginian government could not fail to perceive
the defects of this military system, and they certainly sought
to remedy them by every available means.   They insisted on
maintaining full chests and full magazines, that they might
at any time be able to equip mercenaries.   They bestowed
great care on those elements which among the ancients represented the modern artillery—the construction of machines,
in which we find the Carthaginians regularly superior to the
Siceliots, and the use of elephants, after these had superseded
in warfare the earlier war-chariots : in the casemates of Carthage there were stalls for 300 elephants.   They could not
venture to fortify the dependent cities, and were obliged to
submit to the occupation of the towns and villages as well
as of the open country by any hostile army that landed in
Africa—a thorough contrast to the state of Italy, where most
of the subject towns had retained their walls, and a chain of
Roman fortresses commanded the whole peninsula.   But on
the fortification of the capital they expended all the resources
of money and of art, and on several occasions nothing but
the strength of its walls saved the state ; whereas Rome
held a political and military position so secure that it never
underwent a formal siege.   Lastly, the main bulwark of the
state was their war-marine, on which they lavished the
utmost care.   In the building as well as in the management
of vessels the Carthaginians excelled the Greeks ; it was at
Carthage that ships were first built of more than three banks
of oars, and the Carthaginian war-vessels, at this period
mostly quinqueremes, were ordinarily better sailers than the
Greek ; the rowers, all of them public slaves, who never
stirred from the galleys, were excellently trained, and the
captains were expert and fearless.   In this respect Carthage
was decidedly superior to the Romans, who, with the few
ships of their Greek allies and still fewer of their own, were
unable even to show themselves in the open sea against the

fleet which at that time without a rival ruled the western
Mediterranean.

If, in conclusion, we sum up the results of this comparison of the resources of the two great powers, the judgment
expressed by a sagacious and impartial Greek is perhaps
borne out, that Carthage and Rome were, when the struggle
between them began, on the whole equally matched. But we
cannot omit to add that, while Carthage had put forth all the
efforts of which intellect and wealth were capable to provide
herself with artificial means of attack and defence, she was
unable in any satisfactory way to make up for the fundamental want of a land army of her own and of a symmachy
resting on a self-supporting basis. That Rome could only
be seriously attacked in Italy, and Carthage only in Libya,
no one could fail to see ; as little could anyone fail to perceive that Carthage could not in the long run escape from
such an attack. Fleets were not yet in those times of
the infancy of navigation a permanent heirloom of nations,
but could be fitted out wherever there were trees, iron,
and water. It was clear, and had been several times
tested in Africa itself, that even powerful maritime states
were not able to prevent a weaker enemy from landing.
When Agathocles had shown the way thither, a Roman
general could follow the same course; and while in Italy
the entrance of an invading army simply began the war,
the same event in Libya put an end to it by converting it
into a siege, in which, unless some special accident should
intervene, even the most obstinate and heroic courage must
finally succumb.

CHAPTER II.

THE WAR BETWEEN ROME AND CARTHAGE CONCERNING SICILY.

FOR upwards of a century the feud between the Cartha- State of ginians and the rulers of Syracuse had devastated the beau- Sicily. tiful island of Sicily. On both sides the contest was carried on with the weapons of political proselytism, for, while Carthage kept up communications with the aristocratic-republican opposition in Syracuse, the Syracusan dynasts maintained relations with the national party in the Greek cities that had become tributary to Carthage. On both sides armies of mercenaries were employed to fight their battles —by Timoleon and Agathocles, as well as by the Phoenician generals. And as like means were employed on both sides, so the conflict had been waged on both with a disregard of honour and a perfidy unexampled in the history of the west. The Syracusans were the weaker party. In the peace of 440 Carthage had still limited her claims to the third of   314. the island to the west of Heraclea Minoa and Himera, and had expressly recognized the hegemony of the Syra-cusans over all the cities to the eastward. The expulsion of Pyrrhus from Sicily and Italy (479) left by far the larger   275. half of the island, and especially the important city of Agrigentum, in the hands of Carthage; the Syracusans retained nothing but Tauromenium and the south-east of the island.

In the second great city on the east coast, Messana, a Campa-band of foreign soldiers had established themselves and held nian mer-cenaries. the city, independent alike of Syracusans and Carthaginians. These new rulers of Messana were Campanian mercenaries. The dissolute habits that had become prevalent among the Sabellians settled in and around Capua (i. 389), had made

Campania in the fourth and fifth centuries—what Aetolia, Crete, and Laconia were afterwards—the universal recruiting-field for princes and cities in search of mercenaries. The partial civilization that had been called into existence there by the Campanian Greeks, the barbaric luxury of life in Capua and the other Campanian cities, the political impotence to which the hegemony of Rome condemned them, while yet its rule was not so stern as wholly to withdraw from them the right of self-disposal—all tended to drive the youth of Campania in troops to the standards of the recruiting officers. As a matter of course, this wanton and unscrupulous selling of themselves was here as in all cases attended by estrangement from their native land, habits of military violence and lawlessness, and indifference to the breach of their allegiance. These Campanians could see no reason why a band of mercenaries should not seize on their own behalf any city entrusted to their guardianship, provided only they were in a position to hold it—the Samnites had established their dominion in Capua itself, and the Lucanians in a succession of Greek cities, after a fashion not much more honourable. Nowhere was the state of political relations more inviting for such enterprises than in Sicily. Already the Campanian captains who came to Sicily during the Peloponnesian war had insinuated themselves in this way into Entella and Aetna. Somewhere about the year 470 a Campanian band, which had previously served under Agathocles and after his death (465) took up the trade of freebooters on their own account, established themselves in Messana, the second city of Grecian Sicily, and the chief seat of the anti-Syracusan party in that portion of the island which was still in the power of the Greeks. The citizens were slain or expelled, their wives and children and houses were distributed among the soldiers, and the new masters of the city, the Mamertines or "men of Mars," as they called themselves, soon became the third power in the island, the north-eastern portion of which they reduced to subjection in the times of confusion that succeeded the death of Agathocles. The Carthaginians were no unwilling spectators of these events, which established in the immediate vicinity of the Syracusans a new and powerful adver-

Mamer-
tines.
284.
289.

sary instead of a cognate and ordinarily allied or dependent city. With Carthaginian aid the Mamertines maintained themselves against Pyrrhus, and the untimely departure of the king restored to them all their power.

It is not proper in the historian either to excuse the perfidious crime by which the Mamertines seized their power, or to forget that the God of history does not necessarily punish the sins of the fathers to the fourth generation. He who feels it his vocation to judge the sins of others may condemn the human agents; for Sicily it might be a blessing, that a warlike power, and one belonging to the island, thus began to be formed in it—a power which was already able to bring eight thousand men into the field, and which was gradually putting itself in a position to take up at the proper time and on its own resources that struggle against the foreigners, to the maintenance of which the Hellenes, becoming more and more unaccustomed to arms notwithstanding their perpetual wars, were no longer equal.

In the first instance, however, things took another turn. A young Syracusan officer, who by his descent from the family of Gelo and his intimate relations of kindred with king Pyrrhus as well as by the distinction with which he had fought in the campaigns of the latter, had attracted the notice of his fellow-citizens as well as of the Syracusan soldiery—Hiero, son of Hierocles—was called by military election to command the army, which was at variance with the citizens (479-480). By his prudent administration, the nobility of his character, and the moderation of his views, he rapidly gained the hearts of the citizens of Syracuse—who had been accustomed to the most scandalous lawlessness in their despots—and of the Sicilian Greeks in general. He rid himself—in a perfidious manner, it is true—of the insubordinate army of mercenaries, revived the citizen-militia, and endeavoured, at first with the title of general, afterwards with that of king, to re-establish the deeply sunken Hellenic power by means of his civic troops and of fresh and more manageable recruits. With the Carthaginians, who in concert with the Greeks had driven king Pyrrhus from the island, there was at that time peace. The immediate foes of

Hiero of Syracuse.

275-274.

War between the Syracusans and Mamertines.

the Syracusans were the Mamertines. They were the kinsmen of those hated mercenaries whom the Syracusans had recently extirpated; they had murdered their own Greek hosts; they had curtailed the Syracusan territory; they had oppressed and plundered a number of smaller Greek towns. In league with the Romans who just about this time were sending their legions against the Campanians in Rhegium, the allies, kinsmen, and confederates in crime of the Mamertines (i. 451), Hiero turned his arms against Messana.

270.

By a great victory, after which Hiero was proclaimed king of the Siceliots (484), he succeeded in shutting up the Mamertines within their city, and after the siege had lasted some years, they found themselves reduced to extremity and unable to hold the city longer against Hiero on their own resources. It was evident that a surrender on favourable terms was impossible, and that the axe of the executioner, which had fallen upon the Campanians of Rhegium at Rome, as certainly awaited those of Messana at Syracuse. Their only means of safety lay in delivering up the city either to the Carthaginians or to the Romans, both of whom could not but be so strongly set upon acquiring that important place as to overlook all other scruples. Whether it would be more advantageous to surrender it into the hands of the Phoenicians or into those of the masters of Italy, was doubtful; after long hesitation the majority of the Campanian burgesses at length resolved to offer the possession of their sea-commanding fortress to the Romans.

The Mamertines received into the Italian confederacy.

It was a moment of the deepest significance in the history of the world, when the envoys of the Mamertines appeared in the Roman senate. No one indeed could then anticipate all that was to depend on the crossing of that narrow arm of the sea; but that the decision, however it should go, would involve consequences far other and more important than had attached to any decree hitherto passed by the senate, must have been manifest to every one of the fathers of the city assembled in council. Strictly upright men might indeed ask how it was possible to hesitate at all, and how any one could even think of suggesting that the Romans should not only break their alliance with Hiero, but should, just

after the Campanians of Rhegium had been punished by them
with righteous severity, admit their no less guilty Sicilian
accomplices to the alliance and friendship of the state, and
thereby rescue them from the punishment which they deserved.   Such an outrage on propriety would not only afford
their adversaries matter for declamation, but must seriously
offend all men of moral feeling.   But even the statesman,
with whom political morality was no mere phrase, might ask
in reply, how Roman burgesses, who had broken their military oath and treacherously murdered the allies of Rome,
could be placed on a level with foreigners who had committed
an outrage on foreigners, where no one had constituted the
Romans judges of the one or avengers of the other?   Had
the question been only whether the Syracusans or Mamertines should rule in Messana, Rome might certainly have
acquiesced in the rule of either.   Rome was striving for the
possession of Italy, Carthage for that of Sicily; the designs
of the two powers scarcely then went further.   But that
very circumstance formed a reason why each desired to
have and retain on its frontier an intermediate power—the
Carthaginians for instance reckoning in this way on Tarentum, the Romans on Syracuse and Messana—and why, if
that course was impossible, each preferred to see these
adjacent places given over to itself rather than to its great
rival.   As Carthage had made an attempt in Italy, when
Rhegium and Tarentum were about to be occupied by the
Romans, to acquire these cities for itself, and had only been
prevented from doing so by accident, so in Sicily an opportunity now offered itself for Rome to bring the city of Messana
into its symmachy; should the Romans reject it, it was not
to be supposed that the city would remain independent or
would become Syracusan; they would themselves throw it
into the arms of the Phoenicians.   Were they justified in
allowing an opportunity to escape, such as certainly would
never recur, of making themselves masters of the natural
tête de pont between Italy and Sicily, and of securing it by
means of a brave garrison on which they could, for good
reasons, depend?   Were they justified in abandoning Messana,
and thereby surrendering the command of the last free passage between the eastern and western seas, and sacrificing

the commercial liberty of Italy? It is true that other objections might be urged to the occupation of Messana besides mere scruples of feeling and of honourable policy. That it could not but lead to a war with Carthage, was the least of these; serious as was such a war, Rome might not fear it. But there was the more important objection that by crossing the sea the Romans would depart from the purely Italian and purely continental policy which they had hitherto pursued; they would abandon the system by which their ancestors had founded the greatness of Rome, to enter upon another system the results of which no one could foretell. It was one of those moments when calculation fails, and when faith in men's own and in their country's destiny alone gives them courage to grasp the hand which beckons to them out of the darkness of the future, and to follow it they know not whither. Long and seriously the senate deliberated on the proposal of the consuls to lead the legions to the help of the Mamertines; it came to no decisive resolution. But the burgesses, to whom the matter was referred, were animated by a lively sense of the greatness of the power which their own energy had established. The conquest of Italy encouraged the Romans, as that of Greece encouraged the Macedonians and that of Silesia the Prussians, to enter upon a new political career. A formal pretext for supporting the Mamertines was found in the protectorate which Rome claimed the right to exercise over all Italians. The transmarine Italians were received into the Italian confederacy;* and on the proposal of the consuls the citizens resolved to send them aid (489).

265.

Variance between Rome and Carthage.

Much depended on the way in which the two Sicilian powers, immediately affected by this intervention of the Romans in the affairs of the island, and both hitherto nominally in alliance with Rome, would regard her interference. Hiero had sufficient reason to treat the summons, by which the Romans required him to desist from hostilities against their new confederates in Messana, precisely in the same way as the Samnites and Lucanians in similar circumstances had treated the occupation of Capua and Thurii, and to answer

---

* The Mamertines were admitted into precisely the same position towards Rome as the Italian communities, bound themselves to furnish ships (Cic. *Verr.* v. 19, 50), and, as the coins show, did not possess the privilege of coining silver.

the Romans by a declaration of war. If, however, he remained unsupported, such a war would be folly; and it might be expected from his prudent and moderate policy that he would acquiesce in what was inevitable, if Carthage should be disposed for peace. This seemed not impossible. A Roman embassy was now (489) sent to Carthage, seven years after the attempt of the Phoenician fleet to gain possession of Tarentum, to demand explanations as to that transaction (i. 451). Grievances not unfounded, but half forgotten, once more emerged — it seemed not superfluous amidst other warlike preparations to replenish the diplomatic armoury with reasons for war, and to be able to claim in the coming manifesto, as was the custom of the Romans, the character of the party aggrieved. This much at least might with entire justice be affirmed, that the respective enterprises on Tarentum and Messana stood upon exactly the same footing in point of design and of pretext, and that it was simply the accident of success that made the difference. Carthage avoided an open rupture. The ambassadors carried back to Rome a disavowal on the part of the Carthaginian admiral who had made the attempt on Tarentum, along with the requisite false oaths: the counter-complaints, which of course were not wanting on the part of Carthage, were studiously moderate, and abstained from characterizing the meditated invasion of Sicily as a ground for war. Such, however, it was; for Carthage regarded the affairs of Sicily—just as Rome regarded those of Italy—as internal matters in which an independent power could suffer no interference, and was determined to act accordingly. But Phoenician policy followed a gentler course than that of threatening open war. When the preparations of Rome for sending help to the Mamertines were at length so far advanced that the fleet formed of the war-vessels of Naples, Tarentum, Velia, and Locri, and the vanguard of the Roman land army under the military tribune Gaius Claudius, had appeared at Rhegium (in the spring of 490), unexpected news arrived from Messana that the Carthaginians, having come to an understanding with the anti-Roman party there, had as a neutral power arranged a peace between Hiero and the Mamertines; that the siege had in consequence been raised; and that a Carthaginian

265.

264.
Carthaginians in Messana.

fleet lay in the harbour of Messana, and a Carthaginian garrison in the citadel, both under the command of admiral Hanno. The Mamertine citizens, now under Carthaginian influence, informed the Roman commanders, with due thanks for the federal help so speedily accorded to them, that they were glad that they no longer needed it. The adroit and daring officer who commanded the Roman vanguard nevertheless set sail with his troops. But the Carthaginians warned the Roman vessels to retire, and even made some of them prizes; these, however, the Carthaginian admiral, remembering his strict orders to give no pretext for the outbreak of hostilities, sent back to his good friends on the other side of the straits. It almost seemed as if the Romans had compromised themselves as uselessly before Messana, as the Carthaginians before Tarentum. But Claudius did not allow himself to be deterred, and on a second attempt he succeeded in crossing. Scarcely had he landed when he called a meeting of the citizens; and, at his wish, the admiral also appeared at the meeting, still imagining that he should

Messana seized by the Romans. be able to avoid an open breach. But the Romans seized his person in the assembly itself; and Hanno and the Phoenician garrison in the citadel, weak and destitute of a leader, were pusillanimous enough, the former to give to his troops the command to withdraw, the latter to comply with the orders of their captive general and to evacuate the city

War between the Romans and the Carthaginians and Syracusans. along with him. Thus the *tête de pont* of the island fell into the hands of the Romans. The Carthaginian authorities, justly indignant at the folly and weakness of their general, caused him to be executed, and declared war against the Romans. It was of especial importance to recover the lost place. A strong Carthaginian fleet, led by Hanno, son of Hannibal, appeared off Messana; while the fleet blockaded the straits, the Carthaginian army landing from it began the siege on the north side. Hiero, who had only waited for the Carthaginian attack to begin the war with Rome, again brought up his army, which he had hardly withdrawn, against Messana, and undertook the attack on the south side of the city.

But meanwhile the Roman consul Appius Claudius Caudex had appeared at Rhegium with the main body of his

army, and succeeded in crossing on a dark night in spite
of the Carthaginian fleet. Audacity and fortune were on
the side of the Romans; the allies, not prepared for an
attack by the whole Roman army and consequently not
united, were beaten in detail by the Roman legions issuing
from the city ; and thus the siege was raised. The Roman
army kept the field during the summer, and even made an
attempt on Syracuse; but, when that had failed and the
siege of Echetla (on the confines of the territories of Syracuse and Carthage) had to be abandoned with loss, the Roman
army returned to Messana, and thence, leaving a strong
garrison behind them, to Italy. The results obtained in
this first campaign of the Romans out of Italy probably did
not quite correspond to the expectations formed at home,
for the consul had no triumph ; nevertheless, the energy
which the Romans displayed in Sicily could not fail to make
a great impression on the Sicilian Greeks. In the following
year both consuls and an army twice as large entered the
island unopposed. One of them, Marcus Valerius Maximus,
afterwards called from this campaign the " hero of Messana "
(*Messalla*), achieved a brilliant victory over the allied Carthaginians and Syracusans. After this battle the Phoenician
army no longer ventured to keep the field against the
Romans ; Alaesa, Centuripa, and the smaller Greek towns
generally joined the victors, and Hiero himself abandoned
the Carthaginian side and made peace and alliance with
Rome (491). He pursued a judicious policy in joining the
Romans as soon as it appeared that their interference in
Sicily was in earnest, and while there was still time to
purchase peace without cessions and sacrifices. The intermediate states in Sicily, Syracuse and Messana, which were
unable to follow out a policy of their own and had only the
choice between Roman and Carthaginian hegemony, necessarily preferred the former ; because the Romans had not
probably as yet formed the design of conquering the island
for themselves, but sought merely to prevent its being acquired by Carthage, and at all events Rome might be expected
to substitute a juster treatment and due protection of commercial freedom for the tyrannizing and monopolizing system
that Carthage pursued. Henceforth Hiero continued to be

Peace with
Hiero.

263.

the most important, the steadiest, and the most esteemed ally
of the Romans in the island.

Capture
of Agri-
gentum.
The Romans had thus gained their immediate object.   By
their double alliance with Messana and Syracuse, and the
firm hold which they had on the whole east coast, they
secured the means of landing on the island and of maintaining—which hitherto had been a very difficult matter—their
armies there; and the war, which had previously been doubtful
and hazardous, lost in a great measure its character of risk.
Accordingly, no greater exertions were made for it than for
the wars in Samnium and Etruria; the two legions which
262.
were despatched to the island for the next year (492) sufficed,
in concert with the Sicilian Greeks, to drive the Carthaginians everywhere into their fortresses.   The commander-
in-chief of the Carthaginians, Hannibal son of Gisgo, threw
himself with the flower of his troops into Agrigentum, to
defend to the last that most important of the Carthaginian
inland cities.   Unable to storm a city so strong, the Romans
blockaded it with entrenched lines and a double camp; the
besieged, who numbered 50,000, soon suffered from want of
provisions.   To raise the siege the Carthaginian admiral
Hanno landed at Heraclea, and cut off in turn the supplies
from the Roman besieging force.   On both sides the distress
was great.   At length a battle was resolved on, to put an end to
the state of embarrassment and uncertainty.   In this battle the
Numidian cavalry showed itself just as superior to the Roman
horse as the Roman infantry was superior to the Phoenician
foot; the infantry decided the victory, but the losses even of
the Romans were very considerable.   The result of the
successful struggle was somewhat marred by the circumstance
that, after the battle, during the confusion and fatigue of
the conquerors, the beleaguered army succeeded in escaping
from the city and in reaching the fleet.   The victory was
nevertheless of importance; Agrigentum fell into the hands
of the Romans, and thus the whole island was in their power,
with the exception of the maritime fortresses, in which the
Carthaginian general Hamilcar, Hanno's successor in command, entrenched himself to the teeth, and was not to be
driven out either by force or by famine.   The war was
thenceforth continued only by sallies of the Carthaginians

from the Sicilian fortresses and their descents on the Italian coasts.

In fact, the Romans now for the first time felt the real difficulties of the war. If, as we are told, the Carthaginian diplomatists before the outbreak of hostilities warned the Romans not to push the matter to a breach, because against their will no Roman could even wash his hands in the sea, the threat was well founded. The Carthaginian fleet ruled the sea without a rival, and not only kept the coast towns of Sicily in due obedience and provided them with all necessaries, but also threatened a descent upon Italy, for which reason it was necessary in 492 to retain a consular army there. No invasion on a large scale occurred; but smaller Carthaginian detachments landed on the Italian coasts and levied contributions on the allies of Rome, and, what was worst of all, completely paralyzed the commerce of Rome and her allies. The continuance of such a course for even a short time would suffice entirely to ruin Caere, Ostia, Neapolis, Tarentum, and Syracuse, while the Carthaginians easily consoled themselves for the loss of the tribute of Sicily with the contributions which they levied and the rich prizes of their privateering. The Romans now learned, what Dionysius, Agathocles, and Pyrrhus had learned before, that it was as difficult to conquer the Carthaginians as it was easy to beat them in the field. They saw that everything depended on procuring a fleet, and resolved to form one of twenty triremes and a hundred quinqueremes. The execution, however, of this energetic resolution was not easy. The representation originating in the schools of the rhetoricians, which would have us believe that the Romans then for the first time dipped their oars in water, is no doubt a childish tale; the mercantile marine of Italy must at this time have been very extensive, and there was no want even of Italian vessels of war. But these were war-barks and triremes, such as had been in use in earlier times; quinqueremes, which under the more modern system of naval warfare that had originated chiefly in Carthage were almost exclusively employed in the line, had not yet been built in Italy. The measure adopted by the Romans was therefore much as if a maritime state of the present day

Beginning of the maritime war.

262.

The Romans build a fleet.

were to pass at once from the building of frigates and cutters to the building of ships of the line; and, just as in such a case now a foreign ship of the line would, if possible, be adopted as a pattern, the Romans referred their master shipbuilders to a stranded Carthaginian *penteres* as a model. No doubt the Romans, had they wished, might have sooner attained their object with the aid of the Syracusans and Massiliots; but their statesmen had too much sagacity to desire to defend Italy by means of a fleet not Italian. The Italian allies, however, were largely drawn upon both for the naval officers, who must have been for the most part taken from the Italian mercantile marine, and for the sailors, whose name (*socii navales*) shows that for a time they were exclusively furnished by the allies; along with these, slaves provided by the state and the wealthier families were afterwards employed, and ere long also the poorer class of burgesses. Under such circumstances, and when we take into account, as is but fair, on the one hand the comparatively low state of shipbuilding at that time, and on the other hand the energy of the Romans, there is nothing incredible in the statement that the Romans solved within a year the problem—which baffled Napoleon—of converting a continental into a maritime power, and actually launched their fleet of 120 sail in the spring of 494. It is true, that it was by no means a match for the Carthaginian fleet in numbers and efficiency at sea; and these were points of the greater importance, as the naval tactics of the period consisted mainly in manœuvring. In the maritime warfare of that period hoplites and archers no doubt fought from the deck, and projectile machines were also plied from it; but the ordinary and really decisive mode of action consisted in running foul of the enemy's vessels, for which purpose the prows were furnished with heavy iron beaks: the vessels engaged were in the habit of sailing round each other till one or the other succeeded in giving the thrust, which usually proved decisive. Accordingly the crew of an ordinary Greek trireme, consisting of about 200 men, contained only about 10 soldiers, but on the other hand 170 rowers, from 50 to 60 on each deck; that of a quinquereme numbered about 300 rowers, and soldiers in proportion.

260.

The happy idea occurred to the Romans that they might make up for what their vessels, with their unpractised officers and crews, necessarily lacked in ability of manœuvring, by again assigning a more considerable part in naval warfare to the soldiers. They stationed at the prow of each vessel a flying bridge, which could be lowered in front or on either side; it was furnished on both sides with parapets, and had space for two men in front. When the enemy's vessel was sailing up to strike the Roman one, or was lying alongside of it after the thrust had been evaded, the bridge on deck was suddenly lowered and fastened to its opponent by means of a grappling-iron: this not only prevented the running down, but enabled the Roman marines to pass along the bridge to the enemy's deck and to carry it by assault as in a conflict on land. No distinct body of marines was formed, but land troops were employed, when required, for this maritime service. In one instance as many as 120 legionaries fought in each ship on occasion of a great naval battle; in that case however the Roman fleet had at the same time a landing-army on board.

In this way the Romans created a fleet which was a match for the Carthaginians. Those err, who represent this building of a Roman fleet as a fairy tale, and besides they miss their aim; the feat must be understood in order to be admired. The construction of a fleet by the Romans was in very truth a noble national work—a work through which, by their clear perception of what was needful and possible, by ingenuity in invention, and by energy in resolution and in execution, they rescued their country from a position which was worse than at first it seemed.

The outset, nevertheless, was not favourable to the Romans. The Roman admiral, the consul Gnaeus Cornelius Scipio, who had sailed for Messana with the first seventeen vessels ready for sea (494), fancied, when on the voyage, that he should be able to capture Lipara by a *coup de main*. But a division of the Carthaginian fleet stationed at Panormus blockaded the harbour of the island where the Roman vessels rode at anchor, and captured the whole squadron along with the consul without a struggle. This, however, did not deter the main fleet from likewise sailing, as soon as

Naval victory at Mylae.

260.

its preparations were completed, for Messana. On its voyage
along the Italian coast it fell in with a Carthaginian reconnoitring squadron of less strength, on which it had the good
fortune to inflict a loss more than counterbalancing the first
loss of the Romans ; and thus successful and victorious it
entered the port of Messana, where the second consul Gaius
Duilius took the command in room of his captured colleague.
At the promontory of Mylae, to the north-west of Messana,
the Carthaginian fleet, that advanced from Panormus under
the command of Hannibal, encountered the Roman, which here
underwent its first trial on a great scale. The Carthaginians,
seeing in the ill-sailing and awkward vessels of the Romans an
easy prey, fell upon them in irregular order ; but the newly
invented boarding-bridges proved their thorough efficiency.
The Roman vessels hooked and stormed those of the enemy
as they came up one by one ; they could not be approached
either in front or on the sides without the dangerous bridge
descending on the enemy's deck. When the battle was
over, about fifty Carthaginian vessels, almost the half of the
fleet, were sunk or captured by the Romans; among the
latter was the ship of the admiral Hannibal, formerly
belonging to king Pyrrhus. The gain was great; still
greater the moral effect of the victory. Rome had suddenly
become a naval power, and held in her hand the means of
energetically terminating a war which threatened to be
endlessly prolonged and to involve the commerce of Italy
in ruin.

The war on
the coasts
of Sicily
and
Sardinia.

Two plans were open to the Romans. They might attack
Carthage on the Italian islands and deprive her of the coast
fortresses of Sicily and Sardinia one after another—a scheme
which was perhaps practicable through well-combined operations by land and sea ; and, in the event of its being accomplished, peace might either be concluded with Carthage on the
basis of the cession of these islands, or, should such terms
not be accepted or prove unsatisfactory, the second stage
of the war might be transferred to Africa. Or they might
neglect the islands and throw themselves at once with all
their strength on Africa, not, in the adventurous style of
Agathocles, burning their vessels behind them and staking
all on the victory of a desperate band, but covering with a

strong fleet the communications between the African invading army and Italy; and in that case a peace on moderate terms might be expected from the consternation of the enemy after the first successes, or, if the Romans chose, they might by pushing matters to an extremity compel the enemy to entire surrender.

They chose, in the first instance, the former plan of operations.   In the year after the battle of Mylae (495) the consul Lucius Scipio captured the port of Aleria in Corsica —we still possess the tombstone of the general, which makes mention of this deed—and made Corsica a naval station against Sardinia.   An attempt to establish a footing in Olbia on the northern coast of that island failed, because the fleet wanted troops for landing.   In the succeeding year (496) it was repeated with better success, and the open villages along the coast were plundered; but no permanent establishment of the Romans took place.   Nor was greater progress made in Sicily.   Hamilcar conducted the war with energy and adroitness, not only by force of arms on sea and land, but also by political proselytism.   Of the numerous small country towns some every year fell away from the Romans, and had to be laboriously reclaimed from the Phoenician grasp; while in the coast fortresses the Carthaginians maintained themselves without challenge, particularly in their head-quarters of Panormus and in their new stronghold of Drepana, to which, on account of its easier defence by sea, Hamilcar had transferred the inhabitants of Eryx.   A second great naval engagement off the promontory of Tyndaris (497), in which both parties claimed the victory, made no change in the position of affairs.   In this way no progress was made, whether in consequence of the divided command and the rapid changes in the commanders of the Roman troops, which rendered the concentrated management of a series of operations on a small scale exceedingly difficult, or from the general strategical relations of the case, which certainly, as the science of war then stood, were unfavourable to the attacking party in general (i. 451), and particularly so to the Romans, who were still on the mere threshold of scientific warfare.   Meanwhile, although the pillaging of the Italian coasts had ceased, the commerce of

259.

258.

257.

Italy suffered not much less than it had done before the fleet
was built.

Attack on
Africa.

Weary of a course of operations without results, and
impatient to put an end to the war, the senate resolved to
change its system, and to assail Carthage in Africa. In the

256.

spring of 498 a fleet of 330 ships of the line set sail for the
coast of Libya: at the mouth of the river Himera on the
south coast of Sicily it embarked the army for landing,
consisting of four legions, under the charge of the two
consuls Marcus Atilius Regulus and Lucius Manlius Volso,
both experienced generals. The Carthaginian admiral
suffered the embarkation of the enemy's troops to take place;
but on continuing their voyage towards Africa the Romans
found the Punic fleet drawn up in order of battle off Ecnomus

Naval vic-
tory of
Ecnomus.

to protect its native land from invasion. Seldom have
greater numbers fought at sea than were engaged in the
battle that now ensued. The Roman fleet of 330 sail contained at least 100,000 men in its crews, besides the landing
army of about 40,000; the Carthaginian of 350 vessels was
manned by at least an equal number; so that wellnigh three
hundred thousand men were brought into action on this day
to decide the contest between the two mighty peoples. The
Phoenicians were placed in a single widely-extended line,
with their left wing resting on the Sicilian coast. The
Romans arranged themselves in a triangle, with the ships of
the two consuls as admirals at the apex, the first and second
squadrons drawn out in oblique line to the right and left, and
a third squadron, having the vessels built for the transport of
the cavalry in tow, forming the line which closed the triangle.
They thus bore down in close order on the enemy. A fourth
squadron placed in reserve followed more slowly. The wedge-
shaped attack broke without difficulty the Carthaginian line,
for its centre, which was first assailed, intentionally gave way,
and the battle resolved itself into three separate engagements.
While the admirals with the two squadrons drawn up on the
wings pursued the Carthaginian centre and were closely engaged with it, the left wing of the Carthaginians drawn up
along the coast wheeled round upon the third Roman squadron, which was prevented by the vessels which it had in tow
from following the two others, and by a vehement onset in

superior force drove it against the shore; at the same time
the Roman reserve was turned on the open sea, and assailed
from behind, by the right wing of the Carthaginians.   The
first of these three engagements was soon at an end; the
ships of the Carthaginian centre, manifestly much weaker
than the two Roman squadrons with which they were
engaged, took to flight.   Meanwhile the two other divisions
of the Romans had a severe encounter with the superior
enemy; but in close fighting the dreaded boarding-bridges
stood them in good stead, and by this means they succeeded
in maintaining their ground till the two admirals with their
vessels could come up.   By their arrival the Roman reserve
was relieved, and the Carthaginian vessels of the right wing
retired before the superior force.   And now, when this
conflict had been decided in favour of the Romans, all the
Roman vessels that still could keep the sea fell on the rear
of the Carthaginian left wing, which was obstinately
following up its advantage, so that it was surrounded and
almost all the vessels composing it were taken.   The losses
otherwise were nearly equal.   Of the Roman fleet 24 sail
were sunk; of the Carthaginian 30 were sunk, and 64 were
taken.

Notwithstanding its considerable loss, the Carthaginian
fleet did not give up the protection of Africa, and with that
view returned to the gulf of Carthage, where it expected the
descent to take place and purposed to give battle a second
time.   But the Romans landed, not on the western side of
the peninsula which helps to form the gulf, but on the
eastern side, where the bay of Clupea presented a spacious
harbour affording protection from almost all winds, and the
town, situated close by the sea on a shield-shaped eminence
rising out of the plain, supplied an excellent defence for the
harbour.   They disembarked the troops without hindrance
from the enemy, and established themselves on the hill; in
a short time an entrenched naval camp was constructed, and
the land army was at liberty to commence operations.   The
Roman troops ranged over the country and levied contributions: they were able to send as many as 20,000 slaves to
Rome.   Through the rarest good fortune the bold scheme
had succeeded at the first stroke, and with but slight sacri-

Landing of Regulus in Africa.

fices: the end seemed attained. The feeling of confidence that in this respect animated the Romans is evinced by the resolution of the senate to recall to Italy the greater portion of the fleet and half of the army; Marcus Regulus alone remained in Africa with 40 ships, 15,000 infantry, and 500 cavalry. Their confidence, however, was seemingly not over-strained. The Carthaginian army, which was disheartened, did not venture forth into the plain, but waited to sustain discomfiture in the wooded defiles, in which it could make no use of its two best arms, the cavalry and the ele-phants. The towns surrendered *en masse*; the Numidians rose in insurrection, and overran the open country far and wide. Regulus might hope to begin the next cam-paign with the siege of the capital, and with that view he pitched his camp for the winter in its immediate vicinity at Tunes.

Vain nego-
tiations for
peace.

The spirit of the Carthaginians was broken: they sued for peace. But the conditions which the consul proposed—not merely the cession of Sicily and Sardinia, but the conclusion of an alliance on unequal terms with Rome, which would have bound the Carthaginians to renounce their own war-marine and to furnish vessels for the Roman wars—condi-tions which would have placed Carthage on a level with Neapolis and Tarentum, could not be accepted, so long as a Carthaginian army kept the field and a Carthaginian fleet kept the sea, and the capital stood unshaken.

Prepara-
tions of
Carthage.

The mighty enthusiasm, which kindles into a noble flame among Oriental nations, even the most abased, on the ap-proach of extreme peril—the energy of dire necessity—im-pelled the Carthaginians to exertions, such as were by no means expected from a nation of shopkeepers. Hamilcar, who had carried on the guerilla war against the Romans in Sicily with so much success, appeared in Libya with the flower of the Sicilian troops, who furnished an admirable nucleus for the newly levied force. The connections and gold of the Carthaginians, moreover, brought to them troop after troop of excellent Numidian horse, and also numerous Greek mercenaries; amongst whom was the celebrated captain Xanthippus of Sparta, whose talent for organiza-tion and strategical skill were of great service to his new masters.*   While the Carthaginians were thus making their preparations in the course of the winter, the Roman general remained inactive at Tunes.   Whether it was that he did not anticipate the storm which was gathering over his head, or that a sense of military honour prohibited him from doing what his position demanded—instead of renouncing a siege which he was not in a condition even to attempt, and shutting himself up in the stronghold of Clupea, he remained with a handful of men before the walls of the hostile capital, neglecting even to secure his line of retreat to the naval camp, and neglecting to provide himself with — what above all he wanted, and what might have been so easily obtained through negotiation with the revolted Numidian tribes—a good light cavalry.   He thus wantonly brought himself and his army into a plight similar to that which formerly befel Agathocles in his desperate adventure.

When spring came (499), the state of affairs had so changed, that now the Carthaginians were the first to take the field and to offer battle to the Romans.   It was natural that they should do so, for everything depended on their getting quit of the army of Regulus, before reinforcements could arrive from Italy.   The same reason should have led the Romans to desire delay; but, relying on their invincibleness in the open field, they at once accepted battle notwithstanding their inferiority of strength—for, although the numbers of the infantry on both sides were nearly the same, their 4000 cavalry and 100 elephants gave to the Carthaginians a decided superiority—and notwithstanding the unfavourable nature of the ground where the Carthaginians were drawn up, a broad plain probably not far from Tunes. Xanthippus, who on this day commanded the Carthaginians, first threw his cavalry on that of the enemy, which was stationed, as usual, on the two flanks of the line of battle; the few squadrons of the Romans were scattered like dust in a

255.

Defeat of Regulus.

* The statement, that the military talent of Xanthippus was the primary means of saving Carthage, is probably coloured; the officers of Carthage can hardly have waited for foreigners to teach them that the light African cavalry could be more appropriately employed on the plain than among hills and forests. From such stories, the echo of the talk of Greek guard-rooms, even Polybius is not free.

The statement that Xanthippus was put to death by the Carthaginians after the victory, is a fiction; he departed voluntarily, perhaps to enter the Egyptian service.

moment before the masses of the enemy's horse, and the Roman infantry found itself outflanked by them and surrounded. The legions, unshaken by their apparent danger, advanced to attack the enemy's line; and, although the row of elephants placed as a protection in front of it checked the right wing and centre of the Romans, the left wing at any rate, marching past the elephants, engaged the mercenary infantry on the right of the enemy, and overthrew them completely. But this very success broke up the Roman ranks. The main body indeed, assailed by the elephants in front and by the cavalry on the flanks and in the rear, formed square, and defended itself with heroic courage, but the close masses were at length broken and swept away. The victorious left wing encountered the still fresh Carthaginian centre, where the Libyan infantry prepared a similar fate for it. From the nature of the ground and the superior numbers of the enemy's cavalry, all the combatants in these masses were cut down or taken prisoners; only two thousand men, chiefly, in all probability, the light troops and horsemen who were dispersed at the commencement, gained— while the Roman legions stood to be slaughtered—a start sufficient to enable them with difficulty to reach Clupea. Among the few prisoners was the consul himself, who afterwards died in Carthage; his family, under the idea that he had not been treated by the Carthaginians according to the usages of war, wreaked a most revolting vengeance on two noble Carthaginian captives, till even the slaves were moved to pity, and on their information the tribunes put a stop to the shameful outrage.*

Evacuation of Africa.

When the terrible news reached Rome, the first care of the Romans was naturally directed to the saving of the force shut up in Clupea. A Roman fleet of 350 sail immediately started, and after a noble victory at the Hermaean promontory, in which the Carthaginians lost 114 ships, it reached Clupea

---

* Nothing further is known with certainty as to the end of Regulus; even his mission to Rome—which is sometimes placed in 503, sometimes in 513—is very imperfectly attested. The later Romans, who sought in the fortunes and misfortunes of their forefathers mere materials for school themes, made Regulus the type of heroic misfortune as they made Fabricius the type of heroic poverty, and circulated a number of anecdotes, invented by way of due accompaniment in his name—incongruous embellishments, contrasting ill with serious and sober history.

251.   241.

just in time to deliver from their hard-pressed position the remains of the defeated army which were there entrenched. Had it been despatched before the catastrophe occurred, it might have converted the defeat into a victory that would probably have put an end to the Punic wars. But so completely had the Romans now lost their judgment, that after a successful conflict before Clupea they embarked all their troops and sailed home, voluntarily evacuating that important and easily defended position which secured to them facilities for landing in Africa, and abandoning their numerous African allies without protection to the vengeance of the Carthaginians. The Carthaginians did not neglect the opportunity of filling their empty treasury, and of making their subjects clearly understand the consequences of rebellion. An extraordinary contribution of 1000 talents of silver (£244,000) and 20,000 oxen was levied, and the sheiks in all the communities that had revolted were crucified; it is said that there were three thousand of them, and that this revolting atrocity on the part of the Carthaginian authorities really laid the foundation of the revolution which broke forth in Africa some years later. Lastly, as if to fill up the measure of misfortune to the Romans even as their measure of success had been filled before, on the homeward voyage of the fleet three-fourths of the Roman vessels perished with their crews in a violent storm; only eighty reached their port (July 499). The captains had foretold the impending mischief, but the extemporised Roman admirals had nevertheless given orders to sail.

255.

After successes so immense the Carthaginians were able to resume their offensive operations, which had long been in abeyance. Hasdrubal son of Hanno landed at Lilybaeum with a strong force, which was enabled, particularly by its enormous number of elephants—amounting to 140— to keep the field against the Romans: the last battle had shown that it was possible to make up for the want of good infantry to some extent by elephants and cavalry. The Romans also resumed the war in Sicily; the annihilation of their invading army had, as the voluntary evacuation of Clupea shows, at once restored ascendancy in the senate to the party which was opposed to the war in Africa and was content

Recommencement of the war in Sicily.

with the gradual subjugation of the islands. But for this
purpose too there was need of a fleet; and, since that which
had conquered at Mylae, at Ecnomus, and at the Hermaean
promontory was destroyed, they built a new one. Keels
were at once laid down for 220 new vessels of war—they had
never hitherto undertaken the building of so many simultaneously—and in the incredibly short space of three months

254. they were all ready for sea. In the spring of 500 the Roman
fleet, numbering 300 vessels mostly new, appeared on the
north coast of Sicily ; Panormus, the most important town in
Carthaginian Sicily, was acquired through a successful
attack from the seaboard, and the smaller places there,
Soluntum, Cephaloedium, and Tyndaris, likewise fell into
the hands of the Romans, so that along the whole north
coast of the island Thermae alone was retained by the Carthaginians. Panormus became thenceforth one of the chief
stations of the Romans in Sicily. The war by land, nevertheless, made no progress ; the two armies stood face to face
before Lilybaeum, but the Roman commanders, who knew
not how to encounter the mass of elephants, made no
attempt to compel a pitched battle.

253. In the ensuing year (501) the consuls, instead of pursuing
sure advantages in Sicily, preferred to make an expedition
to Africa, for the purpose not of landing but of plundering
the coast towns. They accomplished their object without
opposition ; but, after having first run aground in the
troublesome, and to their pilots unknown, waters of the
Lesser Syrtis, whence they with difficulty got clear again,
the fleet encountered a storm between Sicily and Italy,
which cost more than 150 ships. On this occasion also the
pilots, notwithstanding their representations and entreaties
to be allowed to take the course along the coast, were obliged
by command of the consuls to steer straight from Panormus
across the open sea to Ostia.

Suspen-
sion of the
maritime
war.
  Despondency now seized the fathers of the city ; they
resolved to reduce their war-fleet to sixty sail, and to confine
the war by sea to the defence of the coasts, and to the convoy of
transports. Fortunately, just at this time, the languishing

252. war in Sicily took a more favourable turn. In the year 502,
Thermae, the last point which the Carthaginians held on the

north coast, and the important island of Lipara, had fallen
into the hands of the Romans, and in the following year
(summer of 503) the consul Gaius Caecilius Metellus achieved   251.
a brilliant victory over the army of elephants under the walls   Roman
of Panormus.   These animals, which had been imprudently   victory at
Panormus.
brought forward, were wounded by the light troops of the
Romans stationed in the moat of the town; some of them fell
into the moat, and others fell back on their own troops, who
crowded in wild disorder along with the elephants towards
the beach, that they might be picked up by the Phoenician
ships.   One hundred and twenty elephants were captured,
and the Carthaginian army, whose strength depended on
these animals, was obliged once more to shut itself up in its
fortresses.   Eryx soon fell into the hands of the Romans
(505), and the Carthaginians retained nothing in the island   249.
but Drepana and Lilybaeum.   Carthage a second time offered peace; but the victory of Metellus and the exhaustion
of the enemy gave to the more energetic party ascendancy in
the senate.

Peace was declined, and it was resolved to prosecute in   Siege of
earnest the siege of the two Sicilian cities and for this pur-   Lilybaeum.
pose to send to sea once more a fleet of 200 sail.   The siege
of Lilybaeum, the first great and regular siege undertaken
by Rome, and one of the most obstinate known in history,
was opened by the Romans with an important success: they
succeeded in introducing their fleet into the harbour of the
city, and in blockading it on the side facing the sea.   The
besiegers, however, were not able to close the sea completely.   In spite of their sunken vessels and their pali-
sades, and in spite of the most careful vigilance, dexterous
mariners, accurately acquainted with the shallows and
channels, maintained with swift-sailing vessels a regular
communication between the besieged in the city and the
Carthaginian fleet in the harbour of Drepana.   In fact, after
a time, a Carthaginian squadron of 50 sail succeeded in
running into the harbour, in throwing a large quantity of
provisions and a reinforcement of 10,000 men into the city,
and in returning unmolested.   The besieging land army was
not much more fortunate.   They began with a regular
attack; machines were erected, and in a short time the bat-

teries had demolished six of the towers flanking the walls, so that the breach soon appeared to be practicable. But the able Carthaginian commander Himilco parried this assault by giving orders for the erection of a second wall behind the breach. An attempt of the Romans to enter into an understanding with the garrison was likewise frustrated in proper time. And, after a first sally made for the purpose of burning the Roman set of machines, had been repulsed, the Carthaginians succeeded during a stormy night in effecting their object. Upon this the Romans abandoned their preparations for an assault, and contented themselves with blockading the city by land and water. The prospect of success in this way was indeed very remote, so long as they were unable wholly to preclude the entrance of the enemy's vessels; and the army of the besiegers was in a condition not much better than that of the besieged in the city, because their supplies were frequently cut off by the numerous and bold light cavalry of the Carthaginians, and their ranks began to be thinned by the diseases indigenous to that unwholesome region. The capture of Lilybaeum, however, was of sufficient importance to induce a patient perseverance in the laborious task, which promised to be crowned in time with the desired success.

Defeat of the Roman fleet before Drepana.

But the new consul Publius Claudius considered the task of maintaining the investment of Lilybaeum too trifling : he preferred to change once more the plan of operations, and with his numerous newly manned vessels suddenly to surprise the Carthaginian fleet which was waiting in the neighbouring harbour of Drepana. With the whole blockading squadron, which had taken on board volunteers from the legions, he started about midnight, and sailing in good order with his right wing by the shore, and his left in the open sea, he safely reached the harbour of Drepana at sunrise. The Phoenician admiral Atarbas commanded there. Although surprised, he did not lose his presence of mind or allow himself to be shut up in the harbour, but as the Roman ships entered the harbour, which opens to the south in the form of a sickle, on the one side, he withdrew his vessels from it by the opposite side which was still free, and stationed them in line on the outside. No other course

remained to the Roman admiral but to recall as speedily as
possible the foremost vessels from the harbour, and to make
his arrangements for battle in like manner in front of it;
but in consequence of this retrograde movement he lost the
free choice of his position, and was obliged to accept battle in
a line, which on the one hand was outflanked by that of the
enemy to the extent of five ships—for there was not time
fully to deploy the vessels as they issued from the harbour—
and on the other hand was crowded so close on the shore
that his vessels could neither retreat, nor sail behind the
line so as to come to each other's aid. Not only was the
battle lost before it began, but the Roman fleet was so completely ensnared that it fell almost wholly into the hands
of the enemy. The consul indeed escaped, for he was the
first who fled; but 93 Roman vessels, more than three
fourths of the blockading fleet, with the flower of the Roman
legions on board, fell into the hands of the Phoenicians. It
was the first and only great naval victory which the Carthaginians gained over the Romans. Lilybaeum was practically
relieved on the side towards the sea, for though the remains
of the Roman fleet returned to their former position, they
were much too weak seriously to blockade a harbour which
had never been wholly closed, and they could only protect
themselves from the attack of the Carthaginian ships with
the assistance of the land army. That single imprudent act
of an inexperienced and criminally thoughtless officer had
thrown away all that had been with so much difficulty
attained by the long and galling warfare around the fortress;
and those war-vessels of the Romans which his presumption
had not forfeited were shortly afterwards destroyed by the
folly of his colleague. The second consul, Lucius Junius
Pullus, who had received the charge of lading at Syracuse
the supplies destined for the army at Lilybaeum, and of
convoying the transports along the south coast of the island
with a second Roman fleet of 120 war-vessels, instead of
keeping his ships together, committed the error of allowing
the first set of transports to depart unattended and of only
following with the second. When the Carthaginian vice-
admiral, Carthalo, who with a hundred select ships blockaded
the Roman fleet in the port of Lilybaeum, received the in-

Annihila-
tion of the
Roman
transport
fleet.

telligence, he proceeded to the south coast of the island, cut off the two Roman squadrons from each other by interposing between them, and compelled them to take shelter in two harbours of refuge on the inhospitable shores of Gela and Camarina. The attacks of the Carthaginians were indeed bravely repulsed by the Romans with the help of the shore batteries, which had for some time been erected there as everywhere along the coast; but, as the Romans could not hope to effect a junction and continue their voyage, Carthalo could leave the elements to finish his work. The next great storm, accordingly, completely annihilated the two Roman fleets in their wretched roadsteads, while the Phoenician admiral easily weathered it on the open sea with his light and well-managed ships. The Romans, however, succeeded in saving the greater part of the crews and cargoes (505).

249. Perplexity of the Romans. The Roman senate was in perplexity. The war had now reached its sixteenth year; and they seemed to be farther from their object in the sixteenth than in the first. In this war four large fleets had perished, three of them with Roman armies on board; a fourth select land army had been destroyed by the enemy in Libya; to say nothing of the numerous losses which had been occasioned by the minor naval engagements, and by the battles, and still more by the guerilla warfare and the diseases, of Sicily. What a multitude of human lives the war swept away may be seen from 252-247. the fact, that the burgess-roll from 502 to 507 alone decreased by about 40,000, a sixth part of the whole; and this does not include the losses of the allies, who bore the whole brunt of the war by sea, and, in addition, at least an equal proportion with the Romans of the warfare by land. Of the financial loss it is not possible to form any conception; but both the direct damage sustained in ships and *matériel*, and the indirect injury through the paralyzing of trade, must have been immense. An evil still greater than this was the exhaustion of all the methods by which they had sought to terminate the war. They had tried a landing in Africa with their forces fresh and in the full career of victory, and had totally failed. They had undertaken to storm Sicily town by town; the lesser places had fallen, but the two

mighty naval strongholds of Lilybaeum and Drepana stood more invincible than ever. What were they to do? In fact, there was to some extent reason for despondency. The fathers of the city became faint-hearted; they allowed matters simply to take their course, knowing well that a war protracted without object or end was more pernicious for Italy than the straining of the last man and the last penny, but without that courage and confidence in the nation and in fortune, which could stimulate new sacrifices in addition to those that had already been lavished in vain. They discarded the fleet; at the most they encouraged privateering, and with that view placed the war-vessels of the state at the disposal of captains who were ready to undertake a piratical warfare on their own account. The war by land was continued nominally, because they could not do otherwise; but they were content with observing the Sicilian fortresses and barely maintaining what they possessed,—measures which, in the absence of a fleet, required a very numerous army and extremely costly preparations.

Now, if ever, the time had come when Carthage was in a position to humble her mighty antagonist. She, too, of course must have felt some exhaustion of resources; but, in the circumstances, the Phoenician finances could not possibly be so disorganized as to prevent the Carthaginians from continuing the war, which cost them little beyond money, offensively and with energy. The Carthaginian government, however, was not energetic, but on the contrary weak and indolent, unless impelled to action by an easy and sure gain or by extreme necessity. Glad to be rid of the Roman fleet, they foolishly allowed their own also to fall into decay, and began after the example of the enemy to confine their operations by land and sea to the petty warfare in and around Sicily.

Thus there ensued six years of uneventful warfare (506–511), the most inglorious in the history of this century for Rome, and inglorious also for the Carthaginian people. One man, however, among the latter thought and acted differently from his nation. Hamilcar, named Barak or Barca (i. e. lightning), a young officer of great promise, was en-

248–243.
Petty war in Sicily.

Hamilcar Barca.

247.

trusted with the supreme command in Sicily in the year 507. His army, like every Carthaginian one, was defective in a trustworthy and experienced infantry; and the government, although it was perhaps in a position to create such an infantry and at any rate was bound to make the attempt, contented itself with passively looking on at its defeats or at most with nailing the defeated generals to the cross. Hamilcar resolved to take the matter into his own hands. He knew well that his mercenaries were as indifferent to Carthage as to Rome, and that he had to expect from his government not Phoenician or Libyan conscripts, but at the best a permission to save his country with his troops in his own way, provided it cost nothing. But he knew himself also, and he knew men. His mercenaries cared nothing for Carthage; but a true general is able to substitute his own person for his country in the affections of his soldiers; and such an one was this young commander. After he had habituated his men to face the legionaries in the warfare of outposts before Drepana and Lilybaeum, he established himself with his force on Mount Ercte (Monte Pellegrino near Palermo), which commands like a fortress the neighbouring country; and making them settle there with their wives and children, levied contributions from the plains, while Phoenician privateers plundered the Italian coast as far as Cumæ. He thus provided his people with copious supplies without asking money from the Carthaginians, and, keeping up the communication with Drepana by sea, he threatened to surprise the important town of Panormus in his immediate vicinity. Not only were the Romans unable to expel him from his stronghold, but after the struggle had lasted awhile at Ercte, Hamilcar formed for himself another similar position at Eryx. This mountain, which bore half way up the city of the same name and on its summit a temple of Aphrodite, had been hitherto in the hands of the Romans, who made it a basis for annoying Drepana. Hamilcar deprived them of the town and besieged the temple, while the Romans in turn blockaded him from the plain. The Celtic deserters from the Carthaginian army who were stationed by the Romans at the forlorn post of the temple—a reckless pack of marauders, who in the course of this siege plundered the temple and perpetrated every sort of outrage—defended the summit of the rock with desperate courage; but Hamilcar did not allow himself to be again dislodged from the town, and kept his communications constantly open by sea with the fleet and the garrison of Drepana. The war in Sicily seemed to be assuming a turn more and more unfavourable to the Romans. The Roman state was losing in that warfare its money and its men, and the Roman generals their honour; it was already clear that no Roman general was a match for Hamilcar, and the time might be calculated when even the Carthaginian mercenary would be able boldly to measure himself against the legionary. The privateers of Hamilcar appeared with ever-increasing audacity on the Italian coast: already a praetor had been obliged to take the field against a band of Carthaginian rovers which had landed there. A few years more, and Hamilcar might with his fleet have accomplished from Sicily what his son subsequently undertook by the land route from Spain.

The Roman senate, however, persevered in its inaction; the desponding party for once had the majority there. At length a number of sagacious and high-spirited men determined to save the state even without the interposition of the government, and to put an end to the ruinous Sicilian war. Successful corsair expeditions, if they had not raised the courage of the nation, had aroused energy and hope in a portion of the people; they had already joined together to form a squadron, burnt down Hippo on the African coast, and sustained a successful naval conflict with the Carthaginians off Panormus. By a private subscription—such as had been resorted to in Athens also, but not on so magnificent a scale—the wealthy and patriotic Romans equipped a war fleet, the nucleus of which was supplied by the ships built for privateering and the practised crews which they contained, and which altogether was far more carefully fitted out than had hitherto been the case in the shipbuilding of the state. This fact—that a number of citizens in the twenty-third year of a severe war voluntarily presented to the state two hundred ships of the line, manned by 60,000 sailors—stands perhaps unparalleled in the annals of history.

A fleet built by the Romans.

The consul Gaius Lutatius Catulus, to whom fell the
honour of conducting this fleet to the Sicilian seas, met
with almost no opposition : the two or three Carthaginian
vessels, with which Hamilcar had made his corsair expeditions, disappeared before the superior force, and almost without resistance the Romans occupied the harbours of Lilybaeum
and Drepana, the siege of which was now undertaken with
energy by water and by land. Carthage was completely
taken by surprise; even the two fortresses, weakly provisioned, were in great danger. A fleet was equipped at
home ; but with all the haste which they displayed, the year
came to an end without any appearance of Carthaginian
sails in the Sicilian waters; and when at length, in the

241.

spring of 513, the hurriedly prepared vessels appeared in the
offing of Drepana, they deserved the name of a fleet of
transports rather than that of a war fleet ready for action.

Victory of
Catulus at
the island
Aegusa.

The Phoenicians had hoped to land undisturbed, to disembark their stores, and to be able to take on board the troops
requisite for a naval battle ; but the Roman vessels intercepted them, and forced them, when about to sail from the
island of Hiera (now Maritima) for Drepana, to accept battle

241.

near the little island of Aegusa (Favignano) (10 March, 513).
The issue was not for a moment doubtful; the Roman fleet,
well built and manned, and admirably handled by the able
praetor Publius Valerius Falto (for a wound received before
Drepana still confined the consul Catulus to his bed),
defeated at the first blow the heavily laden and poorly and
inadequately manned vessels of the enemy; fifty were sunk,
and with seventy prizes the victors sailed into the port of
Lilybaeum. The last great effort of the Roman patriots
had borne fruit ; it brought victory, and with victory
peace.

Conclusion
of peace.

The Carthaginians first crucified the unfortunate admiral—
a step which did not mend the matter—and then despatched
to the Sicilian general unlimited authority to conclude a
peace. Hamilcar, who saw his heroic labours of seven years
undone by the fault of others, magnanimously submitted to
what was inevitable without on that account sacrificing either
his military honour, or his nation, or his own designs.
Sicily indeed could not be retained, seeing that the Romans

had now command of the sea; and it was not to be expected
that the Carthaginian government, which had vainly endeavoured to fill its empty treasury by a state-loan in Egypt,
would make even any further attempt to vanquish the Roman
fleet. He therefore surrendered Sicily. The independence
and integrity of the Carthaginian state and territory, on the
other hand, were expressly recognized in the usual form.
Rome bound herself not to enter into a separate alliance with
the Carthaginian, and Carthage engaged not to enter into
separate alliance with the Roman, symmachy—that is, with
their respective subject or dependent communities; neither
was to make war, or exercise rights of sovereignty, or undertake recruiting within the other's dominions.* The secondary stipulations included, of course, the gratuitous return of
the Roman prisoners of war and the payment of a war-contribution; but the demand of Catulus that Hamilcar should
deliver up his arms and the Roman deserters was resolutely
refused by Hamilcar, and with success. Catulus desisted
from his second request, and allowed the Phoenicians a free
departure from Sicily for the moderate ransom of 18 *denarii*
(11*s.* 6*d.*) per man.

If the continuance of the war appeared to the Carthaginians undesirable, they had reason to be satisfied with
these terms. It may be that the natural wish to bring to
Rome peace as well as triumph, the recollection of Regulus
and of the many vicissitudes of the war, the consideration
that such a patriotic effort as had at last decided the victory
could neither be enjoined nor repeated, perhaps even the personal character of Hamilcar, concurred in influencing the
Roman general to yield so much as he did. It is certain that there was dissatisfaction with the proposals of
peace at Rome, and the assembly of the people, doubtless
under the influence of the patriots who had effected the
equipment of the last fleet, at first refused to ratify it. We
do not know with what view this was done, and therefore we
are unable to decide whether the opponents of the proposed

---

* The statement (Zon. viii. 17) that
the Carthaginians had to promise that
they would not send vessels of war into
the territories of the Roman symmachy
—and therefore not to Syracuse, perhaps
even not to Massilia—sounds credible
enough; but the text of the treaty says
nothing of it (Polyb. iii. 27).

peace in reality rejected it merely for the purpose of exacting some further concessions from the enemy, or whether, remembering that Regulus had summoned Carthage to surrender her political independence, they were resolved to continue the war till they had gained that end—so that it was no longer a question of peace, but a question of conquest. If the refusal took place with the former view, it was probably mistaken; compared with the gain of Sicily every other concession was of little moment, and looking to the determination and the inventive genius of Hamilcar, it was very rash to stake the securing of the principal gain on the attainment of secondary objects. If on the other hand the party opposed to the peace regarded the complete political annihilation of Carthage as the only end of the struggle that would satisfy the Roman community, it showed political tact and anticipation of coming events; but whether the resources of Rome would have sufficed to renew the expedition of Regulus and to follow it up as far as might be required not merely to break the courage but to breach the walls of the mighty Phoenician city, is another question, to which no one now can venture to give either an affirmative or a negative answer.

At last the settlement of the momentous question was entrusted to a commission which was to decide it upon the spot in Sicily. It confirmed the proposal in substance; only, the sum to be paid by Carthage for the costs of the war was raised to 3,200 talents (£790,000), a third of which was to be paid down at once, and the remainder in ten annual instalments. The definitive treaty included, in addition to the surrender of Sicily, the cession also of the islands between Sicily and Italy, but this can only be regarded as an alteration of detail made on revision; for it is self-evident that Carthage, when surrendering Sicily, could hardly desire to retain the island of Lipara which had long been occupied by the Roman fleet, and the suspicion, that an ambiguous stipulation was intentionally introduced into the treaty with reference to Sardinia and Corsica, is unworthy and improbable.

Thus at length they came to terms. The unconquered general of a vanquished nation descended from the mountains which he had defended so long, and delivered to the new masters of the island the fortresses which the Phoenicians had held in their uninterrupted possession for at least four hundred years, and from whose walls all assaults of the Hellenes had recoiled unsuccessful. The west had peace (513).

241.

Remarks on the Roman conduct of the war.

Let us pause for a moment over the conflict, which extended the dominion of Rome beyond the circling sea that encloses the peninsula. It was one of the longest and most severe which the Romans ever waged ; many of the soldiers who fought in the decisive battle were unborn when the contest began. Nevertheless, despite the incomparably noble incidents which it now and again presented, we can scarcely name any war which the Romans managed so wretchedly and with such vacillation, both in a military and in a political point of view. It could hardly be otherwise. The contest occurred amidst a transition in their political system —the transition from an Italian policy, which no longer sufficed, to the policy of a great state, which was not yet matured. The Roman senate and the Roman military system were excellently organized for a purely Italian policy. The wars which such a policy provoked were purely continental wars, and always rested on the capital situated in the middle of the peninsula as the primary basis of operations, and on the chain of Roman fortresses as a secondary basis. The problems to be solved were mainly tactical, not strategical ; marches and operations occupied but a subordinate, battles held the first, place ; siege warfare was in its infancy ; the sea and naval war hardly for a moment crossed men's thoughts. We can easily understand—especially if we bear in mind that in the battles of that period, where the naked weapon predominated, it was really the hand-to-hand encounter that proved decisive—how a deliberative assembly might direct such operations, and how any one who was mayor of the city might command the troops. All this was changed in a moment. The field of battle stretched away to an incalculable distance, to the unknown regions of another continent, and beyond a broad expanse of sea ; every wave was a highway for the enemy, every harbour might send forth an invading fleet. The siege of strong places, particularly maritime fortresses, in which the first tacticians of Greece had failed, had now for the first time to be attempted by the Romans. A land army and the system of a civic militia no longer sufficed. It was necessary to create a fleet, and, what was more difficult, to employ it; it was necessary to find out the true points of attack and defence, to combine and to direct masses, to calculate expeditions extending over long periods and great distances, and to adjust their co-operation; if these things were not attended to, even an enemy far weaker in the tactics of the field might easily vanquish a stronger opponent. Is there any wonder that the reins of government in such an exigency slipped from the hands of a deliberative assembly and of commanding burgomasters?

It was plain, that at the beginning of the war the Romans did not know what they were undertaking; it was only during the course of the struggle that the inadequacies of their system, one after another, forced themselves on their notice —the want of a naval power, the lack of fixed military leadership, the incapacity of their generals, the total uselessness of their admirals. In part these evils were remedied by energy and good fortune; as was the case with the want of a fleet. That mighty creation, however, was but a grand make-shift, and always remained so. A Roman fleet was formed, but it was rendered national only in name, and was always treated with the affection of a stepmother; the naval service continued to be little esteemed in comparison with the high honour of serving in the legions; the naval officers were in great part Italian Greeks; the crews were composed of subjects or even of slaves and outcasts. The Italian farmer was at all times distrustful of the sea; one of the three things in his life which Cato regretted was, that he had travelled by sea when he might have gone by land. This result arose partly out of the nature of the case, for the vessels were oared galleys and the service of the oar can scarcely be ennobled; but the Romans might at least have formed separate legions of marines and taken steps towards the rearing of a class of Roman naval officers. Taking advantage of the impulse of the nation, they should have made it their aim gradually to establish a naval force important not only in numbers but in sailing powers and practice, and for such a purpose they had a valuable nucleus in the privateering that was developed during the long war; but nothing of the sort was done by the government. Nevertheless the Roman fleet with its unwieldy grandeur was the noblest creation of genius in this war, and, as at its beginning, so at its close it was the fleet that turned the scale in favour of Rome.

Far more difficult to be overcome were those deficiencies, which could not be remedied without an alteration of the constitution. That the senate, according to the strength of the contending parties within it, should leap from one system of conducting the war to another, and perpetrate errors so incredible as the evacuation of Clupea and the repeated discontinuance of the fleet; that the general of one year should lay siege to Sicilian towns, and his successor, instead of urging their surrender, should pillage the African coast or think proper to risk a naval battle; and that at any rate the supreme command should by law change hands every year— all these anomalies could not be reformed without stirring constitutional questions the solution of which was more difficult than the building of a fleet, but as little could their retention be reconciled with the requirements of such a war. Above all, moreover, neither the senate nor the generals could at once adapt themselves to the new mode of conducting war. The campaign of Regulus is an instance how singularly they adhered to the idea that superiority in tactics decides everything. There are few generals who have had such successes thrown as it were into their lap by fortune : in the year 498 he stood precisely where Scipio stood fifty years later, with this difference, that he had no Hannibal and no experienced army arrayed against him. But the senate withdrew half the army, as soon as they had satisfied themselves of the tactical superiority of the Romans ; in blind reliance on that superiority the general remained where he was, to be beaten in strategy, and accepted battle when it was offered to him, to be beaten also in tactics. This was the more remarkable, as Regulus was an able and experienced general of his kind. The rustic method of warfare, by which Etruria and Samnium had been won, was the very cause of the defeat in the

256.

plain of Tunes.   The principle, quite right in its own
province, that every citizen is fit for a general, was no longer
applicable ; the new system of war demanded the employment of generals who had a military training and a military
eye, and every burgomaster had not those qualities.   The
arrangement was however still worse, by which the chief
command of the fleet was treated as an appanage to the
chief command of the land army, and any one who chanced
to be president of the city thought himself able to act the
part not of general only, but of admiral too.   The worst
disasters which Rome suffered in this war were due not to
the storms and still less to the Carthaginians, but to the
presumptuous folly of its own citizen-admirals.

Rome was victorious at last.   But her acquiescence in a
gain far less than had at first been demanded and indeed
offered, as well as the energetic opposition which the peace
encountered in Rome, very clearly indicate the indecisive and
superficial character of the victory and of the peace ; and if
Rome was the victor, she was indebted for her victory in
part no doubt to the favour of the gods and to the energy of
her citizens, but still more to the errors of her enemies in
the conduct of the war—errors far surpassing even her
own.

CHAPTER III.

THE EXTENSION OF ITALY TO ITS NATURAL BOUNDARIES.

THE Italian confederacy as it emerged from the crises of the fifth century—or, in other words, the State of Italy—united the various civic and cantonal communities from the Apennines to the Ionian Sea under the hegemony of Rome. But before the close of the fifth century these limits were already overpassed in both directions, and Italian communities belonging to the confederacy had sprung up beyond the Apennines and beyond the sea. In the north the republic, in revenge for ancient and recent wrongs, had already in 471 annihilated the Celtic Senones; in the south, through the great war from 490 to 513, it had dislodged the Phoenicians from the island of Sicily. In the north there belonged to the combination headed by Rome the Latin town of Ariminum (besides the burgess-settlement of Sena), in the south the community of the Mamertines in Messana, and as both were nationally of Italian origin, so both shared in the common rights and obligations of the Italian confederacy. It was probably the pressure of events at the moment rather than any comprehensive political calculation, that gave rise to these extensions of the confederacy; but it was natural that now at least, after the great successes achieved against Carthage, new and wider views of policy should dawn upon the Roman government—views which even otherwise were obviously enough suggested by the physical features of the peninsula. Alike in a political and in a military point of view Rome was justified in shifting its northern boundary from the low and easily crossed Apennines to the mighty mountain-wall that separates northern from southern Europe, the Alps, and in combining with the sovereignty of Italy the sovereignty of the seas and islands on the west and east

Natural boundaries of Italy.

283.

264-241.

of the peninsula ; and now, when by the expulsion of the
Phoenicians from Sicily the most difficult portion of the task
had been already achieved, various circumstances united to
facilitate its completion by the Roman government.

Sicily a de-
pendency
of Italy.

In the western sea which was of far more account for
Italy than the Adriatic, the most important position, the
large and fertile island of Sicily copiously furnished with
harbours, had been by the peace with Carthage transferred
for the most part into the possession of the Romans.   King
Hiero of Syracuse indeed, who during the last twenty-two
years of the war had adhered with unshaken steadfastness
to the Roman alliance, had a fair claim to an extension of
territory ; but, if Roman policy had begun the war with the
resolution of tolerating only secondary states in the island,
the views of the Romans at its close decidedly tended towards
the seizure of Sicily for themselves.   Hiero might be content
that his territory—namely, in addition to the immediate
district of Syracuse, the domains of Elorus, Neetum, Acrae,
Leontini, Megara, and Tauromenium—and his independence
in relation to foreign powers, were (for want of any pretext
to curtail them) left to him in their former compass ; he
might well be content that the war between the two great
powers had not ended in the complete overthrow of the one
or of the other, and that there consequently still remained
at least a possibility of continuance for the intermediate
power in Sicily.   In the remaining and by far the larger
portion of Sicily, at Panormus, Lilybaeum, Agrigentum,
Messana, the Romans effected a permanent settlement.

Sardinia
Roman.

They only regretted that the possession of that beautiful
island was not enough to convert the western waters into a
Roman inland sea, so long as Sardinia still remained Carthaginian.   Soon, however, after the conclusion of the peace
there appeared an unexpected prospect of wresting from the

The Lib-
yan insur-
rection.

Carthaginians the second island of the Mediterranean.   In
Africa, immediately after peace had been concluded with
Rome, the mercenaries and the subjects of the Phoenicians
joined in a common revolt.   The blame of the dangerous
insurrection was mainly chargeable on the Carthaginian
government.   In the last years of the war Hamilcar had
not been able to pay his Sicilian mercenaries as formerly

from his own resources, and he had vainly requested that money might be sent to him from home; he might, he was told, send his forces to Africa to be paid off. He obeyed; but as he knew the men, he prudently embarked them in small subdivisions, that the authorities might pay them off by troops or might at least separate them, and he then laid down his command. But all his precautions were thwarted not so much by the emptiness of the exchequer, as by the bureaucratic mode of transacting business and the folly of the government. They waited till the whole army was once more united in Libya, and then endeavoured to curtail the pay promised to the men. Of course a mutiny broke out among the troops, and the hesitating and cowardly demeanour of the authorities showed the mutineers what they might dare. Most of them were natives of the districts ruled by, or dependent on, Carthage; they knew the feelings which had been provoked throughout these districts by the slaughter decreed by the government after the expedition of Regulus (p. 49) and by the fearful pressure of taxation, and they knew also the character of their government, which never kept faith and never pardoned; they were well aware of what awaited them, should they disperse to their homes with pay exacted by mutiny. The Carthaginians had for long been digging the mine, and they now themselves filled it with men who could not but explode it. Like wildfire the revolution spread from garrison to garrison, from village to village; the Libyan women contributed their ornaments to pay the wages of the mercenaries; a number of Carthaginian citizens, amongst whom were some of the most distinguished officers of the Sicilian army, became the victims of the infuriated multitude; Carthage was already besieged on two sides, and the Carthaginian army marching out of the city was totally routed in consequence of the blundering of its unskilful leader.

When the Romans thus saw their hated and still dreaded foe involved in a greater danger than any ever occasioned by the Roman wars, they began more and more to regret the conclusion of the peace of 513—which, if it was not in reality precipitate, now at least appeared so to all—and to forget how exhausted at that time their own state had been

241.

and how powerful had been their Carthaginian rival. Shame indeed forbade their entering into communication openly with the Carthaginian rebels; in fact, they gave an exceptional permission to the Carthaginians to levy recruits for this war in Italy, and prohibited Italian mariners from dealing with the Libyans. But it may be doubted whether the government of Rome was very earnest in these acts of friendly alliance; for, in spite of them, the dealings between the African insurgents and the Roman mariners continued, and when Hamilcar, whom the extremity of the peril had recalled to the command of the Carthaginian army, seized and imprisoned a number of Italian captains concerned in these dealings, the senate interceded for them with the Carthaginian government and procured their release. The insurgents themselves appeared to recognize in the Romans their natural allies. The garrisons in Sardinia, which like the rest of the army had declared in favour of the insurgents, offered the possession of the island to the Romans, when they saw that they were unable to hold it against the attacks

239.   of the unconquered mountaineers of the interior (about 515); and a similar offer came even from the community of Utica, which had likewise taken part in the revolt and was now hard pressed by the arms of Hamilcar. The latter offer was declined by the Romans, chiefly doubtless because its acceptance would have carried them beyond the natural boundaries of Italy and therefore farther than the Roman government was then disposed to go; on the other hand they entertained the proposals of the Sardinian mutineers, and took over from them the portion of Sardinia which had

238.   been in the hands of the Carthaginians (516). In this instance, more than in the affair of the Mamertines, the Romans were justly liable to the reproach that a great and victorious nation had not disdained to fraternize and share the spoil with a venal pack of mercenaries, and had not sufficient self-denial to prefer the course enjoined by justice and by honour to the gain of the moment. The Carthaginians, whose troubles reached their height just about the period of the occupation of Sardinia, were silent for the time being as to the unwarrantable violence; but, after their peril had been, contrary to the expectations and probably contrary to the

hopes of the Romans, averted by the genius of Hamilcar, and Carthage had been restored to her full sovereignty in Africa (517), Carthaginian envoys immediately appeared at Rome to require the restitution of Sardinia.   But the Romans, not inclined to restore their booty, replied with frivolous or at any rate irrelevant complaints as to all sorts of injuries which they alleged that the Carthaginians had inflicted on the Roman traders, and hastened to declare war; * the principle, that in politics power is the measure of right, appeared in its naked effrontery.   Just resentment urged the Carthaginians to accept that offer of war; had Catulus insisted upon the cession of Sardinia five years before, the war would probably have pursued its course.   But now, when both islands were lost, when Libya was in a ferment, and when the state was weakened to the utmost by its twenty-four years' struggle with Rome and the dreadful civil war that had raged for nearly five years more, they were obliged to submit.   It was only after repeated entreaties, and after the Phoenicians had bound themselves to pay to Rome a ransom of 1200 talents (£292,000) for the warlike preparations which had been wantonly begun, that the Romans reluctantly desisted from war.   Thus the Romans acquired Sardinia almost without a struggle; to which they added Corsica, the ancient possession of the Etruscans, where perhaps some detached Roman garrisons still remained over from the last war (p. 43).   In Sardinia, however, and still more in the rugged Corsica, the Romans restricted themselves, just as the Phoenicians had done, to an occupation of the coasts.   With the natives in the interior they were continually engaged in war or, to speak more correctly, in hunting them like wild beasts; they baited them with dogs, and carried what they captured to the slave market; but they undertook no real conquest. They had occupied the islands not on their own account, but for the security of Italy.   Now that the confederacy possessed the three large islands, it might call the Tyrrhene Sea its own.

237.

Corsica.

---

* That the cession of the islands lying between Sicily and Italy, which the peace of 513 prescribed to the Carthaginians, did not include the cession of Sardinia, is an ascertained fact (p. 60); but the statement, that the Romans made that a pretext for their occupation of the island three years after the peace, is ill attested.   Had they done so, they would merely have added diplomatic folly to political effrontery.

241.

Method of adminis-tration in the trans-marine posses-sions.

The acquisition of the islands in the western sea of Italy introduced into the state administration of Rome a distinc-tion, which to all appearance originated in mere considera-tions of convenience and almost accidentally, but nevertheless came to be of the deepest importance in the sequel—the distinction between the continental and transmarine forms of administration, or to use the appellations afterwards current, the distinction between Italy and the provinces. Hitherto the two chief magistrates of the community, the consuls, had no legally defined sphere of action; on the contrary their field of action extended as far as the Roman government itself. Of course, however, in practice they made a division of functions between them, and of course also they were bound in every particular department of their duties by the existing enactments in regard to it; the jurisdiction, for instance, over Roman citizens had in every case to be left to the praetor, and in the Latin or other autonomous commu-nities the existing treaties had to be respected. The four

267.

quaestors who had been since 487 distributed throughout Italy did not, formally at least, curtail the consular authority, for in Italy, just as in Rome, they were regarded simply as auxiliary magistrates dependent on the consuls. This mode of administration appears to have been at first extended also to the territories taken from Carthage, and Sicily and Sar-dinia were governed for some years by quaestors under the superintendence of the consuls; but the Romans must very soon have become practically convinced that it was indispen-sable to have superior magistrates specially appointed for

Provincial praetors.

the transmarine regions. As they had been obliged to abandon the concentration of the Roman jurisdiction in the person of the praetor as the community extended, and to send to the more remote districts deputy judges (i. 476), so

227.

now (527) the concentration of administrative and military power in the person of the consuls had to be abandoned. For each of the new transmarine regions—viz. Sicily, and Sardinia with Corsica annexed to it—there was appointed a special auxiliary consul, who was in rank and title inferior to the consul and equal to the praetor, but otherwise was—like the consul in earlier times before the praetorship was instituted—in his own sphere of action at once commander-in-chief, chief magistrate, and supreme judge. The direct administration of finance alone was withheld from these new chief magistrates, as from the first it had been withheld from the consuls (i. 277); one or more quaestors were assigned to them, who were in all respects dependent on them and were regarded officially as sons, as it were, in the household of their respective praetors, but had specially to manage the finances and to render account of their administration to the senate after having laid down their office.

This difference in the supreme administrative power was the only legal distinction between the continental and trans-marine possessions. The principles in other respects, on which Rome had organized her dependencies in Italy, were transferred also to the extra-Italian districts. As a matter of course, these communities without exception forfeited their independence in external relations. As to internal intercourse, no provincial could thenceforth acquire valid property in the province out of the bounds of his own community, or perhaps even conclude a valid marriage. On the other hand the Roman government tolerated, at least in Sicily, the federative organization of the cities, which was fraught with little danger, and even the general Sicilian diets with their harmless right of petition and complaint.* In monetary arrangements it was not practicable at once to declare the Roman currency to be the only valid tender in the islands; but it seems from the first to have obtained legal circulation, and in like manner, at least as a rule, the right of coining the precious metals seems to have been with-drawn from the cities in Roman Sicily.† On the other hand not only was the landed property in all Sicily left untouched

Organiza-tion of the provinces.

Commer-cium.

Property.

---

* That this was the case may be gathered partly from the appearance of the "Siculi" against Marcellus (Liv. xxvi. 26, *seq.*), partly from the "con-joint petitions of all the Sicilian com-munities" (Cicero, *Verr.* ii. 42, 102; 45, 114; 50, 146; iii. 88, 204), partly from well-known analogy (Marquardt, *Handb.* iii. 1, 267). Because there was no *commercium* between the different towns, it by no means follows that there was no *concilium*.

† The right of coining gold and silver

was not monopolised by Rome in the provinces so strictly as in Italy, evident-ly because gold and silver money not struck after the Roman standard was of less importance. But in their case too the mints were doubtless, as a rule, restricted to the coinage of copper, or at most silver, small money; even the most favourably treated communities of Roman Sicily, such as the Mamertines, the Centuripans, the Alaesines, the Se-gestans, and the Panormitans also in the main, coined only copper.

—the principle, that the land out of Italy fell by right of war to the Romans as their property, was still unknown in this century—but all the Sicilian and Sardinian communities

Autonomy. retained self-administration and some sort of autonomy. The democratic constitutions were no doubt set aside in all the communities, and in every city the power was transferred to the hands of a council representing the civic aristocracy; and the Sicilian communities, at least, were required to institute a general valuation corresponding to the Roman census every fifth year. But both these measures were only the necessary result of subordination to the Roman senate, which in reality could not govern with Greek *ecclesiae*, or without a view of the financial and military resources of each dependent community; in the various districts of Italy also the same course was in both respects pursued.

Tenths and customs. But, side by side with this essential equality of rights, there was established a distinction between the Italian communities on the one hand, and the transmarine communities on the other—a distinction indeed only *de facto*, but yet very important in its effects. The transmarine communities furnished no fixed contingent to the army or fleet of the Romans;* and they lost the right of arms, at least in so far that they could not be employed otherwise than on the summons of the Roman praetor for the defence of their own homes, and that the Roman government was at liberty to send Italian troops at its pleasure into the islands. In lieu of contingents a tenth of the field-produce of Sicily, and a tax of 5 per cent. on the value on all articles of commerce exported from or imported to the Sicilian harbours, were paid to Rome. Neither tax was in itself new. The imposts levied by the Persian great king and the Carthaginian republic were substantially of the same character with that tenth; and in Greece also such a taxation had for long been, after Oriental precedent, associated with the *tyrannis* and often also with a hegemony. The Sicilians, in particular, had long paid their tenth either to Syracuse or to Carthage, and had long levied customs-dues on account of others.

---

* This is implied in Hiero's expression (Liv. xxii. 37): that he knew that the Romans made use of none but Roman or Latin infantry and cavalry, and employed " foreigners " at most only among the light-armed troops.

"We received," says Cicero, "the Sicilian communities into our clientship and protection in such a way that they continued under the same law under which they had lived before, and obeyed the Roman community in the same manner in which they had obeyed their own rulers." It is fair that this should not be overlooked ; but to continue an injustice is to commit injustice. Viewed in relation not to the subjects, who merely changed masters, but to their new rulers, the abandonment of the equally wise and magnanimous principle of Roman statesmanship—viz., that Rome should accept from her subjects simply military aid, and never pecuniary compensation in lieu of it—was of a fatal importance, in comparison with which all alleviations in the rates and the mode of levying them, as well as all exceptions in detail, were as nothing. Such exceptions were, no doubt, made in various cases. Messana was directly admitted to the confederacy of the *togati*, and, like the Greek cities in Italy, furnished its contingent to the Roman fleet. Various other cities—Segesta and Halicyae, which were the first towns of Carthaginian Sicily that joined the Roman alliance, Centuripa, an inland town in the east of the island, which was destined to keep a watch over the Syracusan territory in its neighbourhood,* Alaesa on the northern coast, which was the first of the free Greek towns to join the Romans, and above all Panormus, hitherto the capital of Carthaginian, and now destined to become that of Roman, Sicily— while not admitted to the Italian military confederacy, yet received in addition to other favours immunity from tribute and tenths, so that their position in a financial point of view was even more favourable than that of the Italian communities. The Romans thus applied to Sicily the ancient principle of their policy, that of subdividing the dependent communities into carefully graduated classes with different privileges ; but the Sardinian and Sicilian communities on the whole occupied a position not of dependent alliance, but of recognized tributary subjection.

Communities exempted.

---

* This is shown at once by a glance at the map, and also by the remarkable exceptional provision which allowed the Centuripans to settle in any part of Sicily. They required, as Roman spies, the utmost freedom of movement. Besides, Centuripa appears to have been among the first cities that went over to Rome (Diodorus, *l.* xxiii. p. 501).

It is true that this thorough distinction between the
communities that furnished contingents and those that paid
tribute, or at least did not furnish contingents, was not in
law necessarily coincident with the distinction between Italy
and the provinces. Transmarine communities might belong
to the Italian confederacy; the Mamertines for example
were substantially on a level with the Italian Sabellians, and
there existed no legal obstacle to the establishment even of
new communities with Latin rights in Sicily and Sardinia
any more than in the country beyond the Apennines. Communities on the mainland might be deprived of the right of
bearing arms and become tributary; this arrangement was
already the case with certain Celtic districts on the Po, and
was introduced to a considerable extent in after times. But,
in reality, the communities that furnished contingents as
decidedly preponderated on the mainland as the tributary
communities in the islands; and while Italian settlements
were not contemplated on the part of the Romans either
in Sicily with its Hellenic civilization or in Sardinia, the
Roman government had beyond doubt already determined
not only to subdue the barbarian land between the Apennines
and the Alps, but also, as their conquests advanced, to establish
in it new communities of Italic origin and Italic rights. Thus
their transmarine possessions were not merely reduced to a
state of subjection, but were destined to remain subject in
all time to come; whereas the official field recently marked
off by law for the consuls, or, which is the same thing, the
continental territory of the Romans, was to become a new
and more extended Italy, which should reach from the Alps
to the Ionian sea. In the first instance, indeed, this essentially geographical conception of Italy was not altogether
coincident with the political conception of the Italian confederacy; it was partly wider, partly narrower. But even
now the Romans regarded the whole space up to the boundary of the Alps as *Italia*, that is, as the present or future
domain of the *togati*, and, just as was and still is the case in
North America, the boundary was provisionally marked off
in a geographical sense, that the field might be gradually

occupied in a political sense also with the advance of colonization.*

In the Adriatic sea, at the entrance of which the impor- Events on
the Adri-
atic coasts.
tant and long-contemplated colony of Brundisium had at
length been founded before the close of the war with Carthage (510), the supremacy of Rome was from the very first   244.
decided. In the western sea Rome had been obliged to rid
herself of rivals; in the eastern, the quarrels of the Hellenes
themselves prevented any of the states in the Grecian peninsula from acquiring or retaining power. The most considerable of them, that of Macedonia, had through the influence of Egypt been dislodged from the upper Adriatic by the
Aetolians and from the Peloponnesus by the Achaeans, and
was scarcely even in a position to defend its northern frontier against the barbarians. How desirous the Romans were
to keep down Macedonia and its natural ally, the king of
Syria, and how closely they associated themselves with the
Egyptian policy directed to that object, is shown by the
remarkable offer which after the end of the war with Carthage they made to king Ptolemy III. Euergetes, to support
him in the war which he waged with Seleucus II. Callinicus
of Syria (who reigned 507–529) on account of the murder   247–225.
of Berenice, and in which Macedonia had probably taken
part with the latter. Generally, the relations of Rome with
the Hellenistic states became closer; the senate already
negotiated even with Syria, and interceded with the Seleu-

---

* This distinction between Italy as
the Roman mainland or consular sphere
on the one hand, and the transmarine
territory or praetorial sphere on the
other, already appears variously applied
in the sixth century. The ritual rule,
that certain priests should not leave
Rome (Val. Max. i. 1, 2), was explained
to mean, that they were not allowed to
cross the sea (Liv. *Ep.* 19, xxxvii. 51.
Tac. *Ann.* iii. 58, 71; Cic. *Phil.* xi. 8, 18;
comp. Liv. xxviii. 38, 44, *Ep.* 59). The
distinction is still more definitely brought
out in the interpretation which was
210. proposed in 544 to be put upon the old
rule, that the consul could nominate the
dictator only on "Roman ground": viz.
that "Roman ground" comprehended
all Italy (Liv. xxvii. 5). The erection
of the Celtic land between the Alps and
Apennines into a special province, distinct from that of the consuls and subject to a separate chief magistrate, was
the work of Sulla. Of course no one
will consider it an objection to this view,
that already in the sixth century Gallia or
Ariminum is very often designated as
the "official district" (*provincia*) ordinarily of one of the consuls. *Provincia*,
as is well known, denoted in the older
language not what we now call *province*,
a definite space assigned as a district to
a standing chief magistrate, but simply
the department of duty prescribed for
the particular magistrate by law, decree
of the senate, or agreement; and in
that sense it was certainly allowable,
and was even for a time the rule, that
one of the consuls should undertake the
government of Northern Italy.

cus just mentioned on behalf of the Ilians with whom the Romans claimed affinity.

No direct interference of the Romans in the affairs of the eastern powers took place for the present, simply because Rome had no need for her own ends to interfere. The Achaean league, the prosperity of which was arrested by the narrow-minded coterie-policy of Aratus, the Aetolian republic of military adventurers, and the decayed Macedonian empire kept down each other's power without the necessity of Roman intervention for the purpose; and the Romans of that time avoided rather than sought transmarine acquisitions. When the Acarnanians, appealing to the ground that they alone of all the Greeks had taken no part in the destruction of Ilion, besought the descendants of Aeneas to help them against the Aetolians, the senate did indeed attempt a diplomatic mediation; but when the Aetolians returned an answer drawn up in their own saucy fashion, the antiquarian interest of the Roman senators by no means provoked them into undertaking a war by which they would have freed the Macedonians from their hereditary foe (about 515).

239.
Illyrian
piracy.

Even the evil of piracy, which was naturally in such a state of matters the only trade that flourished on the Adriatic coast, and from which the commerce of Italy suffered greatly, was submitted to by the Romans with an undue measure of patience,—a patience intimately connected with their radical aversion to maritime war and their wretched marine. But at length it became too flagrant. Favoured by Macedonia, which no longer found occasion to continue its old function of protecting Hellenic commerce from the corsairs of the Adriatic for the benefit of its foes, the rulers of Scodra had induced the Illyrian tribes—nearly corresponding to the Dalmatians, Montenegrins, and northern Albanians of the present day—to unite for joint piratical expeditions on a great scale. With whole squadrons of their swift-sailing vessels with two banks of oars, the well-known "Liburnian" cutters, the Illyrians waged war by sea and along the coasts against all and sundry. The Greek settlements in these regions, the island-towns of Issa (Lissa) and Pharos (Lesina), the important ports of Epidamnus (Durazzo) and Apollonia (to the north of Avlone on the Aous) of course suffered

especially, and were repeatedly beleaguered by the barbarians.
Farther to the south, moreover, the corsairs established
themselves in Phoenice, the most flourishing town of Epirus;
partly voluntarily, partly by constraint, the Epirots and
Acarnanians entered into an unnatural symmachy with the
foreign freebooters; the coast was insecure even as far as
Elis and Messene. In vain the Aetolians and Achaeans
collected what ships they had, with a view to check the evil:
in a battle on the open sea they were beaten by the pirates
and their Greek allies; the corsair fleet was able at length to
take possession even of the rich and important island of
Corcyra (Corfu). The complaints of Italian mariners, the
appeals for aid of their old allies the Apolloniates, and the
urgent entreaty of the besieged Issaeans at length compelled
the Roman senate to send at least ambassadors to Scodra.
The brothers Gaius and Lucius Coruncanius went thither to
demand that king Agron should put an end to the nuisance.
The king answered that according to the national law of the
Illyrians piracy was a lawful trade, and that the government
had no right to put a stop to privateering; whereupon Lucius
Coruncanius replied, that in that case Rome would make it
her business to introduce better law among the Illyrians.
For this certainly not very diplomatic reply one of the envoys
was—by the king's orders, as the Romans asserted—murdered on the way home, and the surrender of the murderers
was refused. The senate had now no choice left to it. In
the spring of 525 a fleet of 200 ships of the line, with a landing-army on board, appeared off Apollonia; the corsair-
vessels were scattered before the former, while the latter
demolished the piratic strongholds; the queen Teuta, who
after the death of her husband Agron conducted the government during the minority of her son Pinnes, besieged in her
last retreat, was obliged to accept the conditions dictated by
Rome. The rulers of Scodra were again confined both on
the north and south to the original limits of their narrow
domain, and had to quit their hold not only on all the Greek
towns, but also on the Ardiaei in Dalmatia, the Parthini
around Epidamnus, and the Atintanes in northern Epirus;
no armed Illyrian vessel, and not more than two unarmed in
company, were to be allowed in future to sail to the south of

229.
Expedition
against
Scodra.

Lissus (Alessio, between Scutari and Durazzo). The maritime supremacy of Rome in the Adriatic was asserted, in the most praiseworthy and effective way, by the rapid and energetic suppression of the evil of piracy.

Acquisition of territory in Illyria. But the Romans went further, and established themselves on the east coast. The Illyrians of Scodra were rendered tributary to Rome; Demetrius of Pharos, who had passed over from the service of Teuta to that of the Romans, was installed, as a dependent dynast and ally of Rome, over the islands and coasts of Dalmatia; the Greek cities Corcyra, Epidamnus, Apollonia, and the communities of the Atintanes and Parthini were attached to Rome under mild forms of symmachy. These acquisitions on the east coast of the Adriatic were not sufficiently extensive to require the appointment of a special auxiliary consul; governors of subordinate rank appear to have been sent to Corcyra and perhaps also to other places, and the superintendence of these possessions seems to have been entrusted to the chief magistrates who administered Italy.* Thus the most important maritime stations in the Adriatic became subject, like Sicily and Impression in Greece and Macedonia. Sardinia, to the authority of Rome. What other result was to be expected? Rome was in want of a good naval station in the upper Adriatic—a want which was not supplied by her possessions on the Italian shore; her new allies, especially the Greek commercial towns, saw in the Romans their deliverers, and doubtless did what they could permanently to secure so powerful a protection; in Greece itself no one was in a position to oppose the movement; on the contrary, the praise of the liberators was on every one's lips. It may be a question whether there was greater rejoicing or shame in

---

* A standing Roman commandant of Corcyra is apparently mentioned in Polyb. xxii. 15, 6 (erroneously translated by Liv. xxxviii. 11, comp. xlii. 37), and a similar one in the case of Issa in Liv. xliii. 9. We have, moreover, the analogy of the *praefectus pro legato insularum Baliarum* (Orelli, 732), and of the governor of Pandataria (*Corp. Inscr. Neapol.* 3528). It appears, accordingly, to have been a rule in the Roman administration to appoint non-senatorial *praefecti* for the more remote islands. But these "deputies" presuppose in the nature of the case the existence of a superior magistrate who nominates and superintends them; and this superior magistracy can only have been at this period that of the consuls. Subsequently, after the erection of Macedonia and Gallia Cisalpina into provinces, the superior administration was committed to one of these two governors; the very territory now in question, the nucleus of the subsequent Roman province of Illyricum, belonged, as is well known, in part to Caesar's district of administration.

Hellas, when, in place of the ten ships of the line of the Achaean league, the most warlike power in Greece, two hundred sail belonging to the barbarians now entered her harbours and accomplished at a blow the task, which properly belonged to the Greeks, but in which they had failed so miserably. But if the Greeks were ashamed that the salvation of their oppressed countrymen had to come from abroad, they accepted the deliverance at least with a good grace; they did not fail to receive the Romans solemnly into the fellowship of the Hellenic nation by admitting them to the Isthmian games and the Eleusinian mysteries.

Macedonia was silent; it was not in a condition to protest in arms, and disdained to do so in words. No resistance was encountered. Nevertheless Rome, by seizing the keys to her neighbour's house, had converted that neighbour into an adversary who, should he recover his power, or should a favourable opportunity occur, might be expected emphatically to break the silence. Had the energetic and prudent king Antigonus Doson lived longer, he would have doubtless taken up the gauntlet which the Romans had flung down, for, when some years afterwards the dynast Demetrius of Pharos withdrew from the hegemony of Rome, prosecuted piracy contrary to the treaty in concert with the Istrians, and subdued the Atintanes whom the Romans had declared independent, Antigonus formed an alliance with him, and the troops of Demetrius fought in the army of Antigonus at the battle of Sellasia (532). But Antigonus died (in the winter   222. 533–4); and his successor Philip, still a boy, allowed the 221. 220. consul Lucius Aemilius Paullus to attack the ally of Macedonia, to destroy his capital, and to drive him from his kingdom into exile (535).   219.

The mainland of Italy proper, south of the Apennines, Northern enjoyed profound peace after the fall of Tarentum: the six Italy. days' war with Falerii (513) was little more than an interlude.   241. But on the north, between the territory of the confederacy and the natural boundary of Italy—the chain of the Alps— there still extended a wide region not absolutely subject to the Romans. Beyond the Apennines they possessed nothing but the narrow space between the Aesis above Ancona and

the Rubico below Cesena,* nearly the modern provinces of
Forli and Urbino.   South of the Po the strong Celtic tribe of
the Boii still held its ground (from Parma to Bologna);
alongside of them, the Lingones on the east and the Anares
on the west (in the region of Parma)—two smaller Celtic
cantons that were probably clients of the Boii—peopled the
plain.   At the western end of the plain the Ligurians began, who, mingled with isolated Celtic tribes, and settled on
the Apennines westward from Arezzo and Pisa, occupied the
region of the sources of the Po.   The eastern portion of the
plain north of the Po, nearly from Verona to the coast, was
possessed by the Veneti, a race different from the Celts and
probably of Illyrian extraction.   Between these and the
western mountains were settled the Cenomani (about Brescia
and Cremona) who rarely acted with the Celtic nation and
were probably largely intermingled with Veneti, and the
Insubres (around Milan).   The latter was the most considerable of the Celtic cantons in Italy, and was in constant communication not merely with the minor communities partly of
Celtic, partly of non-Celtic extraction, that were scattered in
the Alpine valleys, but also with the Celtic cantons beyond
the Alps.   The gates of the Alps, the mighty stream navigable
for 230 miles, and the largest and most fertile plain of the
then civilized Europe, still continued in the hands of hereditary foes of the Italian name, who, humbled indeed and
weakened, but still scarce even nominally dependent and still
troublesome neighbours, persevered in their barbarism, and,
thinly scattered over the spacious plains, continued to pasture their herds and to plunder.   It was to be anticipated
that the Romans would hasten to possess themselves of these
regions; the more so as the Celts gradually began to forget

283.   282. their defeats in the campaigns of 471 and 472 and to bestir
themselves again, and, what was still more dangerous, the
Transalpine Celts began anew to show themselves on the
south of the Alps.

Celtic
wars.
238. In fact the Boii had already renewed the war in 516, and
their chiefs Atis and Galatas had—without, it is true, the

---

* According to the most careful recent investigations of the locality, the
Rubico is the Fiumicino near Savignano,
which however has now changed its
channel in the upper part of its course.

authority of the general diet—summoned the Transalpine
Gauls to make common cause with them.   The latter had
numerously answered the call, and in 518 a Celtic army,   236.
such as Italy had not seen for long, encamped before Ariminum.   The Romans, for the moment much too weak to
attempt a battle, concluded an armistice, and to gain time
allowed envoys from the Celts to proceed to Rome, who ventured in the senate to demand the cession of Ariminum—it
seemed as if the times of Brennus had returned.   But an
unexpected incident put an end to the war before it had
well begun.   The Boii, dissatisfied with their unbidden
allies and afraid probably for their own territory, fell
into variance with the Transalpine Gauls.   An open battle
took place between the two Celtic hosts ; and, after the
chiefs of the Boii had been put to death by their own men,
the Transalpine Gauls returned home.   The Boii were thus
delivered into the hands of the Romans, and the latter were
at liberty to expel them like the Senones, and to advance at
least to the Po ; but they preferred to grant the Boii peace
in return for the cession of some districts of their land
(518).   This was probably done, because they were just at   236.
that time expecting the renewed outbreak of war with
Carthage ; but, after that war had been averted by the cession
of Sardinia, true policy required the Roman government to
take possession as speedily and entirely as possible of the
country up to the Alps.   Accordingly the constant apprehensions of such a Roman invasion on the part of the Celts
were sufficiently justified.   The Romans, however, were in
no haste ; and so the Celts themselves began the war, either
because the Roman assignations of land on the east coast
(522), although not a measure immediately directed against   232.
them, made them apprehensive of danger ; or because they
perceived that a war with Rome for the possession of Lombardy was inevitable ; or, as is perhaps most probable,
because their Celtic impatience was once more weary of
inaction and preferred to arm for a new warlike expedition.
With the exception of the Cenomani, who acted with the
Veneti and declared for the Romans, all the Italian Celts
concurred in the war, and they were joined by the Celts of
the upper valley of the Rhone, or rather by a number of

adventurers belonging to them, under the leaders Concolitanus and Aneroestus.* With 50,000 warriors on foot,
and 20,000 on horseback or in chariots, the leaders of the
225. Celts advanced to the Apennines (529). The Romans had
not anticipated an attack on this side, and had not expected
that the Celts, disregarding the Roman fortresses on the
east coast and the protection of their own kinsmen, would
venture to advance directly against the capital. Not very
long before a similar Celtic swarm had in an exactly similar
way overrun Greece. The danger was serious, and appeared still more serious than it really was. The belief
that Rome's destruction was this time inevitable, and that
the Roman soil was fated to become the property of the
Gauls, was so generally diffused among the multitude in
Rome itself that the government reckoned it not beneath its
dignity to allay the absurd superstitious belief of the mob
by an act still more absurd, and to bury alive a Gaulish man
and a Gaulish woman in the Roman Forum with a view to
fulfil the sentence of destiny. At the same time they made
more serious preparations. Of the two consular armies, each
of which numbered about 25,000 infantry and 1,100 cavalry, one was stationed in Sardinia under Gaius Atilius
Regulus, the other at Ariminum under Lucius Aemilius
Papus. Both received orders to repair as speedily as possible to Etruria, the point of immediate danger. The
Celts had already been under the necessity of leaving a
garrison at home to face the Cenomani and Veneti, who
were allied with Rome; now the levy of the Umbrians was
directed to advance from their native mountains down into
the plain of the Boii, and to inflict all the injury which they
could think of on the enemy upon his own soil. The militia

---

* These, whom Polybius designates as the "Celts in the Alps and on the Rhone, who on account of their character as military adventurers are called Gaesati (free lances)," are in the Capitoline Fasti named *Germani*. It is possible that the contemporary annalists may have here mentioned Celts alone, and that it was the historical speculation of the age of Caesar and Augustus that first induced the editors of these Fasti to treat them as "Germans." If, on the other hand, the mention of the Germans in the Fasti was based on contemporary records—in which case this is the earliest mention of the name—we must regard it as denoting not the Germanic races who were afterwards so called, but a Celtic horde; and this hypothesis may be the more readily adopted, since, according to the view of the best philologists, the name *Germani* is not of Germanic but of Celtic origin, and perhaps signifies "criers."

of the Etruscans and Sabines was to occupy the Apennines, and if possible to obstruct the passage till the regular troops could arrive. A reserve was formed in Rome of 50,000 men. Throughout all Italy, which on this occasion recognized its true champion in Rome, the men capable of service were enrolled, and stores and materials of war were collected.

All this, however, required time. For once the Romans had allowed themselves to be surprised, and it was too late at least to save Etruria. The Celts found the Apennines weakly defended, and plundered unopposed the rich plains of the Tuscan territory, which for long had seen no enemy. They were already at Clusium, three days' march from Rome, when the army of Ariminum, under the consul Papus, appeared on their flank, while the Etruscan militia, which after the passage of the Apennines had assembled in rear of the Gauls, followed the line of the enemy's march. Suddenly one evening, after the two armies had already encamped and the bivouac fires were kindled, the Celtic infantry again broke up and retreated on the road towards Faesulae (Fiesole) : the cavalry occupied the advanced posts during the night, and followed the main force next morning. When the Tuscan militia, who had pitched their camp close upon the enemy, became aware of his departure, they imagined that the host had begun to disperse, and marched hastily in pursuit. The Gauls had reckoned on this very result : their infantry, which had rested and was drawn up in order, awaited on a well-chosen battle-field the Roman militia, which came up from its forced march fatigued and disordered. Six thousand men fell after a furious combat, and the rest of the militia, which had been compelled to seek refuge on a hill, would have perished, had not the consular army appeared just in time. This induced the Gauls to return homeward. Their dexterously contrived plan for preventing the union of the two Roman armies and annihilating the weaker in detail, had only partially been successful; now it seemed to them advisable first of all to place in security their considerable booty. For the sake of an easier line of march they proceeded from the district of Chiusi, where they were, to the level coast, and were marching along the shore, when they found an unexpected obstacle in the way.   It was the Sardinian legions, which had landed at Pisae ; and, when they arrived too late to obstruct the passage of the Apennines, had immediately put themselves in motion and were advancing along the coast in a direction opposite to the march of the Gauls.   Near Telamon (at the mouth of the Ombrone) they met with the enemy.   While the Roman infantry advanced with close front along the great road, the cavalry, led by the consul Gaius Atilius Regulus in person, made a side movement so as to take the Gauls in flank, and to acquaint the other Roman army under Papus as soon as possible with their arrival.   A hot cavalry engagement took place, in which along with many brave Romans Regulus fell; but he had not sacrificed his life in vain : his object was gained.   Papus became aware of the conflict, and guessed how matters stood ; he hastily arrayed his legions, and on both sides the Celtic host was now pressed by the Romans. Courageously it made its dispositions for the double conflict, the Transalpine Gauls and Insubres against the troops of Papus, the Alpine Taurisci and the Boii against the Sardinian legions ; the cavalry combat pursued its course apart on the flank.   The forces were in numbers not unequally matched, and the desperate position of the Gauls impelled them to the most obstinate resistance.   But the Transalpine Gauls, accustomed only to close fighting, gave way before the missiles of the Roman skirmishers ; in the hand-to-hand combat the better temper of the Roman weapons placed the Gauls at a disadvantage ; and at last an attack in flank by the victorious Roman cavalry decided the day.   The Celtic horsemen made their escape ; the infantry, wedged in between the sea and the three Roman armies, had no means of flight.   10,000 Celts, with their king Concolitanus, were taken prisoners ; 40,000 others lay dead on the field of battle ; Aneroestus and his attendants had, after the Celtic fashion, put themselves to death.

The victory was complete, and the Romans were firmly resolved to prevent the recurrence of such surprises by the complete subjugation of the Celts on the south of the Alps. In the following year (530) the Boii submitted without resistance along with the Lingones ; and in the year after that

(marginal notes:)

Battle of Telamon.

224.

(531) the Anares; so that the plain as far as the Po was in the hands of the Romans. The conquest of the northern side of the river cost a more serious struggle. Gaius Flaminius crossed the river in the newly-acquired territory of the Anares (somewhere near Piacenza) in 531; but during the passage, and still more while making good his footing on the other side, he suffered so heavy losses and found himself with the river in his rear in so dangerous a position, that he made a capitulation with the enemy to secure a free retreat, which the Insubres foolishly conceded. Scarce, however, had he escaped when he appeared in the territory of the Cenomani, and, united with them, advanced for the second time from the north into the canton of the Insubres. The Gauls perceived what was now the object of the Romans, when it was too late: they took from the temple of their goddess the golden standards called the "immoveable," and with their whole levy, 50,000 strong, they offered battle to the Romans. The situation of the latter was critical: they were stationed with their back to a river (perhaps the Oglio), separated from home by the enemy's territory, and left to depend for aid in battle as well as for their line of retreat on the uncertain friendship of the Cenomani. There was, however, no choice. The Gauls fighting in the Roman ranks were placed on the left bank of the stream; on the right, opposite to the Insubres, the legions were drawn up, and the bridges were broken down that they might not be assailed, at least in the rear, by their dubious allies.

In this way undoubtedly the river cut off their retreat, and their homeward route lay through the hostile army. But the superiority of the Roman arms and of Roman discipline achieved the victory, and the army cut its way through: once more the Roman tactics had redeemed the blunders of the general. The victory was due to the soldiers and officers, not to the generals, who gained a triumph only through popular favour in opposition to the just decree of the senate. Gladly would the Insubres have made peace; but Rome required unconditional subjection, and things had not yet come to that pass. They tried to maintain their ground with the help of their northern kinsmen; and, with 30,000 mercenaries whom they had raised amongst these and their

223.
The Celts attacked in their own land.

223.

own levy, they received the two consular armies advancing

222. once more in the following year (532) from the territory of
the Cenomani to invade their land. Various obstinate combats took place; in a diversion, attempted by the Insubres
against the Roman fortress of Clastidium (Casteggio, below
Pavia), on the right bank of the Po, the Gallic king Virdu-
marus fell by the hand of the consul Marcus Marcellus. But,
after a battle partially gained by the Celts but ultimately
decided in favour of the Romans, the consul Gnaeus Scipio
took by assault Mediolanum, the capital of the Insubres,
and the capture of that town and of Comum terminated
The Celts their resistance. Thus the Celts of Italy were completely
conquered
by Rome. vanquished, and as, just before, the Romans had shown to the
Hellenes in the war with the pirates the difference between a
Roman and a Greek sovereignty of the seas, so they had now
brilliantly demonstrated that Rome knew how to defend the
gates of Italy against freebooters on land very differently
from the way in which Macedonia had guarded the gates
of Greece, and that in spite of all internal quarrels Italy
presented a united front to the common enemy, while
Greece exhibited distraction and discord.

The boundary of the Alps was reached, in so far as the
whole flat country on the Po was either rendered subject to
the Romans, or, like the territories of the Cenomani and
Veneti, was occupied by dependent allies. It needed time,
however, to reap the consequences of this victory and to
Romanize the land. In this the Romans did not adopt
a uniform mode of procedure. In the mountainous north-
west of Italy and in the more remote districts between the
Alps and the Po they tolerated, on the whole, the former
inhabitants; the numerous wars, as they are called, which

238. were waged with the Ligurians in particular (first in 516)
appear to have been slave-hunts rather than wars, and, often
as the cantons and valleys submitted to the Romans, Roman
sovereignty in that quarter was ordinarily but an empty

221. name. The expedition to Istria also (533) appears not to
have aimed at much more than the destruction of the last
lurking-places of the Adriatic pirates, and the establishment of a communication by land along the coast between
the Italian conquests of Rome and her acquisitions on the

other shore. On the other hand the Celts in the districts
south of the Po were doomed irretrievably to destruction;
for, owing to the looseness of the ties connecting the Celtic
nation, none of the northern Celtic cantons took part with
their Italian kinsmen except for money, and the Romans
looked on the latter not only as their national foes, but
as the usurpers of their natural heritage. The extensive
assignations of land in 522 had already filled the whole   232.
territory between Picenum and Ariminum with Roman colonists; further measures of the same character were taken,
and it was not difficult to dislodge and extirpate a half-
barbarous population like the Celtic, but partially devoted
to agriculture, and destitute of walled towns. The great
northern highway, which had been, probably some eighty
years earlier, carried by way of Otricoli to Narni, and had
shortly before been prolonged to the newly-founded fortress
of Spoletium (514), was now (534) carried, under the name   240.   220.
of the " Flaminian " road, by way of the newly established
market-village Forum Flaminii (near Foligno), through the
pass of Furlo to the coast, and thence along the latter from
Fanum (Fano) to Ariminum; it was the first artificial road
which crossed the Apennines and connected the two Italian
seas. Great zeal was manifested in covering the newly-
acquired fertile territory with Roman townships. Already
on the Po itself the strong fortress of Placentia (Piacenza)
had been founded to cover the passage of the river; already
had Cremona been laid out on the left bank, and the building of the walls of Mutina (Modena), in the territory
acquired from the Boii on the right, had far advanced;
already preparations were being made for further assignations of land and for continuing the highway, when a sudden
event interrupted the Romans in reaping the fruit of their
successes.

CHAPTER IV.

HAMILCAR AND HANNIBAL.

241.
Situation
of Car-
thage after
the peace.
THE treaty with Rome in 513 gave to the Carthaginians peace, but they paid for it dearly. That the tribute of the largest portion of Sicily now flowed into the enemy's exchequer instead of the Carthaginian treasury, was the least part of their loss. They felt a far keener regret when they found that they had to abandon the hope of monopolizing all the lines of traffic between the eastern and the western Mediterranean, just as that hope seemed on the eve of fulfilment. They now beheld their whole system of commercial policy broken up, the south-western basin of the Mediterranean, which they had hitherto exclusively commanded, converted since the loss of Sicily into an open thoroughfare for all nations, and the commerce of Italy rendered completely independent of the Phoenicians. Nevertheless the peaceful Sidonians might perhaps have been induced to acquiesce in this result. They had met with similar blows already; they had been obliged to share with the Massiliots, the Etruscans, and the Sicilian Greeks what they had previously possessed alone; even now the possessions which they retained, Africa, Spain, and the gates of the Atlantic Ocean, were sufficient to confer power and prosperity. But in truth, where was their security that these at least would continue in their hands?

The demands made by Regulus, and his very near approach to the obtaining of what he asked, could only be forgotten by those who were willing to forget; and if Rome should now renew from Lilybaeum the enterprise which she had undertaken with so great success from Italy, Carthage would undoubtedly fall, unless the perversity of the enemy or some special piece of good fortune should intervene to save it. No doubt they had peace for the present; but the ratification of that peace had hung on a thread, and they knew what public opinion in Rome thought of the terms on which it was concluded. It might be that Rome was not yet meditating the conquest of Africa and was content with Italy; but if the existence of the Carthaginian state depended on that contentment, the prospect was but a sorry one; and where was the security that the Romans might not find it even convenient for their Italian policy to extirpate rather than reduce to subjection their African neighbour?

In short, Carthage could only regard the peace of 513 in the light of a truce, and could not but employ it in preparations for the inevitable renewal of the war; not for the purpose of avenging the defeat which she had suffered, nor even with the direct view of recovering what she had lost, but in order to secure for herself an existence that should not be dependent on the good-will of the enemy. But when a war of annihilation is surely, though in point of time indefinitely, impending over a weaker state, the wiser, more resolute, and more devoted men—who would immediately prepare for the unavoidable struggle, accept it at a favourable moment, and thus cover their defensive policy by offensive tactics—always find themselves hampered by the indolent and cowardly mass of the money-worshippers, of the aged and feeble, and of the thoughtless who wish merely to gain time, to live and die in peace, and to postpone at any price the final struggle. So there was in Carthage a party for peace and a party for war, both, as was natural, associating themselves with the political distinction which already existed between the conservatives and the reformers. The former found its support in the governing boards, the council of the Ancients and that of the Hundred, led by Hanno the Great, as he was called; the latter found its support in the leaders of the multitude, particularly the much-respected Hasdrubal, and in the officers of the Sicilian army, whose great successes under the leadership of Hamilcar, although they had been otherwise fruitless, had at least shown to the patriots a method which appeared to promise deliverance from the great danger that beset them. Vehement feud had probably long subsisted between these parties, when the

War party and [241. peace party in Carthage.

Libyan war intervened to suspend the strife. We have already related how that war arose. After the governing party had instigated the mutiny by their incapable administration which frustrated all the precautionary measures of the Sicilian officers, had converted that mutiny into a revolution by the operation of their inhuman system of government, and had at length brought the country to the verge of ruin by their military incapacity—and particularly that of their leader Hanno, the destroyer of their army—Hamilcar Barca, the hero of Ercte, was in the perilous emergency solicited by the government itself to save it from the effects of its blunders and crimes. He accepted the command, and had the magnanimity not to resign it even when they appointed Hanno as his colleague. Indeed, when the indignant army sent the latter home, Hamilcar had the self-control a second time to concede to him, at the urgent request of the government, a share in the command; and, in spite of his enemies and in spite of such a colleague, he was able by his influence with the insurgents, by his dexterous treatment of the Numidian sheiks, and by his unrivalled genius for organization and generalship, in a singularly short time to put down the revolt entirely and to recall rebellious Africa to its allegiance (end of 517).

237.

During this war the patriot party had kept silence; now it spoke out the louder. On the one hand this catastrophe had brought to light the utterly corrupt and pernicious character of the ruling oligarchy, their incapacity, their coterie-policy, their leanings towards the Romans. On the other hand the seizure of Sardinia, and the threatening attitude which Rome on that occasion assumed, showed plainly even to the humblest that a declaration of war by Rome was constantly hanging like the sword of Damocles over Carthage, and that, if Carthage in her present circumstances went to war with Rome, the consequence must necessarily be the downfall of the Phoenician dominion in Libya. Probably there were in Carthage not a few who, despairing of the future of their country, counselled emigration to the islands of the Atlantic; who could blame them? But minds of the nobler order disdain to save themselves apart from their nation, and great natures enjoy the privilege of deriving enthusiasm from circumstances in which the multitude of good men despair. They accepted the new conditions just as Rome dictated them; no course was left but to submit and, adding fresh bitterness to their former hatred, carefully to cherish and husband resentment—that last resource of an injured nation. They then took steps towards a political reform.* They had become sufficiently convinced of the incorrigibleness of the party in power: the fact that the governing lords had even in the last war neither forgotten their spite nor learned greater wisdom, was shown by the effrontery bordering on simplicity with which they now instituted proceedings against Hamilcar as the originator of the mercenary war, because he had without authority from the government promised money to his Sicilian soldiers. Had the club of officers and popular leaders desired to overthrow this rotten and wretched government, it would hardly have encountered much difficulty in Carthage itself; but it would have met with a more formidable obstacle in Rome, with which the chiefs of the government in Carthage already maintained relations that bordered on treason. To all the other difficulties of the position there fell to be added the circumstance, that the means of saving their country had to be created without allowing the Romans, or their own government with its Roman tendencies, to become rightly aware of what was doing.

So they left the constitution untouched, and the chiefs of the government in full enjoyment of their exclusive privileges and of the public property. It was merely proposed and carried, that of the two commanders-in-chief, who at the end of the Libyan war were at the head of the Carthaginian troops, Hanno and Hamilcar, the former should be recalled, and the latter should be nominated commander-in-chief for all Africa during an indefinite period. It was arranged that he should hold a position independent of the governing

Hamilcar commander-in-chief.

---

* Our accounts as to these events are not only imperfect but one sided, for of course it was the version of the Carthaginian peace party which was adopted by the Roman annalists. Even, however, in our mutilated and distorted accounts (the most important are those of Fabius, in Polyb. iii. 8; Appian. *Hisp.* 4; and Diodorus, xxv. p. 567) the relations of the parties appear clearly enough. Of the vulgar gossip by which its opponents sought to blacken the "revolutionary combination" (ἑταιρεία τῶν πονηροτάτων ἀνθρώπων) specimens may be had in Nepos (*Ham.* 3), to which it will be difficult perhaps to find a parallel.

corporations—his antagonists called it an unconstitutional monarchical power, Cato calls it a dictatorship—and that he could only be recalled and placed upon his trial by the popular assembly.* Even the choice of a successor was to be vested not in the authorities of the capital, but in the army, that is, in the Carthaginians serving in the army as Gerusiasts or officers, who were named in treaties also along with the general. Of course the right of confirmation was reserved to the popular assembly. Whether this may or may not have been a usurpation, it clearly indicates that the war party regarded and treated the army as its special domain.

The duties of Hamilcar were modest in form. Wars with the Numidian tribes on the borders never ceased; only a short time previously the " city of a hundred gates," Theveste (Tebessa), in the interior had been occupied by the Carthaginians. The task of continuing this border warfare, which was allotted to the new commander-in-chief of Africa, was not in itself of such importance as to prevent the Carthaginian government, which was allowed to do as it liked in its own immediate sphere, from tacitly conniving at the decrees passed in reference to the matter by the popular assembly; and the Romans did not perhaps recognize its significance at all.

Hamilcar's war projects. Thus there was placed at the head of the army the very man, who had given proof in the Sicilian and in the Libyan wars that fate had destined him, if any one, to be the saviour of his country. Never perhaps was the noble struggle of man with fate waged more nobly than by him. The army was intended to save the state; but what sort of army? The Carthaginian civic militia had fought not badly under Hamilcar's leadership in the Libyan war; but he knew well, that it is one thing to lead out the merchants and manufacturers of a city which is in the extremity of peril for once to battle, and another to form them into soldiers. The patriot party in Carthage furnished him with excellent

The army.

---

* The Barcine family conclude the most important state treaties, and the ratification of the governing board is a formality (Pol. iii. 21). Rome enters her protest before them and before the Senate (Pol. iii. 15). The position of that family towards Carthage in many points resembles that of the Princes of Orange towards the States-General.

officers, but it was of course almost exclusively the cultivated class that was represented in it. He had no citizen-
militia, at most a few squadrons of Libyphoenician cavalry.
The task was to form an army out of Libyan conscripts and
mercenaries; a task possible in the hands of a general like
Hamilcar, but possible even for him only on condition that
he should be able to pay his men punctually and well. But
he had learned, by experience in Sicily, that the state
revenues of Carthage were expended in Carthage itself on
matters much more urgent than the payment of the armies
that fought against the enemy. The warfare which he
waged, accordingly, had to support itself, and he had to carry
out on a great scale, what he had already attempted on a
smaller scale at Monte Pellegrino. But further, Hamilcar
was not only a miliiary chief, he was also a party leader. In
opposition to the implacable governing party, which eagerly
but patiently waited for an opportunity of overthrowing him,
he had to seek support among the citizens; and although
their leaders might be ever so pure and noble, the multitude
was deeply corrupt and accustomed by the unhappy system
of corruption to give nothing without being paid for it. In
particular emergencies, indeed, necessity or enthusiasm might
for the moment prevail, as everywhere happens even with the
most venal corporations; but, if Hamilcar wished to secure the
permanent support of the Carthaginian community for his
plan, which at the best could only be executed after a series
of years, he had to supply his friends at home with regular
consignments of money as the means of keeping the mob in
good humour. Thus compelled to beg or to buy from the
lukewarm and venal multitude permission to save it; compelled to wring from the arrogance of men whom he hated
and whom he had constantly conquered, at the price of humiliation and of silence, the respite indispensable for his
ends; compelled to conceal from those despised traitors to
their country, who called themselves the lords of his native
city, his plans and his contempt—the noble hero stood
with few friends of congenial sentiments between enemies
without and enemies within, building upon the irresolution
of the one and of the other, at once deceiving both and
defying both, if only he might gain means, money, and men

The citi-
zens.

for the contest with a land which, even were the army ready to strike the blow, it seemed difficult to reach and scarce possible to vanquish. He was still a young man, little beyond thirty, but he had apparently, when he was preparing for his expedition, a foreboding that he would not be permitted to attain the end of his labours, or to see otherwise than afar off the promised land. When he left Carthage he enjoined his son Hannibal, nine years of age, to swear at the altar of the supreme God eternal hatred to the Roman name, and reared him and his younger sons Hasdrubal and Mago—the "lion's brood," as he called them—in the camp as the inheritors of his projects, of his genius, and of his hatred.

Hamilcar proceeds to Spain.

236.

The new commander-in-chief of Libya departed from Carthage immediately after the termination of the mercenary war (perhaps in the spring of 518). He apparently meditated an expedition against the free Libyans in the west. His army, which was especially strong in elephants, marched along the coast; by its side sailed the fleet, led by his faithful associate Hasdrubal. Suddenly tidings came that he had crossed the sea at the Pillars of Hercules and had landed in Spain, where he was waging war with the natives—with people who had done him no harm, and without orders from his government, as the Carthaginian authorities complained. They could not complain at any rate that he neglected the affairs of Africa; when the Numidians once more rebelled, his lieutenant Hasdrubal so effectually routed them that for a long period there was tranquillity on the frontier, and several tribes hitherto independent submitted to pay tribute.

Spanish kingdom of the Barcides.

What he personally did in Spain, we are no longer able to trace in detail. His achievements compelled Cato the elder, who, a generation after Hamilcar's death, beheld in Spain the still fresh traces of his working, to exclaim, notwithstanding all his hatred of the Carthaginians, that no king was worthy to be named by the side of Hamilcar Barca. Their results still show to us, at least in a general way, what was accomplished by Hamilcar as a soldier and a statesman in the last nine years of his life

236–228.

(518–526), till in the flower of his age, fighting bravely in the field of battle, he met his death like Scharnhorst just as

his plans were beginning to reach maturity.   During the
next eight years (527-534) the heir of his office and of his   227-220.
plans, his son-in-law Hasdrubal, prosecuted in the spirit of
his master the work which Hamilcar had begun.   Instead
of the small entrepôt for trade, which, along with the protectorate of Gades, was all that Carthage had hitherto possessed on the Spanish coast, and which she had treated as
a dependency of Libya, a Carthaginian kingdom was
founded in Spain by the generalship of Hamilcar, and confirmed by the adroit statesmanship of Hasdrubal.   The
fairest regions of Spain, the southern and eastern coasts,
became Phoenician provinces.   Towns were founded; above
all, " Spanish Carthage " (Cartagena) was established by
Hasdrubal on the only good harbour along the south coast,
containing the splendid " royal castle " of its founder.
Agriculture flourished, and still more mining in consequence
of the fortunate discovery of the silver-mines of Cartagena,
which a century afterwards had a yearly produce of more
than £360,000 (36,000,000 sesterces).   Most of the communities as far as the Ebro became dependent on Carthage
and paid tribute to it.   Hasdrubal skilfully by every means,
even by intermarriage, attached the chiefs to the interests
of Carthage.   Thus Carthage acquired in Spain a rich
market for its commerce and manufactures; and not
only did the revenues of the province sustain the army, but
there remained a balance to be remitted to Carthage and
reserved for future use.   The province at the same time
formed and trained the army; regular levies took place in
the territory subject to Carthage; the prisoners of war were
incorporated with Carthaginian corps.   Contingents and
mercenaries, as many as were desired, were supplied by the
dependent communities.   During his long life of warfare
the soldier found in the camp a second home, and found a
substitute for patriotism in fidelity to his standard and enthusiastic attachment to his great leaders.   Constant conflicts with the brave Iberians and Celts created a serviceable
infantry, to co-operate with the excellent Numidian cavalry.

So far as Carthage was concerned, the Barcides were   The Car-
allowed to go on.   The citizens were not asked for regular   thaginian
                                                                govern-

ment and
the Bar-
cides.

contributions, but on the contrary derived benefit from the acquisition; commerce recovered in Spain what it had lost in Sicily and Sardinia; and the Spanish war and the Spanish army with its brilliant victories and important successes soon became so popular that it was even possible in particular emergencies, such as after Hamilcar's fall, to effect the despatch of considerable reinforcements of African troops to Spain, and the governing party, whether well or ill affected, had to maintain silence, or at any rate to content themselves with complaining to each other or to their friends in Rome regarding the demagogic officers and the mob.

The Ro-
man go-
vernment
and the
Barcides.

On the part of Rome too nothing took place calculated seriously to affect the course of Spanish affairs. The first and chief cause of the inactivity of the Romans was undoubtedly their very want of acquaintance with the circumstances of the remote peninsula—which was certainly also Hamilcar's main reason for selecting Spain and not, as might otherwise have been possible, Africa for the execution of his plan. The explanations with which the Carthaginian generals met the Roman commissioners sent to Spain to procure information on the spot, and their assurances that all this was done only to provide the means of promptly paying the war-contributions to Rome, could not possibly find belief in the senate. But they probably discerned only the immediate object of Hamilcar's plans, viz. to procure compensation in Spain for the tribute and the traffic of the islands which Carthage had lost; and they deemed an aggressive war on the part of the Carthaginians, and in particular an invasion of Italy from Spain—as is evident (both from express statements to that effect and from the whole state of the case—absolute impossibilities. Many, of course, among the peace party in Carthage saw further; but, whatever they might think, they could hardly be much inclined to enlighten their Roman friends as to the impending storm, which the Carthaginian authorities had long been unable to prevent, or that step would accelerate, instead of averting, the crisis; and even if they did so, such denunciations proceeding from partisans would justly be received with great caution

at Rome.   By degrees, certainly, the inconceivably rapid and
mighty extension of the Carthaginian power in Spain could
not but excite the observation and awaken the apprehensions
of the Romans.   In fact, in the course of the later years
before the outbreak of war, they did attempt to set bounds
to it.   About the year 528, mindful of their newborn Hel-   226.
lenism, they concluded an alliance with the two Greek
or semi-Greek towns on the east coast of Spain, Zacynthus or Saguntum (Murviedro, not far from Valencia), and
Emporiae (Ampurias); and when they acquainted the Carthaginian general Hasdrubal that they had done so, they at
the same time warned him not to push his conquests over
the Ebro, with which he promised compliance.   This was
not done to prevent an invasion of Italy by the land route—
no treaty would fetter the general who should undertake
such an enterprise—but partly to set a limit to the material
power of the Spanish Carthaginians which began to be
dangerous, partly to secure, in the free communities between
the Ebro and the Pyrenees whom Rome thus took under
her protection, a basis of operations in case of its being necessary to land and make war in Spain.   In reference to the
impending war with Carthage, which the senate did not fail to
see was inevitable, they hardly apprehended any greater in-
convenience from the events that had occurred in Spain than
that they might be compelled to send some legions thither,
and that the enemy would be somewhat better provided
with money and soldiers than, without Spain, he would have
been; they were at any rate firmly resolved, as the plan
of the campaign of 536 shows and as indeed could not but   218
be the case, to begin and terminate the next war in Africa,
—a course which would at the same time decide the fate of
Spain.   Further grounds for delay were suggested during
the first years by the instalments from Carthage, which a
declaration of war would have cut off, and then by the death
of Hamilcar, which probably induced friends and foes to
think that his projects must have died with him.   Lastly,
during the latter years when the senate certainly began to
apprehend that it was not prudent to delay the renewal of
the war, there was the very intelligible wish to dispose
of the Gauls in the valley of the Po in the first instance,

for these, threatened with extirpation, might be expected to
avail themselves of any serious war undertaken by Rome
to allure the Transalpine tribes once more to Italy, and
to renew those Celtic migrations which were still fraught
with very great peril. That it was not regard either for the
Carthaginian peace party or for existing treaties which withheld the Romans from action, is self-evident; moreover, if they
desired war, the Spanish feuds furnished at any moment a
ready pretext. The conduct of Rome in this view is by no
means unintelligible; but as little can it be denied that the
Roman senate in dealing with this matter displayed shortsightedness and slackness—faults which were still more inexcu-
sably manifested in their mode of dealing at the same epoch
with Gallic affairs. The policy of the Romans was always
more remarkable for tenacity, cunning, and consistency, than
for grandeur of conception or power of rapid organization—
qualities in which the enemies of Rome from Pyrrhus down
to Mithradates often surpassed her.

Hannibal.   Thus the smiles of fortune inaugurated the brilliantly
conceived project of Hamilcar. The means of war were
acquired—a numerous army accustomed to combat and to
conquer, and a constantly replenished exchequer; but in
order that the right moment might be discovered for the
struggle and that the right direction might be given to it
there was wanted a leader. The man, whose head and heart
had in a desperate emergency and amidst a despairing people
paved the way for their deliverance, was no more, when it
became possible to carry out his design. Whether his successor Hasdrubal forbore to make the attack because the
proper moment seemed to him to have not yet arrived, or
whether, a statesman rather than a general, he believed
himself unequal to the conduct of the enterprise, we are
220.   unable to determine. When, at the beginning of 534, he
fell by the hand of an assassin, the Carthaginian officers of
the Spanish army summoned to fill his place Hannibal, the
eldest son of Hamilcar. He was still a young man—born
249.   in 505, and now, therefore, in his twenty-ninth year; but
his life had already been fraught with varied experience. His
first recollections pictured to him his father fighting in a
distant land and conquering on Ercte; he shared that uncon-

quered father's fortunes, and sympathized with his feelings,
on the peace of Catulus, on the bitter return home, and
throughout the horrors of the Libyan war. While yet a
boy, he had followed his father to the camp; and he soon
distinguished himself. His light and firmly built frame
made him an excellent runner and fencer, and a fearless
rider; the privation of sleep did not affect him, and he knew
like a soldier how to enjoy or to want his food. Although
his youth had been spent in the camp, he possessed
such culture as belonged to the Phoenicians of rank in his
day; in Greek, apparently after he had become a general, he
made such progress under the guidance of his intimate friend
Sosilus of Sparta as to be able to compose state papers
in that language. As he grew up, he entered the army of
his father, to perform his first feats of arms under the paternal
eye and to see him fall in battle by his side. Thereafter he
had commanded the cavalry under his sister's husband, Hasdrubal, and distinguished himself by brilliant personal bravery
as well as by his talents as a leader. The voice of his
comrades now summoned him—the tried, although youthful
general—to the chief command, and he could now execute
the designs for which his father and his brother-in-law had
lived and died. He took possession of the inheritance, and
he was worthy of it. His contemporaries tried to cast stains
of various sorts on his character; the Romans charged him
with cruelty, the Carthaginians with covetousness; and it is
true that he hated as only Oriental natures know how to
hate, and that a general who never fell short of money and
stores can hardly have been other than covetous. But though
anger and envy and meanness have written his history, they
have not availed to mar the pure and noble image which it
presents. Laying aside wretched inventions which furnish
their own refutation, and some things which his lieutenants,
particularly Hannibal Monomachus and Mago the Samnite, were guilty of doing in his name, nothing occurs in
the accounts regarding him which may not be justified in the
circumstances, and according to the international law, of the
times; and all agree in this, that he combined in rare per-
fection discretion and enthusiasm, caution and energy. He
was peculiarly marked by that inventive craftiness, which

forms one of the leading traits of the Phoenician character; he was fond of taking singular and unexpected routes; ambushes and stratagems of all sorts were familiar to him; and he studied the character of his antagonists with unprecedented care. By an unrivalled system of espionage— he had regular spies even in Rome—he kept himself informed of the projects of the enemy; he himself was frequently seen wearing disguises and false hair, in order to procure information on some point or other. Every page of the history of the period attests his genius as a general; and his gifts as a statesman were, after the peace with Rome, no less conspicuously displayed in his reform of the Carthaginian constitution, and in the unparalleled influence which as a foreign exile he exercised in the cabinets of the Eastern powers. The power which he wielded over men is shown by his incomparable control over an army of various nations and many tongues—an army which never in the worst times mutinied against him. He was a great man; wherever he went, he riveted the eyes of all.

Rupture between Rome and Carthage. [220.

Hannibal resolved immediately after his nomination (in the spring of 534) to commence the war. The land of the Celts was still in a ferment, and war seemed imminent between Rome and Macedonia: he had good reason now to throw off the mask without delay and to carry the war whithersoever he pleased, before the Romans began it at their own convenience with a descent on Africa. His army was soon ready to take the field, and his exchequer was tolerably filled by means of some razzias; but the Carthaginian government showed itself far from desirous of issuing a declaration of war against Rome. The place of Hasdrubal, the patriotic national leader, was even more difficult to fill in Carthage than that of Hasdrubal the general in Spain; the peace party had now the ascendancy at home, and persecuted the leaders of the war party with political indictments. The rulers who had already cut down and mutilated the plans of Hamilcar were by no means inclined to allow the unknown young man, who now commanded in Spain, to exercise his youthful patriotism at the expense of the state; and Hannibal hesitated personally to declare war in open opposition to the legitimate authorities. He tried to provoke

the Saguntines to break the peace; but they contented
themselves with complaining to Rome.   When the Romans
on receiving their complaint nominated a commission, he
tried to drive it to a declaration of war by treating it rudely;
but the commissioners saw how matters stood: they kept
silence in Spain, with a view to lodge complaints at Carthage,
and with a view to send home the news that Hannibal was
ready to strike and that war was imminent.   Thus the time
passed away; accounts had already come of the death of
Antigonus Doson, who had suddenly died nearly at the
same time with Hasdrubal; in Cisalpine Gaul the establishment of fortresses was carried on by the Romans with re-
doubled rapidity and energy; preparations were made in
Rome for putting a speedy conclusion to the insurrection
in Illyria in the course of the next spring.   Every day was
precious; Hannibal formed his resolution.   He sent summary intimation to Carthage that the Saguntines were making
aggressions on the Torboletes, subjects of Carthage, and he
must therefore attack them; and without waiting for a reply
he began in the spring of 535 the siege of a town which was   219.
in alliance with Rome, or in other words, war against Rome.
We may form some idea of the views and counsels that
would prevail in Carthage from the impression produced in
certain circles by York's capitulation.   All "respectable
men," it was said, disapproved an attack made "without
orders;" there was talk of disavowal, of surrendering the
daring officer.   But whether it was that dread of the army
and of the multitude nearer home outweighed in the Carthaginian council the fear of Rome; or that they perceived the
impossibility of retracing such a step, now that it was taken;
or that mere inertness prevented any definite action, they
determined at length to do nothing, and to suffer the war to go
on, although not prepared to sanction it.   Saguntum defended itself, as only Spanish towns can conduct their defence: had the Romans showed but a tithe of the energy
of their clients, and not trifled away their time during the
eight months' siege of Saguntum in the paltry warfare with
Illyrian brigands, they might, masters as they were of the sea
and of places suitable for landing, have spared themselves the
disgrace of failing to grant the protection which they had

promised, and might perhaps have given a different turn to the war. But they delayed, and the town was at length taken by storm. When Hannibal sent the spoil for distribution to Carthage, patriotism and zeal for war were roused in the hearts of many who had hitherto felt nothing of the kind, and the distribution cut off all prospect of coming to terms with Rome. Accordingly, when after the destruction of Saguntum a Roman embassy appeared at Carthage and demanded the surrender of the general and of the Gerusiasts present in the camp, and when the Roman spokesman, interrupting an attempt at justification, broke off the discussion and, gathering up his robe, declared that he held in it peace and war and that the Gerusia might choose between them, the gerusiasts mustered courage to reply that they left it to the choice of the Roman; and when he offered war, they accepted it (in the spring of 536).

218.

Preparations for attacking Italy.
219–218.

Hannibal, who had lost a whole year through the obstinate resistance of the Saguntines, had as usual retired for the winter of 535-6 to Cartagena, to make all his preparations on the one hand for the attack of Italy, on the other for the defence of Spain and Africa ; for, as he, like his father and his brother-in-law, held the supreme command in both countries, it devolved upon him to take measures also for the protection of his native land. The whole mass of his forces amounted to about 120,000 infantry and 16,000 cavalry ; he had also 58 elephants, 32 quinqueremes manned, and 18 not manned, besides the elephants and vessels remaining at the capital. Excepting a few Ligurians among the light troops, there were no mercenaries in this Carthaginian army ; the troops, with the exception of some Phoenician squadrons, consisted mainly of the Carthaginian subjects called out for service—Libyans and Spaniards. To insure the fidelity of the latter the general, who knew the men with whom he had to deal, gave them as a proof of his confidence a general leave of absence for the whole winter ; while, not sharing the narrow-minded exclusiveness of Phoenician patriotism, he promised to the Libyans on his oath the citizenship of Carthage, should they return to Africa victorious. This mass of troops however was only destined in part for the expedition to Italy. Nearly 20,000 men were sent to Africa, the smaller portion of them proceeding to the

capital and the Phoenician territory proper, the majority to
the western point of Africa. For the protection of Spain
12,000 infantry, 2500 cavalry, and nearly the half of the
elephants were left behind, in addition to the fleet stationed
there; the chief command and the government of Spain
were entrusted to Hannibal's younger brother Hasdrubal.
The immediate territory of Carthage was comparatively
weakly garrisoned, because the capital afforded in case of
need sufficient resources; in like manner a moderate number of infantry sufficed for the present in Spain, where new
levies could be procured with ease, whereas a comparatively
large proportion of the arms specially African—horses and
elephants—was retained there. Great care was taken to
secure the communications between Spain and Africa : with
that view the fleet remained in Spain, and western Africa
was guarded by a very strong body of troops. The fidelity
of the troops was secured not only by hostages collected
from the Spanish communities and detained in the stronghold of Saguntum, but by the removal of the soldiers from
the districts where they were raised to other quarters :
the East African militia were moved chiefly to Spain, the
Spanish to Western Africa, the West African to Carthage.
Adequate provision was thus made for defence. As to offensive
measures, a squadron of 20 quinqueremes with 1000 soldiers
on board was to sail from Carthage for the west coast of
Italy and to pillage it, and a second of 25 sail was, if possible,
to re-establish itself at Lilybaeum ; Hannibal believed that
he might count upon the government making this moderate
amount of exertion. With the main army he determined
in person to invade Italy ; as was beyond doubt part of
the original plan of Hamilcar. A decisive attack on Rome
was only possible in Italy, as a similar attack on Carthage
was only possible in Libya ; as certainly as Rome meant to
begin her next campaign with the latter, so certainly ought
Carthage not to confine herself at the outset to any secondary
object of operations, such as Sicily, or to mere defence—
defeat would in any case involve equal destruction, but victory
would not yield equal fruit.

But how could Italy be attacked ? He might succeed Method of
in reaching the peninsula by sea or by land ; but if the pro- attack.
ject was to be no mere desperate adventure, but a military

expedition with a strategic aim, a nearer basis for its operations was requisite than Spain or Africa. Hannibal could
not rely for support on a fleet and a fortified harbour, for
Rome was now mistress [of the sea. As little did the
territory of the Italian confederacy present any tenable
basis. If in very different times, and in spite of Hellenic
sympathies, it had withstood the shock of Pyrrhus, it was
not to be expected that it would now fall to pieces on the appearance of the Phoenician general; an invading army would
without doubt be crushed between the network of Roman
fortresses and the firmly consolidated confederacy. The land
of the Ligurians and Celts alone could be to Hannibal, what
Poland was to Napoleon in his very similar Russian campaigns. These tribes still smarting under their scarcely
ended struggle for independence, alien in race from the
Italians, and feeling their very existence endangered by the
chain of Roman fortresses and highways whose first coils were
even now being fastened around them, could not but recognize their deliverers in the Phoenician army (which numbered
in its ranks numerous Spanish Celts), and would serve as
a support for it to fall back upon—a source whence it might
draw supplies and recruits. Already formal treaties were concluded with the Boii and the Insubres, by which they bound
themselves to send guides to meet the Carthaginian army,
to procure for it a good reception from the cognate tribes
and supplies along its route, and to rise against the Romans as soon as it should set foot on Italian ground. In
fine, the state of Roman relations with the East led the Carthaginians to this same quarter. Macedonia, which by the
victory of Sellasia had re-established its sovereignty in the
Peloponnesus, was at variance with Rome; Demetrius of
Pharos, who had exchanged the Roman alliance for that of
Macedon and had been dispossessed by the Romans, lived as
an exile at the Macedonian court, and the latter had refused
the demand which the Romans made for his surrender. If it
was possible to combine the armies from the Guadalquivir and
the Karasu anywhere against the common foe, it could only
be done on the Po. Thus everything directed Hannibal to
northern Italy; and that the eyes of his father had already
been turned to that quarter, is shown by the reconnoitring

party of Carthaginians, whom the Romans to their great
surprise encountered in Liguria in 524.

The reason for Hannibal's preference of the land route to
that by sea is less obvious; for that neither the maritime
supremacy of the Romans nor their league with Massilia
could have prevented a landing at Genoa, is evident, and was
shown by the sequel. Our authorities fail to furnish us
with several of the elements, on which a satisfactory answer to
this question would depend, and which cannot be supplied
by conjecture. Hannibal had to choose between two evils.
Instead of exposing himself to the unknown and unforeseen
contingencies of a sea voyage and of naval war, it must have
seemed to him the better course to accept the assurances,
which beyond doubt were seriously meant, of the Boii and
Insubres, and the more so that, even if the army should land
at Genoa, it would still have mountains to cross; he could
hardly know exactly, how much smaller are the difficulties
presented by the Apennines at Genoa than by the main
chain of the Alps. At any rate the route which he took
was the primitive Celtic route, by which many much larger
hordes had crossed the Alps: the ally and deliverer of the
Celtic nation might without temerity venture to traverse it.

So Hannibal collected the troops, destined for the grand
army, in Cartagena at the beginning of the favourable season;
there were 90,000 infantry and 12,000 cavalry, of whom
about two-thirds were Africans and a third Spaniards. The
37 elephants which they took with them were probably
destined rather to make an impression on the Gauls than
for serious warfare. Hannibal's infantry no longer needed,
like that led by Xanthippus, to shelter itself behind a screen
of elephants, and the general had too much sagacity to employ otherwise than sparingly and with caution that two-
edged weapon, which had as often occasioned the defeat of
its own as of the enemy's army. With this force the
general set out in the spring of 536 from Cartagena towards the Ebro. He so far informed his soldiers as to the
measures which he had taken, particularly as to the connections he had entered into with the Celts and the resources
and object of the expedition, that even the common soldier,
whose military instincts lengthened war had developed, felt

Marginal notes:

230.

Departure
of Hanni-
bal.

218.

the clear perception and the steady hand of his leader, and followed him with implicit confidence to the unknown and distant land; and the animated address, in which he laid before them the position of their country and the demands of the Romans, the slavery certainly reserved for their dear native land, and the disgrace of the imputation that they could surrender their beloved general and his staff, kindled a soldierly and patriotic ardour in the hearts of all.

Position of Rome.

The Roman state was in a plight, such as easily occurs even in firmly-established and sagacious aristocracies. The Romans knew doubtless what they wished to accomplish, and they took various steps; but nothing was done rightly or at the right time. They might long ago have been masters of the gates of the Alps and have crushed the Celts; the latter were still formidable, and the former were open. They might either have had friendship with Carthage, had

241.

they honourably kept the peace of 513, or, had they not been disposed for peace, they might long ago have conquered Carthage: the peace was practically broken by the seizure of Sardinia, and they allowed the power of Carthage to recover itself undisturbed for twenty years. There was no great difficulty in maintaining peace with Macedonia; but they had forfeited her friendship for a trifling gain. There must have been a lack of some leading statesman to take a comprehensive view of the position of affairs; on all hands either too little was done, or too much. Now the war began at a time and at a place which they had allowed the enemy

Their uncertain plans for the war

to determine; and, with all their well-founded conviction of military superiority, they were perplexed as to the object to be aimed at and the course to be followed in their first operations. They had at their disposal more than half a million of serviceable soldiers; the Roman cavalry alone was less good, and relatively less numerous, than the Carthaginian, the former constituting about a tenth, the latter an eighth, of the whole number of troops taking the field. None of the states affected by the war had any fleet corresponding to the Roman fleet of 220 quinqueremes, which had just returned from the Adriatic to the western sea. The natural and proper application of this crushing superiority of force was self-evident. It had been long settled

that the war ought to be opened with a landing in Africa.
The subsequent turn taken by events had compelled the
Romans to embrace in their scheme of the war a simultaneous landing in Spain, chiefly to prevent the Spanish army
from appearing before the walls of Carthage.   In accordance
with this plan they ought above all, when the war had
been practically opened by Hannibal's attack on Saguntum in the beginning of 535, to have thrown a Roman army   219.
into Spain before the town fell; but they neglected the
dictates of interest no less than of honour.   For eight
months Saguntum held out in vain: when the town passed
into other hands, Rome had not even equipped her arma-
ment for landing in Spain.   The country, however, between
the Ebro and the Pyrenees was still free, and its tribes were
not only the natural allies of the Romans, but had also, like
the Saguntines, received from Roman emissaries promises of
speedy assistance.   Catalonia may be reached by sea from
Italy in not much longer time than from Cartagena by land:
had the Romans started, like the Phoenicians, in April, after
the formal declaration of war that had taken place in the
interval, Hannibal might have encountered the Roman
legions on the line of the Ebro.

At length, certainly, the greater part of the army and of   Hannibal
the fleet was got ready for the expedition to Africa, and   on the
the second consul Publius Cornelius Scipio was ordered to   Ebro.
the Ebro; but he proceeded leisurely, and when an insurrection broke out on the Po, he allowed the army that was
ready for embarkation to be employed there, and formed new
legions for the Spanish expedition.   So although Hannibal
encountered on the Ebro very vehement resistance, it proceeded only from the natives; and, as under existing circumstances time was still more precious to him than the blood
of his men, he surmounted the opposition after some months
with the loss of a fourth part of his army, and reached the
line of the Pyrenees.   That the Spanish allies of Rome
would be sacrificed a second time by that delay might have
been as certainly foreseen, as the delay itself might have been
easily avoided; but probably even the expedition to Italy
itself, which in the spring of 536 must not have been anti-   218.
cipated in Rome, would have been averted by the timely

appearance of the Romans in Spain. Hannibal had by no means the intention of sacrificing his Spanish " kingdom," and throwing himself like a desperado on Italy. The time which he had spent in the siege of Saguntum and in the reduction of Catalonia, and the considerable corps which he left behind for the occupation of the newly-won territory between the Ebro and the Pyrenees, sufficiently show that, had a Roman army disputed the possession of Spain with him, he would not have been content to withdraw from it; and—which was the main point—had the Romans been able to delay his departure from Spain for but a few weeks, winter would have closed the passes of the Alps before Hannibal reached them, and the African expedition would have departed without hindrance for its destination.

Hannibal in Gaul.   Arrived at the Pyrenees, Hannibal sent home a portion of his troops; a measure which he had resolved on from the first with the view of showing to the soldiers how confident their general was of success, and of counteracting the presentiment that his enterprise was one of those from which there is no return. With an army of 50,000 infantry and 9000 cavalry, entirely veteran soldiers, he crossed the Pyrenees without difficulty, and then took the coast route by Narbonne and Nimes through the Celtic territory, which was opened to the army partly by the connections previously formed, partly by Carthaginian gold, partly by arms. It was not till it arrived in the end of July at the Rhone opposite Avignon, that a serious resistance appeared to await it. The

Scipio at Massilia.   consul Scipio, who on his voyage to Spain had landed at Massilia (about the end of June), had there been informed that he had come too late and that Hannibal had crossed not only the Ebro but the Pyrenees. On receiving these accounts, which appear to have first opened the eyes of the Romans to the course and the object of Hannibal, the consul had temporarily abandoned his expedition to Spain, and had resolved in connection with the Celtic tribes of that region, who were under the influence of the Massiliots and thereby under that *Passage of the Rhone.*   of Rome, to receive the Phoenicians on the Rhone, and to obstruct their passage of the river and their march into Italy. Fortunately for Hannibal, opposite to the point at which he meant to cross, there lay at the moment only the general levy of the Celts, while the consul himself with his army of 22,000 infantry and 2000 horse was still in Massilia, four days' march farther down the stream. The messengers of the Gallic levy hastened to inform him. It was the object of Hannibal to convey his army with its numerous cavalry and elephants across the rapid stream under the eyes of the enemy, and before the arrival of Scipio; and he possessed not a single boat. He immediately gave directions that all the boats belonging to the numerous navigators of the Rhone in the neighbourhood should be bought up at any price, and that the deficiency of boats should be supplied by rafts made from felled trees, so that all the numerous army could be conveyed over in one day. While this was done, a strong division under Hanno, son of Bomilcar, proceeded by forced marches up the stream till they reached a suitable point for crossing, which they found undefended, situated two short days' march above Avignon. Here they crossed the river on hastily constructed rafts, with the view of then moving down on the left bank and taking the Gauls, who were impeding the passage of the main army, in the rear. On the morning of the fifth day after they had reached the Rhone, and of the third after Hanno's departure, the preconcerted smoke-signals, which Hannibal was anxiously expecting from the division that had been detached, arose on the opposite bank. Just as the Gauls, seeing that the enemy's fleet of boats began to move, were hastening to occupy the bank, their camp behind them suddenly burst into flames. Surprised and divided, they were unable either to withstand the attack or to resist the passage, and they dispersed in hasty flight.

Scipio meanwhile held councils of war in Massilia as to the proper mode of occupying the ferries of the Rhone, and was not induced to move even by the urgent messages that came from the leaders of the Celts. He distrusted their accounts, and he contented himself with detaching a weak Roman cavalry division to reconnoitre on the left bank of the Rhone. This detachment found the whole enemy's army already transported to that bank, and occupied in bringing over the elephants which alone remained on the right bank of the stream; and, after it had warmly engaged some Carthaginian squadrons in the district of Avignon, merely for the purpose of enabling it to complete its reconnaissance—the first encounter of the Romans and Phoenicians in this war—it hastily returned to report at head-quarters. Scipio now started in the utmost haste with all his troops for Avignon; but, when he arrived there, even the Carthaginian cavalry that had been left behind to cover the passage of the elephants had already taken its departure three days ago, and nothing remained for the consul but to return with weary troops and little credit to Massilia, and to revile the "cowardly flight" of the Punic leader. Thus the Romans had for the third time through pure negligence abandoned their allies and an important line of defence; and not only so, but they sacrificed the real means of repairing their error by passing after this first blunder from mistaken slackness to mistaken haste, and by still attempting without any prospect of success to do what might have been done with so much certainty a few days before. When once Hannibal was in the Celtic territory on the Roman side of the Rhone, he could no longer be prevented from reaching the Alps; but if Scipio had at the first accounts proceeded with his whole army to Italy—the Po might have been reached by way of Genoa in seven days—and had united with his corps the weak divisions in the valley of the Po, he might have at least prepared a formidable reception for the enemy. But not only did he lose precious time in the march to Avignon, but, able as otherwise he was, he wanted either the political courage or the military sagacity to change the destination of his corps as the change of circumstances required. He sent the main body under his brother Gnaeus to Spain, and returned himself with a few men to Pisae.

Hannibal's passage of the Alps.

Hannibal, who after the passage of the Rhone had assembled the army and explained to his troops the object of his expedition, and had brought forward the Celtic chief Magilus himself, who had arrived from the valley of the Po, to address the army through an interpreter, meanwhile continued his march to the passes of the Alps without obstruction. Which of these passes he should choose, could not be at once determined either by the shortness of the route or by the disposition of the inhabitants, although he had no time to lose either in circuitous routes or in combat. He had necessarily to select a route which should be practicable for his baggage, his numerous cavalry, and his elephants, and in which an army could procure sufficient means of subsistence either by friendship or by force; for, although Hannibal had made preparations to convey provisions after him on beasts of burden, these could only meet for a few days the wants of an army which still, notwithstanding its great losses, amounted to nearly 50,000 men. Leaving out of view the coast route, which Hannibal abstained from taking not because the Romans obstructed it, but because it would have led him away from his destination, there were only two well-known routes leading across the Alps from Gaul to Italy in ancient times : * the pass of the Cottian Alps (Mont Genèvre) leading into the territory of the Taurini (by Susa or Fenestrelles to Turin), and that of the Graian Alps (the Little St. Bernard) leading into the territory of the Salassi (to Aosta and Ivrea). The former route is the shorter; but, after leaving the valley of the Rhone, it passes by the impracticable and unfruitful valleys of the Drac, the Romanche, and the upper Durance, through a difficult and poor mountain country, and requires at least a seven or eight days' mountain march. A military road was first constructed there by Pompeius, to furnish a shorter communication between the provinces of Cisalpine and Transalpine Gaul.

The route by the Little St. Bernard is somewhat longer; but, after crossing the first Alpine wall that forms the eastern boundary of the Rhone valley, it keeps by the valley of the upper Isère, which stretches from Grenoble by Chambéry up to the very foot of the Little St. Bernard or, in other words, of the chain of the higher Alps, and is the broadest, most fertile and most populous of all the Alpine valleys. Moreover, the pass of the Little St. Bernard, while not the lowest of all the natural passes of the Alps, is by far the easiest; although no artificial road was constructed there, an Austrian corps with artillery crossed the Alps by

---

* It was not till the middle ages that the route by Mont Cenis became a military road. The eastern passes, such as that over the Poenine Alps or the Great St. Bernard—which, moreover, was only converted into a military road by Caesar and Augustus—are, of course, in this case out of the question.

that route in 1815. And lastly this route, which only leads
over two mountain ridges, has been from the earliest times
the great military route from the Celtic to the Italian territory. The Carthaginian army had thus in fact no choice.
It was a fortunate coincidence, but not a motive influencing
the decision of Hannibal, that the Celtic tribes allied with
him in Italy inhabited the country up to the Little St.
Bernard, while the route by Mont Genèvre would have brought
him directly into the territory of the Taurini, who were
from ancient times at feud with the Insubres.

So the Carthaginian army marched in the first instance
up the Rhone towards the valley of the upper Isère, not, as
might be presumed, by the nearest route up the left bank of
the lower Isère from Valence to Grenoble, but through the
" island " of the Allobroges, the rich, and even then thickly
peopled, low ground, which is enclosed on the north and
west by the Rhone, on the south by the Isère, and on the
east by the Alps. The reason of this movement was, that
the nearest route would have led them through an impracticable and poor mountain-country, while the " island " was
level and extremely fertile, and was separated by but a single
mountain-wall from the valley of the upper Isère. The march
along the Rhone into, and across, the " island " to the foot
of the Alpine wall was accomplished in sixteen days : it presented little difficulty, and in the " island " itself Hannibal
dexterously availed himself of a feud that had broken out
between two chiefs of the Allobroges to attach to his interests
one of the most important of the chiefs, who not only escorted
the Carthaginians through the whole plain, but also supplied
them with provisions, and furnished the soldiers with arms,
clothing, and shoes. But the expedition narrowly escaped
destruction at the crossing of the first Alpine chain, which
rises precipitously like a wall, and over which only a single
available path leads (over Mont du Chat, near the hamlet
Chevelu). The population of the Allobroges had strongly
occupied the pass. Hannibal learned the state of matters
early enough to avoid a surprise, and encamped at the foot,
until after sunset the Celts dispersed to the houses of the
nearest town : he then seized the pass in the night. Thus
the summit was gained ; but on the extremely steep path,

which leads down from the summit to the lake of Bourget, the mules and horses slipped and fell. The assaults, which at all available points were made by the Celts upon the army in march, were very annoying, by reason not so much of the direct injury which they inflicted, as of the confusion which they occasioned; and when Hannibal with his light troops threw himself from above on the Allobroges, these were chased indeed without difficulty and with heavy loss down the mountain, but the confusion, in the train especially, was still further increased by the noise of the combat. So, when after much loss he arrived in the plain, Hannibal immediately attacked the nearest town, to chastise and terrify the barbarians, and at the same time to repair as far as possible his loss in sumpter animals and horses. After a day's repose in the pleasant valley of Chambéry the army continued its march up the Isère, without being detained either by want of supplies or by attacks so long as the valley continued broad and fertile. It was only when on the fourth day they entered the territory of the Ceutrones (the modern Tarantaise) where the valley gradually contracts, that they had greater occasion to be on their guard. The Ceutrones received the army at the boundary of their country (somewhere about Conflans) with branches and garlands, furnished cattle for slaughter, guides, and hostages; and the Carthaginians marched through their territory as through a friendly land. When, however, the troops had reached the very foot of the Alps, at the point where the path leaves the Isère, and winds by a narrow and difficult defile along the brook Reclus up to the summit of the St. Bernard, all at once the militia of the Ceutrones appeared partly in the rear of the army, partly on the crests of the rocks enclosing the pass on the right and left, in the hope of cutting off the train and baggage. But Hannibal, whose unerring tact had seen in all the courtesies of the Ceutrones nothing but a scheme to secure at once immunity for their territory and a rich spoil, had in expectation of such an attack sent forward the baggage and cavalry, and covered the march with all his infantry. By this means he frustrated the design of the enemy, although he could not prevent them from moving along the mountain slopes parallel to the march of the infantry, and inflicting very considerable

loss by hurling or rolling down stones upon it. At the
" white stone " (still called *la roche blanche*), a high isolated
chalk cliff standing at the foot of the St. Bernard and commanding the ascent to it, Hannibal encamped with his infantry, to cover the march of the horses and sumpter animals
laboriously climbing upward throughout the whole night;
and amidst continual and very bloody conflicts he at length
on the following day reached the summit of the pass. There,
on the sheltered table-land which spreads to the extent of
two and a half miles round a little lake, the source of the
Doria, he allowed the army to rest. Despondency had begun
to seize the minds of the soldiers. The paths that were becoming ever more difficult, the provisions failing, the marching through defiles exposed to the constant attacks of foes
whom they could not reach, the sorely thinned ranks, the
hopeless situation of the stragglers and the wounded, the
object which appeared chimerical to all save the enthusiastic
leader and his immediate staff—all these things began to tell
even on the African and Spanish veterans. But the confidence of the general remained ever the same ; numerous
stragglers rejoined the ranks ; the friendly Gauls were near;
the watershed was reached, and the view of the descending
path, so gladdening to the mountain-pilgrim, opened up :
after a brief repose they prepared with renewed courage
for the last and most difficult undertaking,—the downward
march. In it the army was not materially annoyed by the
enemy ; but the advanced season—it was already the beginning of September—occasioned troubles in the descent,
equal to those which had been occasioned in the ascent by
the attacks of the barbarians. On the steep and slippery
mountain-slope along the Doria, where the recently fallen
snow had concealed and obliterated the paths, men and
animals went astray and slipped, and were precipitated
into the chasms. In fact, towards the end of the first day's
march they reached a portion of the path about two hundred
paces in length, on which avalanches are constantly descending from the precipices of the Cramont that overhang
it, and where in cold summers snow lies throughout the
year. The infantry crossed ; but the horses and elephants
were unable to pass over the smooth masses of ice, on which

there lay but a thin covering of freshly fallen snow, and the general encamped above the difficult spot with the baggage, the cavalry, and the elephants. On the following day the horsemen, by zealous exertion in entrenching, prepared a path for horses and beasts of burden; but it was not until after a further labour of three days with constant reliefs, that the half-famished elephants could at length be conducted over. In this way the whole army was after a delay of four days once more united; and after a further three days' march through the valley of the Doria, which was ever widening and displaying greater fertility, and whose inhabitants the Salassi, clients of the Insubres, hailed in the Carthaginians their allies and deliverers, the army arrived about the middle of September in the plain of Ivrea, where the exhausted troops were quartered in the villages, that by good nursing and a fortnight's repose they might recruit from their unparalleled hardships. Had the Romans placed a corps, as they might have done, of 30,000 men thoroughly fresh and ready for action somewhere near Turin, and immediately forced on a battle, the prospects of Hannibal's great plan would have been very dubious; fortunately for him, once more, they were not where they should have been, and they did not disturb the troops of the enemy in the repose which was so greatly needed.*

---

* The much discussed questions of topography, connected with this celebrated expedition, may be regarded as cleared up and substantially solved by the masterly investigations of Messrs. Wickham and Cramer. Respecting the chronological questions, which likewise present difficulties, a few remarks may be exceptionally allowed to have a place here.

When Hannibal reached the summit of the St. Bernard, "the peaks were already beginning to be thickly covered with snow" (Pol. iii. 54); snow lay on the route (Pol. iii. 55), perhaps for the most part snow not freshly fallen, but proceeding from the fall of avalanches. At the St. Bernard winter begins about Michaelmas, and the falling of snow in September; when the Englishmen already mentioned crossed the mountain at the end of August, they found almost no snow on their road, but the slopes on both sides were covered with it. Hannibal thus appears to have arrived at the pass in the beginning of September; which is quite compatible with the statement that he arrived there "when the winter was already approaching"—for συνάπτειν τὴν τῆς πλειάδος δύσιν" (Pol. iii. 54) does not mean anything more than this, least of all the day of the heliacal setting of the Pleiades (about 26th October); comp. Ideler, Chronol. i. 241.

If Hannibal reached Italy nine days later, and therefore about the middle of September, there is room for the events that occurred from that time up to the battle of the Trebia towards the end of December (περὶ χειμερινὰς τροπὰς, Pol. iii. 72), and in particular for the transporting of the army destined for Africa from Lilybaeum to Placentia. This hypothesis further suits the statement that the day of departure was announced

Results.   The object was attained, but at a heavy cost. Of the
50,000 veteran infantry and the 9,000 cavalry, which the
army had numbered at the crossing of the Pyrenees, more
than half had been sacrificed in the conflicts, the marches,
and the passages of the rivers. Hannibal now, according to
his own statement, numbered not more than 20,000 infantry
--of whom three-fifths were Libyans and two-fifths Spaniards
—and 6,000 cavalry, part of whom were dismounted: the
comparatively small loss of the latter proclaimed the excellence of the Numidian cavalry no less than the consideration
of the general in making a sparing use of troops so select.
A march of 526 miles or about 33 moderate days' marching
—the continuance and termination of which were only rendered possible by unforeseen accidents and still more unforeseen blunders of the enemy, and which, while it was disturbed
by no special misfortunes on a great scale that could not be
anticipated, not only cost such sacrifices, but so fatigued and
demoralized the army, that it needed a long rest in order to
be again ready for action—is a military operation of doubtful value, and it may be questioned whether Hannibal himself regarded it as successful. Only in so speaking we may
not pronounce an absolute censure on the general: we see
well the defects of the plan of operations pursued by him,
but we cannot determine whether he was in a position to
foresee them—his route lay through an unknown land of barbarians—or whether any other plan, such as that of taking
the coast road or of embarking at Cartagena or at Carthage,
would have exposed him to fewer dangers. The cautious and
masterly execution of the plan in its details at any rate deserves our admiration, and to whatever causes the result may
have been due—whether it was due mainly to the favour of
fortune, or mainly to the skill of the general—the grand idea
of Hamilcar, that of taking up the conflict with Rome in

---

at an assembly of the army ὑπὸ τὴν
ἐαρινὴν ὥραν (Pol. iii. 34), and therefore
towards the end of March, and that the
march lasted five (or according to App.
vii. 4, six) months. If Hannibal was thus
at the St. Bernard in the beginning of
September, he must have reached the
Rhone at the beginning of August—for
he spent thirty days in making his way

from the Rhone thither—and in that
case it is evident that Scipio, who embarked at the beginning of summer (Pol.
iii. 41) and so at latest by the commencement of June, must have spent much
time on the voyage or remained for a
considerable period in singular inaction
at Massilia.

Italy, was now realized. It was his genius that projected this expedition; and as the task of Stein and Scharnhorst was more difficult and nobler than that of York and Blucher, so the unerring tact of historical tradition has always dwelt on the last link in the great chain of preparatory steps, the passage of the Alps, with a greater admiration than on the battles of the Trasimene lake and of the plain of Cannae.

CHAPTER V.

THE WAR UNDER HANNIBAL TO THE BATTLE OF CANNAE.

Hannibal
and the
Italian
Celts.

THE appearance of the Carthaginian army on the Roman side of the Alps changed all at once the situation of affairs, and disconcerted the Roman plan of war. Of the two principal armies of the Romans, one had landed in Spain and was already engaged with the enemy there : it was no longer possible to recall it. The second, which was destined for Africa under the command of the consul Tiberius Sempronius, was fortunately still in Sicily : in this instance Roman delay for once proved useful. Of the two Carthaginian squadrons destined for Italy and Sicily, the first was dispersed by a storm, and some of its vessels were captured by the Syracusans near Messana; the second had endeavoured in vain to surprise Lilybaeum, and had thereafter been defeated in a naval engagement off that port. But the continuance of the enemy's squadrons in the Italian waters was so inconvenient, that the consul determined, before crossing to Africa, to occupy the small islands around Sicily, and to dislodge the Carthaginian fleet operating against Italy. The summer passed away in the conquest of Melita, in the chase after the enemy's squadron, which he expected to find at the Lipari islands while it had made a descent near Vibo (Monteleone) and pillaged the Bruttian coast, and, lastly, in gaining information as to a suitable spot for landing on the coast of Africa ; so that the army and fleet were still at Lilybaeum, when orders arrived from the senate that they should return with all possible speed for the defence of their homes.

In this way, while the two great Roman armies, each in itself equal in numbers to that of Hannibal, remained at a great distance from the valley of the Po, the Romans were quite unprepared for an attack in that quarter. No doubt a

Roman army was there, in consequence of an insurrection that had broken out among the Celts even before the arrival of the Carthaginian army. The founding of the two Roman strongholds of Placentia and Cremona, each of which received 6,000 colonists, and more especially the preparations for the founding of Mutina in the territory of the Boii, had already in the spring of 536 driven the Boii to revolt before the time concerted with Hannibal; and the Insubres had immediately joined them. The colonists already settled in the territory of Mutina, suddenly attacked, took refuge in the town. The praetor Lucius Manlius, who held the chief command at Ariminum, hastened with his single legion to relieve the blockaded colonists; but he was surprised in the woods, and no course was left to him after sustaining great loss but to establish himself upon a hill and to submit to a siege there on the part of the Boii, till a second legion sent from Rome under the praetor Lucius Atilius succeeded in relieving army and town, and in suppressing for the moment the Gaulish insurrection. This premature rising of the Boii on the one hand, by delaying the departure of Scipio for Spain, essentially promoted the plans of Hannibal; on the other hand, but for its occurrence he would have found the valley of the Po entirely unoccupied, except the fortresses. But the Roman corps, whose two severely thinned legions did not number 20,000 soldiers, had enough to do to keep the Celts in check, and did not think of occupying the passes of the Alps. The Romans only learned that the passes were threatened, when in August the consul Publius Scipio returned without his army from Massilia to Italy, and perhaps even then they gave little heed to the matter, because, forsooth, the foolhardy attempt would be frustrated by the Alps alone. Thus at the decisive hour and on the decisive spot there was not even a Roman outpost. Hannibal had full time to rest his army, to capture after a three days' siege the capital of the Taurini which closed its gates against him, and to induce or terrify into alliance with him all the Ligurian and Celtic communities in the upper basin of the Po, before Scipio, who had taken the command in the Po valley, encountered him.

Scipio, who, with an army considerably smaller and very

218.

weak in cavalry, had the difficult task of preventing the
advance of the superior force of the enemy and of repressing
the movements of insurrection which everywhere were spreading among the Celts, had crossed the Po probably at Placentia,
and marched up the river to meet the enemy, while Hannibal
after the capture of Turin marched downwards to relieve the
Insubres and Boii. In the plain between the Ticino and the
Sesia, not far from Vercelli, the Roman cavalry, which had
advanced with the light infantry to make a reconnaissance
in force, encountered the Punic cavalry sent out for the like
purpose, both led by the generals in person. Scipio accepted
battle when offered, notwithstanding the superiority of the
enemy; but his light infantry, which was placed in front of
the cavalry, dispersed before the charge of the heavy cavalry
of the enemy, and while the latter engaged the masses of the
Roman horsemen in front, the light Numidian cavalry, after
having pushed aside the broken ranks of the enemy's infantry,
took the Roman horsemen in flank and rear. This decided
the combat. The loss of the Romans was very considerable.
The consul himself, who made up as a soldier for his deficiencies as a general, received a dangerous wound, and owed
his safety entirely to the devotion of his son of seventeen,
who, courageously dashing into the ranks of the enemy,
compelled his squadron to follow him and rescued his father.
Scipio, enlightened by this combat as to the strength of the
enemy, saw the error which he had committed in posting
himself, with a weaker army, in the plain with his back to
the river, and resolved to return to the right bank of the Po
under the eyes of his antagonist. As the operations became
contracted into a narrower space and his illusions regarding
Roman invincibility departed, he recovered the use of his
considerable military talents, which the adventurous boldness
of his youthful opponent's plans had for a moment paralyzed.
While Hannibal was preparing for a pitched battle, Scipio
by a rapidly projected and steadily executed march succeeded
in reaching the right bank of the river which in an evil hour
he had abandoned, and broke down the bridge over the Po
behind his army; the Roman detachment of 600 men charged
to cover the process of destruction were, however, intercepted
and made prisoners. But as the upper course of the river

was in the hands of Hannibal, he could not be prevented from marching up the stream, crossing on a bridge of boats, and in a few days confronting the Roman army on the right bank. The latter had taken a position in the plain in front of Placentia; but the mutiny of a Celtic division in the Roman camp, and the Gallic insurrection breaking out afresh all around, compelled the consul to evacuate the plain and to post himself on the hills behind the Trebia. This was accomplished without much loss, because the Numidian horsemen sent in pursuit lost their time in plundering, and setting fire to, the abandoned camp. In this strong position, with his left wing resting on the Apennines, his right on the Po and the fortress of Placentia, and covered in front by the Trebia—no inconsiderable stream at that season—Scipio was unable to save the rich stores of Clastidium (Casteggio), from which in this position he was cut off by the army of the enemy; nor was he able to avert the insurrectionary movement on the part of almost all the Gallic cantons, excepting the Cenomani who were friendly to Rome; but he completely checked the progress of Hannibal, and compelled him to pitch his camp opposite to that of the Romans. Moreover, the position taken up by Scipio, and the circumstance of the Cenomani threatening the borders of the Insubres, hindered the main body of the Gallic insurgents from directly joining the enemy, and gave to the second Roman army, which meanwhile had arrived at Ariminum from Lilybaeum, the opportunity of reaching Placentia through the midst of the insurgent country without material hindrance, and of uniting itself with the army of the Po.

The armies at Placentia.

Scipio had thus solved his difficult task brilliantly and completely. The Roman army, now close on 40,000 strong, and though not a match for its antagonist in cavalry, at least equal in infantry, had simply to remain in its existing position, in order to compel the enemy either to attempt in the winter season the passage of the river and an attack upon the camp, or to suspend his advance and to test the fickle temper of the Gauls by the burden of winter quarters. Clear, however, as this was, it was no less clear that it was now December, and that under the course proposed the victory might perhaps be gained by Rome, but would not be gained

Battle on the Trebia.

by the consul Tiberius Sempronius, who held the sole command in consequence of Scipio's wound, and whose year of office expired in a few months. Hannibal knew the man, and neglected no means of alluring him to fight. The Celtic villages that had remained faithful to the Romans were cruelly laid waste, and, when this brought on a conflict between the cavalry, Hannibal allowed his opponents to boast of the victory. Soon thereafter on a raw rainy day a general engagement came on, unlooked for by the Romans. From the earliest hour of the morning the Roman light troops had been skirmishing with the light cavalry of the enemy; the latter slowly retreated, and the Romans eagerly pursued it through the deeply swollen Trebia, so as to follow up the advantage which they had gained. Suddenly the cavalry halted; the Roman vanguard found itself face to face with the army of Hannibal drawn up for battle on a field chosen by himself; it was lost, unless the main body should cross the stream with all speed to its support. Hungry, weary, and wet, the Romans came on and hastened to form in order of battle, the cavalry, as usual, on the wings, the infantry in the centre. The light troops, who formed the vanguard on both sides, began the combat : but the Romans had already almost exhausted their missiles against the cavalry, and immediately gave way. In like manner the cavalry gave way on the wings, hard pressed by the elephants in front, and outflanked right and left by the far more numerous Carthaginian horse. But the Roman infantry proved itself worthy of its name : at the beginning of the battle it fought with very decided superiority against the infantry of the enemy, and even when the repulse of the Roman horse allowed the enemy's cavalry and light-armed troops to turn their attacks against the Roman infantry, the latter, although ceasing to advance, obstinately maintained its ground. At this stage a select Carthaginian band of 2,000 men, half infantry, half cavalry, under the leadership of Mago, Hannibal's youngest brother, suddenly emerged from an ambush in the rear of the Roman army, and fell upon the densely entangled masses. The wings of the army and the rear ranks of the Roman centre were broken up and scattered by this attack, while the first division, 10,000 men strong, in compact array broke through the Carthaginian line, and made a passage for itself obliquely through the midst of the enemy, inflicting great loss on the opposing infantry and more especially on the Gallic insurgents. This brave body, pursued but feebly, thus reached Placentia. The remaining mass was for the most part slaughtered by the elephants and light troops of the enemy in attempting to cross the river: only part of the cavalry and some divisions of infantry were able, by wading through the river, to gain the camp whither the Carthaginians did not follow them, and thus they too reached Placentia.* Few battles confer more honour on the Roman soldier than this on the Trebia, and few at the same time furnish graver impeachment of the general in command; although the candid judge will not forget that a commandership-in-chief expiring on a definite day was an unmilitary institution, and that figs cannot be reaped from thistles. The victory came to be costly even to the victors. Although the loss in the battle fell chiefly on the Celtic insurgents, yet a multitude of the veteran soldiers of Hannibal died afterwards from diseases engendered by that raw and wet winter day, and all the elephants perished except one.

The effect of this first victory of the invading army was, *Hannibal master of northern Italy.*

---

* Polybius's account of the battle on the Trebia is quite clear. If Placentia lay on the right bank of the Trebia where it falls into the Po, and if the battle was fought on the left bank, while the Roman encampment was pitched upon the right—both of which points have been disputed, but are nevertheless indisputable—the Roman soldiers must certainly have passed the Trebia in order to gain Placentia as well as to gain the camp. But those who crossed to the camp must have made their way through the disorganized portions of their own army and through the corps of the enemy that had gone round to their rear, and must then have crossed the river almost in hand to hand combat with the enemy. On the other hand the passage near Placentia was accomplished after the pursuit had slackened; the corps was several miles distant from the field of battle, and had arrived within reach of a Roman fortress; it may

even have been the case, although it cannot be proved, that a bridge led over the Trebia at that point, and that the *tête de pont* on the other bank was occupied by the garrison of Placentia. It is evident that the first passage was just as difficult as the second was easy, and therefore with good reason Polybius, military judge as he was, merely says of the corps of 10,000, that in close columns it cut its way to Placentia (iii. 74, 6), without mentioning the passage of the river which in this case was unattended with difficulty.

The erroneousness of the view of Livy, which transfers the Phoenician camp to the right, the Roman to the left bank of the Trebia, has been repeatedly pointed out. We may only further mention, that the site of Clastidium, near the modern Casteggio, has now been established by inscriptions (*Orelli—Henzen*, 5117).

that the national insurrection now spread and assumed shape without hindrance throughout the Celtic territory. The remains of the Roman army of the Po threw themselves into the fortresses of Placentia and Cremona : completely cut off from home, they were obliged to procure their supplies by way of the river. The consul Tiberius Sempronius only escaped, as if by miracle, from being taken prisoner, when with a weak escort of cavalry he went to Rome on account of the elections. Hannibal, who would not hazard the health of his troops by further marches at that inclement season, bivouacked for the winter where he was ; and, as a serious attempt on the larger fortresses would have led to no result, contented himself with annoying the enemy by attacks on the river-port of Placentia and other minor Roman positions. He employed himself mainly in organizing the Gallic insurrection: more than 60,000 foot soldiers and 4,000 horsemen from the Celts are said to have joined his army.

Military and politi- cal [217. position of Hannibal. No extraordinary exertions were made in Rome for the campaign of 537. The senate thought, and not unreasonably, that, despite the lost battle, their position was by no means fraught with serious danger. Besides the coast-garrisons, which were despatched to Sardinia, Sicily, and Tarentum, and the reinforcements which were sent to Spain, the two new consuls Gaius Flaminius and Gnaeus Servilius obtained only as many men as were necessary to restore the four legions to their full complement; additions were made to the strength of the cavalry alone. The consuls had to protect the northern frontier, and stationed themselves accordingly on the two highways which led from Rome to the north, the western of which at that time terminated at Arretium, and the eastern at Ariminum ; Gaius Flaminius occupied the former, Gnaeus Servilius the latter. There they ordered the troops from the fortresses on the Po to join them, probably by water, and awaited the commencement of the favourable season, when they proposed to occupy in the defensive the passes of the Apennines, and then, resuming offensive operations, to descend into the valley of the Po and effect a junction somewhere near Placentia. But Hannibal by no means intended to defend the valley of the Po. He knew

Rome better perhaps than the Romans knew it themselves, and was very well aware how decidedly he was the weaker and continued to be so notwithstanding the brilliant battle on the Trebia ; he knew too that his ultimate object, the humiliation of Rome, was not to be wrung from the unbending Roman pride either by terror or by surprise, but could only be gained by the complete subjugation of the haughty city.   It was clearly apparent that the Italian federation was in political solidity and in military resources infinitely superior to an adversary, who received only precarious and irregular support from home, and who was in the first instance dependent for aid in Italy solely on the vacillating and capricious nation of the Celts; and that the Phoenician foot soldier was, notwithstanding all the pains taken by Hannibal, far inferior in point of tactics to the legionary, had been completely proved by the defensive movements of Scipio and the brilliant retreat of the defeated infantry on the Trebia.   From this conviction flowed the two fundamental principles which determined Hannibal's whole method of operations in Italy—viz., that the war should be carried on, somewhat adventurously, with constant changes in the plan and in the theatre of operations ; and that its favourable issue could only be looked for as the result of political and not of military successes—of the gradual loosening and final breaking up of the Italian federation.   This mode of carrying on the war was necessary, because the single element which Hannibal had to throw into the scale against so many disadvantages—his military genius —only told with its full weight, when he constantly foiled his opponents by unexpected combinations ; he was undone, if the war became stationary.   This aim was the aim dictated to him by right policy, because, mighty conqueror though he was in battle, he saw very clearly that on each occasion he vanquished the generals but not the city, and that after each new battle the Romans remained just as superior to the Carthaginians as he was personally superior to the Roman commanders.   That Hannibal even at the height of his fortune never deceived himself on this point, is a fact more wonderful than his most wondrous battles.

It was these motives, and not the entreaties of the Gauls that he should spare their country—which would not have

Hannibal crosses the Apennines.

influenced him—that induced Hannibal now to forsake, as it were, his newly acquired basis of operations against Italy, and to transfer the scene of war to Italy itself.   Before doing so he gave orders that all the prisoners should be brought before him.   He ordered the Romans to be separated and loaded with chains as slaves—the statement that Hannibal put to death all the Romans capable of bearing arms, who here and elsewhere fell into his hands, is beyond doubt at least strongly exaggerated.   On the other hand, all the Italian allies were released without ransom, and charged to report at home that Hannibal waged war not against Italy, but against Rome; that he promised to every Italian community the restoration of its ancient independence and its ancient boundaries; and that the deliverer was about to follow those whom he had set free, bringing release and revenge.   So, when the winter ended, he started from the valley of the Po to search for a route through the difficult defiles of the Apennines.   Gaius Flaminius, with the Etruscan army, was still for the moment at Arezzo, intending to move from that point towards Lucca in order to protect the vale of the Arno and the passes of the Apennines, so soon as the season should allow.   But Hannibal anticipated him. The passage of the Apennines was accomplished without much difficulty, at a point as far west as possible or, in other words, as distant as possible from the enemy; but the marshy low grounds between the Serchio and the Arno were so flooded by the melting of the snow and the spring rains, that the army had to march four days in water, without finding any other dry spot for resting by night than was supplied by piling the baggage or by the sumpter animals that had fallen.   The troops underwent unutterable sufferings, particularly the Gallic infantry, which marched behind the Carthaginians along tracks already rendered impassable : they murmured loudly and would undoubtedly have dispersed to a man, had not the Carthaginian cavalry under Mago, which brought up the rear, rendered flight impossible.   The horses, assailed by a distemper in their hoofs, fell in heaps ; various diseases decimated the soldiers; Hannibal himself lost an eye in consequence of ophthalmia.

Flaminius.   But the object was attained.   Hannibal encamped at Fiesole, while Gaius Flaminius was still waiting at Arezzo until the roads should become passable that he might blockade them.   After the Roman defensive position had thus been turned, the best course for the consul, who might perhaps have been strong enough to defend the mountain passes but certainly was unable now to face Hannibal in the open field, would have been to wait till the second army, which had now become completely superfluous at Ariminum, should arrive. He himself, however, thought otherwise.   He was a political party leader, raised to distinction by his efforts to limit the power of the senate; indignant at the government in consequence of the aristocratic intrigues concocted against him during his consulship; carried away, through a doubtless justifiable opposition to their beaten track of partisanship, into a scornful defiance of tradition and custom; intoxicated by a blind affection for the common people, and by quite as bitter a hatred towards the party of the nobles; and, in addition to all this, possessed with the fixed idea that he was a military genius.   His campaign against the Insubres of 531, which to unprejudiced judges only showed that good soldiers often repair the errors of bad generals (p. 85), was regarded by him and by his adherents as an irrefragable proof that the Romans had only to put Gaius Flaminius at the head of the army in order to make a speedy end of Hannibal. Talk of this sort had procured for him his second consulship, and hopes of this sort had now brought to his camp so great a multitude of unarmed followers eager for spoil, that their number, according to the assurance of sober historians, exceeded that of the legionaries.   Hannibal based his plan in part on this circumstance.   So far from attacking him, he marched past him, and caused the country all around to be pillaged by the Celts who thoroughly understood plundering, and by his numerous cavalry.   The complaints and indignation of the multitude which had to submit to be plundered under the eyes of the hero who had promised to enrich them, and the protestation of the enemy that they did not believe him possessed of either the power or the resolution to undertake anything before the arrival of his colleague, could not but induce such a man to display his genius for strategy, and to give a sharp lesson to his inconsiderate and haughty foe.

223.

No plan was ever more successful. In haste, the consul followed the line of march of the enemy, who passed by Arezzo
and moved slowly through the rich valley of the Chiana towards Perugia. He overtook him in the district of Cortona,
where Hannibal, accurately informed of his antagonist's
march, had had full time to select his field of battle—a
narrow defile between two steep mountain walls, closed at
its outlet by a high hill, and at its entrance by the Trasimene lake. With the flower of his infantry he barred the
outlet; the light troops and the cavalry placed themselves in
concealment on either side. The Roman columns advanced
without hesitation into the unoccupied pass; the thick
morning mist concealed from them the position of the enemy.
As the head of the Roman line approached the hill, Hannibal
gave the signal for battle; the cavalry, advancing behind the
heights, closed the entrance of the pass, and at the same
time the mist rolling away revealed the Phoenician arms
everywhere along the crests on the right and left. There
was no battle; it was a mere rout. Those that remained out
of the defile were driven by the cavalry into the lake. The
main body was annihilated in the pass itself almost without
resistance, and most of them, including the consul himself,
were cut down in the order of march. The head of the Roman column, formed of 6,000 infantry, cut their way through
the infantry of the enemy, and proved once more the irresistible might of the legions; but, cut off from the rest of
the army and without knowledge of its fate, they marched
on at random, were surrounded on the following day, on a
hill which they had occupied, by a corps of Carthaginian
cavalry, and—as the capitulation, which promised them a
free retreat, was rejected by Hannibal—were all treated as
prisoners of war. 15,000 Romans had fallen, and as many
were captured; in other words, the army was annihilated.
The slight Carthaginian loss—1,500 men—again fell mainly
upon the Gauls.* And, as if this were not enough, immediately after the battle on the Trasimene lake, the cavalry of

---

* The date of the battle, 23rd June according to the uncorrected calendar, must,
according to the rectified calendar, fall
somewhere in April, since Quintus Fabius resigned his dictatorship, after six
months, in the middle of autumn (Liv.

xxii. 31, 7; 32, 1), and must therefore
have entered upon it about the beginning
of May. The confusion of the calendar
(i. 505) in Rome was even at this period
very great.

the army of Ariminum under Gaius Centenius, 4,000 strong, which Gnaeus Servilius had sent forward to the support of his colleague while he himself advanced by slow marches, was likewise surrounded by the Phoenician army, and partly slain, partly made prisoners. All Etruria was lost, and Hannibal might without hindrance march on Rome. The Romans prepared themselves for the worst; they broke down the bridges over the Tiber, and nominated Quintus Fabius Maximus dictator to repair the walls and conduct the defence, for which an army of reserve was formed. At the same time two new legions were summoned under arms in the room of those annihilated, and the fleet, which might become of importance in the event of a siege, was put in order.

But Hannibal was more farsighted than king Pyrrhus. He did not march on Rome ; nor even against Gnaeus Servilius, an able general, who had with the help of the fortresses on the northern road preserved his army hitherto uninjured, and would perhaps have kept his antagonist at bay. Once more a movement occurred which was quite unexpected. Hannibal marched past the fortress of Spoletium, which he attempted in vain to surprise, through Umbria, fearfully devastated the territory of Picenum which was covered all over with Roman farmhouses, and halted on the shores of the Adriatic. The men and horses of his army had not yet recovered from the painful effects of their spring campaign ; here he rested for a considerable time to allow his army to recruit its strength in a pleasant district and at a fine season of the year, and to reorganize his Libyan infantry after the Roman mode, the means for which were furnished to him by the mass of Roman arms among the spoil. From this point, moreover, he resumed his long interrupted communication with his native land, sending his messages of victory by water to Carthage. At length, when his army was sufficiently restored and had been adequately exercised in the use of the new arms, he broke up and marched slowly along the coast into southern Italy.

Hannibal on the east coast.

Reorganization of the Carthaginian army.

He had calculated correctly, when he chose this time for remodelling his infantry. The surprise of his antagonists, who were in constant expectation of an attack on

the capital, allowed him at least four weeks of undisturbed
leisure for the execution of the unprecedentedly bold experiment of changing completely his military system in
the heart of a hostile country and with an army still comparatively small, and of attempting to oppose African legions
to the invincible legions of Italy. But his hope that the
confederacy would now begin to break up was not fulfilled.
In this respect the Etruscans, who had carried on their last
wars of independence mainly with Gallic mercenaries, were
of less moment; the flower of the confederacy, particularly
in a military point of view, consisted—next to the Latins—
of the Sabellian communities, and with good reason Hannibal
had now come into their neighbourhood. But one town
after another closed its gates; not a single Italian community entered into alliance with the Phoenicians. This
result was a great, in fact an all-important, point gained for
Rome. Nevertheless it was felt in the capital that it would
be imprudent to put the fidelity of their allies to such a test,
without a Roman army to keep the field. The dictator
Quintus Fabius combined the two supplementary legions
formed in Rome with the army of Ariminum, and when
Hannibal marched past the Roman fortress of Luceria towards Arpi, the Roman standards appeared on his right flank
at Aeca. Their leader, however, pursued a different course
from his predecessors. Quintus Fabius was a man advanced
in years, of a deliberation and firmness, which to not a
few seemed procrastination and obstinacy. Zealous in his
reverence for the good old times, for the political omnipotence of the senate, and for the command of the burgomasters,
he looked to a methodical prosecution of the war as
—next to sacrifices and prayer—the means of saving the
state. A political antagonist of Gaius Flaminius, and summoned to the head of affairs in virtue of the reaction against
his foolish war-demagogism, Fabius departed for the camp
just as firmly resolved to avoid a pitched battle at any price,
as his predecessor had been determined at any price to fight
one; he was without doubt convinced that the first elements
of strategy would forbid Hannibal to advance so long as the
Roman army confronted him intact, and that accordingly it
would not be difficult to weaken by petty conflicts and gra-

War in
Lower
Italy.

Fabius.

dually to starve out the enemy's army, dependent as it was on foraging for its supplies.

Hannibal, well served by his spies in Rome and in the Roman army, immediately learned how matters stood, and, as usual, adjusted the plan of his campaign in accordance with the individual character of the opposing leader. Passing the Roman army, he marched over the Apennines into the heart of Italy towards Beneventum, took the open town of Telesia on the boundary between Samnium and Campania, and thence turned against Capua, which was the most important of all the Italian cities dependent on Rome, and for that very reason had been oppressed and maltreated in a more vexatious manner than any other community had been by the Roman government. He had formed connections there, which led him to hope that the Campanians might revolt from the Roman alliance; but in this hope he was disappointed. So, retracing his steps, he took the road to Apulia. During all this march of the Carthaginian army the dictator had followed along the heights, and had condemned his soldiers to the melancholy task of looking on with arms in their hands, while the Numidian cavalry plundered the faithful allies far and wide, and the villages over all the plain rose in flames. At length he opened up to the exasperated Roman army the eagerly coveted prospect of attacking the enemy. When Hannibal had begun his retreat, Fabius intercepted his route near Casilinum (the modern Capua), by strongly garrisoning that town on the left bank of the Volturnus and occupying the heights that secured the right bank with his main army, while a division of 4,000 men encamped on the road itself that led along by the river. But Hannibal ordered his light-armed troops to climb the heights which rose immediately alongside of the road, and to drive before them a number of oxen with lighted faggots on their horns, so that it seemed as if the Carthaginian army were thus marching off during the night by torchlight. The Roman division, which blocked up the road, imagining that they were evaded and that further covering of the road was superfluous, marched by a side movement to the same heights. Along the road thus left free Hannibal then retreated with the bulk of his army, without encountering the enemy; next

morning he without difficulty, but with severe loss to the
Romans, disengaged and recalled his light troops. Hannibal
then continued his march unopposed in a north-easterly
direction ; and by a widely-circuitous route, after traversing
and laying under contribution the lands of the Hirpinians,
Campanians, Samnites, Paelignians, and Frentanians without
resistance, he arrived with rich booty and a full chest once
more in the region of Luceria, just as the harvest there was
about to begin. Nowhere in his extensive march had he
met with active opposition, but nowhere had he found allies.

**War in
Apulia.**
Clearly perceiving that no course remained for him but to
take up winter quarters in the open field, he began the
difficult operation of collecting the winter supplies requisite
for the army, by means of its own agency, from the fields of
the enemy. For this purpose he had selected the broad and
mostly flat district of northern Apulia, which furnished grain
and grass in abundance, and which could be completely
commanded by his excellent cavalry. An entrenched camp
was constructed at Gerunium, twenty-five miles to the north
of Luceria. Two-thirds of the army were daily despatched
from it to bring in the stores, while Hannibal with the remainder took up a position to protect the camp and the
detachments sent out.

**Fabius
and Minu-
cius.**
The master of the horse, Marcus Minucius, who held temporary command in the Roman camp during the absence of the
dictator, deemed this a suitable opportunity for approaching
the enemy more closely, and formed a camp in the territory of
the Larinates ; where on the one hand by his mere presence
he checked the sending out of detachments and thereby hindered the provisioning of the enemy's army, and on the other
hand, in the series of successful conflicts in which his troops
encountered isolated Phoenician divisions and even Hannibal
himself, drove the enemy from their advanced positions and
compelled them to concentrate themselves at Gerunium. On
the news of these successes, which of course lost nothing in
the telling, reaching the capital, the storm broke forth against
Quintus Fabius. It was not altogether unwarranted. Prudent as it was on the part of Rome to abide by the defensive
and to expect success mainly from the cutting off of the
enemy's means of subsistence, there was yet something strange

in a system of defence and of starving out, under which the enemy had laid waste all central Italy without opposition beneath the eyes of a Roman army of equal numbers, and had provisioned themselves sufficiently for the winter by an organized method of foraging on the greatest scale. Publius Scipio, when he commanded on the Po, had not adopted this view of a defensive attitude, and the attempt of his successor to imitate him at Casilinum had failed in such a way as to afford a copious fund of ridicule to the scoffers of the city. It was wonderful that the Italian communities had not wavered, when Hannibal so palpably showed them the superiority of the Phoenicians and the nullity of Roman aid; but how long could they be expected to bear the burden of a double war, and to allow themselves to be plundered under the very eyes of the Roman troops and of their own contingents? Finally, it could not be alleged that the condition of the Roman army compelled the general to adopt this mode of warfare. It was composed, indeed, in part of militia called out for the emergency, but the flower of it consisted of the legions of Ariminum accustomed to service; and, so far from being discouraged by the last defeats, it was indignant at the far from honourable task which its general, " Hannibal's lackey," assigned to it, and it demanded with a loud voice to be led against the enemy. In the assemblies of the people the most violent invectives were directed against the obstinate old man. His political opponents, with the former praetor Marcus Terentius Varro at their head, laid hold of the quarrel—for the understanding of which we must not forget that the dictator was practically nominated by the senate, and the office was regarded as the palladium of the conservative party— and, in concert with the discontented soldiers and the possessors of the plundered estates, they carried an unconstitutional and absurd resolution of the people conferring the dictatorship, which was destined to obviate the evils of a divided command in times of danger, on Marcus Minucius,* who had hitherto been the lieutenant of Quintus Fabius, in the same way as on Fabius himself. Thus the Roman army, after its

---

* The inscription of the gift devoted *Hercolei sacrom M. Minuci(us) C. f.* by the new dictator on account of his *dictator vovit*—was found in the year victory at Gerunium to Hercules Victor— 1862 at Rome, near S. Lorenzo.

hazardous division into two separate corps had just been appropriately remedied, was once more divided; and not only so, but the two sections were placed under leaders who notoriously followed quite opposite plans of war.   Quintus Fabius of course adhered more than ever to his methodical inaction; Marcus Minucius, compelled to justify in the field of battle his title of dictator, made a hasty attack with inadequate forces, and would have been annihilated had not his colleague averted greater misfortune by the seasonable interposition of a fresh corps.   This last turn of matters justified in some measure the system of passive resistance.   But in reality Hannibal had completely attained in this campaign all that arms could attain: not a single material operation had been frustrated either by his impetuous or by his deliberate opponent; and his foraging, though not unattended with difficulty, had yet been in the main so successful that the army passed the winter without complaint in the camp at Gerunium. It was not the *Cunctator* that saved Rome, but the compact structure of its confederacy and, not less perhaps, the national hatred with which the Phoenician hero was regarded by the men of the West.

New war-
like prepa-
rations in
Rome.

Despite all its misfortunes, Roman pride stood no less unshaken than the Roman symmachy.   The donations which were offered by king Hiero of Syracuse and the Greek cities in Italy for the next campaign—the war affected the latter less severely than the other Italian allies of Rome, for they sent no contingents to the land army—were declined with thanks; the chieftains of Illyria were informed that they could not be allowed to neglect payment of their tribute; and even the king of Macedonia was once more summoned to surrender Demetrius of Pharos.   The majority of the senate, notwithstanding the semblance of legitimation which recent events had given to the Fabian system of delay, had firmly resolved to depart from a mode of war that was slowly but certainly ruining the state; if the popular dictator had failed in his more energetic method of warfare, they laid the blame of the failure, and not without reason, on the fact that they had adopted a half-measure and had given him too few troops.   This error they determined to avoid and to equip an army, such as Rome had never sent out before— eight le-

gions, each raised a fifth above the normal strength, and a
corresponding number of allies—enough to crush an opponent who was not half so strong.   Besides this, a legion under
the praetor Lucius Postumius was destined for the valley of
the Po, in order, if possible, to draw off the Celts serving in
the army of Hannibal to their homes.   These resolutions
were judicious; everything depended on their coming to an
equally judicious decision respecting the supreme command.
The stiff carriage of Quintus Fabius, and the attacks of the
demagogues which it provoked, had rendered the dictatorship
and the senate generally more unpopular than ever: amongst
the people, not without the connivance of their leaders, the
foolish report circulated that the senate was intentionally prolonging the war.   As, therefore, the nomination of a dictator
was not to be thought of, the senate attempted to procure the
election of suitable consuls; but this only had the effect of
thoroughly rousing suspicion and obstinacy.   With difficulty Paullus
and Varro.
the senate carried one of its candidates, Lucius Aemilius
Paullus, who had with judgment conducted the Illyrian war
in 535 (p. 79); an immense majority of the citizens assigned 219.
to him as colleague the candidate of the popular party,
Marcus Terentius Varro, an incapable man, who was known
only by his bitter opposition to the senate and more especially as the main author of the proposal to elect Marcus
Minucius co-dictator, and who was recommended to the multitude solely by his humble birth and his coarse effrontery.

While these preparations for the next campaign were Battle of
Cannae.
making in Rome, the war had already recommenced in
Apulia.   As soon as the season allowed him to leave his
winter quarters, Hannibal, determining as usual the course
of the war and assuming the offensive, set out from Gerunium
in a southerly direction, and marching past Luceria crossed
the Aufidus and took the citadel of Cannae (between Canosa
and Barletta) which commanded the plain of Canusium, and
had hitherto served the Romans as one of their principal
magazines.   The Roman army which, since Fabius had conformably to the constitution resigned his dictatorship in the
middle of autumn, was now commanded by Gnaeus Servilius
and Marcus Regulus, first as consuls then as proconsuls, had
been unable to avert a loss which they could not but feel.   On

military as well as on political grounds, it became more than
ever necessary to arrest the progress of Hannibal by a pitched
battle. With definite orders to this effect from the senate,
accordingly, the two new commanders-in-chief, Paullus and
Varro, arrived in Apulia in the beginning of the summer of

216.   538. With the four new legions and a corresponding contingent of Italians which they brought up, the Roman
army was raised to 80,000 infantry, half burgesses, half
allies, and 6,000 cavalry, of whom one-third were burgesses
and two-thirds allies ; whereas Hannibal's army numbered
10,000 cavalry, but only about 40,000 infantry. Hannibal
wished nothing so much as a battle, not merely for the
general reasons which we have explained above, but specially
because the wide Apulian plain allowed him to develop the
whole superiority of his cavalry, and because the providing
supplies for his numerous army would soon, in spite of that
excellent cavalry, be rendered very difficult by the proximity
of an enemy twice as strong and resting on a chain of fortresses. The leaders of the Roman forces had also, as we
have said, made up their minds on the general question of
giving battle, and approached the enemy with that view ; but
the more sagacious of them saw the position of Hannibal, and
were disposed accordingly to wait in the first instance and
simply to station themselves in the vicinity of the enemy, so
as to compel him to retire and accept battle on ground less
favourable to him. With this view, confronting the Carthaginian position at Cannae on the right bank of the Aufidus,
Paullus constructed two camps farther up the stream, the
larger likewise on the right bank, the smaller, at a distance
of fully a mile from it and not much more distant from the
enemy's camp, on the left, so as to prevent the foraging of
the enemy on both banks of the river. But such military
pedantry was disapproved by the democratic consul—so
much had been said about men taking the field not to set
sentinels, but to use their swords—and he gave orders accordingly to attack the enemy, wherever and whenever they
found him. According to an old custom foolishly retained,
the decisive voice in the council of war alternated between
the commanders-in-chief day by day ; it was necessary therefore to submit, and to let the hero of the pavement have his

way. Only one division of 10,000 men was left in the principal Roman camp, charged to capture the Carthaginian
encampment during the conflict and thus to intercept the
retreat of the enemy's army across the river. The bulk
of the Roman army, at early dawn on the 2nd August according to the uncorrected, probably in June according to
the correct, calendar, crossed the river which at this season
was shallow and did not materially hamper the movements
of the troops, and took up a position in line near the smaller
Roman camp—which lay nearest to the enemy, intermediate
between the larger Roman camp and that of the Carthaginians, and which had already been the scene of outpost
skirmishes—in the wide plain stretching westward from
Cannae on the left bank of the river. The Carthaginian
army followed and likewise crossed the stream, on which
rested the right Roman as well as the left Carthaginian
wing. The Roman cavalry was stationed on the wings:
the weaker portion consisting of burgesses, led by Paullus,
on the right next the river; the stronger consisting of the
allies, led by Varro, on the left towards the plain. In the
centre was stationed the infantry in unusually deep files,
under the command of the proconsul Gnaeus Servilius. Opposite to this centre Hannibal arranged his infantry in the
form of a crescent, so that the Celtic and Iberian troops in
their national armour formed the advanced centre, and the
Libyans, armed after the Roman fashion, formed the retreating wings on either side. On the side next the river the
whole heavy cavalry under Hasdrubal was stationed, on the
side towards the plain the light Numidian horse. After a
short skirmish between the light troops the whole line was
soon engaged. Where the light cavalry of the Carthaginians
fought against the heavy cavalry of Varro, the conflict was
prolonged, amidst constant charges of the Numidians, without decisive result. In the centre, on the other hand, the
legions completely overthrew the Spanish and Gallic troops
that first encountered them; eagerly the victors pressed on
and followed up their advantage. But meanwhile, on the
right wing, fortune had turned against the Romans. Hannibal had merely sought to occupy the left cavalry wing of the
enemy, that he might bring Hasdrubal with the whole

regular cavalry to bear against the weaker right and to overthrow it first. After a brave resistance, the Roman horse
gave way, and those that were not cut down were chased
across the river and scattered in the plain; Paullus, wounded,
rode to the centre to avert or, if not, to share the fate of the
legions. These, in order the better to follow up the victory
over the advanced infantry of the enemy, had changed their
front disposition into a column of attack, which, in the shape
of a wedge, penetrated the enemy's centre. In this position
they were warmly assailed on both sides by the Libyan infantry wheeling in upon them right and left, and a portion of
them were compelled to halt in order to defend themselves
against the flank attack; by this means their advance was
checked, and the mass of infantry, which was already too
closely crowded, now had no longer room to develop itself at
all. Meanwhile Hasdrubal, after having completed the defeat
of the wing of Paullus, had collected and arranged his cavalry
anew and led them behind the enemy's centre against the wing
of Varro. His Italian cavalry, already sufficiently occupied
with the Numidians, was rapidly scattered before the double
attack, and Hasdrubal, leaving the pursuit of the fugitives
to the Numidians, rallied his squadrons for the third time,
to lead them against the rear of the Roman infantry. This
last charge proved decisive. Flight was impossible, and no
quarter was given. Never, perhaps, was an army of such size
annihilated on the field of battle so completely, and with so
little loss to its antagonist, as was the Roman army at
Cannae. Hannibal had lost not quite 6,000 men, and two-
thirds of that loss fell upon the Celts, who sustained the
first shock of the legions. On the other hand, of the 76,000
Romans who had taken their places in line of battle 70,000
covered the field, amongst whom were the consul Lucius
Paullus, the proconsul Gnaeus Servilius, two-thirds of the
staff-officers, and eighty men of senatorial rank. The consul
Marcus Varro was saved solely by his quick resolution and
his good steed, reached Venusia, and was not ashamed to survive the disaster. The garrison also of the Roman camp, 10,000
strong, were for the most part made prisoners of war; only
a few thousand men, partly of these troops, partly of the line,
escaped to Canusium. Nay, as if in this year Rome was to be

altogether ruined, before its close the legion sent to Gaul
fell into an ambush, and was, with its general Lucius Postumius who was nominated as consul for the next year, totally
destroyed by the Gauls.

This unexampled success appeared at length to mature Conse-
the great political combination, for the sake of which Han- quences of
nibal had come to Italy. He had indeed based his plan of Cannae.
primarily upon his army; but with accurate knowledge of
the power opposed to him he designed that army to be merely
the vanguard, in support of which the powers of the west
and east were gradually to unite their forces, so as to prepare
destruction for the proud city. That support however, which Prevention
seemed the most secure, namely the sending of reinforcements forcements
from Spain, had been frustrated by the boldness and firmness from
of the Roman general sent thither, Gnaeus Scipio. After Spain.
Hannibal's passage of the Rhone Scipio had sailed for Emporiae, and had made himself master first of the coast between
the Pyrenees and the Ebro, and then, after conquering Hanno,
of the interior also (536). In the following year (537) he 218. 217.
had completely defeated the Carthaginian fleet at the mouth
of the Ebro, and after his brother Publius, the brave defender
of the valley of the Po, had joined him with a reinforcement
of 8,000 men, he had even crossed the Ebro, and advanced as
far as Saguntum. Hasdrubal had indeed in the succeeding
year (538), after obtaining reinforcements from Africa, made
an attempt in accordance with his brother's orders to conduct
an army over the Pyrenees; but the Scipios opposed his passage of the Ebro, and totally defeated him, nearly at the same
time that Hannibal conquered at Cannae. The powerful
tribe of the Celtiberians and numerous other Spanish tribes
had joined the Scipios; they commanded the sea, the passes
of the Pyrenees, and, by means of the trusty Massiliots, the
Gallic coast also. Now therefore support to Hannibal was
less than ever to be looked for from Spain.

On the part of Carthage as much had hitherto been done Reinforce-
in support of her general in Italy as could be expected. Africa.
Phoenician squadrons threatened the coasts of Italy and of
the Roman islands and guarded Africa from a Roman landing, and there the matter ended. More substantial assistance
was prevented not so much by the uncertainty as to where

Hannibal was to be found and the want of a port of disembarkation in Italy, as by the fact that for many years the Spanish army had been accustomed to be self-sustaining, and above all by the murmurs of the peace party. Hannibal severely felt the consequences of this unpardonable inaction; in spite of all his saving of his money and of the soldiers whom he had brought with him, his chests were gradually emptied, the pay fell into arrear, and the ranks of his veterans began to thin. But now the news of the victory of Cannae reduced even the factious opposition at home to silence. The Carthaginian senate resolved to place at the disposal of the general considerable assistance in money and men, partly from Africa, partly from Spain, including 4,000 Numidian horse and 40 elephants, and to prosecute the war with energy in Spain as well as in Italy.

Alliance between Carthage and Macedonia.

220–217.

The long-discussed offensive alliance between Carthage and Macedonia had been delayed, first by the sudden death of Antigonus, and then by the indecision of his successor Philip and the unseasonable war waged by him and his Hellenic allies against the Aetolians (534–537). It was only now, after the battle of Cannae, that Demetrius of Pharos found Philip disposed to listen to his proposal to cede to Macedonia his Illyrian possessions—which it was necessary, no doubt, to wrest in the first place from the Romans—and it was only now that the court of Pella came to terms with Carthage. Macedonia undertook to land an invading army on the east coast of Italy, in return for which she received an assurance that the Roman possessions in Epirus should be restored to her.

Alliance between Carthage and Syracuse.

216.

In Sicily king Hiero had during the years of peace maintained a policy of neutrality, so far as he could do so with safety, and he had shown a disposition to accommodate the Carthaginians during the perilous crises after the peace with Rome, particularly by sending supplies of corn. There is no doubt that he saw with the utmost regret a renewed breach between Carthage and Rome; but he had no power to avert it, and when it occurred he adhered with well-considered fidelity to Rome. But soon afterwards (in the autumn of 538) death removed the old man after a reign of fifty-four years. The grandson and successor of the prudent veteran, the young and incapable Hieronymus, entered at once into negotiations with the Carthaginian diplomatists ; and, as they made no difficulty in consenting to secure to him by treaty, first, Sicily as far as the old Carthagino-Sicilian frontier, and then, when he rose in the arrogance of his demands, the possession even of the whole island, he entered into alliance with Carthage, and ordered the Syracusan fleet to unite with the Carthaginian which had come to threaten Syracuse.   The position of the Roman fleet at Lilybaeum, which already had to deal with a second Carthaginian squadron stationed near the Aegates, became all at once very critical, while at the same time the force that was in readiness at Rome for embarkation to Sicily had, in consequence of the defeat at Cannae, to be diverted to other and more urgent objects.

Above all came the decisive fact, that now at length the fabric of the Roman confederacy began to be unhinged, after it had survived unshaken the shocks of two severe years of war.   There passed over to the side of Hannibal Arpi in Apulia, and Uzentum in Messapia, two old towns which had been greatly injured by the Roman colonies of Luceria and Brundisium ; all the towns of the Bruttii—who took the lead —with the exception of the Petelini and the Consentini who had to be besieged before yielding ; the greater portion of the Lucanians ; the Picentes transplanted into the region of Salernum; the Hirpini ; the Samnites with the exception of the Pentri ; lastly and chiefly, Capua the second city of Italy, which was able to bring into the field 30,000 infantry and 4,000 horse, and whose secession determined that of the neighbouring towns Atella and Calatia.   The aristocratic party, indeed, attached by many ties to the interest of Rome everywhere, and more especially in Capua, very earnestly opposed this change of sides, and the obstinate internal conflicts which arose regarding it diminished not a little the advantage which Hannibal derived from these accessions. He found himself obliged, for instance, to have one of the leaders of the aristocratic party in Capua, Decius Magius, who even after the entrance of the Phoenicians obstinately contended for the Roman alliance, seized and conveyed to Carthage ; thus furnishing a demonstration, very inconvenient for himself, of the small value of the liberty and sovereignty

Capua and most of the communities of Lower Italy pass over to Hannibal.

which had just been solemnly guaranteed to the Campanians by the Carthaginian general. On the other hand, the south Italian Greeks adhered to the Roman alliance—a result to which the Roman garrisons no doubt contributed, but which was still more due to the very decided dislike of the Hellenes towards the Phoenicians and towards their new Lucanian and Bruttian allies, and their attachment on the other hand to Rome, which had zealously embraced every opportunity of displaying its Hellenism, and had exhibited towards the Greeks in Italy an unwonted gentleness. Thus the Campanian Greeks, particularly Neapolis, courageously withstood the attack of Hannibal in person : in Magna Graecia Rhegium, Thurii, Metapontum, and Tarentum did the same notwithstanding their very perilous position. Croton and Locri on the other hand were partly carried by storm, partly forced to capitulate, by the united Phoenicians and Bruttians ; and the citizens of Croton were conducted to Locri, while Bruttian colonists occupied that important naval station. The Latin colonies in southern Italy, such as Brundisium, Venusia, Paestum, Cosa, and Cales, of course maintained unshaken fidelity to Rome. They were the strongholds by which the conquerors held in check a foreign land, settled on the soil of the surrounding population, and at feud with their neighbours ; they, too, would be the first to be affected, if Hannibal should keep his word and restore to every Italian community its ancient boundaries. This was likewise the case with all central Italy, the earliest seat of the Roman rule, where Latin manners and language already everywhere preponderated, and the people felt themselves to be the comrades rather than the subjects of their rulers. The opponents of Hannibal in the Carthaginian senate did not fail to appeal to the fact that not one Roman citizen or one Latin community had cast itself into the arms of Carthage. This groundwork of the Roman power could only be broken up, like the Cyclopean walls, stone by stone.

Attitude of the Romans.

Such were the consequences of the day of Cannae, in which the flower of the soldiers and officers of the confederacy, a seventh of the whole number of Italians capable of bearing arms, perished. It was a cruel but righteous punishment for the grave political errors with which not merely some foolish or miserable individuals, but the Roman people themselves, were justly chargeable. A constitution adapted for a small country town was no longer suitable for a great power ; it was simply impossible that the question as to the leadership of the armies of the city in such a war should be left year after year to be decided by the Pandora's box of the ballot-ing-urn. As a fundamental revision of the constitution, if practicable at all, could not at any rate be undertaken now, no course was left but at once to commit the practical super-intendence of the war, and in particular the bestowal and prolongation of the command, to the only authority which was in a position to undertake such a charge—the senate—and to reserve to the comitia the mere formality of confirma-tion. The brilliant successes of the Scipios in the difficult arena of Spanish warfare showed what might in this way be achieved. But political demagogism, which was already gnawing at the aristocratic foundations of the constitution, had seized on the management of the Italian war. The absurd accusation, that the nobles were conspiring with the enemy without, had made an impression on the " people." The heroes to whom political superstition looked for deliver-ance, Gaius Flaminius and Marcus Varro, both " new men " and friends of the people of the purest dye, had accordingly been empowered by the multitude itself to execute the plans of operations which, amidst the approbation of that multitude, they had explained in the Forum ; and the results were the battles of the Trasimene lake and of Cannae. Duty required that the senate, which now of course understood its task better than when it recalled half the army of Regulus from Africa, should take into its hands the management of affairs, and should oppose such mischievous proceedings ; but when the first of those two defeats had for the moment placed the rudder in its hands, it had hardly acted in a manner unbiassed by the interests of party. Little as Quintus Fabius deserves to be compared with these Roman Cleons, he too conducted the war not as a mere military leader, but adhered to his obstinate attitude of defence specially as the political opponent of Gaius Flaminius ; and in the treatment of the quarrel with his subordinate, he did what he could to exasperate at a time when unity was needed. The conse-quence was, first, that the most important instrument which the wisdom of their ancestors had placed in the hands of the senate for such uses—the dictatorship—broke down in his hands; and, secondly—at least indirectly—the battle of Cannae. But the headlong fall of the Roman power was owing not to the fault of Quintus Fabius or Marcus Varro, but to the distrust between the government and the governed —to the variance between the senate and the burgesses. If the deliverance and revival of the state were still possible, the work had to begin with the re-establishment of unity and of confidence at home. To have perceived this and, what is of more importance, to have done it, and done it with an abstinence from all recriminations however justly provoked, constitutes the glorious and imperishable honour of the Roman senate. When Varro—alone of all the generals who had command in the battle—returned to Rome, and the Roman senators met him at the gate and thanked him that he had not despaired of the salvation of his country, this was no empty phraseology concealing under sounding words their real vexation, nor was it bitter mockery over a poor wretch; it was the conclusion of peace between the government and the governed. In presence of the gravity of the time and the gravity of such an appeal, the chattering of demagogues was silent; henceforth the only thought of the Romans was how they might be able jointly to avert the common peril. Quintus Fabius, whose tenacious courage at this decisive moment was of more service to the state than all his feats of war, and the other senators of note took the lead in every movement, and restored to the citizens confidence in themselves and in the future. The senate preserved its firm and unbending attitude, while messengers from all sides hastened to Rome to report the loss of battles, the secession of allies, the capture of posts and magazines, and to ask reinforcements for the valley of the Po and for Sicily at a time when Italy was abandoned and Rome was almost without a garrison. Assemblages of the multitude at the gates were forbidden; onlookers and women were sent to their houses; the time of mourning for the fallen was restricted to thirty days that the service of the gods of joy, from which those clad in mourning attire were excluded, might not be too long interrupted—for so great was the number of the fallen, that there was scarcely a family

which had not to lament its dead.   Meanwhile the remnant
saved from the field of battle had been assembled by two able
military tribunes, Appius Claudius and Publius Scipio the
younger, at Canusium.   The latter managed, by his spirited
bearing and by the brandished swords of his faithful comrades, to change the views of those noble young lords who,
in indolent despair of the salvation of their country, were
thinking of escape beyond the sea.   The consul Marcus
Varro joined them with a handful of men ; about two legions
were gradually collected there ; the senate gave orders that
they should be reorganized and degraded to serve in disgrace
and without pay.   The incapable general was on a suitable
pretext recalled to Rome; the praetor Marcus Claudius
Marcellus, experienced in the Gallic wars, who had been
destined to depart for Sicily with the fleet from Ostia,
assumed the chief command.   The utmost exertions were
made to organize an army capable of taking the field.   The
Latins were summoned to render aid in the common peril.
Rome itself set the example, and called out all the men above
boyhood, armed the debtor-serfs and criminals, and even
incorporated in the army eight thousand slaves purchased by
the state.   As there was a want of arms, they took the old
spoils from the temples, and everywhere set the workshops
and artisans in action.   The senate was completed, not as
timid patriots urged, from the Latins, but from the Roman
burgesses who had the best title.   Hannibal offered a release
of captives at the expense of the Roman treasury ; it was declined, and the Carthaginian envoy who had arrived with the
deputation of captives was not admitted into the city : nothing
should look as if the senate thought of peace.   Not only
were the allies to be prevented from believing that Rome was
disposed to enter into negotiations, but even the meanest
citizen was to be made to understand that for him as for all
there was no peace, and that safety lay only in victory.

CHAPTER VI.

THE WAR UNDER HANNIBAL FROM CANNAE TO ZAMA.

The crisis. THE aim of Hannibal in his expedition to Italy had been to break up the Italian confederacy : after three campaigns that aim had been attained, so far as it was at all attainable. It was clear that the Greek and Latin or Latinized communities of Italy, since they had not been shaken in their allegiance by the day of Cannae, would not yield to terror, but only to force ; and the desperate courage with which even in southern Italy isolated little country towns, such as the Bruttian Petelia, maintained their forlorn defence against the Phoenicians, showed very plainly what awaited them among the Marsians and Latins. If Hannibal had expected to accomplish more in this way and to lead even the Latins against Rome, these hopes had proved vain. But it appears as if even in other respects the Italian coalition had by no means produced the results which Hannibal hoped for. Capua had at once stipulated that Hannibal should not have the right to call Campanian citizens compulsorily to arms ; the citizens had not forgotten how Pyrrhus had acted in Tarentum, and they foolishly imagined that they should be able to withdraw at once from the Roman and from the Phoenician rule. Samnium and Luceria were no longer what they had been, when king Pyrrhus had thought of marching into Rome at the head of the Sabellian youth. Not only did the chain of Roman fortresses everywhere cut the nerves and sinews of the land, but the Roman rule continued for many years had rendered the inhabitants unused to arms—they furnished only a moderate contingent to the Roman armies—had appeased their ancient hatred, and had gained over a number of individuals everywhere to the interest of the ruling community. They joined the conqueror of the Romans, indeed, after the cause of Rome seemed fairly lost, but they felt that the question was no longer one of liberty ; it was simply the exchange of an Italian for a Phoenician master, and it was not enthusiasm, but despair that threw the Sabellian communities into the arms of the victor.   Under such circumstances the war in Italy flagged. Hannibal, who commanded the southern part of the peninsula as far up as the Volturnus and Garganus, and who could not simply abandon these lands again as he had abandoned that of the Celts, had now a frontier to protect, which could not be left uncovered with impunity ; and for the purpose of defending the districts that he had gained against the fortresses which everywhere defied him and the armies advancing from the north, and at the same time of resuming the difficult offensive against central Italy, his forces—an army of about 40,000 men, without reckoning the Italian contingents— were far from sufficient.

Above all, he found that other antagonists were opposed Marcellus. to him.   Taught by fearful experience, the Romans adopted a more judicious system of conducting the war, appointed none but experienced generals to the charge of their armies, and left them, at least where it was necessary, for a longer period in command.   These generals were neither mere spectators of the enemy's movements from the mountains, nor did they throw themselves on their adversary wherever they found him; but, keeping the true mean between inaction and precipitation, they took up their positions in entrenched camps under the walls of fortresses, and accepted battle where victory would lead to results and defeat would not be destruction.   The soul of this new mode of warfare was Marcus Claudius Marcellus.   Instinctively, after the disastrous day of Cannae, the senate and people had turned their eyes to this brave and experienced officer, and entrusted him at once with the actual supreme command.   He had received his training in the troublesome warfare against Hamilcar in Sicily, and had given brilliant evidence of his talents as a leader as well as of his personal valour in the last campaigns against the Celts.   Although far above fifty, he still glowed with all the ardour of the most youthful soldier, and only a few years before this he had, as general, cut down the mounted general of the enemy (p. 86)—the first and only Roman consul who achieved that feat of arms. His life was consecrated to the two divinities, to whom he erected the splendid double temple at the Capene Gate—to Honour and to Valour; and, while the merit of rescuing Rome from the extremity of danger belonged to no single individual, but pertained to the Roman citizens collectively and pre-eminently to the senate, yet no single man contributed more towards the success of the common enterprise than Marcus Marcellus.

Hannibal proceeds to Campania.   From the field of battle Hannibal had turned his steps to Campania. He knew Rome better than the simpletons, who in ancient and modern times have fancied that he might have terminated the struggle by a march on the enemy's capital. Modern warfare, it is true, decides a war on the field of battle; but in ancient times, when the system of attacking fortresses was far less developed than the system of defence, the most complete success in the field was on numberless occasions neutralized by the resistance of the walls of the capitals. The council and citizens of Carthage were not at all to be compared to the senate and people of Rome; the peril of Carthage after the first campaign of Regulus was infinitely more imminent than that of Rome after the battle of Cannae; yet Carthage had made a stand and been completely victorious. With what colour could it be expected that Rome would now deliver her keys to the victor, or even accept an equitable peace? Instead therefore of sacrificing practicable and important successes for the sake of such empty demonstrations, or losing time in the besieging of the two thousand Roman fugitives enclosed within the walls of Canusium, Hannibal had immediately proceeded to Capua before the Romans could throw in a garrison, and by his advance had induced this second city of Italy after long hesitation to join him. He probably hoped that, in possession of Capua, he would be able to seize one of the Campanian ports, where he might disembark the reinforcements which his great victories had wrung from the opposition at home.

Renewal of the war in Campania.   When the Romans learned whither Hannibal had gone, they also left Apulia, where only a weak division was retained, and collected their remaining strength on the right bank of the Volturnus. With the two legions saved from

Cannae Marcus Marcellus marched to Teanum Sidicinum, where he was joined by such troops as were at the moment disposable from Rome and Ostia, and advanced—while the dictator Marcus Junius slowly followed with the main army which had been hastily formed—as far as the Volturnus at Casilinum, with a view if possible to save Capua. That city he found already in the power of the enemy; but on the other hand the attempts of the enemy on Neapolis had been thwarted by the courageous resistance of the citizens, and the Romans were still in good time to throw a garrison into that important port. With equal fidelity the two other large coast towns, Cumae and Nuceria, adhered to Rome. In Nola the struggle between the popular and senatorial parties as to whether they should attach themselves to the Carthaginians or to the Romans, was still undecided. Informed that the former were gaining the superiority, Marcellus crossed the river at Caiatia, and marching along the heights of Suessula so as to evade the enemy's army, he reached Nola in sufficient time to hold it against the foes without and within. In a sally he even repulsed Hannibal in person with considerable loss; a success which, as the first defeat sustained by Hannibal, was of far more importance from its moral effect than from its material results. In Campania indeed, Nuceria, Acerrae, and, after an obstinate siege prolonged into the following year (539), Casilinum also, the key of the Volturnus, were conquered by Hannibal, and the severest punishments were inflicted on the senates of these towns which had ad-hered to Rome. But terror is a bad weapon of proselytism; the Romans succeeded, with comparatively trifling loss, in surmounting the perilous moment of their first weakness. The war in Campania came to a standstill; then winter came on, and Hannibal took up his quarters in Capua, the luxury of which was by no means fraught with benefit to his troops who for three years had not been under a roof. In the next year (539) the war acquired another aspect. The tried general Marcus Marcellus, Tiberius Sempronius Gracchus who had distinguished himself in the campaign of the pre-vious year as master of the horse to the dictator, and the veteran Quintus Fabius Maximus, took—Marcellus as pro-consul, the two others as consuls—the command of the three

215.

215.

Roman armies which were destined to surround Capua and Hannibal; Marcellus resting on Nola and Suessula, Maximus taking a position on the right bank of the Volturnus near Cales, and Gracchus on the coast near Liternum, covering Neapolis and Cumae. The Campanians, who marched to Hamae three miles from Cumae with a view to surprise the Cumaeans, were thoroughly defeated by Gracchus; Hannibal, who had appeared before Cumae to wipe out the stain, was himself worsted in a combat, and when the pitched battle offered by him was declined, retreated in ill humour to Capua. While the Romans in Campania thus not only maintained what they possessed, but also recovered Compulteria and other minor places, loud complaints were heard from the eastern allies of Hannibal. A Roman army under the praetor Marcus Valerius had taken position at Luceria, partly that it might, in connection with the Roman fleet, watch the east coast and the movements of the Macedonians; partly that it might, in connection with the army of Nola, levy contributions on the revolted Samnites, Lucanians, and Hirpinians. To give relief to these, Hannibal turned first against his most active opponent, Marcus Marcellus; but the latter achieved under the walls of Nola no inconsiderable victory over the Phoenician army, and it was obliged to depart, without having cleared off the stain, from Campania for Arpi, in order at length to check the progress of the enemy's army in Apulia. Tiberius Gracchus followed it with his corps, while the two other Roman armies in Campania made arrangements to proceed next spring to the attack of Capua.

The war in Apulia.

The clear vision of Hannibal had not been dazzled by his victories. It became every day more evident that he was not by their means gaining his object. Those rapid marches, that adventurous shifting of the war to and fro, to which Hannibal was mainly indebted for his successes, were at an end; the enemy had become wiser; further enterprises were rendered almost impossible by the inevitable necessity of defending what had been gained. The offensive was not to be thought of; the defensive was difficult, and threatened every year to become more so. He could not conceal from himself that the second half of his great task, the subju-

Hannibal reduced to the defensive.

gation of the Latins and the conquest of Rome, could not be accomplished with his own forces and those of his Italian allies alone. Its accomplishment depended on the council at Carthage, on the head-quarters at Cartagena, on the courts of Pella and of Syracuse. If all the resources of Africa, Spain, Sicily, and Macedonia should now be put forth in earnest against the common enemy; if Lower Italy should become the great rendezvous for the armies and fleets of the west, south, and east; he might hope successfully to finish what the vanguard under his leadership had so brilliantly begun. The most natural and easy course would have been to send to him adequate support from home ; and the Carthaginian state, which had remained almost unaffected by the war and had been raised from its deep decline and brought so close to complete victory by a small band of resolute patriots acting of their own accord and at their own risk, could beyond doubt have done this. That it would have been possible for a Phoenician fleet of any desired strength to effect a landing at Locri or Croton, especially as long as the port of Syracuse remained open to the Carthaginians and the fleet at Brundisium was kept in check by Macedonia, is demonstrated by the unopposed disembarkation at Locri of 4,000 Africans, whom Bomilcar about this time brought over from Carthage to Hannibal, and still more by Hannibal's undisturbed embarkation, when all had been already lost. But after the first impression of the victory of Cannae had died away, the peace party in Carthage, which was at all times ready to purchase the downfall of its political opponents at the expense of its country, and which found faithful support in the shortsightedness and indolence of the citizens, refused the entreaties of the general for more decided support with the half simple, half malicious reply, that he in fact needed no help inasmuch as he was really victor; and thus contributed not much less than the Roman senate to save Rome. Hannibal, reared in the camp and a stranger to the machinery of civic factions, found no popular leader on whose support he could rely, such as his father had found in Hasdrubal ; and he was obliged to seek abroad the means of saving his native country—means which it possessed in rich abundance at home.

His prospects as to reinforcements.

For this purpose he might, at least with more prospect of success, reckon on the leaders of the Spanish patriot army, on the connections which he had formed in Syracuse, and on the intervention of Philip. Everything depended on bringing new forces into the field of war against Rome from Spain, Syracuse, or Macedonia; and for the attainment or for the prevention of this object wars were carried on in Spain, Sicily, and Greece. All of these were but means to an end, and historians have often erred in accounting them of greater importance. So far as the Romans were concerned, they were essentially defensive wars, the proper objects of which were to hold the passes of the Pyrenees, to detain the Macedonian army in Greece, to defend Messana and to prevent the communication between Italy and Sicily. Of course this defensive warfare was, wherever it was possible, carried on by offensive means; and, as circumstances favoured its expansion, it led to the expulsion of the Phoenicians from Spain and Sicily, and to the dissolution of Hannibal's alliances with Syracuse and with Philip. The Italian war in itself fell for the time being into the shade, and resolved itself into conflicts about fortresses and razzias, which had no decisive effect on the main issue. Nevertheless, so long as the Phoenicians retained the offensive at all, Italy always remained the central object of operations; and all efforts were directed towards, as all interest centred in, the removal or the continuance of Hannibal's isolation in southern Italy.

The sending of reinforcements temporarily frustrated.

Had it been possible, immediately after the battle of Cannae, to bring into play all the resources on which Hannibal thought that he might reckon, he might have been tolerably certain of success. But the position of Hasdrubal at that time in Spain after the battle on the Ebro was so critical, that the supplies of money and men, which the victory of Cannae had roused the Carthaginian citizens to furnish, were for the most part expended on Spain, without producing much improvement in the position of affairs there. The Scipios transferred the theatre of war in the following campaign (539) from the Ebro to the Guadalquivir; and in Andalusia, in the very centre of the proper Carthaginian territory, they achieved at Illiturgi and Intibili two brilliant

215.

victories. In Sardinia communications entered into with the natives led the Carthaginians to hope that they should be able to master the island, which would have been of importance as an intermediate station between Spain and Italy. But Titus Manlius Torquatus, who was sent with a Roman army to Sardinia, completely destroyed the Carthaginian landing force, and reassured to the Romans the undisputed possession of the island (539). The legions from Cannae   215. sent to Sicily held their ground in the north and east of the island with courage and success against the Carthaginians and Hieronymus; the latter met his death towards the end of 539 by the hand of an assassin. Even in the case of Mace-   215. donia the ratification of the alliance was delayed, principally because the Macedonian envoys sent to Hannibal were captured on their homeward journey by the Roman vessels of war. In consequence the dreaded invasion of the east coast was temporarily suspended; and the Romans gained time to secure the very important station of Brundisium first by their fleet and then by the land army which before the arrival of Gracchus was employed for the protection of Apulia, and even to make preparations for an invasion of Macedonia in the event of war being declared. While in Italy the war thus came to a stand, out of Italy nothing was done on the part of Carthage to accelerate the movement of new armies or fleets towards the seat of war. The Romans, again, had everywhere with the greatest energy put themselves in a state of defence, and in that defensive attitude had fought for the most part with good results wherever the genius of Hannibal was absent. Thus the short-lived patriotism, which the victory of Cannae had awakened in Carthage, evaporated; the not inconsiderable forces which had been organized there were, either through factious opposition or through a useless attempt to conciliate the different opinions expressed in the council, so frittered away that they were nowhere of any real service, and but a very small portion arrived at the spot where they would have been most useful. At the close of 539 the reflecting Roman   215. statesman might feel that the urgency of the danger was past, and that the resistance so heroically begun had but to persevere in its exertions at all points in order to achieve its object.

War in Sicily.

First of all the war in Sicily was brought to an end. It had formed no part of Hannibal's original plan to excite a war on the island; but partly through accident, chiefly through the boyish vanity of the imprudent Hieronymus, a land war had broken out there, which—doubtless because Hannibal had not planned it—the Carthaginian council took up with especial zeal. After Hieronymus was killed at the close of 539, it seemed more than doubtful whether the citizens would persevere in the policy which he had pursued.

215.

Siege of Syracuse.

If any city had reason to adhere to Rome, that city was Syracuse; for the victory of the Carthaginians over the Romans could not but give to the former, at any rate, the sovereignty of all Sicily, and no one could seriously believe that the promises made by Carthage to the Syracusans would be actually kept. Partly induced by this consideration, partly terrified by the threatening preparations of the Romans—who made every effort to bring once more under their complete control that important island, the bridge between Italy and Africa, and now for the campaign of 540

214.

sent their best general, Marcus Marcellus, to Sicily—the Syracusan citizens showed a disposition to obtain oblivion of the past by a timely return to the Roman alliance. But, amidst the dreadful confusion in the city—which after the death of Hieronymus was agitated alternately by endeavours to restore the ancient freedom of the people and by the *coups de main* of the numerous pretenders to the vacant throne, while the captains of the foreign mercenary troops were the real masters of the place—Hannibal's dexterous emissaries, Hippocrates and Epicydes, found opportunity to frustrate the projects of peace. They stirred up the multitude in the name of liberty; descriptions, exaggerated beyond measure, of the fearful punishment that the Romans were said to have inflicted on the Leontines who had just been re-conquered, awakened doubts even among the better portion of the citizens whether it was not too late to restore their old relations with Rome; while the numerous Roman deserters among the mercenaries, mostly runaway rowers from the fleet, were easily persuaded that a peace on the part of the

citizens with Rome would be their death-warrant. So the
chief magistrates were put to death, the armistice was broken,
and Hippocrates and Epicydes undertook the government of
the city. No course was left to the consul except to undertake a siege; but the skilful conduct of the defence, in which
the Syracusan engineer Archimedes, celebrated as a learned
mathematician, especially distinguished himself, compelled the
Romans after besieging the city for eight months to convert
the siege into a blockade by sea and land.

In the meanwhile Carthage, which hitherto had only sup- Carthagi-
ported the Syracusans with her fleets, on receiving news of nian expedition to
their renewed rising in arms against the Romans had des- Sicily.
patched a strong land army under Himilco to Sicily, which
landed without interruption at Heraclea Minoa and immediately occupied the important town of Agrigentum. To effect a junction with Himilco, the bold and able Hippocrates
marched forth from Syracuse with an army: the position of
Marcellus between the garrison of Syracuse and the two hostile armies began to be critical. With the help of some reinforcements, however, which arrived from Italy, he maintained
his ground in the island and continued the blockade of Syracuse. On the other hand, the greater portion of the small
inland towns were driven into the arms of the Carthaginians
not so much by the armies of the enemy, as by the fearful
severity of the Roman proceedings in the island, more especially the slaughter of the citizens of Enna, suspected of a
design to revolt, by the Roman garrison which was stationed
there. In 542 the besiegers of Syracuse during a festival in   212.
the city succeeded in scaling a portion of the extensive outer
walls that had been deserted by the guard, and in penetrating
into the suburbs which stretched from the "island" and the
city proper on the shore (Achradina) towards the interior. The
fortress of Euryalus, which, situated at the extreme western
end of the suburbs, protected these and the principal road
leading from the interior to Syracuse, was thus isolated and
fell not long afterwards. When the siege of the city thus The Carthaginian
began to assume a turn favourable to the Romans, the two troops de-
armies under Himilco and Hippocrates advanced to its relief, stroyed.
and attempted a simultaneous attack on the Roman position,
combined with an attempt at landing on the part of the Car-

thaginian fleet and a sally of the Syracusan garrison; but the attack was repulsed on all sides, and the two relieving armies were obliged to content themselves with encamping before the city, in the low marshy grounds along the Anapus, which in the height of summer and autumn engender pestilences fatal to those that tarry in them. These pestilences had often saved the city, oftener even than the valour of its citizens; in the times of the first Dionysius, two Phoenician armies in the act of besieging the city had been in this way destroyed under its very walls. Now fate turned the special defence of the city into the means of its destruction; while the army of Marcellus quartered in the suburbs suffered but little, fevers desolated the Phoenician and Syracusan bivouacs. Hippocrates died; Himilco and most of the Africans died also; the survivors of the two armies, mostly natives of Sicily, dispersed into the neighbouring cities. The Carthaginians made a further attempt to save the city from the sea side; but the admiral Bomilcar withdrew, when the Roman fleet offered him battle. Epicydes himself, who commanded in the city, now abandoned it as lost, and made his escape to Agrigentum. Syracuse would gladly have surrendered to the Romans; negotiations had already begun. But for the second time they were thwarted by the deserters: in another mutiny of the soldiers the chief magistrates and a number of respectable citizens were slain, and the government and the defence of the city were entrusted by the foreign troops to their captains. Marcellus now entered into a negotiation with one of these, which gave into his hands one of the two portions of the city that were still free, the "island;" upon which the citizens voluntarily opened to him the gates of Achradina also (in the autumn of 542). If mercy was to be shown in any case, it might, even according to the far from laudable principles of Roman public law as to the treatment of perfidious communities, have been extended to a city which manifestly had not been at liberty to act for itself, and which had repeatedly made the most earnest attempts to get rid of the tyranny of the foreign soldiers. Nevertheless, not only did Marcellus stain his military honour by permitting a general pillage of the wealthy mercantile city, in the course of which Archimedes and many other citizens were

122.
Conquest
of Syra-
cuse.

put to death, but the Roman senate lent a deaf ear to the
complaints which the Syracusans afterwards presented regarding the celebrated general, and neither returned to individuals their property nor restored to the city its freedom.
Syracuse and the towns that had been previously dependent
on it were classed among the communities tributary to Rome
—Tauromenium and Neetum alone obtained the same privileges as Messana, while the territory of Leontini became Roman domain and its former proprietors Roman lessees—and
no Syracusan citizen was henceforth allowed to reside in the
" island," the portion of the city that commanded the harbour.

Sicily thus appeared lost to the Carthaginians; but the
genius of Hannibal exercised even from a distance its influence there.   He despatched to the Carthaginian army, which
remained at Agrigentum in perplexity and inaction under
Hanno and Epicydes, a Libyan cavalry officer Mutines, who
took the command of the Numidian cavalry, and with his
flying squadrons, fanning into an open flame the bitter hatred
which the despotic rule of the Romans had excited over all
the island, commenced a guerilla warfare on the most extensive scale and with the happiest results; so that he even,
when the Carthaginian and Roman armies met on the river
Himera, sustained some conflicts with Marcellus himself successfully.   The relations, however, which prevailed between
Hannibal and the Carthaginian council, were here repeated
on a small scale.   The general appointed by the council pursued with jealous envy the officer sent by Hannibal, and insisted upon giving battle to the proconsul without Mutines
and the Numidians.   The wish of Hanno was carried out,
and he was completely beaten.   Mutines was not induced to
deviate from his course ; he maintained himself in the interior
of the country, occupied several small towns, and was enabled by the not inconsiderable reinforcements which joined
him from Carthage gradually to extend his operations.   His
successes were so brilliant, that at length the commander-in-
chief, who could not otherwise prevent the cavalry officer from
eclipsing him, deprived him summarily of the command of
the light cavalry, and entrusted it to his own son.   The Numidian, who had now for two years preserved the island for

Marginal note: Guerilla war in Sicily.

his Phoenician masters, had the measure of his patience exhausted by this treatment. He and his horsemen who refused to follow the younger Hanno entered into negotiations with the Roman general Marcus Valerius Laevinus, and delivered to him Agrigentum. Hanno escaped in a boat, and went to Carthage to report to his superiors the disgraceful high treason of Hannibal's officer; the Phoenician garrison in the town was put to death by the Romans, and the citizens were sold into slavery (544). To secure the island from such surprises as the landing of 540, the city received a Roman colony; the old and glorious Akragas became the Roman fortress Agrigentum. After the whole of Sicily was thus subdued, the Romans exerted themselves to restore some sort of tranquillity and order to the distracted island. The pack of banditti that haunted the interior were driven together *en masse* and conveyed to Italy, that from their headquarters at Rhegium they might burn and destroy in the territories of Hannibal's allies. The government did its utmost to promote the restoration of agriculture which had been totally neglected in the island. The Carthaginian council more than once talked of sending a fleet to Sicily and renewing the war there; but the project went no further.

Macedonia might have exercised an influence over the course of events more decisive than that of Syracuse. From the Eastern powers neither aid nor resistance was for the moment to be expected. Antiochus the Great, the natural ally of Philip, had, after the decisive victory of the Egyptians at Raphia in 537, to deem himself fortunate in obtaining peace from the indolent Philopator on the basis of the *status quo ante*. The rivalry of the Lagidae and the constant apprehension of a renewed outbreak of the war on the one hand, and insurrections of pretenders in the interior and enterprises of all sorts in Asia Minor, Bactria, and the eastern satrapies on the other, prevented him from joining that great anti-Roman alliance which Hannibal had in view. The Egyptian court was decidedly on the side of Rome, with which it renewed alliance in 544; but it was not to be expected of Ptolemy Philopator, that he would support Rome otherwise than by cargoes of corn. Accordingly there was nothing to prevent Greece and Macedonia from throwing their decisive

Margin notes:

Agrigentum occupied by the Romans.

210.
214.

Sicily tranquillized.

Philip of Macedonia and his delay.

217.

210.

weight into the great Italian struggle except their own discord; they might save the Hellenic name, if they had the self-
control to stand by each other for but a few years against the
common foe.　Such sentiments doubtless were current in
Greece.　The prophetic saying of Agelaus of Naupactus, that
he was afraid that the prize-fights in which the Hellenes
now indulged at home might soon be over; his earnest warning to direct their eyes to the west, and not to allow a
stronger power to impose on all the parties now contending
a peace of equal servitude—such sayings had essentially contributed to bring about the peace between Philip and the
Aetolians (537), and it was a significant proof of the tendency　　217.
of that peace, that the Aetolian league immediately nominated Agelaus as its *strategus*.

National patriotism was bestirring itself in Greece as in
Carthage : for a moment it seemed possible to kindle a
national Hellenic war against Rome.　But the general in
such a crusade could only be Philip of Macedonia ; and he
lacked the enthusiasm and the faith in the nation, which
alone could carry on such a war.　He knew not how to solve
the arduous problem of transforming himself from the oppressor into the champion of Greece.　His very delay in the
conclusion of the alliance with Hannibal damped the first and
best zeal of the Greek patriots ; and when he did enter into
the conflict with Rome, his mode of conducting war was still
less fitted to awaken sympathy and confidence.　His first attempt, which was made in the very year of the battle of Cannae
(538), to obtain possession of the city of Apollonia, failed in a　　216.
way almost ridiculous, for Philip turned back in all haste on
receiving the totally groundless report that a Roman fleet
was steering for the Adriatic.　This took place before there
was a formal breach with Rome ; when the breach at length
ensued, friend and foe expected a Macedonian landing in
Lower Italy.　Since 539 a Roman fleet and army had been　　215.
stationed at Brundisium to meet it ; Philip, who was without
vessels of war, was constructing a flotilla of light Illyrian
barks to convey his army across.　But when the endeavour
had to be made in earnest, his courage failed to encounter
the dreaded quinqueremes at sea ; he broke the promise
which he had given to his ally Hannibal to attempt a landing,

and with the view of still doing something he resolved to make an attack on his own share of the spoil, the Roman possessions in Epirus (540). Nothing would have come of this even at the best; but the Romans, who well knew that offensive was preferable to defensive protection, were by no means content to remain—as Philip probably expected—spectators of the attack from the opposite shore. The Roman fleet conveyed a division of the army from Brundisium to Epirus; Oricum was recaptured from the king, a garrison was thrown into Apollonia, and the Macedonian camp was stormed. Thereupon Philip passed from partial action to total inaction, and notwithstanding all the complaints of Hannibal, who vainly tried to infuse into Philip's halting and shortsighted policy the energy of his own fire and decision, he allowed some years to elapse in armed inactivity.

Rome heads [212 a Greek coalition against Macedonia.

Nor was Philip the first to renew the hostilities. The fall of Tarentum (542), by which Hannibal acquired an excellent port on the coast which was the most convenient for the landing of a Macedonian army, induced the Romans to parry the blow at a distance and to give the Macedonians so much employment at home that they could not think of an attempt on Italy. The national enthusiasm in Greece had of course evaporated long ago. With the help of the old antagonism to Macedonia, and of the fresh acts of imprudence and injustice of which Philip had been guilty, the Roman admiral Laevinus found no difficulty in organizing against Macedonia a coalition of the intermediate and minor powers under the protectorate of Rome. It was headed by the Aetolans, at whose diet Laevinus had personally appeared and had gained its support by a promise of the Acarnanian territory which the Aetolians had long coveted. They concluded with Rome a modest agreement to rob the other Greeks of men and land on the joint account, so that the land should belong to the Aetolians, the men and moveables to the Romans. They were joined by the states of anti-Macedonian, or rather primarily of anti-Achaean, tendencies in Greece proper; in Attica by Athens, in the Peloponnesus by Elis and Messene and especially by Sparta, the antiquated constitution of which had been just about this time overthrown by a daring soldier

Machanidas, in order that he might exercise despotic power under the name of king Pelops, a minor, and might establish a government of military adventurers sustained by bands of mercenaries. The coalition was joined moreover by those steadfast antagonists of Macedonia, the chiefs of the half-barbarous Thracian and Illyrian tribes, and lastly by Attalus king of Pergamus, who followed out his own interest with sagacity and energy amidst the ruin of the two great Greek states which surrounded him, and had the acuteness even now to attach himself as a client to Rome when his assistance was still of some value.

It is neither agreeable nor necessary to follow the vicissitudes of this aimless struggle. Philip, although he was superior to each one of his opponents and repelled their attacks on all sides with energy and personal valour, yet consumed his time and strength in that profitless defensive. Now he had to turn against the Aetolians, who in concert with the Roman fleet annihilated the unfortunate Acarnanians and threatened Locris and Thessaly ; now an invasion of barbarians summoned him to the northern provinces ; now the Achaeans solicited his help against the predatory expeditions of Aetolians and Spartans ; now king Attalus of Pergamus and the Roman admiral Publius Sulpicius with their combined fleets threatened the east coast or landed troops in Euboea. The want of a war fleet paralyzed Philip in all his movements ; he even went so far as to beg vessels of war from his ally Prusias of Bithynia, and even from Hannibal. It was only towards the close of the war that he resolved—as he should have done at first—to order the construction of 100 ships of war ; of these however no use was made, if the order was executed at all. All who understood the position of Greece and sympathized with it lamented the unhappy war, in which the last energies of Greece preyed upon itself and the prosperity of the land was destroyed ; repeatedly the commercial states, Rhodes, Chios, Mitylene, Byzantium, Athens, and even Egypt had attempted a mediation. In fact both parties had an interest in coming to terms. The Aetolians, to whom their Roman allies attached the chief importance, had, like the Macedonians, suffered greatly by the war ; especially after the petty king of the Athamanes had

Resultless warfare.

Peace between Philip and the Greeks.

been gained by Philip, and the interior of Aetolia had thus been laid open to Macedonian incursions. Many Aetolians too had their eyes gradually opened to the dishonourable and pernicious part which the Roman alliance condemned them to play; a cry of horror pervaded the whole Greek nation when the Aetolians in concert with the Romans sold whole bodies of Hellenic citizens, such as those of Anticyra, Oreus, Dyme, and Aegina, into slavery. But the Aetolians were no longer free; they ran a great risk if of their own accord they concluded peace with Philip, and they found the Romans by no means disposed, especially after the favourable turn which matters were taking in Spain and in Italy, to desist from a war, which on their part was carried on with merely a few ships, and the burden and injury of which fell mainly on the Aetolians. At length however the Aetolians resolved to listen to the mediating cities: and, notwithstanding the counter efforts of the Romans, a peace was arranged in the winter of 548–9 between the Greek powers. Aetolia had converted an over-powerful ally into a dangerous enemy; but the Roman senate, which just at that time was summoning all the resources of the exhausted state for the decisive expedition to Africa, did not deem it a fitting moment to resent the breach of the alliance. The war with Philip could not have been carried on by the Romans without considerable exertions of their own after the withdrawal of the Aetolians; and it appeared to them more convenient to terminate it also by a peace, whereby the state of things before the war was substantially restored and Rome in particular retained all her possessions on the coast of Epirus except the worthless territory of the Atintanes. Under the circumstances Philip might deem himself fortunate in obtaining such terms; but the fact proclaimed—what could not indeed be longer concealed—that all the unspeakable misery which ten years of a warfare waged with revolting inhumanity had brought upon Greece had been endured in vain, and that the grand and just combination, which Hannibal had projected and all Greece had for a moment joined, was shattered irretrievably.

In Spain, where the spirit of Hamilcar and Hannibal was powerful, the struggle was more severe. Its progress was

206–205.
Peace between
Philip and
Rome.

Spanish
war.

marked by the singular vicissitudes incidental to the peculiar
nature of the country and the habits of the people.   The
farmers and shepherds, who inhabited the beautiful valley of
the Ebro and the luxuriantly fertile Andalusia as well as the
rough intervening highland region traversed by numerous
wooded mountain ranges, could easily be assembled in arms
as a general levy ; but it was difficult to lead them against the
enemy or even to keep them together at all.   The inhabitants of the towns could just as little be combined for steady
and united action, obstinately as in each case they bade defiance to the oppressor behind their walls.   They all appear
to have made little distinction between the Romans and the
Carthaginians ; whether the troublesome guests who had
established themselves in the valley of the Ebro, or those
who had established themselves on the Guadalquivir, possessed a larger or smaller portion of the peninsula, was probably to the natives very much a matter of indifference ; and
for that reason the tenacity of partisanship so characteristic
of Spain was but little prominent in this war, with isolated
exceptions such as Saguntum on the Roman and Astapa on
the Carthaginian side.   But, as neither the Romans nor the
Africans had brought with them sufficient forces of their own,
the war necessarily became on both sides a struggle to gain
partisans, which was decided rarely by solid attachment, more
usually by fear, money, or accident, and which, when it
seemed at an end, simply resolved itself into an endless series
of fortress-sieges and guerilla conflicts, whence it soon revived with fresh fury.   The armies were as shifting as the
downs on the sea shore ; on the spot where a hill stood
yesterday, not a trace of it remains to-day.   In general the
superiority was on the side of the Romans, partly because
they at first appeared in Spain as the deliverers of the land
from Phoenician despotism, partly because of the fortunate
selection of their leaders and of the stronger nucleus of trustworthy troops which these brought along with them.   It is
hardly possible, however, with the very imperfect and—in
point of chronology especially—very confused accounts which
have been handed down to us, to give a satisfactory view of
a war so conducted.

The two lieutenant-governors of the Romans in the pe-   Successes

M 2

ninsula, Gnaeus and Publius Scipio — both of them, but especially Gnaeus, good generals and excellent administrators — accomplished their task with the most brilliant success. Not only was the barrier of the Pyrenees steadfastly maintained, and the attempt to re-establish the interrupted communication by land between the commander-in-chief of the enemy and his head-quarters sternly repulsed; not only had a Spanish New Rome been created, after the model of the Spanish New Carthage, by means of the comprehensive fortifications and harbour works of Tarraco, but **215.** the Roman armies had already in 539 fought with success in Andalusia (p. 152). Their expedition thither was repeated **214.** in the following year (540) with still greater success. The Romans carried their arms almost to the Pillars of Hercules, extended their protectorate in South Spain, and lastly by regaining and restoring Saguntum secured for themselves an important station on the line from the Ebro to Cartagena, repaying at the same time as far as possible an old debt which the nation owed. While the Scipios thus almost dislodged the Carthaginians from Spain, they knew how to raise up a dangerous enemy to them in western Africa itself in the person of the powerful west African prince Syphax, ruling in the modern provinces of Oran and Algiers, who entered into connections with the Romans (about 541). Had it been possible to supply him with a Roman army, great results might have been expected; but at that time not a man could be spared from Italy, and the Spanish army was too weak to be divided. Nevertheless the troops belonging to Syphax himself, trained and led by Roman officers, excited so serious a ferment among the Libyan subjects of Carthage that the lieutenant-commander of Spain and Africa, Hasdrubal Barca went in person to Africa with the flower of his Spanish troops. His arrival in all likelihood gave another turn to the matter; king Gala—in what is now the province of Constantine—who had long been the rival of Syphax, declared for Carthage, and his brave son Massinissa defeated Syphax, and compelled him to make peace. Little more is related of this Libyan war than the story of the cruel vengeance which Carthage, according to her wont, inflicted on the rebels after the victory of Massinissa.

This turn of affairs in Africa had an important effect on the war in Spain. Hasdrubal was able once more to proceed to that country (543), whither he was soon followed by considerable reinforcements and by Massinissa himself. The Scipios, who during the absence of the enemy's general (541, 542) had continued to plunder and to gain partisans in the Carthaginian territory, found themselves unexpectedly assailed by forces so superior that they were under the necessity of either retreating behind the Ebro or calling out the Spaniards. They chose the latter course, and took into their pay 20,000 Celtiberians; and then, in order the better to encounter the three armies of the enemy under Hasdrubal Barca, Hasdrubal the son of Gisgo, and Mago, they divided their army and did not even keep their Roman troops together. They thus prepared the way for their own destruction. While Gnaeus with his corps, containing a third of the Roman and all the Spanish troops, lay encamped opposite to Hasdrubal Barca, the latter had no difficulty in inducing the Spaniards in the Roman army by means of a sum of money to withdraw — which perhaps to their freelance ideas of morals did not even seem a breach of fidelity, seeing that they did not pass over to the enemies of their paymaster. Nothing was left to the Roman general but hastily to begin his retreat, in which the enemy closely followed him. Meanwhile the second Roman corps under Publius found itself vigorously assailed by the two other Phoenician armies under Hasdrubal son of Gisgo and Mago, and the daring squadrons of Massinissa's horse gave to the Carthaginians a decided advantage. The Roman camp was almost surrounded; if the Spanish auxiliaries already on the way should arrive, the Romans would be completely hemmed in. The bold resolve of the proconsul to encounter with his best troops the advancing Spaniards, before their appearance should fill up the gap in the blockade, ended unfortunately. The Romans indeed had at first the advantage; but the Numidian horse, who were rapidly despatched in pursuit, soon overtook them and prevented them both from following up the victory which they had already half gained, and from marching back, until the Phoenician infantry came up and at length the fall of the general converted

The Scipios defeated and killed. 211.

213. 212.

the lost battle into a defeat.   After Publius had thus fallen, Gnaeus, who slowly retreating had with difficulty defended himself against the one Carthaginian army, found himself suddenly assailed at once by three, and all retreat cut off by the Numidian cavalry.   Hemmed in upon a bare hill, which did not even afford a possibility of pitching a camp, the whole corps were cut down or taken prisoners.   As to the fate of the general himself no certain information was ever obtained.   A small division alone was conducted by Gaius Marcius, an excellent officer of the school of Gnaeus, in safety to the other bank of the Ebro ; and thither the legate Titus Fonteius also succeeded in bringing safely the portion of the corps of Publius that had been left in the camp; most even of the Roman garrisons scattered in the south of Spain

Spain south of the Ebro lost to the Romans.

were enabled to flee thither.   In all Spain south of the Ebro the Phoenicians ruled without opposition; and the moment seemed not far distant, when the river would be crossed, the Pyrenees would be open, and the communication with Italy would be restored.   But the emergency in the Roman camp called the right man to the command.   The choice of the soldiers, passing over older and not incapable officers, summoned that Gaius Marcius to become leader of the army ; and his dexterous management and, quite as much perhaps, the envy and discord among the three Carthaginian generals, wrested from these the further fruits of their important victory.   Such of the Carthaginians as had crossed the river were driven back, and the line of the Ebro was held in the meanwhile, till Rome gained time to send a new army and a

Nero sent to Spain.

new general.   Fortunately the turn of the war in Italy, where Capua had just fallen, allowed this to be done.   A strong legion—12,000 men—arriving under the propraetor Gaius Claudius Nero, restored the balance of arms.   An ex-

210.

pedition to Andalusia in the following year (544) was most successful; Hasdrubal Barca was beset and surrounded, and escaped a capitulation only by ignoble stratagem and open perfidy.   But Nero was not the right general for the Spanish war.   He was an able officer, but a harsh, irritable, unpopular man, who had little skill in the art of renewing old connections or of forming new ones, or in taking advantage of the injustice and arrogance with which the Carthaginians

after the death of the Scipios had treated friend and foe in
Further Spain, and had exasperated all against them.

The senate, which formed a correct judgment as to the Publius
Scipio.
importance and the peculiar character of the Spanish war,
and had learned from the Uticenses brought in as prisoners
by the Roman fleet the great exertions which were making
in Carthage to send Hasdrubal and Massinissa with a numerous army over the Pyrenees, resolved to despatch to Spain
new reinforcements and an extraordinary general of higher
rank, the nomination of whom they deemed it expedient to
leave to the people. For long—so runs the story—nobody
announced himself as a candidate for the perilous and complicated office ; but at last a young officer of twenty-seven,
Publius Scipio (son of the general of the same name that had
fallen in Spain), who had held the offices of military tribune
and aedile, came forward to solicit it. It is incredible that
the Roman senate should have left to accident an election of
such importance in an assembly which it had itself suggested,
and equally incredible that ambition and patriotism should
have so died out in Rome that no tried officer presented himself for the important post. If on the other hand the eyes
of the senate turned to the young, talented, and experienced
officer, who had brilliantly distinguished himself in the hotly
contested days on the Trebia and at Cannae, but who still had
not the rank requisite for his coming forward as the successor
of men who had been praetors and consuls, it was very natural
to adopt this course, which compelled the people out of good
nature to admit the only candidate notwithstanding his defective qualification, and which could not but bring both him
and the Spanish expedition, which was doubtless very unpopular, into favour with the multitude. If the effect of this
ostensibly unpremeditated candidature was thus calculated, it
was perfectly successful. The son, who went to avenge the
death of a father whose life he had saved nine years before at
the Trebia ; the young man of manly beauty and long locks,
who with modest blushes offered himself in the absence of a
better for the post of danger ; the mere military tribune,
whom the votes of the centuries now raised at once to the
roll of the highest magistracies—all this made a wonderful
and indelible impression on the citizens and farmers of Rome.

And in truth Publius Scipio was one, who was himself enthusiastic, and who inspired enthusiasm. He was not one of the few who by their energy and iron will constrain the world to adopt and to move in new paths for centuries, or who at any rate grasp the reins of destiny for years till its wheels roll over them. Publius Scipio gained battles and conquered countries under the instructions of the senate; with the aid of his military laurels he took also a prominent position in Rome as a statesman ; but a wide interval separates such a man from an Alexander or a Cæsar. As an officer, he rendered at least no greater service to his country than Marcus Marcellus ; and as a politician, although not perhaps himself fully conscious of the unpatriotic and personal character of his policy, he injured his country at least as much, as he benefited it by his military skill. Yet a special charm lingers around the form of that graceful hero ; it is surrounded, as with a dazzling halo, by the atmosphere of serene and confident inspiration, in which Scipio with mingled credulity and adroitness always moved. With quite enough of enthusiasm to warm men's hearts, and enough of calculation to follow in every case the dictates of intelligence, while not leaving out of account the vulgar ; not naïve enough to share the belief of the multitude in his divine inspirations, nor straightforward enough to set it aside, and yet in secret thoroughly persuaded that he was a man specially favoured of the gods—in a word, a genuine prophetic nature ; raised above the people, and not less aloof from them ; a man steadfast to his word and kingly in his bearing, who thought that he would humble himself by adopting the ordinary title of a king, but could never understand how the constitution of the republic should in his case be binding ; so confident in his own greatness that he knew nothing of envy or of hatred, courteously acknowledged other men's merits, and compassionately forgave other men's faults ; an excellent officer and a refined diplomatist without presenting offensively the special stamp of either calling, uniting Hellenic culture with the fullest national feeling of a Roman, an accomplished speaker and of graceful manners—Publius Scipio won the hearts of soldiers and of women, of his countrymen and of the Spaniards, of his rivals in the senate and of his greater Carthaginian antagonist. His name was soon on every one's lips, and his was the star which seemed destined to bring victory and peace to his country.

Publius Scipio went to Spain in 544–5, accompanied by the propraetor Marcus Silanus, who was to succeed Nero and to serve as assistant and counsellor to the young commander-in-chief, and by his intimate friend Gaius Laelius as admiral, and furnished with a legion exceeding the usual strength and a well-filled chest. His appearance on the scene was at once signalized by one of the boldest and most fortunate *coups de main* that are known in history. Of the three Carthaginian generals Hasdrubal Barca was stationed at the sources, Hasdrubal son of Gisgo at the mouth, of the Tagus, and Mago at the Pillars of Hercules; the nearest of them was ten days' march from the Phoenician capital New Carthage. Suddenly in the spring of 545, before the enemy's armies began to move, Scipio set out with his whole army of nearly 30,000 men and the fleet for this town, which he could reach by the coast route from the mouth of the Ebro in a few days, and surprised the Phoenician garrison, not above 1,000 men strong, by a combined attack by sea and land. The town, situated on a tongue of land projecting into the harbour, found itself threatened at once on three sides by the Roman fleet, and on the fourth by the legions; and all help was far distant. Nevertheless the commandant Mago defended himself with resolution and armed the citizens, as the soldiers did not suffice to man the walls. A sortie was attempted; but the Romans repelled it with ease and, without taking time to open a regular siege, began the assault on the landward side. Eagerly the assailants pushed their advance along the narrow land approach to the town; new columns constantly relieved those that were fatigued; the weak garrison was utterly exhausted; but the Romans had gained no advantage. Scipio had not expected any; the assault was merely designed to draw away the garrison from the side next to the harbour, where, having been informed that part of the latter was left dry at ebb-tide, he meditated a second attack. While the assault was raging on the landward side, Scipio sent a division with ladders over the shallow bank "where Neptune himself showed them the way," and they had actually the

Scipio goes to Spain. 210–209.

Capture of New Carthage. 209.

good fortune to find the walls at that point undefended. Thus the city was won on the first day; whereupon Mago in the citadel capitulated. With the Carthaginian capital there fell into the hands of the Romans 18 dismantled vessels of war and 63 transports, the whole war-stores, considerable supplies of corn, the war-chest of 600 talents (more than £140,000), the hostages of all the Spanish allies of Carthage, and ten thousand captives, among whom were eighteen Carthaginian gerusiasts or judges. Scipio promised the hostages permission to return home so soon as their respective communities should have entered into alliance with Rome, and employed the resources which the city afforded to reinforce and improve the condition of his army. He ordered the artisans of New Carthage, 2,000 in number, to work for the Roman army, promising to them liberty at the close of the war, and he selected the able-bodied men among the remaining multitude to serve as rowers in the fleet. But the burgesses of the city were spared, and allowed to retain their liberty and former position. Scipio knew the Phoenicians and was aware that they would obey; and it was important that a city possessing the only excellent harbour on the east coast and rich silver-mines should be secured by something more than a garrison.

Success thus crowned the bold enterprise—bold, because it was not unknown to Scipio that Hasdrubal Barca had received orders from his government to advance towards Gaul and was engaged in fulfilling them, and because the weak division left behind on the Ebro was not in a position seriously to oppose that movement, should the return of Scipio be delayed. But he was again at Tarraco, before Hasdrubal made his appearance on the Ebro. The hazard of the game which the young general played, when he abandoned his primary task in order to execute a dashing stroke, was concealed by the fabulous success which Neptune and Scipio had gained in concert. The marvellous capture of the Phoenician capital so abundantly justified all the expectations which had been formed at home regarding the wondrous youth, that none could venture to utter any adverse opinion. Scipio's command was indefinitely prolonged; he himself resolved no longer to confine his efforts to the mere task of guarding the passes of the Pyrenees. Already, in consequence of the fall of New Carthage, not only had the Spaniards on the north of the Ebro completely submitted, but even beyond the Ebro the most powerful princes had exchanged the Carthaginian for the Roman protectorate.

Scipio employed the winter of 545-6 in breaking up his fleet and increasing his land army with the men thus acquired, so that he might at once guard the north and assume the offensive in the south more energetically than before; and he marched in 546 to Andalusia. There he encountered Hasdrubal Barca, who, in the execution of his long cherished plan, was moving northward to the help of his brother. A battle took place at Baecula, in which the Romans claimed the victory and professed to have made 10,000 captives; but Hasdrubal substantially attained his end, although at the sacrifice of a portion of his army. With his chest, his elephants, and the best portion of his troops, he fought his way to the north coast of Spain; marching along the shore, he reached the western passes of the Pyrenees which appear to have been unoccupied, and before the bad season began he was in Gaul, where he took up quarters for the winter. It was evident that the resolve of Scipio to combine offensive operations with the defensive which he had been instructed to maintain was inconsiderate and unwise. The immediate task assigned to the Spanish army, which not only Scipio's father and uncle, but even Gaius Marcius and Gaius Nero had accomplished with much inferior means, was not enough for the arrogance of the victorious general at the head of a numerous army; and he was mainly to blame for the extremely critical position of Rome in the summer of 547, when the plan of Hannibal for a combined attack on the Romans was at length realized. But the gods covered the errors of their favourite with laurels. In Italy the peril fortunately passed over; the Romans were glad to accept the bulletin of the ambiguous victory of Baecula, and, when fresh tidings of victory arrived from Spain, they thought no more of the circumstance that they had had to combat the ablest general and the flower of the Hispano-Phoenician army in Italy.

After the removal of Hasdrubal Barca the two generals who were left in Spain determined for the time being to retire, Hasdrubal son of Gisgo to Lusitania, Mago even to the

Margin notes:

209-208. Scipio goes to Andalusia.

208.

Hasdrubal crosses the Pyrenees.

207.

Spain conquered.

Baleares ; and, until new reinforcements should arrive from Africa, they left the light cavalry of Massinissa alone to wage a desultory warfare in Spain, as Mutines had done so successfully in Sicily. The whole east coast thus fell into the power

207.   of the Romans. In the following year (547) Hanno actually made his appearance from Africa with a third army, whereupon Mago and Hasdrubal returned to Andalusia. But Marcus Silanus defeated the united armies of Mago and Hanno, and captured the latter in person. Hasdrubal upon this abandoned the idea of keeping the open field, and distributed his troops among the Andalusian cities, of which Scipio was during this year able to storm only one, Oringis. The Phoenicians seemed vanquished ; but yet they were able in the

206.   following year (548) once more to send into the field a powerful army, 32 elephants, 4,000 horse, and 70,000 foot, far the greater part of whom, it is true, were hastily collected Spanish militia. Again a battle took place at Baecula. The Roman army numbered little more than half that of the enemy, and was also to a considerable extent composed of Spaniards. Scipio, like Wellington in similar circumstances, disposed his Spaniards so that they should not partake in the fight—the only possible mode of preventing their dispersion—while on the other hand he threw his Roman troops in the first instance on the Spaniards. The day was nevertheless obstinately contested ; but at length the Romans were the victors, and, as a matter of course, the defeat of such an army was equivalent to its complete dissolution—Hasdrubal and Mago singly made their escape to Gades. The Romans were now without a rival in the peninsula ; the few towns that did not submit with good will were subdued one by one, and some of them were punished with cruel severity. Scipio was even able to visit Syphax on the African coast, and to enter into communications with him and also with Massinissa with reference to an expedition to Africa—a foolhardy venture, which was not warranted by any corresponding advantage, however much the report of it might please the curiosity of the citizens of the capital at home. Gades alone, where Mago held command, was still Phoenician. For a moment it seemed as if, after the Romans had entered upon the Carthaginian heritage

and had sufficiently undeceived the expectation cherished
here and there among the Spaniards that after the close of
the Phoenician rule they would get rid of their Roman guests
also and regain their ancient freedom, a general insurrection against the Romans would break forth in Spain, in
which the former allies of Rome would take the lead.   The
sickness of the Roman general and the mutiny of one of
his corps, occasioned by their pay being in arrear for
many years, favoured the rising.   But Scipio recovered
sooner than was expected, and dexterously suppressed the
tumult among the soldiers ; upon which the communities
that had taken the lead in the national rising were subdued at once before the insurrection gained ground.   Seeing *Mago*
that nothing came of this movement and Gades could not *goes to*
be permanently held, the Carthaginian government ordered *Italy.*
Mago to gather together whatever could be got in ships,
troops, and money, and with these, if possible, to give
another turn to the war in Italy.   Scipio could not prevent
this—his dismantling of the fleet now avenged itself—and
he was a second time obliged to leave in the hands of his
gods the defence, with which he had been entrusted, of his
country against new invasions.   The last of Hamilcar's sons
left the peninsula without opposition.   After his departure *Gades*
Gades, the earliest and latest possession of the Phoenicians *becomes*
on Spanish soil, submitted on favourable conditions to the *Roman.*
new masters.   Spain was, after a thirteen years' struggle,
converted from a Carthaginian into a Roman province, in
which the conflict with the Romans was still continued
for centuries by means of insurrections always suppressed and
yet never subdued, but in which at the moment no enemy
stood opposed to Rome.   Scipio embraced the first moment
of apparent peace to resign his command (in the end of 548),   *206.*
and to report at Rome in person the victories which he had
achieved and the provinces which he had won.

While the war was thus terminated in Sicily by Marcel- *Italian*
lus, in Greece by Publius Sulpicius, and in Spain by Scipio, *war.*
the mighty struggle was carried on without interruption in
the Italian peninsula.   There after the battle of Cannae
had been fought and its effects in loss or gain could by degrees be discerned, at the commencement of 540, the fifth   *211.*

Position of the armies.

year of the war, the dispositions of the opposing Romans and Phoenicians were the following. North Italy had been reoccupied by the Romans after the departure of Hannibal, and was protected by three legions, two of which were stationed in the Celtic territory, the third as a reserve in Picenum. Lower Italy, as far as Mount Garganus and the Volturnus, was, with the exception of the fortresses and most of the ports, in the hands of Hannibal. He lay with his main army at Arpi, while Tiberius Gracchus with four legions confronted him in Apulia, resting upon the fortresses of Luceria and Beneventum. In the land of the Bruttians, where the inhabitants had thrown themselves entirely into the arms of Hannibal, and where even the ports—excepting Rhegium, which the Romans protected from Messana—were occupied by the Phoenicians, there was a second Carthaginian army under Hanno, which in the meanwhile had no enemy to face it. The Roman main army of four legions under the two consuls, Quintus Fabius and Marcus Marcellus, was on the point of attempting to recover Capua. To these there fell to be added on the Roman side the reserve of two legions in the capital, the garrisons placed in all the seaports— Tarentum and Brundisium having been reinforced by a legion on account of the Macedonian landing apprehended there—and lastly the strong fleet which had undisputed command of the sea. If we add to these the Roman armies in Sicily, Sardinia, and Spain, the whole number of the Roman forces, even apart from the garrison service in the fortresses of Lower Italy which was provided for by the colonists occupying them, may be estimated at not less than 200,000 men, of whom one-third were newly enrolled for this year, and about one half were Roman citizens. It may be assumed that all the men capable of service from the 17th to the 46th year were under arms, and that the fields, where the war permitted them to be tilled at all, were cultivated by the slaves and the old men, women, and children. Of course, under such circumstances the finances were in the most grievous embarrassment; the land-tax, the main source of revenue, came in but very irregularly. Yet notwithstanding these difficulties as to men and money the Romans were able—slowly indeed and by exerting all their energies, but still surely—to recover what they had so rapidly lost; to increase their armies yearly, while those of the Phoenicians were diminishing; to gain ground year by year on the Italian allies of Hannibal, the Campanians, Apulians, Samnites, and Bruttians, who neither sufficed, like the Roman fortresses in Lower Italy, for their own protection nor were adequately protected by the weak army of Hannibal; and finally, by means of the method of warfare instituted by Marcus Marcellus, to develop the talent of their officers and to bring into play the full superiority of the Roman infantry. Hannibal might doubtless still hope for victories, but no longer such victories as those on the Trasimene lake and on the Aufidus; the times of the citizen-generals were gone by. No course was left to him but to wait till either Philip should execute his long promised descent or his own brothers should join him from Spain, and meanwhile to keep himself, his army, and his clients as far as possible free from harm and in good humour. We hardly recognize in the obstinate defensive system which he now began the same general who had carried on the offensive with almost unequalled impetuosity and boldness; it is marvellous in a psychological as well as in a military point of view, that the same man should have accomplished the two tasks prescribed to him—tasks so diametrically opposite in their character—with equal completeness.

At first the war turned chiefly towards Campania. Hannibal appeared in good time to protect its capital, which he prevented from being invested; but he was unable either to wrest any of the Campanian towns held by the Romans from their strong Roman garrisons, or to prevent—in addition to a number of less important country towns—Casilinum, which secured his passage over the Volturnus, from being taken by the two consular armies after an obstinate defence. An attempt of Hannibal to gain Tarentum, with the view especially of acquiring a safe landing-place for the Macedonian army, proved unsuccessful. Meanwhile the Bruttian army of the Carthaginians under Hanno had various encounters in Lucania with the Roman army of Apulia; in the course of which Tiberius Gracchus fought with favourable results, and after a successful combat not far from

Conflicts in the south of Italy.

Beneventum, in which the slave legions pressed into service distinguished themselves, he bestowed liberty and burgess-rights on his slave-soldiers in the name of the people.

Arpi [213. acquired by the Romans.

In the following year (541) the Romans recovered the rich and important Arpi, whose citizens, after the Roman soldiers had stolen into the town, made common cause with them against the Carthaginian garrison. In general the bonds of the symmachy formed by Hannibal were relaxing; a number of the leading Capuans and several of the Bruttian towns passed over to Rome; even a Spanish division of the Phoenician army, when informed by Spanish emissaries of the course of events in their native land, passed from the Carthaginian into the Roman service.

212. Tarentum taken by Hannibal.

The year 542 was more unfavourable for the Romans in consequence of fresh political and military errors, of which Hannibal did not fail to take advantage. The connections which Hannibal maintained with the towns of Magna Graecia had led to no serious result; save that the hostages from Tarentum and Thurii, who were kept at Rome, were induced by his emissaries to make a foolhardy attempt at escape, in which they were speedily recaptured by the Roman posts. But the injudicious spirit of revenge displayed by the Romans was of more service to Hannibal than his intrigues; the execution of all the hostages who had sought to escape deprived them of a valuable pledge, and the exasperated Greeks thenceforth meditated how they might open their gates to Hannibal. Tarentum was actually occupied by the Carthaginians in consequence of an understanding with the citizens and of the negligence of the Roman commandant; with difficulty the Roman garrison maintained itself in the citadel. The example of Tarentum was followed by Heraclea, Thurii, and Metapontum, from which town the garrison had to be withdrawn in order to save the Tarentine Acropolis. These successes so greatly increased the risk of a Macedonian landing, that Rome felt herself compelled to direct renewed attention and apply renewed exertion to the Greek war, which had been almost totally neglected; and fortunately the capture of Syracuse and the favourable state of the Spanish war enabled her to do so.

Conflicts

At the chief seat of war, Campania, the struggle went on

with very varying success. The legions posted in the neigh- around Capua.
bourhood of Capua had not exactly invested the city,
but had so greatly impeded the cultivation of the soil and
the ingathering of the harvest, that the populous city was
in urgent need of supplies from without. Hannibal accordingly collected a considerable supply of grain, and directed
the Campanians to receive it at Beneventum ; but their tar-
diness gave the consuls Quintus Flaccus and Appius Claudius time to come up, to inflict a severe defeat on Hanno
who protected the grain, and to seize his camp and all
his stores. The two consuls then surrounded the town,
while Tiberius Gracchus stationed himself on the Appian
Way to prevent Hannibal from approaching to relieve it.
But that brave officer fell in consequence of the shameful
stratagem of a perfidious Lucanian ; and his death was
equivalent to a complete defeat, for his army, consisting
mostly of those slaves whom he had manumitted, dispersed
after the fall of their beloved leader. So Hannibal found
the road to Capua open, and by his unexpected appearance
compelled the two consuls to raise the blockade which they
had barely begun. Their cavalry had already, before Hannibal's arrival, been thoroughly defeated by the Phoenician
cavalry, which lay as a garrison in Capua under Hanno and
Bostar, and by the equally excellent Campanian horse. The
total destruction of the regular troops and free bands in
Lucania led by Marcus Centenius, a man imprudently promoted from a subaltern to be a general, and the not much
less complete defeat of the negligent and arrogant praetor
Gnaeus Fulvius Flaccus in Apulia, closed the long series of
the misfortunes of this year. But the tough perseverance of the Romans again neutralized the rapid success of
Hannibal, at least at the most decisive point. As soon as
Hannibal turned his back on Capua to proceed to Apulia,
the Roman armies once more gathered around that city, one
at Puteoli and Volturnum under Appius Claudius, another
at Casilinum under Quintus Fulvius, and a third on the
Nolan road under the praetor Gaius Claudius Nero. The
three camps, well entrenched and connected by fortified lines,
precluded all access to the place, and the large, inadequately
provisioned city could not but find itself compelled by the mere

investment to surrender at no distant time, should no relief
212–211. arrive.   As the winter of 542–3 drew to an end, the provisions
were almost exhausted, and urgent messengers, who were
barely able to steal through the well-guarded Roman lines,
requested speedy help from Hannibal, who was at Tarentum,
occupied with the siege of the citadel.   With 33 elephants
and his best troops he departed by forced marches from
Tarentum for Campania, captured the Roman guard at Calatia, and took up his camp on Mount Tifata close by Capua,
in the confident expectation that the Roman generals would
now raise the siege as they had done the year before.   But
the Romans, who had had time to entrench their camps
and their lines like a fortress, did not stir, and looked on
unmoved from their ramparts, while on one side the Campanian horsemen, on the other the Numidian squadrons, dashed
against their lines.   A serious assault could not be contemplated by Hannibal ; he could foresee that his advance would
soon draw the other Roman armies after him to Campania,
if even before their arrival the scarcity of supplies in a
region so systematically foraged did not drive him away.
Nothing could be done in that quarter.

Hannibal
marches
towards
Rome.

Hannibal tried a further expedient, the last which occurred
to his inventive genius, to save the important city.   After
giving the Campanians information of his intention and ex-
horting them to hold out, he started with the relieving army
from Capua and took the road for Rome.   With the same
dexterous boldness which he had shown in his first Italian
campaigns, he threw himself with a weak army between the
armies and fortresses of the enemy, and led his troops through
Samnium and along the Valerian Way past Tibur to the
bridge over the Anio, which he passed and encamped on the
opposite bank, five miles from the city.   The children's
children of the Romans still shuddered, when they were told
of "Hannibal at the gate ; " real danger there was none.
The country houses and fields in the neighbourhood of the
city were laid waste by the enemy ; the two legions in the
city, who went forth against them, prevented the investment
of the walls.   Besides, Hannibal had never expected to surprise Rome by a *coup de main*, such as Scipio soon afterwards
executed against New Carthage, and still less had he meditated a siege in earnest ; his only hope was that in the first

alarm part of the besieging army of Capua would march to Rome and thus give him an opportunity of breaking up the blockade. Accordingly after a brief stay he departed. The Romans saw in his withdrawal a miraculous intervention of the gods, who by portents and visions had compelled the wicked man to depart, when in truth the Roman legions were unable to compel him; at the spot where Hannibal had approached nearest to the city, at the second milestone on the Appian Way in front of the Capene gate, with grateful credulity the Romans erected an altar to the god " who turned back and protected " (*Rediculus Tutanus*). Hannibal in reality retreated, because this was part of his plan, and directed his march towards Capua. But the Roman generals had not committed the mistake on which their opponent had reckoned; the legions remained unmoved in the lines round Capua, and only a weak corps had been detached on the news of Hannibal's march towards Rome. When Hannibal learned this, he suddenly turned against the consul Publius Galba, who had imprudently followed him from Rome, and with whom he had hitherto avoided an engagement, vanquished him, and took his camp by storm.

But this was a poor compensation for the now inevitable fall of Capua. Long had its citizens, particularly the better classes, anticipated with sorrowful forebodings what was coming; the senate-house and the administration of the city were left almost exclusively to the leaders of the popular party hostile to Rome. Now despair seized high and low, Campanians and Phoenicians alike. Twenty-eight senators chose a voluntary death; the remainder gave over the city to the discretion of an implacably exasperated foe. Of course a bloody retribution had to follow; the only discussion was as to whether the process should be long or short: whether the wiser and more appropriate course was to probe to the bottom the further ramifications of the treason beyond Capua, or to terminate the matter by rapid executions. Appius Claudius and the Roman senate wished to take the former course; the latter view, perhaps the less inhuman, prevailed. Fifty-three of the officers and magistrates of Capua were scourged and beheaded in the market-places of Cales and Teanum by the orders and before the eyes of the proconsul

Capua capitulates.

Quintus Flaccus, the rest of the senators were imprisoned, numbers of the citizens were sold into slavery, and the estates of the more wealthy were confiscated. Similar penalties were inflicted upon Atella and Calatia. These punishments were severe; but, when regard is had to the importance of the revolt of Capua from Rome, and to what was the ordinary if not warrantable usage of war in those times, they were not unnatural. And had not the citizens themselves pronounced their own sentence, when immediately after their defection they put to death all the Roman citizens present in Capua at the time of the revolt? But it was unjustifiable in Rome to embrace this opportunity of gratifying the secret rivalry that had long subsisted between the two largest cities of Italy, and of wholly annihilating, in a political point of view, her hated and envied competitor by abolishing the constitution of the Campanian city.

Superiority of the Romans.

Immense was the impression produced by the fall of Capua, and all the more that it had not been brought about by surprise, but by a two years' siege carried on in spite of all the exertions of Hannibal. It was quite as much a token that the Romans had recovered their ascendancy in Italy, as its defection some years before to Hannibal had been a token that that ascendancy was lost. In vain Hannibal had tried to counteract the impression of this news on his allies by the capture of Rhegium or of the citadel of Tarentum. His forced march to surprise Rhegium had yielded no result. The citadel of Tarentum suffered greatly from famine, after the Tarentino-Carthaginian squadron closed the harbour; but, as the Romans with their much more powerful fleet were able to cut off the supplies from that squadron itself, and the territory, which Hannibal commanded, scarce sufficed to maintain his army, the besiegers on the side next the sea suffered not much less than did the besieged in the citadel, and at length they left the harbour. No enterprise was now successful; Fortune herself seemed to have deserted the Carthaginians. The consequences of the fall of Capua—the deep shock given to the respect and confidence which Hannibal had hitherto enjoyed among the Italian allies, and the endeavours made by every community that was not too deeply compromised to gain readmission on tolerable terms into the

Roman symmachy—affected Hannibal much more sensibly
than the immediate loss. He had to choose one of two
courses ; either to throw garrisons into the wavering towns, in
which case he would weaken still more his army already too
weak and would expose the troops on whom he could rely to
destruction in small divisions or to treachery—500 select
Numidian horse were put to death in this way in 544 on the
defection of the town of Salapia ; or to pull down and burn
the towns which could not be depended on, so as to keep
them out of the enemy's hands—a course which would not
raise the spirits of his Italian clients. On the fall of Capua
the Romans felt themselves once more confident as to the
final issue of the war in Italy ; they despatched considerable
reinforcements to Spain, where the existence of the Roman
army was placed in jeopardy by the fall of the two Scipios ;
and for the first time since the beginning of the war they
ventured on a diminution in the total number of their troops,
which had hitherto been annually augmented notwithstanding the annually increasing difficulty of levying them, and
had risen at last to 23 legions. Accordingly in the next year
(544) the Italian war was prosecuted more remissly than
hitherto by the Romans, although Marcus Marcellus had after
the close of the Sicilian war resumed the command of the
main army ; he applied himself to the besieging of fortresses
in the interior, and had indecisive conflicts with the Carthaginians. The struggle for the Acropolis of Tarentum also
continued without decisive result. In Apulia Hannibal succeeded in defeating the proconsul Gnaeus Fulvius Centumalus
at Herdoneae. In the following year (545) the Romans took
steps to regain possession of the second large city, which had
passed over to Hannibal, the city of Tarentum. While
Marcus Marcellus continued the struggle against Hannibal
in person with his wonted obstinacy and energy, and in a two
days' battle, beaten on the first day, achieved on the second a
costly and bloody victory ; while the consul Quintus Fulvius
induced the already wavering Lucanians and Hirpinians to
change sides and to deliver up their Phoenician garrisons ;
while well-conducted razzias from Rhegium compelled Hannibal to hasten to the aid of the hard-pressed Bruttians ; the
veteran Quintus Fabius, who had once more—for the fifth

210.

210.

209.
Tarentum
capitu-
lates.

time—accepted the consulship and along with it the commission to reconquer Tarentum, established himself firmly in the neighbouring Messapian territory, and the treachery of a Bruttian portion of the garrison surrendered to him the city. Fearful excesses were committed by the exasperated victors. They put to death all of the garrison or of the citizens whom they could find, and pillaged the houses. 30,000 Tarentines are said to have been sold as slaves, and 3000 talents (£730,000) are stated to have been sent to the state treasury. It was the last achievement of the veteran general of eighty; Hannibal arrived to the relief of the city when all was over, and withdrew to Metapontum.

Hannibal driven back.

208.

After Hannibal had thus lost his most important acquisitions and found himself hemmed in by degrees to the south-western point of the peninsula, Marcus Marcellus, who had been chosen consul for the next year (546), hoped that, in connection with his able colleague Titus Quintius Crispinus, he should be able to terminate the war by a decisive attack. The old soldier was not disturbed by the burden of his sixty years; sleeping and waking he was haunted by the one thought of defeating Hannibal and of liberating Italy. But fate reserved that wreath of victory for a younger brow. While engaged in an unimportant reconnaissance in the district of Venusia, both consuls were suddenly attacked by a division of African cavalry. Marcellus maintained the unequal struggle—as he had fought forty years before against Hamilcar and fourteen years before at Clastidium—till he sank dying from his horse; Crispinus escaped, but died of his wounds received in the conflict (546).

Death of Marcellus.

208.

Pressure of the war.

216.

It was now the eleventh year of the war. The danger which some years before had threatened the very existence of the state seemed to have vanished; but all the more the Romans felt the heavy burden—a burden pressing more severely year after year—of the endless war. The finances of the state suffered beyond measure. After the battle of Cannae (538) a special bank-commission (*tres viri mensarii*) had been appointed, composed of the most eminent men, to form a permanent and circumspect board of superintendence for the public finances in these difficult times. It probably did what it could; but the state of things was such as to

baffle all financial sagacity. At the very beginning of the war
the Romans had debased the silver and copper coin, raised
the legal value of the silver currency more than a third, and
issued a gold coinage far above the value of the metal.
This very soon proved insufficient; they were obliged to
take supplies from the contractors on credit, and connived
at their conduct because they needed them, till the scandalous malversation at last induced the aediles to make an
example of some of the worst by impeaching them before the
people. Appeals were often made, and not in vain, to the
patriotism of the wealthy, who in fact were the very persons
that suffered comparatively the most. The soldiers of the
better classes and the subaltern officers and equites in a
body, either voluntarily or constrained by the *esprit de corps*,
declined to receive pay. The owners of the slaves armed
by the state and manumitted after the engagement at Beneventum (p. 176) replied to the bank-commission, which
offered them payment, that they would allow it to stand
over to the end of the war (540). When there was no   214.
longer money in the exchequer for the celebration of the
national festivals and the repairs of the public buildings, the
companies which had hitherto contracted for these matters
declared themselves ready to continue their services for a
time without remuneration (540). A fleet was even fitted out   214.
and manned, just as in the first Punic war, by means of a
voluntary loan among the rich (544). They spent the moneys   210.
belonging to minors; and at length, in the year of the
conquest of Tarentum, they laid hands on the last long-
spared reserve fund (£164,000). The state nevertheless was
unable to meet its most necessary payments; the pay of the
soldiers fell dangerously into arrear, particularly in the more
remote districts. But the embarrassment of the state was
not the worst part of the material distress. Everywhere the
fields lay fallow: even where the war did not make havoc,
there was a want of hands for the hoe and the sickle. The
price of the *medimnus* (a bushel and a half) had risen to 15
denarii (9s. 7d.), at least three times the average price in the
capital; and many would have died of absolute want, if
supplies had not arrived from Egypt, and if, above all, the
revival of agriculture in Sicily (p. 158) had not prevented

the distress from coming to the worst. The effect which
such a state of things must have had in ruining the small
farmers, in eating away the savings which had been so
laboriously acquired, and in converting flourishing villages into
nests of beggars and brigands, is illustrated by similar wars
of which more circumstantial accounts have been preserved.

The allies.   Still more ominous than this material distress was the
increasing aversion of the allies to the Roman war, which
consumed their substance and their blood. In regard to
the non-Latin communities, indeed, this was of less consequence. The war itself showed that they could do nothing,
so long as the Latin nation stood by Rome; their greater or
less measure of dislike was therefore of little moment.
Now, however, Latium also began to waver. Most of the
Latin communes in Etruria, Latium, the territory of the
Marsians, and northern Campania—and so in those very districts of Italy which directly had suffered least from the
209.   war—announced to the Roman senate in 545 that thenceforth they would send neither contingents nor contributions,
and would leave it to the Romans themselves to defray the
costs of a war waged in their interest. The consternation
in Rome was great; but for the moment there were no means
of compelling the refractory. Fortunately all the Latin
communities did not act in this way. The colonies in the
land of the Gauls, in Picenum, and in southern Italy, headed
by the powerful and patriotic Fregellae, declared on the
contrary that they adhered the more closely and faithfully to
Rome; in fact, it was very clearly evident to all of these
that in the present war their existence was, if possible, still
more at stake than that of the capital, and that the war was
really waged not for Rome merely, but for the Latin hegemony in Italy, and in truth for the independence of the
Italian nation. That partial defection itself was certainly
not high treason, but merely the result of shortsightedness
and exhaustion; beyond doubt these same towns would have
rejected with horror an alliance with the Phoenicians. But
still there was a variance between Romans and Latins, which
did not fail injuriously to react on the subject population of
these districts. A dangerous ferment immediately showed
itself in Arretium; a conspiracy organized in the interest of

Hannibal among the Etruscans was discovered, and appeared so perilous that Roman troops were ordered to march thither. The military and police suppressed this movement without difficulty; but it was a significant token of what might happen in those districts, if once the Latin strongholds ceased to inspire terror.

Amidst these difficulties and symptoms of variance, news suddenly arrived that Hasdrubal had crossed the Pyrenees in the autumn of 546, and that the Romans must be prepared to carry on the war next year with both the sons of Hamilcar in Italy. Not in vain had Hannibal persevered at his post throughout the long anxious years; the aid, which the factious opposition at home and the shortsighted Philip had refused him, was at length in the course of being brought to him by his brother, who, like himself, largely inherited the spirit of Hamilcar. Already 8000 Ligurians, enlisted by Phoenician gold, were ready to unite with Hasdrubal; if he gained the first battle, he might hope that like his brother he should be able to bring the Gauls and perhaps the Etruscans into arms against Rome. Italy, moreover, was no longer what it had been eleven years before; the state and its citizens were exhausted, the Latin league was shaken, their best general had just fallen in the field of battle, and Hannibal was not subdued. In reality Scipio might bless the star of his genius, if it averted the consequences of his unpardonable blunder from himself and from his country. *Hasdrubal's approach. 208.*

As in the times of the utmost danger, Rome once more called out twenty-three legions. Volunteers were summoned to arm, and those legally exempt from military service were included in the levy. Nevertheless, they were taken by surprise. Far earlier than either friends or foes expected, Hasdrubal was on the Italian side of the Alps (546); the Gauls, now accustomed to such transits, were readily bribed to open their passes, and furnished what the army required. If the Romans had any intention of occupying the outlets of the Alpine passes, they were again too late; they heard that Hasdrubal was on the Po, that he was calling the Gauls to arms as successfully as his brother had formerly done, and that Placentia was invested. With all haste the consul Marcus Livius proceeded to the northern army; and it was high time that he should appear. Etruria and Umbria were *New armaments.* *Hasdrubal and Hannibal on the march. 207.*

in sullen ferment; volunteers from them reinforced the Phoenician army.   His colleague Gaius Nero summoned the
praetor Gaius Hostilius Tubulus from Venusia to join him,
and hastened with an army of 40,000 men to intercept the
march of Hannibal to the north.   The latter collected all
his forces in the Bruttian territory, and, advancing along the
great road leading from Rhegium to Apulia, encountered the
consul at Grumentum.   An obstinate engagement took place
in which Nero claimed the victory ; but Hannibal was able
at all events, although with some loss, to evade the enemy
by one of his usual adroit flank-marches, and to reach Apulia
without hindrance.   There he halted, and encamped at first
at Venusia, then at Canusium : Nero, who had followed
closely in his steps, encamped opposite to him at both places.
That Hannibal voluntarily halted and was not prevented
from advancing by the Roman army, appears to admit of no
doubt; the reason for his taking up his position exactly at
this point and not farther to the north, must have depended
on arrangements concerted between himself and Hasdrubal, or on conjectures as to the route of the latter's march,
with which we are not acquainted.   While the two armies
thus lay inactive, face to face, the despatch from Hasdrubal
which was anxiously expected in Hannibal's camp was intercepted by the outposts of Nero.   It stated that Hasdrubal
intended to take the Flaminian road, in other words, to
keep in the first instance along the coast and then at Fanum
to turn across the Apennines towards Narnia, at which
place he hoped to meet Hannibal.   Nero immediately ordered the reserve in the capital to proceed to Narnia as the
point selected for the junction of the two Phoenician armies,
while the division stationed at Capua went to the capital,
and a new reserve was formed there.   Convinced that Hannibal was not acquainted with the purpose of his brother and
would continue to await him in Apulia, Nero resolved on the
bold experiment of hastening northward by forced marches
with a small but select corps of 7,000 men and, in connection
with his colleague, compelling Hasdrubal, if possible, to
fight.   He was able to do so, for the Roman army which
he left behind still continued strong enough either to hold
its ground against Hannibal if he should attack it, or to

accompany him and to arrive simultaneously with him at
the decisive scene of action, should he depart.

Nero found his colleague Marcus Livius at Sena Gallica
awaiting the enemy; both consuls at once marched against
Hasdrubal, whom they found occupied in crossing the Me-
taurus. Hasdrubal wished to avoid a battle and to escape
from the Romans by a flank movement, but his guides
abandoned him; he lost his way on the strange ground, and
was at length attacked on the march by the Roman cavalry
and detained until the Roman infantry arrived and a battle
became inevitable. Hasdrubal stationed the Spaniards on
the right wing, with his ten elephants in front of it, and the
Gauls on the left, which he held back. Long the fortune of
battle wavered on the right wing, and the consul Livius who
commanded there was hard pressed, till Nero, repeating his
strategical operation as a tactical manœuvre, allowed the
motionless enemy opposite to him to remain as they stood,
and marching round his own army fell upon the flank of the
Spaniards. This decided the day. The severely bought and
very bloody victory was complete; the army, which had no
retreat, was destroyed, and the camp was taken by assault.
Hasdrubal, when he saw the admirably conducted battle lost,
sought and found like his father an honourable soldier's
death. As an officer and a man, he was worthy to be the
brother of Hannibal. On the day after the battle Nero
started, and after scarcely fourteen days' absence once more
confronted Hannibal in Apulia, whom no message had
reached, and who had not stirred. The consul brought the
message with him; it was the head of Hannibal's brother,
which the Roman ordered to be thrown into the enemy's outposts, repaying in this way his great antagonist, who scorned
to war with the dead, for the honourable burial which he had
given to Paullus, Gracchus, and Marcellus.

Hannibal saw that his hopes had been in vain, and that all
was over. He abandoned Apulia and Lucania, even Metapontum, and retired with his troops to the land of the Bruttians, whose ports formed his only means of withdrawal from
Italy. By the energy of the Roman generals, and still more
by a conjuncture of singular good fortune, a peril was averted
from Rome, the greatness of which justified Hannibal's

Battle of
Sena.

Hannibal
retires to
the Brut-
tian terri-
tory.

tenacious perseverance in Italy, and which fully bears comparison with the magnitude of the peril of Cannae. The joy in Rome was boundless; business was resumed as in time of peace; every one felt that the danger of the war was surmounted.

Stagnation of the war in Italy.

Nevertheless the Romans were in no hurry to terminate the war. The state and the citizens were exhausted by the excessive moral and material strain on their energies; men gladly abandoned themselves to carelessness and repose. The army and fleet were reduced; the Roman and Latin farmers were brought back to their desolate homesteads; the exchequer was filled by the sale of a portion of the Campanian domains. The administration of the state was regulated anew and the disorders which had prevailed were remedied; the repayment of the voluntary war-loan was begun, and the Latin communities that remained in arrears were compelled to fulfil their neglected obligations with heavy interest.

The war in Italy made no progress. It forms a brilliant proof of the strategic talent of Hannibal as well as of the incapacity of the Roman generals now opposed to him, that after this he was still able for four years to keep the field in the Bruttian country, and that all the superiority of his opponents could not compel him either to shut himself up in fortresses or to embark. It is true that he was obliged to retire farther and farther, not so much in consequence of the indecisive engagements which took place with the Romans, as because his Bruttian allies were always becoming more troublesome, and at last he could only reckon on the towns which his army garrisoned. Thus he voluntarily abandoned Thurii; Locri was, on the suggestion of Publius Scipio, re-

205.

captured by an expedition from Rhegium (549). As if at last his projects were to receive a brilliant justification at the hands of the very Carthaginian authorities who had thwarted them, these now, in their apprehension as to the anticipated landing of the Romans, revived of their own accord his plans

206. 205.

(548, 549), and sent reinforcements and subsidies to Hannibal in Italy, and to Mago in Spain, with orders to rekindle the war in Italy so as to achieve some further respite for the trembling possessors of the country houses of Libya and the shops of Carthage. An embassy was likewise sent to Macedonia, to induce Philip to renew the alliance and to land in Italy (549). But it was too late. Philip had made peace with Rome some months before; the impending political annihilation of Carthage was far from agreeable to him, but he took no step openly at least against Rome. A small Macedonian corps proceeded to Africa, the expenses of which, according to the assertion of the Romans, were defrayed by Philip: this may have been the case, but the Romans had at any rate no proof of it, as the subsequent course of events showed. No Macedonian landing in Italy was thought of.

205.

Mago, the youngest son of Hamilcar, set himself to his task more earnestly. With the remains of the Spanish army, which he had conducted in the first instance to Minorca, he landed in 549 at Genoa, destroyed the city, and summoned the Ligurians and Gauls to arms. Gold and the novelty of the enterprise led them now, as always, to come to him in troops; he had formed connections even throughout Etruria, where political prosecutions never ceased. But the troops which he had brought with him were too few for a serious enterprise against Italy proper; and Hannibal likewise was much too weak, and his influence in Lower Italy had fallen too far, to permit him to advance with any prospect of success. The rulers of Carthage were not willing to save their native country, when its salvation was possible; now, when they were willing, it was possible no longer.

Mago in Italy.

205.

Nobody probably in the Roman senate doubted either that the war on the part of Carthage against Rome was at an end, or that the war on the part of Rome against Carthage must now be begun; but unavoidable as was the expedition to Africa, they were afraid to enter on its preparation. They required for it, above all, an able and beloved leader; and they had none. Their best generals had either fallen in the field of battle, or they were, like Quintus Fabius and Quintus Fulvius, too old for such an entirely new and probably tedious war. The victors of Sena, Gaius Nero and Marcus Livius, would perhaps have been equal to the task, but they were both in the highest degree unpopular aristocrats; it was doubtful whether they would succeed in procuring the com-

The African expedition of Scipio.

mand—matters had already reached such a pass that ability,
as such, determined the popular choice only in times of grave
anxiety—and it was more than doubtful whether these were
the men to stimulate the exhausted people to fresh exertions.
At length Publius Scipio returned from Spain, and the
favourite of the multitude, who had so brilliantly fulfilled, or
at any rate seemed to have fulfilled, the task with which it
had entrusted him, was immediately chosen consul for the
205.   next year. He entered on office (549) with the firm determination of now realizing that African expedition which he had
projected in Spain. In the senate, however, not only was
the party favourable to a methodical conduct of the war
unwilling to entertain the project of an African expedition so
long as Hannibal remained in Italy, but the majority was
by no means favourably disposed towards the young general
himself. His Greek refinement and his modern culture and
tone of thought were but little agreeable to the austere and
somewhat boorish fathers of the city; and serious doubts
existed both as to his conduct of the Spanish war and as to
his military discipline. How much ground there was for the
objection that he showed too great indulgence towards his
officers of division, was very soon demonstrated by the disgraceful proceedings of Gaius Flaminius at Locri, the blame
of which certainly was indirectly chargeable to the scandalous
negligence which marked Scipio's supervision. In the proceedings in the senate regarding the organization of the
African expedition and the appointment of a general for
it, the new consul, wherever usage or the constitution came
into conflict with his private views, showed no great reluctance to set such obstacles aside, and very clearly indicated
that in case of need he was disposed to rely for support
against the governing board on his fame and his popularity
with the people. These things could not but annoy the
senate and awaken, moreover, serious apprehension, lest in
the impending decisive war and the eventual negotiations for
peace with Carthage such a general would not be bound by
the instructions which he received—an apprehension which
his arbitrary management of the Spanish expedition was by
no means fitted to allay. Both sides, however, displayed
wisdom enough not to push matters too far. The senate

itself could not fail to see that the African expedition was necessary, and that it was injudicious indefinitely to postpone it; it could not fail to see that Scipio was a very able officer and in so far was well adapted for the leader in such a war, and that he, if any one, would be able to induce the people to protract his command as long as was necessary and to put forth their last energies. The majority came to the resolution not to refuse to Scipio the desired commission, after he had previously observed, at least in form, the respect due to the supreme governing board and had submitted himself beforehand to the decree of the senate. Scipio was to proceed this year to Sicily to superintend the building of the fleet, the preparation of siege materials, and the formation of the expeditionary army, and then in the following year to land in Africa. For this purpose the army of Sicily—still composed of those two legions that were formed from the remnant of the army of Cannae—was placed at his disposal, because a weak garrison and the fleet were quite sufficient for the protection of the island ; and he was permitted moreover to raise volunteers in Italy. It was evident that the senate did not organize the expedition, but merely allowed it : Scipio did not obtain half the resources which had formerly been placed at the command of Regulus, and he got that very corps which for years had been subjected by the senate to intentional degradation. The African army was, in the view of the majority of the senate, a forlorn hope of disrated companies and volunteers, the loss of whom in any event the state had no great occasion to regret.

Any one else than Scipio would perhaps have declared that the African expedition must either be undertaken with other means, or not at all; but Scipio's confidence accepted the terms such as they were solely with the view of attaining the eagerly coveted command. He carefully avoided, as far as possible, the imposition of direct burdens on the people, that he might not injure the popularity of the expedition. Its expenses, particularly those of building the fleet which were considerable, were partly procured by what was termed a voluntary contribution of the Etruscan cities—that is, by a war tribute imposed as a punishment on the Arretines and other communities disposed to favour the Phoenicians—

partly laid upon the cities of Sicily. In forty days the fleet
was ready for sea. The crews were reinforced by volunteers,
of whom seven thousand from all parts of Italy responded
to the call of the beloved officer. So Scipio set sail for

204.

Africa in the spring of 550 with two strong legions of veterans
(about 30,000 men), 40 vessels of war, and 400 transports,
and landed successfully, without meeting the slightest resistance, at the Fair Promontory in the neighbourhood of
Utica.

Prepara-
tions in
Africa.

The Carthaginians, who had long expected that the plundering expeditions, which the Roman squadrons had frequently made during the last few years to the African coast,
would be followed by a more serious invasion, had not only,
in order to ward it off, endeavoured to bring about a revival
of the Italo-Macedonian war, but had also made armed preparation at home to receive the Romans. Of the two rival
Berber kings, Massinissa of Cirta (Constantine), the ruler
of the Massylians, and Syphax of Siga (at the mouth of the
Tafna westward from Oran), the ruler of the Massaesylians,
they had succeeded in attaching the latter, who was far the
more powerful and hitherto had been friendly to the Romans,
by treaty and affinity closely to Carthage, while they cast off
the other, the old rival of Syphax and ally of the Carthaginians. Massinissa had after desperate resistance succumbed
to the united power of the Carthaginians and of Syphax, and
had been obliged to leave his territories a prey to the latter;
he himself wandered with a few horsemen in the desert.
Besides the contingent to be expected from Syphax, a Carthaginian army of 20,000 foot, 6,000 cavalry, and 140 elephants—Hanno had been sent out to hunt elephants for the
very purpose—was ready to fight for the protection of the
capital, under the command of Hasdrubal son of Gisgo, a
general who had gained experience in Spain; in the port there
lay a strong fleet. A Macedonian corps under Sopater, and
a consignment of Celtiberian mercenaries, were immediately
expected.

Scipio
driven
back to
the coast.

On the report of Scipio's landing, Massinissa immediately
arrived in the camp of the general whom not long before he
had confronted as an enemy in Spain; but the landless prince
brought in the first instance nothing beyond his personal

ability to the aid of the Romans, and the Libyans, although heartily weary of levies and tribute, had acquired too bitter experience in similar cases to declare at once for the invaders. So Scipio began the campaign. So long as he was only opposed by the weaker Carthaginian army, he had the advantage, and was enabled after some successful cavalry skirmishes to proceed to the siege of Utica; but when Syphax arrived, according to report with 50,000 infantry and 10,000 cavalry, the siege had to be raised, and a fortified naval camp had to be constructed for the winter on a promontory, which easily admitted of entrenchment, between Utica and Carthage. Here the Roman general passed the winter of 550–1. From the disagreeable situation in which the spring found him he extricated himself by a fortunate *coup de main*. The Africans, lulled into security by proposals of peace suggested by Scipio with more artifice than honour, allowed themselves to be surprised on one and the same night in their two camps; the reed huts of the Numidians burst into flames, and, when the Carthaginians hastened to their help, their own camp shared the same fate; the fugitives were slain without resistance by the Roman divisions. This nocturnal surprise was more destructive than many a battle; nevertheless the Carthaginians did not suffer their courage to sink, and they rejected even the advice of the timid, or rather of the judicious, to recall Mago and Hannibal. Just at this time the expected Celtiberian and Macedonian auxiliaries arrived; it was resolved once more to try a pitched battle on the " Great Plains," five days' march from Utica. Scipio hastened to accept it; with little difficulty his veterans and volunteers dispersed the hastily collected host of Carthaginians and Numidians, and the Celtiberians, who could not reckon on any mercy from Scipio, were cut down after obstinate resistance. After this double defeat the Africans could no longer keep the field. An attack on the Roman naval camp attempted by the Carthaginian fleet, while not unsuccessful, was far from decisive, and was greatly outweighed by the capture of Syphax, which Scipio's singular good fortune threw in his way, and by which Massinissa became to the Romans what Syphax had been at first to the Carthaginians.

204–203.

Surprise of the Carthaginian camp.

Negotiations for peace.

After such defeats the Carthaginian peace party, which had been reduced to silence for sixteen years, was able once more to raise its head and openly to rebel against the government of the Barcides and the patriots. Hasdrubal son of Gisgo was in his absence condemned by the government to death, and an attempt was made to obtain an armistice and peace from Scipio. He demanded the cession of their Spanish possessions and of the islands of the Mediterranean, the transference of the kingdom of Syphax to Massinissa, the surrender of all their vessels of war except 20, and a war contribution of 4,000 talents (nearly £1,000,000)—terms which seem so singularly favourable to Carthage, that the question obtrudes itself whether they were offered by Scipio more in his own interest or in that of Rome. The Carthaginian plenipotentiaries accepted them under reservation of their being ratified by the respective authorities, and accordingly

Machinations of the Carthaginian patriots.

a Carthaginian embassy was despatched to Rome. But the patriot party in Carthage were not disposed to give up the struggle so cheaply; faith in the nobleness of their cause, confidence in their great leader, even the example that had been set to them by Rome herself, stimulated them to persevere, apart from the fact that peace of necessity involved the return of the opposite party to the helm of affairs and their own consequent destruction. The patriotic party had the ascendancy among the citizens; it was resolved to allow the opposition to negotiate for peace, and meanwhile to prepare for a last and decisive effort. Orders were sent to Mago and Hannibal to return with all speed to Africa. Mago,

205–203.

who for three years (549–551) had been labouring to bring about a coalition in Northern Italy against Rome, had just at this time in the territory of the Insubres (about Milan) been defeated by the far superior double army of the Romans. The Roman cavalry had been brought to give way, and the infantry had been thrown into confusion; victory seemed on the point of declaring for the Carthaginians, when a bold attack by a Roman troop on the enemy's elephants, and above all a serious wound received by their beloved and able commander, turned the fortune of the day. The Phoenician army was obliged to retreat to the Ligurian coast, where it

received and obeyed the order to embark; but Mago died of
his wound on the voyage.

Hannibal would probably have anticipated the order, had
not the last negotiations with Philip presented to him a
renewed prospect of rendering better service to his country
in Italy than in Libya; when he received it at Croton,
where he latterly had his head-quarters, he lost no time in
complying with it. He caused his horses to be put to death
as well as the Italian soldiers who refused to follow him
over the sea, and embarked in the transports that had been
long in readiness in the roadstead of Croton. The Roman
citizens breathed freely, when the mighty Libyan lion, whose
departure no one even now ventured to compel, thus voluntarily turned his back on Italian ground. On this occasion
the decoration of a grass wreath was bestowed by the senate
and burgesses on the only surviving Roman general who had
traversed that troubled time with honour, the veteran of
nearly ninety years, Quintus Fabius. To receive this wreath—
which by the custom of the Romans the army that a general
had saved presented to its deliverer—at the hands of the
whole community was the highest distinction which had
ever been bestowed upon a Roman citizen, and the last
honour accorded to the old general, who died in the course of
that same year (551). Hannibal, doubtless not under the
protection of the armistice, but solely through his rapidity of
movement and good fortune, arrived at Leptis without hindrance, and the last of the " lion's brood " of Hamilcar trode
once more, after an absence of thirty-six years, his native
soil. He had left it, when still almost a boy, to enter on that
noble and yet so thoroughly fruitless career of heroism, in
which he had set out towards the west to return homewards
from the east, having described a wide circle of victory
around the Carthaginian sea. Now, when what he had
wished to prevent, and what he would have prevented had
he been allowed, was done, he was summoned to help and
if possible, to save; and he obeyed without complaint or
reproach.

On his arrival the patriot party came forward openly
the disgraceful sentence against Hasdrubal was cancelled;
new connections were formed with the Numidian sheiks

Hannibal recalled to Africa.

203.

Recommencement of hostilities.

through the dexterity of Hannibal; and not only did the assembly of the people refuse to ratify the peace practically concluded, but the armistice was broken by the plundering of a Roman transport fleet driven ashore on the African coast, and by the seizure even of a Roman vessel of war carrying Roman envoys. In just indignation Scipio started from his camp at Tunes (552) and traversed the rich valley of the Bagradas (Mejerda), no longer allowing the townships to capitulate, but causing the inhabitants of the villages and towns to be seized and sold *en masse*. He had already penetrated far into the interior, and was at Naraggara (to the west of Sicca, now Kaf, near Ras o Dschaber), when Hannibal, who had marched out from Hadrumetum, fell in with him. The Carthaginian general attempted to obtain better conditions from the Roman in a personal conference; but Scipio, who had already gone to the extreme verge of concession, could not possibly after the breach of the armistice agree to yield further, and it is improbable that Hannibal had any other object in this step than to show the multitude that the patriots were not absolutely opposed to peace. The conference led to no result.

The two armies accordingly came to a decisive battle at Zama (probably not far from Sicca).* Hannibal arranged his infantry in three lines; in the first division the Carthaginian hired troops, in the second the African militia and the Phoenician civic force along with the Macedonian corps, in the third the veterans who had followed him from Italy. In front of the line were placed the 80 elephants; the cavalry were stationed on the wings. Scipio likewise disposed his legions in three divisions, as was the wont of the Romans, and so arranged them that the elephants could pass through and along the line without breaking it. Not only was this disposition completely successful, but the elephants making their way to the side disordered also the Carthaginian cavalry on the wings, so that Scipio's cavalry—which moreover was by the arrival of Massinissa's troops rendered far

Margin left: 202.

Margin left: Battle of Zama.

---

* Neither the place nor time of the battle is properly determined. The former was probably no other than the well-known Zama regia; the time pro- bably the spring of 552. The fixing of the day as the 19th October, on account of the solar eclipse, is not to be depended on.

superior to the enemy—had little trouble in dispersing them, and were soon engaged in full pursuit. The struggle of the infantry was more severe. The conflict lasted long between the first divisions on both sides; at length in the extremely bloody hand-to-hand encounter both parties fell into confusion, and were obliged to seek a support in the second divisions. The Romans found that support; but the Carthaginian militia showed itself so unsteady and wavering, that the mercenaries believed themselves betrayed and a combat arose between them and the Carthaginian civic force. But Hannibal now hastily withdrew what remained of the first two lines to the flanks, and pushed forward his choice Italian troops along the whole line. Scipio, on the other hand, gathered together in the centre as many of the first line as still were able to fight, and made the second and third divisions close up on the right and left of the first. Once more on the same spot began a still more fearful conflict; Hannibal's old soldiers never wavered in spite of the superior numbers of the enemy, till the cavalry of the Romans and of Massinissa, returning from the pursuit of the beaten cavalry of the enemy, surrounded them on all sides. This not only terminated the struggle, but annihilated the Phoenician army; the same soldiers, who fourteen years before had given way at Cannae, had retaliated on their conquerors at Zama. With a handful of men Hannibal arrived, a fugitive, at Hadrumetum.

After this day folly alone could counsel a continuance of the war on the part of Carthage. On the other hand it was in the power of the Roman general immediately to begin the siege of the capital, which was neither protected nor provisioned, and, unless unforeseen accidents should intervene, now to subject Carthage to the fate which Hannibal had wished to bring upon Rome. Scipio did not do so; he granted peace (533), but no longer upon the former terms. Besides the concessions which had already in the last negotiations been demanded in favour of Rome and of Massinissa, an annual contribution of 200 talents (£48,000) was imposed for fifty years on the Carthaginians; and they had to bind themselves that they would not wage war against Rome or its allies or indeed beyond the bounds of Africa at all,

Peace.

201.

and that in Africa they would not wage war beyond their
own territory without having sought the permission of Rome
—the practical effect of which was that Carthage became
tributary and lost her political independence. It even appears
that the Carthaginians were bound in certain cases to furnish
ships of war to the Roman fleet.

Scipio has been accused of granting too favourable conditions to the enemy, lest he might be obliged to hand over
the glory of terminating the most severe war which Rome
had waged, along with his command, to a successor. The
charge might have had some foundation, had the first proposals been carried out; it seems to have no warrant in
reference to the second. His position in Rome was not
such as to make the favourite of the people, after the victory
of Zama, seriously apprehensive of recall—already before the
victory an attempt to supersede him had been referred by the
senate to the burgesses, and by them decidedly rejected. Nor
do the conditions themselves warrant such a charge. The
Carthaginian city never, after its hands were thus tied
and a powerful neighbour was placed by its side, made even
an attempt to withdraw from Roman supremacy, still less
to enter into rivalry with Rome ; besides, every one who
cared to know knew that the war just terminated had been
undertaken much more by Hannibal than by Carthage, and
that it was absolutely impossible to revive the gigantic plans
of the patriot party. It might seem little in the eyes of
the vengeful Italians, that only the five hundred surrendered ships of war perished in the flames, and not the
hated city itself ; secret spite and official pedantry might
contend for the view, that an opponent is only really vanquished when he is annihilated, and might censure the man
who had disdained rigorously to punish the crime of having
made Romans tremble. Scipio thought otherwise ; and we
have no reason and therefore no right to assume that the
Roman was in this instance influenced by vulgar motives
rather than by the noble and magnanimous impulses which
formed part of his character. It was not the consideration of his own possible recall or of the mutability of
fortune, nor was it any apprehension of the outbreak of a
Macedonian war at certainly no distant date, that prevented

the self-reliant and confident hero, with whom everything had hitherto succeeded beyond belief, from completing the destruction of the unhappy city, which fifty years afterwards his adopted grandson was commissioned to execute, and which might indeed have been equally well accomplished now.   It is much more probable that the two great generals, on whom the decision of the political question now devolved, offered and accepted peace on such terms in order to set just and reasonable limits on the one hand to the furious vengeance of the victors, on the other to the obstinacy and imprudence of the vanquished.   The noble-mindedness and statesmanlike gifts of the great antagonists are no less apparent in the magnanimous submission of Hannibal to what was inevitable, than in the wise abstinence of Scipio from an extravagant and insulting use of victory.   Is it to be supposed that one so generous, unprejudiced, and intelligent should not have asked himself of what benefit it could be to his country, now that the political power of the Carthaginian city was annihilated, utterly to destroy that ancient seat of commerce and of agriculture, and wickedly to overthrow one of the main pillars of the then existing civilization?   The time had not yet come when the first men of Rome lent themselves to destroy the civilization of their neighbours, and frivolously fancied that they could wash away from themselves the eternal infamy of the nation by shedding an idle tear.

Thus ended the second Punic or, as the Romans more correctly called it, the Hannibalic war, after it had devastated the lands and islands from the Hellespont to the Pillars of Hercules for seventeen years.   Before this war the policy of the Romans had no higher aim than to acquire command of the mainland of the Italian peninsula within its natural boundaries, and of the Italian islands and seas; it is clearly proved by their treatment of Africa on the conclusion of peace that they also terminated the war with the impression, not that they had laid the foundation of sovereignty over the states of the Mediterranean or of the so-called universal empire, but that they had rendered a dangerous rival innocuous and had given to Italy agreeable neighbours.   It is true doubtless that the results of the war, the conquest of Spain in particular, little accorded with such an idea; but

Results of the war,

their very successes led them beyond their proper design, and it may in fact be affirmed that the Romans came into possession of Spain accidentally. The Romans achieved the sovereignty of Italy, because they strove for it; the hegemony— and the sovereignty which grew out of it—over the territories of the Mediterranean was to a certain extent thrown into the hands of the Romans by the force of circumstances without intention on their part to acquire it.

Out of Italy. The immediate results of the war out of Italy were, the conversion of Spain into two Roman provinces—which, however, were in perpetual insurrection; the union of the hitherto dependent kingdom of Syracuse with the Roman province of Sicily; the establishment of a Roman instead of a Carthaginian protectorate over the most important Numidian chiefs; and lastly the conversion of Carthage from a powerful commercial state into a defenceless mercantile town. In other words, it established the uncontested hegemony of Rome over the western region of the Mediterranean. Moreover, it brought about that decided contact between the state systems of the East and the West which the first Punic war had only foreshadowed; and thereby gave rise to the proximate decisive interference of Rome in the conflicts of the Alexandrine monarchies.

In Italy. In Italy, first of all the Celts were now doomed to destruction, if indeed their fate had not been decided before; and the execution of the doom was only a question of time. Within the Roman confederacy the effect of the war was to bring into more distinct prominence the ruling Latin nation, whose internal union had been tried and attested by the peril which, notwithstanding isolated instances of wavering, it had surmounted on the whole in faithful fellowship; and to depress still further the non-Latin or Latinized Italians, particularly the Etruscans and the Sabellians of Lower Italy. The heaviest punishment or rather vengeance was inflicted partly on the most powerful, partly on those who were at once the earliest and latest, allies of Hannibal—the community of Capua, and the land of the Bruttians. The Capuan constitution was abolished, and Capua was reduced from the second city into the first village of Italy; it was even proposed to raze the city and level it with the ground. The

whole soil, with the exception of a few possessions of
foreigners or of Campanians well disposed towards Rome,
was declared by the senate to be public domain, and was
thereafter parcelled out to small occupiers on temporary
lease. The Picentes on the Silarus were similarly treated;
their capital was razed, and the inhabitants were dispersed
among the surrounding villages. The doom of the Bruttians
was still more severe; they were converted *en masse* into a
sort of bondsmen to the Romans, and were for ever excluded
from the right of bearing arms. The other allies of Hannibal
also dearly expiated their offence. The Greek cities suffered severely, with the exception of the few which had steadfastly adhered to Rome, such as the Campanian Greeks and
the Rhegines. Punishment not much lighter awaited the
Arpanians and a multitude of other Apulian, Lucanian, and
Samnite communities, most of which lost portions of their
territory. On part of the lands thus acquired new colonies
were settled. Thus in the year 560 a succession of burgess-   194.
colonies was sent to the best ports of Lower Italy, among
which Sipontum (near Manfredonia) and Croton may be
named, as also Salernum placed in the former territory of the
southern Picentes and destined to hold them in check, and
above all Puteoli, which soon became the seat of the fashionable villa-life and of the traffic in Asiatic and Egyptian luxuries.
Thurii became a Latin fortress under the new name of Copia
(560), and the rich Bruttian town of Vibo under the name of   194.
Valentia (562). The veterans of the victorious army of   192.
Africa were settled singly on various patches of land in
Samnium and Apulia; the remainder was retained as public
land, and the pasture stations of the grandees of Rome replaced the gardens and arable fields of the farmers. As
a matter of course, moreover, in all the communities of the
peninsula the persons of note who were not well affected to
Rome were got rid of, so far as this could be accomplished by
political processes and confiscations of property. Everywhere
in Italy the non-Latin allies felt that their name was meaningless, and that they were henceforth subjects of Rome;
the conquest of Hannibal was felt as a second subjugation of
Italy, and all the exasperation and all the arrogance of the
victors vented themselves especially on their Italian allies

who were not Latin.   Even the colourless Roman comedy of
this period, subjected as it was to close censorship, bears
traces of this.   When the subjugated towns of Capua and
Atella were abandoned without restraint to the unbridled wit
of the Roman farce, so that the latter town became its very
stronghold, and when other writers of comedy jested over
the fact that the Campanian serfs had already learned to survive amidst the deadly atmosphere in which even the hardiest
race of slaves, the Syrians, pined away; such unfeeling
mockeries reflected the scorn of the victors, and re-echoed
the cry of distress from the down-trodden nations.   The
position in which matters stood is shown by the anxious
carefulness, which during the ensuing Macedonian war the
senate evinced in the watching of Italy, and by the reinforcements which were despatched from Rome to the most impor-
200.   199.   tant colonies, to Venusia in 554, Narnia in 555, Cosa in 557,
197.   194.   and Cales shortly before 570.

What blanks were produced by war and famine in the
ranks of the Italian population, is shown by the example of
the burgesses of Rome, whose numbers during the war had
fallen almost a fourth.   The statement, accordingly, that the
whole number of Italians who fell in the war under Hannibal
was 300,000, seems not at all exaggerated.   Of course this
loss fell chiefly on the flower of the burgesses, who in fact
furnished the core and mass of the combatants.   How fearfully the senate in particular was thinned, is shown by the
filling up of its complement after the battle of Cannae, when
it had been reduced to 123 persons, and was with difficulty
restored to its normal state by an extraordinary nomination
of 177 senators.   That, moreover, the seventeen years' war,
which had been carried on simultaneously in all districts of
Italy and towards all the four points of the compass abroad,
must have shaken to the very heart the national economy, is
abundantly evident; but our tradition does not suffice to
illustrate this in detail.   The state no doubt gained by the
confiscations, and the Campanian territory in particular
thenceforth remained an inexhaustible source of revenue to
the state; but by this extension of the domain system the
national prosperity of course lost just about as much as at
other times it had gained by the breaking up of the state

lands. Numbers of flourishing townships—four hundred, it was reckoned—were destroyed and ruined; the capital laboriously accumulated was consumed; the population were demoralized by camp life; the good old traditional habits of the burgesses and farmers were undermined from the capital down to the smallest village. Slaves and desperadoes associated themselves in robber-bands, of the dangers of which an idea may be formed from the fact that in a single year (569) 7,000 men had to be condemned for robbery in Apulia alone; the extension of the pastures, with their half-savage slave-herdsmen, favoured this mischievous barbarizing of the land. Italian agriculture saw its very existence endangered by the proof, first afforded in this war, that the Roman people could be supported by grain from Sicily and from Egypt instead of that which they reaped themselves.

185.

Nevertheless the Roman, whom the gods had allowed to survive the close of that gigantic struggle, might look with pride to the past and with confidence to the future. Many errors had been committed, but much suffering had also been endured; the people, whose whole youth capable of arms had for ten years hardly laid aside shield and sword, might excuse many faults. The living of different nations side by side in peace and amity upon the whole, although maintaining an attitude of mutual antagonism—which appears to be the aim of the peoples of modern times—was a thing foreign to antiquity. In ancient times it was necessary to be either anvil or hammer; and in the final struggle between the victors victory remained with the Romans. Whether they would have the judgment to use it rightly—to attach the Latin nation by still closer bonds to Rome, gradually to Latinize Italy, to rule their dependents in the provinces as subjects and not to abuse them as slaves, to reform the constitution, to reinvigorate and to enlarge the tottering middle class—remained to be seen. If they should have the skill to accomplish these results, Italy might hope to see happy times, in which prosperity based on personal exertion under favourable circumstances, and the most decisive political supremacy over the then civilized world, would impart a just self-reliance to every member of the great whole, furnish a worthy aim for every ambition, and open a career for every talent. It would, no doubt, be otherwise, should they fail to use aright their victory.   But for the moment doubtful voices and gloomy apprehensions were silent; from all quarters the warriors and victors returned to their homes; thanksgivings and amusements, and rewards to soldiers and burgesses were the order of the day; the released prisoners of war were sent home from Gaul, Africa, and Greece; and at length the youthful conqueror moved in splendid procession through the decorated streets of the capital, to deposit his laurels in the house of the god by whose direct inspiration, as the pious whispered one to another, he had been guided in counsel and in action.

CHAPTER VII.

THE WEST FROM THE PEACE OF HANNIBAL TO
THE CLOSE OF THE THIRD PERIOD.

THE war waged by Hannibal had interrupted Rome in the extension of her dominion to the Alps or to the boundary of Italy, as was even now the Roman phrase, and in her organization and colonizing of the Celtic territories. It was self-evident that the task would now be resumed at the point where it had been broken off, and the Celts were well aware of this. In the very year of the conclusion of peace with Carthage (553) hostilities had recommenced in the territory of the Boii, who were the most immediately exposed to danger; and a first success obtained by them over the hastily assembled Roman levy, coupled with the persuasions of a Carthaginian officer, Hamilcar, who had been left behind from the expedition of Mago in northern Italy, produced in the following year (554) a general insurrection spreading beyond the two tribes immediately threatened, the Boii and Insubres. The Ligurians were driven to arms by the nearer approach of the danger, and even the youth of the Cenomani on this occasion listened less to the voice of their cautious chiefs than to the urgent appeal of their kinsmen who were in peril. Of the two fortresses constructed with a view to check the raids of the Gauls, Placentia and Cremona, the former was sacked—not more than 2,000 of the inhabitants of Placentia saved their lives—and the second was invested. In haste the legions advanced to save what they could. A great battle took place before Cremona. The dexterous management and the professional skill of the Phoenician leader failed to make up for the deficiencies of his troops; the Gauls were unable to withstand the onset of the legions, and among the numerous dead who covered the field of battle

Subjugation of the valley of the Po.

Celtic wars.

201.

200.

was the Carthaginian officer. The Celts, nevertheless, continued the struggle; the same Roman army which had conquered at Cremona was next year (555), chiefly through the fault of its careless leader, almost destroyed by the Insubres; and it was not till 556 that Placentia could be partially re-established. But the league of the cantons associated for the desperate struggle suffered from intestine discord; the Boii and Insubres quarrelled, and the Cenomani not only withdrew from the national league, but purchased their pardon from the Romans by a disgraceful betrayal of their countrymen; during a battle in which the Insubres engaged the Romans on the Mincius, the Cenomani attacked in rear, and helped to destroy, their allies and comrades in arms (557). Thus humbled and deserted, the Insubres, after the fall of Comum, likewise consented to conclude a separate peace (558). The conditions, which the Romans prescribed to the Cenomani and Insubres, were certainly harder than they had been in the habit of granting to the members of the Italian confederacy; in particular, they were careful to confirm by law the barrier of separation between Italians and Celts, and to enact that no member of these two Celtic tribes should ever be capable of acquiring the citizenship of Rome. But these Transpadane Celtic districts were allowed to retain their existence and their national constitution—so that they formed not townships, but cantons of the several tribes—and no tribute, as it would seem, was imposed on them. They were intended to serve as a bulwark for the Roman settlements south of the Po, and to ward off from Italy the incursions of the migratory northern tribes and the aggressions of the predatory inhabitants of the Alps, who were wont to make regular razzias in these districts. The process of Latinizing, moreover, made rapid progress in these regions; the Celtic nationality was evidently far from able to oppose such resistance as the more civilized nations of Sabellians and Etruscans. The celebrated Latin comic poet Statius Caecilius, who died in 586, was a manumitted Insubrian; and Polybius, who visited these districts towards the close of the sixth century, affirms, not perhaps without some exaggeration, that in that quarter only a few villages among the Alps remained Celtic. The Veneti, on the other hand, appear to have retained their nationality longer.

The chief efforts of the Romans in these regions were naturally directed to check the immigration of the Transalpine Celts, and to make the natural wall, which separates the peninsula from the interior of the continent, also its political boundary. That the terror of the Roman name had already penetrated to the adjacent Celtic cantons beyond the Alps, is shown not only by the totally passive attitude which they maintained during the annihilation or subjugation of their Cisalpine countrymen, but still more by the official disapproval and disavowal which the Transalpine cantons— which term we must suppose primarily to apply to the Helvetii (between the lake of Geneva and the Main) and the Carni or Taurisci (in Carinthia and Styria)—expressed to the envoys from Rome, who complained of the attempts made by isolated Celtic bands to settle peacefully on the Roman side of the Alps. Not less significant was the humble spirit in which these same bands of emigrants first came to the Roman senate entreating an assignment of land, and then without remonstrance obeyed the rigorous order to return over the Alps (568–575), and allowed the town, which they had already founded not far from Aquileia, to be again destroyed. With wise severity the senate permitted no sort of exception to the principle that the gates of the Alps should be henceforth closed against the Celtic nation, and visited with heavy penalties those Roman subjects in Italy, who had instigated any such schemes of immigration. An attempt of this kind which was made on a route hitherto little known to the Romans, in the innermost recess of the Adriatic, and still more, as it would seem, the project of Philip of Macedon for invading Italy from the east as Hannibal had done from the west, gave occasion to the founding of a fortress in the extreme north-eastern corner of Italy—Aquileia, the most northerly of the Italian colonies (571–573)—which was intended not only to close that route for ever against foreigners, but also to secure the command of the gulf which was specially convenient for navigation, and to check the piracy which was still not wholly extirpated in those waters. The establishment of Aquileia led to a war with the Istrians

Measures adopted to check the immigrations of the Transalpine Gauls.

186–179.

183–181.

178. 177. (576, 577), which was speedily terminated by the storming of some strongholds and the fall of the king, Aepulo, and which was remarkable for nothing except for the panic, which the news of the surprise of the Roman camp by a handful of barbarians occasioned in the fleet and throughout Italy.

Colonizing of the region on the south of the Po.

A different course was adopted with the region on the south of the Po, which the Roman senate had determined to incorporate with Italy. The Boii, who were immediately affected by this step, defended themselves with the resolution of despair. They even crossed the Po and made an at-

194. tempt to rouse the Insubres once more to arms (560); they blockaded a consul in his camp, and he was on the point of succumbing; Placentia maintained itself with difficulty against the constant assaults of the exasperated natives. At length the last battle was fought at Mutina; it was long and

193. bloody, but the Romans conquered (561); and thenceforth the struggle was no longer a war, but a slave hunt. The Roman camp soon was the only asylum in the Boian territory; thither the better part of the still surviving population began to take refuge; and the victors were able, without much exaggeration, to report to Rome that nothing remained of the nation of the Boii but old men and children. The nation was thus obliged to resign itself to the fate appointed for it. The Romans demanded the cession of half

191. the territory (563); the demand could not be refused, and even within the diminished district which was left to the Boii, they soon disappeared, amalgamated with their conquerors.*

---

* According to the account of Strabo these Italian Boii were driven by the Romans over the Alps, and from them proceeded that Boian settlement in what is now Hungary between the Neus-ied-lersee and the Plattensee, which was attacked and annihilated in the time of Augustus by the Getae who crossed the Danube, but which bequeathed to this district the name of the Boian desert. This account is far from agreeing with the well-attested representation of the Roman annals, according to which the Romans were content with the cession of half the territory; and, in order to explain the disappearance of the Italian Boii, we have really no need to assume a violent expulsion—the other Celtic peoples, although visited to a far less extent by war and colonization, disappeared not much less rapidly and totally from the ranks of the Italian nations. On the other hand, other accounts suggest the derivation of those Boii on the Plattensee from the main stock of the nation, which formerly had its seat in Bavaria and Bohemia before Germanic tribes pushed it towards the south. But it is altogether very doubtful whether the Boii, whom we find near Bordeaux, on the Po, and in Bohemia, were really scattered branches of one stock, or

After the Romans had thus cleared the ground for themselves, the fortresses of Placentia and Cremona, whose colonists had been mostly swept away or dispersed by the
troubles of the last few years, were reorganized, and new
settlers were sent thither. The new foundations were, in or
near the former territory of the Senones, Potentia (near Re-
canati not far from Ancona, in 570) and Pisaurum (Pesaro,   ·184.
in 570), and, in the newly acquired district of the Boii, the   184.
fortresses of Bononia (565), Mutina (571), and Parma (571) ;   ⎰ 189. 183.
the colony of Mutina had been instituted before the war   ⎱ 183.
under Hannibal, but that war had interrupted the completion of the settlement. The institution of fortresses was
associated, as was always the case, with the construction
of military roads. The Flaminian way was prolonged from
its northern termination at Ariminum, under the name
of the Aemilian way, to Placentia (567). Moreover, the   187.
road from Rome to Arretium or the Cassian way, which
perhaps had already been long a municipal road, was taken
in charge and constructed anew by the Roman community
probably in 583 ; while in 567 the track from Arretium over   187.   171.
the Apennines to Bononia as far as the new Aemilian road
had been put in order, and furnished a shorter communication between Rome and the fortresses on the Po. By these
comprehensive measures the Apennines were practically
superseded as the boundary between the Celtic and Italian
territories, and were replaced by the Po. South of the Po
there henceforth prevailed mainly the civic constitution of
the Italians, beyond it mainly the cantonal constitution of
the Celts ; and, if the district between the Apennines and
the Po was still designated *ager Celticus*, it was but an empty
name.

In the north-western mountain-land of Italy, whose   Liguria.
valleys and hills were occupied chiefly by the much-sub-
divided Ligurian stock, the Romans pursued a similar
course. Those dwelling immediately to the north of the
Arno were extirpated. This fate befel chiefly the Apuani,
who dwelt on the Apennines between the Arno and the

whether this is not an instance of mere   name—an inference such as the ancients
similarity of name. The hypothesis of   drew, often without due reason, in the
Strabo may have rested on nothing else   case of the Cimbri, Veneti, and others.
than an inference from the similarity of

Magra, and incessantly plundered on the one side the territory of Pisae, on the other that of Bononia and Mutina.
Those who did not fall victims in that quarter to the sword
of the Romans were transported into Lower Italy to the
180.   region of Beneventum (574); and by energetic measures the
Ligurian nation, from which the Romans were obliged in
176.   578 to recover the colony of Mutina which it had conquered,
was completely crushed in the mountains which separate
the valley of the Po from that of the Arno.   The fortress of
177.   Luna (not far from Spezzia), established in 577 in the former
territory of the Apuani, protected the frontier against the
Ligurians just as Aquileia did against the Transalpines, and
gave the Romans at the same time an excellent port which
henceforth became the usual station for the passage to
Massilia or to Spain.   The construction of the coast or
Aurelian road from Rome to Luna, and of the cross road
carried from Luca by way of Florence to Arretium between
the Aurelian and Cassian ways, probably belongs to the same
period.

With the more western Ligurian tribes, who held the
Genoese Apennines and the Maritime Alps, there were
incessant conflicts.   They were troublesome neighbours,
accustomed to pillage by land and by sea: the Pisans and
Massiliots suffered no little injury from their incursions and
their piracies.   But no permanent results were gained
amidst these constant hostilities, or perhaps even aimed
at; except apparently that, with a view to have a communication by land with Transalpine Gaul and Spain in addition
to the regular route by sea, the Romans endeavoured to
clear the great coast road from Luna by way of Massilia to
Emporiae, at least as far as the Alps—beyond the Alps it
devolved on the Massiliots to keep the coast navigation open
for Roman vessels and the road along the shore open for
travellers by land.   The interior with its impassable valleys
and its rocky fastnesses, and with its poor but dexterous
and crafty inhabitants, served the Romans mainly as a
school of war for the training and hardening of officers and
soldiers.

Corsica.   Wars as they are called, of a similar character with those
Sardinia.   against the Ligurians, were waged with the Corsicans and

to a still greater extent with the inhabitants of the interior of Sardinia, who retaliated for the predatory expeditions directed against them by sudden attacks on the districts along the coast. The expedition of Tiberius Gracchus against the Sardinians in 577 was specially held in remembrance, not so much because it gave "peace" to the province, as because he asserted that he had slain or captured as many as 80,000 of the islanders, and dragged slaves thence in such multitudes to Rome that " as cheap as a Sardinian" became a proverb.

177.

In Africa the policy of Rome was substantially summed up in the one idea, as short-sighted as it was narrow-minded, that she ought to prevent the revival of the power of Carthage, and ought accordingly to keep the unhappy city constantly oppressed and apprehensive of a declaration of war suspended over it by Rome like the sword of Damocles. The stipulation in the treaty of peace, that the Carthaginians should retain their territory undiminished, but that their neighbour Massinissa should have all those possessions guaranteed to him which he or his predecessor had possessed within the Carthaginian bounds, looks almost as if it had been inserted not to prevent, but to provoke disputes. The same remark applies to the obligation imposed by the treaty of peace on the Carthaginians not to make war upon the allies of Rome ; so that, according to the letter of the treaty, they were not even entitled to expel their Numidian neighbours from their own undisputed territory. With such stipulations and amidst the uncertainty of African frontier questions in general, the situation of Carthage in presence of a neighbour equally powerful and unscrupulous and of a liege lord who was at once umpire and party in the cause, could not but be a painful one ; but the reality was worse than the worst expectations. As early as 561 Carthage found herself suddenly assailed under frivolous pretexts, and saw the richest portion of her territory, the province of Emporiae on the lesser Syrtis, partly plundered by the Numidians, partly even seized and retained by them. Encroachments of this kind were multiplied; the level country passed into the hands of the Numidians, and the Carthaginians with difficulty maintained themselves in the larger towns. Within

Carthage

193.

172.

the last two years alone, the Carthaginians declared in 582, seventy villages had been again wrested from them in opposition to the treaty. Embassy after embassy was despatched to Rome; the Carthaginians adjured the Roman senate either to allow them to defend themselves by arms, or to appoint a court of arbitration with power to enforce their award, or to regulate the frontier anew that they might at least learn once for all how much they were to lose; otherwise it were better to make them Roman subjects at once than thus gradually to deliver them over to the Libyans.

200.

But the Roman government, which already in 554 had held forth a direct prospect of extension of territory to their client, of course at the expense of Carthage, seemed to have little objection that he should himself take the booty destined for him; they moderated at times the too great impetuosity of the Libyans, who now retaliated fully on their old tormentors for their former sufferings; but it was in reality for the very sake of inflicting this torture that the Romans had assigned Massinissa as a neighbour to Carthage. All the requests and complaints had no result, except that Roman commissions made their appearance in Africa and after a thorough investigation came to no decision, or that in the negotiations at Rome the envoys of Massinissa pretended a want of instructions and the matter was adjourned. Phoenician patience alone was able to submit meekly to such a position, and even to exhibit towards the despotic victors every attention and courtesy, solicited or unsolicited, with unwearied perseverance. The Carthaginians especially courted Roman favour by sending supplies of grain.

Hannibal.

This pliability on the part of the vanquished, however, was not mere patience and resignation. There was still in Carthage a patriotic party, and at its head stood the man, who, wherever fate placed him, was still dreaded by the Romans. It had not abandoned the idea of resuming the struggle by taking advantage of those complications that might be easily foreseen between Rome and the eastern powers; and, as the failure of the magnificent scheme of Hamilcar and his sons had been due mainly to the Carthaginian oligarchy, the chief object was internally to reinvigorate the country for this new struggle. The salutary influence of adversity, and the clear, noble, and commanding mind of Hannibal, effected political and financial reforms. The oligarchy, which had filled up the measure of its guilty follies by raising a criminal process against the great general, charging him with having intentionally abstained from the capture of Rome and with embezzlement of the Italian spoil —that rotten oligarchy was, on the proposition of Hannibal, overthrown, and a democratic government was introduced such as was suited to the circumstances of the citizens (before 559). The finances were so rapidly reorganized by the collection of arrears and of embezzled moneys and by the introduction of better control, that the contribution due to Rome could be paid without burdening the citizens with any extraordinary taxes. The Roman government, just then on the point of beginning its critical war with the great king of Asia, observed the progress of these events, as may easily be conceived, with apprehension; it was no imaginary danger that the Carthaginian fleet might land in Italy and a second war under Hannibal might spring up there, while the Roman legions were fighting in Asia Minor. We can scarcely, therefore, censure the Romans for sending an embassy to Carthage (in 559) which was charged, in all probability, to demand the surrender of Hannibal. The spiteful Carthaginian oligarchs, who sent letter after letter to Rome to denounce to the national foe the hero who had overthrown them as having entered into secret communications with the powers unfriendly to Rome, were contemptible, but their information was probably correct; and, true as it was that that embassy involved a humiliating confession of the dread with which the simple shofete of Carthage inspired so powerful a people, and natural and honourable as it was that the proud conqueror of Zama should take exception in the senate to so humiliating a step, still that confession was nothing but the simple truth, and Hannibal was of a genius so extraordinary, that none but sentimental politicians in Rome could tolerate him longer at the head of the Carthaginian state. The marked recognition thus accorded to him by the Roman government scarcely took himself by surprise. As it was Hannibal and not Carthage that had carried on the

Reform of the Carthaginian constitution.

195.

Hannibal's flight.

195.

last war, so it was he who had to bear the fate of the vanquished. The Carthaginians could do nothing but submit
and be thankful that Hannibal, sparing them the greater
disgrace of delivering him up by a speedy and prudent flight
to the East, left to his ancestral city merely the lesser disgrace of banishing its greatest citizen for ever from his
native land, of confiscating his property, and of razing his
house. The profound saying that those are the favourites
of the gods, on whom they lavish infinite joys and infinite
sorrows, thus verified itself in full measure in the case of
Hannibal.

Continued
irritation
in Rome
towards
Carthage.
A graver responsibility than that arising out of their proceedings against Hannibal attaches to the Roman government for their persistence in suspecting and tormenting the
city after his removal. Parties indeed fermented there as
before; but, after the withdrawal of the extraordinary man
who had wellnigh changed the destinies of the world, the
patriot party was not of much more importance in Carthage
than in Aetolia or Achaia. The most rational of the various
ideas which then agitated the unhappy city was beyond
doubt that of attaching themselves to Massinissa, and of
converting him from the oppressor into the protector of the
Phoenicians. But neither the national section of the patriots
nor the section with Libyan tendencies attained the helm;
on the contrary the government remained in the hands of the
oligarchs friendly to Rome, who, so far as they did not
altogether renounce thought of the future, clung to the
single idea of saving the material prosperity and the communal freedom of Carthage under Roman protection.
With this state of matters the Romans might well have
been content. But neither the multitude, nor even the
senators of the average stamp, could rid themselves of the
profound alarm produced by the campaigns of Hannibal;
and the Roman merchants with envious eyes beheld the city
even now, when its political power was gone, possessed
of extensive commercial dependencies and of a firmly esta-
187.   blished wealth which nothing could shake. Already in 567
the Carthaginian government offered to pay up at once the
201.   whole instalments stipulated in the treaty of 553—an offer
which the Romans, who attached far more importance to the

having Carthage tributary than to the sums of money themselves, naturally declined, and only deduced from it the conviction that, in spite of all the trouble they had taken, the
city was not ruined and was not capable of ruin. Fresh
reports were ever circulating through Rome as to the intrigues of the faithless Phoenicians. At one time it was
alleged that Aristo of Tyre had been seen in Carthage as
an emissary of Hannibal, to prepare the citizens for the
landing of an Asiatic war-fleet (561) ; at another, that the   193.
council had, in a secret nocturnal sitting in the temple of
the God of Healing, given audience to the envoys of Perseus
(581) ; at another there was talk of the powerful fleet which   173.
was being equipped in Carthage for the Macedonian war (583).   171.
It is probable that these and similar reports were founded on
nothing more than, at most, individual indiscretions; but
still they were the signal for new diplomatic misrepresent-
ations on the part of Rome, and for new aggressions on the
part of Massinissa, and the idea gained ground the more,
the less sense and reason there was in it, that the Carthaginian question would not be settled without a third Punic
war.

While the power of the Phoenicians was thus declining   Numi-
in the land of their adoption, just as it had long ago sunk in   dians.
their original home, a new state grew up by their side. The
northern coast of Africa has been inhabited from time immemorial, and is inhabited still, by a people, who themselves
assume the name of Shilah or Tamazigt, whom the Greeks
and Romans call Nomades or Numidians, *i.e.* the " pastoral "
people, and the Arabs call Berbers, although they also at
times designate them as " shepherds " (Shâwie), and to
whom we are wont to give the name of Berbers or Kabyles.
This people is, so far as its language has been hitherto in-
vestigated, related to no other known nation. In the Carthaginian period these tribes, with the exception of those
dwelling immediately around Carthage or immediately on
the coast, had on the whole maintained their independence,
and had also substantially retained their pastoral and equestrian life, such as the inhabitants of the Atlas lead at the
present day; although they were not strangers to the Phoenician alphabet and Phoenician civilization generally (p. 12),

and instances occurred in which the Berber sheiks had their sons educated in Carthage and intermarried with the families of the Phoenician nobility. It was not the policy of the Romans to have direct possessions of their own in Africa; they preferred to rear a state there, which should not be of sufficient importance to dispense with Roman protection, and yet should be sufficiently strong to keep down the power of Carthage now that it was restricted to Africa, and to render all freedom of movement impossible for the tortured city. They found what they sought among the native princes. About the time of the Hannibalic war the natives of North Africa were subject to three principal kings, each of whom, according to the custom there, had a multitude of princes bound to follow his banner; Bocchar king of the Mauri, who ruled from the Atlantic Ocean to the river Molochath (now Mluia, on the boundary between Morocco and the French territory); Syphax king of the Massaesyli, who ruled from the last-named point to the "Perforated Promontory," as it was called (Seba Rûs, between Djidjeli and Bona), in what are now the provinces of Oran and Algiers; and Massinissa king of the Massyli, who ruled from the Tretum Promontorium to the boundary of Carthage, in what is now the province of Constantine. The most powerful of these, Syphax king of Siga, had been vanquished in the last war between Rome and Carthage and carried away captive to Rome, where he died in captivity. His wide dominions were mainly given to Massinissa; although Vermina the son of Syphax by humble petition recovered a small portion of his father's territory from the Romans (554), he was unable to deprive the earlier ally of the Romans of his position as the privileged oppressor of Carthage.

200.

Massinissa. Massinissa became the founder of the Numidian kingdom; and seldom has choice or accident hit upon a man so thoroughly fitted for his post. In body sound and supple up to extreme old age; temperate and sober like an Arab; capable of enduring any fatigue, of standing on the same spot from morning to evening, and of sitting four-and-twenty hours on horseback; tried alike as a soldier and a general amidst the romantic vicissitudes of his youth as well as on the battle-fields of Spain, and not less master of the more difficult art of maintaining discipline in his numerous household and order in his dominions; with equal unscrupulousness ready to throw himself at the feet of his powerful protector, or to tread under foot his weaker neighbour; and, in addition to all this, as accurately acquainted with the circumstances of Carthage where he was educated and had been on familiar terms in the noblest houses, as he was filled with an African bitterness of hatred towards his own and his people's oppressors,—this remarkable man became the soul of the revival of his nation, which had seemed on the point of perishing, and of whose virtues and faults he appeared as it were a living embodiment. Fortune favoured him, as in everything, so especially in the fact, that it allowed him time for his work. He died in the ninetieth year of his age (516–605), and in the sixtieth year of his reign, retaining to the last the full enjoyment of his bodily and mental powers, leaving behind him a son one year old, and possessing the reputation of having been the strongest man and the best and most fortunate king of his age.

238–149.

We have already narrated how palpably the Romans in their management of African affairs displayed their studied leaning towards Massinissa, and how zealously and constantly the latter availed himself of the tacit permission to enlarge his territory at the expense of Carthage. The whole interior to the border of the desert fell to the native sovereign as it were of its own accord, and even the upper valley of the Bagradas (Mejerda) with the rich town of Vaga became subject to the king; on the coast also to the east of Carthage he occupied the old Sidonian city of Great Leptis and other districts, so that his kingdom stretched from the Mauretanian to the Cyrenaean frontier, enclosed the Carthaginian territory on every side by land, and everywhere pressed, in the closest vicinity, on the Phoenicians. It admits of no doubt, that he looked on Carthage as his future capital; the Libyan party there was significant. But it was not only by the diminution of her territory that Carthage suffered injury. The roving shepherds were converted by their great king into another people. After the example of the king, who brought the fields under cultivation far and wide and bequeathed to each of his sons considerable landed estates, his

Extension and civilization of Numidia.

subjects also began to settle and to practise agriculture. As he converted his shepherds into settled citizens, he converted also his hordes of plunderers into soldiers who were deemed by Rome worthy to fight side by side with her legions; and he bequeathed to his successors a richly-filled treasury, a well-disciplined army, and even a fleet. His residence Cirta (Constantine) became the stirring capital of a powerful state, and a chief seat of Phoenician civilization, which was zealously fostered at the court of the Berber king—fostered perhaps studiously with a view to the future Carthagino-Numidian kingdom. The hitherto degraded Libyan nationality thus rose in its own estimation, and the native manners and language made their way even into the old Phoenician towns, such as Great Leptis. The Berber began, under the aegis of Rome, to feel himself the equal or even the superior of the Phoenician; Carthaginian envoys at Rome had to submit to be told that they were aliens in Africa, and that the land belonged to the Libyans. The Phoenico-national civilization of North Africa, which still retained life and vigour even under the levelling times of the empire, was far more the work of Massinissa than of the Carthaginians.

The state of culture in Spain.

In Spain the Greek and Phoenician towns along the coast, such as Emporiae, Saguntum, New Carthage, Malaca, and Gades, submitted to the Roman rule the more readily, that, left to their own resources, they would hardly have been able to protect themselves from the natives; as for similar reasons Massilia, although far more important and more capable of self-defence than those towns, did not omit to secure a powerful support in case of need by closely attaching itself to the Romans, to whom it was in return very serviceable as an intermediate station between Italy and Spain. The natives, on the other hand, gave to the Romans endless trouble. It is true that there were not wanting the rudiments of a national Iberian civilization, although of its special character it is scarcely possible for us to acquire any clear idea. We find among the Iberians a widely diffused national writing, which divides itself into two chief kinds, that of the valley of the Ebro, and the Andalusian, and each of these was probably subdivided into various branches: this writing seems to have originated at a very early period, and to be traceable rather

to the old Greek than to the Phoenician alphabet.   There
is a tradition that the Turdetani (round Seville) possessed
lays from very ancient times, a metrical book of laws of
6,000 verses, and even historical records; at any rate this
tribe is described as the most civilized of all the Spanish
tribes, and at the same time the least warlike; indeed, it
regularly carried on its wars by means of foreign mercenaries.   To the same region probably we must refer Polybius' descriptions of the flourishing condition of agriculture and the rearing of cattle in Spain—so that, in the
absence of opportunity of export, grain and flesh were to
be had at nominal prices—and of the splendid royal palaces
with golden and silver jars full of "barley wine."   At least a
portion of the Spaniards, moreover, zealously embraced the
elements of culture which the Romans brought along with
them, so that the process of Latinizing made more rapid progress in Spain than anywhere else in the transmarine provinces.   For example, warm baths after the Italian fashion
came into use even at this period among the natives.   Roman
money, too, was to all appearance not only current in Spain
far earlier than elsewhere out of Italy, but was imitated in
Spanish coins; a circumstance in some measure explained by
the rich silver-mines of the country.   The so-called " silver
of Osca " (now Huesca in Arragon), *i.e.* Spanish *denarii* with
Iberian inscriptions, is mentioned in 559; and the com-   195.
mencement of their coinage cannot be placed much later,
because the impression is imitated from that of the oldest
Roman *denarii*.

But, while in the southern and eastern provinces the
culture of the natives may have so far prepared the way for
Roman civilization and Roman rule that these encountered
no serious difficulties, the west and north on the other hand,
and the whole of the interior, were occupied by numerous
tribes more or less barbarous, who knew little of any kind
of civilization—in Intercatia, for instance, the use of gold
and silver was still unknown about 600—and who were on   150.
no better terms with each other than with the Romans.   A
characteristic trait in these free Spaniards was the chivalrous spirit of the men and, at least to an equal extent, of the
women.   When a mother sent forth her son to battle, she

roused his spirit by the recital of the feats of his ancestors ; and the fairest maiden unasked offered her hand in marriage to the bravest man.   Single combat was common, both with a view to determine the prize of valour, and for the settlement of lawsuits ; even disputes among the relatives of princes as to the succession were settled in this way.   It not unfrequently happened that a well-known warrior confronted the ranks of the enemy and challenged an antagonist by name ; the defeated champion then surrendered his mantle and sword to his opponent, and even entered into relations of friendship and hospitality with him.   Twenty years after the close of the second Punic war, the little Celtiberian community of Complega (in the neighbourhood of the sources of the Tagus) sent a message to the Roman general, that unless he sent to them for every man that had fallen a horse, a mantle, and a sword, it would fare ill with him.   Proud of their military honour, so that they frequently could not bear to survive the disgrace of being disarmed, the Spaniards were nevertheless disposed to follow any one who should enlist their services, and to stake their lives in any foreign quarrel.   The summons was characteristic, which a Roman general well acquainted with the customs of the country sent to a Celtiberian band fighting in the pay of the Turdetani against the Romans—either to return home, or to enter the Roman service with double pay, or to fix time and place for battle.   If no recruiting officer made his appearance, they met of their own accord in free bands, with the view of pillaging the more peaceful districts and even of capturing and occupying towns, quite after the manner of the Campanians. The wildness and insecurity of the inland districts are attested by the fact that the being sent into the interior westward of Cartagena was regarded by the Romans as a severe punishment, and that in periods of any excitement the Roman commandants of Further Spain took with them escorts of as many as 6,000 men.   They are still more clearly shown by the singular relations subsisting between the Greeks and their Spanish neighbours in the Graeco-Spanish double city of Emporiae, at the eastern extremity of the Pyrenees.   The Greek settlers, who dwelt on a peninsula separated on the landward side from the Spanish part of the town by a wall, took care that this wall should be guarded every night by a third of their civic force, and that one of the superior magistrates should constantly superintend the watch at the only gate; no Spaniard was allowed to set foot in the Greek city, and the Greeks conveyed their merchandise to the natives only in numerous and well-escorted companies.

These natives, full of restlessness and fond of war—full of the spirit of the Cid and of Don Quixote—were now to be tamed and, if possible, civilized by the Romans. In a military point of view the task was not difficult. It is true that the Spaniards showed themselves, not only when behind the walls of their cities or under the leadership of Hannibal, but even when left to themselves and in the open field of battle, no contemptible opponents; with their short two-edged sword which the Romans subsequently adopted from them, and their formidable assaulting columns, they not unfrequently made even the Roman legions waver. Had they been able to submit to military discipline and to political combination, they might perhaps have shaken off the foreign yoke imposed on them. But their valour was rather that of the guerilla than of the soldier, and they were utterly void of political judgment. Thus in Spain there was no serious war, but as little was there any real peace; the Spaniards, as Cæsar afterwards very justly pointed out to them, never showed themselves quiet in peace or strenuous in war. Easy as it was for a Roman general to scatter a host of insurgents, it was difficult for the Roman statesman to devise any suitable means of really pacifying and civilizing Spain. In fact, he could only deal with it by palliative measures; because the only really adequate expedient, a comprehensive Latin colonization, was not accordant with the general aim of Roman policy at this period.

Wars between the Romans and Spaniards.

The territory which the Romans acquired in Spain in the course of the second Punic war was from the beginning divided into two masses—the province formerly Carthaginian, which embraced in the first instance the present districts of Andalusia, Granada, Murcia, and Valencia, and the province of the Ebro, or the modern Arragon and Catalonia, the headquarters of the Roman army during the last war. Out of these territories were formed the two Roman provinces of Further and Hither Spain. The Romans sought gradually to reduce

The Romans maintain a standing army in Spain.

to subjection the interior corresponding nearly to the two Castiles, which they comprehended under the general name of Celtiberia, while they were content with checking the incursions of the inhabitants of the western provinces, more especially those of the Lusitanians in the modern Portugal and the Spanish Estremadura, into the Roman territory; with the tribes on the north coast, the Gallaecians, Asturians, and Cantabrians, they did not as yet come into contact at all. The territories thus won, however, could not be maintained and secured without a standing garrison, for the governor of Hither Spain had no small trouble every year with the chastisement of the Celtiberians, and the governor of the more remote province found similar employment in repelling the Lusitanians. It was needful accordingly to maintain in Spain a Roman army of four strong legions, or about 40,000 men, year after year; besides which the general levy had often to be called out in the districts occupied by Rome, to reinforce the legions. This was of great importance for two reasons: it was in Spain that the military occupation of the land first became continuous, at least on any great scale; and it was there consequently that the military service acquired a permanent character. The old Roman custom of sending troops only where the exigencies of war at the moment required them, and of not keeping the men called to serve, except in very serious and important wars, under arms for more than a year, was found incompatible with the retention of the turbulent and remote Spanish provinces beyond the sea; it was absolutely impossible to withdraw the troops from these, and very dangerous even to relieve them extensively. The Roman burgesses began to perceive that dominion over a foreign people is an annoyance not only to the slave, but to the master, and murmured loudly regarding the odious war-service of Spain. While the new generals with good reason refused to allow the relief of the existing corps as a whole, the men mutinied and threatened that, if they were not allowed their discharge, they would take it of their own accord.

The wars themselves, which the Romans waged in Spain, were but of subordinate importance. They began with the very departure of Scipio (p. 173), and continued as long as the war under Hannibal lasted. After the peace with Car-

thage (in 553) there was a cessation of arms in the peninsula;   201.
but only for a short time. In 557 a general insurrection   197.
broke out in both provinces; the commander of the Further
province was hard pressed; the commander of Hither Spain
was completely defeated, and was himself slain. It was
necessary to take up the war in earnest, and although in the
mean time the able praetor Quintus Minucius had mastered
the first danger, the senate resolved in 559 to send the consul   195.
Marcus Cato in person to Spain. On landing at Emporiae he
actually found the whole of Hither Spain overrun by the
insurgents; with difficulty that seaport and one or two
strongholds in the interior were still held for Rome. A
pitched battle took place between the insurgents and the
consular army, in which, after an obstinate conflict man
against man, the Roman military skill at length decided
the day with its last reserve. The whole of Hither Spain
thereupon sent in its submission: so little, however, was
this submission meant in earnest, that on a rumour of the
consul having returned to Rome the insurrection immediately
recommenced. But the rumour was false; and after Cato
had rapidly reduced the communities which had revolted for
the second time and sold them *en masse* into slavery, he
decreed a general disarming of the Spaniards in the Hither
province, and issued orders to all the towns of the natives
from the Pyrenees to the Guadalquivir to pull down their
walls on one and the same day. No one knew how far the
command extended, and there was no time to come to any
understanding; most of the communities complied; and of
the few that were refractory not many ventured, when the
Roman army soon appeared before their walls, to await its
assault.

These energetic measures were certainly not without
permanent effect. Nevertheless the Romans had almost
every year to reduce to subjection some mountain valley or
mountain stronghold in the " peaceful province," and the
constant incursions of the Lusitanians into the Further
province terminated occasionally in the severe defeat of the
Romans. In 563, for instance, a Roman army was obliged   191.
after heavy loss to abandon its camp, and to return by forced
marches into the more tranquil districts. It was not till

after a victory gained by the praetor Lucius Aemilius Paullus in 565, and a second still more considerable gained by the brave praetor Gaius Calpurnius beyond the Tagus over the Lusitanians in 569, that quiet for some time prevailed. In Further Spain the hitherto almost nominal rule of the Romans over the Celtiberian tribes was converted into something more real by Quintus Fulvius Flaccus, who after a great victory over them in 573 compelled at least the adjacent cantons to submission; and especially by his successor Tiberius Gracchus (575, 576), who achieved results of a permanent character not only by his arms, by which he reduced three hundred Spanish townships, but still more by his adroitness in adapting himself to the views and habits of the simple and haughty nation. He induced Celtiberians of note to take service in the Roman army, and so created a class of dependents; he assigned land to the roving tribes, and collected them in towns—the Spanish town Graccurris preserved the Roman's name—and so imposed a serious check on their freebooter habits; he regulated the relations of the several tribes to the Romans by just and wise treaties, and so stopped, as far as possible, the springs of future rebellion. His name was held in grateful remembrance by the Spaniards, and comparative peace henceforth reigned in the land, although the Celtiberians still from time to time winced under the yoke.

The system of administration in the two Spanish provinces was similar to that of the Sicilo-Sardinian province, but not identical. The superintendence was in both instances vested in two auxiliary consuls, who were first nominated in 557, in which year also the regulation of the boundaries and the definitive organization of the two provinces took place. The judicious enactment of the Baebian law (562?), that the Spanish praetors should always be nominated for two years, was not seriously carried out in consequence of the increasing competition for the highest magistracies, and still more in consequence of the jealous supervision exercised over the powers of the magistrates by the senate; and in Spain also, except where deviations occurred in extraordinary circumstances, the Romans adhered to the system of annually chang-

Margin notes:

189.

185.

181.

179. 178. Gracchus.

Administration of Spain.

179.

192.

ing the governors—a system especially injudicious in the case
of provinces so remote and with which it was so difficult to
gain an acquaintance. The dependent communities were universally tributary ; but, instead of the Sicilian and Sardinian
tenths and customs, in Spain fixed payments in money or
other contributions were imposed by the Romans, just as
formerly by the Carthaginians, on the several towns and
tribes : the collection of these by military means was prohibited by a decree of the senate in 583, in consequence of
the complaints of the Spanish communities. Grain was not
furnished in their case except for compensation, and even
then the governor might not levy more than a twentieth ;
besides, conformably to the just-mentioned ordinance of the
supreme authority, he was bound to adjust the compensation
in an equitable manner. On the other hand, the obligation
of the Spanish subjects to furnish contingents to the Roman
armies had an importance very different from that which
belonged to it at least in peaceful Sicily, and it was strictly
regulated in the several treaties. The right, too, of coining
silver money of the Roman standard appears to have been
very frequently conceded to the Spanish towns, and the monopoly of coining seems to have been by no means asserted by
the Roman government with the same strictness as in Sicily.
Rome had too much need of subjects in Spain, not to
proceed with all possible caution and tenderness in the
introduction and the working of the provincial constitution
there. Among the communities specially favoured by Rome
were the great cities along the coast of Greek, Phoenician, or
Roman foundation, such as Saguntum, Gades, and Tarraco,
which, as the natural pillars of the Roman rule in the peninsula, were admitted to alliance with Rome. On the whole,
Spain was in a military as well as financial point of view a
burden rather than a gain to the Roman commonwealth ; and
the question naturally occurs, Why did the Roman government, whose policy at that time evidently did not contemplate the acquisition of countries beyond the sea, not rid
itself of so troublesome a possession ? The not inconsiderable
commercial connections of Spain, her important iron-mines,
and her still more important silver-mines famous from ancient

171.

times even in the far East *—the working of which Rome, like Carthage, took into her own hands, and the management of which was specially regulated by Marcus Cato (559)— must beyond doubt have co-operated to induce its retention ; but the chief reason of the Romans for retaining the peninsula in their own immediate possession was, that there were no states in that quarter of similar character to the Massiliot republic in the land of the Celts and the Numidian kingdom in Libya, and that thus they could not abandon Spain without putting it into the power of any adventurer to revive the Spanish empire of the Barcides.

195.

---

* 1 Maccab. viii. 3. "And Judas heard what the Romans had done in the land of Hispania to become masters of the silver and gold mines there."

CHAPTER VIII.

THE EASTERN STATES AND THE SECOND MACEDONIAN WAR.

THE work, which Alexander king of Macedonia had begun a century before the Romans acquired their first footing in the territory which he had called his own, had in the course of time—while adhering substantially to the great fundamental idea of Hellenizing the East—changed and expanded into the construction of a system of Helleno-Asiatic states. The unconquerable propensity of the Greeks for migration and colonizing, which had formerly carried their traders to Massilia and Cyrene, to the Nile and to the Black Sea, now enabled them to retain what the king had won; and under the protection of the *sarissae*, Greek civilization peacefully domiciled itself everywhere throughout the ancient empire of the Achaemenidae. The officers, who divided the heritage of the great commander, gradually settled their differences, and a system of equilibrium was established whose very oscillations manifest some sort of regularity.

The Hellenic East.

Of the three states of the first rank belonging to this system—Macedonia, Asia, and Egypt—Macedonia under Philip the Fifth, who had occupied the throne since 534, was externally at least very much what it had been under Philip the Second the father of Alexander—a compact military state with its finances in good order. On its northern frontier matters had resumed their former footing, after the waves of the Gallic inundation had rolled away; the guard of the frontier kept the Illyrian barbarians in check without difficulty, at least in ordinary times. In the south, not only was Greece in general dependent on Macedonia, but a large portion of it—including all Thessaly in its widest sense from Olympus to the Spercheius and the peninsula of Magnesia, the large and important island of Euboea, the provinces of

The great states. Macedonia. 220.

Q 2

Locris, Phocis, and Doris, and, lastly, a number of isolated positions in Attica and in the Peloponnesus, such as the promontory of Sunium, Corinth, Orchomenus, Heraea, the Triphylian territory—was directly subject to Macedon and received Macedonian garrisons; more especially the three important fortresses of Demetrias in Magnesia, Chalcis in Euboea, and Corinth, "the three fetters of the Hellenes." But the strength of the state lay above all in its hereditary soil, the province of Macedonia. The population, indeed, of that extensive territory was remarkably scanty; Macedonia, putting forth all her energies, was scarcely able to bring into the field as many men as were contained in an ordinary consular army of two legions; and it was unmistakeably evident that the land had not yet recovered from the depopulation occasioned by the campaigns of Alexander and by the Gallic invasion. But while in Greece proper the moral and political energy of the people had decayed, the day of national vigour seemed to have gone by, life appeared scarce worth living for, and even the better spirits there spent their time over the wine-cup, in fencing with their rapiers, or in study by the midnight lamp; while in the East and Alexandria the Greeks were able perhaps to disseminate elements of culture among the dense native population and to diffuse among that population their language and their loquacity, their science and pseudo-science, but were barely sufficient in point of number to supply the nations with officers, statesmen, and schoolmasters, and were far too few to form even in the cities a middle-class of the pure Greek type; there still existed, on the other hand, in northern Greece a goodly portion of the old national vigour, which had produced the warriors of Marathon. Hence arose the confidence with which the Macedonians, Aetolians, and Acarnanians, wherever they made their appearance in the East, claimed and obtained acknowledgment of their superiority; and hence the transcendent position which they occupied at the courts of Alexandria and Antioch. There is a characteristic story, that an Alexandrian who had lived for a considerable time in Macedonia and had adopted the manners and the dress of that country, on returning to his native city, looked upon himself as a man and upon the Alexandrians as little better than slaves. This sturdy vigour and unimpaired national spirit were turned to peculiarly good account by the Macedonians, as the most powerful and best organized of the states of northern Greece. There, no doubt, absolutism had emerged in opposition to the old constitution, which to some extent recognized different estates ; but sovereign and subject by no means stood towards each other in Macedonia as they stood in Asia and Egypt, and the people still felt itself independent and free.   In stead-fast resistance to the public enemy under whatever name, in un-shaken fidelity towards their native country and their here-ditary government, and in persevering courage amidst the severest trials, no nation in ancient history bears so close a resemblance to the Roman people as the Macedonians ; and the almost miraculous regeneration of the state after the Gallic invasion redounds to the imperishable honour of its leaders and of the people whom they led.

The second of the great states, Asia, was nothing but Asia. Persia superficially remodelled and Hellenized—the empire of " the king of kings," as its master was wont to call him-self in a style characteristic at once of his arrogance and of his weakness—with the same pretensions to rule from the Hellespont to the Punjab, and with the same disjointed orga-nization ; an aggregate of dependent states in various degrees of dependence, of insubordinate satrapies, and of half-free Greek cities.   In Asia Minor more especially, which was nominally included in the empire of the Seleucidae, the whole north coast and the greater part of the eastern interior were practically in the hands of native dynasties or of the Celtic hordes that had penetrated thither from Europe ; a considerable portion of the west was in the possession of the kings of Pergamus, and the islands and coast towns were some of them Egyptian, some of them free ; so that little more was left to the great king than the interior of Cilicia, Phrygia, and Lydia, and a great number of titular claims, not easily made good, against free cities and princes—exactly similar in character to the sovereignty of the German emperor, in his day, beyond his hereditary dominions.   The strength of the empire was expended in vain endeavours to expel the Egyptians from the provinces along the coast ; in frontier strife with the eastern peoples, the Parthians and Bactrians ;

in feuds with the Celts, who to the misfortune of Asia Minor had settled within its bounds; in constant efforts to check the attempts of the eastern satraps and of the Greek cities of Asia Minor to achieve their independence; and in family quarrels and insurrections of pretenders. None indeed of the states founded by the successors of Alexander were free from such attempts, or from the other horrors which absolute monarchy in degenerate times brings in its train; but in the kingdom of Asia these evils were more injurious than elsewhere, because, from the lax composition of the empire, they usually led to the severance of particular portions from it for longer or shorter periods.

Egypt.

In marked contrast to Asia, Egypt formed a consolidated and united state, in which the intelligent statecraft of the first Lagidae, skilfully availing itself of ancient national and religious precedent, had established a completely absolute cabinet government, and in which even the worst misrule failed to provoke any attempt either at emancipation or disruption. Very different from the Macedonians, whose national attachment to royalty was based upon their personal dignity and was its political expression, the rural population in Egypt was wholly passive; the capital on the other hand was everything, and that capital was a dependency of the court. The remissness and indolence of its rulers, accordingly, paralyzed the state in Egypt still more than in Macedonia and in Asia; while on the other hand when wielded by men, like the first Ptolemy and Ptolemy Euergetes, such a state machine proved itself extremely useful. It was one of the peculiar advantages of Egypt as compared with its two great rivals, that its policy did not grasp at shadows, but pursued definite and attainable objects. Macedonia, the home of Alexander, and Asia, the land where he had established his throne, never ceased to regard themselves as direct continuations of the Alexandrine monarchy and more or less loudly asserted their claim to represent it at least, if not to restore it. The Lagidae never tried to found a universal empire, and never dreamt of conquering India; but, by way of compensation, they drew the whole traffic between India and the Mediterranean from the Phoenician ports to Alexandria, and made Egypt the first commercial and maritime state of this epoch, and the mistress of the eastern Mediterranean and of its coasts and islands. It is a significant fact, that Ptolemy III. Euergetes voluntarily restored all his conquests to Seleucus Callinicus except the seaport of Antioch. Partly by this means, partly by its favourable geographical situation, Egypt attained, with reference to the two continental powers, an excellent military position either for defence or for attack. While an opponent even in the full career of success was hardly in a position seriously to threaten Egypt, which was almost inaccessible on any side to land armies, the Egyptians were able by sea to establish themselves not only in Cyrene, but also in Cyprus and the Cyclades, on the Phoenico-Syrian coast, on the whole south and west coast of Asia Minor, and even in Europe on the Thracian Chersonese. By their unexampled skill in turning to account the fertile valley of the Nile for the direct benefit of the treasury, and by a financial system—equally sagacious and unscrupulous—earnestly and adroitly calculated to foster material interests, the court of Alexandria was constantly superior to its opponents even as a moneyed power. Lastly, the intelligent munificence, with which the Lagidae encouraged the tendency of the age towards earnest inquiry in all departments of enterprise and of knowledge, skilfully confining such inquiries within the bounds of absolute monarchy and entwining them with its interests, was productive of direct advantage to the state, whose ship-building and machine-making showed traces of the beneficial influence of Alexandrian mathematics ; and not only so, but also rendered that new development of intellectual power—the most important and the greatest, which the Hellenic nation after its political dismemberment produced—subservient, so far as it would consent to be serviceable at all, to the Alexandrian court. Had the empire of Alexander continued to stand, Greek science and art would have found a state worthy and capable of containing them. Now, when the nation had fallen to pieces, a learned cosmopolitanism grew up in it luxuriantly, and was very soon attracted by the magnet of Alexandria, where scientific appliances and collections were inexhaustible, where kings composed tragedies and ministers wrote commentaries on them, and where pensions and academies flourished.

The mutual relations of the three great states are evident from this description. The maritime power, which ruled the coasts and monopolized the sea, was necessarily led after the first great success—the political separation of the European from the Asiatic continent—to direct its further efforts towards the weakening of the two great states on the mainland, and consequently towards the protection of the several minor states; whereas Macedonia and Asia, while regarding each other as rivals, recognized above all their common adversary in Egypt, and combined, or at any rate should have combined, against it.

The kingdoms of Asia Minor.

Among the states of the second rank, merely an indirect importance, so far as concerned the contact between the East and the West, attached in the first instance to that series of states which, stretching from the southern end of the Caspian Sea to the Hellespont, occupied the interior and the north coast of Asia Minor: Atropatene (in the modern Aderbijan, south-west of the Caspian), next to it Armenia, Cappadocia in the interior of Asia Minor, Pontus on the south-east, and Bithynia on the south-west, shore of the Black Sea. All of these were fragments of the great Persian empire, and were ruled by Oriental, mostly old Persian, dynasties—the remote mountain-land of Atropatene in particular was the true asylum of the ancient Persian system, over which even the expedition of Alexander had swept without leaving a trace —and all were in the same relation of temporary and superficial dependence on the Greek dynasty, which had taken or wished to take the place of the great kings in Asia.

The Celts of Asia Minor.

Of greater importance in its general relations was the Celtic state in the interior of Asia Minor. There, intermediate between Bithynia, Paphlagonia, Cappadocia, and Phrygia, three Celtic tribes—the Tolistobogi, the Tectosages, and Trocmi—had settled, without abandoning either their native language and manners or their constitution and their trade as freebooters. The twelve tetrarchs, one of whom was appointed to preside over each of the four cantons in each of the three tribes, formed, with their council of 300 men, the supreme authority of the nation, and assembled at the "holy place" (*Drunemetum*), especially for the pro-nouncing of capital sentences. Singular as this cantonal constitution of the Celts appeared to the Asiatics, equally strange seemed to them the adventurous and marauding habits of the northern intruders, who on the one hand furnished their unwarlike neighbours with mercenaries for every war, and on the other plundered or levied contributions from the surrounding districts. These rude but vigorous barbarians were the general terror of the effeminate surrounding nations, and even of the great kings of Asia themselves, who, after several Asiatic armies had been destroyed by the Celts and king Antiochus I. Soter had even lost his life in conflict with them (493), agreed at last to pay them tribute.

261.

In consequence of bold and successful measures of opposition to these Gallic hordes, Attalus, a wealthy citizen of Pergamus, received the royal title from his native city and bequeathed it to his posterity. This new court was in miniature what that of Alexandria was on a great scale. Here too the promotion of material interests and the fostering of art and literature formed the order of the day, and the government pursued a cautious and sober cabinet policy, the main object of which was on the one hand to weaken its two dangerous continental neighbours, on the other to establish an independent Greek state in the west of Asia Minor. A well-filled treasury contributed greatly to the importance of these rulers of Pergamus. They advanced considerable sums to the kings of Syria, the repayment of which afterwards formed part of the Roman conditions of peace. They succeeded even in gaining territory in this way; Aegina, for instance, which the allied Romans and Aetolians had wrested in the last war from Philip's allies, the Achaeans, was sold by the Aetolians, to whom it fell in terms of the treaty, to Attalus for 30 talents (£7,300). But, notwithstanding the splendour of the court and the royal title, the commonwealth of Pergamus always retained something of an urban character; and in its policy it usually went along with the free cities. Attalus himself, the Lorenzo de' Medici of antiquity, remained throughout life a wealthy burgher; and the family life of the Attalid house, from which harmony and cordiality were not banished by

Pergamus.

the royal title, formed a striking contrast to the dissolute and scandalous behaviour of more aristocratic dynasties.

Greece.

In European Greece—exclusive of the Roman possessions on the west coast, in the most important of which, particularly Corcyra, Roman magistrates appear to have resided (p. 78), and the territory directly subject to Macedonia— the powers more or less in a position to pursue a policy of their own were the Epirots, Acarnanians, and Aetolians in northern Greece, the Boeotians and Athenians in central Greece, and the Achaeans, Lacedaemonians, Messenians, and

Epirots, Acarnanians, Boeotians.

Eleans in the Peloponnesus. Among these, the republics of the Epirots, Acarnanians, and Boeotians were in various ways closely knit to Macedonia—the Acarnanians more especially, because it was only Macedonian protection that enabled them to escape the destruction with which they were threatened by the Aetolians; none of them were of any consequence. Their internal condition was very various. The state of things may to some extent be illustrated by the fact, that among the Boeotians—where, it is true, matters reached their worst—it had become customary to make over every property, which did not descend to heirs in the direct line, to the *syssitia ;* and, in the case of candidates for the public magistracies, for a quarter of a century the primary condition of election was that they should bind themselves not to allow any creditor, least of all a foreign one, to sue his debtor.

The Athenians.

The Athenians were in the habit of receiving support against Macedonia from Alexandria, and were in close league with the Aetolians. But they too were totally powerless, and hardly anything save the halo of Attic poetry and art distinguished these unworthy representatives of a glorious past from a number of petty towns of the same stamp.

The Aetolians.

The power of the Aetolian confederacy manifested a greater vigour. The energy of the northern Greek character was still unbroken there, although it had degenerated into a reckless impatience of discipline and control. It was a public law in Aetolia, that an Aetolian might serve as a mercenary against any state, even against a state in alliance with his own country; and, when the other Greeks urgently

besought them to redress this scandal, the Aetolian diet declared that Aetolia might sooner be removed from its place
than this principle from their national code. The Aetolians might have been of great service to the Greek nation,
had they not inflicted still greater injury on it by their system
of organized robbery, by their thorough hostility to the
Achaean confederacy, and by their unhappy antagonism to
the great state of Macedonia.

In the Peloponnesus, the Achaean league had united the
best elements of Greece proper in a confederacy based on
civilization, national spirit, and peaceful preparation for self-
defence. But the vigour and more especially the military
efficiency of the league had, notwithstanding its outward
enlargement, been arrested by the selfish diplomacy of
Aratus. The unfortunate variances with Sparta, and the
still more lamentable invocation of Macedonian interference
in the Peloponnesus, had so completely subjected the Achaean
league to Macedonian supremacy, that the chief fortresses of
the country thenceforward received Macedonian garrisons,
and the oath of fidelity to Philip was annually taken
there. The
Achaeans.

The policy of the weaker states in the Peloponnesus, Elis,
Messene, and Sparta, was determined by their ancient enmity
to the Achaean league—an enmity specially fostered by disputes regarding their frontiers—and their tendencies were
Aetolian and anti-Macedonian, because the Achaeans took
part with Philip. The only one of these states possessing any
importance was the Spartan military monarchy, which after
the death of Machanidas had passed into the hands of one
Nabis. With ever-increasing hardihood Nabis leaned on
the support of vagabonds and itinerant mercenaries, to
whom he assigned not only the houses and lands, but also
the wives and children, of the citizens; and he assiduously
maintained connections, and even entered into an association for the joint prosecution of piracy, with the great
refuge of mercenaries and pirates, the island of Crete, where
he possessed some townships. His predatory expeditions
by land, and the piratical vessels which he maintained
at the promontory of Malea, were dreaded far and wide; he
was personally hated for his baseness and cruelty; but his Sparta,
Elis, Mes-
sene.

rule was extending, and about the time of the battle of Zama he had even succeeded in gaining possession of Messene.

League of the Greek cities.

Lastly, the most independent position among the intermediate states was held by the free Greek mercantile cities on the European shore of the Propontis, along the coast of Asia Minor, and on the islands of the Aegean Sea; they formed, at the same time, the brightest elements in the confused and multifarious picture which was presented by the Hellenic state-system. Three of them, in particular, had after Alexander's death regained their full freedom, and by the activity of their maritime commerce had attained to respectable political power and even to considerable territorial possessions; namely, Byzantium the mistress of the Bosporus, rendered wealthy and powerful by the transit dues which she levied and by the important corn trade carried on with the Black Sea; Cyzicus on the Asiatic side of the Propontis, the daughter and heiress of Miletus, maintaining the closest relations

Rhodes.

with the court of Pergamus; and lastly and above all, Rhodes. The Rhodians, who immediately after the death of Alexander had expelled the Macedonian garrison, had, by their favourable position for commerce and navigation, secured the carrying trade of all the eastern Mediterranean; and their well-handled fleet, as well as the tried courage of the citizens in

304.

the famous siege of 450, enabled them in that age of promiscuous and ceaseless hostilities to become the prudent and energetic representatives and, when occasion required, champions of a neutral commercial policy. They compelled the Byzantines, for instance, by force of arms to concede to the vessels of Rhodes exemption from the transit dues of the Bosporus; and they did not permit the dynast of Pergamus to close the Black Sea. On the other hand they kept themselves, as far as possible, aloof from land warfare, although they had acquired no inconsiderable possessions on the opposite coast of Caria; where war could not be avoided, they carried it on by means of mercenaries. With their neighbours on all sides they were in friendly relations—with Syracuse, Macedonia, Syria, but more especially with Egypt— and they enjoyed high consideration at these courts, so that their mediation was not unfrequently invoked in the wars of the great states. But they interested themselves specially on behalf of the Greek maritime cities, which were so numerously spread along the coasts of the kingdoms of Pontus, Bithynia, and Pergamus, as well as on the coasts and islands of Asia Minor that had been wrested by Egypt from the Seleucidae; such as Sinope, Heracleia Pontica, Cius, Lampsacus, Abydos, Mitylene, Chios, Smyrna, Samos, Halicarnassus and various others. All these were in substance free and had nothing to do with the lords of the soil except to request confirmation of their privileges and, at most, to pay a moderate tribute: such encroachments, as from time to time were threatened by the dynasts, they skilfully warded off sometimes by cringing, sometimes by strong measures. In this case the Rhodians were their chief auxiliaries; they emphatically supported Sinope, for instance, against Mithradates of Pontus. How firmly amidst the quarrels, and by means of the very differences, of the monarchs the liberties of these cities of Asia Minor were established, is shown by the fact, that the dispute between Antiochus and the Romans some years after this time related not to the freedom of these cities in itself, but to the question whether they were to ask confirmation of their charters from the king or not. This league of the cities was, in its peculiar attitude towards the lords of the soil as well as in other respects, a formal Hanseatic association, headed by Rhodes, which negotiated and stipulated in treaties for itself and its allies. This league upheld the freedom of the cities against monarchical interests; and while wars raged around their walls, public spirit and civic prosperity were sheltered in comparative peace within, and art and science flourished without the risk of being crushed by the tyranny of a dissolute soldiery or of being corrupted by the atmosphere of a court.

Such was the state of things in the East, at the time when the wall of political separation between the East and the West was broken down and the Eastern powers, Philip of Macedonia leading the way, were induced to interfere in the relations of the West. We have already set forth to some extent the origin of this interference and the course of the first Macedonian war (540-549); and we have pointed out what Philip might have accomplished during the second Punic

Philip, king of Macedonia.

214-205.

war, and how little of all that Hannibal was entitled to expect and to count on was really fulfilled. A fresh illustration had been afforded of the truth, that of all haphazards
none is more hazardous than an absolute hereditary monarchy. Philip was not the man whom Macedonia at that
time required; yet his gifts were far from insignificant. He
was a genuine king, in the best and worst sense of the term.
A strong desire to rule in person and unaided was the fundamental trait of his character; he was proud of his purple,
but he was no less proud of other gifts, and he had reason to
be so. He not only showed the valour of a soldier and the
eye of a general, but he displayed a high spirit in the conduct of public affairs, whenever his Macedonian sense of
honour was offended. Full of intelligence and wit, he won
the hearts of all whom he wished to gain, especially of the
men who were ablest and most refined, such as Flamininus
and Scipio; he was a pleasant boon companion and, not
by virtue of his rank alone, a dangerous wooer. But he was
at the same time one of the most arrogant and flagitious
characters, which that shameless age produced. He was in
the habit of saying that he feared none save the gods; but it
seemed almost as if his gods were those to whom his admiral
Dicaearchus regularly offered sacrifice—ungodliness (*Asebeia*)
and lawlessness (*Paranomia*). The lives of his advisers and
of the promoters of his schemes possessed no sacredness in
his eyes, nor did he disdain to pacify his indignation against
the Athenians and Attalus by the destruction of venerable
monuments and illustrious works of art; it is quoted as one
of his maxims of state, that "whoever puts to death the
father must also kill the sons." Perhaps cruelty was not,
strictly, a pleasure to him; but he was indifferent to the
lives and sufferings of others, and the disposition to relent,
which alone renders men tolerable, found no place in his
hard and stubborn heart. So abruptly and harshly did he
proclaim the principle that no promise and no moral law are
binding on an absolute king, that he thereby interposed the
most serious obstacles to the success of his plans. No one
can deny that he possessed sagacity and resolution, but these
were, in a singular manner, combined with procrastination
and supineness; which is perhaps partly to be explained by

the fact, that he was called in his eighteenth year to the
position of an absolute sovereign, and that his ungovernable
fury against every one who disturbed his autocratic course by
counter-argument or counter-advice scared away from him all
independent counsellors.   What various causes co-operated
to produce the weak and disgraceful management which he
showed in the first Macedonian war, we cannot tell; it may
have been due perhaps to that indolent arrogance which only
puts forth its full energies against danger when it becomes
imminent, or perhaps to his indifference towards a plan which
was not of his own devising and his jealousy of the greatness
of Hannibal which put him to shame.   It is certain that his
subsequent conduct betrayed no further trace of the Philip,
through whose negligence the great scheme of Hannibal suffered shipwreck.

When Philip concluded his treaty with the Aetolians and
Romans in 548-9, he seriously intended to make a lasting
peace with Rome, and to devote himself exclusively in future
to the affairs of the East.   It admits of no doubt that he saw
with regret the rapid subjugation of Carthage ; and it may
be, that Hannibal hoped for a second declaration of war from
Macedonia, and that Philip secretly reinforced the last Carthaginian army with mercenaries (p. 189).   But the tedious
affairs in which he had meanwhile involved himself in the
East, as well as the nature of the alleged support, and especially the total silence of the Romans as to such a breach of
the peace while they were searching for grounds of war,
place it beyond doubt, that Philip was by no means disposed in
551 to make up for what he ought to have done ten years before.

*Macedonia
[206–205.]
and Asia
attack
Egypt.*

203.

He had turned his eyes to an entirely different quarter.
Ptolemy Philopator of Egypt had died in 549.   Philip and
Antiochus, the kings of Macedonia and Asia, had combined
against his successor Ptolemy Epiphanes, a child of five years
old, in order completely to gratify the ancient grudge which
the monarchies of the mainland entertained towards the maritime state.   The Egyptian state was to be broken up;
Egypt and Cyprus were to fall to Antiochus; Cyrene, Ionia,
and the Cyclades to Philip.   Thoroughly in the spirit of
Philip, who ridiculed such considerations, the kings began
the war not merely without cause, but even without pretext,

205.

" just as the large fishes devour the small." The allies, moreover, had made their calculations correctly, especially Philip.
Egypt had enough to do in defending herself against the
nearer enemy in Syria, and was obliged to leave her possessions in Asia Minor and the Cyclades undefended when Philip
threw himself upon these as his share of the spoil. In the

201. year in which Carthage concluded peace with Rome (553),
Philip ordered a fleet equipped by the towns subject to him
to take on board troops, and to sail along the coast of Thrace.
There Lysimachia was taken from the Aetolian garrison, and
Perinthus, which stood in the relation of clientship to Byzantium, was likewise occupied. Thus the peace was broken as
respected the Byzantines; and as respected the Aetolians,
who had just made peace with Philip, the good understanding was at least disturbed. The crossing to Asia was attended with no difficulties, for Prusias king of Bithynia was in
alliance with Macedonia. By way of recompense, Philip
helped him to subdue the Greek mercantile cities in his
territory. Chalcedon submitted. Cius, which resisted, was
taken by storm and levelled with the ground, and its inhabitants were reduced to slavery—a meaningless barbarity,
which annoyed Prusias himself who wished to get possession
of the town uninjured, and which excited profound indignation throughout the Hellenic world. The Aetolians, whose
strategus had commanded in Cius, and the Rhodians, whose
attempts at mediation had been summarily and craftily frustrated by the king, were especially offended.

The
Rhodian
league and
Pergamus
oppose
Philip.
 But even had it not been so, the interests of all Greek
commercial cities were at stake. They could not possibly
allow the mild and almost purely nominal Egyptian rule to
be supplanted by the Macedonian despotism, with which
civic self-government and freedom of commercial intercourse
were not at all compatible ; and the fearful treatment of the
Cians showed that the matter at stake was not the right of
confirming the charters of the towns, but the life or death of
one and all. Lampsacus had already fallen, and Thasos had
been treated like Cius. No time was to be lost. Theophiliscus, the vigilant *strategus* of Rhodes, exhorted his citizens to
avert the common danger by common resistance, and not to
suffer the towns and islands to become one by one a prey to

the enemy.   Rhodes resolved on its course, and declared war against Philip.   Byzantium joined it; as did also the aged Attalus king of Pergamus, personally and politically the enemy of Philip.   While the fleet of the allies was mustering on the Aeolian coast, Philip directed a portion of his fleet to take Chios and Samos.   With the other portion he appeared in person before Pergamus, which however he invested in vain; he had to content himself with traversing the level country and leaving the traces of Macedonian valour on the temples which he destroyed far and wide.   Suddenly he departed and re-embarked, to unite with his squadron which was at Samos.   But the Rhodo-Pergamene fleet followed him, and forced him to accept battle in the straits of Chios.   The number of the Macedonian decked vessels was smaller, but the multitude of their open boats made up for this inequality, and the soldiers of Philip fought with great courage.   But he was at length defeated.   Almost half of his decked vessels, 24 sail, were sunk or taken; 6000 Macedonian sailors and 3000 soldiers perished, amongst whom was the admiral Democrates; 2000 were taken prisoners. The victory cost the allies no more than 800 men and six vessels.   But, of the leaders of the allies, Attalus had been cut off from his fleet and compelled to let his own vessel run aground near Erythrae; and Theophiliscus of Rhodes, whose public spirit had decided the question of war and whose valour had decided the battle, died on the day after it of his wounds.   Thus while the fleet of Attalus went home and the Rhodian fleet remained temporarily at Chios, Philip, who falsely claimed the victory, was enabled to continue his voyage and to turn towards Samos, in order to occupy the Carian towns.   On the Carian coast the Rhodians, on this occasion unsupported by Attalus, gave battle for the second time to the Macedonian fleet under Heraclides, near the little island of Lade in front of the port of Miletus.   The victory, claimed again by both sides, appears to have been this time gained by the Macedonians; for while the Rhodians retreated to Myndus and thence to Cos, the Macedonians occupied Miletus, and a squadron under Dicaearchus the Aetolian occupied the Cyclades.   Philip meanwhile prosecuted the conquest of the Rhodian possessions on the Carian mainland, and of the Greek cities : had he been disposed to attack Ptolemy in person, and had he not preferred to confine himself to the acquisition of his own share in the spoil, he was now in a position to think of an expedition to Egypt. In Caria no army opposed the Macedonians, and Philip traversed without hindrance the country from Magnesia to Mylasa ; but every town in that country was a fortress, and the work of besieging was protracted without furnishing, or giving promise of, any material results. Zeuxis the satrap of Lydia supported the ally of his master with the same lukewarmness as Philip had manifested in promoting the interests of the Syrian king, and the Greek cities gave their support only under the pressure of force or fear. The provisioning of the army became daily more difficult ; Philip was obliged now to plunder those who but lately had voluntarily supplied his wants, and then he had reluctantly to submit to beg afresh. Thus the good season of the year gradually drew to an end, and in the interval the Rhodians had reinforced their fleet and had also been rejoined by that of Attalus, so that they were decidedly superior at sea. It seemed almost as if they might cut off the retreat of the king and compel him to take up winter quarters in Caria, while the state of affairs at home, particularly the threatened intervention of the Aetolians and Romans, urgently demanded his return. Philip saw the danger ; he left garrisons amounting together to 3000 men, partly in Myrina to keep Pergamus in check, partly in the petty towns round Mylasa —Iassus, Bargylia, Euromus, and Pedasa—to secure for him the excellent harbour and a landing place in Caria ; and, owing to the negligence with which the allies guarded the sea, he succeeded in safely reaching the Thracian coast with his fleet and arriving at home before the winter of 553-4.

201–200.

Diplomatic intervention of Rome.

In fact a storm was gathering against Philip in the west, which did not permit him to continue the plundering of defenceless Egypt. The Romans, who had at length in this year concluded peace on their own terms with Carthage, began to give serious attention to these complications in the East. It has often been affirmed, that after the conquest of the West they forthwith proceeded to the subjugation of the East ; a more thorough consideration will lead to a juster

judgment. It is only dull prejudice which fails to see that
Rome at this period by no means grasped at the sovereignty
of the Mediterranean states, but, on the contrary, simply
desired to have neighbours that should not be dangerous in
Africa and in Greece ; and Macedonia was not really dangerous to Rome. Its power certainly was far from small, and it
is evident that the Roman senate only consented with reluctance to the peace of 548–9, which left it in all its integrity ; 206–205.
but how little any serious apprehensions of Macedonia were
or could be entertained in Rome, is best shown by the small
number of troops—who yet were never compelled to fight
against a superior force—with which Rome carried on the
next war.   The senate doubtless would have gladly seen
Macedonia humbled ; but that humiliation would be too
dearly purchased at the cost of a land war carried on in Macedonia with Roman troops : and accordingly, after the withdrawal of the Aetolians, the senate voluntarily concluded
peace at once on the basis of the *status quo*.   It is therefore
far from being demonstrated, that the Roman government
concluded this peace with any definite design of beginning
the war at a more convenient season ; and it is very certain
that, at the moment, from the thorough exhaustion of the
state and the extreme unwillingness of the citizens to enter into
a second transmarine struggle, the Macedonian war was in
a high degree unwelcome to the Romans.   But now it was
inevitable.   They might have been satisfied with the Macedonian state as a neighbour, such as it stood in 549 ; but it   205.
was impossible that they could permit it to acquire the best
part of Asiatic Greece and the important Cyrene, to crush
the neutral commercial states, and thereby to double its
power.   Further, the fall of Egypt and the humiliation,
perhaps the subjugation, of Rhodes could not but inflict deep
wounds on the trade of Sicily and Italy ; and could Rome
remain a quiet spectator, while Italian commerce with the
East was made dependent on the two great continental
powers ? Rome had, moreover, an obligation of honour to fulfil
towards Attalus her faithful ally since the first Macedonian
war, and had to prevent Philip, who had already besieged
him in his capital, from expelling him from his dominions.   Lastly, the claim of Rome to extend her protecting

arm over all the Hellenes was by no means an empty phrase:
the Neapolitans, Rhegines, Massiliots, and Emporienses
could testify that that protection was accorded in earnest,
and there is no question that at this time the Romans stood
in a closer relation to the Greeks than any other nation—one
little more remote than that of the Hellenic Macedonians.
It is strange that any should dispute the right of the Romans
to feel their human, as well as their Hellenic, sympathies
revolted at the scandalous treatment of the Cians and Tha-
sians. Thus in reality all political, commercial, and moral
motives concurred in inducing Rome to undertake the
second war against Philip—one of the most righteous which
the city ever waged. It greatly redounds to the honour of
the senate, that it immediately resolved on its course and
did not allow itself to be deterred from making the necessary
preparations either by the exhaustion of the state or by the
unpopularity of such a declaration of war. The propraetor
Marcus Valerius Laevinus made his appearance as early
as 553 with the Sicilian fleet of 38 sail in the eastern
waters.

201.

The government, however, were at a loss to discover an
ostensible pretext for the war; a pretext which they needed
in order to satisfy the people, even although they had not been
far too sagacious to undervalue, as was the manner of Philip,
the importance of assigning a legitimate ground for hostilities. The support, which Philip was alleged to have granted
to the Carthaginians after the peace with Rome, manifestly
could not be proved. The Roman subjects, indeed, in the
province of Illyria had for a considerable time complained of
the Macedonian encroachments. In 551 a Roman envoy at
the head of the Illyrian levy had driven Philip's troops from
the Illyrian territory; and the senate had accordingly declared to the king's envoys in 552, that if he sought war, he
would find it sooner than was agreeable to him. But these
encroachments were simply the ordinary outrages which
Philip practised towards his neighbours; a negotiation regarding them at the present moment would have led to his
humbling himself and offering satisfaction, but not to war.
With all the belligerent powers in the East the Roman community was nominally in friendly relations, and might have

203.

202.

granted them aid in repelling Philip's attack. But Rhodes and Pergamus, which of course did not fail to request Roman aid, were formally the aggressors; and although Alexandrian ambassadors besought the Roman senate to undertake the guardianship of the boy king, Egypt appears to have been by no means anxious to invoke the direct intervention of the Romans, which would put an end to her difficulties for the moment, but would at the same time open up the eastern seas to the great maritime power of the West. Aid to Egypt, moreover, must have been in the first instance rendered in Syria, and would have entangled Rome simultaneously in a war with Asia and with Macedonia; which the Romans were naturally the more desirous to avoid, as they were firmly resolved not to intermeddle at least in Asiatic affairs. No course was left but to despatch in the meantime an embassy to the East for the purpose, first, of obtaining—what was not in the circumstances difficult—the sanction of Egypt to the interference of Rome in the affairs of Greece; secondly, of pacifying king Antiochus by abandoning Syria to him; and, lastly, of accelerating as much as possible a breach with Philip and promoting a coalition of the minor Graeco-Asiatic states against him (end of 553). At Alexandria they had no difficulty in accomplishing their object; the court had no choice, and was obliged gratefully to receive Marcus Aemilius Lepidus, whom the senate had despatched as "guardian of the king" to uphold his interests, so far as that could be done without an actual intervention. Antiochus did not break off his alliance with Philip, nor did he give to the Romans the definite explanations which they desired; in other respects, however—whether from remissness, or influenced by the declarations of the Romans that they did not wish to interfere in Syria—he pursued his schemes in that direction and left things in Greece and Asia Minor to take their course.

201.

Meanwhile, the spring of 554 had arrived, and the war had recommenced. Philip first threw himself once more upon Thrace, where he occupied all the places on the coast, in particular Maronea, Aenus, Elaeus, and Sestus; he wished to have his European possessions secured against the risk of a Roman landing. He then attacked Abydus on the Asiatic

200.
Continuation of the war.

coast, the acquisition of which was an object of great importance to him, for the possession of Sestus and Abydus would bring him into closer connection with his ally Antiochus, and he would no longer need to be apprehensive lest the fleet of the allies might intercept him in crossing to or from Asia Minor. That fleet commanded the Aegean Sea after the withdrawal of the weaker Macedonian squadron: Philip confined his operations by sea to maintaining garrisons on three of the Cyclades, Andros, Cythnos, and Paros, and fitting out privateers. The Rhodians proceeded to Chios, and thence to Tenedos, where Attalus, who had passed the winter at Aegina and had spent his time in listening to the declamations of the Athenians, joined them with his squadron. The allies might probably have arrived in time to help the Abydenes, who heroically defended themselves; but they stirred not, and so at last the city surrendered, after almost all who were capable of bearing arms had fallen in the struggle before the walls; a large portion of the inhabitants fell by their own hand after the capitulation—the mercy of the victor consisted in allowing the Abydenes a term of three days to die voluntarily. Here, in the camp before Abydus, the Roman embassy, which after the termination of its business in Syria and Egypt had visited and dealt with the minor Greek states, met with the king, and submitted the proposals which it had been charged to make by the senate, viz., that the king should wage no aggressive war against any Greek state, should restore the possessions which he had wrested from Ptolemy, and should consent to an arbitration regarding the injury inflicted on the Pergamenes and Rhodians. The object of the senate, which sought to provoke the king to a formal declaration of war, was not gained; the Roman ambassador, Marcus Aemilius Lepidus, obtained from the king nothing but the polite reply, that he would excuse what the envoy had said because he was young, handsome, and a Roman.

Meanwhile, however, the occasion for declaring war, which Rome desired, had been furnished from another quarter. The Athenians in their silly and cruel vanity had put to death two unfortunate Acarnanians, because these had accidentally strayed into their mysteries. When the Acarnanians, who

were naturally indignant, asked Philip to procure them
satisfaction, he could not refuse the just request of his most
faithful allies, and he allowed them to levy men in Macedonia
and, with these and their own troops, to invade Attica without a formal declaration of war. This, it is true, was no
war in the proper sense of the term ; and, besides, the leader
of the Macedonian band, Nicanor, immediately gave orders
to his troops to retreat, when the Roman envoys, who were
at Athens at the time, used threatening language (in the end
of 553). But it was too late. An Athenian embassy was   201.
sent to Rome to report the attack made by Philip on an
ancient ally of the Romans; and, from the way in which the
senate received it, Philip saw clearly what awaited him ; so
that he at once, in the very spring of 554, directed Philocles,   200.
his general in Greece, to lay waste the Attic territory and to
reduce the city to extremities.

The senate now had what they wanted; and in the summer   Declara-
of 554 they were able to propose to the comitia a declaration   tion [200.
of war " on account of an attack on a state in alliance with   Rome.
Rome." It was rejected on the first occasion almost unanimously : foolish or evil-disposed tribunes of the people complained that the senate would allow the citizens no rest; but
the war was necessary and, in strictness, was already begun,
so that the senate could not possibly recede. The burgesses
were induced to yield by representations and concessions. It
is remarkable that these concessions were made mainly at the
expense of the allies. The garrisons of Gaul, Lower Italy,
Sicily, and Sardinia, amounting in all to 20,000 men, were
exclusively taken from the allied contingents that were in
active service—quite contrary to the former principles of the
Romans. All the burgess troops, on the other hand, that
had continued under arms from the Hannibalic war, were
discharged ; volunteers alone, it was alleged, were to be
enrolled for the Macedonian war, but they were, as was
afterwards found, for the most part forced volunteers—a fact
which in the autumn of 555 gave rise to a dangerous mili-   199.
tary revolt in the camp of Apollonia. Six legions were
formed of the men newly called out ; of these two remained
in Rome and two in Etrucia, and only two embarked at

Brundisium for Macedonia, led by the consul Publius Sulpicius Galba.

Thus it was once more clearly demonstrated, that the sovereign burgess assemblies, with their shortsighted resolutions dependent often on mere accident, were no longer at all fitted to deal with the complicated and difficult relations into which Rome was drawn by her victories; and that their mischievous intervention in the working of the state machine led to dangerous modifications of the measures which in a military point of view were necessary, and to the still more dangerous course of treating the Latin allies as inferiors.

The Roman league.

The position of Philip was very disadvantageous. The eastern states, which ought to have acted in unison against all interference of Rome and probably under other circumstances would have done so, had been mainly by Philip's fault so incensed at each other, that they were not inclined to hinder, or were inclined even to promote, the Roman invasion. Asia, the natural and most important ally of Philip, had been neglected by him, and was moreover prevented from any immediate active interference by being entangled in the quarrel with Egypt and the Syrian war. Egypt had an urgent interest in keeping the Roman fleet out of the eastern waters; even now an Egyptian embassy intimated at Rome very plainly, that the court of Alexandria was ready to relieve the Romans from the trouble of intervention in Attica. But the treaty for the partition of Egypt concluded between Asia and Macedonia threw that important state thoroughly into the arms of Rome, and compelled the cabinet of Alexandria to declare that it would only intermeddle in the affairs of European Greece with consent of the Romans. The Greek commercial cities, with Rhodes, Pergamus, and Byzantium at their head, were in a position similar, but of still greater perplexity. They would under other circumstances have beyond doubt done what they could to close the eastern seas against the Romans; but the cruel and destructive policy of conquest pursued by Philip had driven them to an unequal struggle, in which for their self-preservation they were obliged to use every effort to obtain the interference of the great Italian power. In Greece proper also the Roman envoys, who were commissioned to organize a second league against Philip there, found the way already substantially paved for them by the enemy. Of the anti-Macedonian party—the Spartans, Eleans, Athenians, and Aetolians—Philip might perhaps have gained the latter, for the peace of 548 had made a deep, and far from healed, breach in their friendly alliance with Rome; but apart from the old differences which subsisted between Aetolia and Macedonia regarding the Thessalian towns withdrawn by Macedonia from the Aetolian confederacy —Echinus, Larissa Cremaste, Pharsalus, and Thebes in Phthiotis—the expulsion of the Aetolian garrisons from Lysimachia and Cius had produced fresh exasperation against Philip in the minds of the Aetolians. If they delayed to join the league against him, the chief reason doubtless was the ill-feeling that continued to prevail between them and the Romans.

206.

It was a circumstance still more ominous, that even among the Greek states firmly attached to the interests of Macedonia —the Epirots, Acarnanians, Boeotians, and Achaeans—the Acarnanians and Boeotians alone stood steadfastly by Philip. With the Epirots the Roman envoys negotiated not without success; Amynander, king of the Athamanes, in particular closely attached himself to Rome. Even among the Achaeans, Philip had offended many by the murder of Aratus; while on the other hand he had thereby paved the way for a more free development of the confederacy. Under the leadership of Philopoemen (502–571, for the first time *strategus* in 546) it had reorganized its military system, recovered confidence in itself by successful conflicts with Sparta, and no longer blindly followed, as in the time of Aratus, the policy of Macedonia. The Achaean league, which had to expect neither profit nor immediate injury from the thirst of Philip for aggrandizement, alone in all Hellas looked at this war from an impartial and national Hellenic point of view. It perceived—what there was no difficulty in perceiving—that the Hellenic nation was thereby surrendering itself to the Romans even before they wished or desired its surrender, and attempted accordingly to mediate between Philip and the Rhodians; but it was too late. The national patriotism, which had formerly terminated the federal war

252–183.

208.

and had mainly contributed to the first war between Macedonia and Rome, was extinguished; the Achaean mediation remained fruitless, and in vain Philip visited the cities and islands to rekindle the zeal of the nation—its apathy was the Nemesis for Cius and Abydus. The Achaeans, as they could effect no change and were not disposed to render help to either party, remained neutral.

200.
Landing
of the
Romans
in Mace-
donia.

In the autumn of 554 the consul, Publius Sulpicius Galba, landed with his two legions and 1000 Numidian cavalry accompanied even by elephants derived from the spoils of Carthage, at Apollonia; on receiving accounts of which the king returned in haste from the Hellespont to Thessaly. But, owing partly to the far advanced season, partly to the sickness of the Roman general, nothing was undertaken by land that year except a reconnaissance in force, in the course of which the places in the vicinity, and in particular the Macedonian colony Antipatreia, were occupied by the Romans. For the next year a joint attack on Macedonia was concerted with the northern barbarians, especially with Pleuratus, the then ruler of Scodra, and Bato, prince of the Dardani, who of course were eager to profit by the favourable opportunity.

More importance attached to the enterprises of the Roman fleet, which numbered 100 decked and 80 light vessels. While the rest of the ships took their station for the winter at Corcyra, a division under Gaius Claudius Cento proceeded to the Piraeeus to render assistance to the hard-pressed Athenians. But, as Cento found the Attic territory already sufficiently protected against the raids of the Corinthian garrison and the Macedonian corsairs, he sailed on and appeared suddenly before Chalcis in Euboea, the chief stronghold of Philip in Greece, where his magazines, stores of arms, and prisoners were kept, and where the commandant Sopater was far from expecting a Roman attack. The undefended walls were scaled, and the garrison was put to death; the prisoners were liberated and the stores were burnt; unfortunately, there was a want of troops to hold the important position. On receiving news of this invasion, Philip immediately in vehement indignation started from Demetrias in Thessaly for Chalcis, and when he found no trace of the enemy there save the scene of ruin, he went on to Athens to retaliate. But his attempt to surprise the city was a failure, and even the assault was in vain, greatly as the king exposed his life; the approach of Gaius Claudius from the Piraeeus, and of Attalus from Aegina, compelled him to depart. Philip still tarried for some time in Greece; but in a political and in a military point of view his successes were equally insignificant. In vain he tried to induce the Achaeans to take up arms in his behalf; and equally fruitless were his attacks on Eleusis and the Piraeeus, as well as a second attempt on Athens itself. Nothing remained for him but to gratify his natural exasperation in an unworthy manner by laying waste the country and destroying the trees of Academus, and then to return to the north.

Thus the winter passed away. With the spring of 555, the proconsul Publius Sulpicius broke up from his winter camp, determined to conduct his legions from Apollonia by the shortest route into Macedonia proper. This principal attack from the west was to be supported by three subordinate attacks; on the north by an invasion of the Dardani and Illyrians; on the east by an attack on the part of the combined fleet of the Romans and allies, which assembled at Aegina; while lastly the Athamanes, and the Aetolians also, if the attempt to induce them to share in the struggle should prove successful, were to advance from the south. After Galba had crossed the mountains intersected by the Apsus (now the Beratinó), and had marched through the fertile plain of the Dassaretae, he reached the mountain range which separates Illyria from Macedonia, and crossing it, entered the proper Macedonian territory. Philip had marched to meet him; but in the extensive and thinly peopled regions of Macedonia the antagonists for a time sought each other in vain; at length they met in the province of Lyncestis, a fertile but marshy plain not far from the north-western frontier, and encamped not 1000 paces apart. Philip's army, after he had been joined by the corps detached to occupy the northern passes, numbered about 20,000 infantry and 2000 cavalry; the Roman army was nearly as strong. The Macedonians however had the great advantage, that, fighting in their native land and well

Attempt of the Romans to invade Macedonia. [198.

acquainted with its highways and byways, they had little
trouble in procuring supplies of provisions, while they had
encamped so close to the Romans that the latter could not
venture to disperse for any extensive foraging. The consul
repeatedly offered battle, but the king persisted in declining
it; and the combats between the light troops, although the
Romans gained some advantages in them, produced no material alteration. Galba was obliged to break up his camp
and to pitch another eight miles off at Octolophus,
where he conceived that he could more easily procure
supplies. But here too the divisions sent out were destroyed
by the light troops and cavalry of the Macedonians; the
legions were obliged to come to their help, whereupon
the Macedonian van-guard, which had advanced too far,
were driven back to their camp with heavy loss; the king
himself lost his horse in the action, and only saved his
life through the magnanimous self-devotion of one of his
troopers. From this perilous position the Romans were
liberated through the better success of the subordinate attacks which Galba had directed the allies to make, or rather
through the weakness of the Macedonian forces. Although
Philip had instituted levies as large as possible in his own
dominions, and had enlisted Roman deserters and other
mercenaries, he had not been able to bring into the field
(over and above the garrisons in Asia Minor and Thrace)
more than the army, with which in person he confronted
the consul; and besides, in order to form even this, he had
been obliged to leave the northern passes in the Pelagonian
territory undefended. For the protection of the east coast
he relied partly on the orders which he had given for the laying waste of the islands of Sciathus and Peparethus, which
might have furnished a station to the enemy's fleet, partly
on the garrisoning of Thasos and the coast and on the fleet
organized at Demetrias under Heraclides. For the south
frontier he had been obliged to reckon solely upon the more
than doubtful neutrality of the Aetolians. These now suddenly joined the league against Macedonia, and immediately
in conjunction with the Athamanes penetrated into Thessaly,
while simultaneously the Dardani and Illyrians overran the
northern provinces, and the Roman fleet under Lucius

Apustius, departing from Corcyra, appeared in the eastern waters, where the ships of Attalus, the Rhodians, and the Istrians joined it.

Philip, on learning this, voluntarily abandoned his position and retreated in an easterly direction: whether he did so in order to repel the probably unexpected invasion of the Aetolians, or to draw the Roman army after him with a view to its destruction, or to take either of these courses according to circumstances, cannot well be determined. He managed his retreat so dexterously that Galba, who adopted the rash resolution of following him, lost his track, and Philip was enabled to reach by a flank movement, and to occupy, the narrow pass which separates the provinces of Lyncestis and Eordaea, with the view of awaiting the Romans and giving them a warm reception there. A battle took place on the spot which he had selected; but the long Macedonian spears proved unserviceable on the wooded and uneven ground. The Macedonians were partly turned, partly broken, and lost many men.

But, although Philip's army was after this unfortunate action no longer able to prevent the advance of the Romans, the latter were themselves afraid to encounter further unknown dangers in an impassable and hostile country; and returned to Apollonia, after they had laid waste the fertile provinces of Upper Macedonia—Eordaea, Elymaea, and Orestis. Celetrum, the most considerable town of Orestis (now Kastoria, on a peninsula in the lake of the same name), had surrendered to them: it was the only Macedonian town that opened its gates to the Romans. In the Illyrian land Pelium, the city of the Dassaretae, on the upper confluents of the Apsus, was taken by storm and strongly garrisoned to serve as a future basis for a similar expedition. *Return of the Romans.*

Philip did not disturb the Roman main army in its retreat, but turned by forced marches against the Aetolians and Athamanians who, in the belief that the legions were occupying the attention of the king, were fearlessly and recklessly plundering the rich vale of the Peneius, defeated them completely, and compelled such as did not fall to make their escape singly through the well-known mountain paths. The effective strength of the confederacy was not a little diminished by this defeat, and not less by the numerous enlistments made in Aetolia on Egyptian account. The Dardani were chased back over the mountains by Athenagoras, the leader of Philip's light troops, without difficulty and with severe loss. The Roman fleet also did not accomplish much; it expelled the Macedonian garrison from Andros, visited Euboea and Sciathus, and then made attempts on the Chalcidian peninsula, which were, however, vigorously repulsed by the Macedonian garrison at Mende. The rest of the summer was spent in the capture of Oreus in Euboea, which was long delayed by the resolute defence of the Macedonian garrison. The weak Macedonian fleet under Heraclides remained inactive at Heraclea, and did not venture to dispute the possession of the sea with the enemy. The latter went early to winter quarters, the Romans proceeding to the Piraeeus and Corcyra, the Rhodians and Pergamenes going home.

Philip might on the whole congratulate himself upon the results of this campaign. The Roman troops, after an extremely troublesome campaign, stood in autumn precisely on the spot whence they had started in spring; and, but for the well-timed interposition of the Aetolians and the unexpected success of the battle at the pass of Eordaea, perhaps not a man of their entire force would have again seen the Roman territory. The fourfold assault had everywhere failed in its object, and not only did Philip in autumn see his whole dominions cleared of the enemy, but he was able to make an attempt—which, however, miscarried—to wrest from the Aetolians the strong town of Thaumaci, situated on the Aetolo-Thessalian frontier and commanding the plain of the Peneius. If Antiochus, for whose coming Philip vainly supplicated the gods, should unite with him in the next campaign, he might anticipate great successes. For a moment it seemed as if Antiochus was disposed to do so; his army appeared in Asia Minor, and occupied some places belonging to king Attalus, who requested military protection from the Romans. The latter, however, were not anxious to urge the great king at this time to a breach; they sent envoys, who in fact obtained an evacuation of the dominions of Attalus. From that quarter Philip had nothing to hope for.

But the fortunate issue of the last campaign had so raised
the courage or the arrogance of Philip, that, after having
assured himself afresh of the neutrality of the Achaeans
and the fidelity of the Macedonians by the sacrifice of some
strong places and of the detested admiral Heraclides, he next
spring (556) assumed the offensive and advanced into the
territory of the Atintanes, with a view to form a well-en-
trenched camp in the narrow pass, where the Aous (Viosa)
winds its way between the mountains Aeropus and Asnaus.
Opposite to him encamped the Roman army reinforced by
new arrivals of troops, and commanded first by the consul of
the previous year, Publius Villius, and then from the summer
of 556 by that year's consul, Titus Quinctius Flamininus.
Flamininus, a talented man just thirty years of age, belonged
to the younger generation, who began to lay aside the patriotism as well as the habits of their forefathers and, though
not unmindful of their fatherland, were still more mindful of
themselves and of Hellenism.   A skilful officer and a better
diplomatist, he was in many respects admirably adapted for
the management of the troubled affairs of Greece.   Yet it
would perhaps have been better both for Rome and for
Greece, if the choice had fallen on one less full of Hellenic
sympathies, and if the general despatched thither had been a
man, who would neither have been bribed by delicate flattery
nor stung by pungent sarcasm; who would not amidst literary and artistic reminiscences have overlooked the pitiful
condition of the constitutions of the Hellenic states; and
who, while treating Hellas according to its deserts, would
have spared the Romans the trouble of striving after unat-
tainable ideals.

The new commander-in-chief immediately had a conference
with the king, while the two armies lay face to face inactive.
Philip made proposals of peace ; he offered to restore all his
own conquests, and to submit to an equitable arbitration
regarding the damage inflicted on the Greek cities ; but the
negotiations broke down, when he was asked to give up
ancient possessions of Macedonia and particularly Thessaly.
For forty days the two armies lay in the narrow pass of the
Aous ; Philip would not retire, and Flamininus could not
make up his mind whether he should order an assault, or

*Philip en-
camps on
the Aous.*

198.

198.

*Flami-
ninus.*

leave the king alone and reattempt the expedition of the
previous year.   At length the Roman general was helped out
of his perplexity by the treachery of some chiefs among the
Epirots, who were otherwise well-disposed to Macedon, and
especially of Charops.   They conducted a Roman corps of
4000 infantry and 300 cavalry by mountain paths to the
heights above the Macedonian camp; and, when the consul
attacked the enemy's army in front, the advance of that
Roman division, unexpectedly descending from the mountains
commanding the position, decided the battle.   Philip lost
his camp and entrenchments and nearly 2000 men, and
hastily retreated to the pass of Tempe, the gate of Macedonia
proper.   He gave up everything which he had held except
the fortresses; the Thessalian towns, which he could not
defend, he destroyed; Pherae alone closed its gates against
him and thereby escaped destruction.   The Epirots, induced
partly by these successes of the Roman arms, partly by the
judicious moderation of Flamininus, were the first to secede
from the Macedonian alliance.   On the first accounts of the
Roman victory the Athamanes and Aetolians immediately
invaded Thessaly, and the Romans soon followed; the open
country was easily overrun, but the strong towns, which were
friendly to Macedonia and received support from Philip, fell
only after a brave resistance or withstood even the superior
foe—especially Atrax on the left bank of the Peneius, where
the phalanx stood in the breach as a substitute for the wall.
Except these Thessalian fortresses and the territory of the
faithful Acarnanians, all northern Greece was thus in the
hands of the coalition.

The south, on the other hand, was still in the main retained
under the power of Macedonia by the fortresses of Chalcis
and Corinth, which maintained communication with each
other through the territory of the Boeotians who were
friendly to the Macedonians, and by the Achaean neutrality;
and as it was too late to advance into Macedonia this year,
Flamininus resolved to direct his land army and fleet in the
first place against Corinth and the Achaeans.   The fleet,
which had again been joined by the Rhodian and Pergamene
ships, had hitherto been employed in the capture and pillage
of two of the smaller towns in Euboea, Eretria and Carystus;

Philip
driven
back to
Tempe.

Greece in
the power
of the Ro-
mans.

both however, as well as Oreus, were thereafter abandoned, and reoccupied by Philocles the Macedonian commandant of Chalcis. The united fleet proceeded thence to Cenchreae, the eastern port of Corinth, to threaten that strong fortress. On the other side Flamininus advanced into Phocis and occupied the country, in which Elatea alone sustained a somewhat protracted siege : this district and Anticyra in particular on the Corinthian gulf were chosen as winter quarters. The Achaeans, who thus saw the Roman legions approaching and the Roman fleet already on their own coast, abandoned their morally honourable, but politically untenable, neutrality. After the deputies from the towns most closely attached to Macedonia—Dyme, Megalopolis, and Argos—had left the diet, it resolved to join the coalition against Philip. Cycliades and other leaders of the Macedonian party went into exile ; the troops of the Achaeans immediately united with the Roman fleet and hastened to invest Corinth by land, which city—the stronghold of Philip against the Achaeans—had been guaranteed to them on the part of Rome in return for their joining the coalition. Not only, however, did the Macedonian garrison, which was 1300 strong and consisted chiefly of Italian deserters, defend with determination the almost impregnable city, but Philocles also arrived from Chalcis with a division of 1500 men, which after relieving Corinth invaded the territories of the Achaeans and, in concert with the citizens who were favourable to Macedonia, wrested from them Argos. But the recompense of such devotedness was, that the king delivered over the faithful Argives to the reign of terror of Nabis of Sparta. Philip hoped, after the accession of the Achaeans to the Roman coalition, to gain over Nabis who had hitherto been the ally of the Romans ; for his chief reason for joining the Roman alliance was, that he was opposed to the Achaeans and since 550 had been even at open war with them. But the affairs of Philip were in too desperate a condition for any one to feel satisfaction in joining him now. Nabis accepted Argos from Philip, but he betrayed the traitor and remained in alliance with Flamininus, who, in his perplexity at being now allied with two powers that were at war with each other, had in the mean

The Achaeans enter into alliance with Rome.

204.

time arranged an armistice of four months between the Spartans and Achaeans.

Vain attempts to arrange a peace.
Thus winter came on; and Philip once more availed himself of it to obtain if possible an equitable peace. At a conference held at Nicaea on the Maliac gulf the king appeared in person, and endeavoured to come to an understanding with Flamininus. With haughty politeness he repelled the forward arrogance of the petty chiefs, and by marked deference to the Romans, as the only antagonists on an equality with him, he sought to obtain from them tolerable terms. Flamininus was sufficiently refined to feel himself flattered by the urbanity of the vanquished prince towards himself and his haughtiness in reference to the allies, whom the Roman as well as the king had learned to despise; but his powers were not ample enough to meet the king's wishes. He granted him a two months' armistice in return for the evacuation of Phocis and Locris, and referred him, as to the main matter, to his government. The Roman senate had long been of opinion that Macedonia must give up all her possessions abroad; accordingly, when the ambassadors of Philip appeared in Rome, they were simply asked whether they had full powers to renounce all Greece and in particular Corinth, Chalcis, and Demetrias, and when they said that they had not, the negotiations were immediately broken off, and it was resolved that the war should be prosecuted with vigour. With the help of the tribunes of the people, the senate succeeded in preventing a change in the chief command—which had often proved so injurious—and in prolonging the command of Flamininus; he obtained considerable reinforcements, and the two former commanders, Publius Galba and Publius Villius, were instructed to place themselves at his disposal. Philip resolved once more to risk a pitched battle. To secure Greece, where all the states except the Acarnanians and Boeotians were now in arms against him, the garrison of Corinth was augmented to 6000 men, while he himself, straining the last energies of exhausted Macedonia and enrolling children and old men in the ranks of the phalanx, brought into the field an army of about 26,000 men, of whom 16,000 were Macedonian *phalangitae*.

197.
Thus the fourth campaign, that of 557, began. Flamin-

inus despatched a part of the fleet against the Acarnanians, Philip proceeds to Thessaly. who were besieged in Leucas; in Greece proper he became by stratagem master of Thebes, the capital of Boeotia, in consequence of which the Boeotians were compelled to join at least nominally the alliance against Macedonia. Content with having thus interrupted the communication between Corinth and Chalcis, he proceeded to the north, where alone a decisive blow could be struck. The great difficulties of provisioning the army in a hostile and for the most part desolate country, which had often hampered its operations, were now to be obviated by the fleet accompanying the army along the coast and carrying after it supplies sent from Africa, Sicily, and Sardinia. The decisive blow came, however, earlier than Flamininus had expected. Philip, impatient and confident as he was, could not endure to await the enemy on the Macedonian frontier: after assembling his army at Dium, he advanced through the pass of Tempe into Thessaly, and encountered the army of the enemy advancing to meet him in the district of Scotussa.

The Macedonian and Roman armies—the latter of which Battle of Cynoscephalae. had been reinforced by the contingents of the Apolloniates and the Athamanes, by the Cretans sent by Nabis, and especially by a strong band of Aetolians—contained nearly equal numbers of combatants, each about 26,000 men; the Romans, however, had the superiority in cavalry. In front of Scotussa, on the plateau of the Karadagh, during a gloomy day of rain, the Roman vanguard unexpectedly encountered that of the enemy, which occupied a high and steep hill named Cynoscephalae, that lay between the two camps. Driven back into the plain, the Romans were reinforced from the camp by the light troops and the excellent corps of Aetolian cavalry, and now in turn forced the Macedonian vanguard back upon and over the height. But here the Macedonians again found support in their whole cavalry and the larger portion of their light infantry; the Romans, who had ventured forward imprudently, were pursued with great loss almost to their camp, and would have wholly taken to flight, had not the Aetolian horsemen prolonged the combat in the plain until Flamininus brought up his rapidly arranged legions. The king yielded to the impetuous cry of his victorious troops demanding the continuance of the conflict, and hastily drew up his heavy-armed soldiers for the battle, which neither general nor soldiers had expected on that day. It was important to occupy the hill, which for the moment was quite denuded of troops. The right wing of the phalanx, led by the king in person, arrived early enough to form without trouble in battle order on the height; the left had not yet come up, when the light troops of the Macedonians, put to flight by the legions, rushed up the hill. Philip quickly pushed the crowd of fugitives past the phalanx into the middle division, and, without waiting till Nicanor had arrived on the left wing with the other half of the phalanx which followed more slowly, he ordered the right phalanx to couch their spears and to charge down the hill on the legions, and the rearranged light infantry simultaneously to turn them and take them in flank. The attack of the phalanx, irresistible on so favourable ground, shattered the Roman infantry, and the left wing of the Romans was completely beaten. Nicanor on the other wing, when he saw the king give the attack, ordered the other half of the phalanx to advance in all haste; by this movement it was thrown into confusion, and while the first ranks were already rapidly following the victorious right wing down the hill, and were still more thrown into disorder by the inequality of the ground, the last files were just gaining the height. The right wing of the Romans under these circumstances soon overcame the enemy's left; the elephants alone, stationed upon this wing, made sad havoc in the broken Macedonian ranks. While a fearful slaughter was taking place at this point, a resolute Roman officer collected twenty companies, and with these threw himself on the victorious Macedonian wing, which had advanced so far in pursuit of the Roman left that the Roman right came to be in its rear. Against an attack from behind the phalanx was defenceless, and this movement ended the battle. From the complete breaking up of the two phalanxes we may well believe that the Macedonian loss amounted to 13,000, partly prisoners, partly fallen—but chiefly the latter, because the Roman soldiers were not acquainted with the Macedonian sign of surrender, the raising of the *sarissae*. The loss of the victors was slight. Philip escaped to Larissa, and, after burning all his papers that nobody might be compromised, evacuated Thessaly and returned home. Simultaneously with this great defeat, the Macedonians suffered other discomfitures at all the points which they still occupied; in Caria the Rhodian mercenaries defeated the Macedonian corps stationed there and compelled it to shut itself up in Stratonicea; the Corinthian garrison was defeated by Nicostratus and his Achaeans with severe loss, and Leucas in Acarnania was taken by assault after a heroic resistance. Philip was completely vanquished; his last allies, the Acarnanians, yielded on the news of the battle of Cynoscephalae.

It was completely in the power of the Romans to dictate peace; they used their power without abusing it. The empire of Alexander might be annihilated; at a conference of the allies this proposal was actually brought forward by the Aetolians. But what would be the effect of such a course, save to demolish the rampart protecting Hellenic culture from the Thracians and Celts? Already during the war just ended the flourishing Lysimachia on the Thracian Chersonese had been totally destroyed by the Thracians—a serious warning for the future. Flamininus, who had clearly perceived the bitter animosities subsisting among the Greek states, could never consent that the great Roman power should carry into execution the spiteful projects of the Aetolian confederacy, even if his Hellenic sympathies had not been as much won by the polished and chivalrous king as his Roman national feeling was offended by the boastings of the Aetolians, the "victors of Cynoscephalae," as they called themselves. He replied to the Aetolians that it was not the custom of Rome to annihilate the vanquished, and that, besides, they were their own masters and were at liberty to put an end to Macedonia if they could. The king was treated with all possible respect, and, on his declaring himself ready now to entertain the demands formerly made, an armistice for a considerable term was agreed to by Flamininus in return for the payment of a sum of money and the furnishing of hostages, among whom was the king's son Demetrius,—an armistice which Philip greatly needed in order to expel the Dardani out of Macedonia.

Preliminaries of peace.

Peace with Macedonia.

The final regulation of the complicated affairs of Greece was entrusted by the senate to a commission of ten persons, the head and soul of which was Flamininus. Philip obtained from it terms similar to those granted to Carthage. He lost all his foreign possessions in Asia Minor, Thrace, Greece, and in the islands of the Aegean Sea; while he retained Macedonia proper undiminished, with the exception of some unimportant tracts on the frontier and the province of Orestis, which was declared free—a stipulation which Philip felt very keenly, but which the Romans could not avoid prescribing, for with his known character it was impossible to leave him free to dispose of subjects who had once revolted from their allegiance. Macedonia was further bound not to conclude any foreign alliances without the previous knowledge of Rome, and not to send garrisons abroad; she was bound, moreover, not to make war out of Macedonia against civilized states or against any allies of Rome at all, and she was to maintain no army exceeding 5,000 men, no elephants, and not more than five decked ships; the rest were to be given up to the Romans. Lastly, Philip entered into symmachy with the Romans, which obliged him to send a contingent when requested; indeed, Macedonian troops immediately afterwards fought side by side with the legions. Moreover, he paid a contribution of 1000 talents (£244,000).

Greece free.

After Macedonia had thus been reduced to complete political nullity and was left in possession of only as much power as was needful to guard the frontier of Hellas against the barbarians, the Romans proceeded to dispose of the possessions ceded by the king. The Romans, who just at that time were learning by experience in Spain that transmarine provinces were a very dubious gain, and who had by no means begun the war with a view to the acquisition of territory, took none of the spoil for themselves, and thus compelled their allies also to moderation. They resolved to declare all the states of Greece, which had previously been under Philip, free; and Flamininus was commissioned to read the decree to that effect to the Greeks assembled at the Isthmian games

196.

(558). Thoughtful men doubtless might ask whether freedom was a blessing capable of being thus bestowed, and what was the value of freedom to a nation apart from union and unity; but the rejoicing was great and sincere, as the intention of the senate was sincere in conferring the freedom.*

The only exceptions to this general rule were, the Illyrian provinces eastward of Epidamnus, which fell to Pleuratus the ruler of Scodra, and rendered that state of robbers and pirates, which a century before had been humbled by the Romans (p. 77), once more one of the most powerful of the petty principalities in those regions; some districts in western Thessaly, which Amynander had occupied and was allowed to retain; and the three islands of Paros, Scyros, and Imbros, which were presented to Athens in return for the many hardships which she had suffered, and her still more numerous addresses of thanks and courtesies of all sorts. The Rhodians, of course, retained their Carian possessions, and the Pergamenes retained Aegina. The remaining allies were only indirectly rewarded by the accession of the newly liberated cities to the several confederacies. The Achaeans were the best treated, although they were the latest in joining the coalition against Philip; apparently for the honourable reason, that this federation was the best organized and most respectable of all the Greek states. All the possessions of Philip in the Peloponnesus and on the Isthmus, and consequently Corinth in particular, were incorporated with their league. With the Aetolians on the other hand the Romans used little ceremony; they were allowed to receive the towns of Phocis and Locris into their symmachy, but their attempts to extend it also to Acarnania and Thessaly were in part decidedly rejected, in part postponed, and the Thessalian cities were organized into four small independent confederacies. The Rhodian city-league reaped the benefit of the liberation of Thasos, Lemnos, and the towns of Thrace and Asia Minor.

The regulation of the affairs of the Greek states, as respected both their mutual relations and their internal condi-

Side notes: Scodra.

The Achaean league enlarged.

The Aetolians.

War against Nabis of Sparta.

---

* There are still extant gold staters, with the head of Flamininus and the inscription " *T. Quincti*(*us*)," struck in Greece under the government of the liberator of the Hellenes. The use of the Latin language is a significant compliment.

tion, was attended with difficulty. The most urgent matter
was the war which had been carried on between the Spartans
234.   and Achaeans since 550, in which the duty of mediating necessarily fell to the Romans. But after various attempts to
induce Nabis to yield, and particularly to give up the city of
Argos belonging to the Achaean league, which Philip had
surrendered to him, no course at last was left to Flamininus
but to have war declared against the obstinate petty robber-
chieftain, who reckoned on the well-known grudge of the
Aetolians against the Romans and on the advance of Antiochus into Europe, and pertinaciously refused to restore Argos.
This was done, accordingly, by all the Hellenes at a great
diet in Corinth, and Flamininus advanced into the Peloponnesus accompanied by the fleet and the Romano-allied army,
which included a contingent sent by Philip and a division
of Lacedaemonian emigrants under Agesipolis, the legitimate
195.   king of Sparta (559). In order to crush his antagonist
immediately by an overwhelming superiority of force, no
less than 50,000 men were brought into the field, and, the
other towns being disregarded, the capital itself was at once
invested; but the desired result was not attained. Nabis
had sent into the field a considerable army amounting to
15,000 men, of whom 5,000 were mercenaries, and he had
confirmed his rule afresh by a complete reign of terror—
by the execution *en masse* of the officers and inhabitants of
the country whom he suspected. Even when he himself
after the first successes of the Roman army and fleet resolved to yield and to accept the comparatively favourable
terms of peace proposed by Flamininus, " the people," that
is to say the gang of robbers whom Nabis had domiciled
in Sparta, not without reason apprehensive of a reckoning
after the victory, and deceived by accompanying lies as to
the nature of the terms of peace and as to the advance of the
Aetolians and Asiatics, rejected the peace offered by the
Roman general, so that the struggle began anew. A battle
took place in front of the walls and an assault was made upon
them; they were already scaled by the Romans, when the
setting on fire of the captured streets compelled the assailants
to retire.

Settle-   At last the obstinate resistance came to an end. Sparta retained its independence and was neither compelled to receive back the emigrants nor to join the Achaean league; even the existing monarchical constitution, and Nabis himself, were left intact.   On the other hand Nabis had to cede his foreign possessions, Argos, Messene, the Cretan cities, and the whole coast besides; to bind himself neither to conclude foreign alliances, nor to wage war, nor to keep any other vessels than two open boats; and lastly to disgorge all his plunder, to give to the Romans hostages, and to pay to them a war-contribution.   The towns on the Laconian coast were given to the Spartan emigrants, and this new community, who named themselves the "free Laconians," in contrast to the monarchically governed Spartans, were directed to enter the Achaean league.   The emigrants did not receive back their property, as the district assigned to them was regarded as a compensation for it; it was stipulated on the other hand, that their wives and children should not be detained in Sparta against their will.   The Achaeans, although by this arrangement they gained the accession of the free Laconians as well as Argos, were yet far from content; they had expected that the dreaded and hated Nabis would be superseded, that the emigrants would be brought back, and that the Achaean symmachy would be extended to the whole Peloponnesus.   Unprejudiced persons, however, will not fail to see that Flamininus managed these difficult affairs as fairly and justly as it was possible to manage them where two political parties, both chargeable with unfairness and injustice, stood opposed to each other.   With the old and deep hostility subsisting between the Spartans and Achaeans, the incorporation of Sparta into the Achaean league would have been equivalent to placing Sparta under the Achaean yoke, a course no less contrary to equity than to prudence.   The restitution of the emigrants, and the complete restoration of a government that had been set aside for twenty years, would only have substituted one reign of terror for another; the plan adopted by Flamininus was the right one, just because it failed to satisfy either of the extreme parties.   At length thorough provision appeared to be made that the Spartan system of robbery by sea and land should cease, and that the government there, such as it was, should prove troublesome only to its own subjects. It is possible that Flamininus, who knew Nabis and could not but be aware how desirable it was that he should personally be superseded, omitted to take such a step from the mere desire to have done with the matter and not to mar the fair impression of his successes by complications that might be prolonged beyond all calculation; it is possible, moreover, that he sought to preserve Sparta as a counterpoise to the power of the Achaean confederacy in the Peloponnesus. But the former objection relates to a point of secondary importance; and as to the latter view, it is far from probable that the Romans condescended to fear the Achaeans.

Final regulation of Greece. Peace was thus established, externally at least, among the petty Greek states. But the internal condition of the several communities also furnished employment to the Roman arbiter. The Boeotians openly displayed their Macedonian tendencies, even after the expulsion of the Macedonians from Greece; although Flamininus had at their request allowed the Boeotians who were in the service of Philip to return home, Brachyllas, the most decided partisan of Macedonia, was elected to the presidency of the Boeotian confederacy, and Flamininus was otherwise irritated in every way. He bore it with unparalleled patience; but the Boeotians friendly to Rome, who knew what awaited them after the departure of the Romans, determined to put Brachyllas to death, and Flamininus, whose permission they deemed it necessary to ask, at least did not forbid them. Brachyllas was accordingly killed; upon which the Boeotians were not content with prosecuting the murderers, but lay in wait for the Roman soldiers passing singly or in small parties through their territories, and killed about 500 of them. This was too much to be endured; Flamininus imposed on them a fine of a talent for every soldier; and when they did not pay it, he collected the nearest troops and besieged Coronea **196.** (558). Now they betook themselves to entreaty; Flamininus in reality desisted on the intercession of the Achaeans and Athenians, exacting but a very moderate fine from those who were guilty; and although the Macedonian party remained continuously at the helm in the petty province, the

Romans met their puerile opposition simply with the for-
bearance of superior power.. In the rest of Greece Flamininus contented himself with exerting his influence, so far
as he could do so without violence, over the internal affairs
especially of the newly-freed communities; with placing the
councils and courts in the hands of the more wealthy and bringing the anti-Macedonian party to the helm; and with attaching
as much as possible the civic commonwealths to the Roman
interest, by adding everything, which in each community
should have fallen by martial law to the Romans, to the
common property of the city concerned. The work was
finished in the spring of 560; Flamininus once more as-   194.
sembled the deputies of all the Greek communities at
Corinth, exhorted them to a rational and moderate use of
the freedom conferred on them, and requested as the only
return for the kindness of the Romans, that they would
within thirty days send to him the Italian captives who had
been sold into Greece during the Hannibalic war. Then
he evacuated the last fortresses in which Roman garrisons were stationed, Demetrias, Chalcis along with the
smaller forts dependent upon it in Euboea, and Acrocorin-
thus—thus practically giving the lie to the assertion of the
Aetolians that Rome had inherited from Philip the "fetters"
of Greece—and departed homeward with all the Roman troops
and the liberated captives.

It is only contemptible disingenuousness or weakly senti-   Results.
mentality, which can fail to perceive that the Romans were
entirely in earnest in the liberation of Greece; and the reason why the plan so nobly projected resulted in so wretched
a structure, is to be sought only in the complete moral and
political disorganization of the Hellenic nation. It was no
small matter, that a mighty nation should have suddenly
with its powerful arm brought the land, which it had been
accustomed to regard as its primitive home and as the
shrine of its intellectual and higher interests, into the possession of full freedom, and should have conferred on every
community in it deliverance from foreign taxation and
foreign garrisons and the unlimited right of self-government;
it is mere paltriness that sees in this nothing save political calculation. Political calculation suggested to the

Romans the possibility of liberating Greece; it was converted into a reality by the Hellenic sympathies that were
at that time indescribably powerful in Rome, and above all
in Flamininus himself. If the Romans are liable to any reproach, it is that all of them, and in particular Flamininus
who overcame the well-founded scruples of the senate,
allowed the magic charm of the Hellenic name to prevent
them from perceiving in all its extent the wretched character
of the Greek states of that period, and from putting a stop
at once to the proceedings of communities who, owing to the
impotent antipathies that prevailed alike in their internal
and their mutual relations, neither knew how to act nor
how to keep quiet. As things stood, it was really necessary
at once to put an end to such a freedom, equally pitiful and
pernicious, by means of a superior power permanently present on the spot; the feeble policy of sentiment, with all its
apparent humanity, was far more cruel than the sternest occupation would have been. In Boeotia for instance Rome
had, if not to instigate, at least to permit, a political murder
because the Romans had resolved to withdraw their troops
from Greece and, consequently, could not prevent the
Greeks friendly to Rome from seeking their remedy in the
usual manner of the country. But Rome herself also suffered from the effects of this indecision. The war with Antiochus would not have arisen but for the political blunder
of liberating Greece, and it would not have been dangerous but for the military blunder of withdrawing the
garrisons from the principal fortresses on the European
frontier. History has a Nemesis for every sin—for an
impotent craving after freedom, as well as for an injudicious
generosity.

CHAPTER IX.

THE WAR WITH ANTIOCHUS OF ASIA.

In the kingdom of Asia the diadem of the Seleucidae had *Antiochus the Great. 223.* been worn since 531 by king Antiochus the Third, the great-great-grandson of the founder of the dynasty. He had, like Philip, begun to reign at nineteen years of age, and had displayed sufficient energy and enterprise, especially in his first campaigns in the East, to warrant his being without ludicrous impropriety addressed in courtly style as "the Great." He had succeeded—more, however, through the negligence of his opponents and of the Egyptian Philopator in particular, than through any ability of his own—in restoring in some degree the integrity of the monarchy, and in reuniting with his crown first the eastern satrapies of Media and Parthyene, and then the separate state which Achaeus had founded on this side of the Taurus in Asia Minor. A first attempt to wrest from the Egyptians the coast of Syria, the loss of which he sorely felt, had, in the year of the battle of the Trasimene lake, met with a bloody repulse from Philopator at Raphia; and Antiochus had taken good care not to resume the contest with Egypt, so long as a man—even though he were but an indolent one—occupied the Egyptian throne. But, after Philopator's death (549), the right moment for *205.* crushing Egypt appeared to have arrived; with that view Antiochus entered into concert with Philip, and had thrown himself upon Coele-Syria, while Philip attacked the cities of Asia Minor. When the Romans interposed in that quarter, it seemed for a moment as if Antiochus would make common cause with Philip against them—the course dictated by the position of affairs, as well as by the treaty of alliance. But, not far-seeing enough to repel at once with all his energy any interference whatever by the Romans in the affairs of the East, Antiochus thought that his best course was to take advantage of the subjugation of Philip by the Romans (which might easily be foreseen), in order to secure the kingdom of Egypt, which he had previously been willing to share with Philip, for himself alone. Notwithstanding the intimate relations of Rome with the court of Alexandria and her royal ward, the senate by no means intended to be in reality, what it was in name, his "guardian;" firmly resolved to give itself no concern about Asiatic affairs except in case of extreme necessity, and to limit the sphere of the Roman power by the Pillars of Hercules and the Hellespont, it allowed the great king to take his course. He himself did not probably contemplate in earnest the conquest of Egypt proper—which was more easily talked of than achieved—but he contemplated the subjugation of the foreign possessions of Egypt one after another, and at once attacked those in Cilicia as well as in Syria and Palestine. The great victory, which he

198.   gained in 556 over the Egyptian general Scopas at Mount Panium near the sources of the Jordan, not only gave him complete possession of that region as far as the frontier of Egypt proper, but so terrified the Egyptian guardians of the young king that, to prevent Antiochus from invading Egypt, they submitted to a peace and sealed it by the betrothal of their ward to Cleopatra the daughter of Antiochus. When he had thus achieved his first object, he proceeded in the following year, that of the battle of Cynoscephalae, with a strong fleet of 100 decked and 100 open vessels to Asia Minor, to take possession of the districts that formerly belonged to Egypt on the south and west coasts of Asia Minor—it is probable that the Egyptian government had ceded these districts, which were actually in the hands of Philip, to Antiochus under the peace, and had renounced their foreign possessions generally in Antiochus' favour—and to recover the Greeks of Asia Minor as a whole to his empire. At the same time a strong Syrian land-army assembled in Sardes.

Difficulties with Rome.   This enterprise had an indirect bearing on the Romans, who from the first had demanded that Philip should withdraw his garrisons from Asia Minor and should leave to the Rhodians and Pergamenes their territory and to the free cities their former constitution unimpaired, and who had now to witness Antiochus taking possession of them in Philip's place. Attalus and the Rhodians found themselves now directly threatened by Antiochus with precisely the same danger as had driven them a few years before into the war with Philip; and they naturally sought to involve the Romans in this war as well as in that which had just terminated. Already in 555–6 Attalus had requested from the Romans military aid against Antiochus, who had occupied his territory while the troops of Attalus were employed in the Roman war. The more energetic Rhodians even declared to king Antiochus, when in the spring of 557 his fleet appeared off the coast of Asia Minor, that they would regard its passing beyond the Chelidonian islands (off the Lycian coast) as a declaration of war; and, when Antiochus did not regard the threat, they, emboldened by the accounts that had just arrived of the battle of Cynoscephalae, had immediately begun the war and had actually protected against the king the most important of the Carian cities, Caunus, Halicarnassus, and Myndus, and the island of Samos. Most of the half-free cities had submitted to Antiochus, but some of them, more especially the important cities of Smyrna, Alexandria Troas, and Lampsacus, had, on learning the discomfiture of Philip, likewise taken courage to resist the Syrian; and their urgent entreaties were combined with those of the Rhodians.

199-198.

197.

It admits of no doubt, that Antiochus, so far as he was at all capable of forming a resolution and adhering to it, had already made up his mind not only to attach to his empire the Egyptian possessions in Asia, but also to make conquests on his own behalf in Europe and, if not to seek, at any rate to risk on that account a war with Rome. The Romans had thus every reason to comply with that request of their allies, and to interfere directly in Asia; but they showed little inclination to do so. They not only delayed as long as the Macedonian war lasted, and gave to Attalus nothing but the protection of diplomacy (which, so far, proved in the first instance effective); but even after their victory, while they doubtless spoke as though the cities which had been in the hands of Ptolemy and Philip ought not to be taken possession of by Antiochus, and while the freedom of the Asiatic cities,

Abydus, Cius, and Myrina, figured in Roman documents, they took not the smallest step to give effect to it, and allowed king Antiochus to employ the favourable opportunity presented by the withdrawal of the Macedonian garrisons to introduce his own.   In fact, they even went so far as to submit

196. to his landing in Europe in the spring of 558 and invading the Thracian Chersonese, where he occupied Sestus and Madytus and spent a considerable time in the chastisement of the Thracian barbarians and the restoration of the destroyed Lysimachia, which he had selected as his chief stronghold and as the capital of the newly instituted satrapy of Thrace. Flamininus indeed, who was entrusted with the conduct of these affairs, sent to the king at Lysimachia envoys, who talked of the integrity of the Egyptian territory and of the freedom of all the Hellenes; but nothing came of it.   The king talked in reply of his undoubted legal title to the ancient kingdom of Lysimachus conquered by his ancestor Seleucus, explained that he was employed not in making territorial acquisitions but only in preserving the integrity of his hereditary dominions, and declined the intervention of the Romans in his disputes with the cities subject to him in Asia Minor.   With justice he was enabled to add that peace had already been concluded with Egypt, and that the Romans were thus deprived of any formal pretext for interfering.*   The sudden return of the king to Asia occasioned by a false report of the death of the young king of Egypt, and the projects which it suggested of a landing in Cyprus or even at Alexandria, led to the breaking off of the conferences without coming to any conclusion, still less producing any result.   In

195. the following year, 559, Antiochus returned to Lysimachia with his fleet and army reinforced, and employed himself in organizing the new satrapy which he destined for his son Seleucus.   Hannibal, who had been obliged to flee from Carthage, came to him at Ephesus; and the singularly honourable reception accorded to the exile was equivalent to a

---

* The definite testimony of Hieronymus, who places the betrothal of the Syrian princess Cleopatra with Ptolemy Epiphanes in 556, taken in connection with the hints in Liv. xxxiii. 40 and Appian. *Syr.* 3, and with the actual accomplishment of the marriage in 561, puts it beyond a doubt that the interference of the Romans in the affairs of Egypt was in this case formally uncalled for.

declaration of war against Rome. Nevertheless Flamininus
in the spring of 560 withdrew all the Roman garrisons from   194.
Greece. This was under the existing circumstances at least
a mischievous error, if not a criminal acting in opposition
to his own better knowledge; for we cannot dismiss the idea
that Flamininus, in order to carry home with him the undiminished glory of having wholly terminated the war and
liberated Hellas, contented himself with superficially covering up for the moment the smouldering embers of revolt and
war. The Roman statesman might perhaps be right, when
he pronounced any attempt to bring Greece directly under
the dominion of the Romans, and any intervention of the Romans in Asiatic affairs, to be a political blunder; but the
opposition fermenting in Greece, the feeble arrogance of the
Asiatic king, the residence, at the Syrian head-quarters, of
the bitter enemy of the Romans who had already raised the
West in arms against Rome—all these were clear signs of
the approach of a fresh appeal to arms on the part of the
Hellenic East, which would necessarily seek at least to
transfer Greece from the clientship of Rome to that of the
states opposed to Rome, and, if this object should be attained, would immediately extend the circle of its operations.
It is plain that Rome could not allow this to take place.
When Flamininus, ignoring all these sure indications of war,
withdrew the garrisons from Greece, and yet at the same
time made demands on the king of Asia which he had no intention of employing his army to support, he overdid his
part in words as much as he fell short in action, and forgot
his duty as a general and as a citizen in the indulgence of
his personal vanity—a vanity which wished to enjoy the
credit of having conferred peace on Rome and freedom on
the Greeks of both continents.

Antiochus employed the unexpected respite in strengthen-   Prepara-
ing his position at home and his relations with his neighbours   tions of
before beginning the war—in which he was the more re-   Antiochus
solved to engage, the more the enemy appeared to procrasti-   for war
nate. He now (561) gave his daughter Cleopatra, previously   with Rome.
betrothed, in marriage to the young king of Egypt. That   193.
he at the same time promised to restore the provinces wrested
from his son-in-law, was afterwards affirmed on the part of

Egypt, but probably without warrant; at any rate the land
remained actually attached to the Syrian kingdom.* He
197. offered to restore to Eumenes, who had in 557 succeeded his
father Attalus on the throne of Pergamus, the towns taken
from him, and to give him also one of his daughters in
marriage, if he would abandon the Roman alliance. In like
manner he bestowed a daughter on Ariarathes, king of Cappadocia, and gained the Galatians by presents, while he
reduced by arms the Pisidians who were constantly in revolt,
and other small tribes. Extensive privileges were granted to
the Byzantines; respecting the cities in Asia Minor, the king
declared that he would concede the independence of the old
free cities such as Rhodes and Cyzicus, and would be content
in the case of the others with a mere formal recognition of
his supremacy; he even gave them to understand that he was
ready to submit to the arbitration of the Rhodians. In European Greece he could safely count on the Aetolians, and he
hoped to induce Philip again to take up arms. In fact, a plan
of Hannibal obtained the royal approval, according to which
he was to receive from Antiochus a fleet of 100 sail and a
land army of 10,000 infantry and 1000 cavalry, and was to
employ them in kindling first a third Punic war in Carthage,
and then a second Hannibalic war in Italy; Tyrian emissaries
proceeded to Carthage to pave the way for an appeal to arms
there (p. 215). Finally, good results were anticipated from
the Spanish insurrection, which, at the time when Hannibal
left Carthage, was at its height (p. 223).

Aetolian
intrigues
against
Rome.

While the storm was thus gathering from far and wide
against Rome, it was on this, as on all occasions, the Hellenes implicated in the enterprise, who, while they were of
least moment, took the most important steps and acted with
the utmost impatience. The exasperated and arrogant Aetolians began by degrees to persuade themselves that Philip
had been vanquished by them and not by the Romans, and

* For this we have the testimony of
Polybius (xxviii. 1), which the sequel
of the history of Judaea completely
confirms; Eusebius (p. 117, Mai) is
mistaken in making Philometor ruler of
Syria. We certainly find that about
187. 567 farmers of the Syrian taxes made
their payments at Alexandria (Joseph.
xii. 4, 7); but this doubtless took place
without detriment to the rights of sovereignty, simply because the dowry of
Cleopatra constituted a charge on those
revenues; and from this very circumstance probably arose the subsequent
dispute.

could not even wait till Antiochus should advance into Greece. Their policy is briefly expressed in the reply, which their *strategus* gave soon afterwards to Flamininus, when he requested a copy of the declaration of war against Rome: that he would deliver it to him in person, when the Aetolian army should encamp by the Tiber. The Aetolians acted as the agents of the Syrian king in Greece and deceived both parties, by representing to the king that all the Hellenes were waiting with open arms to receive him as their true deliverer, and by telling those in Greece who were disposed to listen to them that the landing of the king was nearer than it was in reality. Thus they actually succeeded in inducing the foolish obstinacy of Nabis to break the peace and to rekindle in Greece the flame of war two years after Flamininus's departure, in the spring of 562; but in doing so they missed their aim. Nabis   192. attacked Gythium, one of the towns of the free Laconians that by the last treaty had been annexed to the Achaean league, and took it; but the experienced *strategus* of the Achaeans, Philopoemen, defeated him at the Barbosthenian mountains, and the tyrant brought back barely a fourth part of his army to his capital, in which Philopoemen shut him up. As such a commencement was no sufficient inducement for Antiochus to come to Europe, the Aetolians resolved to possess themselves of Sparta, Chalcis, and Demetrias, and by gaining these important towns to prevail upon the king to embark. In the first place they thought to become masters of Sparta, by arranging that the Aetolian Alexamenus should march with 1000 men into the town under pretext of bringing a contingent in terms of the alliance, and should embrace the opportunity of making away with Nabis and of occupying the town. This was done, and Nabis was killed at a review of the troops; but, when the Aetolians dispersed to plunder the town, the Lacedaemonians found time to rally and slew them to a man. The city was then induced by Philopoemen to join the Achaean league. This laudable project of the Aetolians had thus not only deservedly failed, but had precisely the opposite effect of uniting almost the whole Peloponnesus in the hands of the other party. It fared little better with them at Chalcis, for the Roman party there called in the citizens of Eretria and Carystus in Euboea, who

were favourable to Rome, to render seasonable aid against
the Aetolians and the Chalcidian exiles.   On the other hand
the occupation of Demetrias was successful, for the Magnetes
to whom the city had been assigned were, not without reason,
apprehensive that it had been promised by the Romans to
Philip as a prize in return for his aid against Antiochus;
several squadrons of Aetolian horse moreover managed to
steal into the town under the pretext of escorting Eury-
lochus, the recalled head of the opposition to Rome.   Thus
the Magnetes passed over, partly of their own accord, partly
by compulsion, to the side of the Aetolians, and the latter
did not fail to make good use of the fact at the court of the
Seleucid.

Rupture
between
Antiochus.
and the
Romans.
193.
Antiochus took his resolution.   A rupture with Rome, in
spite of endeavours to postpone it by the diplomatic expedient of embassies, could no longer be avoided.   As early as
the spring of 561 Flamininus, who continued to have the
decisive voice in the senate as to Eastern affairs, had expressed
the Roman ultimatum to the envoys of the king, Menippus
and Hegesianax; viz., that he should either evacuate Europe
and dispose of Asia at his pleasure, or retain Thrace and
submit to the Roman protectorate over Smyrna, Lampsacus,
and Alexandria Troas.   These demands had been again discussed at Ephesus, the chief stronghold and head-quarters of
192.
the king in Asia Minor, in the spring of 562, between Antiochus and the envoys of the senate, Publius Sulpicius and
Publius Villius; and they had separated with the conviction
on both sides that a peaceful settlement was no longer possible.   Thenceforth war was resolved on in Rome.   In that
192.
very summer of 562 a Roman fleet of 30 sail, with 3000
soldiers on board, under Aulus Atilius Serranus appeared off
Gythium, where their arrival accelerated the conclusion of the
treaty between the Achaeans and Spartans; the eastern
coasts of Sicily and Italy were strongly garrisoned, so as to
be secure against any attempts at a landing; a land army
was expected in Greece in the autumn.   In the spring of
562 Flamininus, by direction of the senate, had visited
Greece to thwart the intrigues of the opposite party, and to
counteract as far as possible the evil effects of the ill-timed
evacuation of the country.   The Aetolians had already gone

so far as formally to declare war in their diet against Rome. But Flamininus succeeded in preserving Chalcis to the Romans by throwing into it a garrison of 500 Achaeans and 500 Pergamenes. He made an attempt also to recover Demetrias; and the Magnetes wavered. Though some towns in Asia Minor, which Antiochus had proposed to subdue before beginning the great war, still held out, he could no longer delay his landing, unless he was willing to let the Romans recover all the advantages which they had surrendered two years before by withdrawing their garrisons from Greece. He collected the vessels and troops which were at hand—he had but 40 decked vessels and 10,000 infantry, along with 500 horse and 6 elephants—and started from the Thracian Chersonese for Greece, where he landed in the autumn of 562 at Pteleum on the Pagasaean gulf, and immediately occupied the adjoining Demetrias. About the same time a Roman army of nearly 25,000 men under the praetor Marcus Baebius landed at Apollonia. The war was thus begun on both sides.

192.

Everything depended on the extent to which that comprehensively planned coalition against Rome, of which Antiochus came forward as the head, might be realized. As to the plan, first of all, of stirring up enemies to the Romans in Carthage and Italy, it was the fate of Hannibal at the court of Ephesus, as through his whole career, to have projected his noble and lofty schemes for the behoof of people narrow-minded and mean. Nothing was done towards their execution, except that some Carthaginian patriots were compromised; no choice was left to the Carthaginians but to show unconditional submission to Rome. The camarilla would have nothing to do with Hannibal—he was too inconveniently great for court cabals; and, after having tried all sorts of absurd expedients—such as accusing the general, with whose name the Romans frightened their children, of concert with the Roman envoys—they succeeded in persuading Antiochus the Great, who like all insignificant monarchs plumed himself greatly on his independence and was influenced by nothing so easily as by the fear of being ruled, into the wise belief that he ought not to allow himself to be thrown into the shade by so illustrious a man. Accordingly

Attitude of the minor powers. Carthage and Hannibal.

it was in solemn council resolved that the Phoenician should be employed in future only for subordinate enterprises and for giving advice—with the reservation, of course, that that advice should never be followed. Hannibal revenged himself on the mob of courtiers by accepting every commission and brilliantly executing all.

States of Asia Minor.

In Asia Cappadocia adhered to the great king; Prusias of Bithynia on the other hand took, as usual, the side of the stronger. King Eumenes remained faithful to the old policy of his house, which was now at length to yield to him its true fruit. He had not only persisted in refusing the offers of Antiochus, but had constantly urged the Romans to a war, from which he anticipated the aggrandisement of his kingdom. The Rhodians and Byzantines likewise joined their old allies. Egypt too took the side of Rome and offered support in supplies and men; which, however, the Romans did not accept.

Macedonia.

In Europe the result mainly depended on the position which Philip of Macedonia would take up. True policy ought perhaps to have induced him, notwithstanding all the injuries or short-comings of the past, to unite with Antiochus. But Philip was ordinarily influenced not by such considerations, but by his likings and dislikings; and his hatred was naturally directed much more against the faithless ally, who had left him to contend alone with the common enemy, had sought merely to seize his own share in the spoil, and had become a burdensome neighbour to him in Thrace, than against the conqueror, who had treated him respectfully and honourably. Antiochus had, moreover, given deep offence to the hot temper of Philip by the setting up of absurd pretenders to the Macedonian crown, and by the ostentatious burial of the Macedonian bones bleaching at Cynoscephalae. Philip therefore placed his whole force with cordial zeal at the disposal of the Romans.

The lesser Greek states.

The second power of Greece, the Achaean league, adhered no less decidedly than the first to the alliance with Rome. Of the smaller powers, the Thessalians and the Athenians held by Rome; among the latter an Achaean garrison introduced by Flamininus into the citadel brought the patriotic party, which was somewhat numerous, to reason. The Epirots exerted themselves to keep on good terms, if possible, with both parties. Thus, in addition to the Aetolians and the Magnetes who were joined by a portion of the neighbouring Perrhaebians, Antiochus was supported only by Amynander, the weak king of the Athamanes, who allowed himself to be dazzled by foolish designs on the Macedonian crown; by the Boeotians, among whom the party opposed to Rome was still at the helm; and by the Eleans and Messenians in the Peloponnesus, who were in the habit of taking part with the Aetolians against the Achaeans. This was indeed a hopeful beginning; and the title of commander-in-chief with absolute power, which the Aetolians decreed to the great king, seemed insult added to injury. There had been, just as usual, deception on both sides. Instead of the countless hordes of Asia, the king brought up a force scarcely half as strong as an ordinary consular army; and instead of the open arms with which all the Hellenes were to welcome their deliverer from the Roman yoke, one or two bands of klephts and some dissolute bodies of citizens fraternized with the king.

For the moment, indeed, Antiochus anticipated the Romans in Greece proper. Chalcis was garrisoned by the Greek allies of the Romans, and refused the first summons; but the fortress surrendered when Antiochus advanced with all his force; and a Roman division, which arrived too late to occupy it, was annihilated by Antiochus at Delium. Euboea was thus lost to the Romans. Antiochus also made an attempt in winter, in concert with the Aetolians and Acarnanians, to gain Thessaly; Thermopylae was occupied, Pherae and other towns were taken, but Appius Claudius came up with 2,000 men from Apollonia, relieved Larisa, and took up his position there. Antiochus, tired of the winter campaign, preferred to return to his pleasant quarters at Chalcis, where the time was spent merrily, and the king even, in spite of his fifty years and his warlike schemes, married a fair Chalcidian. So the winter of 562-3 passed, without Antiochus doing much more than sending letters hither and thither through Greece: he waged war—a Roman officer remarked—by means of pen and ink.

In the beginning of spring 563 the Roman staff arrived at

Antiochus in Greece.

192-191.

191

Apollonia. The commander-in-chief was Manius Acilius Glabrio, a man of humble origin, but an able general feared
both by his soldiers and by the enemy; the admiral was
Gaius Livius; and among the military tribunes were Marcus
Porcius Cato, the conqueror of Spain, and Lucius Valerius
Flaccus, who after the old Roman wont did not disdain, although they had been consuls, to re-enter the army as simple
commanders of legions. They brought with them reinforcements in ships and men, including Numidian cavalry and
Libyan elephants sent by Massinissa, and the permission of
the senate to accept auxiliary troops to the number of 5,000
from the extra-Italian allies, so that the whole number of the
Roman forces were raised to about 40,000 men. The king,
who in the beginning of spring had gone to the Aetolians
and had thence made an aimless expedition to Acarnania, on
learning the arrival of Glabrio, returned to his head-quarters
to begin the campaign in earnest. But through his own in-
conceivable negligence and that of his lieutenants in Asia no
reinforcements reached him, so that he had nothing but the
weak army—now further decimated by sickness and deser-
tion in its dissolute winter-quarters—with which he had
landed at Pteleum in the autumn of the previous year.
The Aetolians too, who had professed to send such enormous
numbers into the field, now, when their support was of
moment, brought to their commander-in-chief no more
than 4,000 men. The Roman troops had already begun
operations in Thessaly, where the vanguard in concert with
the Macedonian army drove the garrisons of Antiochus
out of the Thessalian towns and occupied the territory
of the Athamanes. The consul with the main army
followed; the whole force of the Romans assembled at
Larisa.

Instead of returning with all speed to Asia and evacuating
the field before an enemy in every respect superior, Antiochus resolved to entrench himself at Thermopylae, which
he had occupied, and there to await the arrival of the great
army from Asia. He himself took up a position in the
principal pass, and commanded the Aetolians to occupy the
mountain-path, by which Xerxes had formerly succeeded in
turning the Spartans. But only half of the Aetolian contin-

gent thought fit to comply with this command of the commander-in-chief; the other 2,000 men threw themselves into
the neighbouring town of Heraclea, where they took no other
part in the battle than that of attempting during its progress
to surprise and plunder the Roman camp.   Even the Aetolians
posted on the heights discharged their duty of watching with
remissness and reluctance; their post on the Callidromus
allowed itself to be surprised by Cato, and the Asiatic phalanx, which the consul had meanwhile assailed in front,
dispersed, when the Romans hastening down the mountain
fell upon its flank.   As Antiochus had made no provision for
any case and had not thought of retreat, the army was destroyed partly on the field of battle, partly during its flight;
with difficulty a small band reached Demetrias, and the
king himself escaped to Chalcis with 500 men.   He embarked in haste for Ephesus; Europe was lost to him all
but his possessions in Thrace, and even the fortresses could
be no longer defended.   Chalcis surrendered to the Romans,   Greece oc-
and Demetrias to Philip, who received permission—as a com-   cupied by
pensation for the conquest of the town of Lamia in Achaia   the
Romans.
Phthiotis which he was on the point of accomplishing and
then abandoned by orders of the consul—to make himself
master of all the communities that had gone over to Antiochus in Thessaly proper, and even of the territories bordering on Aetolia, the districts of Dolopia and Aperantia.
All the Greeks that had pronounced in favour of Antiochus hastened to make their peace; the Epirots humbly
besought pardon for their ambiguous conduct, the Boeotians
surrendered at discretion, the Eleans and Messenians, the
latter after some struggle, submitted to the Achaeans.   The
prediction of Hannibal to the king was fulfilled, that no
dependence at all could be placed upon the Greeks, who
would submit to any conqueror.   Even the Aetolians, when   Resistance
their corps shut up in Heraclea had been compelled after   of the
Aetolians.
obstinate resistance to capitulate, attempted to make their
peace with the sorely provoked Romans; but the stringent
demands of the Roman consul, and a consignment of money
seasonably arriving from Antiochus, emboldened them once
more to break off the negotiations and to sustain for two
whole months a siege in Naupactus.   The town was already

reduced to extremities, and its capture or capitulation could
not have been long delayed, when Flamininus, constantly
striving to save every Hellenic community from the worst
consequences of its own folly and from the severity of his
ruder colleagues, interposed and arranged in the first instance an armistice on tolerable terms. This terminated, at
least for the moment, all resistance in Greece.

Maritime
war, and
prepara-
tions for
crossing to
Asia.
A more serious war was impending in Asia—a war which
appeared of a very hazardous character on account not so
much of the enemy as of the great distance and the insecurity of the communications with home, while yet, owing
to the short-sighted obstinacy of Antiochus, the struggle
could not well be terminated otherwise than by an attack on
the enemy in his own country. The first object was to
secure the sea. The Roman fleet, which during the campaign in Greece was charged with the task of interrupting
the communication between Greece and Asia Minor, and
which had been successful about the time of the battle
at Thermopylae in seizing a strong Asiatic transport fleet
near Andros, was thenceforth employed in making preparations for the crossing of the Romans to Asia next year and
first of all in driving the enemy's fleet out of the Aegean
Sea. It lay in the harbour of Cyssus on the southern shore
of the tongue of land that projects from Ionia towards
Chios; thither the Roman fleet proceeded in search of it,
consisting of 75 Roman, 24 Pergamene, and 6 Carthaginian,
decked vessels under the command of Gaius Livius. The
Syrian admiral, Polyxenidas, a Rhodian emigrant, had only
70 decked vessels to oppose to it; but, as the Roman fleet
still expected the ships of Rhodes, and as Polyxenidas relied
on the superior seaworthiness of his vessels, those of Tyre
and Sidon in particular, he immediately accepted battle.
At the outset the Asiatics succeeded in sinking one of the
Carthaginian vessels; but, when they came to grapple,
Roman valour prevailed, and it was owing solely to the
swiftness of their rowing and sailing that the enemy lost
no more than 23 ships. During the pursuit the Roman
fleet was joined by 25 ships from Rhodes, and the superiority of the Romans in those waters was now doubly
decisive. The enemy's fleet thenceforth kept the shelter of

the harbour of Ephesus, and, as it could not be induced to risk a second battle, the fleet of the Romans and allies broke up for the winter; the Roman ships of war proceeded to the harbour of Cane in the neighbourhood of Pergamus.

Both parties were busy during the winter in preparing for the next campaign. The Romans sought to gain over the Greeks of Asia Minor; Smyrna, which had perseveringly resisted all the attempts of the king to get possession of it, received the Romans with open arms, and the Roman party gained the ascendancy in Samos, Chios, Erythrae, Clazomenae, Phocaea, Cyme, and other places. Antiochus was resolved, if possible, to prevent the Romans from crossing to Asia, and with that view he made zealous naval preparations—employing Polyxenidas to fit out and augment the fleet stationed at Ephesus, and Hannibal to equip a new fleet in Lycia, Syria, and Phoenicia; while he further collected in Asia Minor a powerful land army from all regions of his extensive empire. Early next year (564) the Roman fleet resumed its operations. Gaius Livius left the Rhodian fleet —which had appeared in good time this year, numbering 36 sail—to observe that of the enemy in the offing of Ephesus, and went with the greater portion of the Roman and Pergamene vessels to the Hellespont in accordance with his instructions, to pave the way for the passage of the land army by the capture of the fortresses there. Sestus was already occupied and Abydus reduced to extremities, when the news of the defeat of the Rhodian fleet recalled him. The Rhodian admiral Pausistratus, lulled into security by the representations of his countryman that he wished to desert from Antiochus, had allowed himself to be surprised in the harbour of Samos; he himself fell, and all his vessels were destroyed except five Rhodian and two Coan ships; Samos, Phocaea, and Cyme on hearing the news went over to Seleucus, who held the chief command by land in those provinces for his father. But when the Roman fleet arrived partly from Cane, partly from the Hellespont, and was after some time joined by twenty new ships of the Rhodians at Samos, Polyxenidas was once more compelled to shut himself up in the harbour of Ephesus. As he declined the offered naval battle, and

190.

as, owing to the small numbers of the Roman force, an attack by land was out of the question, nothing remained for the Roman fleet but to take up its position in like manner at Samos. A division meanwhile proceeded to Patara on the Lycian coast, partly to relieve the Rhodians from the very troublesome attacks that were directed against them from that quarter, partly and chiefly to prevent the hostile fleet, which Hannibal was expected to bring up, from entering the Aegean Sea. When the squadron sent against Patara achieved nothing, the new admiral Lucius Aemilius Regillus, who had arrived with 20 war-vessels from Rome and had relieved Gaius Livius at Samos, was so indignant that he proceeded thither with the whole fleet; his officers with difficulty succeeded, while they were on their voyage, in making him understand that the primary object was not the conquest of Patara but the command of the Aegean Sea, and in inducing him to return to Samos. On the mainland of Asia Minor Seleucus had in the meanwhile begun the siege of Pergamus, while Antiochus with his chief army ravaged the Pergamene territory and the possessions of the Mytilenaeans on the mainland; they hoped to crush the hated Attalids, before Roman aid appeared. The Roman fleet went to Elaea and the port of Adramyttium to help their ally; but, as the admiral wanted troops, he accomplished nothing. Pergamus seemed lost; but the laxity and negligence with which the siege was conducted allowed Eumenes to throw into the city Achaean auxiliaries under Diophanes, whose bold and successful sallies compelled the Gallic mercenaries, whom Antiochus had entrusted with the siege, to raise it. In the southern waters too the projects of Antiochus were frustrated. The fleet equipped and led by Hannibal, after having been long detained by the constant westerly winds, attempted at length to reach the Aegean; but at the mouth of the Eurymedon, off Aspendus in Pamphylia, it encountered a Rhodian squadron under Eudamus; and in the battle, which ensued between the two fleets, the excellence of the Rhodian ships and naval officers carried the victory over Hannibal's tactics and his numerical superiority. It was the first naval battle, and the last battle against Rome, fought by the great Carthaginian. The vic-

torious Rhodian fleet then took its station at Patara, and
there prevented the intended junction of the two Asiatic
fleets. In the Aegean Sea the Romano-Rhodian fleet at
Samos, after being weakened by detaching the Pergamene
ships to the Hellespont to support the land army which
had arrived there, was in its turn attacked by that of
Polyxenidas, who now numbered nine sail more than his
opponents. On December 23 of the uncorrected calendar,
according to the corrected calendar about the end of
August, in 564, the battle took place at the promontory of   190.
Myonnesus between Teos and Colophon; the Romans broke
through the line of the enemy, and totally surrounded the
left wing, so that they took or sank 42 ships. An inscription in Saturnian verse over the temple of the Lares Per-
marini, which was built in the Campus Martius in memory
of this victory, for many centuries thereafter proclaimed to
the Romans how the fleet of the Asiatics had been defeated
before the eyes of king Antiochus and of all his land army,
and how the Romans thus "settled the mighty strife and
subdued the kings." Thenceforth the enemy's ships no
longer ventured to show themselves on the open sea, and
made no further attempt to obstruct the crossing of the
Roman land army.

The conqueror of Zama had been selected at Rome to   Expedition
conduct the war on the Asiatic continent; he practically   to Asia.
exercised the supreme command for the nominal commander-
in-chief, his brother Lucius Scipio, whose intellect was
insignificant, and who had no military capacity. The
reserve hitherto stationed in Lower Italy was destined
for Greece, the army under Glabrio for Asia: when it
became known who was to command it, 5,000 veterans from
the Hannibalic war voluntarily enrolled, to fight once more
under their beloved leader. In the Roman July, but according to the true time in March, the Scipios arrived at the
army to commence the Asiatic campaign; but they were
disagreeably surprised to find themselves involved, in the first
instance, in an endless struggle with the desperate Aetolians.
The senate, finding that Flamininus pushed his boundless
consideration for the Hellenes too far, had left the Aetolians
to choose between paying an utterly exorbitant war contri-

bution and unconditional surrender, and thus had driven
them anew to arms; none could tell when this warfare among
mountains and strongholds would come to an end. Scipio
got rid of the inconvenient obstacle by concerting a six-
months' armistice, and then entered on his march to Asia.
As the one fleet of the enemy was only blockaded in the
Aegean Sea, and the other, which was coming up from the
south, might daily arrive there in spite of the squadron
charged to intercept it, it seemed advisable to take the
land route through Macedonia and Thrace and to cross the
Hellespont. In that direction no real obstacles were to be
anticipated; for Philip of Macedonia might be entirely
depended on, Prusias king of Bithynia was in alliance
with the Romans, and the Roman fleet could easily establish itself in the straits. The long and weary march along
the coast of Macedonia and Thrace was accomplished without material loss; Philip made provision on the one hand for
supplying their wants, on the other for their friendly reception
by the Thracian barbarians. They had lost so much time however, partly with the Aetolians, partly on the march, that the
army only reached the Thracian Chersonese about the time
of the battle of Myonnesus. But the marvellous good
fortune of Scipio now in Asia, as formerly in Spain and
Africa, cleared his path of all difficulties.

Passage of
the Helles-
pont by
the Ro-
mans.
On the news of the battle at Myonnesus Antiochus so completely lost his judgment, that in Europe he caused the
strongly-garrisoned and well-provisioned fortress of Lysimachia to be evacuated by the garrison and by the inhabitants who were faithfully devoted to the restorer of their
city, but forgot even to withdraw in like manner the garrisons
or to destroy the rich magazines at Aenus and Maronea;
and on the Asiatic coast he opposed not the slightest resistance to the landing of the Romans, but on the contrary,
while it was taking place, spent his time at Sardes in
upbraiding destiny. It is scarcely doubtful that, had he but
provided for the defence of Lysimachia down to the no
longer distant close of the summer, and moved forward his
great army to the Hellespont, Scipio would have been compelled to take up winter quarters on the European shore, in a
position far from being, in a military or political point of
view, secure.

While the Romans, after disembarking on the Asiatic shore, paused for some days to refresh themselves and to await their leader who was detained behind by religious duties, ambassadors from the great king arrived in their camp to negotiate for peace. Antiochus offered half the expenses of the war, and the cession of his European posses-sions as well as of all the Greek cities in Asia Minor that had gone over to Rome; but Scipio demanded the whole costs of the war and the surrender of all Asia Minor. The former terms, he declared, might have been accepted, had the army still been before Lysimachia, or even on the Euro-pean side of the Hellespont; but they did not suffice now, when the steed felt the bit and knew its rider. The attempts of the great king to purchase peace from his antagonist after the Oriental manner by sums of money—he offered the half of his year's revenues!—failed as they deserved; the proud burgess, in return for the gratuitous restoration of his son who had fallen a captive, rewarded the great king with the friendly advice to make peace on any terms. This was not in reality necessary: had the king possessed the resolution to prolong the war and to draw the enemy after him by retreating into the interior, a favourable issue was still by no means impossible. But Antiochus, irritated by the probably intentional arrogance of his antagonist, and too indolent for any persevering and consistent warfare, hastened with the utmost eagerness to expose his unwieldy, heterogeneous, and undisciplined mass of an army to the shock of the Roman legions.

In the valley of the Hermus, near Magnesia at the foot of Mount Sipylus not far from Smyrna, the Roman troops fell in with the enemy late in the autumn of 564. The force of Antiochus numbered close on 80,000 men, of whom 12,000 were cavalry; the Romans—who had along with them about 5,000 Achaeans, Pergamenes, and Macedonian volunteers—had not nearly half that number, but they were so sure of victory, that they did not wait for the re-covery of their general who had remained behind sick at Elaea; Gnaeus Domitius took the command in his stead. Antiochus, in order to be able even to place his immense mass of troops, formed two divisions. In the first were

Battle of Magnesia.

190.

placed the mass of the light troops, the peltasts, bowmen, slingers, the mounted archers of the Mysians, Dahae, and Elymaeans, the Arabs on their dromedaries, and the scythe-chariots. In the second division the heavy cavalry (the Cataphractae, a sort of cuirassiers) were stationed on the flanks; next to these, in the intermediate division, the Gallic and Cappadocian infantry; and in the very centre the phalanx armed after the Macedonian fashion, 16,000 strong, the flower of the army, which, however, had not room in the narrow space and had to be drawn up in double files 32 deep. In the space between the two divisions were placed 54 elephants, distributed among the companies of the phalanx and of the heavy cavalry. The Romans stationed but a few squadrons on the left wing, where the river gave protection; the mass of the cavalry and all the light armed were placed on the right, which was led by Eumenes; the legions stood in the centre. Eumenes began the battle by despatching his archers and slingers against the scythe-chariots with orders to shoot at the teams; in a short time not only were these thrown into disorder, but the camel-riders stationed next to them were also carried away, and even in the second line the left wing of heavy cavalry placed behind fell into confusion. Eumenes now threw himself with all the Roman cavalry, numbering 3,000 horse, on the mercenary infantry, which was placed in the second line between the phalanx and the left wing of heavy cavalry, and, when these gave way, the cuirassiers who had already fallen into disorder also fled. The phalanx, which had just allowed the light troops to pass through and was preparing to advance against the Roman legions, was hampered by the attack of the cavalry in flank, and compelled to stand still and to form front on both sides—a movement which the depth of its disposition favoured. Had the heavy Asiatic cavalry been at hand, the battle might have been restored; but the left wing was shattered, and the right, led by Antiochus in person, had driven before it the little division of Roman cavalry opposed to it, and had reached the Roman camp, which was with great difficulty defended from its attack. In this way the cavalry were at the decisive moment absent from the scene of action. The Romans were careful not to assail the phalanx with their legions, but sent against it the archers and slingers, not one of whose missiles failed to take effect on the densely crowded mass. The phalanx nevertheless retired slowly and in good order, till the elephants stationed in the interstices became frightened and broke the ranks. Then the whole army dispersed in tumultuous flight; an attempt to hold the camp failed, and only increased the number of the dead and the prisoners. The estimate of the loss of Antiochus at 50,000 men is, considering the infinite confusion, not incredible; the legions of the Romans had never been engaged, and the victory, which gave them a third continent, cost them 24 horsemen and 300 foot soldiers. Asia Minor submitted; including even Ephesus, whence the admiral hastily withdrew his fleet, and Sardes the residence of the court.

The king sued for peace and consented to the terms proposed by the Romans, which, as usual, were just the same as those offered before the battle and consequently included the cession of Asia Minor. Till they were ratified, the army remained in Asia Minor at the expense of the king; which came to cost him not less than 3,000 talents (£730,000). Antiochus himself in his careless fashion soon got over the loss of half his kingdom; it was in keeping with his character, that he declared himself grateful to the Romans for saving him the trouble of governing too large an empire. But with the day of Magnesia Asia was erased from the list of great states; and never perhaps did a great power fall so rapidly, so thoroughly, and so ignominiously as the kingdom of the Seleucidae under this Antiochus the Great. He himself was soon afterwards (567) slain by the indignant inhabitants of Elymais at the head of the Persian gulf, on occasion of the plundering of a temple of Bel, with the treasures of which he had sought to replenish his empty coffers.

Conclusion of peace.

187.

After having obtained the victory, the Roman government had to regulate the affairs of Asia Minor and of Greece. In the former Antiochus was conquered, but his allies and satraps in the interior, the Phrygian, Cappadocian, and Paphlagonian dynasts, trusting to their dis-

Expedition against the Celts of Asia Minor.

tance, delayed their submission, and the Celts of Asia Minor, who had not strictly been in alliance with Antiochus but had merely after their custom allowed him to raise mercenaries in their land, in like manner saw no reason why they should trouble themselves about the Romans. To the new Roman commander-in-chief, Gnaeus Manlius Volso, who in the spring of 565 relieved Lucius Scipio in Asia Minor, this afforded a welcome pretext for performing in his turn a service to his country and asserting the Roman protectorate over the Hellenes in Asia, just as had been done already in Spain and Gaul; although the more austere men in the senate failed to see either the ground or the object of such a war. The consul started from Ephesus, levied contributions from the cities and princes on the upper Maeander and in Pamphylia without cause and without measure, and then turned northward against the Celts. The most westerly canton of these, the Tolistobogi, had retired with their property to Mount Olympus, and the middle canton, the Tectosages, to Mount Magaba, in the hope that they would be able to defend themselves there, till winter should compel the foreigners to retire. But the missiles of the Roman slingers and archers—which so often turned the scale against the Celts unacquainted with such weapons, somewhat in the same way as in modern times fire-arms have turned the scale against savage tribes—forced the heights, and the Celts succumbed in a battle, such as was often paralleled both before and afterwards on the Po and on the Seine, but which in Asia appears no less singular than the whole phenomenon of this northern race emerging amidst the Greek and Phrygian nations. The number of the slain at both places was very great, and that of the prisoners still greater. The survivors escaped over the Halys to the third Celtic canton of the Trocmi, whom the consul did not disturb, as he did not venture to cross the frontier agreed on in the preliminaries between Scipio and Antiochus.

Regulation of Asiatic affairs. [189.   The affairs of Asia Minor were regulated partly by the peace with Antiochus (565), partly by the ordinances of a Roman commission presided over by the consul Volso. Antiochus had to furnish hostages, one of whom was his younger son of the same name, and to pay a war-contribution—proportional in amount to the treasures of Asia—of 15,000 Euboic talents (£3,600,000), a fifth of which was to be paid at once and the remainder in twelve annual instalments. He was compelled, moreover, to cede all his possessions in Europe, and all the territory in Asia Minor to the west of the river Halys throughout its course, and of the mountain-chain of the Taurus, which separates Cilicia and Lycaonia, so that he retained nothing in the Anatolian peninsula but Cilicia. His protectorate over the kingdoms and principalities of Asia Minor of course ceased. Even beyond the Roman frontier Cappadocia assumed an independent attitude towards Asia or Syria, as the kingdom of the Seleucidae was now more commonly and appropriately called; and not only so, but the satraps of the two Armenias, Artaxias and Zariadris, became transformed, under the influence of Rome if not exactly in conformity to the Roman treaty of peace, into independent kings and founders of new dynasties. The Syrian king forfeited the right of waging aggressive war against the states of the West, and, in the event of a defensive war, of acquiring territory from them on the conclusion of peace. He was prohibited from navigating the sea to the west of the mouth of the Calycadnus in Cilicia with ships of war, except for the conveyance of envoys, hostages, or tribute; from keeping more than ten decked vessels, except in the event of a defensive war; from taming war-elephants; and finally, from levying mercenaries in the western states, or receiving political refugees and deserters from these states at his court. He gave up the vessels of war which he possessed beyond the prescribed number, the elephants, and the political refugees who had taken shelter with him. The great king received, by way of compensation, the title of a friend of the Roman commonwealth. The state of Syria was thus by land and sea completely and for ever dislodged from the West; it is a significant indication of the feeble and loose organization of the kingdom of the Seleucidae, that it alone, of all the great states conquered by Rome, never after the first conquest made a second appeal to the decision of arms.

Ariarathes, king of Cappadocia, whose land lay beyond the boundary laid down by the Romans for their protecto-

rate, escaped with a money fine of 600 talents (£146,000) ;
which was afterwards, on the intercession of his son-in-law
Eumenes, abated to half that sum.

Prusias, king of Bithynia, retained his territory as it stood,
and so did the Celts ; but they were obliged to promise that
they would no longer send armed bands beyond their bounds
—a step which put an end to the disgraceful payments of
tribute which many of the towns of Asia Minor made to
them.   Rome thus conferred on the Asiatic Greeks a real
benefit, which they did not fail to repay with golden chaplets
and transcendental panegyrics.

The free Greek cities.
In the western portion of Asia Minor the regulation of
the territorial arrangements was not without difficulty, especially as the dynastic policy of Eumenes there came into collision with that of the Greek Hansa.   At last an understanding was arrived at to the following effect.   All the Greek
cities, which were free and had joined the Romans on the day
of the battle of Magnesia, had their liberties confirmed, and
all of them, excepting those previously tributary to Eumenes,
were relieved from the payment of tribute to the different
dynasts for the future.   In this way the towns of Dardanus
and Ilium, whose ancient affinity with the Romans was
traced to the times of Aeneas, became free, along with
Cyme, Smyrna, Clazomenae, Erythrae, Chios, Colophon,
Miletus, and other names of old renown.   Phocaea also,
which in spite of its capitulation had been plundered by
the soldiers of the Roman fleet—although it did not fall
under the category designated in the treaty—received back
by way of compensation its territory and its freedom.   Most
of the cities of the Graeco-Asiatic Hansa acquired additions
of territory and other advantages.   Rhodes of course received most consideration ; it obtained Lycia exclusive of
Telmissus, and the greater part of Caria south of the Maeander ; besides, Antiochus guaranteed the property and the
claims of the Rhodians within his kingdom, as well as the exemption from customs-dues which they had hitherto enjoyed.

Extension of the kingdom of Pergamus.
All the rest, forming by far the largest share of the spoil,
fell to the Attalids, whose ancient fidelity to Rome, as well
as the hardships endured by Eumenes in the war and his
personal merit in connection with the issue of the decisive

battle, were rewarded by Rome as no king ever rewarded
his ally.   Eumenes received, in Europe, the Chersonese with
Lysimachia ; in Asia—in addition to Mysia which he already
possessed—the provinces of Phrygia on the Hellespont, Lydia
with Ephesus and Sardes, the northern district of Caria to
the Maeander with Tralles and Magnesia, Great Phrygia and
Lycaonia along with a portion of Cilicia, the district of
Milyas between Phrygia and Lycia, and, as a port on the
southern sea, the Lycian town Telmissus.   There was a dispute afterwards between Eumenes and Antiochus regarding
Pamphylia, whether it lay on this side of or beyond the
Taurus, and whether accordingly it belonged to the former
or to the latter.   He further acquired the protectorate over,
and the right of receiving tribute from, those Greek cities
which did not receive absolute freedom; but it was stipulated in this case that the cities should retain their charters,
and that the tribute should not be heightened.   Moreover,
Antiochus had to bind himself to pay to Eumenes the 350
talents (£85,000) which he owed to his father Attalus,
and likewise to pay a compensation of 127 talents (£31,000)
for arrears in the supplies of corn.   Lastly, Eumenes obtained the royal forests and the elephants delivered up
by Antiochus, but not the ships of war, which were burnt :
the Romans tolerated no naval power by the side of their
own.   By these means the kingdom of the Attalids became
in the east of Europe and Asia what Numidia was in Africa,
a powerful state with an absolute constitution dependent on
Rome, destined and able to keep in check both Macedonia and
Syria without needing, except in extraordinary cases, Roman
support.   With this creation dictated by policy the Romans
had as far as possible combined the liberation of the Asiatic
Greeks, which was dictated by republican and national sympathy and by vanity.   About the affairs of the more remote
East beyond the Taurus and Halys they were firmly resolved
to give themselves no concern.   This is clearly shown by the
terms of the peace with Antiochus, and still more decidedly
by the peremptory refusal of the senate to guarantee to the
town of Soli in Cilicia the freedom which the Rhodians
requested for it.   With equal fidelity they adhered to the
fixed principle of acquiring no direct transmarine possessions.

After the Roman fleet had made an expedition to Crete and
had accomplished the release of the Romans sold thither into
slavery, the fleet and land army left Asia towards the end of
188.   the summer of 566; on which occasion the land army, which
again marched through Thrace, in consequence of the negligence of the general suffered greatly on the route from the
attacks of the barbarians. The Romans brought nothing
home from the East but honour and gold, which were even at
this period usually conjoined in the practical shape assumed
by the address of thanks—the golden chaplet.

Settlement   European Greece also had been agitated by this Asiatic
of Greece.   war, and needed re-organization. The Aetolians, who had
not yet learned to reconcile themselves to their insignifi-
cance, had, after the armistice concluded with Scipio in the
190.   spring of 564, rendered intercourse between Greece and
Conflicts   Italy difficult and unsafe by means of their Cephallenian
and peace
with the   corsairs; and not only so, but even perhaps while the armis-
Aetolians.   tice yet lasted, they, deceived by false reports as to the state
of things in Asia, had the folly to place Amynander once
more on his Athamanian throne, and to carry on a desultory
warfare with Philip in the districts occupied by him on the
borders of Aetolia and Thessaly, in the course of which
Philip suffered several discomfitures. After this, as a matter
of course, Rome replied to their request for peace by the
landing of the consul Marcus Fulvius Nobilior. He arrived
189.   among the legions in the spring of 565, and after fifteen
days' siege gained possession of Ambracia by a capitulation
honourable for the garrison; while simultaneously the Macedonians, Illyrians, Epirots, Acarnanians, and Achaeans fell
upon the Aetolians. There was no such thing as resistance
in the strict sense; after repeated entreaties of the Aetolians
for peace the Romans at length desisted from the war, and
granted conditions which must be reckoned reasonable
when viewed with reference to such pitiful and malicious
opponents. The Aetolians lost all cities and territories
which were in the hands of their adversaries, more especially
Ambracia which afterwards became free and independent
in consequence of an intrigue concocted in Rome against
Marcus Fulvius, and Oenia[dae] which was given to the
Acarnanians; they likewise ceded Cephallenia. They lost the

right of making peace and war, and were in that respect
dependent on the foreign relations of Rome. Lastly, they
paid a large sum of money. Cephallenia opposed this treaty
on its own account, and only submitted when Marcus Fulvius landed on the island. In fact, the inhabitants of Same,
who feared that they would be dispossessed from their well-
situated town by a Roman colony, revolted after their first
submission and sustained a four months' siege; the town,
however, was finally taken and the whole inhabitants were
sold into slavery.

In this case also Rome adhered to the principle of con- Macedonia.
fining herself to Italy and the Italian islands. She took no
portion of the spoil for herself, except the two islands of
Cephallenia and Zacynthus, which formed a desirable supplement to the possession of Corcyra and other naval stations
in the Adriatic. The rest of the territorial gain went to
the allies of Rome. But the two most important of these,
Philip and the Achaeans, were by no means content with
the share of the spoil granted to them. Philip felt himself
aggrieved, and not without reason. He could safely affirm
that the chief difficulties in the last war—difficulties which
arose not from the character of the enemy, but from the
distance and the uncertainty of the communications—had
been overcome mainly by his loyal aid. The senate recognized this by remitting his arrears of tribute and sending
back his hostages; but he did not receive those additions to
his territory which he expected. He got the territory of the
Magnetes, with Demetrias which he had taken from the
Aetolians; besides, there practically remained in his hands
the districts of Dolopia and Athamania and a part of
Thessaly, from which also the Aetolians had been expelled
by him. In Thrace the interior remained under Macedonian protection, but nothing was fixed as to the coast
towns and the islands of Thasos and Lemnos which were *de
facto* in Philip's hands, while the Chersonese was even expressly given to Eumenes; and it was not difficult to see
that Eumenes received possessions in Europe, simply that
he might in case of need keep not only Asia but Macedonia
in check. The exasperation of the proud and in many
respects chivalrous king was natural it was not chicane,

however, but an unavoidable political necessity that induced the Romans to take this course.   Macedonia suffered for having once been a power of the first rank, and for having waged war on equal terms with Rome ; there was much better reason in her case than in that of Carthage for guarding against the revival of her former attitude of power.

The Achaeans.

It was otherwise with the Achaeans. They had, in the course of the war with Antiochus, gratified their long che-rished wish to include the whole Peloponnesus within their confederacy ; for first Sparta, and then, after the ex-pulsion of the Asiatics from Greece, Elis and Messene also had more or less reluctantly joined it. The Romans had allowed this to take place, and had even tolerated the in-tentional disregard of Rome which marked their proceed-ings.   When Messene declared that she wished to submit to the Romans but not to enter the confederacy, and the latter thereupon employed force, Flamininus had not failed to remind the Achaeans that such separate arrangements as to the disposal of a part of the spoil were in themselves unjust, and were, in the relation in which the Achaeans stood to the Romans, more than unseemly ; and yet in his very impolitic complaisance towards the Hellenes he had sub-stantially allowed the Achaeans their will.   But the matter did not end there.   The Achaeans, tormented by their dwarfish thirst for aggrandizement, would not relax their hold on the town of Pleuron in Aetolia which they had oc-cupied during the war, but compelled it to become a mem-ber of their league ; they bought Zacynthus from Amynander the lieutenant of the last possessor, and would gladly have acquired Aegina also.   It was with reluctance that they gave up the former island to Rome, and they heard with great displeasure the good advice of Flamininus that they should content themselves with their Peloponnesus.

The Achaean patriots.

The Achaeans believed it their duty to display the inde-pendence of their state all the more, the less they really had; they talked of the rights of war, and of the faithful aid of the Achaeans in the wars of the Romans ; they asked the Roman envoys at the Achaean diet why Rome should concern herself about Messene when Achaia put no questions as to Capua ; and the spirited patriot, who had thus spoken, was applauded and was sure of votes at the elections.   All this would have been very right and very dignified, had it not been much more ridiculous.   There was a profound justice and a still more profound melancholy in the fact, that Rome, however earnestly she endeavoured to establish the freedom and to earn the thanks of the Hellenes, yet gave them nothing but anarchy and reaped nothing but ingratitude.   Undoubtedly very generous sentiments lay at the bottom of the Hellenic antipathy to the protecting power, and the personal bravery of some of the men who took the lead in the movement was unquestionable; but this Achaean patriotism remained not the less a folly and a genuine historical caricature.   With all that ambition and all that national susceptibility the whole nation was, from the highest to the lowest, pervaded by the most thorough sense of impotence.   Every one was constantly listening to learn the sentiments of Rome, the liberal man no less than the servile; they thanked heaven, when the dreaded decree was not issued; they were sulky, when the senate gave them to understand that they would do well to yield voluntarily in order that they might not need to be compelled; they did what they were obliged to do, if possible, in a way offensive to the Romans, " to save forms; " they reported, explained, delayed, equivocated, and when all this would no longer avail yielded with a patriotic sigh.   Their proceedings might have claimed indulgence at any rate, if not approval, had their leaders been resolved to fight, and had they preferred the destruction of the nation to its bondage; but neither Philopoemen nor Lycortas thought of any such political suicide—they wished, if possible, to be free, but they wished above all to live.   Besides all this, the dreaded intervention of Rome in the internal affairs of Greece was not the arbitrary act of the Romans, but was always invoked by the Greeks themselves, who, like boys, brought down on their own heads the rod which they feared.   The reproach repeated *ad nauseam* by the mass of the learned in Hellenic and post-Hellenic times—that the Romans strove to stir up internal discord in Greece—is one of the most foolish absurdities which scholars dealing in politics have ever invented.   It was not the Romans that carried strife to Greece—which in truth would have been " carrying owls to

Athens "—but the Greeks that carried their dissensions to
Rome.

Quarrels
between
the
Achaeans
and
Spartans.

The Achaeans in particular, who, in their eagerness to
enlarge their territory, totally failed to see how much it would
have been for their own good that Flamininus had not incorporated the towns of Aetolian sympathies with their league,
acquired in Lacedaemon and Messene a very hydra of intestine strife. Members of these communities were incessantly
at Rome, entreating and beseeching to be released from the
odious connection; and amongst them, characteristically
enough, were even those who were indebted to the Achaeans
for their return to their native land. The Achaean league
was incessantly occupied in the work of reformation and restoration at Sparta and Messene; the wildest refugees from
these quarters dictated the measures of the diet. Four years
after the nominal admission of Sparta to the confederacy
matters came to an open war and to an insanely thorough
restoration, in which all the slaves on whom Nabis had conferred citizenship were once more sold into slavery, and a
colonnade was built from the proceeds in the Achaean city
of Megalopolis; the old state of property in Sparta was re-
established, the laws of Lycurgus were superseded by Achaean

188.

laws, and the walls were pulled down (566). At last the
Roman senate was summoned by all parties to arbitrate in
reference to the whole matter—an annoying task, which was
the righteous punishment of the sentimental policy that the
senate had pursued. Far from mixing itself up too much in
these affairs, the senate not only bore the sarcasms of Achaean
conceit with exemplary composure, but even manifested a
culpable indifference while the worst outrages were committed. There was cordial rejoicing in Achaia when, after
that restoration, the news arrived from Rome that the senate
had found fault with it, but had not annulled it. Nothing
was done for the Lacedaemonians by Rome, except that the
senate, shocked at the judicial murder of from sixty to eighty
Spartans committed by the Achaeans, deprived the diet of
criminal jurisdiction over the Spartans—truly a heinous interference with the internal affairs of an independent state!
The Roman statesmen gave themselves as little concern as
possible about this tempest in a nut-shell, as is best shown

y the many complaints regarding the superficial, contradic-
ory, and obscure decisions of the senate ; in fact, how could
ts decisions be expected to be clear, when there were four
parties from Sparta simultaneously speaking against each
other at its bar ? Then the personal impression, which most
of these Peloponnesian statesmen produced in Rome, was
not favourable ; even Flamininus shook his head, when one
of them showed him on the one day how to perform some
dance, and on the next entertained him with affairs of
state. Matters went so far, that the senate at last lost
patience and informed the Peloponnesians that it could no
longer listen to them, and that they might do what they
chose (572). This was natural enough, but it was not right ; 182.
situated as the Romans were, they were under a moral and
political obligation earnestly and consistently to rectify this
melancholy state of things. Callicrates the Achaean, who
went to the senate in 575 to enlighten it as to the state of 179.
matters in the Peloponnesus and to demand a consistent
and sustained intervention, may have had somewhat less
worth as a man than his countryman Philopoemen who was
the main founder of that patriotic policy ; but he was in the
right.

Thus the protectorate of the Roman community now em- Death of
braced all the states from the eastern to the western end of Hannibal.
the Mediterranean. There nowhere existed a state that the
Romans would have deemed it worth while to fear. But
there still lived a man to whom Rome accorded this rare
honour—the homeless Carthaginian, who had raised in arms
against Rome first all the West and then all the East, and
whose schemes had been frustrated solely perhaps by infamous aristocratic policy in the one case, and by stupid court
policy in the other. Antiochus had been obliged to bind
himself in the treaty of peace to deliver up Hannibal ; but
the latter had escaped, first to Crete, then to Bithynia,* and
now lived at the court of Prusias king of Bithynia, employed
in aiding the latter in his wars with Eumenes, and victorious

---

* The story that he went to Armenia
and at the request of king Artaxias built
the town of Artaxata on the Araxes
(Strabo, xi. p. 528 ; Plutarch, *Luc.* 31),
is certainly a fiction ; but it is a striking
circumstance that Hannibal should have
become mixed up, almost like Alexander,
with Oriental fables.

as ever by sea and by land. It is affirmed that he was desirous of stirring up Prusias also to make war on Rome; a
folly, which, as it is told, sounds very far from credible. It
is more certain that, while the Roman senate deemed it beneath its dignity to have the old man hunted out in his last
asylum—for the tradition which inculpates the senate appears
to deserve no credit—Flamininus, whose restless vanity sought
after new opportunities for great achievements, undertook on
his own part to deliver Rome from Hannibal as he had delivered the Greeks from their chains, and, if not to wield—
which was not diplomatic—at any rate to whet and to point,
the dagger against the greatest man of his time. Prusias
the most pitiful among the pitiful princes of Asia, was de-
lighted to grant the little favour which the Roman envoy in
ambiguous terms requested; and, when Hannibal saw his
house beset by assassins, he took poison. He had long been
prepared to do so, adds a Roman, for he knew the Romans
and the faith of kings. The year of his death is uncertain;
probably he died in the latter half of the year 571, at the
age of sixty-seven. When he was born, Rome was contending with doubtful success for the possession of Sicily; he had
lived long enough to see the West wholly subdued, and to
fight his own last battle with the Romans against the vessels
of his native city which had itself become Roman; and he
was constrained at last to remain a mere spectator while Rome
overpowered the East as the tempest overpowers the ship that
has no one at the helm, and to feel that he alone was the pilot
that could have weathered the storm. There was left to him
no further hope to be disappointed, when he died; but he had
honestly, through fifty years of struggle, kept the oath which
he had sworn when a boy.

Death of Scipio.

About the same time, probably in the same year, died also
the man whom the Romans were wont to call his conqueror,
Publius Scipio. On him fortune had lavished all the successes which she denied to his antagonist—successes which
did belong to him, and successes which did not. He had
added to the empire Spain, Africa, and Asia; and Rome,
which he had found merely the first community of Italy, was
at his death mistress of the civilized world. He himself had
so many titles of victory, that some of them were made over

183. (margin)

to his brother and his cousin.* And yet he too spent his last years in bitter vexation, and died when little more than fifty years of age in voluntary banishment, leaving orders to his relatives not to bury his remains in the city for which he had lived and in which his ancestors reposed. It is not exactly known what drove him from the city. The charges of corruption and embezzlement, which were directed against him and still more against his brother Lucius, were beyond doubt empty calumnies, which do not satisfactorily account for such irritation of feeling; although it was characteristic of the man, that instead of simply vindicating himself by means of his account-books, he tore them in pieces in presence of the people and of his accusers, and summoned the Romans to accompany him to the temple of Jupiter and to celebrate the anniversary of his victory at Zama. The people left the accusers on the spot, and followed Scipio to the Capitol; but this was the last glorious day of that illustrious man. His proud spirit, his belief that he was different from, and better than, other men, his very decided family-policy, which in the person of his brother Lucius especially brought forward a clumsy man of straw as a hero, gave offence to many, and not without reason. While genuine pride protects the heart, arrogance lays it open to every blow and every sarcasm, and corrodes even an originally noble-minded spirit. It is throughout, moreover, the distinguishing characteristic of such natures as that of Scipio—strange mixtures of genuine gold and glittering tinsel—that they need the good fortune and the brilliance of youth in order to exercise their charm, and, when this charm begins to fade, it is the charmer himself that is most painfully conscious of the change.

---

* Africanus, Asiagenus, Hispallus.

CHAPTER X.

THE THIRD MACEDONIAN WAR.

Dissatis-
faction of
Philip with
Rome.

PHILIP OF MACEDONIA was greatly annoyed by the treatment which he met with from the Romans after the peace with Antiochus; and the subsequent course of events was not fitted to appease his wrath. His neighbours in Greece and Thrace, mostly communities that had once trembled at the Macedonian name not less than now they trembled at the Roman, made it their business, as was natural, to retaliate on the fallen great power for all the injuries which since the times of Philip the Second they had received at the hands of Macedonia. The empty arrogance and venal anti-Macedonian patriotism of the Hellenes of this period found vent at the diets of the different confederacies and in ceaseless complaints addressed to the Roman senate. Philip had been allowed by the Romans to retain what he had taken from the Aetolians; but in Thessaly the confederacy of the Magnetes alone had formally joined the Aetolians, while those towns which Philip had wrested from the Aetolians in two of the other Thessalian confederacies — the Thessalian in its narrower sense, and the Perrhaebian—were demanded back by the latter on the ground that Philip had only liberated these towns, not conquered them. The Athamanes conceived that they might request their freedom; and Eumenes demanded the maritime cities which Antiochus had possessed in Thrace proper, especially Aenus and Maronea, although in the peace with Antiochus the Thracian Chersonese alone had been expressly promised to him. All these complaints and numerous minor ones from all the neighbours of Philip as to his supporting king Prusias against Eumenes, as to competition in trade, as to the violation of contracts and the seizing of cattle, were poured forth at Rome. The king of Mace-

donia had to submit to be accused by the sovereign rabble
before the Roman senate, and to accept justice or injustice as
the senate chose; he was compelled to witness judgment constantly going against him; he had to submit to withdraw
his garrisons from the Thracian coast and from the Thessalian and Perrhaebian towns, and courteously to receive the
Roman commissioners, who came to see whether everything
required had been properly done. The Romans were not so
indignant against Philip as they had been against Carthage;
in fact, they were in many respects even favourably disposed
to the Macedonian ruler; there was not in his case so reckless a violation of forms as in that of Libya; but the situation
of Macedonia was at bottom substantially the same as that
of Carthage. Philip, however, was by no means the man to
submit to this infliction with Phoenician patience. Passionate as he was, he had after his defeat been more indignant
with his faithless ally than with his honourable antagonist;
and, long accustomed to pursue a policy not Macedonian but
personal, he had regarded the war with Antiochus simply as
an excellent opportunity of instantaneously revenging himself
on the ally who had disgracefully deserted and betrayed him.
This object he had attained; but the Romans, who saw very
clearly that the Macedonian was influenced not by friendship
for Rome, but by enmity to Antiochus, and who were by no
means in the habit of regulating their policy by such feelings
of liking and disliking, had carefully abstained from bestow-
ing any material advantages on Philip, and had preferred to
confer their favours on the Attalids. From their first elevation the Attalids had been at vehement feud with Macedonia,
and were politically and personally the objects of Philip's
bitterest hatred; of all the Eastern powers they had contributed most to maim Macedonia and Syria, and to extend the
protectorate of Rome in the East; and in the last war, when
Philip had voluntarily and loyally embraced the side of
Rome, they had been obliged to take part with Rome for the
sake of their very existence. The Romans had made use of
these Attalids for the purpose of reconstructing in all essential points the kingdom of Lysimachus—the destruction of
which had been the most important achievement of the
Macedonian rulers after Alexander—and of placing alongside

of Macedonia a state, which was its equal in point of power and was at the same time a client of Rome. In the special circumstances a wise sovereign, devoted to the interests of his people, would perhaps have resolved not to resume the unequal struggle with Rome ; but Philip, in whose character the sense of honour was the most powerful of all noble, and the thirst for revenge the most potent of all ignoble, motives, was deaf to the voice of timidity or of resignation, and nourished in the depths of his heart a determination once more to try the hazard of the game. When he received the report of fresh invectives, such as were wont to be launched against Macedonia at the Thessalian diets, he replied with the line of Theocritus, that his last sun had not yet set.*

The latter years of Philip.

Philip displayed in the preparation and the concealment of his designs a calmness, earnestness, and perseverance which, had he shown them in better times, would perhaps have given a different turn to the destinies of the world. In particular the submissiveness towards Rome, by which he purchased the time indispensable for his objects, formed a severe trial for the fierce and haughty man ; nevertheless he courageously endured it, although his subjects and the innocent occasions of the quarrel, such as the unfortunate Maronea, paid severely for the suppression of his resentment. It seemed as if war could not but break out as early as 571; but by Philip's instructions, his younger son, Demetrius, effected a reconciliation between his father and Rome, where he had lived some years as a hostage and was a great favourite. The senate, and particularly Flamininus who managed Greek affairs, sought to form a Roman party in Macedonia that would be able to paralyse the exertions of Philip, which of course were not unknown to the Romans; and had selected as its head, and perhaps as the future king of Macedonia, the younger prince who was passionately attached to Rome. With this view they gave it clearly to be understood that the senate forgave the father for the sake of the son; the natural effect of which was, that dissensions arose in the royal household itself, and that the king's elder

183.

* Ἤδη γὰρ φράσδει πάνθ᾽ ἅλιον ἄμμι δεδύκειν.

son, Perseus, who, although the offspring of a marriage of disparagement, was destined by his father for the succession, sought to ruin his brother as his future rival.　It does not appear that Demetrius was a party to the Roman intrigues; it was only when he was falsely suspected that he was forced to become guilty, and even then he intended, apparently, nothing more than flight to Rome.　But Perseus took care that his father should be duly informed of this design; an intercepted letter from Flamininus to Demetrius did the rest, and induced the father to give orders that his son should be put to death.　Philip learned, when it was too late, the intrigues which Perseus had concocted; and death overtook him, as he was meditating the punishment of the fratricide and his exclusion from the throne.　He died in 575 at Demetrias, in his fifty-ninth year.　He left behind him a shattered kingdom and a distracted household, and with a broken heart confessed to himself that all his toils and all his crimes had been in vain.

179.

His son Perseus then entered on the government, without encountering opposition either in Macedonia or in the Roman senate.　He was a man of stately aspect, expert in all gymnastic exercises, reared in the camp and accustomed to command, imperious like his father and unscrupulous in the choice of his means.　Wine and women, which too often led Philip to forget the duties of government, had no charm for Perseus; he was as steady and persevering as his father had been thoughtless and impulsive.　Philip, a king while still a boy, and attended by success during the first twenty years of his reign, had been spoiled and ruined by destiny; Perseus ascended the throne in his thirty-first year, and, as he had while yet a boy borne a part in the unhappy war with Rome and had grown up under the pressure of humiliation and under the idea that a revival of the state was at hand, so he inherited along with the kingdom the troubles, resentments, and hopes of his father.　In fact he entered with the utmost determination on the continuance of his father's work, and prepared more zealously than ever for war against Rome; he was stimulated, moreover, by the reflection, that he was by no means indebted to the goodwill of the Romans for his wearing the diadem of Macedonia.　The proud Macedonian nation looked with pride upon the prince whom they had been

King Perseus.

accustomed to see marching and fighting at the head of their youth; his countrymen, and many Hellenes of every variety of lineage, conceived that in him they had found the proper general for the impending war of liberation. But he was not what he seemed. He wanted Philip's genius and Philip's elasticity—those truly royal qualities, which success obscured and tarnished, but which under the purifying power of adversity recovered their lustre. Philip was self-indulgent, and allowed things to take their course; but, when there was occasion, he found within himself the vigour necessary for speedy and earnest action. Perseus devised comprehensive and subtle plans, and prosecuted them with unwearied perseverance; but, when the moment arrived for action and his plans and preparations confronted him in stern reality, he was frightened at his own work. As is the wont of narrow minds, the means became to him the end; he heaped up treasures on treasures for war with the Romans, and, when the Romans were in the land, he was unable to part with his golden pieces. It is a significant indication of character that after defeat the father first hastened to destroy the papers in his cabinet that might compromise him, whereas the son took his treasure-chests and embarked. In ordinary times he might have made an average king, as good as or better than many others; but he was not adapted for the conduct of an enterprise, which was from the first a hopeless one unless some extraordinary man should become the soul of the movement.

Resources of Macedonia.

The power of Macedonia was far from inconsiderable. The devotion of the land to the house of the Antigonids was unimpaired; in this one respect the national feeling was not paralyzed by the dissensions of political parties. A monarchical constitution has the great advantage, that every change of sovereign supersedes old resentments and quarrels and introduces a new era of different men and fresh hopes. The king had judiciously availed himself of this, and had begun his reign with a general amnesty, with the recall of fugitive bankrupts, and with the remission of arrears of taxes. The hateful severity of the father thus not only yielded benefit, but conciliated affection, to the son. Twenty-six years of peace had partly of themselves filled up the blanks in the Macedonian population, partly given opportunity to the government to take serious steps towards rectifying this which was really the weak point of the land. Philip urged the Macedonians to marry and raise up children; he occupied the coast towns, whose inhabitants he carried into the interior, with Thracian colonists of reliable valour and fidelity. He formed a barrier on the north to check once for all the desolating incursions of the Dardani, by converting the space intervening between the Macedonian frontier and the barbarian territory into a desert, and by founding new towns in the northern provinces. In short he took step by step the same course in Macedonia, as Augustus afterwards took when he laid afresh the foundations of the Roman empire. The army was numerous—30,000 men without reckoning contingents and hired troops—and the younger men were well exercised in the constant border warfare with the Thracian barbarians. It is strange that Philip did not try, like Hannibal, to organize his army after the Roman fashion; but we can understand it when we recollect the value which the Macedonians set upon their phalanx, often conquered, but still believed to be invincible. Through the new sources of revenue which Philip had created in mines, customs, and tenths, and through the flourishing state of agriculture and commerce, he had succeeded in replenishing his treasury, granaries, and arsenals. When the war began, there was in the Macedonian treasury money enough to pay the existing army and 10,000 hired troops for ten years, and there were in the public magazines stores of grain for as long a period (18,000,000 *medimni* or 27,000,000 bushels), and arms for an army of three times the strength of the existing one. In fact, Macedonia had become a very different state from what it was when surprised by the outbreak of the second war with Rome. The power of the kingdom was in all respects at least doubled: with a power in every point of view far inferior Hannibal had been able to shake Rome to its foundations.

Its external relations were not in so favourable a position. Attempted The nature of the case required that Macedonia should now coalition take up the plans of Hannibal and Antiochus, and should try against to place herself at the head of a coalition of all oppressed Rome. states against the supremacy of Rome; and certainly threads

of intrigue ramified in all directions from the court of
Pydna. But their success was slight. It was indeed asserted that the allegiance of the Italians was wavering; but
neither friend nor foe could fail to see that an immediate
resumption of the Samnite wars was not at all probable.
The nocturnal conferences likewise between Macedonian
deputies and the Carthaginian senate, which Massinissa
denounced at Rome, could occasion no alarm to serious and
sagacious men, even if they were not, as is very possible,
an utter fiction. The Macedonian court sought to attach
the kings of Syria and Bithynia to its interests by intermarriages; but nothing further came of it, except that the
immortal simplicity of the diplomacy which seeks to gain political ends by matrimonial means once more exposed itself to
derision. Eumenes, whom it would have been ridiculous to
attempt to gain, the agents of Perseus would have gladly put
out of the way: he was to have been murdered at Delphi
on his way homeward from Rome, where he had been active
against Macedonia; but the dastardly project miscarried.

Bastarnae.   Of greater moment were the efforts made to stir up the
northern barbarians and the Hellenes to rebellion against
Rome. Philip had conceived the project of crushing the
old enemies of Macedonia, the Dardani in what is now
Servia, by means of another still more barbarous horde of
Germanic descent brought from the left bank of the
Danube, the Bastarnae, and of then marching in person with
these and with the whole avalanche of peoples thus set in
motion by the land route to Italy and invading Lombardy, the Alpine passes leading to which he had already
sent spies to reconnoitre—a grand project, worthy of Hannibal, and doubtless immediately suggested by Hannibal's
passage of the Alps. It is more than probable that this
gave occasion to the founding of the Roman fortress of Aquileia (p. 207), which was formed towards the end of the reign
181.   of Philip (573), and did not harmonize with the system followed elsewhere by the Romans in the establishment of
fortresses in Italy. The plan, however, was thwarted by the
desperate resistance of the Dardani and of the adjoining
tribes concerned; the Bastarnae were obliged to retreat, and
the whole horde were drowned in returning home by the

giving way of the ice on the Danube. The king then sought Genthius.
at least to extend his clientship among the chieftains of the
Illyrian land, the modern Dalmatia and northern Albania.
One of these who faithfully adhered to Rome, Arthetaurus,
perished, not without the cognizance of Perseus, by the
hand of an assassin. The most considerable of the whole,
Genthius the son and heir of Pleuratus, was, like his father,
nominally in alliance with Rome ; but the ambassadors of
Issa, a Greek town on one of the Dalmatian islands, informed the senate, that Perseus had a secret understanding with the young, weak, and drunken prince, and that
the envoys of Genthius served as spies for Perseus in Rome.

In the regions on the east of Macedonia towards the Cotys.
lower Danube the most powerful of the Thracian chieftains,
the brave and sagacious Cotys, prince of the Odrysians and
ruler of all eastern Thrace from the Macedonian frontier on
the Hebrus (Maritza) down to the fringe of coast covered
with Greek towns, was in the closest alliance with Perseus.
Of the other minor chiefs who in that quarter took part with
Rome, one, Abrupolis prince of the Sagaei, was, in consequence of a predatory expedition directed against Amphipolis on the Strymon, defeated by Perseus and driven out of
the country. From these regions Philip had drawn numerous
colonists, and mercenaries were to be had there at any time
and in any number.

Among the unhappy nation of the Hellenes Philip and Greek
national
party.
Perseus had, long before declaring war against Rome, carried
on a double system of proselytizing, attempting to gain over
to the side of Macedonia on the one hand the national, and
on the other—if we may be permitted the expression—the
communistic party. As a matter of course, the whole national party among the Asiatic as well as the European Greeks
was now favourable at heart to Macedonia ; not on account
of isolated unrighteous acts on the part of the Roman deliverers, but because the restoration of Hellenic nationality by a foreign power involved a contradiction in terms,
and now, when it was in truth too late, every one perceived
that the most detestable form of Macedonian rule was less
fraught with evil for Greece than a free constitution originating in the noblest intentions of honourable foreigners.

That the most able and upright men throughout Greece
should be opposed to Rome was to be expected; the venal
aristocracy alone was favourable to the Romans, and here
and there an isolated man of worth, who, unlike the great
majority, was under no delusion as to the circumstances and
the future of the nation. This was most painfully experienced
by Eumenes of Pergamus, who was the main supporter of
that extraneous liberty among the Greeks. In vain he treated
the cities subject to him with every sort of consideration;
in vain he sued for the favour of the communities and diets
by fair-sounding words and still better-sounding gold; he
learned with pain that his presents were declined, and that
all the statues that had formerly been erected to him were
broken in pieces and the honorary tablets were melted down,
in accordance with a decree of the diet, simultaneously
170.   throughout the Peloponnesus (584). The name of Perseus,
again, was on every one's lips; even the states that formerly
were most decidedly anti-Macedonian, such as the Achaeans,
deliberated as to the abolition of the laws directed against
Macedonia; Byzantium, although situated within the kingdom of Pergamus, sought and obtained protection and a garrison against the Thracians not from Eumenes, but from
Perseus, and in like manner Lampsacus on the Hellespont
joined the Macedonian: the powerful and prudent Rhodians
escorted the Syrian bride of king Perseus from Antioch with
their whole magnificent war-fleet—for the Syrian war-vessels
were not allowed to appear in the Aegean—and returned
home highly honoured and furnished with rich presents,
more especially with wood for ship-building; commissioners
from the Asiatic cities, and consequently subjects of Eumenes,
held secret conferences with Macedonian deputies in Samothrace. That sending of the Rhodian war-fleet had at least
the aspect of a demonstration; and such, certainly, was the
object of king Perseus, when he exhibited himself and all his
army before the eyes of the Hellenes under pretext of performing a religious ceremony at Delphi. That the king
should appeal to the support of this national partisanship in
the impending war, was natural and reasonable. But it was
wrong in him to take advantage of the fearful economic
disorganization of Greece for the purpose of attaching to

Macedonia all those who desired a revolution in matters of property and of debt. It is difficult to form any adequate idea of the unparalleled extent to which the commonwealths as well as individuals in European Greece—excepting the Peloponnesus, which was in a somewhat better position in this respect—were involved in debt. Instances occurred of one city attacking and pillaging another merely to get money—the Athenians, for example, thus attacked Oropus—and among the Aetolians, Perrhaebians, and Thessalians formal battles took place between those that had property and those that had none. Under such circumstances the worst outrages were perpetrated as a matter of course; among the Aetolians, for instance, a general amnesty was proclaimed and a new public peace was made up solely for the purpose of entrapping and putting to death a number of emigrants. The Romans attempted to mediate; but their envoys returned without success, and announced that both parties were equally bad and that their animosities were not to be restrained. In this case there was, in fact, no other remedy than that of the officer and the executioner; sentimental Hellenism began to be as repulsive as from the first it had been ridiculous. Yet king Perseus sought to gain the support of this party, if it deserve to be called such—of people who had nothing, and least of all an honourable name, to lose—and not only issued edicts in favour of Macedonian bankrupts, but also caused placards to be put up at Larisa, Delphi, and Delos, which summoned all Greeks that were exiled on account of political or other offences or on account of their debts to come to Macedonia and to expect full restitution of their former honours and estates. As may easily be supposed, they came; the social revolution smouldering throughout northern Greece now broke out into open flame, and the national-social party there sent to Perseus for help. If Hellenic nationality was to be saved only by such means, the question might well be asked, with all respect for Sophocles and Phidias, whether the object was worth the cost.

The senate saw that it had delayed too long already, and that it was time to put an end to such proceedings. The expulsion of the Thracian chieftain Abrupolis who was in alliance with the Romans, and the alliances of Macedonia

Rupture with Perseus.

with the Byzantines, Aetolians, and part of the Boeotian
cities, were equally violations of the peace of 557, and sufficed for the official war-manifesto : the real ground of war
was that Macedonia was seeking to convert her formal
sovereignty into a real one, and to supplant Rome in the
protectorate of the Hellenes. As early as 581 the Roman
envoys at the Achaean diet stated pretty plainly, that an
alliance with Perseus was equivalent to casting off the
alliance of Rome. In 582 king Eumenes came in person
to Rome with a long list of grievances and laid open to the
senate the whole situation of affairs ; upon which the senate
unexpectedly in a secret sitting resolved on an immediate
declaration of war, and furnished the ports of Epirus with
garrisons. For the sake of form an embassy was sent to
Macedonia, but its message was of such a nature that Perseus,
perceiving that he could not recede, replied that he was
ready to conclude with Rome a new alliance on really equal
terms, but that he looked upon the treaty of 557 as cancelled ; and he bade the envoys leave the kingdom within
three days. Thus war was practically declared. This was
in the autumn of 582. Perseus, had he wished, might have
occupied all Greece and brought the Macedonian party
everywhere to the helm, and he might perhaps have crushed
the Roman division of 5000 men stationed under Gnaeus
Sicinius at Apollonia and opposed the landing of the Romans. But the king, who already began to tremble at the
serious aspect of affairs, engaged in discussions with the
consular Quintus Marcius Philippus, with whom he stood
in relations of hospitality, as to the frivolousness of the
Roman declaration of war, and allowed himself to be induced in this way to postpone the attack and once more to
make an effort for peace with Rome : to which the senate, as
might have been expected, only replied by the dismissal of
all Macedonians from Italy and the embarkation of the
legions. Senators of the older school no doubt censured
the "new wisdom" of their colleague, and his un-Roman
artifice ; but the object was gained and the winter passed
away without any movement on the part of Perseus. The
Roman diplomatists made all the more zealous use of the
interval to deprive Perseus of any support in Greece. They
were sure of the Achaeans. Even the patriotic party among

197.

173.

172.

197.

172.

them—who had neither agreed with those social movements, nor had manifested aught more than a longing after a prudent neutrality—had no idea of throwing themselves into the arms of Perseus; and, besides, the opposition party there had now been brought by Roman influence into power, and attached itself absolutely to Rome. The Aetolian league had doubtless asked aid from Perseus in its internal troubles; but the new *strategus*, Lyciscus, chosen under the eyes of the Roman ambassadors, was more of a Roman partisan than the Romans themselves. Among the Thessalians also the Roman party retained the ascendancy. Even the Boeotians, old partisans as they were of Macedonia, and sunk in the utmost financial disorder, had not in their collective capacity declared openly for Perseus; nevertheless at least two of their cities, Haliartus and Coronea, had of their own accord entered into engagements with him. When on the complaint of the Roman envoy the government of the Boeotian confederacy communicated to him the position of things, he declared that it would best appear which cities adhered to Rome, and which did not, if they would severally pronounce their decision in his presence; and thereupon the Boeotian confederacy fell at once to pieces. It is not true that the great structure of Epaminondas was destroyed by the Romans; it actually collapsed before they touched it, and thus indeed became the prelude to the dissolution of the other still more firmly consolidated leagues of Greek cities.* With the forces of the Boeotian towns friendly to Rome the Roman envoy Publius Lentulus laid siege to Haliartus, even before the Roman fleet appeared in the Aegean.

Chalcis was occupied with Achaean, and the province of Orestis with Epirot, forces: the fortresses of the Dassaretae and Illyrians on the west frontier of Macedonia were occupied by the troops of Gnaeus Sicinius; and as soon as the navigation was resumed, Larisa received a garrison of 2000 men. Perseus during all this remained inactive and had not a foot's breadth of land beyond his own territory, when in the spring, or according to the official calendar in June, of 583, the Roman legions landed on the west coast. It is doubtful whether Perseus would have found allies of any

Preparations for war.

171.

---

* The legal dissolution of the Boeotian confederacy, however, took place not at this time, but only after the destruction of Corinth (Pausan. vii. 14, 4; xvi. 6).

mark, even had he shown as much energy as he displayed remissness ; but, as circumstances stood, he remained of course
completely isolated, and those prolonged attempts at proselytism led, for the time at least, to no result. Carthage,
Genthius of Illyria, Rhodes and the free cities of Asia
Minor, and even Byzantium hitherto so very friendly with
Perseus, offered to the Romans vessels of war ; which they,
however, declined. Eumenes put his land army and his
ships on a war footing. Ariarathes king of Cappadocia
sent hostages, unsolicited, to Rome. The brother-in-law of
Perseus, Prusias II. king of Bithynia, remained neutral.
No one stirred in all Greece. Antiochus IV. king of Syria,
designated in court style " the God, the brilliant bringer
of victory," to distinguish him from his father the " Great,"
bestirred himself, but only to wrest the Syrian coast during
this war from the entirely impotent Egypt.

Beginning
of the war.

But, though Perseus stood almost alone, he was no contemptible antagonist. His army numbered 43,000 men ; of
these 21,000 were phalangites, and 4,000 Macedonian and
Thracian cavalry; the rest were chiefly mercenaries. The
whole force of the Romans in Greece amounted to between
30,000 and 40,000 Italian troops, besides more than 10,000
men belonging to Numidian, Ligurian, Greek, Cretan, and
especially Pergamene contingents. To these was added the
fleet, which numbered only 40 decked vessels, as there was no
fleet of the enemy to oppose it—Perseus, who had been prohibited from building ships of war by the treaty with Rome,
was just erecting docks at Thessalonica—but it had on board
10,000 troops, as it was destined chiefly to co-operate in
sieges. The fleet was commanded by Gaius Lucretius, the
land army by the consul Publius Licinius Crassus.

The
Romans
invade
Thessaly.

The consul left a strong division in Illyria to harass Macedonia from the west, while with the main force he started,
as usual, from Apollonia for Thessaly. Perseus did not
think of disturbing their arduous march, but contented himself with advancing into Perrhaebia and occupying the nearest
fortresses. He awaited the enemy at Ossa, and not far from
Larisa the first conflict took place between the cavalry and
light troops on both sides. The Romans were decidedly
beaten. Cotys with the Thracian horse had defeated and

broken the Italian, and Perseus with his Macedonian horse
the Greek, cavalry; the Romans had 2000 foot and 200 horsemen killed, and 600 horsemen made prisoners, and might
deem themselves fortunate in being allowed to cross the
Peneius without hindrance. Perseus employed the victory
to ask peace on the same terms which Philip had obtained:
he was ready even to pay the same sum. The Romans refused his request: they never concluded peace after a defeat,
and in this case the conclusion of peace would certainly have
been followed by the loss of Greece.

The wretched Roman commander, however, knew not how
or where to attack; the army marched to and fro in Thessaly,
without accomplishing anything of importance. Perseus
might have assumed the offensive; he saw that the Romans
were badly led and dilatory; the news had passed like wildfire through Greece, that the Greek army had been brilliantly victorious in the first engagement; a second victory
might lead to a general rising of the patriot party, and, by
commencing a guerilla warfare, might produce incalculable
results. But Perseus, while a good soldier, was not a
general like his father; he had made his preparations for
a defensive war, and, when things took a different turn, he
felt himself as it were paralyzed. He made an unimportant success, which the Romans obtained in a second cavalry
combat near Phalanna, a pretext for reverting, as is the
habit of narrow and obstinate minds, to his first plan and
evacuating Thessaly. This was of course equivalent to renouncing all idea of a Hellenic insurrection: what might
have been attained by a different course was shown by the
fact that, notwithstanding what had occurred, the Epirots
changed sides. Thenceforth nothing serious was accomplished on either side. Perseus subdued king Genthius,
chastised the Dardani, and, by means of Cotys, expelled from
Thrace the Thracians friendly to Rome and the Pergamene
troops. On the other hand the western Roman army took
some Illyrian towns, and the consul busied himself in clearing
Thessaly of the Macedonian garrisons and making sure of the
turbulent Aetolians and Acarnanians by occupying Ambracia.
But the heroic courage of the Romans was most severely
felt by the two unhappy Boeotian towns which took part

Their lax and unsuccessful management of the war.

with Perseus ; Haliartus was captured by the Roman admiral Gaius Lucretius, and the inhabitants were sold into slavery ; Coronea was treated in the same manner by the consul Crassus in spite of its capitulation. Never had a Roman army exhibited such wretched discipline as the force under these commanders. They had so disorganized the army that, even in the next campaign of 584, the new consul Aulus Hostilius could not think of undertaking anything serious, especially as the new admiral Lucius Hortensius showed himself to be as incapable and unprincipled as his predecessor. The fleet visited the towns on the Thracian coast without result. The western army under Appius Claudius, whose head-quarters were at Lychnidus in the territory of the Dassaretae, sustained one defeat after another : after an expedition to Macedonia had been utterly unsuccessful, the king in turn towards the beginning of winter assumed the aggressive with the troops which were no longer needed on the south frontier in consequence of the deep snow blocking up all the passes, took from Appius numerous places and a multitude of prisoners, and entered into connections with king Genthius ; he was able in fact to attempt an invasion of Aetolia, while Appius allowed himself to be once more defeated in Epirus by the garrison of a fortress which he had vainly besieged. The Roman main army made two attempts to penetrate into Macedonia : first, over the Cambunian mountains, and then through the Thessalian passes ; but they were negligently planned, and both were repulsed by Perseus.

170.

Abuses in the army. 170.

The consul employed himself chiefly in the reorganization of the army—a work which was above all things needful, but which required a sterner man and an officer of greater mark. Discharges and furloughs might be bought, and therefore the divisions were never up to their full numbers ; the men were put into quarters in summer, and, as the officers plundered on a great, the common soldiers plundered on a small, scale. Friendly peoples were subjected to the most shameful suspicions : for instance, the blame of the disgraceful defeat at Larisa was imputed to the pretended treachery of the Aetolian cavalry, and, what was hitherto unprecedented, its officers were sent to be criminally tried at Rome ; and the Molossians in Epirus were forced by false suspicions into actual revolt.

he allied states had war-contributions imposed upon them as
if they had been conquered, and if they appealed to the Roman
ᴣnate, their citizens were executed or sold into slavery:
his was done, for instance, at Abdera, and similar out-
ᴨges were committed at Chalcis. The senate interfered in
ᴀrnest: it enjoined the liberation of the unfortunate Coro-
ᴇans and Abderites, and forbade the Roman magistrates
ᴏ ask contributions from the allies without leave of the
ᴇnate. Gaius Lucretius was unanimously condemned by
ᴴe burgesses. But such steps could not alter the fact, that the
ᴨilitary result of these first two campaigns had been null,
ᴡhile the political result had been a foul stain on the Romans,
ᴡhose extraordinary successes in the East were based in no
ᴍall degree on their reputation for moral purity and sound-
ᴫess as compared with the scandals of Hellenic adminis-
ᴛation. Had Philip commanded instead of Perseus, the
ᴡar would probably have begun with the destruction of the
ᴿoman army and the defection of most of the Hellenes; but
ᴿome was fortunate enough to be constantly outstripped in her
ᴘlunders by her antagonists. Perseus was content with en-
ᴛrenching himself in Macedonia—which towards the south and
ᴡest is a true mountain-fortress—as in a beleaguered town.

The third commander-in-chief also, whom Rome sent to
Macedonia in 585, Quintus Marcius Philippus, already men-
ᴛioned as having honourable relations of hospitality with the
ᴋing, was not at all equal to his far from easy task. He was
ᴀmbitious and enterprising, but a bad officer. His hazard-
ᴏus scheme of crossing Olympus by the pass of Lapathus
ᴡestward of Tempe, leaving behind one division to face the
ᴦarrison of the pass, and making his way with his main force
ᴛhrough impracticable defiles to Heracleum, was not justified
ᴃy the fact of its success. Not only might a handful of reso-
ᴌute men have blocked up the route, in which case retreat was
ᴏut of the question; but even after the passage, when he
ᴤtood with the Macedonian main force in front and the
ᴤtrongly fortified mountain-fortresses of Tempe and Lapa-
ᴛhus behind him, wedged into a narrow plain on the sea-
ᴤhore and without supplies or the possibility of foraging for
them, his position was no less desperate than when, in his
first consulate, he had allowed himself to be similarly sur-

Marcius
en-   [169.
ters Mace-
donia
through
the pass of
Tempe.

rounded in the Ligurian defiles which thenceforth bore hi
name. But as an accident saved him then, so the incapacit
of Perseus saved him now. As if he could not comprehend th
idea of defending himself against the Romans otherwise tha
by the blockading of the passes, he strangely gave himsel
over as lost as soon as he saw the Romans on the Mace
donian side of them, fled in all haste to Pydna, and ordered
his ships to be burnt and his treasures to be sunk. But ever
this voluntary retreat of the Macedonian army did not rescu
the consul from his painful position. He advanced indeed
without hindrance, but he was obliged after four days' march
to turn back for want of provisions; and, when the king
came to his senses and returned in all haste to resume the
position which he had abandoned, the Roman army would
have been in great danger, had not the impregnable Tempe
surrendered at the right moment and handed over its rich
stores to the enemy. The communication with the south
was by this means secured to the Roman army; but Perseus
had strongly barricaded himself in his former well-chosen
position on the bank of the little river Elpius, and there
checked the farther advance of the Romans. So the Roman
army remained, during the rest of the summer and the winter, hemmed in in the farthest corner of Thessaly; and, while
the crossing of the passes was certainly a success and the
first substantial one in the war, it was due not to the ability
of the Roman, but to the blundering of the Macedonian,
general. The Roman fleet in vain attempted the capture of
Demetrias, and performed no exploit whatever. The light
ships of Perseus boldly cruised between the Cyclades, protected the corn-vessels destined for Macedonia, and attacked
the transports of the enemy. With the western army matters were still worse: Appius Claudius could do nothing
with his reduced division, and the contingent which he asked
from Achaia was prevented from coming to him by the
jealousy of the consul. Moreover, Genthius had allowed
himself to be bribed by Perseus with the promise of a great
sum of money to break with Rome, and to imprison the Roman
envoys; whereupon the frugal king deemed it superfluous
to pay the money which he had promised, since Genthius
was now forsooth compelled, independently of it, to substi-

The armies on the Elpius.

tute an attitude of decided hostility to Rome for the ambiguous position which he had hitherto maintained. Accordingly the Romans had a further petty war by the side of the great one, which had already lasted three years. In fact had Perseus been able to part with his money, he might easily have aroused enemies still more dangerous to the Romans. A Celtic host under Clondicus—10,000 horsemen and as many infantry—offered to take service with him in Macedonia itself; but they could not agree as to the pay. In Hellas too there was such a ferment that a guerilla warfare might easily have been kindled with a little dexterity and a full exchequer; but, as Perseus had no desire to give and the Greeks did nothing gratuitously, the land remained quiet.

At length the Romans resolved to send the right man to Greece. This was Lucius Aemilius Paullus, son of the consul of the same name that fell at Cannae; a man of the old nobility but of humble means, and therefore not so successful in the comitia as on the battle-field, where he had remarkably distinguished himself in Spain and still more so in Liguria. The people elected him for the second time consul in the year 586 on account of his merits—a course which was at that time rare and exceptional. He was in all respects the fitting man: an excellent general of the old school, strict as respected both himself and his troops, and, notwithstanding his sixty years, still hale and vigorous; an incorruptible magistrate—" one of the few Romans of that age to whom one could not offer money," as a contemporary says of him— and a man of Hellenic culture, who, when commander-in-chief, embraced the opportunity of travelling through Greece to inspect its works of art.

As soon as the new general arrived in the camp at Heracleum, he gave orders for the ill-guarded pass at Pythium to be surprised by Publius Nasica, while skirmishes between the outposts occupied the attention of the Macedonians in the channel of the river Elpius; the enemy was thus turned, and was obliged to retreat to Pydna. There, on the Roman 4th of September, 586, or on the 22nd of June of the Julian calendar—an eclipse of the moon, which a scientific Roman officer announced beforehand to the army that it might not be regarded as a bad omen, affords in this case the means

Margin notes:

Paullus.

168.

Perseus is driven back to Pydna.

Battle of Pydna. 168.

of determining the date—the outposts accidentally fell into conflict as they were watering their horses after midday; and both sides determined at once to give the battle, which it was originally intended to postpone till the following day.   Passing through the ranks in person, without helmet or shield, the grey-headed Roman general arranged his men.   Scarce were they in position, when the formidable phalanx assailed them; the general himself, who had witnessed many a hard fight, afterwards acknowledged that he had trembled.   The Roman vanguard dispersed; a Paelignian cohort was overthrown and almost annihilated; the legions themselves hurriedly retreated till they reached a hill close upon the Roman camp.   Here the fortune of the day changed. The uneven ground and the hurried pursuit had disordered the ranks of the phalanx; the Romans in single cohorts entered at every gap, and attacked it on the flanks and in rear; the Macedonian cavalry which alone could have rendered aid looked calmly on, and soon fled in a body, the king among the foremost; and thus the fate of Macedonia was decided in less than an hour.   The 3000 select phalangites allowed themselves to be cut down to a man; as if the phalanx, which fought its last great battle at Pydna, had itself wished to perish there.   The overthrow was fearful; 20,000 Macedonians lay on the field of battle, 11,000 were prisoners. The war was at an end, on the fifteenth day after Paullus had assumed the command; all Macedonia submitted in two days. The king fled with his gold—he still had more than 6000 talents (£1,460,000) in his chest—to Samothrace, accompanied by a few faithful attendants.   But he himself put to death one of these, Evander of Crete, who was to be called to account as instigator of the attempted assassination of Eumenes; and then his pages and remaining comrades also deserted him.   For a moment he hoped that the right of asylum would protect him; but he soon perceived that he was clinging to a straw.   An attempt to take flight to Cotys failed. So he wrote to the consul; but the letter was not received, because he had designated himself in it as king.   He recognized his fate, and surrendered to the Romans at discretion with his children and his treasures, pusillanimous and weeping so as to disgust even his conquerors.   With a grave satisfac-

Perseus
taken
prisoner.

tion, and with thoughts turning rather on the mutability
of fortune than on his own present success, the consul received the most illustrious captive whom Roman general had
ever brought home.   Perseus died a few years after, as a
state prisoner, at Alba on the Fucine lake ;* his son in after
years earned a living in the same Italian country town as a
clerk.

Thus perished the empire of Alexander the Great, which
had subdued and Hellenized the East, 144 years after his
death.

That the tragedy, moreover, might not be without its accompaniment of farce, at the same time the war against
" king " Genthius of Illyria was also begun and ended by the
praetor Lucius Anicius within thirty days.   The piratical fleet
was taken, the capital Scodra was captured, and the two
kings, the heir of Alexander the Great and the heir of Pleuratus, entered Rome side by side as prisoners.

*Defeat and
capture of
Genthius.*

The senate had resolved that the peril, which the unseasonable gentleness of Flamininus had brought on Rome,
should not recur.   Macedonia was abolished.   In the conference at Amphipolis on the Strymon the Roman commission ordained that the compact, thoroughly monarchical, and
united state should be broken up into four republican federative leagues moulded on the system of the Greek confederacies, viz., that of Amphipolis in the eastern provinces, that
of Thessalonica with the Chalcidian peninsula, that of Pella
on the frontiers of Thessaly, and that of Pelagonia in the interior.   Intermarriages between persons belonging to different
confederacies were to be invalid, and no one might be a free-
holder in more than one of them.   All who had held office under the king, as well as their grown-up sons, were obliged to
leave the country and proceed to Italy on pain of death ; the
Romans still dreaded, and with reason, the throbbings of
the ancient loyalty.   The law of the land and the former constitution otherwise remained in force ; the magistrates were
of course nominated by election in each community, and the
power in the communities as well as in the confederacies was

*Macedonia
broken up.*

---

* The story, that the Romans, in order at once to keep the promise which
had guaranteed his life and to take vengeance on him, put him to death by depriving him of sleep, is certainly a fable.

placed in the hands of the upper class. The royal domains and
royalties were not granted to the confederacies, and these were
specially prohibited from working the gold and silver mines,
a chief source of the national wealth ; but in 596 they were
again permitted to work at least the silver-mines.* The importation of salt, and the exportation of timber for ship-building, were prohibited. The land-tax hitherto paid to the king
ceased, and the confederacies and communities were left to tax
themselves ; but these had to pay to Rome half of the former
land-tax, according to a rate fixed once for all, amounting in
all to 100 talents annually (£24,000).† The whole land was
for ever disarmed, and the fortress of Demetrias was razed ;
on the northern frontier alone a chain of posts was to be
retained to guard against the incursions of the barbarians.
Of the arms given up, the copper shields were sent to Rome,
and the rest were burnt.

The Romans gained their object. The Macedonian land
still on two occasions took up arms at the call of princes of
the old reigning house ; but otherwise from that time to the
present day it has remained without a history.

Illyria broken up.

Illyria was treated in a similar way. The kingdom of
Genthius was split up into three small free states. There too
the freeholders paid the half of the former land-tax to their
new masters, with the exception of the towns, which had
adhered to Rome and in return obtained exemption from the
tax—an exception which there was no opportunity to make
in the case of Macedonia. The Illyrian piratic fleet was confiscated, and presented to the more reputable Greek com-

---

* The statement of Cassiodorus, that
the Macedonian mines were reopened in
596, receives its more exact interpretation by means of the coins. No gold
coins of the four Macedonias are extant ;
either therefore the gold-mines remained
closed, or the gold extracted was converted into bars. On the other hand
there certainly exist silver coins of Macedonia *prima* (Amphipolis) in which
district the silver-mines were situated.
For the brief period, during which they
must have been struck (596-608), the
number of them is remarkably great,
and proves either that the mines were
very energetically wrought, or that the
old royal money was recoined in large
quantity.

† The statement that the Macedonian
commonwealth was "relieved of seignorial imposts and taxes" by the Romans
(Polyb. xxxvii. 4) does not necessarily
require us to assume a subsequent remission of these taxes : it is sufficient,
for the explanation of Polybius' words,
to assume that the hitherto seignorial
tax now became a public one. The continuance of the constitution granted to
the province of Macedonia by Paullus
down to at least the Augustan age (Liv.
xlv. 32 ; Justin xxxiii. 2), would, it is
true, be compatible also with the remission of the taxes.

munities along that coast.   The constant annoyances, which
the Illyrians inflicted on their neighbours by means of their
corsairs, were in this way put an end to, at least for a lengthened period.

Cotys in Thrace, who was difficult to be reached and might   Cotys.
conveniently be used against Eumenes, obtained pardon and
received back his captive son.

Thus the affairs of the north were settled, and Macedonia
also was at last released from the yoke of monarchy.   In
fact Greece was more free than ever ; a king no longer existed
anywhere.

But the Romans did not confine themselves to cutting the   Humilia-
nerves and sinews of Macedonia.   The senate resolved at   tion of the
                                                           Greeks in
once to render all the Hellenic states, friend and foe, for   general.
ever incapable of harm, and to reduce all of them alike to
the same humble state of dependence.   The course pursued
may itself admit of justification ; but the mode in which it was
carried out in the case of the more powerful of the Greek
dependent states was unworthy of a great power, and showed
that the epoch of the Fabii and the Scipios was at an end.

The state most affected by this change in the position of   Course pur-
parties was the kingdom of the Attalids, which had been   sued with
                                                          Pergamus.
created and fostered by Rome to keep Macedonia in check,
and which now, after the destruction of Macedonia, was forsooth no longer needed.   It was not easy to find a tolerable
pretext for depriving the prudent and considerate Eumenes of his privileged position, and allowing him to fall into
disgrace.   All at once, about the time when the Romans
were encamped at Heracleum, strange reports were circulated regarding him—that he was in secret intercourse with
Perseus ; that his fleet had been suddenly, as it were, wafted
away ; that 500 talents had been offered for his non-partici-
pation in the campaign and 1500 for his mediation to procure peace, and that the agreement had only broken down
through the avarice of Perseus.   As to the Pergamene fleet,
the king, after having paid his respects to the consul, went
home with it at the same time that the Roman fleet went into
winter quarters.   The story about corruption was as certainly
a fable as any newspaper *canard* of the present day ; for that
the rich, cunning, and consistent Attalid, who had primarily

occasioned the breach between Rome and Macedonia by his
journey in 582 and had been on that account wellnigh assassi-
nated by the banditti of Perseus, should—at the moment when
the real difficulties of the war were overcome and its final
issue, if ever seriously doubted at all, was doubtful no longer
—have sold to the instigator of his murder his share in the
spoil for a few talents, and should have perilled the work of
long years for so pitiful a consideration, may be set down not
merely as a fabrication, but as a very silly one.   That no
proof was found either in the papers of Perseus or elsewhere, is sufficiently certain ; for even the Romans did not
venture to express those suspicions aloud.   But they gained
their object.   Their intentions were shown in the behaviour
of the Roman grandees towards Attalus, the brother of
Eumenes, who had commanded the Pergamene auxiliary
troops in Greece.   Their brave and faithful comrade was
received in Rome with open arms and invited to ask not for
his brother, but for himself—the senate would be glad to
give him a kingdom of his own.   Attalus asked nothing but
Aenus and Maronea.   The senate thought that this was
only a preliminary request, and granted it with great politeness.   But when he took his departure without having
made any further demands, and the senate came to perceive
that the reigning family in Pergamus did not live on such
terms with each other as were usual in princely houses,
Aenus and Maronea were declared free cities.   The Pergamenes obtained not a single foot of territory out of the spoil of
Macedonia ; if after the victory over Antiochus the Romans
had still saved forms as respected Philip, they were now disposed to hurt and to humiliate.   About this time the senate
appears to have declared Pamphylia, for the possession of
which Eumenes and Antiochus had hitherto contended, independent.   What was of more importance, the Galatians
—who had been substantially in the power of Eumenes, ever
since he had expelled the king of Pontus by force of arms
from Galatia and had on making peace extorted from him
the promise that he would maintain no further communication with the Galatian princes—now, reckoning beyond
doubt on the variance that had taken place between Eumenes
and the Romans, if not directly instigated by the latter, rose

172.

against Eumenes, overran his kingdom, and brought him into
great danger.   Eumenes besought the mediation of the
Romans; the Roman envoy declared his readiness to mediate, but thought it better that Attalus, who commanded
the Pergamene army, should not accompany him lest the barbarians might be put in ill humour.   Singularly enough, he
accomplished nothing; in fact, he told on his return that
his mediation had only exasperated the barbarians.   No long
time elapsed before the independence of the Galatians was
expressly recognized and guaranteed by the senate.   Eumenes
determined to proceed to Rome in person, and to plead his
cause in the senate.   But the latter, as if troubled by an evil
conscience, suddenly decreed that in future no kings should
be allowed to come to Rome; and despatched a quaestor to
meet him at Brundisium, to lay before him this decree of the
senate, to ask him what he wanted, and to hint to him that
they would be glad to hear of his speedy departure.   The king
was long silent; at length he said that he desired nothing
farther, and re-embarked.   He saw how matters stood : the
epoch of half-powerful and half-free alliance was at an end ;
that of impotent subjection began.

Similar treatment befel the Rhodians.   They had been
singularly favoured : their relation to Rome assumed the
form not of symmachy properly so called, but of friendship
and equality ; they were not prevented from entering into
alliances of any kind, and they were not compelled to supply
the Romans with a contingent on demand.   This very circumstance was probably the real reason why their good
understanding with Rome had already for some time been
impaired.   The first dissensions with Rome had arisen in
consequence of the rising of the Lycians, who were handed
over to Rhodes after the defeat of Antiochus, against their
oppressors who had (576) cruelly reduced them to slavery as
revolted subjects ; the Lycians, however, asserted that they
were not subjects but allies of the Rhodians, and prevailed
with this plea in the Roman senate, which was invited
to settle the doubtful meaning of the instrument of peace.
But in this result a justifiable sympathy with the victims of
grievous oppression had perhaps the chief share ; at least
nothing further was done on the part of the Romans, who

*Humilia-
tion of
Rhodes.*

178.

left this as well as other Hellenic quarrels to take their
course. When the war with Perseus broke out, the Rhodians, like all other sensible Greeks, viewed it with regret,
and blamed Eumenes in particular as the instigator of it,
so that his festal embassy was not even permitted to be
present at the festival of Helios in Rhodes. But this did
not prevent them from adhering to Rome and keeping the
Macedonian party, which existed in Rhodes as well as
everywhere else, aloof from the helm of affairs. The permission given to them in 585 to export grain from Sicily
shows the continuance of the good understanding with Rome.
All of a sudden, shortly before the battle of Pydna, Rhodian
envoys appeared at the Roman head-quarters and in the
Roman senate, announcing that the Rhodians would no
longer tolerate this war which was injurious to their Macedonian traffic and the revenues of their ports, that they were
disposed themselves to declare war against the party which
should refuse to make peace, and that with this view they
had already concluded an alliance with Crete and with the
Asiatic cities. Many caprices are possible in a republic
governed by popular assemblies; but this insane intervention
on the part of a commercial city—which can only have been
resolved on after the fall of the pass of Tempe was known at
Rhodes—requires special explanation. The key to it is furnished by the well-attested account that the consul Quintus
Marcius, that master of the " new-fashioned diplomacy," had
in the camp at Heracleum (and therefore after the occupation of the pass of Tempe) loaded the Rhodian envoy Age-
polis with civilities and made an underhand request to him
to mediate a peace. Republican vanity and folly did the
rest; the Rhodians fancied that the Romans had abandoned
all hope of success; they were eager to play the part of
mediator among four great powers at once; communications were entered into with Perseus; Rhodian envoys with
Macedonian sympathies said more than they should have
said; and they were caught. The senate, which doubtless
was itself for the most part unaware of such intrigues, heard
the strange announcement with natural indignation, and
was glad of the favourable opportunity to humble the
haughty merchant city. A warlike praetor went even so

far as to propose to the people a declaration of war against
Rhodes. In vain the Rhodian ambassadors repeatedly on
their knees adjured the senate to think of the friendship
of a hundred and forty years rather than of the one offence;
in vain they sent the heads of the Macedonian party to the
scaffold or to Rome; in vain they sent a massive wreath of
gold in token of their gratitude for the non-declaration of
war. The honourable Cato indeed showed that strictly the
Rhodians had committed no offence, and asked whether the
Romans were desirous to undertake the punishment of wishes
and thoughts, and whether they could blame the nations for
being apprehensive that Rome might allow herself all licence
if she had no longer any one to fear? His words and warn-
ings were in vain. The senate deprived the Rhodians of
their possessions on the mainland, which yielded a yearly
produce of 120 talents (£29,000). Still heavier were the
blows aimed at the Rhodian commerce. The prohibition of
the import of salt to, and of the export of ship-building
timber from, Macedonia appears to have been directed
against Rhodes. Rhodian commerce was still more directly
affected by the erection of the free port at Delos; the
Rhodian customs-dues, which hitherto had produced 1,000,000
drachmae (£41,000) annually, sank in a very brief period to
150,000 *drachmae* (£6,180). Generally, the Rhodians were
paralyzed in their freedom of action and in their liberal and
bold commercial policy, and the state began to languish.
Even the alliance asked for was at first refused, and was
only renewed in 590 after urgent entreaties. The equally   164.
guilty but powerless Cretans escaped with a sharp rebuke.

  With Syria and Egypt the Romans could go to work more   Interven-
summarily. War had broken out between them; and Coele-   tion in the
syria and Palaestina formed once more the subject of dispute.   Syro-
                                                            Egyptian
According to the assertion of the Egyptians, those provinces   war.
had been ceded to Egypt on the marriage of the Syrian
Cleopatra: this however the court of Babylon, which was
in actual possession, disputed. Apparently the charging of
her dowry on the taxes of the Coelesyrian cities gave occasion to the quarrel, and the Syrian side was in the right;
the breaking out of the war was occasioned by the death of
Cleopatra in 581, with which at latest the payments of   173.

revenue terminated. The war appears to have been begun by Egypt; but king Antiochus Epiphanes gladly embraced the opportunity of once more—and for the last time—endeavouring to achieve the traditional aim of the policy of the Seleucidae, the acquisition of Egypt, while the Romans were employed in Macedonia. Fortune seemed favourable to him. The king of Egypt at that time, Ptolemy VI. Philometor, the son of Cleopatra, had hardly passed the age of boyhood and had bad advisers; after a great victory on the Syro-Egyptian frontier Antiochus was able to advance into the territories of his nephew in the same year in which the legions landed in Greece (583), and soon had the person of the king in his power. Matters began to look as if Antiochus wished to possess himself of all Egypt in Philometor's name; Alexandria accordingly closed its gates against him, deposed Philometor, and nominated as king in his stead his younger brother, Euergetes II., named the Fat. Disturbances in his own kingdom recalled the Syrian king from Egypt; when he returned, he found that the brothers had come to an understanding during his absence; and he then continued the war against both. Just as he lay before Alexandria, not long after the battle of Pydna (586), the Roman envoy Gaius Popillius, a harsh rude man, arrived, and intimated to him the command of the senate that he should restore all that he had conquered and should evacuate Egypt within a set term. Antiochus asked time for consideration; but the consular drew with his staff a circle round the king, and bade him declare his intentions before he stepped beyond the circle. Antiochus replied that he would comply; and marched off to his capital that he might there, in his character of "the god, the brilliant bringer of victory," celebrate in Roman fashion his conquest of Egypt and parody the triumph of Paullus.

Egypt voluntarily submitted to the Roman protectorate; and thereupon the kings of Babylon also desisted from the last effort to maintain their independence against Rome. Like Macedonia in the war waged by Perseus, the Seleucidae in the war regarding Coelesyria had made a final effort to recover their earlier power; but it is a significant indication of the difference between the two kingdoms, that in the former case the legions, in the latter the abrupt language of a diplomatist, decided the controversy.

In Greece itself, as the two Boeotian cities had already paid more than a sufficient penalty, the Molottians alone remained to be punished as allies of Perseus. Acting on secret orders from the senate, Paullus in one day gave up seventy townships in Epirus to plunder, and sold the inhabitants, 150,000 in number, into slavery. The Aetolians lost Amphipolis, and the Acarnanians Leucas, on account of their equivocal behaviour; whereas the Athenians, who continued to play the part of the begging poet in their own Aristophanes, not only obtained a gift of Delos and Lemnos, but were not ashamed even to petition for the deserted site of Haliartus, which was assigned to them accordingly. Thus something was done for the Muses; but more had to be done for justice.   There was a Macedonian party in every city, and therefore trials for high treason began in all parts of Greece. Whoever had served in the army of Perseus was immediately executed; whoever was compromised by the papers of the king or the statements of political opponents who flocked to lodge informations, was despatched to Rome ; the Achaean Callicrates and the Aetolian Lyciscus distinguished themselves in the trade of informers.   In this way the more conspicuous patriots among the Thessalians, Aetolians, Acarnanians, Lesbians and so forth, were removed from their native land ; and, in particular, more than a thousand Achaeans were thus disposed of—a step taken with the view not so much of prosecuting those who were carried off, as of silencing the childish opposition of the Hellenes.   To the Achaeans, who, as usual, were not content till they got the answer which they anticipated, the senate, wearied by constant requests for the commencement of the investigation, at length roundly declared that till further orders the persons concerned were to remain in Italy.   There they were placed in country towns in the interior, and tolerably well treated ; but attempts to escape were punished with death.   The position of the former officials removed from Macedonia was, in all probability, similar. This expedient, violent as it was, was still, as things stood, the most lenient, and the enraged Greeks of the Roman party were far from

Measures
of security
in Greece.

content with the paucity of the executions. Lyciscus had accordingly deemed it proper to have some 500 of the leading men of the Aetolian patriotic party slain at the meeting of the diet; the Roman commission, which had occasion for the man, suffered the deed to pass unpunished, and merely censured the employment of Roman soldiers in the execution of such Hellenic justice. We may presume, however, that the Romans instituted the system of deportation to Italy partly in order to prevent such horrors. As in Greece proper no power existed even of such importance as Rhodes or Pergamus, there was no need in its case for any further humiliation; the steps taken were taken only in the exercise of justice—in the Roman sense, no doubt, of that term—and for the prevention of the most scandalous and palpable outbreaks of party discord.

Rome and her dependencies.

All the Hellenistic states had thus been completely subjected to the protectorate of Rome, and the whole empire of Alexander the Great had fallen to the Roman commonwealth just as if the city had inherited it from his heirs. From all sides kings and ambassadors flocked to Rome to congratulate her; and they showed that fawning is never more abject than when kings are in the antechamber. King Massinissa, who only desisted from presenting himself in person on being expressly prohibited from doing so, ordered his son to declare that he regarded himself as merely the usufructuary, and the Romans as the true proprietors, of his kingdom, and that he would always be content with what they were willing to leave to him. There was at least truth in this. But Prusias king of Bithynia, who had to atone for his neutrality, bore off the palm in this contest of flattery; he fell on his face when he was conducted into the senate, and did homage to "the delivering gods." As he was so thoroughly contemptible, Polybius tells us, they gave him a courteous reply, and presented him with the fleet of Perseus.

The moment was at least well chosen for such homage. Polybius dates from the battle of Pydna the full establishment of the universal empire of Rome. It was in fact the last battle in which a civilized state confronted Rome in the field on a footing of equality with her as a great power; all

ubsequent struggles were rebellions or wars with peoples
beyond the pale of the Romano-Greek civilization—the barbarians, as they were called. The whole civilized world
henceforth recognized in the Roman senate the supreme
tribunal, whose commissioners decided in the last resort
between kings and nations; and to acquire its language and
manners foreign princes and youths of quality resided in
Rome. A clear and earnest attempt to get rid of her dominion was in reality made only once—by the great Mithradates of Pontus. The battle of Pydna, moreover, marks the
last occasion on which the senate still adhered to the state-
maxim that they should, if possible, hold no possessions
and maintain no garrisons beyond the Italian seas, but
should keep the numerous states dependent on them in order
by a mere political supremacy. The aim of their policy was
that these states should neither decline into utter weakness
and anarchy, as had nevertheless happened in Greece, nor
emerge out of their half-free position into complete independence, as Macedonia had attempted to do not without success. No state was to be allowed utterly to perish, but no
one was to be permitted to stand on its own resources. Accordingly the vanquished foe held at least an equal, often a
better, position with the Roman diplomatists than the faithful ally; and, while a defeated opponent was reinstated, those
who attempted to reinstate themselves were abased—as the
Aetolians, Macedonia after the Asiatic war, Rhodes, and
Pergamus learned by experience. But not only did this part
of protector soon prove as irksome to the masters as to the
servants; the Roman protectorate, with its ungrateful Sisy-
phian toil that continually needed to be begun afresh, showed
itself to be intrinsically untenable. Indications of a change
of system, and of an increasing disinclination on the part
of Rome to tolerate by its side intermediate states even
in such independence as was possible for them, were very
clearly given in the destruction of the Macedonian monarchy
after the battle of Pydna. The more and more frequent and
more and more unavoidable intervention in the internal
affairs of the petty Greek states through their misgovernment
and their political and social anarchy; the disarming of
Macedonia, where the northern frontier at any rate urgently

required a defence different from that of mere posts; and
lastly, the introduction of the payment of land-tax to Rom
from Macedonia and Illyria, were so many symptoms of th
approaching conversion of the client states into subjects o
Rome.

The Ita-
lian and
extra-Ita-
lian policy
of Rome.

If, in conclusion, we glance back at the career of Rom
from the union of Italy to the dismemberment of Macedonia
the universal empire of Rome, far from appearing as a gigan
tic plan contrived and carried out by an insatiable thirs
for territorial aggrandisement, appears to have been a re
sult which forced itself on the Roman government without
and even in opposition to, its wish. It is true that the
former view naturally suggests itself. Sallust is right when
he makes Mithradates say that the wars of Rome with tribes
cities, and kings originated in one and the same prime cause
the insatiable longing after dominion and riches; but it is an
error to give forth this judgment—shaped thus by passion
and the issue—as an historical fact. It is evident to every
one whose observation is not superficial, that the Roman
government during this whole period wished and desired
nothing but the sovereignty of Italy; that they were simply
desirous not to have too powerful neighbours alongside of
them; and that—not out of humanity towards the vanquished, but from the very sound view that they ought not to
suffer the kernel of their empire to be crushed by the shell—
they earnestly opposed the introduction first of Africa, then
of Greece, and lastly of Asia into the pale of the Roman protectorate, till circumstances in each case compelled, or at
least suggested with irresistible force, the extension of that
pale. The Romans always asserted that they did not pursue
a policy of conquest, and that they were always the assailed
rather than the assailants; and this was something more, at
any rate, than a mere phrase. They were in fact driven to
all their great wars with the exception of that concerning
Sicily—to those with Hannibal and Antiochus, no less than
to those with Philip and Perseus—either by a direct aggres-
sion or by an unparalleled disturbance of the existing political relations; and hence they were ordinarily taken by
surprise on their outbreak. That they did not after victory
exhibit the moderation which they ought to have done in the

nterest more especially of Italy itself; that the retention of pain, for instance, the undertaking of the guardianship of Africa, and above all the half-fanciful scheme of conferring berty everywhere on the Greeks, were in the light of Italian olicy grave errors, is sufficiently clear. But the causes of hese errors were, on the one hand a blind dread of Carthage, on the other a still blinder enthusiasm for Hellenistic liberty; o little did the Romans exhibit during this period the lust f conquest, that they, on the contrary, displayed a very judicious dread of its effects. The policy of Rome throughout was not projected by a single mighty intellect and bequeathed by tradition from generation to generation; it was the policy of a very able but somewhat narrow-minded deliberative assembly, which had far too little power of grand combination, and far too much of an instinctive desire for the preservation of its own commonwealth, to devise projects in the spirit of a Cæsar or a Napoleon. The universal empire of Rome had its ultimate ground in the political development of antiquity in general. The ancient world knew nothing of a balance of power among nations; and therefore every nation which had attained internal unity strove either directly to subdue its neighbours, as did the Hellenic states, or at any rate to render them innocuous, as Rome did,—an effort, it is true, which also issued at last in subjugation. Egypt was perhaps the only great power in antiquity which seriously pursued the system of equilibrium: on the opposite system Seleucus and Antigonus, Hannibal and Scipio came into collision. And, however melancholy may seem the fact that all the other richly endowed and highly developed nations of antiquity had to perish in order to enrich a single people, as if the ultimate object of their existence had simply been to contribute to the greatness of Italy and to the decay involved in that greatness; yet historical justice must acknowledge that this result was not produced by the military superiority of the legion over the phalanx, but was the necessary consequence of the international relations of antiquity generally— so that the issue was not decided by provoking chance, but was the fulfilment of an unchangeable, and therefore endurable, destiny.

CHAPTER XI.

THE GOVERNMENT AND THE GOVERNED.

Formation of new parties.

THE fall of the patriciate by no means divested the Roman commonwealth of its aristocratic character. We have already (i. 336) indicated that the plebeian party carried within it that character from the first as well as, and in some sense still more decidedly than, the patriciate; for, while in the old body of burgesses an absolute equality of rights prevailed, the new constitution set out with a distinction between the senatorial houses who were privileged in point of burgess rights and of burgess usufructs, and the mass of the other citizens. Immediately, therefore, on the abolition of the patriciate and the formal establishment of civic equality, a new aristocracy and a corresponding opposition were formed; and we have already shown how the former engrafted itself as it were on the fallen patriciate, and how, accordingly, the first movements of the new party of progress were mixed up with the last movements of the old plebeian opposition (i. 337). The formation of these new parties began in the fifth century, but they assumed their definite shape only in the century which followed. The development of this change is, as it were, drowned amidst the noise of the great wars and victories, and the process of formation is in this case more concealed from our view than in any other in Roman history. Like a crust of ice gathering imperceptibly over the surface of a stream and imperceptibly confining it more and more, this new Roman aristocracy silently arose; and not less imperceptibly, like the concealed current slowly swelling beneath, there arose in opposition to it the new party of progress. It is very difficult to sum up in a general historical view the several, individually insignificant, traces of these two antagonistic movements which do not for the present culminate in any distinct practical catas-

trophe. But the freedom hitherto enjoyed in the commonwealth was undermined, and the foundation for future revolutions was laid, during this epoch; and the delineation of
these as well as of the development of Rome in general would
remain imperfect, if we should fail to give some idea of the
thickness and strength of that encrusting ice, and of the
fearful moaning and cracking that foretold the mighty breaking up which was at hand.

The Roman nobility attached itself, in form, to earlier
institutions belonging to the times of the patriciate. Persons
who once had filled the highest ordinary magistracies of the
state not only, as a matter of course, practically enjoyed
all along a higher honour, but also had at an early period
certain honorary privileges associated with their position.
The most ancient of these was doubtless the permission given
to the descendants of such magistrates to place the wax images
of these illustrious ancestors after their death in the family
hall, along the wall where the pedigree was painted, and
to have these images carried, on occasion of the death of
members of the family, in the funeral procession (i. 319).
To appreciate the importance of this distinction, we must
recollect that the honouring of images was regarded in
the Italo-Hellenic view as unrepublican, and on that account
the Roman state-police did not at all tolerate the exhibition
of effigies of the living, and strictly superintended that
of effigies of the dead. With this privilege were associated
various external insignia, reserved by law or custom for such
magistrates and their descendants; the stripe of purple on
the tunic and the golden finger-ring of the men, the silver-
mounted trappings of the youths, the purple border on the
toga and the golden amulet-case of the boys*—trifling mat-

Germs of
the nobi-
lity in the
patriciate.

---

* All these insignia probably belonged
at first only to the nobility proper, *i. e.*
to the agnate descendants of curule magistrates; although, after the manner of
such decorations, all of them in course
of time were extended to a wider circle.
This can be distinctly proved in the case
of the gold finger-ring, which in the fifth
century was worn only by the nobility
(Plin. *H. N.*, xxxiii. 1, 18), in the sixth
by every senator and senator's son (Liv.
xxvi. 36), in the seventh by every one of
equestrian rank, under the empire by every

one who was of free birth. So also with
the silver trappings, which still, in the
second Punic war, formed a badge of the
nobility alone (Liv. xxvi. 36); and with
the purple border of the *toga*, which at
first was granted only to the sons of
curule magistrates, then to the sons of
equites, afterwards to those of all free-
born persons, lastly—yet as early as the
time of the second Punic war—even to
the sons of freedmen (Macrob. *Sat.* i. 6).
The purple stripe (*clavus*) on the tunic
can only be shown to have been a badge

ters, but still important in a community where civic equality in external appearance was so strictly adhered to (i. 335), and where, even during the second Punic war, a burgess was arrested and kept for years in prison because he had appeared in public, in a manner not sanctioned by law, with a garland of roses upon his head.*

Patricio-
plebeian
nobility.

These distinctions probably already existed in the main in the time of the patrician government, and, so long as families of higher and lower rank were distinguished within the patriciate, served as external insignia for the former. But they only acquired political importance in consequence of

367.

the change of constitution in 387, by which the plebeian families that attained the consulate were placed on a footing of equal privilege with the patrician families, all of whom were now probably entitled to carry images of their ancestors. Moreover, it was now settled that the offices of state to which these hereditary privileges were attached should include neither the lower nor the extraordinary magistracies nor the tribunate of the plebs, but merely the consulship, the praetorship which stood on the same level with it (i. 328), and the curule aedileship, which bore a part in the administration of public justice and consequently in the exercise of the sovereign powers of the state.† Although this plebeian nobility, in the strict sense of the term, could only be formed after the curule offices were opened to plebeians, yet it exhibited in a short time, if not at the very first, a certain

---

of the senators (i. 86) and equites, the former wearing it broad, the latter narrow: in like manner the golden amulet-case (*bulla*) is only mentioned as a badge of the children of senators in the time of the second Punic war (Macrob. *l.c.*; Liv. xxvi. 36), in that of Cicero as the badge of the children of the equestrian order (Cic. *Verr.* i. 58, 152), whereas children of inferior rank wore the leathern amulet (*lorum*). But these seem to be merely accidental gaps in tradition, and the *clavus* and *bulla* also appear at first to have been peculiar to the nobility strictly so-called alone.

* Plin. *H. N.* xxi. 3, 6. The right to appear crowned in public was acquired by distinction in war (Polyb. vi. 39, 9; Liv. x. 47); consequently, the wearing a crown without warrant was an offence

similar to the assumption, in the present day, of the badge of a military order of merit without due title.

† Thus there remained excluded the military tribunate with consular powers (i. 318), the proconsulship, the quaestorship, the tribunate of the people, and several others. As to the censorship, it does not appear, notwithstanding the curule chair of the censors (Liv. xl. 45; comp. xxvii. 8), to have been reckoned a curule office; for the later period, however, when only a man of consular standing could be made censor, the question has no practical importance. The plebeian aedileship certainly was not reckoned originally one of the curule magistracies (Liv. xxiii. 23); it may, however, have been subsequently included amongst them.

compactness of organization—doubtless because the germs
of such a nobility had long existed in the old senatorial plebeian families.   The result of the Licinian laws in reality
therefore amounted nearly to what we would now call the
creation of a batch of peers.   Now that the plebeian families ennobled by their curule ancestors were united into
one body with the patrician families and acquired a distinctive position and distinguished power in the commonwealth, the Romans had again arrived at the point whence
they had started; there was once more not merely a governing aristocracy and a hereditary nobility—both of which in
fact had never disappeared—but there was a governing
hereditary nobility, and the feud between the *gentes* in possession of the government and the commons rising in
revolt against the *gentes* could not but begin afresh.   And
matters very soon reached that stage.   The nobility was
not content with its honorary privileges which were matters
of comparative indifference, but strove after exclusive and
sole political power, and sought to convert the most important institutions of the state—the senate and the equestrian
order—from organs of the commonwealth into organs of the
plebeio-patrician aristocracy.

The dependence *de jure* of the Roman senate of the republic,
more especially of the larger patricio-plebeian senate, on the
magistracy had rapidly become lax, and had in fact been converted into independence.   The subordination of the public
magistracies to the state-council, introduced by the revolution
of 244 (i. 290) ; the transference of the right of summoning men
to the senate from the consul to the censor (i. 321) ; lastly,
and above all, the legal recognition of the right of those who
had been curule magistrates to a seat and vote in the senate
(i. 348), had converted the senate from a council summoned
by the magistrates and in many respects dependent on them
into a governing corporation virtually independent, and in a
certain sense filling up its own ranks ; for the two modes by
which its members obtained admission—election to a curule
office and summoning by the censor—were both virtually in
the power of the governing board itself.   The burgesses, no
doubt, at this epoch were still too independent to allow the
entire exclusion of non-nobles from the senate, and the nobility

The no-
bility in
possession
of the
senate.

510.

were perhaps still too prudent even to wish for this; but, owing to the strictly aristocratic gradations in the senate itself—in which those who had been curule magistrates were sharply distinguished, according to their respective classes of *consulares*, *praetorii*, and *aedilicii*, from the senators who had not entered the senate through a curule office and were therefore excluded from debate—the non-nobles, although they probably sat in considerable numbers in the senate, were reduced to an insignificant and comparatively uninfluential position in it, and the senate became substantially a mainstay of the nobility.

The nobility in possession of the equestrian centuries.

The institution of the equites was developed into a second, less important but yet far from unimportant, organ of the nobility. As the new hereditary nobility had not the power to usurp sole possession of the comitia, it necessarily became in the highest degree desirable that it should obtain at least a distinctive position in the representation of the community. In the assembly of the tribes there was no method of managing this; but the equestrian centuries under the Servian organization seemed as it were created for the very purpose. The 1800 horses which the community furnished *

---

* The current hypothesis, according to which the six centuries of the nobility alone amounted to 1200, and the whole equestrian force accordingly to 3600 horse, is not tenable. The method of determining the number of the equites by the number of duplications specified by the annalists is mistaken: in fact, each of these statements has originated and is to be explained by itself. But there is no evidence either for the first number, which is only found in the passage of Cicero, *De Rep.* ii. 20, acknowledged as erroneous even by the champions of this view, or for the second, which does not appear at all in ancient authors. In favour, on the other hand, of the hypothesis set forth in the text, we have, first of all, the number as indicated not by authorities, but by the institutions themselves; for it is certain that the century numbered 100 men, and there were originally three (i. 79), then six (i. 94), and lastly after the Servian reform eighteen (i.103), equestrian centuries. The deviations of the authorities from this view are only apparent. The one self-consistent tradition, which Becker has developed (ii. 1, 243), reckons not the eighteen patricio-plebeian, but the six patrician, centuries at 1800 men; and this has been manifestly followed by Livy, i. 36 (according to the reading which alone has manuscript authority, and which ought not to be corrected from Livy's particular estimates), and by Cicero *l. c.* (according to the only reading grammatically admissible, MDCCC.; see Becker, ii. 1, 244). But Cicero at the same time indicates very plainly, that in that statement he intended to describe the then existing amount of the Roman equites in general. The number of the whole body has therefore been transferred to the most prominent portion of it by a prolepsis, such as is common in the case of annalists not too much given to reflection: just in the same way 300 equites instead of 100 are assigned to the parent-community, including, by anticipation, the contingents of the Tities and the Luceres (Becker, ii. 1, 238). Lastly, the proposition of Cato (p. 66, Jordan), to raise the number of the horses of the equites to 2200, is as distinct a confirmation of the view proposed above, as it is a distinct refutation of the opposite view.

With this view what is known of the equestrian order under the empire very

were constitutionally disposed of likewise by the censors. It was, no doubt, the duty of these to make the selection on purely military grounds and at their musters to insist that all horsemen incapacitated by age or otherwise, or at all unserviceable, should surrender their public horse; but the very nature of the institution implied that the cavalry-horses should be given especially to men of means, and it

well accords. It was divided into *turmae*, that is, divisions of 30 or 33 men (Marquardt, iii. 2, 258). The slight traces of a division of the cavalry not merely by *turmae*, but at the same time also by tribes (Becker, ii. 1, 261, note 538; and Zonaras, x. 35, p. 421, Bonn: ἵλαρχος τῆς φυλῆς = *sevir eq. R.*), cannot be satisfactorily cleared up; the relation too of the *turma* to the centuries is not quite clear, but cannot well be conceived otherwise than that three *turmae* went to the century. This would accordingly give 54 *turmae*, which number, as all the Roman equites were certainly divided into *turmae*, is doubtless rather too small than too large. Moreover it is self-evident that we have here to do merely with the normal number; by the addition of supernumeraries the number of the equites subsequently far exceeded that normal one. The whole number of the *turmae* is not given by tradition; for, while inscriptions exhibit only the earlier numbers as far as the fifth or sixth, the prominence of these is to be explained simply from the special repute in which the first *turmae* were held—a circumstance which may be compared with the fact that in inscriptions we meet only with the *tribunus a populo* and *laticlavius*, and the *iudex quadringenarius*, never with the *tribunus rufulus* and *angusticlavius*, or the *iudex ducenarius*. There is no reasonable ground for assuming an aggregate number of six *turmae*, and the fact that it is nevertheless the usual hypothesis (Becker, ii. 1, 261, 288) is solely due to an inference—not at all warranted —from the name of the leaders of the *turmae*, the *seviri equitum Romanorum*, to the number of *turmae* led by them. The Roman burgess-cavalry certainly had for a time six centuries under as many centurions or *tribuni celerum* (p. 79, 94); but, even if we should assume that this number was retained after the increase of the centuries from six to eighteen, the *seviri eq. Rom.* could not reasonably be regarded as identical with these *tribuni celerum*, since on the monuments throughout they appear in relation not to the cavalry in general, but to the individual *turmae*, as *seviri eq. Rom. turmae primae*, and so forth, in Greek ἵλαρχοι (Zonaras, x. 35, p. 421 Bonn), and are therefore to be explained not from the arrangement of the centuries, but from that of the *turmae*. In the latter accordingly we find what we are in search of: the six commanders assigned by the military arrangement to each *turma* (Polyb. vi. 25. 1), the *decuriones* and *optiones* of Cato (*Fr.* p. 39 Jordan), must just have been these *seviri*, and there must consequently have been six times as many *seviri* as the cavalry numbered squadrons. There is no evidence, although it is now usually assumed, that there was only one *sevir* in each *turma*: this hypothesis would in fact be decidedly opposed to the turmal arrangement. The objection stated by Henzen (Annali dell' Instituto, 1862, p. 142), that M. Aurelus gave the Seviral games as *sevir "cum collegis,"* by no means excludes the large number of *seviri* which we have assumed, for the colleagues mentioned might in fact very well be merely those of the same *turma*. It may be even reckoned probable that the *seviri* of the first *turma* enjoyed a special distinction, and the *principes iuventutis* were simply nothing else than the imperial princes acting as *seviri* of the first *turma*; the Seviral games, it may be conjectured, devolved exclusively on this *turma*. It is possible too that in later times the first *turmae* alone were formally organised and provided with *seviri*, while in the case of the other *equites equo publico* this subdivision was discontinued.

Leaving out of view the contingents of the Italian and extra-Italian subjects, the *equites equo publico* or *equites legionarii* alone composed the ordinary cavalry of the Roman army; where *equites equo privato* occur, the expression denotes bands of volunteers or of persons disrated.

was not at all easy to hinder the censors from looking to superior birth more than to capacity, and from allowing men of standing who were once admitted, senators particularly, to retain their horse beyond the proper time.   Accordingly it became practically the rule for the senators to vote in the eighteen equestrian centuries, and the other places in these were assigned chiefly to the younger men of the nobility. The military system, of course, suffered from this not so much through the unfitness for effective service of no small part of the legionary cavalry, as through the destruction of military equality to which the change gave rise; the young men of rank more and more withdrew from serving in the infantry, and the legionary cavalry became a close aristocratic corps.   This enables us in some degree to understand why the equites during the Sicilian war refused to obey the order of the consul Gaius Aurelius Cotta that they should work at

252.   the trenches with the legionaries (502), and why Cato, when commander of the army in Spain, found himself under the necessity of addressing a severe reprimand to his cavalry. But this conversion of the burgess-cavalry into a mounted guard of nobles redounded not more decidedly to the injury of the commonwealth than to the advantage of the nobility, which acquired in the eighteen equestrian centuries a suffrage not merely distinct but giving the key-note to the rest.

Separation of the orders in the theatre.

194.

Of a kindred character was the formal separation of the places assigned to the senatorial order from those occupied by the rest of the multitude as spectators at the national festivals.   It was the great Scipio, who effected this change in his second consulship in 560.   The national festival was as much an assembly of the people as were the centuries convoked for voting; and the circumstance that the former had no decrees to issue made the official announcement of a distinction between the ruling order and the body of subjects —which the separation implied—all the more significant. The innovation accordingly met with much censure even from the ruling class, because it was simply invidious and of no benefit, and because it gave a very obvious contradiction to the efforts of the wiser portion of the aristocracy to conceal their exclusive government under the forms of civil equality.

These circumstances explain, why the censorship became the pivot of the later republican constitution; why an office, originally unimportant and on a level with the quaestorship, came to be invested with external insignia which did not at all naturally belong to it and with an altogether unique aristocratico-republican glory, and was viewed as the crown and completion of a well-conducted public career; and why the government looked upon every attempt of the opposition to introduce their men into this office, or even to hold the censor responsible to the people for his administration during or after his term of office, as an attack on their palladium, and presented a united front of resistance to every such attempt. It is sufficient in this respect to mention the storm which the candidature of Cato for the censorship provoked, and the measures, so extraordinarily reckless and in violation of all form, by which the senate prevented the judicial prosecution of the two unpopular censors of the year 550. But with that enhancement of the glory of the censorship the government combined a characteristic distrust of this, their most important and for that very reason most dangerous, instrument. It was thoroughly necessary to leave to the censors absolute control over the personal composition of the senate and the equites; for the right of exclusion could not well be separated from the right of summoning, and it was desirable to retain such a right of exclusion not so much for the purpose of removing from the senate the able men of the opposition—a course which the smooth-going government of that age prudently avoided—as for the purpose of preserving around the aristocracy that moral halo, without which it must have speedily become a prey to the opposition. The right of rejection was retained; but what they chiefly needed was the glitter of the naked blade—the edge of it, which they feared, they took care to blunt. Besides the check involved in the nature of the office—under which the lists of the members of the aristocratic corporations were liable to revision not as formerly at any time, but only at intervals of five years—and besides the limitations resulting from the right of veto vested in the colleague and the right of cancelling vested in the successor, there was added a farther check which operated very powerfully; a

The censorship a prop of the nobility.

204

usage equivalent to law made it the duty of the censor, on erasing from the list any senator or knight, to specify in writing the grounds for his decision, and thus ordinarily to adopt what was tantamount to a judicial procedure.

Remodelling of the constitution according to the views of the nobility.

In this political position—mainly based on the senate, the equites, and the censorship—the nobility not only usurped in substance the government, but also remodelled the constitution according to their own views. It was part of their policy, with a view to keep up the importance of the public magistracies, to add to the number of these as little as possible, and to keep it far below what was required by the extension of territory and the increase of business. The most urgent exigencies were barely met by the division of the judicial functions hitherto discharged by a single praetor between two judges—one of whom tried the lawsuits between Roman burgesses, and the other those that arose between non-burgesses or between burgess and non-burgess—in 511, and by the nomination of four auxiliary consuls for the four transmarine provinces of Sicily (527), Sardinia including Corsica (527), and Hither and Further Spain (557). The far too summary mode of instituting processes in Rome, as well as the increasing influence of the official staff, are probably traceable in great measure to the practically inadequate numbers of the Roman magistracy.

Inadequate number of magistrates.

243.

227.

227. 197.

Election of officers in the comitia.

Among the innovations originated by the government—which were none the less innovations, that in general they changed not the letter, but merely the practice of the existing constitution—the most prominent were the measures by which the appointment of officers as well as of civil magistrates was made to depend not, as the letter of the constitution allowed and its spirit required, simply on merit and ability, but on birth and seniority. As regards the nomination of staff-officers this was done not in form, but in substance. It had already, during the previous period, been in great part transferred from the general to the burgesses (i. 340); during this period the whole staff-officers of the regular yearly levy—the twenty-four military tribunes of the four ordinary legions—came to be nominated in the *comitia tributa*. Thus a line of demarcation more and more insurmountable was drawn between the subalterns, who gained their promotion from the general by punctual and brave service, and the staff, which obtained its privileged position by canvassing the burgesses (i. 482). With a view to check simply the worst abuses in this respect and to prevent young men quite untried from holding these important posts, it became necessary to require, as a preliminary to the bestowal of staff appointments, evidence of a certain number of years of service. Nevertheless, when once the military tribunate, the true pillar of the Roman military system, was prescribed as the first stepping-stone in the political career of the young aristocrats, the obligation of service inevitably came to be frequently eluded, and the election of officers became liable to all the evils of democratic canvassing and of aristocratic exclusiveness. It was a bitter commentary on the new institution, that in serious wars (as in 583) it was found necessary to suspend the democratic mode of electing officers, and to recommit to the general the appointment of his staff.

171.

In the case of civil officers, the first and chief object was to limit re-election to the supreme magistracies. This was certainly necessary, if the presidency of annual kings was not to be an empty name; and even in the preceding period re-election to the consulship was not permitted till after the lapse of ten years, while in the case of the censorship it was altogether forbidden (i. 344). No farther law was passed in the period before us; but an increased stringency in its application is obvious from the fact that, while the law as to the ten years' interval was suspended in 537 during the continuance of the war in Italy, there was no farther dispensation from it afterwards, and indeed towards the close of this period re-election seldom occurred at all. Moreover, towards the end of this epoch (574) a decree of the people was issued, binding the candidates for public magistracies to apply for them in a fixed order of succession, and to observe certain intervals between the offices and certain limits of age. Custom, indeed, had long prescribed both of these; but it was a sensibly felt restriction of the freedom of election, when the customary qualification was raised into a legal requirement, and the liberty of disregarding such requirements in extraordinary cases was withdrawn from the electors. In general, admission to the senate was thrown open to persons belonging to the ruling families without distinction as to

Restrictions on the election of consuls and censors.

217.

180.

ability, while not only were the poorer and humbler ranks of the population utterly precluded from access to the offices of government, but all Roman burgesses not belonging to the hereditary aristocracy were practically excluded not indeed exactly from the senate, but from the two highest magistracies, the consulship and the censorship. After the case of Manius Curius (i. 337), no instance can be pointed out of a consul who did not belong to the social aristocracy, and probably no instance of the kind occurred at all. But the number of the *gentes* which appear for the first time in the lists of consuls and censors in the half-century from the beginning of the war with Hannibal to the close of that with Perseus is extremely limited; and by far the most of these, such as the Flaminii, Terentii, Porcii, Acilii, and Laelii, may be referred to elections by the opposition, or are traceable to special aristocratic connections. The election of Gaius Laelius in 564, for instance, was evidently due to the Scipios. The exclusion of the poorer classes from the government was, no doubt, required by the altered circumstances of the case. Now that Rome had ceased to be a purely Italian state and had adopted Hellenic culture, it was no longer possible to take a small farmer from the plough and to set him at the head of the community. But it was neither necessary nor beneficial that the elections should almost without exception be confined to the narrow circle of the curule houses, and that a " new man " should only be able to make his way into that circle by a sort of usurpation.* No doubt a cer-

190.

---

* The stability of the Roman aristocracy may be clearly traced, more especially in the case of the patrician *gentes*, by means of the consular and aedilician Fasti. As is well known, the consulate was held by one patrician and one plebeian in each year from 388 to 581 (with the exception of the years 399, 400, 401, 403, 405, 409, 411, in which both consuls were patricians). Moreover, the colleges of curule aediles were composed exclusively of patricians in the odd years of the Varronian reckoning, at least down to the close of the sixth century, and they are known for sixteen years, viz., 541, 545, 547, 549, 551, 553, 555, 557, 561, 565, 567, 575, 585, 589, 591, 593. These patrician consuls and aediles are, as respects their *gentes*, distributed as follows:—

	Consuls 388-500	Consuls 501-581	Curule aediles of those 16 patrician colleges
Cornelii . . .	15	15	14
Valerii . . .	10	8	4
Claudii . . .	4	8	2
Aemilii . . .	9	6	2
Fabii	6	6	1
Manlii . . .	4	6	1
Postumii . .	2	6	2
Servilii . . .	3	4	2
Quinctii. . .	2	3	1
Furii	2	3	—
Sulpicii . . .	6	2	2
Veturii . . .	—	2	—
Papirii . . .	3	1	—
Nautii . . .	2	—	—
Julii	1	—	1
Foslii	1	—	—
	70	70	32

tain hereditary character was inherent not merely in the institution of the senate, in so far as it rested from the first on
a representation of the clans (i. 84), but in the nature of
the aristocracy generally, in so far as statesmanly wisdom
and statesmanly experience are bequeathed from the able
father to the able son, and the inspiring spirit of an illustrious ancestry fans every noble spark within the human
breast into a speedier and more brilliant flame. In this
sense the Roman aristocracy had been at all times hereditary; in fact, it had displayed its hereditary character with
great naïveté in the old custom of the senator taking his sons
with him to the senate, and of the public magistrate deco-
rating his sons, as it were by anticipation, with the insignia
of the highest official honour—the purple border of the consular, and the golden amulet case of the triumphator. But,
while in the earlier period the hereditary character of the
outward dignity had been to a certain extent borne out by
the inheritance of intrinsic worth, and the senatorial aristocracy had guided the state not primarily by virtue of hereditary right, but by virtue of the highest of all rights of
representation—the right of the superior, as contrasted with
the mere ordinary, man—it sank in this epoch (and with
specially great rapidity after the end of the Hannibalic war)
from its original high position, as the aggregate of those in
the community who were most experienced in counsel and
action, into an order of lords filling up its ranks by hereditary succession, and exercising collegiate misrule.

Indeed, matters had already at this period reached such
a height, that out of the evil of oligarchy there emerged
the still worse evil of usurpation of power by particular
families. We have already spoken (p. 301) of the offensive
family-policy of the conqueror of Zama, and of his unhappily
successful efforts to cover with his own laurels the incapacity
and pitifulness of his brother; and the nepotism of the

Usurpation of power by certain families.

Thus the fifteen or sixteen houses of the
high nobility, that were powerful in the
state at the time of the Licinian laws,
maintained their ground without material
change in their relative numbers—which
no doubt were partly kept up by adoption—for the next two centuries, or, in
fact, down to the end of the republic.

To the circle of the plebeian nobility new
gentes doubtless were from time to time
added; but in the plebeian Fasti also
the old houses, such as the Licinii, Ful-
vii, Atilii, Domitii, Marcii, Junii, pre-
dominate very decidedly throughout three
centuries.

Flaminini was, if possible, still more shameless and offensive than that of the Scipios. Absolute freedom of election in fact turned to the advantage of such coteries far more than of the electors. The election of Marcus Valerius Corvus to the consulship at twenty-three had doubtless been for the benefit of the state; but now, when Scipio obtained the aedileship at twenty-three and the consulate at thirty, and Flamininus, while not yet thirty years of age, rose from the quaestorship to the consulship, such proceedings involved serious danger to the republic. Things had already reached such a pass, that the only effective barrier against family rule and its consequences had to be sought in a government strictly oligarchical; and this was the reason why even the party otherwise opposed to the oligarchy agreed to the restriction imposed on absolute freedom of election.

Govern-
ment of
the no-
bility.

The government bore the stamp of this gradual change in the spirit of the governing class. It is true that the administration of external affairs was still pervaded at this epoch by the consistency and energy which had established the dominion of the Roman community over Italy. During the severe disciplinary period of the Sicilian war the Roman aristocracy had gradually raised itself to the height of its new position; and if it unconstitutionally usurped for the senate powers which by right fell to be shared between the magistrates and the *comitia* alone, it vindicated the step by its certainly far from brilliant, but sure and steady, pilotage of the vessel of the state during the Hannibalic storm and the complications thence arising, and showed to the world that the Roman senate was alone able, and in many respects alone deserved, to rule the wide circle of the Italo-Hellenic

Internal
adminis-
tration.

states. But admitting the noble attitude of the ruling Roman senate in opposition to the external foe—an attitude crowned with the noblest results—we may not overlook the fact, that in the less conspicuous, but far more important and far more difficult, administration of the internal affairs of the state both the treatment of the existing arrangements and the new institutions betray an almost opposite spirit, or, to speak more correctly, indicate that the opposite tendency has already acquired the predominance in this field.

Decline in

In relation, first of all, to the individual burgess the go-

vernment was no longer what it had been.   The term "ma-   the admin-istration.
gistrate " meant a man who was more than other men ; and,
if he was the servant of the community, he was for that very
reason the master of every burgess.   But the tightness of
the rein was now visibly relaxed.   Where coteries and
canvassing flourish as they did in the Rome of that age, men
are chary of forfeiting the good services of their fellows or
the favour of the multitude by stern words and straightforward action.   If now and then magistrates appeared who
displayed the gravity and the sternness of the olden time, they
were ordinarily, like Cotta (502) and Cato, new men who   252.
had not sprung from the bosom of the ruling class.   It was
even deemed something singular, when Paullus, who had
been named commander-in-chief against Perseus, instead of
tendering his thanks in the usual manner to the burgesses,
declared to them that he presumed they had chosen him as
general because they accounted him the most capable of
command, and requested them accordingly not to help him
to command, but to be silent and obey.

The supremacy and hegemony of Rome in the territories of   As to mili-tary disci-pline and justice.
the Mediterranean rested not least on the strictness of her
military discipline and administration of justice.   Undoubtedly she was still, on the whole, at that time infinitely superior
in these respects to the Hellenic, Phoenician, and Oriental
states, which were without exception thoroughly disorganized ; nevertheless grave abuses were already occurring in
Rome.   We have previously (p. 315 *et seq.*) pointed out how
the wretched character of the commanders-in-chief—and that
not merely in the case of demagogues chosen perhaps by the
opposition, like Gaius Flaminius and Gaius Varro, but of
men who were good aristocrats—had already in the third
Macedonian war imperilled the interests of the state.   And
the mode in which justice was occasionally administered is
shown by the scene in the camp of the consul Lucius
Quinctius Flamininus at Placentia (562).   To compensate a   192.
favourite youth for the gladiatorial games of the capital, which
through his attendance on the consul he had missed the
opportunity of seeing, that great lord had ordered a Boian of
rank who had taken refuge in the Roman camp to be summoned, and had killed him at a banquet with his own hand.

Still worse than the occurrence itself, to which many parallels might be adduced, was the fact that the perpetrator was not brought to trial; and not only so, but when the censor Cato on account of it erased his name from the roll of the senate, his fellow-senators invited the expelled to resume his senatorial stall in the theatre. He was, no doubt, a brother of the liberator of the Greeks, and one of the most powerful coterie-leaders in the senate.

As to the management of the finances.

The financial system of the Roman community also retrograded rather than advanced during this epoch. The amount of their revenues, indeed, was visibly on the increase. The indirect taxes—there were no direct taxes in Rome—increased in consequence of the enlargement of the Roman territory, which rendered it necessary, for example, to institute new customs-offices along the Campanian and Bruttian coasts at

199. 179.

204.

Puteoli, Castra (Squillace), and elsewhere, in 555 and 575. The same reason led to the new salt-tariff of 550 fixing the scale of prices at which salt was to be sold in the different districts of Italy, as it was no longer possible to furnish salt at one and the same price to the Roman burgesses now scattered throughout the land; but, as the Roman government probably supplied the burgesses with salt at cost price, if not below it, this financial measure yielded no gain to the state. Still more considerable was the increase in the produce of the domains. The land-tax indeed, which of right was payable to the treasury from the Italian domain-lands granted for occupation, was in the great majority of cases neither demanded nor paid. On the other hand the *scriptura* was retained; and not only so, but the domains recently acquired in the second Punic war, particularly the greater portion of the territory of Capua and that of Leontini (p. 157, 201), instead of being given up to occupation, were parcelled out and let to petty temporary lessees, and the attempts at occupation made in these cases were opposed with more than usual energy by the government; by which means the state acquired a considerable and secure source of income. The mines of the state also, particularly the important Spanish mines, were turned to profit on lease. Lastly, the revenue was augmented by the tribute of the transmarine subjects. From extraordinary sources very considerable

sums accrued during this epoch to the state treasury, particularly the produce of the spoil in the war with Antiochus,
200 millions of sesterces (£2,000,000), and that of the war
with Perseus, 210 millions of sesterces (£2,100,000)—the
latter, the largest sum in cash which ever came at one time
into the Roman treasury.

But this increase of revenue was for the most part counter-
balanced by the increasing expenditure. The provinces,
Sicily perhaps excepted, probably cost nearly as much as they
yielded ; the expenditure on highways and other structures
rose in proportion to the extension of territory ; the repayment
also of the advances (*tributa*) received from the freeholder
burgesses during times of severe war formed a burden for
many a year on the Roman treasury. To these fell to be added
very considerable losses occasioned to the revenue by the
mismanagement, negligence, or connivance of the supreme
magistrates. Of the conduct of the officials in the provinces,
of their luxurious living at the expense of the public purse, of
their embezzlement more especially of the spoil, of the incipient system of bribery and extortion, we shall speak in the
sequel. How the state fared generally as regarded the farming of its revenues and the contracts for supplies and buildings, may be inferred from the circumstance, that the senate
resolved in 587 to desist from the working of the Macedonian   167.
mines that had fallen to Rome, because the lessees of the
minerals would either plunder the subjects or cheat the
exchequer—truly a naïve confession of impotence, in which
the controlling board pronounced its own censure. Not only
was the land-tax of the occupied domain-land allowed tacitly
to fall into abeyance, as has been already mentioned, but private buildings in the capital and elsewhere were suffered to
encroach on the public property, and the water from the public aqueducts was diverted to private purposes : great dissatisfaction was created on one occasion when the censor took
serious steps against such trespassers, and compelled them
either to desist from this exclusive use of the public property,
or to pay the legal rate for the ground and water. The
conscience of the Romans, otherwise in economic matters so
scrupulous, showed, so far as the state was concerned, a remarkable laxity. " He who steals from a burgess," said Cato,

"ends his days in chains and fetters; but he who steals from the community ends them in gold and purple." If, notwithstanding the fact that the public property of the Roman community was fearlessly and with impunity plundered by officials and speculators, Polybius still lays stress on the rarity of embezzlement in Rome, while Greece could hardly produce a single official who had not touched the public money, and on the honesty with which a Roman commissioner or magistrate would upon his simple word of honour administer enormous sums, while in the case of the paltriest sum in Greece ten letters were sealed and twenty witnesses were required and yet everybody cheated, this merely implies that social and economic demoralization had advanced much further in Greece than in Rome, and, in particular, that direct and palpable peculation was not as yet so flourishing in the one case as in the other. The general financial result is most clearly exhibited to us by the state of the public buildings, and by the amount of cash in the treasury. We find in times of peace a fifth, in times of war a tenth, of the revenues expended on public buildings; which, in the circumstances, does not seem to have been a very large outlay. With these sums, as well as with fines which were not directly payable into the treasury, much was doubtless done for the repair of the highways in and near the capital, for the formation of the chief Italian roads,* and for the construction of public buildings. Perhaps the most important of the building operations in the capital, known to belong to this period, was the great repair and extension of the network of sewers throughout the city, contracted for probably in 570, for which 24,000,000 sesterces (£240,000) were set apart at once, and to which it may be presumed that the portions of the *cloacae* still extant, at least in the main, belong. To all appearance however, even apart from the severe pressure of war, this period was inferior to the last section of the preceding epoch in respect of public buildings; between 482 and 607 no new aqueduct was con-

184.

272–147.

* The expenses of these were, however, thrown mainly in all probability on the adjoining inhabitants. The old system of making requisitions of task-work was not abolished: it must not unfrequently have happened that the slaves of the landholders were called away to be employed in the construction of roads. (Cato, *de R. R.* 2.)

structed at Rome. The treasure of the state, no doubt, increased; the last reserve in 545, when they found themselves under the necessity of laying hands on it, amounted only to 4000 pounds of gold (£164,000; p. 183), whereas a short time after the close of this period (597) close on £860,000 in precious metals were stored in the treasury. But, when we take into account the enormous extraordinary revenues which in the generation after the close of the Hannibalic war came into the Roman treasury, the latter sum surprises us rather by its smallness than by its magnitude. So far as with the extremely meagre statements before us it may be allowable to speak of results, the finances of the Roman state exhibit doubtless an excess of income over expenditure, but are far from presenting a brilliant sum total.

The change in the spirit of the government was most distinctly apparent in the treatment of the Italian and extra-Italian subjects of the Roman community. Formerly there existed in Italy four distinct classes; the ordinary, and the Latin, allied communities, the Roman burgesses *sine suffragio*, and the burgesses with the full franchise. The third of these four classes disappeared during the course of this period, for the communities of passive burgesses either —as was the case with Capua especially—lost their Roman citizenship in consequence of the Hannibalic war, or one after another acquired the full franchise; so that at the close of this period there were no passive burgesses of Rome, except isolated individuals who were for special reasons excluded from the right of voting.

On the other hand there emerged a new class in a position of peculiar inferiority, deprived of municipal freedom and of the right to carry arms and to some extent treated almost like public slaves (*peregrini dediticii*); to which, in particular, the members of the former Campanian, southern Picentine, and Bruttian communities, that had been in alliance with Hannibal (p. 201), belonged. To these were added the Celtic tribes tolerated on the south side of the Alps, whose position in relation to the Italian confederacy is indeed only known imperfectly, but is sufficiently characterized as inferior by the clause embodied in their treaties of alliance with Rome, that

Marginal notes: 209. · 157. · Italian subjects. · Passive burgesses. · Dediticii.

no member of these communities should ever be allowed to acquire Roman citizenship (p. 206).

Allies.   The position of the non-Latin allies had, as we have mentioned before (p. 201), undergone a change greatly to their disadvantage in consequence of the Hannibalic war. Only a few communities in this category, such as Neapolis, Nola, and Heraclea, had during all the vicissitudes of that war remained steadfastly on the Roman side, and therefore retained their former rights as allies unaltered; by far the greater portion were obliged in consequence of having changed sides to acquiesce in a revision of the existing treaties to their disadvantage. The reduced position of the non-Latin allies is attested by the emigration that set in from these towards the 177.   Latin communities: when in 577 the Samnites and Paelignians applied to the senate for a reduction of their contingents, their request was based on the ground that of late years 4000 Samnite and Paelignian families had migrated to the Latin colony of Fregellae.

Latins.   That the Latins—which term now denoted the few towns in old Latium that were not included in the Roman burgess-union, such as Tibur and Praeneste, the allied cities placed in law on the same footing with them, such as several of the Hernican towns, and the Latin colonies dispersed throughout Italy—were still at this time in a better position, is implied in their very name; but they too suffered, in proportion, not much less injuriously. The burdens imposed on them were unjustly increased, and the pressure of military service was more and more transferred from the burgesses to the Latin 218.   and other Italian allies. For instance, in 536, nearly twice as many of the allies were called out as of the burgesses: after the end of the Hannibalic war all the burgesses received their discharge, but not all the allies; the latter were chiefly employed for garrison duty and for the odious service in Spain. 177.   In the triumphal largess of 577 the allies received not as formerly an equal share with the burgesses, but only the half, so that amidst the unrestrained rejoicing of that soldiers' carnival the divisions thus treated as inferior followed the chariot of victory in sullen silence: in the assignations of land in northern Italy the burgesses received ten *iugera* of arable land each, the non-burgesses three *iugera* each. That liberty of migration was no longer granted to the Latin communities founded after 486, has been already observed (i. 462). It was retained in law by the older Latin cities; but the crowding of their burgesses to Rome, and the complaints of their magistrates as to the increasing depopulation of the cities and the impossibility under such circumstances of furnishing the due contingent, led the Roman government to allow those Latins only to exercise their right of migration when the emigrant left behind children of his own in his native city; and, in conformity with this principle, police-ejections from the capital were carried out to a great extent (567, 577). The measure might be unavoidable, but it was none the less felt as a material restriction of the right of free migration accorded by treaty to the allied cities. Moreover, the towns founded by Rome in the interior of Italy began towards the close of this period to receive instead of Latin rights the full franchise, which previously had only been given to the maritime colonies; and the enlargement of the Latin body by the accession of new communities, which hitherto had gone on so regularly, thus came to an end. Aquileia, the establishment of which began in 571, was the latest of the Italian colonies of Rome that received Latin rights; the full franchise was given to the colonies, sent forth nearly at the same time, of Potentia, Pisaurum, Parma, Mutina, and Luna (570–577). The reason for this evidently lay in the decline of the Latin as compared with the Roman franchise. The colonists conducted to the new settlements were always, and now more than ever, chosen in preponderating number from the Roman burgesses; and among the very poorer class of these there was no longer found any one willing, even for the acquisition of considerable material advantages, to exchange his rights as a burgess for those of a Latin.

Lastly, in the case of non-burgesses—communities as well as individuals—admission to the Roman franchise was almost completely foreclosed. The earlier course of incorporating the subject communities in that of Rome had been dropped about 400, that the Roman burgess-body might not be too much decentralized by its undue extension; and therefore communities of half-burgesses were instituted (i. 463). Now the centralization of the community was abandoned, partly through

Margin notes: 268. 187, 177. 183. 184-177. Roman franchise more difficult of acquisition. 350.

the admission of the half-burgess communities to the full franchise, partly through the accession of numerous more remote burgess-colonies to its ranks; but the older system of incorporation was not resumed. It cannot be shown that after the complete subjugation of Italy even a single Italian community exchanged its position as an ally for the Roman franchise; probably none after that date in reality acquired it. But even the transition of individual Italians to the Roman franchise was at this epoch rendered considerably more difficult, especially by the limitation of the liberty of migration which was in law associated with the passive franchise; and it was confined almost wholly to the case of magistrates of the Latin communities (i. 462) and of non-burgesses admitted, by special favour towards themselves individually, on the founding of burgess-colonies.*

It cannot be denied that these changes *de facto* and *de jure* in the relations of the Italian subjects exhibit at least an intimate connection and consistency. The situation of the subject classes was throughout deteriorated in proportion to the gradations previously subsisting, and, while the government had formerly endeavoured to soften the distinctions and to provide means of transition from one to another, now the intermediate links were everywhere set aside and the connecting bridges were broken down. As within the Roman burgess-body the ruling class separated itself from the people, uniformly evaded public burdens, and uniformly appropriated honours and advantages, so the burgesses in their turn asserted their distinction from the Italian confederacy, and excluded it more and more from the joint enjoyment of power, while transferring to it a double or triple share in the common burdens. As the nobility, in relation to the plebeians, returned to the close exclusiveness of the declining patriciate, so did

---

* Thus, as is well known, Ennius of Rudiae received burgess-rights from one of the triumvirs, Q. Fulvius Nobilior, on occasion of the founding of the burgess-colonies of Potentia and Pisaurum (Cic. *Brut.* 20, 79); whereupon, according to the well-known custom, he adopted the *praenomen* of the latter. The non-burgesses who were sent to take part in the foundation of a burgess-colony, did not, at least in this epoch, through that circumstance acquire *de jure* Roman citizenship, although they frequently laid claim to it (Liv. xxxiv. 42); but the magistrates charged with the founding of a colony were empowered, by a clause in the decree of the people relative to each case, to confer burgess-rights on a certain number of persons (Cic. *pro Balb.* 21, 48).

the burgesses in relation to the non-burgesses; the plebeiate, which had become great through the liberality of its institutions, now wrapped itself up in the rigid maxims of patricianism.   The abolition of the passive burgesses cannot in itself be censured, and, so far as concerned the motive which led to it, belonged in all probability to another category to be mentioned afterwards; but through its abolition an inter-mediate connecting link was lost.   Far more fraught with peril, however, was the disappearance of the distinction between the Latin and the other Italian communities.   The privileged position of the Latin nation in Italy was the foundation of the Roman power; that foundation gave way, when the Latin towns began to feel that they were no longer privileged partakers in the dominion of the powerful cognate community, but substantially subjects of Rome like the rest, and when all the Italians began to find their position equally intolerable.   It is true, that there were still distinctions: the Bruttians and their companions in misery were treated exactly like slaves and conducted themselves accordingly, deserting, for instance, from the fleet in which they served as galley-slaves, whenever they could, and gladly taking service against Rome; and the Celtic, and above all the transmarine, subjects formed a class still more oppressed than the Italians were—a class intentionally abandoned by the government to contempt and maltreatment at the hands of the Italians. But such distinctions, while implying a gradation of classes among the subjects, could not in reason afford a compensation for the earlier contrast between the cognate, and the alien, Italian subjects.   A profound dissatisfaction prevailed through the whole Italian confederacy, and fear alone prevented it from finding expression.   The proposal made in the senate after the battle at Cannae, to give the Roman franchise and a seat in the senate to two men from each Latin community, was made at an unseasonable time, and was rightly rejected; but it shows the apprehension with which men in the ruling community even then viewed the relations between Latium and Rome. Had a second Hannibal now carried the war into Italy, it may be doubted whether he would have again been thwarted by the steadfast resistance of the Latin name to a foreign domination.

But by far the most important institution which this epoch introduced into the Roman commonwealth, and that at the same time which involved the most decided and fatal deviation from the course hitherto pursued, was the new provincial magistracies. The earlier state-law of Rome knew nothing of tributary subjects: the conquered communities were either sold into slavery, or merged in the Roman commonwealth, or admitted to an alliance which secured to them at least communal independence and freedom from taxation. But the Carthaginian possessions in Sicily, Sardinia, and Spain, as well as the kingdom of Hiero, had paid tithe and tribute to their former masters: if Rome was desirous of retaining these possessions at all, it was in the judgment of the short-sighted the most judicious, and undoubtedly the most convenient, course to manage the new territories entirely in accordance with the rules heretofore observed. Accordingly the Romans simply retained the Carthagino-Hieronic provincial constitution, and organized in accordance with it those provinces also, such as Hither Spain, which they wrested from the barbarians. It was the shirt of Nessus which they inherited from the enemy. Beyond doubt at first the Roman government intended, in imposing taxes on their subjects, not strictly to enrich themselves, but only to cover the cost of administration and defence; but they deviated from this course, when they made Macedonia and Illyria tributary without undertaking the government or the guardianship of the frontier there. The fact, however, that they still maintained moderation in the imposition of burdens was of little consequence as compared with the conversion of their sovereignty into a profitable privilege at all; the fall was the same, whether a single apple was taken or the tree was plundered.

Punishment followed in the steps of wrong. The new provincial system necessitated the appointment of governors, whose position was absolutely incompatible not only with the welfare of the provinces, but with the Roman constitution. As the Roman community in the provinces took the place of the former rulers of the land, so the governor appeared there in the position of a king; the Sicilian praetor, for example, resided in the palace of Hiero at Syracuse. It is true, that

the governor was nevertheless bound by law to administer his
office with republican honesty and frugality. Cato, when
governor of Sardinia, appeared in the towns subject to him
on foot and attended by a single servant who carried his coat
and sacrificial ladle; and, when he returned from his Spanish
governorship, he sold his war horse beforehand, because he
did not hold himself entitled to charge the state with the expenses of its transport. There is no question that the Roman
governors—although certainly but few of them pushed their
conscientiousness, like Cato, to the verge of being niggardly
and ridiculous—made in many cases a powerful impression on
the subjects, more especially on the frivolous and unstable
Greeks, by their ancestral piety, by the reverential quietness
prevailing at their assemblies, by their comparatively upright
administration of office and of justice, especially by their proper severity towards the worst oppressors of the provincials—
the Roman revenue-farmers and bankers—and in general by
the gravity and dignity of their deportment. The provincials
found their government comparatively tolerable. They had
not been pampered by their former Carthaginian governors
and Syracusan masters, and they were soon to find occasion
for recalling with gratitude the present rods as compared with
the coming scorpions: it is easy to understand how, in later
times, the sixth century of the city appeared as the golden
era of provincial rule. But it was not practicable for any
length of time to be at once republican and king. Playing
the part of governors demoralized the Roman ruling class with
fearful rapidity. Haughtiness and arrogance towards the
provincials were so natural in the circumstances, as scarcely
to form matter of reproach against the individual magistrate.
But already it was a rare thing—and the rarer, because the
government adhered rigidly to the old principle of not paying
public officials—that a governor returned with quite clean
hands from his province; it was already remarked upon as
something singular that Paullus, the conqueror of Pydna, did
not take money. The bad custom of delivering to the
governor "honorary wine" and other "voluntary" gifts
seems as old as the provincial constitution itself, and may
perhaps have been a legacy from the Carthaginians; even
Cato in his administration of Sardinia in 556 had to content

198.

himself with regulating and moderating such dues. The right of the magistrates, and of those travelling on the business of the state generally, to free quarters and free conveyance was already employed as a pretext for exactions. The more important right of the magistrate to make requisitions of grain from his province—partly for the maintenance of himself and his retinue (*in cellam*), partly for the provisioning of the army in case of war or on other special occasions—at a fair valuation was already so scandalously abused, that on the complaint of the Spaniards the senate in 583 found it necessary to withdraw from the governors the right of fixing the price of the supplies for either purpose (p. 225). Requisitions had begun to be made on the subjects even for the popular festivals in Rome; the unmeasured vexatious demands made on the Italian as well as extra-Italian communities by the aedile Tiberius Sempronius Gracchus, for the festival which he had to provide, induced the senate officially to interfere (572). The liberties which Roman magistrates at the close of this period allowed themselves to take not only with the unhappy subjects, but even with the dependent free-states and kingdoms, are illustrated by the raids of Gaius Volso in Asia Minor (p. 290), and especially by the scandalous proceedings in Greece during the war with Perseus (p. 315 *et seq.*).

171.

182.

Control over the governors.

The government had no right to be surprised at such things, for it provided no serious check on the excesses of this capricious military administration. Judicial control, it is true, was not entirely wanting. Although, according to the universal but more than questionable rule of allowing no complaint to be brought against a commander-in-chief during his term of office (i. 278), the Roman governor could ordinarily be called to account only after the mischief had been done, yet he was amenable both to a criminal and to a civil prosecution. In order to the institution of the former, some Roman magistrate who possessed criminal jurisdiction had to undertake the case and bring it before the bar of the people; the civil action was remitted by the senator who administered the corresponding praetorship to a jury appointed, according to the constitution of the tribunal in those times, from the ranks of the senate. In both cases, therefore, the control lay in the hands of the ruling class, and, although the

latter was still sufficiently upright and honourable not absolutely to set aside well-founded complaints, and the senate
even in several instances, at the call of those aggrieved, condescended itself to order the institution of a civil process,
yet the complaints of poor men and foreigners against
‚powerful members of the ruling aristocracy—submitted to
judges and jurymen far remote from the scene and, if not involved in the like guilt, at least belonging to the same order
as the accused—could from the first only reckon on success
in the event of the wrong being clear and crying; and to complain in vain was almost certain destruction.   The aggrieved
no doubt found a sort of support in the hereditary relations
of clientship, which the subject cities and provinces were
wont to enter into with their conquerors and other Romans
who had been brought into contact with them.   The Spanish
governors felt that no one could with impunity maltreat the
clients of Cato; and the circumstance that the representatives of the three nations conquered by Paullus—the Spaniards, Ligurians, and Macedonians—would not forego the
privilege of carrying his bier to the funeral pile, was the
noblest dirge in honour of that noble man.   But not only
did this special protection give the Greeks opportunity to
display in Rome all their talent for abasing themselves
in presence of their masters, and to demoralize even
those masters by their ready servility—the decrees of the
Syracusans in honour of Marcellus, after he had destroyed
and plundered their city and they had complained of his
conduct to the senate in vain, form one of the most scandalous pages in the far from honourable annals of Syracuse—
but, in connection with the dangers of a family policy, this
patronage on the part of great houses had also its politically
perilous side.   In this way the result was that the Roman
magistrates in some degree feared the gods and the senate,
and for the most part were moderate in their plundering; but
still they plundered, and did so with impunity provided
they observed such moderation.   The mischievous rule
became established, that in the case of minor exactions and
moderate violence the Roman magistrate acted in some
measure within his sphere and was in law exempt from punishment, so that those who were aggrieved had to keep silence;

and from this rule succeeding ages did not fail to draw the fatal consequences.

Super-
vision of
the senate
over the
provinces
and their
governors.
Nevertheless, even though the tribunals had been as strict as they were lax, the liability to a judicial reckoning could only check the worst evils. The true security for a good administration lay in a strict and uniform supervision by the supreme administrative authority : and this the senate utterly failed to provide. It was in this respect that the laxity and helplessness of the collegiate government became earliest apparent. By right the governors ought to have been subjected to an oversight far more strict and more special than had sufficed for the Italian municipal administration ; and now, when the empire embraced great transmarine territories, the arrangements, through which the government preserved to itself the supervision of the whole, ought to have undergone a corresponding expansion. In both respects the reverse was the case. The governors ruled virtually as sovereign ; and the most important of the institutions serving for the latter purpose, the census of the empire, was extended to Sicily alone, not to any of the provinces subsequently acquired. This emancipation of the supreme administrative officials from the central authority was more than hazardous. The Roman governor, placed at the head of the armies of the state, and in possession of considerable financial resources ; subject to but a lax judicial control, and practically independent of the supreme administration ; and impelled by a sort of necessity to separate the interests of himself and of the people whom he governed from those of the Roman community and to treat them as conflicting, far more resembled a Persian satrap than one of the commissioners of the Roman senate at the time of the Samnite wars. The man, moreover, who had just conducted a legalized military tyranny abroad, could with difficulty find his way back to the common civic level, which distinguished between those who commanded and those who obeyed, but not between masters and slaves. Even the government felt that their two fundamental principles—equality within the aristocracy, and the subordination of the power of the magistrates to the senatorial college —began in this instance to give way in their hands. The aversion of the government to the acquisition of new pro-

vinces and to the whole provincial system ; the institution of
the provincial quaestorships, which were intended to take at
least the financial power out of the hands of the governors ;
and the abolition of the arrangement—in itself so judicious—
for lengthening the tenure of such offices (p. 224), very clearly
evince the anxiety felt by the more far-seeing of the Roman
statesmen as to the fruits of the seed thus sown.   But diag-
nosis is not cure.   The internal government of the nobility
continued to follow the direction once given to it ; and the
decay of the administration and of the financial system—the
precursor of future revolutions and usurpations—steadily
pursued its course, if not unnoticed, yet unchecked.

If the new nobility was less strictly defined than the old   The oppo-
aristocracy of the clans, and if, while the one encroached on   sition.
the rest of the burgesses as respected the joint enjoyment
of political rights *de jure,* the other only did so *de facto,* the
second form of inferiority was for these very reasons worse to
bear and worse to throw off than the first.   Attempts were,
as a matter of course, made to throw it off.   The opposition
rested on the support of the public assembly, as the nobility
did on the senate : in order to understand the opposition, we
must first describe the spirit of the burgesses during this
period and their position in the commonwealth.

Whatever could be demanded of an assembly of burgesses   Character
like the Roman, which was not the motive power, but the   of the
firm foundation, of the whole machinery—a sure perception   Roman
of the common good, a sagacious deference towards the   burgess-
right leader, a steadfast spirit in prosperous and evil days,   body.
and, above all, the capacity of sacrificing the individual for
the general welfare and the comfort of the present for
the advantage of the future—all these qualities the Roman
community exhibited in so high a degree that, when we look
to its conduct as a whole, all censure is lost in reverent
admiration.   Even now good sense and discretion still
thoroughly predominated.   The whole conduct of the burgesses with reference to the government as well as to the
opposition shows very clearly that the same mighty patriotism
before which even the genius of Hannibal had to quit the field
prevailed also in the Roman comitia.   No doubt they often
erred ; but their errors originated not in the mischievous

impulses of a rabble, but in the narrow-minded views of burgesses and farmers. The machinery, however, by means of which the burgesses influenced the course of public affairs became certainly more and more unwieldy, and the circumstances in which they were placed through their own great deeds far outgrew their power to deal with them. We have already stated, that in the course of this epoch most of the former communities of passive burgesses, as well as a considerable number of newly established colonies, received the full Roman franchise (p. 351, 353). At the close of this period the Roman burgess-body, in a tolerably compact mass, occupied Latium in its widest sense, Sabina, and a part of Campania, so that it reached on the west coast northward to Caere and southward to Cumae; within this district there were only a few cities not included in it, such as Tibur, Praeneste, Signia, Norba, and Ferentinum. To this fell to be added the maritime colonies on the coasts of Italy which uniformly possessed the full Roman franchise, the Picenian and Trans-Apennine colonies of most recent foundation to which the franchise had to be conceded (p. 353), and a very considerable number of Roman burgesses, who, without forming separate communities in a strict sense, were dispersed throughout Italy in market-villages and hamlets (*fora et conciliabula*). To some extent the unwieldiness of a civic community so constituted was remedied, as regarded purposes of justice * and of administration, by the deputy judges previously mentioned (i. 463); and already perhaps the maritime (i. 476) and the new Picenian and Trans-Apennine colonies exhibited at least the first lineaments of the system under which afterwards smaller urban communities were organized within the great city-commonwealth of Rome. But in all political questions the general assembly in the Roman Forum was alone entitled to act. It is obvious at a glance, that this assembly was no longer, in its composition or in its collective action, what it

---

* In Cato's treatise on husbandry, which, as is well known, primarily relates to an estate in the district of Venafrum, the judicial discussion of such processes as might arise is referred to Rome only as respects one definite case; namely, that in which the landlord leases the winter pasture to the owner of a flock of sheep, and thus has to deal with a lessee who, as a rule, is not domiciled in the district (c. 149). It may be inferred from this, that in ordinary cases, where the contract was with a person domiciled in the district, such processes as might arise were even in Cato's time decided not at Rome, but before the local judges.

had been when all the persons entitled to vote could exercise
their privilege as citizens by leaving their farms in the
morning and returning home the same evening.   Moreover
the government—whether from want of judgment, from
negligence, or from any evil design, we cannot tell—no longer
enrolled the communities admitted to the franchise after 513   241.
in newly instituted tribes, but entered them in the old; so
that gradually each tribe came to be composed of different
townships scattered over the whole Roman territory.   Tribes
such as these, containing on an average 8000—the urban
naturally having more, the rural fewer—persons entitled to
vote, without local connection or inward unity, no longer
admitted of any definite leading or of any satisfactory previous
deliberation; disadvantages which must have been the more
felt, that the voting itself was not preceded by any free debate.
Moreover, while the burgesses had quite sufficient capacity to
discern their municipal interests, it was foolish and utterly
ridiculous to leave the decision of the highest and most difficult questions which the power that ruled the world had
to solve to a well-disposed but fortuitous concourse of Italian
farmers, and to allow the nomination of generals and the
conclusion of treaties of state to be finally judged of by
people who understood neither the grounds nor the consequences of their decrees.   In all matters transcending mere
municipal affairs the Roman popular assemblies accordingly
played a childish and even silly part.   As a rule, the people
stood and assented to all proposals; and, when in exceptional
instances they of their own impulse refused their sanction,
as on occasion of the declaration of war against Macedonia
in 554 (p. 247), the policy of the market-place certainly   200.
made a pitiful opposition—and with a pitiful issue—to the
policy of the state.

   At length the rabble of clients assumed a position, formally   Rise of a
of equality and often even, practically, of superiority, along-   city rabble.
side of the class of independent burgesses.   The institutions
in which it originated were of great antiquity.   From time
immemorial the Roman of quality exercised a sort of government over his freedmen and dependents, and was consulted
by them in all their more important affairs; a client, for
instance, was careful not to give his children in marriage

without having obtained the consent of his patron, and very often the latter directly arranged the match. But as the aristocracy became converted into a special ruling class concentrating in its hands not only power but wealth, the clients became parasites and beggars; and these new partisans of the rich undermined outwardly and inwardly the burgess class. The aristocracy not only tolerated this sort of clientship, but worked it financially and politically for their own advantage. Thus, for instance, the old penny collections, which hitherto had taken place chiefly for religious purposes or in connection with the burial of men of merit, were now employed by lords of high standing—for the first time by Lucius Scipio, in 568, on pretext of a popular festival which he had in contemplation—for the purpose of levying on extraordinary occasions a contribution from the public. Presents were specially placed under legal restriction (in 550), because the senators began under that name to take regular tribute from their clients. But the retinue of clients was above all serviceable to the ruling class as a means of commanding the comitia; and the issue of the elections shows clearly how powerfully the dependent rabble already at this epoch counteracted the influence of the independent middle class.

The very rapid increase of the rabble in the capital particularly, which these facts serve to indicate, is also demonstrable otherwise. The increasing number and importance of the freedmen are shown by the very serious discussions that arose in the previous century (i. 339), and were continued during the present, as to their right to vote in the public assemblies, and by the remarkable resolution, adopted by the senate during the Hannibalic war, to admit honourable freedwomen to a participation in the public collections, and to grant to the legitimate children of manumitted fathers the insignia hitherto belonging only to the children of the free-born (p. 335). The majority of the Hellenes and Orientals who settled in Rome were probably little better than the freedmen, for national servility clung as indelibly to the former as legal servility to the latter.

But not only did these natural causes operate to produce a metropolitan rabble: neither the nobility nor the dema-

Systematic corruption of the multitude.

gogues, moreover, can be acquitted from the reproach of
having systematically nursed its growth, and of having undermined, so far as in them lay, the old public spirit by flattery
of the people and things still worse.   The electors as a body
were still too respectable to admit of direct electoral corruption showing itself on a great scale ; but the favour of those
entitled to vote was indirectly courted by methods far from
commendable.   The old obligation of the magistrates, particularly of the aediles, to see that corn could be procured
at a moderate price and to superintend the games, began to
degenerate into the state of things which at length gave
rise to the horrible cry of the city populace under the empire,
" Bread for nothing and games for ever ! "   Large supplies   Distribu-
of grain, either placed by the provincial governors at the   tions of
grain.
disposal of the Roman market officials, or delivered at Rome
free of cost by the provinces themselves for the purpose of
procuring   favour   with   particular   Roman   magistrates,
enabled the aediles, from the middle of the sixth century,
to furnish grain to the population of the capital at very low
prices.   " It was no wonder," Cato considered, " that the
burgesses no longer listened to good advice—the belly had no
ears."

Popular amusements increased to an alarming extent.   Festivals.
For five hundred years the community had been content
with one festival in the year, and with one circus.   The first
Roman demagogue by profession, Gaius Flaminius, added
a second festival and a second circus (534) ; * and by these   220.
institutions—the tendency of which is sufficiently indicated
by the very name of the new festival, " the plebeian games "—
he probably purchased the permission to give battle at the
Trasimene lake.   When the path was once opened, the evil
made rapid progress.   The festival in honour of Ceres, the
goddess who protected the plebeian order (i. 304), must have
been but little, if at all, later than the plebeian games.   On
the suggestion of the Sibylline and Marcian prophecies,

---

* The building of the circus is attested. Respecting the origin of the
plebeian games there is no ancient tradition (for what is said by the Pseudo-
Asconius, p. 143, *Orell.* is not such);
but seeing that they were celebrated in
the Flaminian circus (Val. Max. i. 7, 4),
and first certainly occur in 538, four
years after it was built (Liv. xxiii. 30),
what we have stated above is sufficiently
proved.

216.

212.
204.

173.

moreover, a fourth festival was added in 542 in honour of
Apollo, and a fifth in 550 in honour of the " Great Mother "
recently transplanted from Phrygia to Rome. These were
the severe years of the Hannibalic war—on the first celebration of the Apollinarian games the burgesses were summoned
from the circus itself to arms; the superstitious fear peculiar
to Italy was feverishly excited, and persons were not wanting
who took advantage of the opportunity to circulate Sibylline
and prophetic oracles and to recommend themselves to the
people through the medium of their contents and advocacy:
we can scarcely blame the government, which was obliged to
call for so enormous sacrifices from the burgesses, for
yielding in such matters. But what was once conceded
had to be continued; indeed, even in more peaceful times
(581) there was added another festival, although of minor
importance—the games in honour of Flora. The cost of
these new festal amusements was defrayed by the magistrates entrusted with the exhibition of the respective festivals
from their own means: thus the curule aediles had, over
and above the old national festival, those of the Mother of
the Gods and of Flora; the plebeian aediles had the plebeian
festival and that of Ceres, and the urban praetor the Apollinarian games. Those who sanctioned the new festivals perhaps excused themselves in their own eyes by the reflection that they were not at any rate a burden on the public
purse; but it would have been in reality far less injurious to
burden the public budget with a number of useless expenses,
than to allow the furnishing of an amusement for the people
to become practically a qualification for holding the highest
office in the state. The future candidates for the consulship
soon entered into a mutual rivalry in their expenditure on
these games, which incredibly increased their cost; and of
course it was no injury to the interests of the consul expect-
ant, if he gave, over and above this as it were legal contribution, a voluntary " performance " (munus), a gladiatorial
show at his own expense for the public benefit. The splendour of the games became gradually the standard by which
the electors measured the fitness of the candidates for the
consulship. The nobility had, in truth, to pay dear for their
honours—a gladiatorial show on a respectable scale cost

720,000 sesterces (£7200)—but they paid willingly, since by this means they absolutely precluded men who were not wealthy from a political career.

Corruption, however, was not restricted to the Forum; it was transferred even to the camp. The old burgess militia had reckoned themselves fortunate when they brought home a compensation for their labour in war, and, in the event of success, a trifling gift as a memorial of victory. The new generals, with Scipio Africanus at their head, lavishly scattered amongst their troops the money of Rome as well as the proceeds of the spoil: it was on this point, that Cato quarrelled with Scipio during the last campaigns against Hannibal in Africa. The veterans of the second Macedonian and the Asiatic war already returned home throughout as wealthy men : even the better class began to commend a general, who did not appropriate the gifts of the provincials and the gains of war entirely to himself and his immediate followers, and from whose camp not a few men returned with gold, and many with silver, in their pockets : men began to forget that the moveable spoil was the property of the state. When Lucius Paullus again dealt with it in the old mode, his own soldiers, especially the volunteers who had been allured in numbers by the prospect of rich plunder, were on the point of refusing to decree to the victor of Pydna the honour of a triumph—an honour which they threw away on every one who had subjugated three Ligurian villages.

Squandering of the spoil,

How much the military discipline and the martial spirit of the burgesses suffered from this conversion of war into a traffic in plunder, may be traced in the campaigns against Perseus; and the spread of cowardice was manifested in a way almost scandalous during the insignificant Istrian war (in 576). On occasion of a trifling skirmish magnified by rumour to gigantic dimensions, the land army and the naval force of the Romans, and even the Italians at home, took to flight, and Cato found it necessary to address a special reproof to his countrymen for their cowardice. In this too the youth of quality took precedence. Already during the Hannibalic war (545) the censors found occasion to visit with severe penalties the indolence of those who were bound to serve in the equestrian ranks. Towards the close

Decay of warlike spirit.

178.

209.

180.

of this period (574?) a decree of the people prescribed evidence of ten years' service as a qualification for holding any public magistracy, with a view to compel the sons of the nobility to enter the army.

Title-hunting.

But perhaps nothing so clearly evinces the decline of genuine pride and genuine honour in high and low alike as the hunting after insignia and titles, which appeared under different forms of expression, but with substantial identity of character, among all ranks and classes. So urgent was the demand for the honour of a triumph that there was difficulty in upholding the old rule, which accorded a triumph only to the ordinary supreme magistrate who augmented the power of the state in open battle, and thus, it is true, not unfrequently excluded from that honour the very authors of the most important successes. There was a necessity for acquiescence, while those generals, who had in vain solicited, or had no prospect of attaining, a triumph from the senate or the burgesses, marched in triumph on their own account

231.

at least to the Alban Mount (first in 523). No combat with a Ligurian or Corsican horde was too insignificant to be made a pretext for demanding a triumph. In order to put an end to the trade of peaceful triumphators, such as were

181.

the consuls of 573, the granting of a triumph was made to depend on the producing proof of a pitched battle which had cost the lives of at least 5000 of the enemy; but this proof was frequently evaded by false bulletins—already in houses of quality many an enemy's armour might be seen to glitter, which had by no means come thither from the field of battle. While formerly the commander-in-chief of the one year had been proud in that which followed to enter the staff of his successor, the fact that the consular Cato took service as a

194.
191.

military tribune under Tiberius Sempronius Longus (560) and Manius Glabrio (563; p. 280), was now regarded as a demonstration against the new-fashioned arrogance. Formerly the thanks of the community once for all had sufficed for service rendered to the state: now every meritorious act seemed to demand a permanent distinction. Already Gaius

260.

Duilius, the victor of Mylae (494), had gained an exceptional permission that, when he walked in the evening through the streets of the capital, he should be preceded by a torchbearer and a piper.   Statues and monuments, very often erected at the expense of the person whom they purported to honour, became so common, that it was ironically pronounced a distinction to have none.   But such merely personal honours did not long suffice.   A custom came into vogue, by which the victor and his descendants derived a permanent surname from the victories they had won—a custom mainly established by the victor of Zama who got himself designated as the hero of Africa, his brother as the hero of Asia, and his cousin as the hero of Spain.*   The example set by the higher was followed by the humbler classes.   When the ruling order did not disdain to settle the funeral arrangements for different ranks and to decree to the man who had been censor a purple winding-sheet, it could not complain of the freedmen for desiring that their sons at any rate might be decorated with the much envied purple border.   The robe, the ring, and the amulet-case distinguished not only the burgess and the burgess's wife from the foreigner and the slave, but also the person who was free-born from one who had been a slave, the son of free-born, from the son of manumitted, parents, the son of the knight and the senator from the common burgess, the descendant of a curule house from the common senator (p. 335)—and this in a community where all that was great and good was the work of civil equality!

The dissension in the community was reflected in the ranks of the opposition.   Resting on the support of the farmers, the patriots raised a loud cry for reform ; resting on the support of the mob in the capital, demagogism began its work.   Although the two tendencies do not admit of being wholly separated but in various respects go hand in hand, it will be necessary to consider them apart.

The party of reform emerges, as it were, personified in Marcus Porcius Cato (520-605).   Cato, the last statesman of note belonging to that earlier system which restricted its ideas to Italy and was averse to schemes of universal empire, was for that reason accounted in after times the model

The party of reform. Cato. 234–149.

335.

---

* P. 301.   The first certain instance of such a surname is that of Manius Valerius Maximus, consul in 491, who, as conqueror of Messana, assumed the name Messalla (p. 371) : that the consul of 419 was, in a similar manner, called Calenus, is an error.   The surname of Maximus in the Valerian *gens* (i. 290) is not precisely analogous with the same surname in the Fabian (i. 340).

of a genuine Roman of the antique stamp; he may with greater justice be regarded as the representative of the opposition of the Roman middle class to the new Hellenico-cosmopolite nobility. Brought up at the plough, he was induced to enter on a political career by a neighbouring proprietor, one of the few nobles who kept aloof from the tendencies of the age, Lucius Valerius Flaccus. That upright patrician deemed the rough Sabine farmer the proper man to stem the current of the times; and he was not deceived in his estimate. Beneath the aegis of Flaccus, and after the good old fashion serving his fellow-citizens and the commonwealth in counsel and action, Cato fought his way up to the consulate and a triumph, and even to the censorship. Having in his seventeenth year entered the burgess-army, he had passed through the whole Hannibalic war from the battle on the Trasimene lake to that of Zama; had served under Marcellus and Fabius, under Nero and Scipio; and at Tarentum and Sena, in Africa, Sardinia, Spain, and Macedonia, had shown equal ability as a soldier, a staff-officer, and a general. He was the same in the Forum, as in the battle-field. His prompt and intrepid address, his rough but pungent rustic wit, his knowledge of Roman law and Roman affairs, his incredible activity and his iron frame, first brought him into notice in the neighbouring towns; and, when at length he made his appearance on the greater arena of the Forum and the senate-house in the capital, constituted him the most influential pleader and political orator of his time. He took up the key-note first struck by Manius Curius, his ideal among Roman statesmen (i. 336): throughout his long life he made it his task honestly, to the best of his judgment, to assail on all hands the prevailing declension; and even in his eighty-fifth year he battled in the Forum with the new spirit of the times. He was anything but comely—he had green eyes, his enemies alleged, and red hair—and he was not a great man, still less a far-seeing statesman. Thoroughly narrow in his political and moral views, and having the ideal of the good old times always before his eyes and on his lips, he cherished an obstinate contempt for everything new. Deeming himself entitled by virtue of his own austere life to manifest an unrelenting severity and harshness towards everything and everybody; upright and honourable, but without a glimpse of any duty beyond the sphere of police discipline and of mercantile integrity; an enemy to all villany and vulgarity as well as to all genius and refinement, and above all things a foe to those who were his foes; he never made an attempt to stop evils at their source, but waged war throughout life against mere symptoms, and especially against persons. The ruling lords, no doubt, looked down with a lofty disdain on the ignoble barker, and believed, not without reason, that they were far superior; but fashionable corruption in and out of the senate secretly trembled in the presence of the old censor of morals with his proud republican bearing, of the scar-covered veteran of the Hannibalic war, and of the highly influential senator who was the protector of the Roman farmers. He publicly laid before his noble colleagues, one after another, his list of their sins; certainly without being remarkably particular as to the proofs, and certainly also with a peculiar relish in the case of those who had personally crossed or provoked him. With equal fearlessness he reproved and publicly scolded the burgesses for every new injustice and every fresh disorder. His angry attacks provoked numerous enemies, and he lived in declared and irreconcilable hostility with the most powerful aristocratic coteries of the time, particularly the Scipios and Flaminini; he was publicly accused forty-four times. But the farmers—and it is a significant indication how powerful still in the Roman middle class was the spirit which had enabled them to survive the day of Cannae—never allowed the unsparing champion of reform to lack the support of their votes. Indeed when in 570 Cato and his like-minded patrician colleague, Lucius Flaccus, solicited the censorship, and announced beforehand that it was their intention when in that office to undertake a thorough purification of all ranks and classes, the two men so greatly dreaded were elected by the burgesses notwithstanding all the exertions of the nobility; and the latter were obliged to submit, while the great purgation actually took place and erased among others the brother of Africanus from the roll of the equites, and the brother of the deliverer of the Greeks from the roll of the senate.

184.

This warfare directed against individuals, and the various

Police reform.

attempts to repress the spirit of the age by means of justice
and of police, however deserving of respect might be the sentiments in which they originated, could only at most stem
the current of corruption for a short time ; and, while it is
remarkable that Cato was enabled in spite of that current
or rather by means of it to play his political part, it is
equally significant that he was as little successful in getting
rid of the leaders of the opposite party as they were in getting
rid of him.   The processes of count and reckoning instituted
by him and by those who shared his views before the burgesses
uniformly remained, at least in the cases that were of political
importance, quite as ineffectual as the counter-accusations
directed against him.   Nor was much more effect produced
by the police-laws, which were issued at this period in
unusual numbers, especially with a view to the restriction of
luxury and the introduction of a frugal and orderly house-
keeping, and some of which have still to be noticed in our
view of the national economics.

Assigna-
tions of
land.

Far more practical and more useful were the attempts
made to counteract the spread of decay by indirect means ;
among which, beyond doubt, the assignations of new farms
out of the domain land occupy the first place.   These
assignations were made in great numbers and of considerable
extent in the period between the first and second war with
Carthage, and again from the close of the latter till towards
the end of this epoch.   The most important of them were the
distribution of the Picenian possessions by Gaius Flaminius

232.

194.

in 522 (p. 87) ; the foundation of eight new maritime
colonies in 560 (p. 201) ; and above all the comprehensive
colonization of the district between the Apennines and the
Po by the establishment of the Latin colonies of Placentia,
Cremona (p. 87), Bononia (p. 209), and Aquileia (p. 207),
and of the burgess-colonies, Potentia, Pisaurum, Mutina,

218.
189-177.

Parma, and Luna (p. 209) in the years 536 and 565-577.
By far the greater part of these valuable foundations may be
ascribed to the reforming party.   Cato and those who shared
his opinions demanded such measures, pointing, on the
one hand, to the devastation of Italy by the Hannibalic
war and the alarming decrease of the farms and of the
free Italian population generally, and, on the other, to the

widely extended possessions of the nobles—occupied along with, and similarly to, property of their own—in Cisalpine Gaul, in Samnium, and in the Apulian and Bruttian districts; and although the rulers of Rome did not probably comply with his demands to the extent to which they might and should have complied with them, yet they did not remain deaf to the warning voice of so judicious a man.

Of a kindred character was the proposal, which Cato made in the senate, to remedy the decline of the burgess cavalry by the institution of four hundred new equestrian stalls (p. 338). The exchequer cannot have wanted means for the purpose; but the proposal appears to have been defeated by the exclusive spirit of the nobility and their endeavour to expel from the burgess cavalry those who were troopers merely and not knights. On the other hand, the serious emergencies of the war, which soon induced the Roman government to make an attempt—fortunately unsuccessful—to recruit their armies after the Oriental fashion from the slave-market (p. 145, 176), compelled them to modify the qualifications hitherto required for service in the burgess army, viz., a minimum census of 11,000 *asses* (£43), and free birth. Apart from the fact that they took up for service in the fleet the persons of free birth rated between 4000 *asses* (£17) and 1500 *asses* (£6) and all the freedmen, the minimum census for the legionary was reduced to 4000 *asses* (£17); and, in case of need, both those who were bound to serve in the fleet and the free-born rated between 1500 *asses* (£6) and 375 *asses* (£1 10*s.*) were enrolled in the burgess infantry. These innovations, which belong probably to the end of the preceding or beginning of the present epoch, doubtless did not originate in party efforts any more than did the Servian military reform; but they gave a material impulse to the democratic party, in so far as those who bore civic burdens necessarily claimed and eventually obtained equalization of civic rights. The poor and the freedmen began to be of some importance in the commonwealth from the time when they served it; and chiefly from this cause arose one of the most important constitutional changes of this epoch—the remodelling of the *comitia centuriata*, which most probably took place in the same year in which the war concerning Sicily terminated (513).

Reforms in the military service.

241.

Reform of
the cen-
turies.

According to the order of voting hitherto followed in the
centuriate comitia, the wealthy had the preponderance,
although the freeholders were no longer—as down to the
reform of Appius Claudius (i. 339) they had been—the sole
voters. The equites, or in other words the patricio-plebeian
nobility, voted first, then those of the highest rating, or in
other words those who had exhibited to the censor an estate
of at least 100,000 *asses* (£420) ;* and these two divisions,
when they concurred, had decided every vote. The suffrage
of those assessed under the four following classes had been
of doubtful weight ; that of those whose valuation remained
below the standard of the lowest class, 11,000 *asses* (£43),
had been virtually illusory, and the freedmen had with
few exceptions been totally destitute of the suffrage.
According to the new arrangement the right of priority
in voting was withdrawn from the equites, although they
retained their separate divisions, and it was transferred
to a voting division chosen from the first class by lot;
the freedman was placed on an equal footing with the
freeborn ; and lastly the same number of votes was conceded
to each of the five classes,† so that, even if the burgesses

---

* As to the original rates of the Roman census it is difficult to lay down
anything definite. Afterwards, as is
well known, 100,000 *asses* was regarded
as the minimum census of the first
class ; to which the census of the other
four classes stood in the (at least approxi-
mate) ratio of $\frac{3}{4}$, $\frac{1}{2}$, $\frac{1}{4}$, $\frac{1}{9}$. But these rates
are understood already by Polybius, as by
all later authors, to refer to the light *as* ($\frac{1}{10}$
of the *denarius*), and apparently this
view must be adhered to, although in
reference to the Voconian law the same
sums are reckoned as heavy *asses* ($\frac{1}{4}$ of
the *denarius*: *Geschichte des Röm. Münz-
wesens*, p. 302). But Appius Claudius,
who first in 442 expressed the census-
rates in money instead of in land,
(p. 339), cannot in this have made
use of the light *as*, which only came
into existence in 485 (i. 493). Either
therefore he expressed the same
amounts in heavy *asses*, and these were
at the reduction of the coinage converted
into light ; or he proposed the later
figures, and these remained the same
notwithstanding the reduction of the

coinage, which in this case would have
involved a lowering of the class-rates by
more than the half. Grave doubts may
be raised in opposition to either hypothesis ; but the former appears the more
credible, for so exorbitant an advance in
democratic development is neither probable at the end of the fifth century nor
as an incidental consequence of a mere
administrative measure, and besides it
would hardly have disappeared wholly
from tradition. 100,000 light *asses*, or
40,000 sesterces, may, moreover, be reasonably regarded as the equivalent of the
original Roman full hide of perhaps 20
iugera (p. 107) ; so that according to this
view the rates of the census as a whole
have changed merely in expression, and
not in value.

† The adjustment of the five class-rates
at 100,000, 75,000, 50,000, 25,000, 11,000
asses (£420, £315, £210, £105, £43), in
combination with the hypothesis that
each class gave an equal number of
votes, suggests the possibility that the
whole number of those rated in a higher
class, especially the first, exceeded the

312.

269.

were at one, it was only by the voting of the third class that
the majority was decided.   This reform of the centuries
was the first important constitutional change which the
new opposition won from the nobility, the first victory of
democracy proper.   It thereby obtained on the one hand the
abolition of the priority of voting vested in the nobility, and
on the other hand equality of rights in the matter of election.
The importance of that aristocratic right of prior voting
cannot be estimated too highly, especially at an epoch in
which practically the influence of the nobility on the burgesses
at large was constantly on the increase.   Even the patrician
order proper were still at this epoch powerful enough to
fill the second consulship and the second censorship, which
stood open in law alike to patricians and plebeians, solely
with men of their own body, the former up to the close
of this period (till 582), the latter even for a generation
longer (till 623) ; and in fact, at the most perilous moment
which the Roman republic ever experienced—in the crisis
after the battle of Cannae—they cancelled the duly and
legally conducted election of the officer who was in all respects
the ablest—the plebeian Marcellus—to the consulship va-
cated by the death of the patrician Paullus, solely on account
of his plebeian origin.   At the same time it is a significant
token of the nature even of this reform that the right of precedence in voting was withdrawn from the nobility alone,
not from those of the highest rating ; the right withdrawn
from the equestrian centuries passed not to a division chosen
incidentally by lot from the whole burgesses, but exclusively
to the first class.   Still more trenchant in theory at least
was the equalization of the suffrage for the rich and for
the poor, for the freeborn and the freedmen, who were as-
sessable, so that, instead of the half, only about a fifth of the

172.

131.

---

number of those entitled to vote in the
next following class. But this suspicion,
in itself not without ground, carries no
great weight, inasmuch as the censors, in
fixing the limits of the voting divisions,
acted with an arbitrariness which appears
to our views astonishing; it may be conjectured that, when this case occurred,
they added those of lowest valuation
in the higher class to the roll of the
following, till the number of persons was
at least equal, and probably this is the
reason why the census of the first class
is stated sometimes at 100,000, sometimes at 110,000 and 125,000 *asses*. The
tendency of the measure doubtless was
to grant to those entitled to vote at all,
more especially the first three classes, a
suffrage equal in kind.

whole number of votes remained in the hands of those of the highest rating.   But one of the most important, perhaps practically the most important, of these innovations—the equalizing of the freedmen with the free-born—was set aside again twenty years later (534) by one of the most notable men of the reform party itself, the censor Gaius Flaminius, and the freedmen were removed from the centuries — a measure which the censor Tiberius Sempronius Gracchus, the father of the two authors of the Roman revolution, fifty years afterwards (585) renewed and enforced against the freedmen who were always intruding afresh.   The abiding fruit therefore of the reform of the centuries, apart from the enactment directed against the prerogative of the equestrian order, was the political abolition of the distinction as to estate among the burgesses whose valuation exceeded the lowest rating—equality in point of suffrage for the burgesses entitled to vote at all.   Substantially in this way all free-holder burgesses of free birth had long enjoyed equality of suffrage in the *comitia tributa,* while the votes of the non-freeholders and freedmen had there been rendered almost practically worthless by being crowded into four of the thirty-five tribes.   The general result accordingly was the remodelling of the *comitia centuriata* according to the principle already recognized in the *comitia tributa*; a change which recommended itself by the circumstance, that elections, pro-posals of laws, criminal charges, and generally all affairs requiring the co-operation of the burgesses, came to be uni-formly brought before the *comitia tributa*, and the more unwieldy centuries were seldom convoked except when it was constitutionally necessary to do so for electing the censors, con-suls, and praetors, or for decreeing an aggressive war.   It thus appears that this reform did not introduce a new principle into the constitution, but only brought into general application the principle that had long regulated the working of the practi-cally more frequent and more important form of the burgess-assemblies.   Its democratic, but by no means demagogic, tendency is clearly apparent in the circumstance that the proper supports of every really revolutionary party—the proletariate and the freedmen—still continued as before to hold an inferior position in the centuries as well as in the tribes. For that reason the practical significance of this alteration in the order of voting regulating the popular assemblies must not be estimated too highly. The new law of election doubtless completed in theory civil equality, but did not prevent, and perhaps did not even materially impede, the contemporary formation of a new politically privileged order. It is certainly not owing to the mere imperfection of tradition, defective as it undoubtedly is, that we are nowhere able to point to a practical influence exercised by this much-discussed reform on the course of political affairs. An intimate connection, we may add, subsisted between this reform which equalized the suffrages of the burgesses entitled to vote at all, and the already-mentioned abolition of the Roman burgess-communities *sine suffragio* which were gradually merged in the community of full burgesses. The levelling spirit of the party of progress suggested the abolition of distinctions within the burgess-body, while the chasm between burgesses and non-burgesses was at the same time deepened and widened.

Reviewing what the reform party of this age aimed at and obtained, we find that it undoubtedly exerted itself with patriotism and energy to check, and to a certain extent succeeded in checking, the spread of decay—more especially the falling off of the farmer class and the relaxation of the old strict and frugal habits—as well as the preponderating political influence of the new nobility. But we fail to discover any higher political aim. The discontent of the multitude and the moral indignation of the better classes found doubtless in this opposition their appropriate and powerful expression ; but we do not find either a clear insight into the sources of the evil, or any definite and comprehensive plan of remedying it. A certain want of purpose pervaded all these efforts otherwise so deserving of respect, and the purely defensive attitude of the defenders foreboded little good in the issue. Whether the disease could be remedied at all by human skill, remains fairly open to question ; the Roman reformers of this period seem to have been good citizens rather than good statesmen, and to have conducted the great struggle between the old civism and the new cosmopolitanism on their part in a somewhat inadequate and narrow spirit.

Results of the efforts at reform.

Demagog-
ism.

But, as this period witnessed the rise of a rabble by the side of the burgesses, so it witnessed also the emergence of a demagogism that flattered the populace alongside of the respectable and useful party of opposition. Cato was already acquainted with men who made a trade of demagogism; who had a morbid propensity for speechifying, as others had for drinking or for sleeping; who hired listeners, if they could find no willing audience otherwise; and whom people heard as they heard the market-crier, without attending to their words or, when needing help, entrusting themselves to their care. In his caustic fashion the old man describes these fops formed after the model of the Greek talkers of the *agora*, dealing in jests and witticisms, singing and dancing, ready for anything; such an one was, in his opinion, good for nothing but to exhibit himself as harlequin in a procession and to bandy talk with the public—he would sell his talk or his silence for a bit of bread. In truth these demagogues were the worst enemies of reform. While the reformers insisted above all things and in every direction on moral amendment, demagogism preferred to insist on the limitation of the powers of the government and the extension of those of the burgesses.

Abolition
of the dic-
tatorship.
217.

216.

202.

Under the former head the most important innovation was the practical abolition of the dictatorship. The crisis occasioned by Quintus Fabius and his popular opponents in 537 (p. 133) gave the death-blow to this all-along unpopular institution. Although the government once afterwards, in 538, under the immediate impression produced by the battle of Cannae, nominated a dictator invested with active command, it could not again venture to do so in more peaceful times. On several occasions subsequently (the last in 552), sometimes after a previous indication by the burgesses of the person to be nominated, a dictator was appointed for urban business; but the office, without being formally abolished, fell practically into desuetude. Through its abeyance the Roman constitutional system, so artificially constructed, lost a corrective which was very desirable with reference to its peculiar feature of collegiate magistrates (i. 280); and the government, which was vested with the sole power of creating a dictatorship or in other words of suspending the consuls, and ordinarily designated also the person who was to be nominated as dictator, lost one of its most important instruments. Its place was but very imperfectly supplied by the power—which the senate thenceforward claimed—of conferring in extraordinary emergencies, particularly on the sudden outbreak of revolt or war, a quasi-dictatorial power on the supreme magistrates for the time being, by instructing them " to take measures for the safety of the commonwealth at their discretion," and thus creating a state of things similar to the modern martial law.

Along with this change the formal powers of the people in the nomination of magistrates as well as in questions of government, administration, and finance, received a hazardous extension. The priesthoods—particularly those politically most important, the colleges of men of lore—according to ancient custom filled up the vacancies in their ranks, and nominated also their own presidents, where these corporations had presidents at all ; and in fact, for such institutions destined to transmit the knowledge of divine things from generation to generation, the only form of election in keeping with their spirit was cooptation. It was therefore—although not of great political importance—an indication of the incipient disorganization of the republican arrangements, that at this time (before 542), while election into the colleges themselves was left on its former footing, the designation of the presidents—the *curiones* and *pontifices*—from the ranks of those corporations was transferred from the colleges to the community. In this case, however, with a pious regard for forms that is genuinely Roman, in order to avoid any error, only a minority of the tribes, and therefore not the " people," completed the act of election.

Of greater importance was the growing interference of the burgesses in questions as to persons and things belonging to the sphere of military administration and external policy. To this head belong the transference of the nomination of the ordinary staff-officers from the general to the burgesses, which has been already mentioned (p. 342) ; the elections of the leaders of the opposition as commanders in chief against Hannibal (p. 127, 135) ; the unconstitutional and irrational decree of the people in 537, which divided the

Election of priests by the community.

212.

Interference of the community in war and administration.

217.

supreme command between the unpopular generalissimo and his popular lieutenant who opposed him in the camp as well as at home (p. 133) ; the tribunician complaint laid before the burgesses, charging an officer like Marcellus with injudicious and dishonest management of the war (545), which even compelled him to come from the camp and to demonstrate his military capacity before the public of the capital; the still more scandalous attempts to refuse to the victor of Pydna his triumph by a decree of the burgesses (p. 367) ; the investiture —suggested, it is true, by the senate—of a private man with extraordinary consular authority (544 ; p. 167) ; the dangerous threat of Scipio that, if the senate should refuse him the chief command in Africa, he would seek the sanction of the burgesses (549 ; p. 190) ; the attempt of a man half crazy with ambition to extort from the burgesses, against the will of the government, a declaration of war in every respect unwarranted against the Rhodians (587 ; p. 327) ; and the new constitutional axiom, that every state treaty acquired validity only through the ratification of the people.

Interference of the community with the finances.

This joint action of the burgesses in governing and in commanding was fraught in a high degree with peril. But still more dangerous was their interference with the finances of the state; not only because any attack on the oldest and most important right of the government—the exclusive administration of the public property—struck at the root of the power of the senate, but because the placing of the most important business of this nature—the distribution of the public domains—in the hands of the public assemblies of the burgesses necessarily dug the grave of the republic. To allow the public assembly to decree the transference of public property without limit to its own pocket was not only wrong, but was the beginning of the end ; it demoralized the best-disposed citizens, and gave to the proposer a power incompatible with a free commonwealth. Salutary as was the distribution of the public land, and doubly blameable as was the senate accordingly for omitting to cut off this most dangerous of all weapons of agitation by voluntarily distributing the occupied lands, yet Gaius Flaminius, when he came to the burgesses in 522 with the proposal to distribute the domains of Picenum, undoubtedly injured the com-

(marginal references: 219. 210. 215. 167. 232.)

monwealth more by the means than he benefited it by the
end.   Cassius had doubtless two hundred and fifty years
earlier proposed the same thing (i. 309) ; but the two
measures, closely as they coincided in the letter, were yet
wholly different, inasmuch as Cassius submitted a matter
affecting the community to that community while still in
its vigour and conducting its own government, whereas
Flaminius submitted a public question to the popular assembly
of a great state.

Not the party of the government only, but the party of
reform also, very properly regarded the military, executive,
and financial government as the legitimate domain of the
senate, and carefully abstained from making full use of, to
say nothing of augmenting, the formal power vested in popular assemblies that were inwardly doomed to inevitable
dissolution.   Never even in the most limited monarchy was
a part so completely null assigned to the monarch as was
allotted to the sovereign Roman people : this was no doubt in
more than one respect to be regretted, but it was, owing to
the existing state of the comitial machinery, even in the view
of the friends of reform a matter of necessity.   For this
reason Cato and those who shared his views never submitted
to the burgesses a question, which interfered with the
government strictly so called ; and never, directly or indirectly, by decree of the people extorted from the senate the
political or financial measures which they wished, such as
the declaration of war against Carthage and the assignations
of land.   The government of the senate might be bad ; the
popular assemblies could not govern at all.   Not that an
evil-disposed majority predominated in them ; on the contrary the counsel of a man of standing, the loud call of
honour, and the louder call of necessity were still, as a rule,
listened to in the comitia, and averted the most injurious
and disgraceful results.   The burgesses, before whom Marcellus pleaded his cause, ignominiously dismissed his accuser,
and elected the accused as consul for the following year :
they suffered themselves also to be persuaded of the
necessity of the war against Philip, terminated the war
against Perseus by the election of Paullus, and accorded to
the latter his well-deserved triumph.   But in order to such

Nullity of the comitia.

elections and such decrees there was needed some special stimulus; in general the mass having no will of its own followed the first impulse, and folly or accident dictated the decision.

Disorganization of government.   In the state, as in every organism, an organ which no longer discharges its functions is injurious. The nullity of the sovereign assembly of the people involved no small danger. Any minority in the senate might constitutionally appeal against the majority to the comitia. To every individual who possessed the easy art of addressing untutored ears or of merely throwing away money a path was opened up for his acquiring a position or procuring a decree in his favour, to which the magistrates and the government were formally bound to do homage. Hence sprang those citizen-generals, accustomed to sketch plans of battle on the tables of taverns and to look down on the regular service with compassion by virtue of their inborn genius for strategy; hence those staff-officers, who owed their command to the canvassing intrigues of the capital and, whenever matters looked serious, had at once to get leave of absence *en masse*; and hence the battles of the Trasimene lake and of Cannae, and the disgraceful management of the war with Perseus. At every step the government was thwarted and led astray by those unaccountable decrees of the burgesses, and as was to be expected, most of all in the very cases where it was most in the right.

But the weakening of the government and the weakening of the community itself were among the lesser dangers that sprang from this demagogism. Still more directly the factious violence of individual ambition pushed itself forward under the aegis of the constitutional rights of the burgesses. That which formally issued forth as the will of the supreme authority in the state was in reality very often the mere personal pleasure of the mover; and what was to be the fate of a commonwealth in which war and peace, the nomination and deposition of the general and his officers, the public chest and the public property, were dependent on the caprices of the multitude and its accidental leaders? The thunder-storm had not yet burst; but the clouds were gathering in denser masses, and occasional peals of thunder were already rolling through the sultry air. It was a circumstance, moreover, fraught with double danger, that the tendencies which were apparently most opposite met together at their extremes both as regarded ends and as regarded means. Family policy and demagogism carried on a similar and equally dangerous rivalry in patronizing and worshipping the rabble. Gaius Flaminius was regarded by the statesmen of the following generation as the initiator of that course from which proceeded the reforms of the Gracchi and—we may add—the democratico-monarchical revolution that ensued. But Publius Scipio also, although setting the fashion to the nobility in arrogance, title-hunting, and client-making, sought support for his personal and almost dynastic policy of opposition to the senate in the multitude, which he not only charmed by the dazzling effect of his personal qualities, but also bribed by his largesses of grain; in the legions, whose favour he courted by all means whether right or wrong; and above all in the body of clients, high and low, that personally adhered to him. Only the dreamy mysticism, on which the charm as well as the weakness of that remarkable man so largely depended, never suffered him to awake at all or allowed him to awake but imperfectly out of the belief that he was nothing, and that he desired to be nothing, but the first burgess of Rome.

To assert the possibility of a reform would be as rash as to deny it: this much is certain, that a thorough amendment of the state in all its departments was urgently required, and that in no quarter was any serious attempt made to accomplish it. Various alterations in details, no doubt, were made on the part of the senate as well as on the part of the popular opposition. The majorities in each were still well disposed, and still frequently, notwithstanding the chasm that separated the parties, united in a common endeavour to effect the removal of the worst evils. But, while they did not stop the evil at its source, it was to little purpose that the better disposed listened with anxiety to the dull murmur of the swelling flood and worked at dikes and dams. Contenting themselves with palliatives, and failing to apply even these—especially such as were the most important, the improvement of justice, for instance, and the distribution of the domains—in proper

season and due measure, they helped to prepare evil days for
their posterity. By neglecting to break up the field at the
proper time, they propagated weeds even when they had no
desire to do so.   To the later generations who survived the
storms of revolution the period after the Hannibalic war appeared the golden age of Rome, and Cato seemed the model
of the Roman statesman.   It was in reality the calm before
the storm and the epoch of political mediocrities, an age like
that of the government of Walpole in England; and no
Chatham was found in Rome to infuse fresh energy into the
stagnant life of the nation.   Wherever we cast our eyes,
chinks and rents are yawning in the old building; we see
workmen busy sometimes in filling them up, sometimes in
enlarging them; but we nowhere perceive any trace of preparations for thoroughly rebuilding or renewing it, and the
question is no longer whether, but simply when, the structure
will fall. During no epoch did the Roman constitution remain
formally so stable as in the period from the Sicilian to the
third Macedonian war and for a generation beyond it; but the
stability of the constitution was here, as everywhere, not a sign
of the health of the state, but a token of incipient sickness
and the harbinger of revolution.

CHAPTER XII.

THE MANAGEMENT OF LAND AND OF CAPITAL.

It is in the sixth century of the city that we first find ma- Roman
terials for a history of the times exhibiting in some measure economics.
the mutual connection of events; and it is in that century
also that the economic condition of Rome emerges into view
more clearly and distinctly. It was at this epoch that the
wholesale system, as regards both the cultivation of land and
the management of capital, became first established under the
form, and on the scale, which afterwards prevailed; although
we cannot exactly discriminate how much of that system is
traceable to earlier precedent, how much to an imitation of
the methods of husbandry and of speculation among peoples
that were earlier civilized, especially the Phoenicians, and how
much to the growth of capital and the growth of intelligence
in the nation. A summary outline of these economic relations
will conduce to a more accurate understanding of the internal
history of Rome.

Roman husbandry* applied itself either to the farming of

---

* In order to gain a true idea of ancient
Italy, it is necessary for us to bear in
mind the great changes which have been
produced there by modern cultivation.
Of the *cerealia*, rye was not cultivated in
antiquity; and the Romans of the empire were astonished to find that oats,
with which they were well acquainted as
a weed, was used by the Germans for
making porridge. Rice was first cultivated in Italy at the end of the fifteenth,
and maize at the beginning of the seventeenth, century. Potatoes and tomatoes
were brought from America; artichokes
seem to be nothing but a cultivated
variety of the cardoon which was known
to the Romans, although the peculiar
character superinduced by cultivation
appears of more recent origin. The
almond, again, or " Greek nut," the

peach, or " Persian nut," and also the
" soft nut" (*nux mollusca*), although
originally foreign to Italy, are met with
there at least 150 years before Christ.
The date-palm, introduced into Italy
from Greece as into Greece from the
East, and forming a living attestation of
the primitive commercial-religious intercourse between the West and the
East, was already cultivated in Italy 300
years before Christ (Liv. x. 47; Pallad.
v. 5, 2; xi. 12, 1) not for its fruit (Plin.
H. N. xiii. 4, 26), but, just as in the
present day, as a handsome plant, and
for the sake of the leaves which were
used at public festivals. The cherry, or
fruit of Cerasus on the Black Sea, was
later in being introduced, and only began
to be planted in Italy in the time of
Cicero, although the wild cherry is indi-

estates, to the occupation of pasture lands, or to the tillage of petty holdings. A very distinct view of the first of these is presented to us in the description given by Cato.

Farming of estates. Their size. The Roman estates were, considered as larger holdings, uniformly of limited extent. That described by Cato had an area of 240 *iugera*; a very common measure was the so-called *centuria* of 200 *iugera*. Where the laborious culture of the vine was pursued, the unit of husbandry was made still less; Cato assumes in that case an area of 100 *iugera*. Any one who wished to invest more capital in farming did not enlarge his estate, but acquired several estates; accordingly the quantity of 500 *iugera* (i. 326), fixed as the maximum which it was allowable to occupy, has been conceived to represent the contents of two or three estates.

Management of the estate. Heritable leases were not recognized in law, and leases for life occurred as a substitute only in the case of communal land. Leases for shorter periods, granted either for a fixed sum of money or on condition that the lessee should bear all the costs of tillage and should receive in return a share, ordinarily one half, of the produce,[*] were not unknown, but they were exceptional and a makeshift; so that no distinct class of tenant-farmers grew up in Italy.[†] Ordinarily there-

---

genous there; still later, perhaps, came the apricot, or "Armenian plum." The citron-tree was not cultivated in Italy till the later ages of the empire; the orange was only introduced by the Moors in the twelfth or thirteenth, and the aloe (*Agave Americana*) from America only in the sixteenth, century. Cotton was first cultivated in Europe by the Arabs. The buffalo also and the silkworm belong only to modern, not to ancient Italy.

It is obvious that the products which Italy had not originally are for the most part those very products which seem to us truly "Italian;" and if modern Germany, as compared with the Germany visited by Caesar, may be called a southern land, Italy has since in no less degree acquired a more "southern" aspect.

[*] According to Cato, *de R. R.* 137 (comp. 16), in the case of a lease with division of the produce the gross produce of the estate, after deduction of the fodder necessary for the oxen that drew the plough, was divided between lessor and lessee (*colonus partiarius*) in the proportions agreed upon between them. That the shares were ordinarily equal may be conjectured from the analogy of the French *bail à cheptel* and the similar Italian system of half-and-half leases, as well as from the absence of all trace of any other scheme of partition. It is erroneous to refer to the case of the *politor*, who got the fifth of the grain or, if the division took place before thrashing, from the sixth to the ninth sheaf (Cato, 136, comp. 5); he was not a lessee sharing the produce, but a labourer assumed in the harvest season, who received his daily wages according to that contract of partnership (p. 390).

[†] There existed no appropriate form for such a lease even in law; for that the contract of *locatio* first applied to the letting of houses, and was only transferred to the leasing of land, is shown very clearly by the rule—applicable to the letting of a house, but not to the leasing of land—that the payment

fore the proprietor himself superintended the cultivation of his estates; he did not, however, manage them strictly in person, but only appeared from time to time on the property in order to settle the plan of operations, to look after its execution, and to audit the accounts of his servants. He was thus enabled on the one hand to work a number of estates at the same time, and on the other hand to devote himself, as circumstances might require, to public affairs.

The grain cultivated consisted especially of spelt and wheat, with some barley and millet; turnips, radishes, garlic, poppies, were also grown, and—particularly as fodder for the cattle—lupines, beans, pease, vetches, and other leguminous plants. The seed was sown ordinarily in autumn, only in exceptional cases in spring. Much activity was displayed in irrigation and draining; and drainage by means of covered ditches was early in use. Meadows also for supplying hay were not wanting, and even in the time of Cato they were frequently irrigated artificially. Of equal, if not of greater, economic importance than grain and vegetables were the olive and the vine, of which the former was planted among the crops, the latter in vineyards appropriated to itself.* Figs, apples, pears, and other fruit trees were cultivated; and likewise elms, poplars, and other leafy trees and shrubs, partly for the felling of the wood, partly for the sake of the leaves which were useful as litter and as fodder for cattle. The rearing of cattle, on the other hand, held a far less important place in the economy of the Italians than it holds in modern times, for vegetables formed the general fare, and animal food made its appearance at table only exceptionally; where it did appear, it consisted almost solely of the flesh of swine or lambs.

Objects of husbandry.

---

of the tenant must necessarily consist in money; in consequence of which the produce-lease among the Romans comes under the category of contingencies occurring in practical life but not falling within the theory of jurisprudence. The lease first assumed real importance when the Roman capitalists began to acquire transmarine possessions on a great scale; then indeed they knew how to value it, when a temporary lease was continued through several generations (Colum. i. 7, 3).

* That the space between the vines

was occupied not by grain, but only at the most by such fodder plants as easily grew in the shade, is evident from Cato (33, comp. 137), and accordingly Columella (iii. 3) calculates on no other accessory gain in the case of a vineyard except the produce of the young shoots sold. On the other hand, the orchard (*arbustum*) was sown like any corn field (Colum. ii. 9, 6). It was only where the vine was trained on living trees that corn was cultivated in the intervals between them.

Although the ancients did not fail to perceive the economic connection between agriculture and the rearing of cattle, and in particular the importance of producing manure, the modern combination of the growth of corn with the rearing of cattle was a thing foreign to antiquity. The larger cattle were kept only so far as was requisite for the tillage of the fields, and they were fed not on pasture set apart for the purpose, but, wholly during summer and mostly during winter also, in the stall. Sheep, again, were driven out on the stubble pasture; Cato allows 100 head to 240 *iugera*. Frequently, however, the proprietor preferred to let his winter pasture to a large sheep-owner, or to hand over his flock of sheep to a lessee who was to share the produce, stipulating for the delivery of a certain number of lambs and of a certain quantity of cheese and milk. Swine—Cato assigns to a large estate ten sties—poultry, and pigeons were kept in the farmyard, and fed as there was need; and, where opportunity offered, a small hare-preserve and a fish-pond were constructed—the modest commencement of that nursing and rearing of game and fish which was after-wards prosecuted to so enormous an extent.

Means of hus-bandry. Cattle.

The labours of the field were performed by means of oxen which were employed for ploughing, and of asses, which were used specially for the carriage of manure and for driving the mill; perhaps a horse also was kept, apparently for the use of the master. These animals were not reared on the estate, but were purchased; the oxen and horses at any rate were generally castrated. Cato assigns to an estate of 100 *iugera* one, to one of 240 *iugera* three, yoke of oxen; a later writer on agriculture, Saserna, assigns two yoke to the 200 *iugera*. Three asses were, according to Cato's estimate, required for the smaller, and four for the larger, estate.

Rural slaves.

The human labour on the farm was regularly performed by slaves. At the head of the body of slaves on the estate (*familia rustica*) stood the steward (*vilicus*, from *villa*), who received and expended, bought and sold, went to obtain the instructions of the landlord, and in his absence issued orders and administered punishment. Under him were placed the stewardess (*vilica*), who took charge of the house, kitchen and larder, poultry-yard and dovecot; a number of plough-men (*bubulci*) and common serfs, an ass-driver, a swineherd, and, where a flock of sheep was kept, a shepherd. The number, of course, varied according to the method of husbandry pursued. An arable estate of 200 *iugera* without orchards was estimated to require two ploughmen and six serfs; a similar estate with orchards two ploughmen and nine serfs; an estate of 240 *iugera* with olive plantations and sheep, three ploughmen, five serfs, and three herdsmen. A vineyard naturally required a larger expenditure of labour: an estate of 100 *iugera* with vine-plantations was supplied with one ploughman, eleven ordinary slaves, and two herdsmen. The steward of course occupied a freer position than the other slaves: the treatise of Mago advised that he should be allowed to marry, to rear children, and to have funds of his own, and Cato advises that he should be married to the stewardess; he alone had some prospect, in the event of good behaviour, of obtaining liberty from his master. In other respects all formed a common household. The slaves were, like the larger cattle, not bred on the estate, but purchased at an age capable of labour in the slave-market; and, when through age or infirmity they had become incapable of working, they were again sent with other refuse to the market.* The farm-buildings (*villa rustica*) supplied at once stabling for the cattle, storehouses for the produce, and a dwelling for the steward and the slaves; while a separate country house (*villa urbana*) for the master was frequently erected on the estate. Every slave, even the steward himself, had all the necessaries of life delivered to him on the master's behalf at certain times and according to fixed rates; and upon these he had to subsist. He received in this way clothes and shoes, which were purchased in the market, and which the recipients had merely to keep in repair; a quantity of wheat

---

* Mago, or his translator (in Varro, *R. R.*, i. 17, 3), advises that slaves should not be bred, but should be purchased not under 22 years of age; and Cato must have had a similar course in view, as the personal staff of his model farm clearly shows, although he does not exactly say so. Cato (2) expressly counsels the sale of old and diseased slaves. The slave-breeding described by Columella (i. 8), under which female slaves who had three sons were exempted from labour, and the mothers of four sons were even manumitted, was doubtless an independent speculation rather than a part of the regular management of the estate—similar to the trade pursued by Cato himself of purchasing slaves to be trained and sold again (Plutarch, *Cat. Mai.* 21). The characteristic taxation mentioned in this same passage probably has reference to the body of servants properly so called (*familia urbana*).

monthly, which each had to grind for himself; as also salt, olives or salted fish to form a relish to their food, wine, and oil. The quantity was regulated by the labour; on which account the steward, who had easier work than the common slaves, got scantier measure than these. The stewardess attended to all the baking and cooking; and all partook of the same fare. It was not the ordinary practice to place chains on the slaves; but when any one had incurred punishment or was thought likely to attempt an escape, he was set to work in chains and was shut up during the night in the slaves' prison.*

Other la-
bourers.

Ordinarily these slaves belonging to the estate were sufficient; in case of need neighbours, as a matter of course, helped each other with their slaves for day's wages. Otherwise labourers from without were not usually employed, except in peculiarly unhealthy districts, where it was found advantageous to limit the amount of slaves and to employ hired persons in their room, and for the ingathering of the harvest, for which the regular supply of labour on the farm did not suffice. At the corn and hay harvests they took in hired reapers, who often instead of wages received from the sixth to the ninth sheaf of the produce reaped, or, if they also thrashed, the fifth of the grain: Umbrian labourers, for instance, went annually in great numbers to the vale of Rieti, to help to gather in the harvest there. The grape and olive harvest was ordinarily let to a contractor, who by means of

---

* In this restricted sense the chaining of slaves, and even of the sons of the family (Dionys. ii. 26), was very old; and accordingly chained field-labourers are mentioned by Cato as exceptions, to whom, as they could not themselves grind, bread had to be supplied instead of grain (56). Even in the times of the empire the chaining of slaves uniformly presents itself as a punishment inflicted definitively by the master, provisionally by the steward (Colum. i. 8; Gai. i. 13; Ulp. i. 11). If, notwithstanding, the tillage of the fields by means of chained slaves appeared in subsequent times as a distinct system, and the labourers' prison (*ergastulum*)—an underground cellar with window-apertures numerous but narrow and not to be reached from the ground by the hand (Colum. i. 6)—

became a necessary part of the farm-buildings, this state of matters was occasioned by the fact that the position of the rural serfs was harder than that of other slaves and therefore those slaves were chiefly placed in it who had, or seemed to have, committed some offence. That cruel masters, moreover, applied the chains without any occasion to do so, we do not mean to deny, and it is clearly indicated by the circumstance that the law-books do not decree the penalties applicable to slave transgressors against those in chains, but prescribe the punishment of the half-chained. It was precisely the same with branding; it was meant to be, strictly, a punishment, but the whole flock was probably marked (Diodor. xxxv. 5; Bernays, *Phokylides*, p. xxxi.).

his men—hired free labourers, or slaves of his own or of others—conducted the gleaning and pressing under the inspection of persons appointed by the landlord for the purpose, and delivered the produce to the master;* very frequently the landlord sold the harvest on the tree or branch, and left the purchaser to look after the ingathering.

The whole system was pervaded by the utter unscrupulousness characteristic of the power of capital. Slaves and cattle were placed on the same level; a good watchdog, it is said in a Roman writer on agriculture, must not be on too friendly terms with his "fellow-slaves." The slave and the ox were fed properly so long as they could work, because it would not have been good economy to let them starve; and they were sold like a worn-out ploughshare when they became unable to work, because in like manner it would not have been good economy to retain them longer. In earlier times religious considerations had exercised an alleviating influence, and had released the slave and the plough-ox from labour on the days enjoined for festivals and for rest.† Nothing is more characteristic of the spirit of Cato and those who shared his sentiments than the way in which they inculcated the observance of the holiday in the letter, and evaded it in reality, by advising that, while the plough should certainly be allowed to rest on these days, the slaves should even then be incessantly occupied with other labours not expressly prohibited. On principle no freedom of movement whatever was allowed to them—a slave, so runs one of Cato's maxims, must either work or sleep—and no attempt was ever made to attach the slaves to the estate or to

Spirit of the system.

---

* Cato does not expressly say this as to the vintage, but Varro does so (i. 17), and it is implied in the nature of the case. It would have been economically an error to fix the number of the slaves on a property by the standard of the labours of harvest; and least of all, had such been the case, would the grapes have been sold on the tree, which yet was frequently done (Cato, 147).

† Columella (ii. 12, 9) reckons to the year on an average 45 rainy days and holidays; with which accords the statement of Tertullian (*De Idolol.* 14), that the number of the heathen festival days did not come up to the fifty days of the Christian festal season from Easter to Whitsunday. To these fell to be added the time of rest in the middle of winter after the completion of the autumnal sowing, which Columella estimates at thirty days. Within this time, doubtless, the moveable "festival of seed-sowing" (*feriae sementivae*; comp. i. 210 and Ovid. *Fast.* i. 661) uniformly occurred. This month of rest must not be confounded with the holidays for holding courts in the season of the harvest (Plin. *Ep.* viii. 21, 2, *et al.*) and vintage.

their master by any bond of human sympathy. The letter
of the law in all its naked hideousness regulated the relation, and the Romans indulged no illusions as to the consequences. " So many slaves, so many foes," said a Roman
proverb. It was an economic maxim, that dissensions among
the slaves ought rather to be fostered than suppressed. In
the same spirit Plato and Aristotle, and no less strongly the
oracle of the landlords, the Carthaginian Mago, caution masters against bringing together slaves of the same nationality,
lest they should originate combinations and perhaps con-
spiracies of their fellow-countrymen. The landlord, as we
have already said, governed his slaves exactly in the same
way as the Roman community governed its subjects in the
" country estates of the Roman people," the provinces; and
the world learned by experience, that the ruling state had
modelled its new system of government on that of the slave-
holder. If, moreover, we have risen to that little-to-be
envied elevation of thought which values no feature of an
economy save the capital invested in it, we cannot deny
to the management of the Roman estates the praise of consistency, energy, punctuality, frugality, and solidity. The
sound practical husbandman is reflected in Cato's description of the steward, as he ought to be. He is the first on the
farm to rise and the last to go to bed; he is strict in dealing
with himself as well as with those under him, and knows
more especially how to keep the stewardess in order, but
is also careful of his labourers and his cattle, and in particular of the ox that draws the plough; he puts his hand
frequently to work and to every kind of it, but never works
himself weary like a slave; he is always at home, never
borrows nor lends, gives no entertainments, troubles himself
about no other worship than that of the gods of the hearth
and the field, and like a true slave leaves all dealings with
the gods as well as with men to his master; lastly and
above all, he modestly meets that master and faithfully
and simply, without carelessness and without excess of
care, conforms to the instructions which that master has
given. He is a bad husbandman, it is elsewhere said, who
buys what he can raise on his own land; a bad father of
a household, who takes in hand during the day what can

be done by candle-light, unless the weather be bad; a still
worse, who does on a working-day what might be done on
a holiday; but worst of all is he, who in good weather
allows work to go on within doors instead of in the open
air. The characteristic enthusiasm too of high farming is
not wanting; and the golden rules are laid down, that
the soil was given to the husbandman not to be scoured
and swept but to be sown and reaped, and that the farmer
therefore ought first to plant vines and olives and only
thereafter, and that not too early in life, to build himself
a villa. A certain boorishness marks the system, and,
instead of the rational investigation of causes and effects, the
well-known rules of rustic experience are uniformly brought
forward; yet there is an evident endeavour to appropriate
the experience of others and the products of foreign lands:
in Cato's list of the sorts of fruit trees, for instance, Greek,
African, and Spanish species appear.

The husbandry of the petty farmer differed from that of
the estate-holder only or chiefly in its being on a smaller scale.
The owner himself and his children in this case laboured
along with the slaves or in their room. The quantity of
cattle was reduced, and, where an estate no longer covered
the expenses of the plough and of the yoke that drew it, the
hoe formed the substitute. The culture of the olive and
the vine was less prominent, or was entirely wanting.

Husban-
dry of the
petty
farmers.

In the vicinity of Rome and of other large seats of consumption there existed also carefully irrigated gardens for
flowers and vegetables, somewhat similar to those which one
now sees around Naples; and these yielded a very abundant
return.

Pastoral husbandry was practised on a far greater scale
than agriculture. An estate in pasture land (*saltus*) had
of necessity in every case an area considerably greater than
an arable estate—the least allowance was 800 *iugera*—and
it might with advantage to the business be almost indefinitely extended. Italy is so situated in respect of climate that
the summer pasture in the mountains and the winter pasture
in the plains supplement each other: already at that period,
just as at the present day, and for the most part probably
along the same paths, the flocks and herds were driven in

Pastoral
husban-
dry.

spring from Apulia to Samnium, and in autumn back again from Samnium to Apulia. The winter pasturage, however, as has been already observed, did not consist entirely of ground kept for the purpose, but was partly the grazing of the stubbles. Horses, oxen, asses, and mules were reared, chiefly to supply the animals required by the landowners, carriers, soldiers, and so forth; herds of swine and of goats also were not neglected. But the almost universal habit of wearing woollen stuffs gave a far greater independence and far higher development to the breeding of sheep. The management was in the hands of slaves, and was on the whole similar to the management of the arable estate, the cattle-master (*magister pecoris*) coming in room of the steward. Throughout the summer the shepherd-slaves lived for the most part not under a roof, but, often miles remote from human habitations, under sheds and sheepfolds; it was necessary therefore that the strongest men should be selected for this employment, that they should be provided with horses and arms, and that they should be allowed far greater freedom of movement than was granted to the slaves on arable estates.

Results. Competition of transmarine corn.

In order to form some estimate of the economic results of this system of husbandry, we must consider the state of prices, and particularly the prices of grain at this period. On an average these were alarmingly low; and that in great measure through the fault of the Roman government, which in this important question was led into the most fearful blunders not so much by its short-sightedness, as by an unpardonable disposition to favour the proletariate of the capital at the expense of the farmers of Italy. The main question here was that of the competition between transmarine and Italian corn. The grain which was delivered by the provincials to the Roman government, sometimes gratuitously, sometimes for a moderate compensation, was in part applied by the government to the maintenance of the Roman official staff and of the Roman armies on the spot, partly given up to the lessees of the *decumae* on condition of their either paying a sum of money for it or of their undertaking to deliver certain quantities of grain at Rome or wherever else it should be required. From the time of the second

Macedonian war the Roman armies were uniformly supported by transmarine corn, and, though this tended to the
benefit of the Roman exchequer, it cut off the Italian
farmer from an important field of consumption for his produce. This however was the least part of the mischief.
The government had long, as was reasonable, kept a watch-
ful eye on the price of grain, and, when there was a
threatening of dearth, had interfered by well-timed purchases
abroad; and now, when the corn-deliveries of its subjects
brought into its hands every year large quantities of grain
—larger probably than were needed in times of peace—and
when, moreover, opportunities were presented to it of
acquiring foreign grain in almost unlimited quantity at
moderate prices, there was a natural temptation to glut
the markets of the capital with such grain, and to dispose
of it at rates which either in themselves or as compared
with the Italian rates were ruinously low. Already in the
years 551-554, and in the first instance apparently at the
suggestion of Scipio, 6 *modii* (1½ bush.) of Spanish and
African wheat were sold on public account to the citizens
of Rome at 24 and even at 12 *asses* (1*s.* 8*d.* or 10*d.*). Some
years afterwards (558), more than 240,000 bushels of Sicilian grain were distributed at the latter illusory price in
the capital. In vain Cato inveighed against this short-
sighted policy: the rise of demagogism had a part in
it, and these extraordinary, but probably very frequent,
distributions of grain under the market price by the government or individual magistrates became the germs of the subsequent corn-laws. But, even where the transmarine corn
did not reach the consumers in this extraordinary mode, it
injuriously affected Italian agriculture. Not only were the
masses of grain which the state sold off to the lessees of
the tenths beyond doubt acquired under ordinary circumstances by these so cheaply that, when re-sold, it could
be disposed of under the price of production; but it is
probable that in the provinces, particularly in Sicily—in consequence partly of the favourable nature of the soil, partly
of the extent to which wholesale farming and slave-holding
were pursued on the Carthaginian system (p. 9.)—the price
of production was in general considerably lower than in

203-200.

196.

Italy, while the transport of Sicilian and Sardinian corn to Latium was at least as cheap as, if not cheaper than, its transport thither from Etruria, Campania, or even northern Italy. In the natural course of things therefore transmarine corn could not but flow to the peninsula, and lower the price of the grain produced there. Under the unnatural disturbance of relations occasioned by the lamentable system of slave-labour, it would perhaps have been justifiable to impose a duty on transmarine corn for the protection of the Italian farmer; but the very opposite course seems to have been pursued, and with a view to favour the import of transmarine corn to Italy, a prohibitive system seems to have been applied in the provinces—for though the Rhodians were allowed to export a quantity of corn from Sicily by way of special favour, the exportation of grain from the provinces must probably, as a rule, have been free only as regarded Italy, and the transmarine corn must thus have been monopolized for the benefit of the mother-country.

Prices of Italian corn. 250.

The effects of this system are clearly evident. A year of extraordinary fertility like 504—when the people of the capital paid for 6 Roman *modii* (1½ bush.) of spelt not more than ⅗ of a *denarius* (about 5*d*.), and at the same price there were sold 180 Roman pounds (a pound = 11 oz.) of dried figs, 60 pounds of oil, 72 pounds of meat, and 6 *congii* (= 4½ gallons) of wine—is scarcely by reason of its very singularity to be taken into account; but other facts speak more distinctly. Even in Cato's time Sicily was called the granary of Rome. In productive years Sicilian and Sardinian corn was disposed of in the Italian ports for the freight. In the richest corn districts of the peninsula—the modern Romagna and Lombardy—during the time of Polybius victuals and lodgings in an inn cost on an average half an *as* (⅓*d*.) per day; a bushel and a half of wheat was there worth half a *denarius* (4*d*.). The latter average price, about the twelfth part of the normal price elsewhere,*

---

* The medium price of grain in the capital may be assumed at least for the seventh and eighth centuries of Rome at one *denarius* for the Roman *modius*, or 2*s*. 8*d*. per bushel of wheat, for which there is now paid (according to the average of the prices in the provinces of Brandenburg and Pomerania from 1816

shows undeniably that the producers of grain in Italy were wholly destitute of a market for their produce, and in consequence corn and corn-land there were almost valueless.

In a great industrial state, whose agriculture cannot feed its population, such a result might perhaps be regarded as useful or at any rate as not absolutely injurious; but a country like Italy, where manufactures were inconsiderable and agriculture was altogether the mainstay of the state, was in this way systematically ruined, and the welfare of the nation as a whole was sacrificed in the most shameful fashion to the interests of the essentially unproductive population of the capital, to which in fact bread could never become too cheap. Nothing perhaps evinces so clearly as this, how wretched was the constitution and how incapable was the administration of this so-called golden age of the republic. Any representative system, however meagre, would have led at least to serious complaints and to a perception of the seat of the evil; but in those collective assemblages of the burgesses anything was listened to sooner than the warning voice of a foreboding patriot. Any government that deserved the name would of itself have interfered; but the mass of the Roman senate probably with well-meaning credulity regarded the low prices of grain as a real blessing for the people, and the Scipios and Flamininuses had, forsooth, more important things to do—to emancipate the Greeks, and to exercise the functions of republican kings. So the ship drove on unhindered towards the breakers.

Revolution in Roman agriculture.

When the small holdings ceased to yield any substantial clear return, the farmers were irretrievably ruined, and

Decay of the farmers.

---

to 1841) about 3*s.* 5*d.* Whether this not very considerable difference between the Roman and the modern prices depends on a rise in the value of corn or on a fall in the value of silver, can hardly be decided.

It is very doubtful, perhaps, whether in the Rome of this and of later times the prices of corn really fluctuated more than is the case in modern times. If we compare prices like those quoted above, of 4*d.* and 5*d.* for the bushel and a half, with those of the worst times of

war-dearth and famine—such as in the second Punic war when the same quantity rose to 9*s.* 7*d.* (1 *medimnus* = 15 *drachmae*; Polyb. ix. 44), in the civil war to 19*s.* 2*d.* (1 *modius* = 5 *denarii*; Cic. *Verr.* iii. 92, 214), in the great dearth under Augustus, even to 21*s.* 3*d.* (5 *modii* = 27½ *denarii*; Euseb. *Chron. p. Chr.* 7, *Scal.*) —the difference is indeed immense; but such extreme cases are but little instructive, and might in either direction be found recurring under the like conditions at the present day.

the more so that they gradually, although more slowly than the other classes, lost the moral tone and frugal habits of the earlier ages of the republic. It was merely a question of time, how rapidly the hides of the Italian farmers would, by purchase or by resignation, become merged in the larger estates. The landlord was better able to maintain himself than the farmer. The former produced at a cheaper rate than the latter, when, instead of letting his land according to the older system to petty temporary lessees, he caused it according to the newer system to be cultivated by his slaves. Accordingly, where this course had not been adopted even at an earlier period (i. 485), the competition of Sicilian slave-corn compelled the Italian landlord to adopt it, and to have the work performed by slaves without wife or child instead of families of free labourers. The landlord, moreover, could hold his ground better against competitors by means of improvements or changes in cultivation, and he could content himself with a smaller return from the soil than the farmer, who wanted capital and intelligence and who merely had what was requisite for his subsistence. Hence the Roman landholder comparatively neglected the culture of grain—which in many cases seems to have been restricted to the raising of the quantity required for the staff of labourers*—and gave increased attention to the production of oil and wine as well as to the breeding of cattle. These, under the favourable climate of Italy, had no need to fear foreign competition; Italian wine, Italian oil, Italian wool not only commanded the home markets, but were soon sent abroad; the valley of the Po, which could find no consumption for its corn, provided the half of Italy with swine and bacon. With this the statements that have reached us as to the economic results of Roman husbandry very well agree.

Culture of oil and wine, and rearing of cattle.

---

* Accordingly Cato calls the two estates, which he describes, summarily "olive-plantation" (*olivetum*) and "vineyard" (*vinea*), although not wine and oil merely, but grain also and other products were cultivated there. If indeed the 800 *culei*, for which the possessors of the vineyard are directed to provide themselves with casks (11), formed the maximum of a year's vintage, the whole of the 100 *iugera* must have been planted with vines, because a produce of 8 *culei* per *iugerum* was almost unprecedented (Colum. iii. 3); but Varro (i. 22) understood, and evidently with reason, the estimate to apply to the case of the possessor of a vineyard who found it necessary to make the new vintage before he had sold the old.

There is some ground for assuming that capital invested in land was reckoned to yield a good return at 6 per cent.; this appears to accord with the average rate of interest at this period, which was about twice as much. The rearing of cattle yielded on the whole better results than arable husbandry: in the latter the vineyard gave the best return, next came the vegetable garden and the olive orchard, while meadows and corn-fields yielded least.* It is of course presumed that each species of husbandry was prosecuted under the conditions that suited it, and on the soil which was adapted to its nature. These circumstances were already in themselves suf-

---

* That the Roman landlord made on an average 6 per cent. on his capital, we infer from Colum. iii. 3, 9. We have a precise estimate of the expense and produce only in the case of the vineyard, for which Columella gives the following calculation of the cost per *iugerum*:—

Price of the ground . . 1000 sesterces.
Price of the slaves who
   work it (proportion to
   iugerum) 1143   „
Vines and stakes . . . 2000   „
Loss of interest during
   the first two years . . 497 „

Total 4640 sesterces = £47.

He calculates the produce as, at any rate, 60 *amphorae*, worth at least 900 sesterces (9*l*.), which would thus represent a return of 17 per cent. But this is somewhat illusory, as, apart from bad harvests, the cost of gathering in the produce (p. 390), and the expenses of the maintenance of the vines, stakes, and slaves, are omitted from the estimate.

The gross produce of meadow, pasture, and forest is estimated by the same agricultural writer as, at most, 100 sesterces per *iugerum*, and that of corn land as less rather than more: in fact, the average return of 25 *modii* of wheat per *iugerum* gives, according to the average price in the capital of 1 *denarius* per *modius*, not more than 100 sesterces for the gross proceeds, and at the seat of production the price must have been still lower. Varro (iii. 2) reckons as a good ordinary gross return for a larger estate 150 sesterces per *iugerum*. Estimates of the corresponding expense have not reached us: as a matter of course, the management in this instance cost much less than in that of a vineyard.

All these statements, moreover, date from a century or more after Cato's death. From him we have only the general statement that the breeding of cattle yielded a better return than agriculture (*ap.* Cicero, *De Off.* ii. 25, 89; Colum. vi. *præf.* 4, comp. ii. 16, 2; Plin. *H. N.* xviii. 5, 30; Plutarch, *Cato*, 21); which of course is not meant to imply that it was everywhere advisable to convert arable land into pasture, but is to be understood relatively as signifying that the capital invested in the rearing of flocks and herds on mountain pastures and other suitable grounds yielded, as compared with capital invested in cultivating suitable corn land, a higher interest. Perhaps the circumstance has been also taken into account in the calculation, that the want of energy and intelligence in the landlord operates far less injuriously in the case of pasture land than in the highly developed culture of the vine and olive. On an arable estate, according to Cato, the returns of the soil stood as follows in a descending series:—1, vineyard; 2, vegetable garden; 3, osier copse, which yielded a large return in consequence of the culture of the vine; 4, olive plantation; 5, meadow yielding hay; 6, corn fields; 7, copse; 8, wood for felling; 9, oak forest for forage to the cattle; all of which nine elements enter into the scheme of husbandry for Cato's model estates.

The higher net return of the culture of the vine as compared with that of corn is attested also by the fact, that under the award pronounced in the arbitration between the city of Genua and the villages tributary to it in 637 the city received a sixth of wine, and a twentieth of grain, as quitrent.

117.

ficient to supersede the husbandry of the petty farmer gradually by the system of farming on a great scale; and it was difficult by means of legislation to counteract them. But an injurious effect was produced by the Claudian law to be **218.** mentioned afterwards (shortly before 536), which excluded the senatorial houses from mercantile speculation, and thereby artificially compelled them to invest their enormous capitals mainly in land or, in other words, to replace the old homesteads of the farmers by estates under the management of land-stewards and by pastures for cattle. Moreover special circumstances tended to favour the growth of pastoral husbandry as contrasted with agriculture, although the former was far more injurious to the state. First of all, this form of extracting profit from the soil—the only one which in reality demanded and rewarded operations on a great scale—alone corresponded to the vast capital and to the enterprising spirit of the capitalists of this age. An estate under cultivation, although not demanding the presence of the master constantly, required his frequent appearance on the spot, while the circumstances did not well admit of his enlarging such an estate or of his multiplying his possessions except within narrow limits; whereas an estate under pasture admitted of unlimited enlargement, and claimed little of the owner's attention. For this reason men already began to convert good arable land into pasture even at an economic loss—a practice which was prohibited by legislation (we know not when, perhaps about this period) but hardly with success. The growth of pastoral husbandry was favoured also by the occupation of the domain land. As the portions so occupied were ordinarily large, the system gave rise almost exclusively to great estates; and not only so, but the occupiers of these possessions, which might be resumed by the state at pleasure and were in law always insecure, were afraid to invest any considerable amount in their cultivation—by planting vines for instance, or olives. The consequence was, that these lands were mainly turned to account as pasture.

Manage-
ment of
money.
　　We are prevented from giving a similar comprehensive view of the moneyed economy of Rome, partly by the want of special treatises descending from Roman antiquity on the

subject, partly by its very nature which was far more complex and varied than that of the Roman husbandry. So far as can be ascertained, its principles were, still less perhaps than those of husbandry, the peculiar property of the Romans; on the contrary, they were the common heritage of all ancient civilization, under which, as under that of modern times, the operations on a great scale naturally were everywhere much alike. The system of mercantile and moneyed speculation appears to have been established in the first instance by the Greeks, and to have been simply adopted by the Romans. Yet the precision with which it was carried out and the magnitude of the scale on which its operations were conducted were so peculiarly Roman, that the spirit of the Roman economy and its grandeur whether for good or evil are preeminently conspicuous in its monetary transactions.

The starting-point of the Roman moneyed economy was of course money-lending; and no branch of commercial industry was more zealously prosecuted by the Romans than the trade of the professional money-lender (*fenerator*) and of the money-dealer or banker (*argentarius*). The transference of the charge of the larger monetary transactions from the individual capitalists to the mediating banker, who receives and makes payments for his customers, invests and borrows money, and conducts their money dealings at home and abroad—which is the mark of a developed system of capital—was already completely carried out in the time of Cato. The bankers, however, were not only the cashiers of the rich in Rome, but everywhere insinuated themselves into minor branches of business and settled in ever-increasing numbers in the provinces and dependent states. Already throughout the whole range of the empire the business of making advances to those who wanted money began to be, so to speak, monopolized by the Romans. *Money-lending.*

Closely connected with this was the immeasurable field of speculative enterprise. The system of transacting business through the medium of contract pervaded the whole dealings of Rome. The state took the lead by letting all its more complicated revenues and all contracts for furnishing supplies and executing buildings to capitalists, or associations of capitalists, for a fixed sum to be given or received. But private *Speculation of contractors.*

persons also uniformly contracted for whatever admitted of being done by contract—for buildings, for the ingathering of the harvest (p. 390), and even for the partition of an inheritance among the heirs or the winding up of a bankrupt estate; in which case the contractor—usually a banker—received the whole assets, and engaged on the other hand to settle the liabilities in full or up to a certain percentage and to pay the balance as the circumstances required.

Commerce.   The prominence of transmarine commerce at an early period in the Roman national economy has already been adverted to in its proper place. The further stimulus, which it received during the present period, is attested by the increased importance of the Italian customs-duties in the Roman financial system (p. 348). In addition to the causes of this increase in the importance of transmarine commerce which need no further explanation, it was artificially promoted by the privileged position which the ruling Italian nation assumed in the provinces, and by the exemption from customs-dues which was probably even now in many of the dependent states conceded by treaty to the Romans and Latins.

Manufacturing industry.   On the other hand, industrial art remained comparatively undeveloped. Trades were no doubt indispensable, and there appear indications that to a certain extent they were concentrated in Rome; Cato, for instance, advises the Campanian landowner to purchase the slaves' clothing and shoes, the ploughs, vats, and locks, which he may require, in Rome. From the great consumption of woollen stuffs the manufacture of cloth must have been extensive and lucrative.* But no endeavours were apparently made to transplant to Italy any such professional industry as existed in Egypt and Syria, or even to carry it on abroad with Italian capital. Flax indeed was cultivated in Italy and purple dye was prepared there, but the latter branch of industry at least belonged mainly to the Greek Tarentum, and probably the importation of Egyptian linen and Milesian or Tyrian purple even now preponderated everywhere over the native manufacture.

Under this category, however, falls to some extent the

---

* The industrial importance of the Roman cloth-making is evident from the remarkable part which is played by the fullers in Roman comedy. The profitable nature of the fullers' pits is attested by Cato (ap. Plutarch. Cat. 21).

leasing or purchase by Roman capitalists of landed estates beyond Italy, with a view to carry on the cultivation of grain and the rearing of cattle on a great scale. This species of speculation, which afterwards developed itself to proportions so enormous, probably began within the period now before us; particularly in Sicily, where the commercial restrictions imposed on the Siceliots (p. 72), if not introduced for the very purpose, must have at least tended to give to the Roman speculators who were exempt from such restrictions a sort of monopoly of the profits derivable from land.

Business in all these different branches was uniformly carried on by means of slaves. The money-lenders and bankers instituted, throughout the range of their business, additional counting-houses and branch banks under the direction of their slaves and freedmen. The company which had leased the customs-duties from the state appointed chiefly their slaves and freedmen to levy them at each custom-house. Every one who took contracts for buildings bought architect-slaves; every one who undertook to provide spectacles or gladiatorial games on behalf of those to whom that duty pertained purchased or trained a company of slaves skilled in acting, or a band of serfs expert in the trade of fighting. The merchant imported his wares in vessels of his own under the charge of slaves or freedmen, and disposed of them by the same means in wholesale or retail. We need hardly add that the working of mines and manufactories was conducted entirely by slaves. The situation of these slaves was, no doubt, far from enviable, and was throughout less favourable than that of slaves in Greece; but, if we leave out of account the classes last mentioned, the industrial slaves found their position on the whole more tolerable than the rural serfs. They had more frequently a family and a practically independent household, with no remote prospect of obtaining their freedom and property of their own. Hence such positions formed the true training school of those upstarts from the servile class, who by menial virtues and often by menial vices rose to the rank of Roman citizens and not unfrequently attained great prosperity, and who morally, economically, and politically contributed at least as much as the slaves themselves to the ruin of the Roman commonwealth.

Management of business by slaves.

Extent of
Roman
mercantile
transac-
tions.
The Roman mercantile transactions of this period fully kept
pace with the contemporary development of political power,
and were no less grand of their kind. In order to gain a clear
idea of the activity of the traffic with other lands, we have
only to look into the literature, more especially into the
comedies of this period, in which the Phoenician merchant is
brought on the stage speaking Phoenician, and the dialogue
Coins and
moneys.
swarms with Greek and half Greek words and phrases. But
the extent and energy of the Roman traffic may be traced
most distinctly by means of coins and monetary relations.
The Roman *denarius* kept pace with the Roman legions. We
have already mentioned (p. 71) that the Sicilian mints—last
212.
of all that of Syracuse in 542—were closed or at any rate
restricted to small money in consequence of the Roman conquest, and that in Sicily and Sardinia the *denarius* obtained
legal circulation at least side by side with the older silver
currency and probably very soon became the exclusive legal
tender. With equal if not greater rapidity the Roman silver
coinage penetrated into Spain, where the great silver-mines
existed and there was virtually no earlier national coinage; at
a very early period the Spanish towns even began to coin after
the Roman standard (p. 225). On the whole, as Carthage
coined only to a very limited extent (p. 21), there existed not
a single important mint in addition to that of Rome in the
region of the western Mediterranean, with the exception of
the mint of Massilia and perhaps also those of the Illyrian
Greeks at Apollonia and Dyrrhachium. Accordingly, when
the Romans began to establish themselves in the region of the
220.
Po, these mints were about 225 subjected to the Roman standard in such a way, that, while they retained the right of
coining silver, they uniformly—and the Massiliots in particular—were led to adjust their *drachma* to the weight of the
Roman three-quarter *denarius*, which the Roman government
on its part began to coin, primarily for the use of Upper Italy,
under the name of the "coin of victory" (*victoriatus*). This
new system, based on the Roman, prevailed throughout the
Massiliot, Upper Italian, and Illyrian territories; and these
coins even penetrated into the barbarian lands on the north,
those of Massilia, for instance, into the Alpine districts along
the whole basin of the Rhone, and those of Illyria as far as

the modern Transylvania. The eastern half of the Mediterranean was not yet reached by the Roman money, as it had
not yet fallen under the direct sovereignty of Rome ; but its
place was filled by gold, the true and natural medium for international and transmarine commerce. It is true that the
Roman government, in conformity with its strictly conservative character, adhered—with the exception of a temporary
coinage of gold occasioned by the financial embarrassment
during the Hannibalic war (p. 183)—steadfastly to the rule
of coining silver only in addition to the national-Italian
copper ; but commerce had already assumed such dimensions,
that it was able in the absence of money to conduct its
transactions with gold by weight. Of the sum in cash, which
lay in the Roman treasury in 597, scarcely a sixth was coined
or uncoined silver, five-sixths consisted of gold in bars,* and
beyond doubt the precious metals were found in all the chests
of the larger Roman capitalists in substantially similar proportions. Already therefore gold held the first place in great
transactions ; and, as may be inferred from this fact,
the preponderance of traffic was maintained with foreign
lands, and particularly with the East, which since the times of
Philip and Alexander the Great had adopted a gold currency.

157.

The whole gain from these immense transactions of the
Roman capitalists flowed in the long run to Rome ; for,
much as they went abroad, they were not easily induced to
settle permanently there, but sooner or later returned to
Rome, either realizing their gains and investing them in
Italy, or continuing to carry on business from Rome as a
centre by means of the capital and connections which they
had acquired. The moneyed superiority of Rome as compared with the rest of the civilized world was, accordingly,
quite as decided as its political and military ascendancy.
Rome in this respect stood towards other countries somewhat
as the England of the present day stands towards the Continent—a Greek, for instance, observes of the younger Scipio
Africanus, that he was not rich " for a Roman." We may
form some idea of what was considered as riches in the

Roman
wealth.

---

* There were in the treasury 17,410   silver. The legal ratio of gold to silver
Roman pounds of gold, 22,070 pounds of   was : 1 pound of gold = 4000 sesterces, or
uncoined, and 18,230 pounds of coined,   1 : 11·91.

Rome of those days from the fact, that Lucius Paullus with
an estate of 60 talents (£14,000) was not reckoned a wealthy
senator, and that a dowry—such as each of the daughters of
the elder Scipio Africanus received—of 50 talents (£12,000)
was regarded as a suitable portion for a maiden of quality,
while the estate of the wealthiest Greek of this century was
not more than 300 talents (£72,000).

Mercantile
spirit.

It was no wonder, accordingly, that the mercantile spirit
took possession of the nation, or rather—for that was no new
thing in Rome—that the spirit of the capitalist now penetrated
and pervaded all aspects and stations of life, and agriculture
as well as the government of the state began to become
enterprises of capitalists. The preservation and increase of
wealth positively formed a part of public and private morality.
"A widow's estate may diminish;" Cato wrote in the practical
instructions which he composed for his son, " a man must
augment his substance, and he is deserving of praise and full
of a divine spirit, whose account-books at his death show that
he has gained more than he has inherited." Wherever,
therefore, there was giving and counter-giving, every transaction although concluded without any sort of formality was
held as valid, and in case of necessity the right of action was
accorded to the party aggrieved if not by the law, at any
rate by mercantile custom and judicial usage;* but the promise of a gift without due form was null alike in legal theory
and in practice. In Rome, Polybius tells us, nobody gives
to any one unless he must do so, and no one pays a penny
before it falls due, even among near relatives. The very
legislation yielded to this mercantile morality, which regarded
all giving away without recompense as squandering; the
giving of presents and bequests and the undertaking of
sureties were subjected to restriction at this period by decree
of the people, and heritages which did not fall to the nearest
relatives were at any rate taxed. In the closest connection with
such views mercantile punctuality, honour, and respectability
pervaded the whole of Roman life. Every ordinary man was
morally bound to keep an account-book of his income and ex-

---

* On this was based the actionable
character of contracts of buying, hiring,
and partnership, and, in general, the
whole system of non-formal actionable
contracts.

penditure—in every well-arranged house, accordingly, there
was a separate record-chamber (*tablinum*)—and every one took
care that he should not leave the world without having made
his will: it was one of the three matters in his life which
Cato declares that he regretted, that he had been a single
day without a testament. Those household books were universally by Roman usage admitted as valid evidence in a court of
justice, nearly in the same way as we admit the evidence of a
merchant's ledger. The word of a man of unstained repute
was admissible not merely against himself, but in his own
favour; nothing was more common than to settle differences
between persons of integrity by means of an oath demanded by
the one party and given by the other—a mode of settlement
which was reckoned valid even in law; and a traditional rule
enjoined the jury, in the absence of evidence, to give their
verdict in favour of the man of unstained character when
opposed to one who was less reputable, and only in the event
of both parties being of equal repute to give it in favour of
the defendant.* The conventional respectability of the
Romans was especially apparent in the more and more strict
enforcement of the rule, that no respectable man should allow
himself to be paid for the performance of personal services.
Accordingly magistrates, officers, jurymen, guardians, and
generally all respectable men entrusted with public functions,
received no recompense for the services which they rendered
except, at most, a compensation for their bare outlay; and
not only so, but the services which intimate acquaintances
(*amici*) rendered to each other—such as giving security,
representation in law-suits, custody (*depositum*), lending of
objects not intended to be let on hire (*commodatum*), the
managing and attending to business in general (*procuratio*)
—were treated according to the same principle, so that it was
improper to receive any compensation for them and an action
was not allowable even where a compensation had been pro-

---

* The chief passage as to this point is
the fragment of Cato in Gellius, xiv. 2.
In the case of the *obligatio litteris* also,
i. e., a claim based solely on the entry
of a debt in the account-book of the creditor, this legal recognition of the
personal credibility of the party, even
where his testimony in his own cause is
concerned, affords the key of explanation;
and hence it happened that in later
times, when this mercantile honour had
vanished from Roman life, the *obligatio
litteris*, while not exactly abolished, fell
of itself into desuetude.

mised. How entirely the man was merged in the merchant, appears most distinctly perhaps in the substitution of a money-payment and an action at law for the duel—even for the political duel—in the Roman life of this period. The usual form of settling questions of personal honour was this : a wager was laid between the offender and the party offended as to the truth or falsehood of the offensive assertion, and under the shape of an action for the stake the question of fact was submitted with all the forms of law to a jury ; the acceptance of such a wager when offered by the offended or offending party was, just like the acceptance of a challenge to a duel at the present day, left open in law, but in point of honour it could seldom be refused.

Associations.

One of the most important consequences of this mercantile spirit, which displayed itself with an intensity hardly conceivable by those not engaged in business, was the extraordinary impulse given to the formation of associations. In Rome this was especially fostered by the system already often mentioned as adopted by the government in the transaction of its business—the system of middlemen : for from the extent of the transactions it was natural, and it was probably often required by the state for the sake of greater security, that capitalists should undertake such leases and contracts not individually, but in partnership. All great transactions were organized on the model of these state-contracts. Indications are even found of the occurrence among the Romans of that feature so characteristic of the system of association—a coalition of rival companies in order jointly to establish monopolist prices.* In transmarine transactions more especially and such as were otherwise attended with considerable risk, the system of partnership was so extensively adopted, that it practically took the place

---

* In the remarkable model contract given by Cato (141) for the letting of the olive-harvest, there is the following paragraph :—

"None [of the persons desirous to contract on the occasion of letting] shall withdraw, for the sake of causing the gathering and pressing of the olives to be let at a dearer rate; except when [the joint bidder] immediately names [the other bidder] as his partner. If this rule shall appear to have been infringed, all the partners [of the company with which the contract has been concluded] shall, if desired by the landlord or the overseer appointed by him, take an oath [that they have not conspired in this way to prevent competition]. If they do not take the oath, the stipulated price is not to be paid." It is tacitly assumed that the contract is taken by a company, not by an individual capitalist.

of insurances, which were unknown to antiquity. Nothing was more common than the nautical loan, as it was called— the modern "bottomry"—by which the risk and gain of transmarine traffic were proportionally distributed among the owners of the vessel and cargo and all the capitalists who had advanced money for the voyage. It was, however, a general rule of Roman economy that one should rather take small shares in many speculations than speculate independently; Cato advised the capitalist not to fit out a single ship with his money, but to enter into concert with forty-nine other capitalists so as to send out fifty ships and to take an interest in each, to the extent of a fiftieth share. The greater complication thus introduced into business was overcome by the Roman merchant through his punctual laboriousness and his system of management by slaves and freedmen, which, regarded from the point of view of the pure capitalist, was far preferable to our counting-house system. Thus these mercantile companies, with their hundred ramifications, largely influenced the economy of every Roman of note. There was, according to the testimony of Polybius, hardly a man of means in Rome who had not been concerned as an avowed or silent partner in leasing the public revenues; and much more must each have invested on an average a considerable portion of his capital in mercantile associations generally.

All this laid the foundation for that endurance of Roman wealth, which was perhaps still more remarkable than its magnitude. The phenomenon, unique perhaps of its kind, to which we have already called attention (p. 344)—that the condition of the great houses remained almost the same for several centuries—finds its explanation in the somewhat narrow but solid principles on which they managed their mercantile property.

In consequence of the one-sided prominence assigned to capital in the Roman economy, the evils inseparable from a pure capitalist system could not fail to appear. *Moneyed aristocracy.*

Civil equality, which had already received a fatal wound through the rise of the ruling order of lords, suffered an equally severe blow in consequence of the line of social demarcation becoming more and more distinctly drawn between the rich and the poor. Nothing more effectually promoted this separation in a downward direction than the already-mentioned rule—apparently a matter of indifference, but in reality involving the deepest arrogance and insolence on the part of the capitalists—that it was disgraceful to take money for work; a wall of partition was thus raised not merely between the common day-labourer or artisan and the respectable landlord or manufacturer, but also between the soldier or subaltern and the military tribune, and between the clerk or messenger and the magistrate. In an upward direction a similar barrier was raised by the Claudian law suggested by Gaius Flaminius (shortly before 536), which prohibited senators and senators' sons from possessing sea-going vessels except for the transport of the produce of their estates, and probably also from participating in public contracts—forbidding them generally from carrying on whatever the Romans included under the head of "speculation" (*quaestus*).* It is true that this enactment was not called for by the senators; it was on the contrary a work of the democratic opposition, which perhaps desired in the first instance merely to prevent the evil of members of the governing class personally entering into dealings with the government. It may be, moreover, that the capitalists in this instance, as so often afterwards, made common cause with the democratic party, and seized the opportunity of diminishing competition by the exclusion of the senators. The former object was, of course, only very imperfectly attained, for the system of partnership opened up to the senators ample facilities for continuing to speculate in secret; but this decree of the people drew a legal line of demarcation between those men of quality who did not speculate at all or at any rate not openly and those who did, and it placed alongside of the aristocracy which was primarily political an aristocracy which was purely moneyed—the equestrian order, as it was afterwards called, whose rivalries with the senatorial order fill the history of the following century.

---

* Livy (xxi., 63; comp. Cic. *Verr.* v. 18, 45) mentions only the enactment as to the sea-going vessels; but Asconius (*in Or. de Toga Cand.* p. 94. *Orell.*) and Dio (lv. 10, 5) state that the senator was also forbidden by law to undertake state-contracts (*redemptiones*); and, as according to Livy "all speculation was considered indecorous in a senator," the Claudian law probably went further than he states.

A further consequence of the one-sided power of capital
was the disproportionate prominence of those branches of
business which were the most sterile and the least productive to the national economy as a whole. Industrial art,
which ought to have held the highest place, in fact occupied
the lowest. Commerce flourished; but it was universally
non-reciprocal. Even on the northern frontier the Romans
do not seem to have been able to give merchandise in
exchange for the slaves who were brought in numbers from
the Celtic and probably even from the Germanic territories
to Ariminum and the other markets of northern Italy; at
least as early as 523 the export of silver money to the
Celtic territory was prohibited by the Roman government.
In the intercourse with Greece, Syria, Egypt, Cyrene, and
Carthage, the balance of trade was necessarily unfavourable
to Italy. Rome began to become the capital of the Mediterranean states, and Italy to become the suburbs of Rome;
the Romans had no wish to be anything more, and in their
opulent indifference were satisfied with a non-reciprocal
commerce, such as every city which is nothing more than a
capital necessarily carries on — they possessed, forsooth,
money enough to pay for everything which they needed or
did not need. On the other hand the most unproductive
of all sorts of business, the traffic in money and the
farming of the revenue, formed the true mainstay and
stronghold of the Roman economy. And, lastly, whatever
elements that economy had contained for the production
of a prosperous middle class and of a lower one provided
with sufficient subsistence were extinguished by the unhappy
system of employing slaves, or, at the best, contributed to
the multiplication of the troublesome order of freedmen.

But above all the deep-rooted immorality, which is inherent in an economy of pure capital, ate into the heart of
society and of the commonwealth, and substituted an absolute selfishness for humanity and patriotism. The better
portion of the nation were very clearly aware of the seeds of
corruption which lurked in that pursuit of speculation; and
the instinctive hatred of the great multitude, as well as the
displeasure of the well-disposed statesman, was especially
directed against the trade of the professional money-lender,

which for long had been subjected to penal laws and still continued under the letter of the law amenable to punishment. In a comedy of this period the money-lender is told that the class to which he belongs is on a parallel with the *lenones*—

> *Eodem hercle vos pono et paro ; parissumi estis ibus.*
> *Hi saltem in occultis locis prostant : vos in foro ipso :*
> *Vos fenore, hi male suadendo et lustris lacerant homines.*
> *Rogationes plurimas propter vos populus scivit,*
> *Quas vos rogatas rumpitis : aliquam reperitis rimam.*
> *Quasi aquam ferventem frigidam esse, ita vos putatis leges.*

Cato the leader of the reform party expresses himself still more emphatically than the comedian. " Lending money at interest," he says in the preface to his treatise on agriculture, " has various advantages ; but it is not honourable. Our forefathers accordingly ordained, and inscribed it among their laws, that the thief should be bound to pay two-fold, but the man who takes interest four-fold, compensation ; whence we may infer how much worse a citizen they deemed the usurer than the thief." There is no great difference, he elsewhere considers, between a money-lender and a murderer ; and it must be allowed that his acts did not fall short of his words—when governor of Sardinia, by his rigorous administration of the law he drove the Roman bankers to their wits' end. The great majority of the ruling senatorial order regarded the system of the speculators with dislike, and not only conducted themselves in the provinces on the whole with more integrity and honour than these moneyed men, but frequently acted as a check on them. The frequent changes of the supreme magistrates, however, and the inevitable inequality in their mode of handling the laws, necessarily rendered the effort to check such proceedings in great measure ineffectual.

Reaction of the capitalist system on agriculture.

The Romans perceived moreover—as it was not difficult to perceive—that it was of far more consequence to give a different direction to the whole national economy than to exercise a police control over speculation ; it was such views mainly that men like Cato enforced by precept and example on the Roman agriculturist. " When our forefathers," continues Cato in the preface just quoted, " pronounced the eulogy of a worthy man, they praised him as a worthy farmer and a worthy landlord; one who was thus commended was thought to have received the highest praise. The merchant I deem energetic and diligent in the pursuit of gain; but his calling is too much exposed to perils and mischances. On the other hand farmers furnish the bravest men and the ablest soldiers; no calling is so honourable, safe, and inoffensive as theirs, and those who occupy themselves with it are least liable to evil thoughts." He was wont to say of himself, that his property was derived solely from two sources—agriculture and frugality; and, though this was neither very logically expressed nor strictly conformable to the truth,* yet Cato was not unjustly regarded by his contemporaries and by posterity as the model of a Roman landlord. Unhappily it is a truth as remarkable as it is painful, that this husbandry, commended so much and certainly with so entire good faith as a remedy, was itself pervaded by the poison of the capitalist system. In the case of pastoral husbandry this was obvious; for that reason it was most in favour with the public and least in favour with the party desirous of moral reform. But how stood the case with agriculture itself? The warfare, which from the third to the fifth century U.C. capital had waged against labour, by withdrawing under the form of interest on debt the revenues of the soil from the working farmers and bringing them into the hands of the idly consuming fund-holder, had been settled chiefly by the extension of the Roman economy and the transference of the capital which existed in Latium to the field of mercantile activity opened up throughout the range of the Mediterranean. Now even the extended field of business was no longer able to contain the increased mass of capital; and an insane legislation laboured simultaneously to compel the investment of senatorial capital by artificial means in Italian estates, and systematically to depreciate the arable land of Italy by

---

* Cato, like every other Roman, invested a part of his means in the breeding of cattle, and in commercial and other undertakings. But it was not his habit directly to violate the laws; he neither speculated in state-leases—which as a senator he was not allowed to do— nor practised usury. It is an injustice to charge him with a practice in the latter respect at variance with his theory; the *fenus nauticum*, in which he certainly engaged, was not a branch of usury prohibited by the law; it really formed an essential part of the business of chartering and freighting vessels.

interference with the prices of grain. Thus there began a second campaign of capital against free labour or—what was substantially the same thing in antiquity—against the small farmer system ; and, if the first had been bad, it yet seemed mild and humane as compared with the second. The capitalists no longer lent to the farmer at interest—a course which in itself was not now practicable because the petty landholder no longer produced any surplus of consequence, and was moreover not sufficiently simple and radical—but they bought up the farms and converted them, at the best, into estates managed by stewards and wrought by slaves. This also was called agriculture; it was in reality the application of the capitalist system to the produce of the soil. The description of the husbandmen, which Cato gives, is excellent and quite just; but how does it correspond to the system itself which he portrays and recommends? If a Roman senator, as must not unfrequently have been the case, possessed four such estates as that described by Cato, the same space, which in the olden time when small holdings prevailed had supported from 100 to 150 farmers' families, was now occupied by one family of free persons and about 50, for the most part unmarried, slaves. If this was the remedy by which the decaying national economy was to be restored to vigour, it bore, unhappily, an aspect of extreme resemblance to the disease.

Deve'op-
ment of
Italy.

The general result of this system is only too clearly obvious in the changed proportions of the population. It is true that the condition of the various districts of Italy was very unequal, and some were even prosperous. The farms, instituted in great numbers in the region between the Apennines and the Po at the time of its colonization, did not so speedily disappear. Polybius, who visited that quarter not long after the close of the present period, commends its numerous, handsome, and vigorous population : with a just legislation as to corn it would doubtless have been possible to make the basin of the Po, and not Sicily, the granary of the capital. In like manner Picenum and the so-called *ager Gallicus* acquired a numerous body of farmers through the distributions of domain-land consequent on the Flaminian law

232.

of 522—a body, however, which was sadly reduced in the

Hannibalic war. In Etruria, and perhaps also in Umbria, the internal condition of the subject communities was unfavourable to the flourishing of a class of free farmers. Matters were better in Latium—which could not be entirely deprived of the advantages of the market of the capital, and which had on the whole been spared by the Hannibalic war —as well as in the secluded mountain-valleys of the Marsians and Sabellians. On the other hand the Hannibalic war had fearfully devastated southern Italy and had ruined, in addition to a number of smaller places, its two largest cities, Capua and Tarentum, both once able to send into the field armies of 30,000 men. Samnium had recovered from the severe wars of the fifth century: according to the census of 529 it was in a position to furnish as many men capable of arms as all the Latin towns, and it was probably at that time, next to the *ager Romanus*, the most flourishing region of the peninsula. But the Hannibalic war had desolated the land afresh, and the assignations of land in that quarter to the soldiers of Scipio's army, although considerable, probably did not cover the loss. Campania and Apulia, both hitherto well-peopled regions, were still worse treated in the same war by friend and foe. In Apulia, no doubt, assignations of land were made afterwards, but the colonies instituted there were not successful. The beautiful plain of Campania remained better peopled; but the territory of Capua and of the other communities broken up in the Hannibalic war became public property, and the occupants of it were uniformly not proprietors, but petty temporary lessees. Lastly, in the wide Lucanian and Bruttian territories the population, which was already very thin before the Hannibalic war, was visited by the whole severity of the war itself and of the penal executions that followed in its train; nor was much done on the part of Rome to revive the agriculture there—with the exception perhaps of Valentia (Vibo, now Monteleone), none of the colonies established there attained any real prosperity.

225.

With every allowance for the inequality in the political and economic circumstances of the different districts and for the comparatively flourishing condition of several of them, the retrogression is yet on the whole unmistakeable, and it is confirmed by the most indisputable testimonies as to the

Falling off in the population.

general condition of Italy. Cato and Polybius agree in
stating that Italy was at the end of the sixth century far
weaker in population than at the end of the fifth, and was
no longer able to furnish armies so large as in the first
Punic war. The increasing difficulty of the levy, the necessity of lowering the qualification for service in the legions,
and the complaints of the allies as to the magnitude of the
contingents to be furnished by them, confirm these statements; and, in the case of the Roman burgesses, the num-
252. bers tell the same tale. In 502, shortly after the expedition
of Regulus to Africa, they amounted to 298,000 men capable
of bearing arms; thirty years later, shortly before the com-
220. mencement of the Hannibalic war (534), they had fallen off
to 270,000, or by a tenth, and again twenty years after that,
204. shortly before the end of the same war (550), to 214,000,
or by a fourth; and a generation afterwards—during which
no extraordinary losses occurred, but the institution of the
great burgess-colonies in the plain of northern Italy in particular occasioned a perceptible and exceptional increase—the
numbers of the burgesses had hardly again reached the point
at which they stood at the commencement of this period. If
we had similar statements regarding the Italian population
generally, they would beyond all doubt exhibit a deficit relatively still more considerable. The decline of the national
vigour less admits of proof; but it is stated by the writers on
agriculture that flesh and milk disappeared more and more
from the diet of the common people. At the same time the
slave population increased, as the free population declined.
In Apulia, Lucania, and the Bruttian land, pastoral husbandry must even in the time of Cato have preponderated
over agriculture; the half-savage slave-herdsmen had in reality
the command of the country. Apulia was rendered so insecure by them that a strong force had to be stationed there;
185. in 569 a slave-conspiracy planned on the largest scale, and
mixed up with the proceedings of the Bacchanalia, was discovered there, and nearly 7000 men were judicially condemned. In Etruria also Roman troops were obliged to
196. take the field against a band of slaves (558), and even in
Latium there were instances in which towns like Setia and
Praeneste were in danger of being surprised by a band of

198.

runaway serfs (556). The nation was visibly diminishing, and the community of free burgesses was resolving itself into a body composed of masters and slaves; and, although it was in the first instance the two long wars with Carthage which decimated and ruined both the burgesses and the allies, the Roman capitalists beyond doubt contributed quite as much as Hamilcar and Hannibal to the decline in the vigour and the numbers of the Italian people.   No one can say whether the government could have rendered help; but it was an alarming and discreditable fact, that the circles of the Roman aristocracy, well-meaning and energetic as for the most part they were, never once showed any insight into the real gravity of the situation or any foreboding of the full magnitude of the danger.   When a Roman lady belonging to the high nobility, the sister of one of the numerous citizen-admirals who in the first Punic war had ruined the fleets of the state, one day got among a crowd in the Roman Forum, she said aloud in the hearing of those around, that it was high time to place her brother once more at the head of the fleet and to relieve the pressure in the market-place by bleeding the citizens afresh (508). Those who thus thought and spoke were, no doubt, a small minority; nevertheless this outrageous speech was simply a forcible expression of the criminal indifference with which the whole noble and rich world looked down on the common citizens and farmers. They did not exactly desire their destruction, but they allowed it to run its course; and so desolation advanced with gigantic steps over the flourishing land of Italy, where countless numbers of free men had lately rejoiced in moderate and merited prosperity.

CHAPTER XIII.

FAITH AND MANNERS.

Roman
austerity
and
Roman
pride.

LIFE in the case of the Roman was spent under conditions of austere restraint, and, the nobler he was, the less he was a free man. All-powerful custom restricted him to a narrow range of thought and action; and to have led a serious and strict or, to use the characteristic Latin expressions, a grave and severe life, was his glory. Nothing more or less was expected of him than that he should keep his household in good order and unflinchingly bear his part of counsel and action in public affairs. But, while the individual had neither the wish nor the power to be aught else than a member of the community, the glory and the might of that community were felt by every individual burgess as a personal possession to be transmitted along with his name and his homestead to his posterity; and thus, as one generation after another was laid in the tomb and each in succession added its fresh contribution to the stock of ancient honours, the collective sense of dignity in the noble families of Rome swelled into that mighty pride of Roman citizenship, to which the earth has never perhaps witnessed a parallel, and the traces of which, as strange as they are grand, seem to us whenever we meet them to belong as it were to another world. It was one of the characteristic peculiarities of this powerful pride of citizenship, that, while not suppressed, it was yet compelled by the rigid simplicity and equality that prevailed among the citizens to remain locked up within the breast during life, and was only allowed to find expression after death; but it was displayed in the funeral of the man of distinction so conspicuously and intensely, that this ceremonial is better fitted than any other phenomenon of Roman life to give to us who live in other times a glimpse of that wonderful spirit of the Romans.

It was a singular procession, at which the citizens were A Roman funeral.
invited to be present by the summons of the public crier:
" Yonder warrior is dead; whoever can, let him come to escort Lucius Aemilius; he is borne forth from his house."
It was opened by bands of wailing women, musicians, and
dancers; one of the latter was dressed out and furnished
with a mask in imitation of the deceased, and by gesture
doubtless and action recalled once more to the multitude the
appearance of the well-known man.   Then followed the most
magnificent and peculiar part of the solemnity—the procession of ancestors—before which all the rest of the pageant so
faded in comparison, that men of rank of the true Roman
type enjoined their heirs to restrict the funeral pomp to that
procession alone.   We have already mentioned that the face-
masks of those ancestors who had filled the curule aedileship
or any higher ordinary magistracy, wrought in wax and
painted—modelled as far as possible after life, but not wanting even for the earlier ages up to and beyond the time of
the kings—were wont to be placed in wooden niches along
the walls of the family hall, and were regarded as the chief
ornament of the house.   When a death occurred in the
family, suitable persons, chiefly actors, were dressed up with
these face-masks and the corresponding official costume to
take part in the funeral ceremony, so that the ancestors—
each in the principal dress worn by him in his lifetime, the
triumphator in his gold-embroidered, the censor in his purple, and the consul in his purple-bordered, robe, with their
lictors and the other insignia of office—all in chariots gave
the final escort to the dead.   On the bier overspread with
massive purple and gold-embroidered coverlets and fine linen
cloths lay the deceased himself, likewise in the full costume
of the highest office which he had filled, and surrounded by
the armour of the enemies whom he had slain and by the
chaplets which in jest or earnest he had won.   Behind the
bier came the mourners, all dressed in black and without ornament, the sons of the deceased with their heads veiled, the
daughters without veil, the relatives and clansmen, the
friends, the clients and freedmen.   Thus the procession
passed on to the Forum.   There the corpse was placed in
an erect position; the ancestors descended from their cha-

riots and seated themselves in the curule chairs; and the son
or nearest gentile kinsman of the deceased ascended the rostra,
in order to announce to the assembled multitude in simple
recital the names and deeds of each of the men sitting in
a circle around him and, last of all, those of him who had recently died.

This may be called a barbarous custom, and a nation of
artistic feelings would certainly not have tolerated the continuance of this odd resurrection of the dead down to an
epoch of fully developed civilization; but even Greeks who
were very dispassionate and but little disposed to reverence,
such as Polybius, acknowledged the imposing effect produced
by the naïve pomp of this funeral ceremony. It was a conception essentially in keeping with the grave solemnity, the
uniform movement, and the proud dignity of Roman life,
that departed generations should continue to walk, as it
were, corporeally among the living, and that, when a burgess weary of labours and of honours was gathered to his
fathers, these fathers themselves should appear in the Forum
to receive him among their number.

The new
Hellenism.

But the Romans had now reached a crisis of transition.
Now that the power of Rome was no longer confined to Italy
but had spread far and wide to the west and to the east, the
days of the old home life of Italy were over, and a Hellenizing civilization came in its room. It is true that Italy had
been subject to the influence of Greece, ever since it had a
history at all. We have formerly shown how the youthful
Greece and the youthful Italy—both of them with some
measure of simplicity and originality—gave and received intellectual impulses; and how at a later period Rome endeavoured after a more external manner to appropriate to practical use the language and inventions of the Greeks. But
the Hellenism of the Romans of the present period was, in
its causes as well as its consequences, something essentially
new. The Romans began to feel the lack of a richer intellectual life, and to be startled as it were at their own utter
want of mental culture; and, if even nations of artistic gifts,
such as the English and Germans, have not disdained in the
pauses of their own productiveness to avail themselves of the
miserable French culture for filling up the gap, it need excite

no surprise that the Italian nation now flung itself with eager
zeal on the glorious treasures as well as on the dissolute filth
of the intellectual development of Hellas.   But it was an impulse still more profound and deep-rooted, which carried the
Romans irresistibly into the Hellenic vortex.   Hellenic civilization still doubtless assumed that name, but it was Hellenic no longer; it was, in fact, humanistic and cosmopolitan.
It had solved the problem of moulding a mass of different
nations into one whole completely in the field of intellect,
and to a certain extent also in that of politics; and, now
when the same task on a wider scale devolved on Rome, she
entered on the possession of Hellenism along with the rest of
the inheritance of Alexander the Great.   Hellenism therefore was no longer a mere stimulus or accessory influence; it
penetrated the Italian nation to the very core.   Of course,
the vigorous home life of Italy strove against the foreign
element.   It was only after a most vehement struggle that
the Italian farmer abandoned the field to the cosmopolite of
the capital; and, as in Germany the French coat called forth
the national Germanic frock, so the reaction against Hellenism aroused in Rome a tendency which opposed the influence
of Greece on principle, in a fashion altogether foreign to the
earlier centuries, and in doing so fell pretty frequently into
downright follies and absurdities.

No department of human action or thought remained
unaffected by this struggle between the old fashion and the
new.   Even political relations were largely influenced by
it.   The whimsical project of emancipating the Hellenes, the
well-deserved failure of which has already been described, the
kindred, likewise Hellenic, idea of a combination of republics
in opposition to kings, and the desire of propagating Hellenic polity at the expense of eastern despotism—which were
the two principles that regulated, for instance, the treatment
of Macedonia—were fixed ideas of the new school, just as dread
of the Carthaginians was the fixed idea of the old ; and, if Cato
pushed the latter to a ridiculous excess, Philhellenism now
and then indulged in extravagances at least as foolish.   For
example, the conqueror of king Antiochus not only had a
statue of himself in Greek costume erected on the Capitol,
but also, instead of calling himself in good Latin *Asiaticus*,

Hellenism
in politics.

assumed the unmeaning and anomalous, but yet magnificent and almost Greek, surname of *Asiagenus*.* A more important consequence of this attitude of the ruling nation towards Hellenism was, that the process of Latinizing gained ground everywhere in Italy except where it encountered the Hellenes. The cities of the Greeks in Italy, so far as the war had not destroyed them, remained Greek. Apulia, about which, it is true, the Romans gave themselves little concern, appears at this very epoch to have been thoroughly pervaded by Hellenism, and the local civilization there seems to have attained the level of the decaying Hellenic culture by its side. Tradition is silent on the matter; but the numerous coins of cities, uniformly furnished with Greek inscriptions, and the manufacture of painted vases after the Greek style, which was carried on alone in that part of Italy with more ambition and gaudiness than taste, show that Apulia had completely adopted Greek habits and Greek art.

But the real struggle between Hellenism and its national antagonists during the present period was carried on in the field of faith, of manners, and of art and literature ; and we must not omit to attempt some delineation of this great strife of principles, however difficult it may be to present a summary view of the myriad forms and aspects which the conflict assumed.

The national religion and unbelief.

The extent to which the old simple faith still retained a living hold on the Italians is shown very clearly by the admiration or astonishment which this problem of Italian piety excited among the contemporary Greeks. On occasion of the quarrel with the Aetolians it was reported of the Roman commander-in-chief that during battle he was solely occupied in praying and sacrificing like a priest ; whereas Polybiu with his somewhat stale moralizing calls the attention of his countrymen to the political usefulness of this piety, and admonishes them that a state cannot consist of wise men alone, and that such ceremonies are very convenient for the sake of the multitude.

---

* That *Asiagenus* was the original title of the hero of Magnesia and of his descendants, is established by coins and inscriptions ; the fact that the Capitoline Fasti call him *Asiaticus* is one of several traces indicating that these have undergone a non-contemporaneous revision. The former surname can only be a corruption of Ἀσιαγένης—the form which later authors substituted for it—which signifies not a conqueror of Asia, but an Asiatic by birth.

But if Italy still possessed—what had long been a mere Religious economy. antiquarian curiosity in Hellas—a national religion, it was already visibly beginning to be ossified into theology. The torpor creeping over faith is nowhere perhaps so distinctly apparent as in the alterations in the economy of divine service and of the priesthood. The public service of the gods became not only more tedious, but above all more and more costly. In 558 there was added to the three old colleges of the augurs, pontifices, and keepers of oracles, a fourth consisting of three " banquet-masters " (*tres viri epulones*), solely for the important purpose of superintending the banquets of the gods. The priests, as well as the gods, were in fairness entitled to feast; new institutions, however, were not needed with that view, as every college applied itself with zeal and devotion to its convivial affairs. The clerical banquets were accompanied by the claim of clerical immunities. The priests even in times of grave embarrassment claimed the right of exemption from public burdens, and only after very troublesome controversy submitted to make payment of the taxes in arrear (558). To the individual, as well as to the community, piety became a more and more costly article. The custom of instituting endowments, and generally of undertaking permanent pecuniary obligations, for religious objects prevailed among the Romans in a manner similar to its prevalence in Roman Catholic countries at the present day. These endowments— particularly after they came to be regarded by the supreme spiritual and at the same time the supreme juristic authority in the state, the pontifices, as a real burden devolving *de jure* on every heir or other person acquiring the estate—began to form an extremely oppressive charge on property; "inheritance without sacrificial obligation " was a proverbial saying among the Romans somewhat similar to our " rose without a thorn." The dedication of a tenth of their substance became so common, that twice every month a public entertainment was given from the proceeds in the Forum Boarium at Rome. With the Oriental worship of the Mother of the Gods there was imported to Rome among other pious nuisances the practice, annually recurring on certain fixed days, of demanding penny-collections from house to house (*stipem cogere*).

196.

196.

Lastly, the subordinate class of priests and soothsayers, as was reasonable, rendered no service without being paid for it; and beyond doubt the Roman dramatist sketched from life, when in the curtain-conversation between husband and wife he represents the account for pious services as ranking with the accounts for the cook, the nurse, and other customary presents :—

> Da mihi, vir, ——— quod dem Quinquatribus
> Praecantrici, conjectrici, hariolae atque haruspicae;
> Tum piatricem clementer non potest quin munerem.
> Flagitium est, si nil mittetur, quo supercilio spicit.

The Romans did not create a god of Gold, as they had formerly created one of Silver (i. 479) ; nevertheless he reigned in reality alike over the highest and lowest spheres of religious life. The old pride of the Latin national religion—the moderation of its economic demands—was irrevocably gone.

Theology. At the same time its ancient simplicity also departed. Theology, the spurious offspring of reason and faith, was already occupied in introducing its own tedious prolixity and solemn inanity into the old homely national faith, and thereby expelling the true spirit of that faith. The catalogue of the duties and privileges of the priest of Jupiter, for instance, might well have a place in the Talmud. They pushed the natural rule—that no religious service can be acceptable to the gods unless it is free from flaw—to such an extent in practice, that a single sacrifice had to be repeated thirty times in succession on account of mistakes again and again committed, and that the games, which also formed a part of divine service, were regarded as undone if the presiding magistrate had committed any slip in word or deed or if the music even had paused at a wrong time, and so had to be begun afresh, frequently for several, even as many as seven, times in succession.

Irreligious spirit. This exaggeration of conscientiousness was already a symptom of its incipient torpor; and the reaction against it—indifference and unbelief—appeared without delay. Even in the first Punic war (505) an instance occurred in which the consul himself made an open jest of consulting the auspices before battle—a consul, it is true, belonging to the peculiar clan of the Claudii, which alike in good and evil was ahead of its

age.   Towards the end of this epoch complaints were loudly
made that the lore of the augurs was neglected, and that, to
use the language of Cato, a number of ancient auguries and
auspices were falling into oblivion through the indolence of
the college.   An augur like Lucius Paullus, who regarded the
priesthood as a science and not as a mere title, was already a
rare exception, and could not but be so, when the government more and more openly and unhesitatingly employed
the auspices for the accomplishment of its political designs,
or, in other words, treated the national religion in accordance
with the view of Polybius as a superstition useful for imposing
on the public at large.   Where the way was thus paved,
the Hellenistic irreligious spirit found free course.   In connection with the incipient taste for art the sacred images
of the gods began as early as the time of Cato to be
employed, like other furniture, in adorning the apartments
of the rich.   More dangerous wounds were inflicted on
religion by the rising literature.   It could not indeed venture on open attacks, and such direct additions as were
made by its means to religious ideas—*e.g.* the Pater Caelus
formed by Ennius from the Roman Saturnus in imitation of
the Greek Uranos—were, while Hellenistic, of no great importance.   But the diffusion of the doctrines of Epicharmus
and Euhemerus in Rome was fraught with momentous consequences.   The poetical philosophy, which the later Pytha-
goreans had extracted from the writings of the old Sicilian
comedian Epicharmus of Megara (about 280), or rather had,   470.
at least for the most part, circulated under cover of his
name, regarded the Greek gods as natural substances, Zeus
as the atmosphere, the soul as a particle of sun-dust, and so
forth.   This philosophy of nature, like the Stoic doctrine in
later times, had in its most general outlines a certain affinity
with the Roman religion, and was, in so far, calculated
to undermine the national religion by resolving it into allegory.
A historical analysis of religion was given in the "Sacred
Memoirs" of Euhemerus of Messene (about 450), which,   300.
under the form of a narrative of the travels of the author
among the marvels of foreign lands, subjected to a thorough
and searching investigation the accounts current as to the
so-called gods, and resulted in the conclusion that there

neither were nor are gods at all. To indicate the character
of the book, it may suffice to mention the one fact, that
the story of Kronos devouring his children is explained as
arising out of the existence of cannibalism in the earliest
times and its abolition by king Zeus.   Notwithstanding, or
even by virtue of, its insipidity and destructive tendency the
production had an undeserved success in Greece, and helped,
in concert with the current philosophies there, to bury the
dead religion.   It is a remarkable indication of the expressed
and conscious antagonism between religion and the new
philosophy that Ennius already translated into Latin those
notoriously destructive writings of Epicharmus and Euhemerus.   The translators may have justified themselves at the
bar of Roman police by pleading that the attacks were
directed only against the Greek, and not against the Latin,
gods ; but the evasion was tolerably transparent.   Cato was,
from his own point of view, quite right in assailing these
tendencies indiscriminately, wherever they met him, with his
own peculiar bitterness, and in calling even Socrates a cor-
rupter of morals and offender against religion.

Home and
foreign
supersti-
tion.

Thus the old national religion was visibly on the decline ;
and, as the great trees of the primeval forest were uprooted,
the soil became covered with a rank growth of thorns and
briars and with weeds that had never been seen before.
Native superstitions and foreign impostures of the most
various hues mingled, competed, and conflicted with each
other.   No Italian stock remained exempt from this trans-
muting of old faith into new superstition.   As the lore of
entrails and of lightning was cultivated among the Etruscans,
so the liberal art of observing birds and conjuring serpents
flourished luxuriantly among the Sabellians and more particularly the Marsians.   Even among the Latin nation, and in
fact in Rome itself, we meet with similar phenomena, although
they are, comparatively speaking, less conspicuous.   Such for
instance were the lots of Praeneste, and the remarkable

81.

discovery at Rome in 573 of the tomb and posthumous writings
of king Numa.   These were alleged to prescribe religious
rites altogether strange and unheard of ; but the credulous
were to their regret not permitted to learn more than this,
coupled with the fact that the books looked very new ; for the

senate laid hands on the treasure and ordered the rolls to be
summarily thrown into the fire. The home manufacture was
quite sufficient to meet such demands of folly as might
reasonably be expected; but the Romans were far from being
content with it. The Hellenism of that epoch, already
denationalized and pervaded by Oriental mysticism, introduced not only unbelief but also superstition in its most
offensive and dangerous forms to Italy; and these vagaries
moreover had a special charm, precisely because they were
foreign.

Chaldaean astrologers and casters of nativities were already   Worship of
in the sixth century spread throughout Italy; but a still   Cybele.
more important event — one making in fact an epoch in
history—was the reception of the Phrygian Mother of the
Gods among the publicly recognized divinities of the Roman
state, to which the government had been obliged to give
their consent during the last weary years of the Hannibalic
war (550). A special embassy was sent for the purpose to   204.
Pessinus, a city in the territory of the Celts of Asia Minor;
and the rough field-stone, which the priests of the place
liberally presented to the foreigners as the real Mother
Cybele, was received by the community with unparalleled
pomp. Indeed, by way of perpetually commemorating the
joyful event, clubs in which the members entertained each
other in rotation were instituted among the higher classes,
and seem to have materially stimulated the rising tendency
to the formation of cliques. With the permission thus
granted for the *cultus* of Cybele the worship of the Orientals
gained a footing officially in Rome; and, though the government strictly insisted that the emasculate priests of the
new gods should remain Celts (*Galli*) as they were called,
and that no Roman burgess should devote himself to this
pious eunuchism, yet the barbaric pomp of the " Great
Mother "—her priests clad in Oriental costume with the
chief eunuch at their head, marching in procession through
the streets to the foreign music of fifes and kettledrums,
and begging from house to house—and the whole character
of the system, half sensuous, half monastic, must have exercised a most material influence over the sentiments and
views of the people.

Worship of
Bacchus.
186.

The effect was only too rapidly and fearfully apparent. A few years later (568) rites of the most abominable character came to the knowledge of the Roman authorities: a secret nocturnal festival in honour of the god Bacchus had been first introduced into Etruria through a Greek priest, and, spreading like a cancer, had rapidly reached Rome and propagated itself over all Italy, everywhere corrupting families and giving rise to the most heinous crimes, unparalleled unchastity, falsifying of testaments, and murdering by poison. More than 7000 men were sentenced to punishment, most of them to death, on this account, and rigorous enactments were issued as to the future; yet they did not succeed in repressing the system, and six years later (574) the magistrate to whom the matter fell complained that 3000 men more had been condemned and still there appeared no end of the evil.

180.

Repressive
measures.

Of course all rational men were agreed in the condemnation of these spurious forms of religion—as absurd as they were injurious to the commonwealth: the pious adherents of the olden faith and the partisans of Hellenic enlightenment concurred in their ridicule of, and indignation at, this superstition. Cato made it an instruction to his steward, "that he was not to present any offering, or to allow any offering to be presented on his behalf, without the knowledge and orders of his master, except at the domestic hearth and on the wayside-altar at the Compitalia, and that he should consult no *haruspex*, *hariolus*, or *Chaldaeus*." The well-known question as to how a priest could contrive to suppress laughter when he met his colleague originated with Cato, and was primarily applied to the Etruscan *haruspex*. Much in the same spirit Ennius censures in true Euripidean style the mendicant soothsayers and their adherents:

> Sed superstitiosi vates impudentesque arioli,
> Aut inertes aut insani aut quibus egestas imperat,
> Qui sibi semitam non sapiunt, alteri monstrant viam,
> Quibus divitias pollicentur, ab eis drachumam ipsi petunt.

But in such times reason from the first plays a losing game against unreason. The government, no doubt, interfered; the pious impostors were punished and expelled by the police; every foreign worship not specially sanctioned was

forbidden; even the consulting of the comparatively innocent
lot-oracle of Praeneste was officially prohibited in 512; and,
as we have already said, those who took part in the Bacchanalia were rigorously prosecuted. But, when once men's
heads are thoroughly turned, no command of the higher authorities avails to set them right again. How much the
government was obliged to concede, or at any rate did concede, is obvious from what has been stated. The Roman
custom under which the state consulted Etruscan sages in
certain emergencies and the government accordingly took
steps to secure the traditional transmission of Etruscan lore
in the noble families of Etruria, as well as the permission of
the secret worship of Demeter which was not immoral and
was restricted to women, may probably be ranked with the
earlier innocent and comparatively indifferent adoption of
foreign rites. But the admission of the worship of the
Magna Dea was a bad sign of the weakness which the government felt in presence of the new superstition, perhaps
even of the extent to which it was itself pervaded by it;
and it showed in like manner either an unpardonable
negligence or something still worse, that the authorities
only took steps against such proceedings as the Bacchanalia at so late a stage, and even then on an accidental information.

The picture, which has been handed down to us of the
life of Cato the Elder, enables us in substance to perceive
how, according to the ideas of the respectable Roman
citizens of that period, the private life of the Roman should
be spent. Active as Cato was as a statesman, pleader,
author, and mercantile speculator, family life always formed
with him the central object of existence; it was better, he
thought, to be a good husband than a great senator. His
domestic discipline was strict. The servants were not allowed to leave the house without orders, nor to talk of what
occurred in the household to strangers. The more severe
punishments were not inflicted capriciously, but sentence
was pronounced and executed after a quasi-judicial procedure: the strictness with which offences were punished
may be inferred from the fact, that one of his slaves who
had concluded a purchase without orders from his master

242.

Austerity
of man-
ners.

hanged himself on the matter coming to Cato's ears. For slight offences, such as mistakes committed in waiting at table, the consular was wont after dinner to administer to the culprit the proper number of lashes with a thong wielded by his own hand. He kept his wife and children in order no less strictly, but by other means; for he declared it sinful to lay hands on a wife or grown-up children in the same way as on slaves. In the choice of a wife he disapproved marrying for money, and recommended men to look to good descent; but he himself married in old age the daughter of one of his poor clients. Moreover he adopted views in regard to continence on the part of the husband similar to those which everywhere prevail in slave countries; a wife was throughout regarded by him as simply a necessary evil. His writings abound in invectives against the chattering, finery-loving, ungovernable fair sex; it was the opinion of the old lord that " all women are plaguy and proud," and that, " were men quit of women, their life would probably be less godless." On the other hand the rearing of his children born in wedlock was a matter which touched his heart and his honour, and the wife in his eyes existed strictly and solely for the children's sake. She nursed them ordinarily herself, or, if she allowed her children to be suckled by female slaves, she also allowed their children in return to draw nourishment from her own breast; one of the few traits, which indicate an endeavour to mitigate the institution of slavery by ties of human sympathy—the common impulses of maternity and the bond of foster-brotherhood. The old general was present in person, whenever it was possible, at the washing and swaddling of his children. He watched with reverential care over their childlike innocence; he assures us that he was as careful lest he should utter an unbecoming word in presence of his children as if he had been in presence of the Vestal Virgins, and that he never before the eyes of his daughters embraced their mother, except when she had become alarmed during a thunder-storm. The education of his son was perhaps the noblest portion of his varied and variously honourable activity. True to his maxim, that a ruddy-cheeked boy was worth more than a pale one, the old soldier in person initiated his son into all bodily exercises, and taught him to wrestle, to ride, to swim, to box, and to endure heat and cold. But he felt very justly, that the time had gone by when it sufficed for a Roman to be a good farmer and soldier; and he felt also that it could not but have an injurious influence on the mind of his boy, if he should subsequently learn that the teacher, who had rebuked and punished him and had won his reverence, was a mere slave. Therefore he in person taught the boy what a Roman was wont to learn, to read and write and know the law of the land; and even in his later years he worked his way so far into the general culture of the Hellenes, that he was able to deliver to his son in his native tongue whatever in that culture he deemed to be of use to a Roman. All his writings were primarily intended for his son, and he wrote his historical work for that son's use with large distinct letters in his own hand. He lived in a homely and frugal style. His strict parsimony tolerated no expenditure on luxuries. He allowed no slave to cost him more than 1500 *denarii* (£65) and no dress more than 100 *denarii* (£4 6s.); no carpet was to be seen in his house, and for a long time there was no whitewash on the walls of the rooms. Ordinarily he partook of the same fare with his servants, and did not suffer his outlay in cash for the meal to exceed 30 *asses* (2s.); in time of war even wine was uniformly banished from his table, and he drank water or, according to circumstances, water mixed with vinegar. On the other hand, he was no enemy to hospitality; he was fond of associating both with his club in town and with the neighbouring landlords in the country; he sat long at table, and, as his varied experience and his shrewd and ready wit made him a pleasant companion, he disdained neither the dice nor the wine-flask: among other receipts in his book on husbandry he even gives a tried recipe for the case of a too hearty meal and too deep potations. His life up to extreme old age was one of ceaseless activity. Every moment was apportioned and occupied; and every evening he was in the habit of turning over in his mind what he had heard, said, or done during the day. Thus he found time for his own affairs as well as for those of his friends and of the state, and time also for conversation and pleasure; everything was done quickly and without many words, and his genuine spirit of activity hated nothing so much as bustle or a great ado about trifles.

So lived the man who was regarded by his contemporaries and by posterity as the true model of a Roman burgess, and who appeared as it were the living embodiment of the— certainly somewhat coarse-grained—energy and honesty of Rome as opposed to Greek indolence and Greek immorality; as a later Roman poet says:

> *Sperne mores transmarinos, mille habent offucias.*
> *Cive Romano per orbem nemo vivit rectius.*
> *Quippe malim unum Catonem, quam trecentos Socratas.*

Such judgments will not be absolutely adopted by history; but every one who carefully considers the revolution which the degenerate Hellenism of this age accomplished in the modes of life and thought among the Romans, will be inclined to deepen rather than to modify that condemnation of the foreign manners.

New manners.

184.

234.

10.

The ties of family life became relaxed with fearful rapidity. The evil of grisettes and boy-favourites spread like a pestilence, and, as matters stood, it was not possible to take any material steps in the way of legislation against it. The high tax, which Cato as censor (570) laid on this most abominable species of slaves kept for luxury, would not be of much moment, and besides fell practically into disuse a year or two afterwards along with the property-tax generally. Celibacy—as to which grave complaints were made as early as 520—and divorces naturally increased in proportion. Horrible crimes were perpetrated in the bosom of families of the highest rank; for instance, the consul Gaius Calpurnius Piso was poisoned by his wife and his stepson, in order to occasion a supplementary election to the consulship and so to procure the supreme magistracy for the latter —a plot which was successful (574). Moreover the emancipation of women began. According to old custom the married woman was subject in law to the marital power which was parallel with the paternal, and the unmarried woman to the guardianship of her nearest male *agnati* which fell little short of the paternal power; the wife had no property of her own, the virgin and widow had at any rate no right of management. But now women began to aspire to independence in respect to property, and, getting quit of the guardianship of their *agnati* by evasive lawyers' expedients —particularly through mock marriages—they took the management of their property into their own hands, or, in the event of being married, sought by means not much better to withdraw themselves from the marital power, which under the strict letter of the law was necessary. The mass of capital which was collected in the hands of women appeared to the statesmen of the time so dangerous, that they resorted to the extravagant expedient of prohibiting by law the testamentary nomination of women as heirs (585), and even sought by a highly arbitrary practice to deprive women for the most part of those collateral inheritances which fell to them without testament. In like manner the family jurisdiction over women, which was connected with that marital and tutorial power, became practically more and more antiquated. Even in public matters women already began to have a will of their own and occasionally, as Cato thought, " to rule the rulers of the world; " their influence might be traced in the comitia, and already statues were erected in the provinces to Roman ladies.

Luxury prevailed more and more in dress, ornaments, and furniture, in buildings and at table. Especially after the expedition to Asia Minor in 564 Asiatico-Hellenic luxury, such as prevailed at Ephesus and Alexandria, transferred its empty refinement and its petty trifling, destructive alike of money, time, and pleasure, to Rome. Here too women took the lead : in spite of the zealous invective of Cato they managed to procure the abolition, after the peace with Carthage (559), of the decree of the people passed soon after the battle of Cannae (539), which forbade them to use gold ornaments, variegated dresses, or chariots ; no course was left to their zealous antagonist but to impose a high tax on those articles (570). A multitude of new and for the most part frivolous articles—silver plate elegantly figured, tablecouches with bronze mounting, Attalic dresses as they were called, and carpets of rich gold brocade—now found their way to Rome. Above all, this new luxury appeared in the appliances of the table. Hitherto without exception the Romans had only partaken of hot dishes once a day; now hot dishes were not unfrequently produced at the second

169.

Luxury.

190.

195.

215.

184.

meal (*prandium*), and for the principal meal the two courses
formerly in use no longer sufficed. Hitherto the women of
the household had themselves attended to the baking of
bread and cooking; and it was only on occasion of entertainments that a professional cook was specially hired, who
in that case superintended alike the cooking and the baking.
Now, on the other hand, a scientific cookery began to prevail.
In the better houses a special cook was kept. A division of
labour became necessary, and the trade of baking bread and
cakes branched off from that of cooking—the first bakers'
171.   shops in Rome appeared about 583. Poems on the art of
good eating, with long lists of the most palatable fishes and
other marine products, found their readers: and the theory
was reduced to practice. Foreign delicacies—anchovies from
Pontus, wine from Greece—began to be esteemed in Rome,
and Cato's receipt for giving to the ordinary wine of the
country the flavour of Coan by means of brine would hardly
inflict any considerable injury on the Roman wine-merchants.
The old decorous singing and reciting of the guests and
their boys were supplanted by Asiatic *sambucistriae*. Hitherto
the Romans had perhaps drunk pretty deeply at supper, but
drinking-banquets in the strict sense were unknown; now
formal revels came into vogue, on which occasions the wine
was little or not at all diluted and was drunk out of large
cups, and the drinking of healths, in which each was bound
to follow his neighbour in regular succession, formed the
leading feature—" drinking after the Greek style " (*Graeco
more bibere*) or " playing the Greek " (*pergraecari, congraecare*)
as the Romans called it. In consequence of this debauchery
dice-playing, which had long been in use among the Romans,
reached such a height that it was necessary for legislation
to interfere. The aversion to labour and the habit of idle
lounging were visibly on the increase.* Cato proposed to

---

* A sort of *parabasis* in the Curculio
of Plautus describes what went on in the
leading thoroughfares of the capital, with
little humour perhaps, but with life-like
distinctness.

*Commonstrabo, quo in quemque hominem
    facile inveniatis loco,
Ne nimio opere sumat operam, si quem
    conventum velit,*

*Vel vitiosum vel sine vitio, vel probum vel
    improbum.
Qui perjurum convenire volt hominem,
    mitto in comitium;
Qui mendacem et gloriosum, apud Cloa-
    cinae sacrum.
[Ditis damnosos maritos sub Basilica
    quaerito.
Ibidem erunt scorta exoleta, quique stipu-
    lari solent.]*

have the market paved with pointed stones, in order to put a stop to the habit of idling; the Romans laughed at the jest and went on to enjoy the pleasure of loitering and gazing around them.

We have already noticed the alarming increase of the popular amusements during this epoch. At the beginning of it, apart from some unimportant foot and chariot races which should rather be ranked with religious ceremonies, only a single general festival was held in the month of September, lasting four days and having a definitely fixed maximum of cost (i. 502). At the close of the epoch, this popular festival had a duration of at least six days; and besides this there were celebrated at the beginning of April the festival of the Mother of the Gods or the so-called Megalensia, towards the end of April that of Ceres and that of Flora, in June that of Apollo, in November the Plebeian games—all of them probably occupying already more days than one. To these fell to be added the numerous cases where the games were celebrated afresh — in which pious scruples probably often served as a mere pretext—and the incessant extraordinary festivals. Among these the already-mentioned banquets furnished from the dedicated tenths (p. 423), the feasts of the gods, the triumphal and funeral festivities, were conspicuous; and above all the festal games which were celebrated—for the first time in 505—at the close of one of those longer periods which were marked off in the Etrusco-Roman religion, the *saecula*, as they were called. At the

Increase of amusements.

249.

Symbolarum collatores apud forum piscarium.
In foro infimo boni homines atque dites ambulant.
In medio propter Canalem, ibi ostentatores meri.
Confidentes garrulique et malevoli supra Lacum,
Qui alteri de nihilo audacter dicunt contumeliam.
Et qui ipsi sat habent quod ipsis vere possit dicier.
Sub Veteribus, ibi sunt, qui dant quique accipiunt foenori.
Pone aedem Castoris, ibi sunt, subito quibus credas male.
In Tusco vico, ibi sunt homines, qui ipsi sese venditant.

In Velabro vel pistorem, vel lanium, vel haruspicem,
Vel qui ipsi vorsant, vel, qui aliis subvorsentur, praebeant.
Ditis damnosos maritos apud Leucadiam Oppiam.

The verses in brackets are a subsequent addition, inserted after the building of the first Roman bazaar (570). The business of the baker (*pistor*, literally miller) embraced at this time the sale of delicacies and the providing accommodation for revellers (Festus, *Ep. v. alicariae*, p. 7, Müll.; Plautus, *Capt.* 160; *Poen.* i. 2, 54; *Trin.* 407). The same was the case with the butchers. Leucadia Oppia probably kept a house of bad fame.

184.

same time domestic festivals were multiplied. During the second Punic war there were introduced, among people of quality, the already-mentioned banquetings on the anniversary of the entrance of the Mother of the Gods (after

204. 550), and, among the lower orders, the similar Saturnalia
217. (after 537), both under the influence of the powers henceforth closely allied—the foreign priest and the foreign cook. A very near approach was made to that ideal condition in which every idler should know where he might kill the time every day; and this in a commonwealth where formerly action had been with all and sundry the very object of existence, and idle enjoyment had been proscribed by custom as well as by law! The bad and demoralizing elements in these festal observances, moreover, daily acquired greater ascendancy. It is true that still as formerly the chariot races formed the brilliant finale of the national festivals; and a poet of this period describes very vividly the straining expectancy with which the eyes of the multitude were fastened on the consul, when he was on the point of giving the signal for the chariots to start. But the former amusements no longer sufficed; there was a craving for new and more varied spectacles. Greek athletes now made their appearance

186. (for the first time in 568) alongside of the native wrestlers and boxers. Of the dramatic exhibitions we shall speak hereafter: the introduction of Greek comedy and tragedy to Rome was a gain perhaps of doubtful value; but it formed at any rate the best of their acquisitions at this time. The Romans had probably long indulged in the sport of coursing hares and hunting foxes in presence of the public; now these innocent hunts were converted into formal baitings of wild animals, and the wild beasts of Africa—lions and panthers—

186. were (first so far as can be proved in 568) transported at great cost to Rome, in order that by killing or being killed they might serve to glut the eyes of the gazers of the capital. The still more revolting gladiatorial games, which prevailed in Campania and Etruria, now gained admission to Rome; human blood was first shed for sport in the Roman

264. Forum in 490. Of course these demoralizing amusements
268. encountered severe censure: the consul of 486, Publius Sempronius Sophus, sent a divorce to his wife, because she had

attended funeral games ; the government managed to procure a decree of the people prohibiting the importation of
wild beasts to Rome, and strictly insisted that no gladiators
should appear at the public festivals. But here too it wanted
either the proper power or proper energy : it succeeded, apparently, in checking the practice of baiting animals, but
the appearance of sets of gladiators at private festivals, particularly at funeral celebrations, was not suppressed. Still
less could the public be prevented from preferring the gladiator
to the rope-dancer, the rope-dancer to the comedian, the
comedian to the tragedian ; or the stage be prevented from
revelling by choice amidst the pollution of Hellenic life.
Whatever elements of culture were contained in the scenic
and artistic entertainments were from the first thrown aside ;
it was by no means the object of the givers of the Roman
festivals to elevate—though it should be but temporarily—
the whole body of spectators through the power of poetry to
the level of feeling of the best, as the Greek stage did in the
period of its prime, or to prepare an artistic treat for a select
circle, as our theatres endeavour to do. The character of
the managers and spectators in Rome is illustrated by a
scene at the triumphal games in 587, where the first Greek   167.
flute-players, on their melodies failing to please, were instructed by the director to box with one another instead of
playing, upon which the delight knew no bounds.

Nor was the evil confined to the corruption of Roman
manners by Hellenic contagion ; conversely the scholars
began to demoralize their instructors. Gladiatorial games,
which were unknown in Greece, were first introduced by
king Antiochus Epiphanes (575–590), a professed imitator   175–164.
of the Romans, at the Syrian court, and, although they
excited at first greater horror than pleasure in the Greek
public, which was more humane and had more of a taste for
art than the Romans, they yet held their ground and gradually came more and more into vogue.

As a matter of course, this revolution in life and manners
brought an economic revolution in its train. Residence in
the capital became more and more coveted as well as more
costly. Rents rose to an unexampled height. Extravagant
prices were paid for the new articles of luxury ; a barrel of

anchovies from the Black Sea cost 1600 sesterces (£16)—
more than the price of a rural slave; a beautiful boy cost
24,000 sesterces (£240)—more than many a farmer's homestead. Money therefore, and nothing but money, became
the watchword with high and low. In Greece it had long
been the case that nobody did anything without being paid
for it, as the Greeks themselves with discreditable candour
allowed : after the second Macedonian war the Romans
began in this respect also to imitate the Greeks. Respectability had to provide itself with legal buttresses; pleaders,
for instance, had to be prohibited by decree of the people from
taking money for their services; the jurisconsults alone
formed a noble exception, and needed no decree of the people
to compel their adherence to the honourable custom of giving
their good advice gratuitously. Men did not, if possible, steal
outright; but all shifts seemed allowable in order to attain
rapidly to riches—plundering and begging, cheating on the
part of contractors and swindling on the part of speculators, usurious trading in money and in grain, even the turning
of purely moral relations such as friendship and marriage to
economic account. Marriage especially became on both sides
a matter of mercantile speculation; marriages for money were
common, and it appeared necessary to refuse legal validity to
the presents which the spouses made to each other. That,
under such a state of things, plans for setting fire on all sides
to the capital came to the knowledge of the authorities, need
excite no surprise. When man no longer finds enjoyment in
work, and works merely in order to attain as quickly as
possible to enjoyment, it is a mere accident that he does not
become a criminal. Destiny lavished all the glories of power
and riches with liberal hand on the Romans; but, in truth,
the Pandora's box was a gift of doubtful value.

CHAPTER XIV.

LITERATURE AND ART.

THE influences which stimulated the growth of Roman literature were of a character altogether peculiar and hardly paralleled in any other nation. To estimate them correctly, it is necessary in the first place that we should glance at the national education and national recreations of this period.

Language lies at the root of all mental culture ; and this was especially the case in Rome.   In a community where so much importance was attached to speeches and documents, and where the citizen, at an age which is still according to modern ideas regarded as boyhood, was already entrusted with the uncontrolled management of his property and might find himself under the necessity of formally addressing the public assembly, not only was great value set all along on the fluent and polished use of the mother-tongue, but efforts were early made to acquire a command of it in the years of boyhood. The Greek language also was already generally diffused in Italy in the time of Hannibal.   In the higher circles a knowledge of that language, which was the general medium of intercourse for ancient civilization, had long been a far from uncommon accomplishment ; and now, when the change in the position of Rome had so enormously increased the intercourse with foreigners and the foreign traffic, such a knowledge was, if not necessary, yet in all probability of very material importance to the merchant as well as the statesman.   By means of the Italian slaves and freedmen, a very large portion of whom were Greek or half-Greek by birth, the Greek language and Greek knowledge to a certain extent reached even the lower ranks of the population, especially in the capital. The comedies of this period indicate that even the humbler classes of the capital were familiar with a sort of Latin, which could no more be properly understood without a knowledge of Greek

Knowledge of languages.

than the English of Sterne or the German of Wieland without a knowledge of French.* Men of senatorial families, however, not only addressed a Greek audience in Greek, but even published their speeches—Tiberius Gracchus (consul in 577 and 591) so published a speech which he had given at Rhodes—and in the time of Hannibal wrote their chronicles in Greek, as we shall have occasion to mention more particularly in the sequel. Individuals went still farther. The Greeks honoured Flamininus by complimentary demonstrations in the Roman language (p. 263), and he returned the compliment; the "great general of the Aeneiades" dedicated his votive gifts to the Greek gods after the Greek fashion in Greek distichs.† Cato reproached another senator with the fact, that he had the effrontery to deliver Greek recitations with the due modulation at Greek revels.

Under the influence of such circumstances Roman education developed itself. It is a mistaken opinion, that antiquity was materially inferior to our own times in the general diffusion of elementary attainments. Even among the lower classes and slaves there was considerable knowledge of reading, writing, and counting : in the case of a slave steward, for instance, Cato, following the example of Mago, takes for granted the ability to read and write. Elementary instruction, as well as instruction in Greek, must have been long before this period imparted to a very considerable extent

---

* A distinct set of Greek expressions, such as *stratioticus, machaera, nauclerus, trapezita, danista, drapeta, oenopolium, bolus, malacus, morus, graphicus, logus, apologus, techna, schema*, forms quite a special feature in the language of Plautus. Translations are seldom attached, and that only in the case of words not included in the circle of ideas to which those which we have cited belong; for instance, in the *Truculentus* —in a verse, however, that is perhaps a later addition (i. 1, 60)—we find the explanation: φρόνησις est sapientia. Fragments of Greek also are common, as in the *Casina* (iii. 6, 9):

Πράγματά μοι παρέχεις—*Dabo* μέγα κακὸν, ut opinor.

Greek puns likewise occur, as in the *Bacchides* (240):

opus est chryso Chrysalo.

Ennius in the same way takes for granted that the etymological meaning of Alexandros and Andromache is known to the spectators (Varro, *de L.L.* vii. 82). Most characteristic of all are the half-Greek formations, such as *ferritribax, plagipatida, pugilice*, or in the *Miles Gloriosus* (213):

Euge! euscheme hercle astitit sic dulice et commoedice!

† One of these epigrams composed in the name of Flamininus runs thus:

Ζηνὸς ἰὼ κραιπναῖσι γεγαȣότες ἱπποσύναισι
Κοῦροι, ἰὼ Σπάρτας Τυνδαρίδαι βασιλεῖς,
Αἰνεάδας Τίτος ὕμμιν ὑπέρτατον ὥπασε δῶρον
Ἑλλήνων τεύξας παισὶν ἐλευȣερίαν.

in Rome. But the epoch now before us initiated an education, the aim of which was to communicate not merely an
outward expertness, but a real mental culture.   Hitherto a
knowledge of Greek had conferred on its possessor as little
superiority in civil or social life, as a knowledge of French
perhaps confers at the present day in a hamlet of German
Switzerland; and the earliest writers of Greek chronicles
probably held a position among the senators similar to that
of the farmer in the fens of Holstein who has been a student
and in the evening, when he comes home from the plough,
takes down his Virgil from the shelf.   A man who assumed
airs of greater importance by reason of his Greek, was
reckoned a bad patriot and a fool; and certainly even in
Cato's time one who spoke Greek ill or not at all might still
be a leading man and become senator and consul.   But a
change was already taking place.   The internal decomposition
of Italian nationality had already, particularly in the aristocracy, advanced so far as to render the substitution of a
broader human culture for that nationality inevitable : and
the craving after a more advanced civilization was already
powerfully stirring the minds of men.   Instruction in the
Greek language as it were spontaneously met this craving.
The classical literature of Greece, the Iliad and still more the
Odyssey, had all along formed the basis of that instruction ;
the overflowing treasures of Hellenic art and science were
already by this means spread before the eyes of the Italians.
Without any outward revolution, strictly speaking, in the
character of the instruction the natural result was, that the
empirical study of the language became converted into a
higher study of the literature ; that the general culture connected with such literary studies was communicated in increased measure to the scholars ; and that these availed
themselves of the knowledge thus acquired to dive into that
Greek literature which most powerfully influenced the spirit
of the age—the tragedies of Euripides and the comedies of
Menander.

   In a similar way greater importance came to be attached
to the study of Latin.   The higher society of Rome began to
feel the need, if not of exchanging their mother-tongue for
Greek, at least of refining it and adapting it to the changed

state of culture; and for this purpose too they found themselves in every respect dependent on the Greeks. The economic arrangements of the Romans placed the work of elementary instruction in the mother-tongue—like every other work held in little estimation and performed for hire—chiefly in the hands of slaves, freedmen, or foreigners, or in other words chiefly in the hands of Greeks or half-Greeks;* which was attended with the less difficulty, because the Latin alphabet was almost identical with the Greek and the two languages possessed a close and striking affinity. But this was the least part of the matter; the importance of the study of Greek in a formal point of view exercised a far deeper influence over the study of Latin. Any one who knows how singularly difficult it is to find suitable matter and suitable forms for the higher intellectual culture of youth, and how much more difficult it is to set aside the matter and forms once found, will understand how it was that the Romans knew no mode of supplying the want of a more advanced Latin instruction except that of simply transferring the solution of this problem, which the study of the Greek language and literature furnished, to the study of Latin. In the present day a process entirely analogous goes on under our own eyes in the transference of the methods of instruction from the dead to the living languages.

But unfortunately the chief requisite for such a transference was wanting. The Romans could, no doubt, learn to read and write Latin by means of the Twelve Tables; but a Latin culture presupposed a literature, and no such literature existed in Rome.

The stage under Greek influence.

To this want there was added another. We have already described the multiplication of the amusements of the Roman people. The stage had long played an important part in these recreations; the chariot-races formed strictly the principal amusement in all of them, but these races uniformly took place only on one, viz. the concluding, day, while the earlier days were substantially devoted to stage-entertainments. But for long these stage-representations consisted chiefly of dances and jugglers' feats; the impro-

---

* Such, *e. g.*, was Chilo, the slave of Cato the Elder, who earned money on his master's behalf as a teacher of children (Plutarch, *Cato Mai.* 20).

vised chants, which were produced on these occasions, had
neither dialogue nor plot (i. 502). It was only now that the
Romans looked around them for a real drama. The Roman
popular festivals were throughout under the influence of the
Greeks, whose talent for amusing and for killing time naturally rendered them the purveyors of pleasure to the Romans. Now no national amusement was a greater favourite
in Greece, and none was more varied, than the theatre; it
could not but speedily attract the attention of those who provided the Roman festivals and their staff of assistants. The
earlier Roman stage-chant contained within it a dramatic
germ capable perhaps of development; but to develop the
drama from that germ required on the part of the poet and
the public a genial power of imparting and receiving, such
as was not to be found among the Romans at all, and least
of all at this period; and, had it been possible to find it, the
impatience of those entrusted with the amusement of the
multitude would hardly have allowed to the noble fruit peace
and leisure to ripen. In this case too there was an outward
want, which the nation was unable to satisfy; the Romans
desired a theatre, but the pieces were wanting.

On these elements Roman literature was based; and its
defective character was from the first and necessarily the
result of such an origin. All real art has its root in individual freedom and a cheerful enjoyment of life, and the germs
of such an art were not wanting in Italy; but, when Roman
life substituted for freedom and joyousness the sense of public
obligation and the consciousness of duty, art was arrested
and, instead of growing, necessarily pined away. The cul-
minating point of Roman development was the period which
had no literature. It was not till Roman nationality began
to give way and Hellenico-cosmopolite tendencies began to
prevail, that literature made its appearance at Rome in their
train. Accordingly from the beginning, and by stringent internal necessity, it took its stand on Greek ground and in
broad antagonism to the distinctively Roman national spirit.
Roman poetry in particular had its immediate origin not in
the inward impulse of the poet, but in the outward demands
of the school, which needed Latin manuals, and of the stage,
which needed Latin dramas. Now both institutions—the

*Rise of a
Roman
literature.*

school and the stage—were thoroughly anti-Roman and revolutionary. The gaping and staring idleness of the theatre
was utterly offensive to the sober earnestness and the spirit
of activity which animated the Romans of the olden type;
and—inasmuch as it was the deepest and noblest conception
lying at the root of the Roman commonwealth, that within
the circle of Roman burgesses there should be neither master
nor slave, neither *millionnaire* nor beggar, but that above all a
like faith and a like culture should signalize all Romans—
the school and the necessarily exclusive school-culture were
far more dangerous still, and were in fact utterly destructive
of the sense of equality. The school and the theatre became
the most effective levers in the hands of the new spirit of the
age, and all the more so that they used the Latin tongue.
Men might perhaps speak and write Greek and yet not cease
to be Romans; but in this case they were in the habit of
speaking in the Roman language, while the whole inward
being and life were Greek. It is not one of the most pleasing, but it is one of the most remarkable and in a historical
point of view most instructive, facts in this brilliant era of
Roman conservatism, that during its course Hellenism struck
root in the whole field of intellect not immediately political,
and that the schoolmaster and the *maître de plaisir* of the
great public in close alliance created a Roman literature.

Livius An-
dronicus.

272. 207.

272.

219. 207.

In the very earliest Roman author the later development
appears, as it were, in embryo. The Greek Andronikos
(born before 482, and lived till after 547), afterwards as a
Roman burgess called Lucius * Livius Andronicus, came to
Rome at an early age in 482 among the other captives taken
at Tarentum (i. 450) and passed into the possession of the
conqueror of Sena (p. 187) Marcus Livius Salinator (consul
535, 547). He was employed as a slave, partly in acting
and copying texts, partly in giving instruction in the Latin
and Greek languages, which he taught both to the children
of his master and to other boys of wealthy parents in and
out of the house. He distinguished himself so much in this
way that his master gave him freedom, and even the autho-

---

* The later rule, by which the freed-　his patron, was not yet applied in
man necessarily bore the *praenomen* of　republican Rome.

rities, who not unfrequently availed themselves of his services
—commissioning him, for instance, to prepare a thanksgiving-
chant after the fortunate turn taken by the Hannibalic war
in 547—out of regard for him conceded to the guild of poets   272.
and actors a place for their common worship in the temple
of Minerva on the Aventine. His authorship arose out of
his double occupation. As schoolmaster he translated the
Odyssey into Latin, in order that the Latin text might form
the basis of his Latin, as the Greek text was the basis of his
Greek, instruction; and this earliest of Roman school-books
maintained its place in education for centuries. As an actor,
he not only like every other wrote the texts themselves for
his own use, but he also published them as books, that is, he
read them in public and diffused them by copies. What was
still more important, he substituted the Greek drama for the
old essentially lyrical stage poetry. It was in 514, a year   240.
after the close of the first Punic war, that the first play was
exhibited on the Roman stage. This creation of an epos, a
tragedy, and a comedy in the Roman language, and that by
a man who was more Roman than Greek, was historically a
remarkable event; but we cannot speak of his labours as
having any artistic value. They make no sort of claim to
originality; viewed as translations, they are characterized
by a barbarism which is all the more conspicuous, that his
poetry does not naïvely display its own native simplicity,
but pedantically labours to imitate the high artistic culture
of the neighbouring people. The wide deviations from the
original are due not to the freedom, but to the rudeness of
the imitation; the treatment is sometimes insipid, sometimes
turgid, the language harsh and quaint.* We have no diffi-

---

* One of the tragedies of Livius
presented the line—
Quem ego néfrendem alui lácteam immul-
géns opem.
The verses of Homer (*Odyssey*, xii. 16):

οὐδ᾽ ἄρα Κίρκην
ἐξ Ἀίδεω ἐλθόντες ἐλήθομεν, ἀλλὰ μάλ᾽
ὦκα
ἦλθ᾽ ἐντυναμένη· ἅμα δ᾽ ἀμφίπολοι φέρον
αὐτῇ
σῖτον καὶ κρέα πολλὰ καὶ αἴθοπα οἶνον
ἐρυθρόν.

are thus interpreted:

Tópper citi ad aédis—vénimus Circae
Simul dúona córam (?)—pórtant ad
návis,
Milia ália in isdem—inserinúntur.

The most remarkable feature is not so
much the barbarism as the thoughtless-
ness of the translator, who, instead of
sending Circe to Ulysses, sends Ulysses to
Circe. Another still more ridiculous mistake is the translation of αἰδοίοισιν ἔδωκα
(Odyss. xv. 373) by *lusi* (Festus, *Ep. v.
affatim*, p. 11, *Müller*). Such traits are
not in a historical point of view matters
of indifference; we recognize in them

culty in believing the statement of the old critics of art, that, apart from the compulsory perusal in school, none of the poems of Livius were taken up a second time. Yet these labours were in various respects models for succeeding times. They formed the commencement of the Roman translation-literature, and naturalized the Greek metres in Latium. The reason why these were adopted only in the dramas, while the Odyssey of Livius was written in the national Saturnian measure, evidently was that the iambuses and trochees of tragedy and comedy far more easily admitted of imitation in Latin than the epic dactyls.

But this preliminary stage of literary development was soon passed. The epics and dramas of Livius were regarded by posterity, and undoubtedly with perfect justice, as resembling the rigid statues of Daedalus destitute of emotion or expression—curiosities rather than works of art. But in the following generation, now that the foundations were once laid, there arose a lyric, epic, and dramatic art; and it is of great importance, even in a historical point of view, to trace this poetical growth.

Drama.

Both as respects extent of production and influence over the public, the drama stood at the head of the poetry thus developed in Rome. In antiquity there was no permanent theatre with fixed charges for admission; in Greece as in Rome dramas made their appearance only as an element in the annually recurring or extraordinary amusements of the citizens. Among the measures by which the government counteracted or imagined that they counteracted that extension of the popular festivals which they justly regarded with anxiety, they refused to permit the erection of a stone building for a theatre.* Instead of this there was erected for each festival a scaffolding of boards with a stage for the actors (*proscaenium, pulpitum*) and a decorated background (*scaena*); and in a semicircle in front of it was staked off the space for the spectators (*cavea*), which was merely sloped

Theatre.

---

the level of intellectual culture which marked these earliest Roman verse-making schoolmasters, and we at the same time perceive that, although Andronicus was born in Tarentum, Greek cannot have been properly his mother-tongue.

* Such a building was, no doubt, constructed for the Apollinarian games in the Flaminian circus in 575 (Liv. xl. 51; Becker, *Top.* p. 605); but it was probably soon afterwards pulled down again (Tertull. *de Spect.* 10).

without steps or seats, so that, if the spectators had not chairs brought along with them, they squatted, reclined, or stood.* The women were probably separated at an early period, and were restricted to the upper and worst places; otherwise there was no distinction of places in law till 560, after which, as already mentioned (p. 340), the lowest and best positions were reserved for the senators.

194.

The audience was anything but genteel. The better classes, it is true, did not keep aloof from the general recreations of the people; the fathers of the city seem even to have been bound for decorum's sake to appear on these occasions. But the very nature of a burgess festival implied that, while slaves and probably foreigners also were excluded, admittance free of charge was given to every burgess with his wife and children;† and accordingly the body of spectators cannot have differed much from what one sees in the present day at public fireworks and *gratis* exhibitions. Naturally, therefore, the proceedings were not of the most orderly character; children cried, women talked and shrieked, now and then a wench prepared to make her way to the stage; the attendants whose duty it was to keep order had on these festivals anything but a holiday, and found frequent occasion to confiscate a mantle or to ply the rod.

Audience.

The introduction of the Greek drama increased the demands on the dramatic staff, and there seems to have been no redundance in the supply of capable actors: on one occasion for want of actors a piece of Naevius had to be performed by amateurs. But this produced no change in the position of the artist; the poet or, as he was at this time called, the "writer," the actor, and the composer not only belonged

---

* In 599 there were still no seats in the theatre (Ritschl, *Parerg.* i. p. xviii. xx. 214; comp. Ribbeck, *Trag.* p. 285); but, as not only the authors of the Plautine prologues, but Plautus himself on various occasions, make allusions to a sitting audience (*Mil. Glor.* 82, 83; *Aulul.* iv. 9, 6; *Trucul. ap. fin.; Epid. ap. fin.*), most of the spectators must have brought stools with them or have seated themselves on the ground.

† Women and children appear to have been at all times admitted to the Roman theatre (Val. Max. vi. 3, 12; Plutarch. *Quaest. Rom.* 14; Cicero, *de Har. Resp.* 12, 24; Vitruv. v. 3, 1; Suetonius, *Aug.* 44, &c.); but slaves were *de jure* excluded (Cicero, *de Har. Resp.* 12, 26; Ritschl, *Parerg.* i. p. xix. 223), and the same must doubtless have been the case with foreigners, excepting of course the guests of the community, who took their places among or by the side of the senators (Varro, v. 155; Justin. xliii. 5, 10; Sueton. *Aug.* 44).

still, as formerly, to the despised class of labourers for hire (p. 407), but were still, as formerly, placed in the most marked way under the ban of public opinion, and subjected to police maltreatment (i. 503). Of course all reputable persons kept aloof from such an occupation. The manager of the company (*dominus gregis, factionis,* also *choragus*), who was ordinarily also the chief actor, was generally a freedman, and its members were ordinarily his slaves; the composers, whose names have reached us, were all of them non-free. The remuneration was not merely small—a *honorarium* of 8000 sesterces (£80) given to a dramatist is described shortly after the close of this period as unusually high—but was, moreover, only paid by the magistrates providing the festival, if the piece was not a failure. With the payment the matter ended; dramatic competitions and honorary prizes, such as took place in Attica, were not yet heard of in Rome —the Romans at this time appear to have simply applauded or hissed as we now do, and to have brought forward only a single piece for exhibition each day.* Under such circumstances, where art went for days' wages and the artist instead of receiving due honour was subjected to disgrace, the new national theatre of the Romans could exhibit no original or at all artistic development; and, while the noble rivalry of the noblest Athenians had called into life the Attic drama, the Roman drama taken as a whole could be nothing but a spoiled copy of its predecessor, in which the only wonder is that it has been able to display so much grace and wit in the details.

Comedy.

In the dramatic world comedy greatly preponderated over

---

* It is not necessary to infer from the prologues of Plautus (*Cas.* 17; *Amph.* 65) that there was a distribution of prizes (Ritschl, *Parerg.* i. 229); even the passage *Trin.* 706, may very well belong to the Greek original, not to the translator; and the total silence of the *didascaliae* and prologues, as well as of all tradition, on the point of prize adjudications and prizes is decisive.

That only one piece was produced each day we infer from the fact, that the spectators come from home at the beginning of the piece (*Poen.* 10), and return home after its close (*Epid. Pseud. Rud.*

Stich. Truc. ap. fin.). They went, as these passages show, to the theatre after the second breakfast, and were at home again for the midday meal; the performance thus lasted, according to our reckoning, from about noon till half-past two o'clock, and a piece of Plautus, with music in the intervals between the acts, would probably occupy nearly that length of time (comp. Horat. *Ep.* ii. 1, 189). The passage in which Tacitus (*Ann.* xiv. 20) makes the spectators spend "whole days" in the theatre refers to the state of matters at a later period.

tragedy: the spectators knit their brows, when instead of
the expected comedy a tragedy began. Thus it happened
that, while this period exhibits poets who devoted themselves specially to comedy, such as Plautus and Caecilius, it
presents none who cultivated tragedy alone; and among
the dramas of this epoch known to us by name there occur
three comedies for one tragedy. Of course the Roman comic
poets, or rather translators, laid hands in the first instance
on the pieces which had possession of the Hellenic stage
at the time; and thus they found themselves exclusively*
confined to the range of the newer Attic comedy, and
chiefly to its best-known poets, Philemon of Soli in Cilicia
(394?–492) and Menander of Athens (412–462). This
comedy came to be of so great importance as regards the
development not only of Roman literature, but even of the
nation at large, that history has reason to pause and consider it.

{360–262.
{342–292.

The pieces are of tiresome monotony. Almost without
exception the plot turns on helping a young man, at the
expense either of his father or of some *leno*, to obtain possession of a sweetheart of undoubted charms and of very
doubtful morals. The path to success in love regularly lies
through some sort of pecuniary fraud; and the crafty servant,
who provides the needful sum and performs the requisite
swindling while the lover is mourning over his amatory and
pecuniary distresses, is the real mainspring of the piece.
There is no want of befitting reflections on the joys and .
sorrows of love, of tearful parting-scenes, of lovers who in
the anguish of their hearts threaten to do themselves a mischief; love or rather amorous intrigue was, as the old critics
of art say, the very life-breath of the Menandrian poetry.
Marriage forms, at least with Menander, the inevitable finale;
on which occasion, for the greater edification and satisfaction

Character
of the
newer
Attic
comedy.

---

* The scanty use made of what is
called the middle Attic comedy does not
require notice in a historical point of
view, since it was nothing but the Menandrian comedy in a less developed form.
There is no trace of any employment of
the older comedy. The Roman tragi-
comedy—after the type of the *Amphitruo*
of Plautus—was no doubt styled by the
Roman literary historians *fabula Rhin-
thonica*; but the newer Attic comedians
also composed such parodies, and it is
difficult to see why the Romans should
have resorted for their translations to
Rhinthon and the older writers rather
than to those who were nearer to their
own times.

of the spectators, the virtue of the heroine usually comes forth
almost if not wholly untarnished, and the heroine herself
proves to be the lost daughter of some rich man and so in
every respect an eligible match.   Along with these love-pieces
we find others of a pathetic kind.   Among the comedies of
Plautus, for instance, the *Rudens* turns on a shipwreck and the
right of asylum ; while the *Trinummus* and the *Captivi* contain
no amatory intrigue, but depict the generous devotedness of
the friend to his friend and of the slave to his master.
Persons and situations recur down to the very details like
patterns on a carpet ; we never get rid of the asides of unseen
listeners, of knocking at the house-doors, and of slaves scour-
ing the streets on some errand or other.   The standing masks,
of which there was a certain fixed number—*e. g.* eight masks
for old men, and seven for servants—from which alone in ordinary cases at least the poet had to make his choice, further
favoured a stock-model treatment.   Such a comedy almost of
necessity rejected the lyrical element in the older comedy—
the chorus—and confined itself from the first to conversation,
or at most recitation ; it was devoid not of the political
element only, but of all true passion and of all poetical
elevation.   The pieces judiciously made no pretension to any
grand or really poetical effect ; their charm resided primarily
in furnishing occupation for the intellect, not only through
their subject-matter—in which respect the newer comedy was
distinguished from the old as much by the greater intrinsic
emptiness as by the greater outward complication of the plot
—but more especially through their execution in detail, in
which the point and polish of the dialogue more particularly
formed the triumph of the poet and the delight of the audience.
Complications and confusions of one person with another,
which very readily allowed scope for extravagant, often licen-
tious, practical jokes—as in the *Casina*, which winds up with
the retiring of the two bridegrooms and of the soldier dressed
up as bride in genuine Falstaffian style—jests, drolleries, and
riddles, which in fact for want of real conversation furnished
the staple materials of entertainment at the Attic table of
the period, fill up a large portion of these comedies.   The
authors of them wrote not like Eupolis and Aristophanes
for a great nation, but rather for a cultivated society which,

like other circles whose ingenuity finds no more fitting field
for its exercise, spent its time in guessing riddles and playing
at charades. They give us, therefore, no picture of their
times; of the great historical and intellectual movements of
the age no trace appears in these comedies, and we need to
recall, in order to realize, the fact that Philemon and Menander
were really contemporaries of Alexander and Aristotle. But
they give us a picture, equally elegant and faithful, of that
refined Attic society beyond the circles of which comedy never
travels. Even in the dim Latin copy, through which we
chiefly know it, the grace of the original is not wholly
obliterated; and more especially in the pieces which are
imitated from Menander, the most talented of these poets,
the life which the poet beheld and shared is delicately
reflected not so much in its aberrations and distortions as
in its amiable every-day course. The friendly domestic
relations between father and daughter, husband and wife,
master and servant, with their love-affairs and other little in-
teresting incidents, are portrayed with so broad a truthful-
ness, that even now they do not miss their effect: the servants'
feast, for instance, with which the *Stichus* concludes is, in
the circumscribed character of its relations and the harmony
of the two lovers and the one sweetheart, of unsurpassed
gracefulness in its kind. The elegant grisettes, who make
their appearance perfumed and adorned, with their hair
fashionably dressed and in variegated, gold-embroidered,
sweeping robes, or even perform their toilette on the stage,
are very effective. In their train come the procuresses,
sometimes of the most vulgar sort, such as one who appears
in the *Curculio*, sometimes duennas like Goethe's old Barbara,
such as Scapha in the *Mostellaria*; and there is no lack of
brothers and comrades ready with their help. There is great
abundance and variety of parts representing the old: there
appear in turn the austere and avaricious, the fond and ten-
der-hearted, and the indulgent accommodating, papas, the
amorous old man, the easy old bachelor, the jealous aged
matron with her old maid-servant who takes part with her
mistress against her master; whereas the young men's parts
are less prominent, and neither the first lover, nor the vir-
tuous model son who here and there occurs, claim any great

452 LITERATURE AND ART. [Book III.

significance. The servant-world—the crafty valet, the stern
house-steward, the old vigilant tutor, the rural slave redolent
of garlic, the impertinent page—forms a transition to the
very numerous professional characters. A standing figure
among these is the jester (*parasitus*) who, in return for permission to feast at the table of the rich, has to entertain the
guests with drolleries and charades, or, according to circumstances, to submit to have the potsherds flung at his
head. This was at that time a formal trade in Athens; and
it is certainly no mere poetical fiction which represents
such a parasite as expressly preparing himself for his work
by means of his books of witticisms and anecdotes. Favourite
characters, moreover, are those of the cook, who understands
not only how to bully in an unrivalled style, but also how
to pilfer like a professional thief; the shameless *leno*, com-
placently confessing to the practice of every vice, of whom
Ballio in the *Pseudolus* is a model specimen; the military
braggadocio, in whom we trace a very distinct embodiment
of the free-lance habits that prevailed under Alexander's
successors; the professional sharper or sycophant, the
stingy money-changer, the solemnly silly physician, the
priest, mariner, fisherman, and the like. To these fall to be
added, lastly, the parts delineative of character in the strict
sense, such as the superstitious man of Menander and the
miser in the *Aulularia* of Plautus. The national-Hellenic
poetry has preserved, even in this its last creation, its
indestructible plastic vigour; but the delineation of character
is here copied from without rather than reproduced from inward experience, and the more so, the more the task
approaches to the really poetical. It is a significant circumstance that, in the parts illustrative of character to which we
have just referred, the psychological truth is for the most
part represented by its logical embodiment; the miser here
collects the parings of his nails and laments the tears which
he sheds as a waste of water. But the blame of this want of
depth in the portraying of character, and generally of the
whole poetical and moral hollowness of this newer comedy,
lay less with the comic writers than with the nation as a
whole. Everything distinctively Greek was expiring: fatherland, national faith, domestic life, all nobleness of action and

sentiment were gone ; poetry, history, and philosophy were inwardly exhausted ; and nothing remained to the Athenian save the school, the fish-market, and the brothel. It is no matter of wonder and hardly a matter of blame, that poetry, which is destined to shed a glory over human existence, could make nothing more out of such a life than the Menandrian comedy presents to us. It is at the same time very remarkable that the poetry of this period, wherever it was able to turn away in some degree from the corrupt Attic life without falling into schoolboy imitation, immediately gathers strength and freshness from the ideal. In the only remnant of the mock-heroic comedy of this period—the *Amphitruo* of Plautus —there breathes throughout a purer and more poetical air than in all the other remains of the contemporary stage. The good-natured gods treated with gentle irony, the noble forms from the heroic world, and the ludicrously cowardly slaves present the most wonderful mutual contrasts ; and, after the comical course of the plot, the birth of the son of the gods amidst thunder and lightning forms an almost grand concluding effect. But this task of turning the myths into irony was innocent and poetical, as compared with that of the ordinary comedy depicting the Attic life of the period. No special accusation may be brought from a historico-moral point of view against poets in general, nor ought it to be made matter of individual reproach to the particular poet that he occupies the level of his epoch : comedy was not the cause, but the effect of the corruption that prevailed in the national life. But it is necessary, more especially with a view to estimate correctly the influence of these comedies on the life of the Roman people, to point out the abyss which yawned beneath all that polish and elegance. The coarsenesses and obscenities, which Menander indeed in some measure avoided, but of which there is no lack in the other poets, are the least part of the evil. Features far worse are, the dreadful aspect of life as a desert in which the only oases are lovemaking and intoxication ; the fearfully prosaic monotony, in which anything resembling enthusiasm is to be found only among the sharpers whose heads have been turned by their own swindling, and who prosecute the trade of cheating with some sort of zeal ; and

above all that immoral morality, with which the pieces of
Menander in particular are garnished. Vice is chastised,
virtue is rewarded, and any peccadilloes are covered by conversion at or after marriage. There are pieces, such as the
Trinummus of Plautus and several of Terence, in which all
the characters down to the slaves possess some admixture
of virtue ; all swarm with honest men who allow deception on
their behalf, with maidenly virtue wherever possible, with
lovers equally favoured and making love in company ; moral
commonplaces and well-turned ethical maxims abound. A
finale of reconciliation such as that of the *Bacchides*, where
the swindling sons and the swindled fathers by way of a
good conclusion all go to carouse together in the brothel, presents a corruption of morals thoroughly worthy of Kotzebue.

Roman
comedy.

Such were the foundations, and such the elements which
shaped the growth, of Roman comedy. Originality was in
its case excluded not merely by want of aesthetic freedom,
but still more directly, it is probable, by virtue of its liability

Its Helle-
nism a ne-
cessary re-
sult of the
law.

to police control. Among the considerable number of Latin
comedies of this sort which are known to us, there is not one
that did not announce itself as an imitation of a definite
Greek model ; the title was only complete when the names
of the Greek piece and of its author were also given, and if,
as occasionally happened, the "novelty" of a piece was disputed, the point in dispute was merely whether it had been
previously translated. Comedy laid the scene of its plot
abroad not only frequently, but regularly and under the pressure of necessity ; and the special name of that form of art
(*fabula palliata*) was derived from the fact, that the scene
was laid out of Rome, usually in Athens, and that the *dramatis
personae* were Greeks or at any rate not Romans. The
foreign costume is strictly carried out even in detail, especially in those things in which the uncultivated Roman was
distinctly sensible of the contrast. Thus the names of Rome
and the Romans are avoided, and, where they are referred to,
they are called in good Greek "foreigners" (*barbari*) ; in
like manner among the appellations of moneys and coins
that so frequently occur there does not once appear a Roman
coin. We form a strange idea of men of so great and so ver-
satile talent as Naevius and Plautus, if we refer such caprices

to their free choice: this strange and clumsy outlandish aspect of the Roman comedy was undoubtedly occasioned by causes very different from aesthetic considerations. The transference of such a state of social matters as is uniformly delineated in the new Attic comedy to the Rome of the Hannibalic period would have been a direct outrage on its civil order and morality. But, as the dramatic spectacles at this period were regularly given by the aediles and praetors who were entirely dependent on the senate, and even extraordinary festivals, funeral games for instance, could not take place without permission of the government; and as the Roman police, moreover, was not in the habit of standing on ceremony in any case, and least of all in dealing with comedies; the reason is self-evident why this comedy, even after it was admitted as one of the Roman national amusements, still was not allowed to bring forward a Roman on the stage, and remained as it were relegated to foreign lands.

The compilers were still more decidedly prohibited from naming any living person in terms either of praise or censure, as well as from any captious allusion to the circumstances of the times. In the whole range of the Plautine and post-Plautine comedy, there is not, so far as we know, matter for a single action of damages. In like manner— if we leave out of view some wholly harmless jests—we meet hardly any trace of invectives levelled at communities (invectives which, owing to the lively municipal spirit of the Italians, would have been specially dangerous), except the significant scoff at the unfortunate Capuans and Atellans (p. 202) and, what is remarkable, various sarcasms on the arrogance and the bad Latin of the Praenestines.* In general no references to the events or circumstances of the present occur in the pieces of Plautus. The only exceptions are, good wishes for the progress of the war† or for peaceful

Political neutrality.

---

* *Bacch.* 24; *Trin.* 609; *Truc.* iii. 2, 23. Naevius also, who in fact was generally less scrupulous, ridicules the Praenestines and Lanuvini (*Com.* 21, *Ribb.*). There are indications more than once of a certain variance between the Praenestines and Romans (Liv. xxiii. 20, xlii. 1); and the executions in the time of Pyrrhus (i. 434) as well as the catastrophe in that of Sulla, were certainly connected with this variance.—Innocent jokes, such as *Capt.* 160, 881, of course passed uncensured. —The compliment paid to Massilia in *Cas.* v. 4, 1, deserves notice.

† Thus the prologue of the *Cistellaria* concludes with the following words,

times; general sallies directed against usurious dealings in grain or money, against extravagance, against bribery ⸗ candidates, against the frequency of triumphs, against thos who made a trade of collecting forfeited fines, against farmers of the revenue distraining for payment, against the dear prices of the oil-dealers; and once—in the *Curculio*—a more lengthened diatribe as to the doings in the Roman market, resembling the *parabases* of the older Attic comedy, and but little likely to cause offence (p. 434). But even in the midst of such patriotic endeavours, which from a police point of view were entirely in order, the poet interrupts himself;

> *Sed sumne ego stultus, qui rem curo publicam*
> *Ubi sunt magistratus, quos curare oporteat?*

and taken as a whole, we can hardly imagine a comedy politically tamer than the comedy of Rome in the sixth century.* The oldest Roman comic writer of note, Gnaeus Naevius, alone forms a remarkable exception. Although he did not write exactly original Roman comedies, the few fragments of his, which we possess, are full of references to circumstances and persons in Rome. Among other liberties he not only ridiculed one Theodotus a painter by name, but even directed against the victor of Zama the following verses, of which Aristophanes need not have been ashamed:

> *Etiam qui res magnas manu saepe gessit gloriose,*
> *Cujus facta viva nunc vigent, qui apud gentes solus praestat,*
> *Eum suus pater cum pallio uno ab amica abduxit.*

As he himself says,

> *Libera lingua loquemur ludis Liberalibus,*

---

which may have a place here as the only contemporary mention of the Hannibalic war in the literature that has come down to us:—

Haec res sic gesta est. Bene valete, et vincite
Virtute vera, quod fecistis antidhac;
Servate vostros socios, veteres et novos;
Augete auxilia vostris justis legibus;
Perdite perduelles: parite laudem et lauream
Ut vobis victi Poeni poenas sufferant.

* For this reason we can hardly be too cautious in assuming allusions on the part of Plautus to the events of the times.

Recent investigation has set aside many instances of mistaken acuteness of this sort; but might not the reference to the Bacchanalia, which is found in *Cas.* v. 4, 11 (Ritschl, *Parerg.* i. 192), have been expected to incur censure? We may perhaps reverse the case and infer from the notices of the festival of Bacchus in the *Casina* and some other pieces (*Amph.* 703; *Aul.* iii. 1, 3; *Bacch.* 53, 371; *Mil. Glor.* 1016; and especially *Men.* 836), that these were written at a time when it was not yet dangerous to speak of the Bacchanalia.

he probably often wrote offensively and put dangerous questions, such as:

Cedo qui vestram rem publicam tantam amisistis tam cito?

which he answered by an enumeration of political sins, such as:

Proveniebant oratores novi, stulti adulescentuli.

But the Roman police was not disposed like the Attic to hold stage-invectives and political diatribes as privileged, or even to tolerate them at all. Naevius was put in prison for these and similar sallies, and was obliged to remain there, till he had publicly made amends and recantation in other comedies. These quarrels, apparently, drove him from his native land; but his successors took warning from his example—one of them indicates very plainly, that he has no desire whatever to incur an involuntary gagging like his colleague Naevius. Thus the result was accomplished—not much less unique of its kind than the conquest of Hannibal —that, during an epoch of the most feverish national excitement, there arose a national stage utterly destitute of political tinge.

But the restrictions thus stringently and laboriously imposed by custom and police on Roman poetry stifled its very breath. Not without reason might Naevius declare the position of the poet under the sceptre of the Lagidae and Seleucidae enviable as compared with his position in free Rome.* The degree of success in individual instances was of course determined by the quality of the original which was followed, and by the talent of the individual editor; but amidst all their individual variety the whole range of translations must have agreed in certain leading features, inasmuch as all the comedies were adapted to similar conditions of exhibition and a similar audience. The treatment of the whole as well as of the details was uniformly in the highest degree free; and it was necessary that it should be so. While the original pieces were performed in presence of that society which they copied, and in this very fact lay their

Character of the editing of Roman comedy.

Persons and situations.

---

* The remarkable passage in the *Tarentilla* can have no other meaning:—
Quae ego in theatro hic meis probavi plausibus,
Ea non audere quemquam regem rumpere:
Quanto libertatem hanc hic superat servitus!

principal charm, the Roman audience of this period was so
different from the Attic, that it was not even able properly
to understand that foreign world. The Roman comprehended
neither the grace and courtesy, nor the sentimentalism and
the whitened emptiness of the domestic life of the Hellenes.
The slave-world was utterly different; the Roman slave was
a piece of household furniture, the Attic slave was a servant.
Where marriages of slaves occur or a master carries on a
kindly conversation with his slave, the Roman translators
ask their audience not to take offence at such things which
are usual in Athens;* and, when at a later period comedies
began to be written in Roman costume, the part of the crafty
servant had to be rejected, because the Roman public did not
tolerate slaves of this sort overlooking and controlling their
masters. The professional figures and those illustrative of
character, which were sketched more broadly and farcically,
bore the process of transference better than the polished
figures of every-day life; but even of those delineations the
Roman editor had to lay aside several—and these probably
the very finest and most original, such as the Thais, the
match-maker, the moon-conjuress, and the mendicant priest
of Menander—and to keep chiefly to those foreign trades,
with which the Greek luxury of the table, already very generally diffused in Rome, had made his audience familiar.
The delineation of the professional cook and the parasite in
the comedy of Plautus with so striking a vividness and relish
finds its explanation in the fact, that Greek cooks at that
time daily offered their services in the Roman market, and
that Cato found it necessary to give orders even to his steward
not to keep a parasite. In like manner the translator could
make no use of a very large portion of the elegant Attic conversation in his originals. The Roman citizen or farmer
stood in much the same relation to the refined revelry and
debauchery of Athens, as the German of a provincial town
to the mysteries of the Palais Royal. A science of cookery,

*Parts of comedy
attic which
had the
neglected.*

---

* The ideas of the modern Hellas on   ᾽Εν γάρ τι τοῖς δούλοισιν αἰσχύνην φέρει,
the point of slavery are illustrated by the   Τοὔνομα· τὰ δ' ἄλλα πάντα τῶν ἐλευθέρων.
passage in Euripides (*Ion*, 854; comp.   Οὐδεὶς κακίων δοῦλος, ὅστις ἐσθλὸς ᾗ.
Helena, 728):—

in the strict sense, never entered into his thoughts; the
dinner-parties no doubt continued to be very numerous in
the Roman imitation, but everywhere the plain Roman roast
pork predominated over the variety of baked meats and the
refined sauces and dishes of fish. Of the riddles and drinking
songs, of the Greek rhetoric and philosophy, which played so
great a part in the originals, we meet only a stray trace now
and then in the Roman adaptation.

The havoc, which the Roman editors were compelled in
deference to their audience to make in the originals, drove
them inevitably into methods of cancelling and amalgamating
incompatible with artistic construction. It was usual not
only to throw out whole parts occurring in the original, but
also to insert others taken from other comedies of the same
or of another poet; a treatment indeed which, owing to the
outwardly methodical construction of the originals and the
recurrence of standing figures and incidents, was not quite
so bad as it might seem. Moreover the poets, at least in
the earlier period, allowed themselves the most singular
liberties in the construction of the plot. The plot of the
Stichus (performed in 554) otherwise so excellent turns upon
the circumstance, that two sisters, whom their father urges
to abandon their absent husbands, play the part of Pene-
lopes, till the husbands return home with rich mercantile
gains and with a beautiful damsel as a present for their
father-in-law. In the *Casina*, which was received with altogether peculiar favour by the public, the bride, from whom
the piece is named and around whom the plot revolves, does
not make her appearance at all, and the *dénouement* is quite
naïvely described by the epilogue as " about to be enacted
within." Very often the plot as it thickens suddenly breaks
off, the connecting thread is allowed to drop, and other similar signs of an unfinished art appear. The reason of this lay
probably far less in the unskilfulness of the Roman editors,
than in the indifference of the Roman public to aesthetic
laws. Taste, however, gradually formed itself. In the later
pieces Plautus has evidently bestowed more care on their
construction, and the *Captivi* for instance, the *Pseudolus*, and
the *Bacchides* are executed in a masterly manner after their
kind. His successor Caecilius, none of whose pieces are ex-

Construc-
tion of the
plot.

200.

tant, is said to have especially distinguished himself by the
more artistic treatment of the subject.

Roman
barbarism.

In the treatment of details the endeavour of the poet to
bring matters as far as possible home to his Roman hearers,
and the rule of police which required that the pieces should
retain a foreign character, produced the most singular contrasts.   The Roman gods, the ritual, military, and legal terms
of the Romans, present a strange appearance amid the
Greek world; Roman *aediles* and *tresviri* are grotesquely
mingled with *agoranomi* and *demarchi*; pieces whose scene is
laid in Aetolia or Epidamnus send the spectator without
scruple to the Velabrum and the Capitol.   Such a patchwork of Roman local tints distributed over the Greek ground
is barbarous enough; but interpolations of this nature, which
are often in their naïve way very ludicrous, are far more
tolerable than that thorough alteration of the pieces into a
ruder shape, which the editors deemed necessary to suit the
far from Attic culture of their audience.   It is true that
several even of the new Attic poets probably needed no
accession to their coarseness; pieces like the *Asinaria* of
Plautus cannot owe their unsurpassed dullness and vulgarity
solely to the translator.   Nevertheless coarse incidents so
prevail in the Roman comedy, that the translators must
either have interpolated them or at least have made a very
one-sided selection.   In the endless abundance of cudgelling
and in the lash ever suspended over the back of the slaves
we recognize very clearly the household-government inculcated by Cato, just as we recognize the Catonian opposition
to women in the never-ending disparagement of wives.
Among the jokes of their own invention, with which the
Roman editors deemed it proper to season the elegant Attic
dialogue, several are almost incredibly unmeaning and barbarous.*

---

* For instance, in the otherwise very
graceful examination which in the *Stichus*
of Plautus the father and his daughters
institute into the qualities of a good wife,
the irrelevant question—whether it is
better to marry a virgin or a widow—is
inserted, merely in order that it may be
answered by a no less irrelevant and, in
the mouth of the interlocutrix, altogether

absurd commonplace against women.
But that is a trifle compared with the
following specimen. In Menander's *Plo-
cium* a husband bewails his troubles to
his friend:—

Ἔχω δ' ἐπίκληρον Λάμιαν· οὐκ εἴρηκά σοι
Τοῦτ'; εἶτ' ἄρ' οὐχί; κυρίαν τῆς οἰκίας
Καὶ τῶν ἀγρῶν καὶ πάντων ἀντ' ἐκείνης

So far as concerns metrical treatment on the other hand, Metrical treatment.
the flexible and sounding verse on the whole does all honour
to the composers. The fact that the iambic trimeters, which
predominated in the originals and were alone suitable to
their moderate conversational tone, were very frequently
replaced in the Latin edition by iambic or trochaic tetrame-
ters, is to be attributed not so much to any want of skill on
the part of the editors who knew well how to handle the
trimeter, as to the uncultivated taste of the Roman public
which was pleased with the sonorous magnificence of the
long verse even where it was not appropriate.

Lastly, the arrangements for the exhibition of the pieces Scenic arrange-
bore the like stamp of indifference to aesthetic requirements ments.
on the part of the managers and the public. The stage of
the ancients—which on account of the extent of the theatre
and from the performances taking place by day made no pretension to acting properly so called, employed men to represent female characters, and absolutely required an artificial
strengthening of the voice of the actor—was entirely dependent, in a scenic as well as acoustic point of view, on the use
of facial and resonant masks. These were well known in
Rome; in amateur performances the players appeared without exception masked. But the actors who were to perform
the Greek comedies were not supplied with the masks—beyond doubt much more artificial—that were necessary for
them; a circumstance which, in connection with the defective acoustic arrangements of the stage,* not only compelled
the actor to exert his voice unduly, but drove Livius to the
highly inartistic but inevitable expedient of having the portions which were to be sung performed by a singer not belonging to the staff of actors, and accompanied by the mere

---

Ἔχομεν, Ἄπολλον, ὡς χαλεπῶν χαλεπώτα-
τον.
Ἅπασι δ' ἀργαλέα 'στίν, οὐκ ἐμοὶ μόνῳ,
Υἱῷ, πολὺ μᾶλλον θυγατρί.—πραγμ' ἄμαχον
λέγεις·
Εὖ οἶδα.

In the Latin edition of Caecilius, this
conversation, so elegant in its simplicity,
is converted into the following uncouth
dialogue:—

Sed tua morosane uxor quaeso est?—
 Quam rogas?—

Qui tandem?—Taedet mentionis, quae
 mihi
Ubi domum adveni adsedi, extemplo
 savium
Dat jejuna anima.—Nil peccat de savio:
Ut devomas volt, quod foris potaveris.

* Even when the Romans built stone
theatres, these had not the sounding-
apparatus by which the Greek architects
supported the efforts of the actors (Vitruv.
v. 5, 8).

dumb show of the actor within whose part they fell. As
little were the givers of the Roman festivals disposed to put
themselves to any material expense for decorations and machinery. The Attic stage regularly presented a street with
houses in the background, and had no shifting decorations;
but, besides various other apparatus, it possessed more especially a contrivance for pushing forward on the chief stage a
smaller one representing the interior of a house. The Roman theatre, however, was not provided with this; and we
can hardly therefore throw the blame on the poet, if everything, even childbirth, was represented on the street.

Aesthetic
result.
Such was the nature of the Roman comedy of the sixth
century. The process by which the Greek dramas were
transferred to Rome furnishes us with a picture, historically
invaluable, of the diversity in the culture of the two nations;
but in an aesthetic and a moral point of view the original did
not stand high, and the imitation stood still lower. The world
of beggarly rabble, to whatever extent the Roman editors
might take possession of it under the benefit of the inven-
tory, presented in Rome a forlorn and strange aspect, shorn
as it were of its delicate characteristics: comedy no longer
rested on the basis of reality, but persons and incidents
seemed capriciously or carelessly mingled as in a game of
cards; in the original a picture from life, it became in the
reproduction a caricature. Under a management which
could announce a Greek *agon* with flute-playing, choirs of
dancers, tragedians, and athletes, and eventually convert it
into a boxing-match (p. 437); and in presence of a public
which, as later poets complain, ran away *en masse* from the
play, if there were pugilists, or rope-dancers, or even gladiators to be seen; poets such as the Roman composers were
—workers for hire and of inferior social position—were
obliged even perhaps against their own better judgment
and their own better taste to accommodate themselves more
or less to the prevailing frivolity and rudeness. It was quite
possible, nevertheless, that there might arise among them
individuals of lively and vigorous talents, who were able at
least to repress the foreign and factitious element in poetry,
and, when they had found their fitting sphere, to produce
pleasing and even important creations.

At the head of these stood Gnaeus Naevius, the first
Roman who deserves to be called a poet, and, so far as the
accounts preserved regarding him and the few fragments of
his works allow us to form an opinion, to all appearance one
of the most remarkable and most important names in the
whole range of Roman literature.　He was a younger contemporary of Andronicus—his poetical activity began considerably before, and probably did not end till after, the
Hannibalic war—and felt in a general sense his influence;
he was, as is usually the case in artificial literatures, a
worker in all the forms of art produced by his predecessor,
in epos, tragedy, and comedy, and closely adhered to him in
the matter of metres.　Nevertheless, an immense chasm
separates the poets and their poems.　Naevius was neither
freedman, schoolmaster, nor actor, but a citizen of unstained
character although not of noble descent, belonging probably
to one of the Latin communities of Campania, and a soldier
in the first Punic war.*　In thorough contrast to the language
of Livius, that of Naevius is easy and clear, free from stiffness
and affectation, and seems even in tragedy to avoid pathos
as it were on purpose; his verses, in spite of the not un-
frequent *hiatus* and several other licences afterwards dis-
allowed, have a smooth and graceful flow.†　While the
quasi-poetry of Livius proceeded, somewhat like that of

---

* The personal notices of Naevius are
sadly confused.　Seeing that he fought
in the first Punic war, he cannot have
been born later than 495　Dramas, probably the first, were exhibited by him in
519 (Gell. xii. 21, 45).　That he died
in 550, as is usually stated, was doubted
by Varro (*ap.* Cic. *Brut.* 15, 60), and
certainly with reason; if it were so, he
must have made his escape during the
Hannibalic war to the soil of the enemy.
The sarcastic verses on Scipio (p. 456)
cannot have been written before the battle of Zama.　We may place his life
between 490 and 560, so that he was contemporary of the two Scipios who fell in
543 (Cic. *de Rep.* iv. 10), ten years
younger than Andronicus, and perhaps
ten years older than Plautus.　His Campanian origin is indicated by Gellius, and
his Latin nationality, if proof of it were
needed, by himself in his epitaph.　The
hypothesis that he was not a Roman

citizen, but possibly a burgess of Cales
or of some other Latin town in Campania,
renders the fact that the Roman police
treated him so unscrupulously the more
easy of explanation.　At any rate he was
not an actor, for he served in the army.

† Compare, *e. g.* with the verse of
Livius the fragment from Naevius' tragedy of *Lycurgus* :—

*Vos qui regalis corporis custodias
Agitatis, ite actutum in frundiferos locos,
Ingenio arbusta ubi nata sunt, non obsita ;*

or the famous words, which in the
Hector Profisciscens Hector addresses to
Priam : —

*Laetus sum, laudari me abs te, pater, a
　laudato viro ;*

and the charming verse from the *Tarentilla* :—

*Alii adnutat, alii adnictat ; alium amat,
　alium tenet.*

Gottsched in Germany, from purely external impulses and
moved wholly in the leading-strings of the Greeks, his
successor emancipated Roman poetry, and with the true
divining-rod of the poet struck those springs out of which
alone in Italy a native poetry could well up—national history
and comedy. Epic poetry no longer merely furnished the
schoolmaster with a lesson-book, but appealed on its own
merits to the hearing and reading public. Composing for
the stage had been hitherto, like the preparation of the
stage costume, a subsidiary employment of the actor or a
mechanical service performed for him; with Naevius the
relation was inverted, and the actor now became the servant
of the composer. His poetical activity is marked throughout by a national stamp. This stamp is most distinctly
impressed on his grave national drama and on his national
epos, of which we shall have to speak hereafter; but it
also appears in his comedies, which of all his poetic performances seem to have been the best adapted to his talents
and the most successful. It was probably, as we have
already said (p. 455), external considerations alone that
induced the poet to adhere in comedy so much as he did to
the Greek originals; and this did not prevent him from far
outstripping his successors and probably even the insipid
originals in the freshness of his mirth and in the fulness of
his living interest in the present; indeed in a certain sense
he reverted to the paths of the Aristophanic comedy. He
felt full well, and in his epitaph expressed, what he had been
to his nation:

> Mortales immortales flere si foret fas,
> Flerent Divae Camenae Naevium poetam;
> Itaque, postquam est Orcino traditus thesauro,
> Obliti sunt Romae loquier Latina lingua.

Such proud language on the part of the man and the poet
well befitted one who had witnessed and had personally taken
part in the struggles with Hamilcar and with Hannibal, and
who had discovered for the thoughts and feelings of that age
—so full of deep excitement and so elevated by mighty joy—
a poetical expression which, if not exactly the highest, was
sound, adroit, and national. We have already mentioned
(457) the troubles into which his licence brought him with
the authorities, and how, driven in all probability by these

troubles from Rome, he ended his life at Utica. In his instance likewise the individual life was sacrificed for the common weal, and the beautiful for the useful.

His younger contemporary, Titus Maccius Plautus (500 ?– 570), appears to have been far inferior to him both in outward position and in the conception of his poetical calling. A native of the little town of Sassina, which was originally Umbrian but was perhaps by this time Latinized, he earned his livelihood in Rome at first as an actor, and then —after he had lost in mercantile speculations what he had gained by his acting—as a theatrical composer reproducing Greek comedies, without occupying himself with any other department of literature and probably without making any pretension to authorship properly so called. There seems to have been at that time a considerable number of persons who made a trade of thus editing comedies in Rome; but their names, especially as they did not perhaps in general publish their works,* were virtually forgotten, and the pieces belonging to this stock of plays, which were preserved, passed in after times under the name of the most popular of them, Plautus. The *litteratores* of the following century reckoned up as many as 130 such "Plautine pieces;" but of these a large portion at any rate were merely revised by Plautus or had no connection with him at all; the best of them are still extant. To form a proper judgment, however, regarding the poetical character of the editor is very difficult, if not impossible, where the originals have not been preserved. That the editors reproduced good and bad pieces without selection; that they were subject and subordinate both to the police and to the public; that they were as indifferent to aesthetical requirements as their audience, and to please the latter, lowered the originals to a farcical and vulgar tone—are objections which apply rather to the whole manufacture of translations than to the individual remodeller. On the other hand we may regard as characteristic of

Plautus.
254-184.

---

* This hypothesis appears necessary, because otherwise the ancients could not have hesitated in the way they did as to the genuineness or spuriousness of the pieces of Plautus: in the case of no author, properly so-called, of Roman antiquity, do we find anything like a similar uncertainty as to his literary property. In this respect, as in so many other external points, there exists a most remarkable analogy between Plautus and Shakespeare.

Plautus, the masterly handling of the language and of the varied rhythms, a rare skill in adjusting and working the situation for dramatic effect, the almost always clever and often excellent dialogue, and, above all, a broad and fresh humour, which produces an irresistible comic effect with its happy jokes, its rich vocabulary of nicknames, its whimsical coinage of words, its pungent, often mimic, descriptions and situations—excellences, in which we seem to recognize the former actor. Undoubtedly the editor even in these respects retained what was successful in the originals rather than furnished contributions of his own. Those portions of the pieces which can with certainty be traced to the translator are, to say the least, mediocre ; but they enable us to understand why Plautus came to be and continued the true popular poet of Rome and the true mainstay of the Roman stage, and why even after the passing away of the Roman world the theatre has repeatedly reverted to his plays.

Caecilius.

Still less are we able to form a special opinion as to the third and last—for though Ennius wrote comedies, he did so altogether unsuccessfully—comedian of note in this epoch, Statius Caecilius. He resembled Plautus in his position in life and his profession. Born in Cisalpine Gaul in the district of Mediolanum, he was brought among the Insubrian prisoners of war (pp. 86, 206) to Rome, and earned a livelihood, first as a slave, afterwards as a freedman, by remodelling Greek comedies for the theatre down to his probably early death (586). His language was not pure, as was to be expected from his origin ; on the other hand, he directed his efforts, as we have already said (p. 459), to a more artistic construction of the plot. His pieces experienced but a dull reception from his contemporaries, and the public of later times laid aside Caecilius for Plautus and Terence. The critics of the true literary age of Rome—the Varronian and Augustan epoch—assigned to Caecilius the first place among the Roman editors of Greek comedies ; but this verdict appears due to the fact, that the mediocrity of the connoisseur gladly prefers a kindred spirit of mediocrity to any special features of excellence in the poet. These art-critics probably took Caecilius under their wing, simply because he was more

168.

regular than Plautus and more vigorous than Terence; not-withstanding which he may very well have been far inferior to both.

If therefore the literary historian, while fully acknow-ledging the very respectable talents of the Roman comedians, cannot recognize in their mere stock of translations a pro-duct either artistically important or artistically pure, the judgment of history respecting its moral aspects must necessarily be far more severe. The Greek comedy which formed its basis was morally of little consequence, inasmuch as it was simply on the same level of corruption with its audience; but the Roman drama was, at this epoch when men were wavering between the old austerity and the new corruption, the great school at once of Hellenism and of vice. This Attico-Roman comedy, with its prostitution of body and soul usurping the name of love—equally immoral in shamelessness and in sentimentality—with its offensive and unnatural magnanimity, with its uniform glorification of a life of debauchery, with its mixture of rustic coarseness and foreign refinement, was one continuous lesson of Romano-Hellenic demoralization, and was felt as such. A proof of this is preserved in the epilogue of the *Captivi* of Plautus:—

Moral result.

> Spectatores, ad pudicos mores facta haec fabula est:
> Neque in hac subagitationes sunt neque ulla amatio,
> Nec pueri suppositio neque argenti circumductio;
> Neque ubi amans adulescens scortum liberet clam suom patrem.
> Hujusmodi paucas poetae reperiunt comoedias,
> Ubi boni meliores fiant.   Nunc vos, si vobis placet,
> Et si placuimus neque odio fuimus, signum hoc mittite.
> Qui pudicitiae esse voltis praemium, plausum date!

We see here the opinion entertained regarding the Greek comedy by the party of moral reform; and it may be added, that even in the rare instances of moral comedies the mo-rality was of a character only adapted to ridicule innocence more surely. Who can doubt that these dramas gave a practical impulse to corruption? When Alexander the Great derived no pleasure from a comedy of this sort which its author read before him, the poet excused himself by say-ing that the fault lay not with him, but with the king; that, in order to relish such a piece, a man must be in the habit of holding revels and of giving and receiving blows in an intrigue. The man knew his trade: if, therefore, the Roman burgesses gradually acquired a taste for these Greek comedies, we see at what a price it was bought. The Roman government was to blame not for doing so little in behalf of this poetry, but even for tolerating it at all. Vice no doubt is powerful without a pulpit; but that is no excuse for the erection of a pulpit to proclaim it. To debar the Hellenic comedy from immediate contact with the persons and institutions of Rome, was a subterfuge rather than a serious means of defence. In fact, comedy would probably have been much less injurious morally, had they allowed it to have free course, so that the calling of the poet might have been ennobled and a Roman poetry in some measure independent might have been developed; for poetry is a moral power, and, if it inflicts deep wounds, it is largely able also to heal them. As it was, in this field also the government erred both in omission and commission; the political neutrality and moral hypocrisy of its stage-police contributed their part to the fearfully rapid breaking up of the Roman nation.

National comedy.

But, while the government did not allow the Roman comedian to depict the state of things in his native city or to bring his fellow-citizens on the stage, a national Latin comedy was not absolutely precluded from springing up; for the Roman burgesses at this period were not yet identified with the Latin nation, and the poet was at liberty to lay the plot of his pieces in the Italian towns of Latin rights just as in Athens or Massilia. In this way, in fact, the original Latin comedy arose (*fabula togata*)*: the earliest

---

* *Togatus* denotes, in juristic and generally in technical language, the Italian in contradistinction not merely to the foreigner, but also to the Roman burgess. Thus especially *formula togatorum* (*Corp. Inscr. Lat.*, I. n. 200, v. 21, 50) is the list of those Italians bound to render military service, who do not serve in the legions. The designation also of Cisalpine Gaul as *Gallia togata*, which first occurs in Hirtius and not long after disappears again from the ordinary *usus loquendi*, describes this region in all probability according to its legal position, in so far as in the epoch from 665 to 705 the great majority of its communities possessed Latin rights. Virgil appears likewise in the *gens togata*, which he mentions along with the Romans (*Aen.* i. 282), to have thought of the Latin nation.

According to this view we shall have to recognize in the *fabula togata* the comedy which laid its plot in Latium, as the *fabula palliata* had its plot in Greece; the transference of the scene of action to a foreign land is common to both, and the comic writer is wholly forbidden to bring on the stage the city or the burgesses of Rome. That in

known composer of such pieces, Titinius, flourished probably Titinius. about the close of this period.*

This comedy was also based on the new Attic intrigue-piece; it was not translation, however, but imitation; the scene of the piece lay in Italy, and the actors appeared in the national dress (i. 469), the *toga*. Here the Latin life and habits were brought out with peculiar freshness. The pieces delineate the civil life of the middling towns of Latium; the very titles, such as *Psaltria* or *Ferentinatis, Tibicina, Iurisperita, Fullones*, indicate this; and many particular incidents, such as that of the townsman who has his shoes made after the model of the sandals of the Alban kings, tend to confirm it. The female characters preponderate in a remarkable manner over the male.† With genuine national pride the poet recalls the great times of the Pyrrhic war, and looks down on his new Latin neighbours,—

Qui Obsce et Volsce fabulantur ; nam Latine nesciunt.

This comedy belongs to the stage of the capital quite as much as did the Greek; but it was probably pervaded by something of that rustic antagonism to the ways and the evils of a great town, which appeared contemporaneously in Cato and afterwards in Varro. As in the German comedy,

---

reality the *togata* could only have its plot laid in the towns of Latin rights, is shown by the fact that all the towns in which, to our knowledge, pieces of Titinius and Afranius had their scene— Setia, Ferentinum, Velitrae, Brundisium—demonstrably had Latin rights down to the Social war. By the extension of the franchise to all Italy the writers of comedy lost this Latin localisation for their pieces, for Cisalpine Gaul, which *de jure* took the place of the Latin communities, lay too far off for the dramatists of the capital, and so the *fabula togata* also seems in fact to have disappeared. But the *de jure* suppressed communities of Italy, such as Capua and Atella, stepped into the gap (pp. 202, 455), and thus the *fabula Atellana* was in some measure the continuation of the *togata*.

　* Respecting Titinius there is an utter want of literary information ; except that, to judge from a fragment of

Varro, he seems to have been older than Terence (558–595, Ritschl, *Parerg.* i. 194), for in all probability no more can be inferred from that passage, and though, of the two groups there compared, the second (Trabea, Atilius, Caecilius) is on the whole older than the first (Titinius, Terentius, Atta), it does not exactly follow that the oldest of the junior group is to be deemed younger than the youngest of the elder. 196–519.

　† Of the fifteen comedies of Titinius, with which we are acquainted, six are named after male characters (*baratus*? *coccus, fullones, Hortensius, Quintus, varus*), and nine after female (*Gemina, iurisperita, prilia*? *privigna, psaltria* or *Ferentinatis, Setina, tibicina, Veliterna, Ulubrana*?), two of which, the *iurisperita* and the *tibicina*, are evidently parodies of men's occupations. The feminine world preponderates also in the fragments.

which proceeded from the French in much the same way as the Roman comedy from the Attic, the French Lisette was very soon superseded by the *Frauenzimmerchen* Franziska, so the Latin national comedy sprang up, if not with equal poetical power, at any rate with the same tendency and perhaps with similar success, by the side of the Hellenizing comedy of the capital.

Tragedies.

Greek tragedy as well as Greek comedy came in the course of this epoch to Rome. It was a more valuable, and in some respects also an easier, acquisition than comedy. The Greek and particularly the Homeric epos, which was the basis of tragedy, was not unfamiliar to the Romans, and was already interwoven with their own national legends; and the susceptible foreigner found himself far more at home in the ideal world of the heroic myths than in the fish-market of Athens. Nevertheless tragedy also promoted, only with less abruptness and less vulgarity, the anti-national and Hellenizing spirit; and in this point of view it was a circumstance of the most decisive importance, that the Greek tragic stage of this period was chiefly under the sway of Euripides (274–348). This is

Euripides.
480–406.

not the place for a thorough delineation of that remarkable man and of his still more remarkable influence on his contemporaries and posterity; but the intellectual movements of the later Greek and the Graeco-Roman epoch were to so great an extent affected by him, that it is indispensable to sketch at least the leading outlines of his character. Euripides was one of those poets who raise poetry to a higher level, but in doing so manifest far more the true sense of what ought to be than the power of poetically realizing it. The profound saying which morally as well as poetically sums up all tragic art—that action is passion—holds true no doubt as to ancient tragedy; it exhibits man in action, but it makes no real attempt to individualize him. The unsurpassed grandeur with which the struggle between man and destiny fulfils its course in Aeschylus depends substantially on the circumstance, that each of the contending powers is only conceived broadly and generally; the essential humanity in Prometheus and Agamemnon is but slightly tinged by poetical individualizing. Sophocles seizes human nature in its broader types, the king, the old man, the sister; but not one of his figures displays the microcosm of man in all his aspects—the features of individual character. A high stage was thereby reached, but not the highest; the delineation of man in his entireness and the entwining of the individual—in themselves finished—figures into a higher poetical whole form a greater achievement, and therefore, as compared with Shakespeare, Aeschylus and Sophocles represent imperfect stages of development. But, when Euripides undertook to present man as he is, the advance was logical and in a certain sense historical rather than poetical. He was able to destroy the ancient tragedy, but not to create the modern. Everywhere he halted half way. Masks, through which the expression of the life of the soul is, as it were, translated from the particular into the general, were as necessary for the typical tragedy of antiquity as they are incompatible with the tragedy of character; but Euripides retained them. With remarkably delicate tact the older tragedy never presented the dramatic element, to which it was unable to allow free scope, unmixed, but constantly fettered it in some measure by the epic subjects from the superhuman world of gods and heroes and by the lyrical choruses. One feels that Euripides was impatient under these fetters: in his subjects he descended at least to semi-historic times, and his choral chants were of so subordinate importance, that they were frequently omitted from the performance in after times and hardly perhaps to the injury of the pieces; but yet he has neither placed his figures wholly on the basis of reality, nor entirely thrown aside the chorus. Throughout and on all sides he is the full exponent of an age in which, on the one hand, the grandest historical and philosophical movement was going forward, but in which, on the other hand, the primitive fountain of all poetry—a pure and homely national life—had become turbid. While the reverential piety of the older tragedians sheds over their pieces as it were a reflected radiance of heaven; while the limitation of the narrow horizon of the older Hellenes exercises its satisfying power over the hearer; the world of Euripides appears in the pale glimmer of speculation as much denuded of the gods as it is pervaded by the element of reflection, and gloomy passions shoot like lightnings athwart the gray clouds. The old deeply-rooted faith in destiny has disappeared; fate governs as an outwardly despotic power, and the slaves gnashing their teeth wear its fetters. The unbelief, which is the despair of faith, speaks in this poet with superhuman power. Of necessity therefore the poet never attains a plastic conception overpowering himself, and never reaches a truly poetic effect on the whole ; for which reason he was in some measure careless as to the construction of his tragedies, and indeed not unfrequently altogether spoiled them in this respect by providing no central interest either of plot or person—the slovenly fashion of weaving the plot in the prologue, and of unravelling it by a *Deus ex machinâ* or some other platitude, was in reality brought into vogue by Euripides. All the effect in his case lies in the details ; and with great art certainly every effort has in this respect been made to conceal the irreparable want of poetic completeness. Euripides is a master in what are called effects ; these, as a rule, have a sensuous sentimental colouring, and often moreover stimulate the sensuous impression by a special high seasoning, such as the interweaving of murder or incest with subjects relating to love. The delineations of Polyxena willing to die and of Phaedra pining away under the grief of secret love, above all the splendid picture of the mystic ecstasies of the Bacchae, are of the greatest beauty in their kind; but they are neither artistically nor morally pure, and the reproach of Aristophanes, that the poet was unable to paint a Penelope, was thoroughly well founded. Of a kindred character is the introduction of common compassion into the tragedy of Euripides. While his stunted heroes or heroines, such as Menelaus in the *Helena*, Andromache, Electra as a poor peasant's wife, the sick and ruined merchant Telephus, are repulsive or ridiculous and ordinarily both, the pieces, on the other hand, which confine themselves more to the atmosphere of common reality and exchange the character of tragedy for that of the touching family picture or that almost of sentimental comedy, such as the *Iphigenia in Aulis*, the *Ion*, the *Alcestis*, produce perhaps the most pleasing effect of all his numerous works. With equal frequency, but with less success, the poet attempts to bring into play an intellectual interest. Hence springs the complicated plot, which is calculated not like the older tragedy to move the feelings, but rather to keep curiosity on the rack ; hence the dialectically pointed dialogue, to us non-Athenians often absolutely intolerable; hence the apophthegms, which are scattered throughout the pieces of Euripides like flowers in a pleasure-garden; hence above all the psychology of Euripides, which by no means rests on direct human experience, but on logical reflection. His Medea is certainly in so far painted from life, that she is before departure properly provided with money for her voyage; but of the struggle in the soul between maternal love and jealousy the unbiassed reader will not find much in Euripides. But, above all, poetic effect is replaced in the tragedies of Euripides by moral or political aim. Without strictly or directly entering on the questions of the day, and having in view throughout social rather than political questions, Euripides in the legitimate issues of his principles coincided with the contemporary political and philosophical radicalism, and was the first and chief apostle of that new cosmopolitan humanity which broke up the old Attic national life. This was the ground at once of that opposition which the ungodly and un-Attic poet encountered among his contemporaries, and of that marvellous enthusiasm, with which the younger generation and foreigners devoted themselves to the poet of emotion and of love, of apophthegm and of tendency, of philosophy and of humanity. Greek tragedy in the hands of Euripides stepped beyond its proper sphere and consequently broke down; but the success of the cosmopolitan poet was only promoted by this, since at the same time the nation also stepped beyond its sphere and broke down likewise. The criticism of Aristophanes probably hit the truth exactly both in a moral and in a poetical point of view; but poetry influences the course of history not in proportion to its absolute value, but in proportion as it is able to anticipate the spirit of the age, and in this respect Euripides was unsurpassed. And thus it happened, that Alexander read him diligently; that Aristotle developed the idea of the tragic poet with special reference to him; that the latest poetic and plastic art in Attica as it were originated from him (for the new Attic comedy did nothing but transfer Euripides into a comic form, and the school of painters which we meet with in the designs of the later vases derived their subjects no longer from the old epics, but from the

Euripidean tragedy) ; and lastly that, the more the old
Hellas gave place to the new Hellenism, the more the fame and
influence of the poet increased, and Greek life abroad, in Egypt
as well as in Rome, was directly or indirectly moulded in the
main by Euripides.

Roman
tragedy.
The Hellenism of Euripides flowed to Rome through very
various channels, and probably produced a speedier and deeper
effect there by indirect means than in the form of direct
translation.   The tragic drama in Rome was not exactly later
in its rise than comedy (p. 445) ; but the far greater expense of
bringing a tragedy on the stage—which was undoubtedly felt
as a consideration of moment, at least during the Hannibalic
war—as well as the nature of the audience (p. 447) retarded
the development of tragedy.   In the comedies of Plautus the
allusions to tragedies are not very frequent, and most references of this kind may have been taken from the originals.
The first and only influential tragedian of this epoch was the
younger contemporary of Naevius and Plautus, Quintus
239-169.
Ennius (515-585), whose pieces were already travestied
by contemporary comic writers, and were exhibited and de-
claimed by posterity down to the days of the empire.

The tragic drama of the Romans is far less known to us
than the comic : on the whole the same features, which have
been noticed in the case of comedy, are presented by tragedy
also.   The dramatic stock, in like manner, was mainly formed
by translations of Greek pieces.   The preference was given
to subjects derived from the siege of Troy and the legends
immediately connected with it, evidently because this cycle
of myths alone was rendered familiar to the Roman public by
their instruction at school.   Incidents of striking horror pre-
dominate, such as matricide or infanticide in the *Eumenides*,
the *Alcmaeon*, the *Cresphontes*, the *Melanippe*, the *Medea*, and
the immolation of virgins in the *Polyxena*, the *Erechthides*,
the *Andromeda*, the *Iphigenia*—we cannot avoid recalling
the fact, that the public for which these tragedies were prepared was in the habit of witnessing gladiatorial games.   The
female characters and ghosts appear to have made the deepest
impression.   In addition to the rejection of masks, the most
remarkable deviation of the Roman edition from the original
related to the chorus.   The Roman theatre, fitted up doubt-

less in the first instance for comic plays without chorus, had
not the special dancing-stage (*orchestra*) with the altar in the
middle, on which the Greek chorus performed its part, or, to
speak more correctly, the space thus appropriated among the
Greeks served with the Romans as a sort of pit; accordingly
the choral dance at least, with its artistic alternations and
intermixture of music and declamation, must have been
omitted in Rome, and, even if the chorus was retained, it had
but little importance. Of course there were various alterations of detail, changes in the metres, curtailments, and
mutilations; in the Latin edition of the *Iphigenia* of Euripides,
for instance, the chorus of women was—either after the
model of another tragedy, or by the editor's own device—
converted into a chorus of soldiers. The Latin tragedies of
the sixth century cannot be pronounced good translations
in our sense of the word;* yet it is probable that a tragedy
of Ennius gave a far less imperfect image of the original of
Euripides than a comedy of Plautus gave of the original of
Menander.

The historical position and influence of Greek tragedy in
Rome were entirely analogous to those of Greek comedy;
and while, as the difference in the two kinds of composition
necessarily implied, the Hellenistic tendency appeared in
tragedy under a purer and more spiritual form, the tragic
drama of this period and its principal representative Ennius

Marginal note: Moral effect of tragedy.

---

* We subjoin, for comparison, the
opening lines of the *Medea* in the origi-

Εἴθ' ὤφελ' Ἀργοῦς μὴ διαπτάσθαι σκάφος
Κόλχων ἐς αἶαν κυανέας Συμπληγάδας,
Μηδ' ἐν νάπαισι Πηλίου πεσεῖν ποτε
Τμηθεῖσα πεύκη, μηδ' ἐρετμῶσαι χέρας

Ἀνδρῶν ἀρίστων, οἳ τὸ πάγχρυσον δέρος

Πελίᾳ μετῆλθον· οὐ γὰρ ἂν δέσποιν' ἐμὴ
Μήδεια πύργους γῆς ἔπλευσ' Ἰωλκίας
Ἐρωτι θυμὸν ἐκπλαγεῖσ' Ἰάσονος.

The variations of the translation from
the original are instructive—not only its
tautologies and periphrases, but also the
omission or explanation of the less familiar mythological names, *e.g.* the Sym-

nal of Euripides and in the version of
Ennius:—

Utinam ne in nemore Pelio securibus
Caesa accidisset abiegna ad terram
  trabes,
Neve inde navis inchoandae exordium
Coepisset, quae nunc nominatur nomine
Argo, quia Argivi in ea dilecti viri
Vecti petebant pellem inauratam arietis

Colchis, imperio regis Peliae, per dolum.
Nam nunquam era errans mea domo effer-
  ret pedem
Medea, animo aegra, amore saevo saucia.

plegades, the Iolcian land, the Argo.
But the instances in which Ennius has
really misunderstood the original are
rare.

displayed far more decidedly an anti-national and consciously
propagandist aim. Ennius, hardly the most important but
certainly the most influential poet of the sixth century, was
not a Latin by birth, but on the contrary by virtue of his
origin half a Greek. Of Messapian descent and Hellenic
culture, he settled in his thirty-fifth year at Rome, and lived
there—at first as a resident alien, but after 570 as a burgess
(p. 354)—in straitened circumstances, supported partly by
giving instruction in Latin and Greek, partly by the proceeds of his pieces, partly by the donations of those Roman
grandees, who, like Publius Scipio, Titus Flamininus, and
Marcus Fulvius Nobilior, were inclined to promote the
modern Hellenism and to reward the poet who sang their
own and their ancestors' praises and even accompanied
some of them to the field in the character, as it were, of a
poet laureate nominated beforehand to celebrate the great
deeds which they were to perform. He has himself elegantly
described the client-like qualities requisite for such a calling.*
From the outset and by virtue of the whole tenor of his life a
cosmopolite, he had the skill to appropriate the distinctive
features of the nations among which he lived—Greek, Latin,
and even Oscan—without devoting himself absolutely to any
one of them ; and while the Hellenism of the earlier Roman
poets was the result rather than the conscious aim of their
poetic activity, and accordingly they at least attempted more
or less to take their stand on national ground, Ennius on the

---

* Beyond doubt the ancients were
right in recognizing a sketch of the
poet's own character in the passage in
the seventh book of the Annals, where
the consul calls to his side the confi-
dant,

    quocum bene saepe libenter
Mensam sermonesque suos rerumque
  suarum
Congeriem partit, magnam cum lassus
  diei
Partem fuisset de summis rebus regundis
Consilio indu foro lato sanctoque senatu:
Cui res audacter magnas parvasque jo-
  cumque
Eloqueretur, cuncta simul malaque et bona
  dictu
Evomeret, si qui vellet, tutoque locaret.
Quocum multa volup ac gaudia clamque
  palamque.

Ingenium cui nulla malum sententia
  suadet
Ut faceret facinus lenis aut malus, doctus
  fidelis
Suavis homo facundus suo contentus
  beatus
Scitus secunda loquens in tempore com-
  modus verbum
Paucum, multa tenens antiqua sepulta,
  vetustas
Quem fecit mores veteresque novosque te-
  nentem,
Multorum veterum leges divumque homi-
  numque,
Prudenter qui dicta loquive tacereve possit.

In the line before the last we should
probably read *multarum rerum leges
divumque hominumque.*

contrary is very distinctly conscious of his revolutionary tendency, and evidently labours with zeal to bring into vogue
neological Hellenic ideas among the Italians. His most serviceable instrument was tragedy. The remains of his tragedies show that he was well acquainted with the whole range
of the Greek tragic drama and with Aeschylus and Sophocles
in particular; it is the less therefore the result of accident,
that he has moulded the great majority of his pieces, and all
those that attained celebrity, after the model of Euripides.
In the selection and treatment he was doubtless influenced
partly by external considerations. But these alone cannot
account for his bringing forward so decidedly the Euripidean
element in Euripides; for his neglecting the choruses still
more than did his original; for his laying still stronger emphasis on sensuous effect than the Greek; nor for his taking
up pieces like the *Thyestes* and the *Telephus* so well known
from the immortal ridicule of Aristophanes, with their
princes' woes and woful princes, and even such a piece as
Menalippa the Female Philosopher, in which the whole plot
turns on the absurdity of the national religion, and the
tendency to make war on it from the physicist point of view
is at once apparent. The sharpest arrows are everywhere—
and that partly in passages which can be proved to have
been inserted *—directed against faith in the miraculous,
and we almost wonder that the censorship of the Roman
stage allowed such tirades to pass as the following :—

> *Ego deum genus esse semper dixi et dicam coelitum,*
> *Sed eos non curare opinor, quid agat humanum genus ;*
> *Nam si curent, bene bonis sit, male malis, quod nunc abest.*

We have already remarked (p. 426) that Ennius scientifically inculcated the same irreligion in a didactic poem; and
it is evident that he was in earnest with this freethinking.
With this trait other features are in harmony—his political
opposition tinged with radicalism, that here and there ap-

---

* Comp. p. 428. Euripides (*Iph. in
Aul.* 956) defines the soothsayer as a
man,

"Ὃς ὀλίγ' ἀληθῆ, πολλὰ δὲ ψευδῆ λέγει
Τυχὼν, ὅταν δὲ μὴ τύχῃ, διοίχεται.

This is turned by the Latin translator
into the following diatribe against the
casters of horoscopes :—

Astrologorum signa in coelo quaesit, ob-
  servat, Jovis
Cum capra aut nepa aut exoritur lumen
  aliquod beluae.
Quod est ante pedes, nemo spectat : coeli
  scrutantur plagas.

pears ; * his singing the praises of the Greek pleasures of the
table (p. 434) ; above all his setting aside the last national
element in Latin poetry, the Saturnian measure, and substi-
tuting for it the Greek hexameter.   That the "multiform"
poet executed all these tasks with equal neatness, that he
elaborated hexameters out of a language of by no means
dactylic structure, and that without checking the natural
flow of his style he moved with confidence and freedom
amidst unwonted measures and forms—are so many evi-
dences of his extraordinary plastic talent, which was in fact
more Greek than Roman ; † where he offends us, the offence
is owing much more frequently to Greek alliteration ‡ than
to Roman ruggedness.   He was not a great poet, but a man
of graceful and sprightly talent, throughout possessing the
vivid sensibilities of a poetic nature, but needing the tragic
buskin to feel himself a poet and wholly destitute of the
comic vein.   We can understand the pride with which the
Hellenizing poet looked down on those rude strains

———————*quos olim Faunei vatesque canebant,*

and the enthusiasm with which he celebrates his own artistic poetry :

---

* In the *Telephus* we find him saying—

Palam mutire plebeis piaculum est.

† The following verses, excellent in
matter and form, belong to the adaptation of the *Phoenix* of Euripides :—

*Sed virum virtute vera vivere animatum
  addecet,
Fortiterque innoxium (?) vocare adversum
  adversarios.
Ea libertas est, qui pectus purum et fir-
  mum gestitat :
Aliae res obnoxiosae nocte in obscura la-
  tent.*

In the *Scipio,* which was probably
incorporated in the collection of miscellaneous poems, the graphic lines occurred :—

*— — mundus coeli vastus constitit si-
  lentio,
Et Neptunus saevus undis asperis pausam
  dedit.
Sol equis iter repressit ungulis volanti-
  bus ;*

*Constitere amnes perennes, arbores vento
  vacant.*

This last passage affords us a glimpse
of the way in which the poet worked up
his original poems.   It is simply an expansion of the words which occur in
the tragedy *Hectoris Lustra* (the original
of which was probably by Sophocles) as
spoken by a spectator of the combat between Hephaestus and the Scamander:—

*Constitit credo Scamander, arbores vento
  vacant.*

and the incident is derived from the Iliad
(xxi. 381).

‡ Thus in the *Phoenix* we find the
line :—

*— — stultust, qui cupita cupiens cu-
  pienter cupit.*

and this is not the most absurd specimen
of such recurring assonances.   He also
indulged in acrostic verses (Cic. *de Div.*
ii. 54, 111).

Enni poeta salve, qui mortalibus
Versus propinas flammeos medullitus.

The genius of Ennius instinctively assured him that he had spread his sails to a prosperous breeze; Greek tragedy became, and thenceforth remained, a possession of the Latin nation.

Through less frequented paths, and with a less favourable wind, a bolder mariner pursued a higher aim. Naevius not only like Ennius—although with far less success—adapted Greek tragedies for the Roman stage, but also attempted to create, independently of the Greeks, a grave national drama (*fabula praetextata*). No outward obstacles here stood in the way; he brought forward subjects both from Roman legend and from the contemporary history of the country on the stage of his native land. Such were his *Nursing of Romulus and Remus* or the *Wolf*, in which Amulius king of Alba appeared, and his *Clastidium*, which celebrated the victory of Marcellus over the Celts in 532 (p. 86). After his example, Ennius in his *Ambracia* described from personal observation the siege of that city by his patron Nobilior in 565 (p. 294). But the number of these national dramas remained small, and that species of composition soon disappeared from the stage; the scanty legend and the colourless history of Rome were unable permanently to compete with the Hellenic mythology. Respecting the poetic value of the pieces we have no longer the means of judging; but, if we may take account of the general poetical intention, there were in Roman literature few such strokes of genius as the creation of a Roman national drama. Only the Greek tragedians of that earliest period which still felt its nearness to the gods—only poets like Phrynichus and Aeschylus—had the courage to bring the great deeds which they had witnessed, and in which they had borne a part, on the stage by the side of those of legendary times; and here, if anywhere, we are enabled vividly to realize what the Punic wars were and how powerful was their effect, when we find a poet, who like Aeschylus had himself fought in the battles which he sang, introducing the kings and consuls of Rome upon that stage on which men had hitherto been accustomed to see none but gods and heroes.

National dramas.

222.

189.

Recitative
poetry.

Recitative poetry also took its rise during this epoch at Rome. Livius naturalized the custom which among the ancients held the place of our modern publication—the public reading of new works by the author—in Rome, at least to the extent of reciting them in his school. As poetry was not in this instance practised with a view to a livelihood, or at any rate not directly so, this branch of it was not regarded by public opinion with such disfavour as writing for the stage: towards the end of this epoch one or two noble Romans had publicly come forward in this manner as poets.* Recitative poetry however was chiefly cultivated by those poets who occupied themselves with writing for the stage, and the former held a subordinate place as compared with the latter; in fact, a public to which read poetry might address itself can have existed only to a very limited extent at this period in Rome.

Satura.

Lyrical, didactic, and epigrammatic poetry in particular were feebly represented. The religious festival chants—of which the annals of this period certainly have already thought it worth while to mention the author—as well as the monumental inscriptions on temples and tombs, for which the Saturnian remained the regular measure, hardly belong to literature in its proper sense. So far as the minor poetry makes its appearance at all, it is classed ordinarily, and that as early as the time of Naevius, under the name of *satura*. This term was originally applied to the old stage-poem without action which from the time of Livius was driven off the stage by the Greek drama; but in its application to recitative poetry it corresponds in some measure to our " miscellaneous poems," and like the latter denotes not any positive species or style of art, but simply poems not of an epic or dramatic kind, treating of any matters (mostly subjective), and written in any form, at the pleasure of the author. In addition to Cato's " poem on Morals " to be noticed afterwards, which was probably written in Saturnian verses after the precedent of the earlier attempts at a na-

---

183.

* Besides Cato, we find the names of two " consulars and poets" belonging to this period (Sueton. *Vita Terent.* 4)— Quintus Labeo, consul in 571, and Marcus Popillius, consul in 581. But it remains uncertain whether they published their poems. Even in the case of Cato this may be doubted.

tional didactic poetry (i. 504), there came under this category the minor poems of Ennius, which that writer, who was
very fertile in this department, published partly in his collection of *saturae*, partly separately.   Among these were brief
narrative poems relating to the legendary or contemporary
history of his country ; editions of the religious romance of
Euhemerus (p. 426), of the physical poems circulated in the
name of Epicharmus (p. 426), and of the gastronomics of
Archestratus of Gela, a poet who treated of the higher
cookery ; as also a dialogue between Life and Death, fables
of Aesop, a collection of moral maxims, parodies and epigrammatic trifles—small matters, but indicative of the versa-
tile powers as well as the neological didactic tendencies of
the poet, who evidently allowed himself the freest range in
this field, which the censorship did not reach.

The attempts at a metrical treatment of the national   Metrical
annals lay claim to greater poetical and historical importance.   annals.
Here too it was Naevius who gave poetic form to so much   Naevius.
of the legendary as well as of the contemporary history as
admitted of connected narrative ; and who, more especially,
recorded in the half-prosaic Saturnian national metre the
story of the first Punic war simply and distinctly, with a
straightforward adherence to fact, without disdaining anything as unpoetical, and without at all, especially in the
description of historical times, going in pursuit of poetical
flights or embellishments—maintaining throughout his narrative the present tense.*   What we have already said of

---

* The following fragments will give
some idea of its tone. Of Dido he says :

*Blande et docte percontat—Aeneas quo
   pacto
Troiam urbem liquerit.*

Again of Amulius :

*Manusque susum ad coelum—sustulit
   suas rex
Amulius ; gratulatur—divis.*

Part of a speech where the indirect construction is remarkable :

*Sin illos deserant for—tissumos viro-
   rum*

*Magnum   stuprum   populo—fieri   per
   gentis.*

With reference to the landing at Malta   256.
in 498 :

*Transit Melitam Romanus—insulam in-
   tegram omnem
Urit populatur vastat—rem hostium con-
   cinnat.*

Lastly, as to the peace which terminated
the war concerning Sicily :

*Id quoque paciscunt moenia—sint Luta-
   tium quae
Reconcilient ; captivos—plurimos idem
Sicilienses paciscit—obsides ut reddant.*

the national drama of the same poet, applies substantially to the work of which we are now speaking. The epic poetry of the Greeks, like their tragedy, had wholly reference to the heroic period ; it was an altogether new and, at least in design, an enviably grand idea—to light up the present with the brilliance of poetry. Although in point of execution the chronicle of Naevius was probably not much better than the rhyming chronicles of the middle ages, which are in various respects of kindred character, yet the poet was certainly justified in regarding this work of his with an altogether peculiar complacency. It was no small achievement, in an age when there was absolutely no historical literature except official records, to have composed for his countrymen a connected account of the deeds of their own times and of earlier ages, and in addition to have placed before their eyes the noblest incidents of their history in a dramatic form.

Ennius.   Ennius proposed to himself the very same task as Naevius ; but the similarity of the subject only brings out into stronger relief the political and poetical contrast between the national and the anti-national poet. Naevius sought out for the new subject a new form ; Ennius fitted or forced it into the forms of the Hellenic epos. The hexameter replaced the Saturnian verse ; the ornate style of the Homeridae, striving after plastic vividness of delineation, replaced the homely historic narrative. Wherever the circumstances admit, Homer is directly translated ; e.g. the burial of those that fell at Heraclea is described after the model of the burial of Patroclus, and under the helmet of Marcus Livius Stolo, the military tribune who fights with the Istrians, lurks none other than the Homeric Ajax ; the reader is not even spared the Homeric invocation of the Muse. The epic machinery is fully set agoing ; after the battle of Cannae, for instance, Juno in a full council of the gods pardons the Romans, and Jupiter after obtaining the consent of his wife promises them a final victory over the Carthaginians. Nor do the "Annals" fail to betray the neological and Hellenistic tendencies of the author. The very employment of the gods for the mere purpose of decoration bears this stamp. The remarkable vision, with which the poem opens, tells in good Pythagorean style how the soul now inhabiting Quintus Ennius had previously been domiciled in Homer and still earlier in a peacock, and then in good physicist style explains the nature of things and the relation of the body to the mind. Even the choice of the subject serves the same purpose—at any rate the Hellenic literati of all ages have found an especially suitable handle for their Graeco-cosmopolite tendencies in this very rehabilitation of Roman history. Ennius lays stress on the circumstance that the Romans were reckoned Greeks:

Contendunt Graecos, Graios memorare solent sos.

The poetical value of the greatly celebrated Annals may easily be estimated after the remarks which we have already made regarding the excellences and defects of the poet in general. A poet of lively sympathies, he naturally felt himself elevated by the enthusiastic impulse which the great age of the Punic wars gave to the national sensibilities of Italy, and he not only often succeeds in imitating Homeric simplicity, but also and still more frequently makes his lines strikingly echo the solemnity and decorum of the Roman character. But the construction of his epic was defective; indeed it must have been very lax and indifferent, when it was possible for the poet to insert a special book by way of supplement to please an otherwise forgotten hero and patron. On the whole the Annals were beyond question the work in which Ennius fell farthest short of his aim. The plan of making an Iliad pronounces its own condemnation. It was Ennius, who in this poem for the first time introduced into literature that changeling compound of epos and of history, which from that time up to the present day has haunted it like a ghost, unable either to live or to die. But the poem certainly had its success. Ennius claimed to be the Roman Homer with still greater ingenuousness than Klopstock claimed to be the German, and was received as such by his contemporaries and still more so by posterity. The veneration for the father of Roman poetry was transmitted from generation to generation; even the polished Quintilian says, "Let us revere Ennius as we revere an ancient sacred grove, whose mighty oaks of a thousand years are more venerable than beautiful;" and, if any one is disposed to wonder at this, he may recall analogous phenomena in the successes of the Aeneid, the Henriad, and the Messiad. A mighty poetical development of the nation would indeed have set aside that almost comic official parallel between the Homeric Iliad and the Ennian Annals as easily as we have set aside the parallels of Sappho and Karschin and of Pindar and Willamov; but no such development took place in Rome. Owing to the interest of the subject especially for aristocratic circles, and the great plastic talent of the poet, the Annals remained the oldest Roman original poem which appeared to the culture of later generations readable or worth reading; and thus, singularly enough, posterity came to honour this thoroughly anti-national epos of a half-Greek *littérateur* as the true model poem of Rome.

Prose lite-
rature.

A prose literature arose in Rome not much later than Roman poetry, but in a very different way. It experienced neither the artificial stimulus, by which the school and the stage prematurely forced the growth of Roman poetry, nor the artificial restraint, to which Roman comedy in particular was subjected by the strict and narrow-minded censorship of the stage. Nor was this form of literary activity placed from the first under the ban of good society by the stigma which attached to the " ballad-singer." Accordingly the prose literature, while far less extensive and less active than the contemporary poetical authorship, had a far more natural growth. While poetry was almost wholly in the hands of men of humble rank and not a single Roman of quality appears among the celebrated poets of this age, there is, on the contrary, among the prose writers of this period hardly a name that is not senatorial; and it is from the circles of the highest aristocracy, from men who had been consuls and censors—the Fabii, the Gracchi, the Scipios—that this litera-ture throughout proceeds. The conservative and national tendency, in the nature of the case, accorded better with this prose authorship than with poetry; but here too—and par-ticularly in the most important branch of this literature, historical composition—the Hellenistic tendency had a powerful, in fact a preponderant, influence both on matter and form.

Down to the period of the Hannibalic war there was no

historical composition in Rome ; for the entries in the book Writing of of Annals were of the nature of records and not of literature, history. and never made any attempt to develop the connection of events. It is a significant illustration of the peculiarity of Roman character, that notwithstanding the extension of Roman power far beyond the bounds of Italy, and notwithstanding the constant contact of the noble society of Rome with the Greeks who were so full of literary activity, it was not till the middle of the sixth century that there sprang up any desire to impart a knowledge of the deeds and fortunes of the Roman people, by means of authorship, to the contemporary world and to posterity. When at length this desire was felt, there were neither literary forms ready at hand for the use of Roman history, nor was there a public prepared to read it, and great talent and considerable time were required to create both. In the first instance, accordingly, these difficulties were in some measure evaded by writing the national history either in the mother tongue and in that case in verse, or in prose and in that case in Greek. We have already spoken of the metrical Annals of Naevius (written about 550 ?) 204. and of Ennius (written about 581) ; both belong to the earliest 173. historical literature of the Romans, and those of Naevius may be regarded as the oldest of all Roman historical works. At nearly the same period were composed the Greek " Histories " of Quintus Fabius Pictor * (after 553), a man of noble family 201. who took an active part in state affairs during the Hannibalic war, and of Publius Scipio, the son of Scipio Africanus, (who died about 590). In the former case they availed them- 164.

---

* That this oldest prose work on the history of Rome was composed in Greek, is established beyond a doubt by Dionys. i. 6, and Cicero, *de Div.* i. 21, 43. The Latin Annals quoted under the same name by Quintilian and later grammarians remain involved in mystery, and the difficulty is increased by the circumstance, that there is also quoted under the same name a very complete exposition of the pontifical law in the Latin language. But the latter treatise will not be attributed by any one, who has traced the development of Roman literature in its connection, to an author of the age of the Hannibalic war; and Latin annals from that age appear problematical, although it must remain a moot question whether there has been a confusion of the earlier with a later annalist, Quintus Fabius Maximus Servilianus (consul in 612), or whether 142. there existed an old Latin edition of the Greek Annals of Fabius as well as of those of Acilius and Albinus, or whether there were two annalists of the name of Fabius Pictor.

The historical work likewise written in Greek, ascribed to Lucius Cincius Alimentus a contemporary of Fabius, seems spurious and a compilation of the Augustan age.

selves of the poetical art which was already to a certain
extent developed, and addressed themselves to a public with
a taste for poetry, which was not altogether wanting; in the
latter case they found the Greek forms ready to their hand,
and addressed themselves—as the interest of their subject
stretching far beyond the bounds of Latium naturally
suggested—primarily to the cultivated foreigner. The
former plan was adopted by the plebeian authors, the latter by
those of quality; just as in the time of Frederick the Great
an aristocratic literature in the French language subsisted
side by side with the native German authorship of pastors
and professors, and, while men like Gleim and Ramler wrote
war-songs in German, kings and generals wrote military
histories in French. Neither the metrical chronicles nor
the Greek annals by Roman authors constituted Latin
historical composition in the proper sense of the term;
this only began with Cato, whose "Origines," not published
before the close of this epoch, formed at once the oldest
historical work written in Latin and the first important
prose work in Roman literature.*

All these works, while not coming up to the Greek conception of history,† were, as contrasted with the mere
detached notices of the book of Annals, systematic histories
with a connected narrative and a more or less regular
structure. They all, so far as we can see, embraced the
national history from the building of Rome down to the
time of the writer, although in point of title the work of
Naevius related only to the first war with Carthage, and that
of Cato only to the early history. They were thus naturally
divided into the three sections of the legendary period, of
earlier, and of contemporary, history.

History of the origin of Rome. In the legendary period the history of the origin of the
city was set forth with great minuteness; and in its case
the peculiar difficulty had to be surmounted, that there were,

* Cato's whole literary activity belonged to the period of his old age
(Cicero, Cat. 11, 38; Nepos, Cato, 3);
the composition even of the earlier books
of the "Origines" falls not before, and
yet probably not long subsequent to, 586
(Plin. H. N., iii. 14, 114).

† It is evidently by way of contrast
with Fabius that Polybius (xl. 6, 4) calls
attention to the fact, that Albinus, the
passionate admirer of everything Greek,
endeavoured to write a systematic history [πραγματικὴν ἱστορίαν].

168,

as we have already shown (i. 508), two wholly irreconcileable versions of it in circulation: the national version, which, in its leading outlines at least, was probably already embodied in the book of Annals, and the Greek version of Timaeus, which cannot have remained unknown to these Roman chroniclers. The object of the former was to connect Rome with Alba, that of the latter to connect Rome with Troy; in the former accordingly the city was built by Romulus son of the Alban king, in the latter by the Trojan prince Aeneas. To the present epoch, probably either to Naevius or to Pictor, belongs the amalgamation of the two stories. The Alban prince Romulus remains the founder of Rome, but becomes at the same time the grandson of Aeneas; Aeneas does not found Rome, but is represented as bringing the Roman Penates to Italy and building Lavinium as their shrine, while his son Ascanius founds Alba Longa, the mother-city of Rome and the ancient metropolis of Latium. All this was a sorry and unskilful patchwork. The view that the original Penates of Rome were preserved not, as had hitherto been believed, in their temple in the Roman Forum, but in the shrine at Lavinium, could not but be offensive to the Romans; and the Greek fiction was a still worse expedient, inasmuch as under it the gods only bestowed on the grandson what they had adjudged to the grandsire. But the amalgamation served its object: without exactly denying the national origin of Rome, it yet deferred to the Hellenizing tendency, and legalized in some degree that desire to claim kindred with Aeneas which was already at this epoch greatly in vogue (p. 440); and thus it became the stereotyped, and was soon accepted as the official, account of the origin of the mighty community.

With the exception of the story of the origin of the city, the Greek historiographers had given themselves little or no concern as to the Roman commonwealth; so that the recital of the further course of the national history must have been chiefly derived from native sources. But the scanty information that has been transmitted to us does not enable us to discern distinctly what sort of traditions, in addition to the book of Annals, were at the command of the earliest chroniclers, and what they may possibly have added of their own. The tales inserted from Herodotus * were probably still foreign to these earliest annalists, and a direct borrowing of Greek materials for this section cannot be proved. The more remarkable, therefore, is the tendency, which is everywhere, even in the case of Cato the enemy of Hellenism, very distinctly apparent, not only to connect Rome with Hellas, but to represent the Italian and Greek nations as having been originally identical. To this tendency we owe the primitive Italians or aborigines who were immigrants from Greece, and the primitive Greeks or Pelasgians whose wanderings brought them to Italy.

The earlier history.

The current story presented some sort of connection, though the connecting thread was but weak and loose, throughout the regal period down to the institution of the republic; but at that point the stream of legend dried up, and it was not merely difficult but altogether impossible to form a narrative, in any degree connected and readable, out of the lists of magistrates and the scanty notices appended to them. The poets were the most sensible of the blank. Naevius appears for that reason to have passed at once from the regal period to the war regarding Sicily: Ennius, who in the third of his eighteen books was still occupied with the regal period and in the sixth had already reached the war with Pyrrhus, must have treated the first two centuries of the republic merely in the most general outline. How the annalists who wrote in Greek managed the matter, we do not know. Cato adopted a peculiar course. He felt no pleasure, as he himself says, " in relating what was set forth on the tablet in the house of the Pontifex Maximus, how often wheat had been dear, and when the sun or moon had been eclipsed;" and so he devoted the second and third books of his historical work to accounts of the origin of the other Italian communities and of their admission to the Roman confederacy. He thus got rid of the fetters of chronicle, which reports events year by year under the heading of the magistrates for the time being; the state-

---

* For instance the history of the siege of Gabii is compiled from the anecdotes as to Zopyrus and the tyrant Thrasybulus in Herodotus, and one version of the story of the exposure of Romulus is framed on the model of the history of the youth of Cyrus as Herodotus relates it.

ment, that Cato's historical work narrated events "sectionally," must refer to this feature of his method. This attention bestowed on the other Italian communities, which surprises us in a Roman work, had a bearing on the political position of the author, who leaned throughout on the support of the municipal Italy in his opposition to the proceedings of the capital; while it furnished a sort of substitute for the missing history of Rome from the expulsion of king Tarquinius down to the Pyrrhic war, by presenting in its own way the main result of that history—the union of Italy under the hegemony of Rome.

Contemporary history, again, was treated in a connected and detailed manner. Naevius described the first, and Fabius the second, war with Carthage from their own knowledge; Ennius devoted at least thirteen out of the eighteen books of his Annals to the epoch from Pyrrhus down to the Istrian war (p. 207); Cato narrated in the fourth and fifth books of his historical work the wars from the first Punic war down to that with Perseus, and in the two last books, which probably were on a different and more copious plan, he related the events of the last twenty years of his life. For the Pyrrhic war Ennius may have employed Timaeus or other Greek authorities; but on the whole the accounts given were based, partly on personal observation or communications of eye-witnesses, partly on each other. *Contemporary history.*

Contemporaneously with historical literature, and in some sense as an appendage to it, arose the literature of speeches and letters. This in like manner was commenced by Cato; for the Romans possessed nothing of an earlier age except some funeral orations, most of which probably were only brought to light at a later period from family archives, such as that which the veteran Quintus Fabius, the opponent of Hannibal, delivered when an old man over his son who had died in his prime. Cato on the other hand committed to writing in his old age such of the numerous orations which he had delivered during his long and active public career as were historically important, as a sort of political memoirs, and published them partly in his historical work, partly, it would seem, as independent supplements to it. There also existed a collection of his letters. *Speeches and letters.*

History of other nations. With non-Roman history the Romans concerned themselves so far, that a certain knowledge of it was deemed indispensable for the cultivated Roman; even old Fabius is said to have been familiar not merely with the Roman, but also with foreign, wars, and it is distinctly testified that Cato diligently read Thucydides and the Greek historians in general. But, if we leave out of view the collection of anecdotes and maxims which Cato compiled for himself as the fruits of this reading, no trace is discernible of any literary activity in this field.

Uncritical treatment of history These first essays in historical literature were all of them, as a matter of course, pervaded by an easy, uncritical spirit; neither authors nor readers readily took offence at inward or outward inconsistencies. King Tarquinius the Second, although he was already grown up at the time of his father's death and did not begin to reign till thirty-nine years afterwards, is nevertheless still a young man when he ascends the throne. Pythagoras, who came to Italy about a generation before the expulsion of the kings, is nevertheless set down by the Roman historians as a friend of the wise Numa. The state-envoys sent to Syracuse in the year 262 transact business with Dionysius the elder, who ascended the throne eighty-six years afterwards (348). This naïve uncritical spirit is especially apparent in the treatment of Roman chronology. Since according to the Roman reckoning—the outlines of which were probably fixed in the previous epoch—the foundation of Rome took place 240 years before the consecration of the Capitoline temple (i. 510) and 360 years before the burning of the city by the Gauls (i. 505), and the latter event, which is mentioned in Greek historical works, fell according to these in the year of the Athenian archon Pyrgion 388 B.C. Ol. 98, 1, the building of Rome accordingly fell on Ol. 8, 1. This was, according to the chronology of Eratosthenes which was already recognized as canonical, the year 436 after the fall of Troy; nevertheless the common story retained as the founder of Rome the grandson of the Trojan Aeneas. Cato, who like a good financier checked the calculation, no doubt drew attention in this instance to the incongruity; but he does not appear to have proposed any mode of getting over

492.

406.

the difficulty—the list of the Alban kings, which was afterwards inserted with this view, certainly did not proceed from
him.

The same uncritical spirit, which prevailed in the early
history, prevailed also to a certain extent in the representation of historical times.　The accounts certainly without
exception bore that strong party colouring, for which the
Fabian narrative of the origin of the second war with Carthage is censured by Polybius with the calm severity so
peculiar to him.　Mistrust, however, is more appropriate in
such circumstances than reproach.　It would be somewhat
ridiculous to expect from the Roman contemporaries of
Hannibal a just judgment of their antagonist; but no intentional misrepresentation of the facts, except such as a simple-
minded patriotism of itself involves, has been proved against
the fathers of Roman history.

The beginnings of scientific culture, and even of authorship relating to it, also fall within this epoch.　The instruction hitherto given had been substantially confined to reading and writing and a knowledge of the law of the land.*
But a closer contact with the Greeks gradually suggested to
the Romans the idea of a more general culture ; and stimulated the endeavour, if not directly to transplant this Greek
culture to Rome, at any rate to modify the Roman culture to
some extent after its model.

First of all, the knowledge of the mother-tongue began to
shape itself into Latin grammar ; Greek philology transferred its methods to the kindred idiom of Italy.　The active
study of grammar began nearly at the same time with
Roman authorship.　About 520 Spurius Carvilius, a teacher
of writing, appears to have regulated the Latin alphabet, and
to have given to the letter *g*, which was not previously included in it (i. 517), the place of the *z* which could be dis-
pensed with—the place which it still holds in the modern
alphabets of the West.　The Roman schoolmasters must have
been constantly working at the adjustment of orthography ;
the Latin Muses too never disowned their scholastic Hippo-
crene, and at all times applied themselves to orthography

Marginal notes: Partiality. Science. Grammar. 234.

---

* Plautus (*Mostell.* 126) says of *litteras, iura, leges*; and Plutarch (*Cato*
parents, that they teach their children　*Mai.* 20) testifies to the same effect.

side by side with poetry. Ennius especially—resembling Klopstock in this respect also—not only practised an etymological play on assonance quite after the Alexandrian style ;* but also introduced, in place of the simple signs for the double consonants that had hitherto been usual, the more accurate Greek double writing. Of Naevius and Plautus, it is true, nothing of the kind is known ; the popular poets in Rome must have treated orthography and etymology with the carelessness which poets usually manifest in such matters.

Rhetoric and philosophy.

The Romans of this epoch still remained strangers to rhetoric and philosophy. Public speaking in their case was too decidedly the mainspring of public life to be accessible to the handling of the foreign schoolmaster; the genuine orator Cato poured forth all the vials of his indignant ridicule over the Isocratean folly of ever learning and yet never being able to speak. The Greek philosophy, although it acquired a certain influence over the Romans through the medium of didactic and especially of tragic poetry, was nevertheless viewed with an apprehension compounded of boorish ignorance and of instinctive misgiving. Cato bluntly called Socrates a talker and a revolutionist, who was justly put to death as an offender against the faith and the laws of his country ; and the opinion, which even Romans addicted to philosophy entertained regarding it, probably finds expression in the words of Ennius :

> Philosophari est mihi necesse, at paucis, nam omnino haut placet.
> Degustandum ex câ, non in eam ingurgitandum censeo.

Nevertheless the poem on Morals and the instructions in Oratory, which were found among the writings of Cato, may be regarded as the Roman quintessence or, if the expression be preferred, the Roman *caput mortuum* of Greek philosophy and rhetoric. The immediate sources whence Cato drew were, in the case of the poem on Morals, probably the Pythagorean writings on morals (coupled of course with due commendation of the simple ancestral manners), and, in the case of the book on Oratory, the speeches in Thucydides and more especially the orations of Demosthenes, all of which

---

* Thus in his Epicharmian poems the name of Jupiter is derived from the circumstance *quod iuvat* ; that of Ceres from the fact *quod gerit fruges.*

Cato zealously studied. Of the spirit of these manuals we may form some idea from the golden oratorical rule, oftener quoted than followed by posterity, " to think of the matter and leave the words to follow of themselves." *

Similar manuals of a general elementary character were Medicine. composed by Cato on the Art of Healing, the Science of War, Agriculture, and Jurisprudence—all of which studies were likewise more or less under Greek influence. Physics and mathematics were not much studied in Rome ; but the applied sciences connected with them received a certain measure of attention. This was most of all true of medicine. In 535 the first Greek physician, the Peloponnesian Archa-   219. gathus, settled in Rome and there acquired such repute by his surgical operations, that a residence was assigned to him on the part of the state and he received the freedom of the city ; and thereafter his colleagues flocked in crowds to Italy. Cato no doubt not only reviled the foreign medical practitioners with a zeal worthy of a better cause, but attempted, by means of his medical manual compiled from his own experience and probably in part also from the medical literature of the Greeks, to revive the good old fashion under which the father of the family was at the same time the family physician. The physicians and the public gave themselves, as was reasonable, but little concern about his obstinate invectives : at any rate the profession, one of the most lucrative which existed in Rome, continued a monopoly in the hands of the foreigners, and for centuries there were none but Greek physicians in Rome.

Hitherto the measurement of time had been treated in Mathema- Rome with barbarous indifference, but matters were now at   tics. least in some degree improved. With the erection of the first sundial in the Roman Forum in 491 the Greek hour (ὥρα,   263. hora) began to come into use at Rome : it happened, how- ever, that the Romans erected a sundial which had been pre- pared for Catana situated four degrees farther to the south, and were guided by this for a whole century. Towards the end of this epoch we find several persons of distinction taking an interest in mathematical studies. Manius Acilius Glabrio

---

* Rem tene, verba sequentur.

191. (consul in 563) attempted to check the confusion of the calendar by a law, which allowed the pontifical college to insert or omit intercalary months at discretion: if the measure failed in its object and in fact aggravated the evil, the failure was probably owing more to the unscrupulousness than to the want of intelligence of the Roman theologians.

189. Marcus Fulvius Nobilior (consul in 565), a man of Greek culture, endeavoured at least to make the Roman calendar more generally known. Gaius Sulpicius Gallus (consul in

166. 588), who not only predicted the eclipse of the moon in

168. 586 but also calculated the distance of the moon from the earth, and who appears to have come forward even as an astronomical writer, was regarded on this account by his contemporaries as a prodigy of diligence and acuteness.

Agricul-
ture and
the art
of war.
Agriculture and the art of war were, of course, primarily regulated by the standard of traditional and personal experience, as is very distinctly apparent in that one of the two treatises of Cato on Agriculture which has reached our time. But the results of Graeco-Latin, and even of Phoenician, culture were brought to bear on these subordinate fields just as on the higher provinces of intellectual activity, and for that reason the foreign literature relating to them cannot but have attracted some measure of attention.

Jurispru-
dence.
Jurisprudence, on the other hand, was only in a subordinate degree affected by foreign elements. The activity of the jurists of this period was still mainly devoted to the answering of parties consulting them and to the instruction of younger listeners; but this oral instruction contributed to form a traditional groundwork of rules, and literary activity was not wholly wanting. A work of greater importance for jurisprudence than the short sketch of Cato was the treatise

Aelius
Paetus.
promulgated by Sextus Aelius Paetus, surnamed the "subtle" (*catus*), who was the first practical jurist of his time, and, in consequence of his exertions for the public benefit in this

198. respect, rose to the consulship (556) and to the censorship

194. (560). His treatise—the "*Tripartita*" as it was called—was a work on the Twelve Tables, which appended to each sentence of the text an explanation—chiefly, it is probable, of the antiquated and unintelligible expressions—and the corresponding formula of action. While this process of annota-

tion undeniably indicated the influence of Greek grammatical studies, the portion treating of the formulae of action, on the contrary, was based on the older collection of Appius (i. 515) and on the general system of procedure as developed by national usage and precedent.

The state of science generally at this epoch is very distinctly exhibited in the collection of manuals composed by Cato for his son which, as a sort of encyclopaedia, were designed to set forth in short maxims what a " proper man " (*vir bonus*) ought to be as orator, physician, husbandman, warrior, and jurist. No distinction was yet drawn between an elementary and a special study of the sciences ; but so much of science generally as seemed necessary or useful was required of every true Roman. The work did not include Latin grammar, which consequently cannot as yet have attained that formal development which is implied in a properly scientific instruction in language ; and it excluded music and the whole cycle of the mathematical and physical sciences. Throughout it was the directly practical element in science which alone was to be handled, and that with as much brevity and simplicity as possible. The Greek literature was doubtless made use of, but only to furnish some serviceable maxims of experience culled from the mass of chaff and rubbish : it was a favourite saying of Cato, that " Greek literature must be looked into, but not thoroughly studied." Thus arose those household manuals of necessary information, which, while rejecting Greek subtlety and obscurity, banished also Greek acuteness and depth, but through that very peculiarity moulded the position of the Romans towards Greek science for all ages.

Cato's encyclopaedia.

Thus poetry and literature came to Rome along with the sovereignty of the world, or, to use the language of a poet of the age of Cicero :

Character and historical position of Roman literature.

> *Poenico bello secundo Musa pennato gradu*
> *Intulit se bellicosam Romuli in gentem feram.*

In the districts using the Sabellian and Etruscan dialects also there must have been at the same period no want of intellectual movement. Tragedies in the Etruscan language are mentioned, and vases with Oscan inscriptions show that the makers of them were acquainted with Greek comedy. The question accordingly presents itself, whether, contemporarily with Naevius and Cato, a Hellenizing literature like the Roman may not have been in course of formation on the Arnus and Volturnus. But all information on the point is lost, and history can in such circumstances only indicate the blank.

Helle-nizing literature. The Roman literature is the only one as to which we can still form an opinion; and, however problematical its absolute worth may appear to the aesthetic judge, for those who wish to apprehend the history of Rome it remains of unique value as the reflection of the inner mental life of Italy in that sixth century—so full of the din of arms and so pregnant with the destinies of the future—during which the distinctive development of Italian life closed, and the land began to enter into the broader career of ancient civilization. In it too there prevailed that antagonism, which everywhere during this epoch pervaded the life of the nation and characterized the age of transition. No one of unprejudiced mind, and who is not misled by the venerable rust of two thousand years, can be deceived as to the defectiveness of the Hellenistico-Roman literature. Roman literature by the side of that of Greece resembles a German orangery by the side of a grove of Sicilian orange-trees; both may give us pleasure, but it is impossible even to conceive them as parallel. This holds true of the literature in the mother-tongue of the Latins still more decidedly, if possible, than of the Roman literature in a foreign tongue; to a very great extent the former was not the work of Romans at all, but of foreigners, of half-Greeks, Celts, and ere long even Africans, whose knowledge of Latin was only acquired by study. Among those who in this age came before the public as poets, none, as we have already said, can be shown to have been persons of rank; and not only so, but none can be shown to have been natives of Latium proper. The very name given to the poet was foreign; even Ennius emphatically calls himself a *poeta*.*

* See the lines already quoted at p. 479. The formation of the name *poeta* from the vulgar Greek ποητής instead of ποιητής—as ἐπόησεν was in use among the Attic potters—is characteristic. We may add that *poeta* technically denotes only the author of epic or recitative poems, not the composer for the stage, who at this time was styled *scriba* (p. 447. Festus, *s. v.*, p. 333 *M.*).

But not only was this poetry foreign; it was also liable to all those defects which are found to occur where schoolmasters become authors and the great multitude forms the public. We have shown how comedy was artistically debased out of regard to the multitude, and in fact sank into vulgar coarseness; we have further shown that two of the most influential Roman authors were schoolmasters in the first instance and only became poets in the sequel, and that, while the Greek philology which only sprang up after the decline of the national literature experimented merely on the dead body, in Latium grammar and literature had their foundations laid simultaneously and went hand in hand, almost as in the case of modern missions to the heathen. In fact, if we view with an unprejudiced eye this Hellenistic literature of the sixth century – that mechanical poetry destitute of all productive power of its own, that uniform imitation of the very shallowest forms of foreign art, that stock of translations, that changeling of an epos—we are tempted to reckon it simply one of the diseased symptoms of the epoch before us.

But such a judgment, if not unjust, would yet be just only in a very partial sense. We must first of all consider that this artificial literature sprang up in a nation which not only did not possess any national poetic art, but could never attain any such art. In antiquity, which knew nothing of the modern poetry of individual life, creative poetical activity fell mainly within the mysterious period when a nation was experiencing the fears and pleasures of growth : without prejudice to the greatness of the Greek epic and tragic poets we may assert that their poetry mainly consisted in reproducing the primitive stories of human gods and divine men. This basis of ancient poetry was totally wanting in Latium : where the world of gods remained shapeless and legend remained barren, the golden apples of poetry could not voluntarily ripen. To this falls to be added a second and more important consideration. The inward mental development and the outward political evolution of Italy had equally reached a point at which it was no longer possible to retain the Roman nationality based on the exclusion of all higher and individual mental culture, and to repel the encroachments of Hellenism. The propagation of Hellenism in Italy had certainly a

revolutionary and a denationalizing tendency, but it was
indispensable for the necessary intellectual equalization of the
nations; and this primarily constitutes the historical and even
the poetical justification of the Romano-Hellenistic literature.
Not a single new and genuine work of art issued from its
workshop, but it brought Italy within the intellectual horizon
of Hellas. Viewed even in its mere outward aspect, Greek
poetry presumes in the hearer a certain amount of positive
knowledge. That self-contained completeness, which is one
of the most essential peculiarities of the dramas of Shakespeare for instance, was foreign to ancient poetry; a person
unacquainted with the cycle of Greek legend would fail to
discover the background and often even the ordinary meaning of every rhapsody and every tragedy. If the Roman
public of this period was in some degree familiar, as the
comedies of Plautus show, with the Homeric poems and the
legends of Herakles, and was acquainted with at least the
more generally current of the other myths,* this knowledge
must have found its way to the public primarily through the
stage and the school, and thus have formed at least a first
step towards the understanding of the Hellenic poetry. But
still deeper was the effect—on which the most ingenious literary critics of antiquity justly laid emphasis—produced by the
naturalization of the Greek poetic language and the Greek
metres in Latium. If "conquered Greece vanquished her
rude conqueror by art," the victory was primarily accomplished by elaborating from the unpliant Latin idiom a
cultivated and elevated poetical language, so that instead of
the monotonous and hackneyed Saturnian the senarius
flowed and the hexameter rushed, and the mighty tetra-
meters, the jubilant anapaests, and the artfully intermingled
lyrical rhythms fell on the Latin ear in the mother-tongue.
Poetical language is the key to the ideal world of poetry,
poetic measure the key to poetical feeling; for the man, to
whom the eloquent epithet is dumb and the living image is
dead, and in whom the times of dactyls and iambuses awaken

---

* Even subordinate figures from the
legends of Troy and of Herakles make
their appearance, e. g. Talthybius (Stich.
305), Autolycus (Bacch. 275), Parthaon
(Men. 745). Moreover the most general
outlines must have been known in the
case of the Theban and the Argonautic
legends, and of the stories of Bellerophon
(Bacch. 810), Pentheus (Merc. 467),
Procne and Philomela (Rud. 604),
Sappho and Phaon (Mil. 1247).

no inward echo, Homer and Sophocles have composed in vain.
Let it not be said that poetical and rhythmical feeling comes
spontaneously. The ideal feelings are no doubt implanted by
nature in the human breast, but they need favourable sun-
shine in order to germinate; and especially in the Latin
nation, which was but little susceptible of poetic impulses,
they needed external nurture. Nor let it be said, that, by
virtue of the widely diffused acquaintance with the Greek
language, its literature might have sufficed for the susceptible
Roman public. The mysterious charm which language
exercises over man, and which poetical language and rhythm
only exercise in a higher degree, attaches not to any tongue
learnt accidentally, but only to the mother-tongue. From
this point of view, we shall form a juster judgment of the
Hellenistic literature, and particularly of the poetry, of the
Romans of this period. If it was the tendency of that
literature to transplant the radicalism of Euripides to Rome,
to resolve the gods either into deceased men or into mental
conceptions, to place a denationalized Latium by the side of
a denationalized Hellas, and to merge all purely and distinctly
developed national peculiarities into the questionable idea
of general civilization, every one is at liberty to approve or
disapprove this tendency, but none can doubt its historical
necessity. From this point of view the very defectiveness
of the Roman poetry, which cannot be denied, may be explained and so may in some degree be justified. It is no
doubt pervaded by a disproportion between the trivial and
often mutilated contents and the comparatively finished form;
but the real significance of this poetry lay precisely in its
formal features, especially those of language and metre. It
was not seemly that poetry in Rome was principally in
the hands of schoolmasters and foreigners and was chiefly
translation or imitation; but, if the primary object of poetry
was simply to form a bridge from Latium to Hellas, Livius
and Ennius had certainly a vocation to the poetical pontifi-
cate in Rome, and a translated literature was the simplest
means to the end. It was still less seemly that Roman poetry
preferred to lay its hands on the most prolix and trivial originals; but in this view it was appropriate. No one will
desire to place the poetry of Euripides on a level with that of

Homer; but, historically viewed, Euripides and Menander were quite as much the oracles of cosmopolitan Hellenism as the Iliad and Odyssey were the oracles of national Hellenism, and in so far the representatives of the new school had good reason for introducing their audience especially to this cycle of literature. The instinctive consciousness also of their limited poetical powers may partly have induced the Roman composers to keep mainly by Euripides and Menander and to leave Sophocles and even Aristophanes untouched.; for, while poetry is essentially national and difficult to transplant, intellect and wit, on which the poetry of Euripides as well as of Menander is based, are in their nature cosmopolitan. Moreover the fact always deserves to be honourably acknowledged, that the Roman poets of the sixth century did not attach themselves to the Hellenic literature of the day or what is called Alexandrinism, but sought their models solely in the older classical literature, although not exactly in its richest or purest fields. On the whole, however innumerable may be the false accommodations and sins against the rules of art which we can point out in them, these were just the offences which were by stringent necessity attendant on the far from scrupulous efforts of the missionaries of Hellenism; and they are, in a historical and even aesthetical point of view, outweighed in some measure by the zeal of faith equally inseparable from propagandism. We may form a different opinion from Ennius as to the value of his new gospel; but, if in the case of faith it does not matter so much what, as how, men believe, we cannot refuse recognition and admiration to the Roman poets of the sixth century. A fresh and strong sense of the power of the Hellenic world-literature, a sacred longing to transplant the marvellous tree to the foreign land, pervaded the whole poetry of the sixth century, and coincided in a peculiar manner with the thoroughly elevated spirit of that great age. The later refined Hellenism looked down on the poetical performances of this period with some degree of contempt; it should rather perhaps have looked up to the poets, who with all their imperfections yet stood in an intimate relation to Greek poetry, and approached nearer to genuine poetical art than their more cultivated successors. In the bold emulation, in the sounding rhythms, even in the mighty

professional pride of the poets of this age there is, more than
in any other epoch of Roman literature, an imposing grandeur; and even those who are under no illusion as to the weak
points of this poetry may apply to it the proud language in
which Ennius celebrates its praise :

> *Enni poeta, salve, qui mortalibus*
> *Versus propinas flammeos medullitus.*

As the Hellenico-Roman literature of this period was
essentially marked by a dominant tendency, so was also its
antithesis, the contemporary national authorship. While
the former aimed at neither more nor less than the annihilation of Latin nationality by the creation of a poetry
Latin in language but Hellenic in form and spirit, the best
and purest part of the Latin nation was driven to reject and
place under the ban of outlawry the literature of Hellenism
along with Hellenism itself. The Romans in the time of
Cato stood opposed to Greek literature, very much as in the
time of the Caesars they stood opposed to Christianity ;
freedmen and foreigners formed the main body of the poetical,
as they afterwards formed the main body of the Christian,
community ; the nobility of the nation and above all the
government saw in poetry as in Christianity an absolutely
hostile power ; Plautus and Ennius were ranked with the
rabble by the Roman aristocracy for reasons nearly the
same as those for which the apostles and bishops were put
to death by the Roman government. In this field too it
was Cato, of course, who took the lead as the vigorous
champion of his native country against the foreigners. The
Greek literati and physicians were in his view the most
dangerous scum of the radically corrupt Greek people,* and

National opposition.

---

* " As to these Greeks," he says to
his son Marcus, " I shall tell at the
proper place, what I came to learn regarding them at Athens; and shall
show that it is useful to look into their
writings, but not to study them thoroughly. They are an utterly corrupt
and ungovernable race—believe me, this
is true as an oracle ; if that people
bring hither its culture, it will ruin
everything, and most especially if it
send hither its physicians. They have
conspired to despatch all barbarians by
their physicking, nevertheless they get
themselves paid for it, that people may

trust them and that they may the more
easily bring us to ruin. They call us also
barbarians, and indeed revile us by the
still more vulgar name of Opicans. I
interdict thee, therefore, from all dealings
with the practitioners of the healing
art."

Cato in his zeal was not aware that
the name of Opicans, which had in Latin
an objectionable sense, was in Greek
quite free from this, and that the Greeks
had in the most innocent way come to
designate the Italians by that term
(i. 147).

the Roman "ballad-singers" are treated by him with in-
effable contempt (i. 503). He and those who shared his
sentiments have been often and harshly censured on this
account, and certainly the expressions of his displeasure are
not unfrequently characterized by the bluntness and narrow-
ness peculiar to him; but on a closer consideration we
must not only confess him to have been in individual points
substantially right, but we must also acknowledge that the
national opposition in this field, more than anywhere else,
abandoned the manifestly inadequate line of mere negative defence. When his younger contemporary, Aulus
Postumius Albinus, who was an object of ridicule to the
Hellenes themselves by his offensive Hellenizing, and who
even manufactured Greek verses—when this Albinus in
the preface to his historical treatise pleaded in excuse for
his defective Greek that he was by birth a Roman—was not
the question quite in place, whether he had been condemned
by legal authority to meddle with things which he did not
understand? Were the trades of the professional translator
of comedies and of the poet celebrating heroes for bread and
protection more honourable, perhaps, two thousand years
ago than they are now? Had Cato not reason to make it a
reproach against Nobilior, that he took Ennius—who, we
may add, glorified in his verses the Roman potentates without respect of persons, and overloaded Cato himself with praise
—along with him to Ambracia as the celebrator of his future
achievements? Had he not reason to revile the Greeks, with
whom he had become acquainted in Rome and Athens, as an
incorrigibly wretched pack? This opposition to the culture of
the age and the Hellenism of the day was well warranted;
but Cato was by no means chargeable with an opposition to
culture and to Hellenism in general. On the contrary it is the
highest merit of the national party, that they comprehended
very clearly the necessity of creating a Latin literature and
of bringing the stimulating influences of Hellenism to bear
on it; only their intention was, that Latin literature should
not be a mere copy taken from the Greek and intruded on
the national feelings of Rome, but should, while quickened by
Greek influences, be developed in a manner conformable to
Italian nationality. With a genial instinct, which attests

not so much the sagacity of individuals as the general elevation of the epoch, they perceived that in the case of Rome,
owing to the total want of earlier poetical productiveness,
history furnished the only materials for the development of
a distinctive intellectual life. Rome was, what Greece was
not, a state; and the mighty consciousness of this truth
lay at the root both of the bold attempt which Naevius made
to form by means of history a Roman epos and a Roman
drama, and of the creation of Latin prose by Cato. It is true
that the endeavour to replace the gods and heroes of legend
by the kings and consuls of Rome resembles the attempt
of the giants to storm heaven by means of mountains piled
one above another : without a mythologic world there is no
ancient epos and no ancient drama, and poetry knows no
substitutes. With greater moderation and good sense Cato
left poetry proper, as a thing irremediably lost, to the party
opposed to him; although his attempt to create a didactic
poetry in national measure after the model of the earlier
Roman productions—the Appian poem on Morals and the
poem on Agriculture—remains significant and deserving of
respect, if not in point of success, yet in point of intention.
Prose afforded him a more favourable field, and accordingly
he applied the whole varied power and energy peculiar
to him to the creation of a prose literature in his native
tongue. This effort was all the more Roman and all the
more deserving of respect, that the public which he primarily addressed was the family circle, and that in such an
effort he stood almost alone in his time. Thus arose his
" Origines," his remarkable state-speeches, his treatises on
special branches of science. They are certainly pervaded
by a national spirit, and turn on national subjects; but they
are far from anti-Hellenic : in fact they originated essentially
under Greek influence, although in a different sense from
that in which the writings of the opposite party so originated.
The idea and even the title of his chief work were borrowed
from the Greek " foundation-histories " (κτίσεις). The same
is true of his oratorical authorship; he ridiculed Isocrates,
but he tried to learn from Thucydides and Demosthenes.
His encyclopaedia is substantially the result of his study of
Greek literature. Of all the undertakings of that active and

patriotic man none was more fruitful of results and none more
useful to his country than this literary activity, little esteemed
in comparison as it probably was by himself. He found
numerous and worthy successors in oratorical and scientific
authorship ; and though his original historical treatise, which
of its kind may be compared with the Greek logography, was
followed by no Herodotus or Thucydides, yet he was the
means of establishing the principle that literary occupation
in connection with the useful sciences as well as with history
was not merely becoming but honourable in a Roman.

Architec-
ture.   Let us glance, in conclusion, at the state of the arts of
architecture, sculpture, and painting. So far as concerns the
former, the traces of growing luxury were less observable
in public than in private buildings. It was not till towards
the close of this period, and especially from the time of the
184. censorship of Cato (570), that the Romans began in the case
of the former to have respect to public convenience as well as
to public exigency ; to line with stone the basins (*lacus*) sup-
184. 179. plied from the aqueducts (570) ; to erect colonnades (575,
174. 580) ; and above all to transfer to Rome the Attic halls for
courts and business—the *basilicae* as they were called. The
first of these buildings, somewhat corresponding to our modern
bazaars—the Porcian or silversmiths' hall—was erected by
184. Cato in 570 alongside of the senate-house ; others were soon
associated with it, till gradually along the sides of the Forum
the private shops were replaced by these splendid columnar
halls. Every-day life, however, was more deeply influenced
by the revolution in domestic architecture which must, at
latest, be placed in this period. The dwelling-room (*atrium*),
court (*cavum aedium*), garden and garden colonnade (*peri-
stylium*), the record-chamber (*tablinum*), chapel, kitchen, and
bedrooms were by degrees severally provided for ; and, as to
the internal fittings, the column began to be applied both in
the court and in the dwelling-room for the support of the
open roof and also for the garden colonnades : throughout
these arrangements it is probable that Greek models were
copied or at any rate made use of. Yet the materials used
in building remained simple ; " our ancestors," says Varro,
" dwelt in houses of brick, and laid merely a moderate
foundation of stone to keep away damp."

Of Roman plastic art we scarcely encounter any other trace than, perhaps, the embossing in wax of the images of ancestors. Painters and painting are mentioned somewhat more frequently. Manius Valerius caused the victory which he obtained over the Carthaginians and Hiero in 491 off Messana (p. 37) to be depicted on the side wall of the senate-house—the first historical frescoes in Rome, which were followed by many of similar character, and which were in the domain of the arts of design what the national epos and the national drama became not much later in the domain of poetry. We find named as painters, one Theodotus who, as Naevius scoffingly said,

Plastic art and painting.

263.

> Sedens in cella circumtectus tegetibus
> Lares ludentis peni pinxit bubulo;

Marcus Pacuvius of Brundisium, who painted in the temple of Hercules in the Forum Boarium—the same who, when more advanced in life, made himself a name as an editor of Greek tragedies; and Marcus Plautius Lyco, a native of Asia Minor, whose beautiful paintings in the temple of Juno at Ardea procured for him the freedom of that city.* But these very facts clearly indicate, not only that the exercise of art in Rome was altogether of subordinate importance and more of a manual occupation than an art, but also that it fell, probably still more exclusively than poetry, into the hands of Greeks and half Greeks.

On the other hand there appeared in genteel circles the first traces of the tastes subsequently displayed by the dilettante and the collector. They admired the magnificence of the Corinthian and Athenian temples, and regarded with contempt the old-fashioned terra-cotta figures on the roofs of those of Rome: even a man like Lucius Paullus, who shared the feelings of Cato rather than of Scipio, viewed and judged the Zeus of Phidias with the eye of a connoisseur. The custom of carrying off the treasures of art from the conquered Greek cities was first introduced on a large scale

---

* Plautius belongs to this or to the beginning of the following period, for the inscription on his pictures (Plin. H. N. xxxv. 10, 115), being hexametrical, cannot well be older than Ennius, and the bestowal of the citizenship of Ardea must have taken place before the Social War through which Ardea lost its independence.

212.   by Marcus Marcellus after the capture of Syracuse (542).
The practice met with severe reprobation from men of the
old school of training, and the stern veteran Quintus Fabius,
209.   for instance, on the capture of Tarentum (545) gave orders
that the statues in the temples should not be touched, but
that the Tarentines should be allowed to retain their indignant gods.   Yet the plundering of temples in this way became
of more and more frequent occurrence.   Titus Flamininus
194. 187. in particular (560) and Marcus Fulvius Nobilior (567), two
leading champions of Roman Hellenism, and Lucius Paullus
167.   (587) were the means of filling the public buildings of Rome
with the master-pieces of the Greek chisel.   In taking such
steps the Romans had a dawning consciousness of the truth
that an interest in art as well as an interest in poetry formed
an essential part of Hellenic culture or, in other words, of
modern civilization; but, while the appropriation of Greek
poetry was impossible without some sort of poetical activity, in
the case of art the mere beholding and procuring of its productions seemed to suffice, and therefore, while a native literature
was formed in an artificial way in Rome, no attempt even was
made to develop a native art.

Note to Page 224, Line 2.

The following decree of the praetor Lucius Aemilius Paullus has recently been discovered on a copper tablet found in the neighbourhood of Gibraltar, and now preserved in the Paris Museum: *L. Aimilius L. f. inpeirator decreivit, utei quei Hastensiun* [Hasta Regia, not far from Jerez de la Frontera] *servei in turri Lascutana* [known from coins and Plin. iii. 1, 15, but site uncertain] *habitarent, leiberei essent. Agrum oppidumqu[e], quod ea tempestate posedissent, item possidere habereque iousit, dum poplus senatusque Romanus vellet. Act. in castreis, a.d. XII. k. Febr.* [12th Jan. 564 or 565 of the city]. This is the oldest Roman document which we possess in the original, drawn up two years earlier than the well-known edict of the consuls of 568 in reference to the affair of the Bacchanalia.

END OF THE SECOND VOLUME.

LONDON: PRINTED BY
SPOTTISWOODE AND CO., NEW-STREET SQUARE
AND PARLIAMENT STREET